THE
ORGANIZATION
OF AMERICAN
STATES

THE
ORGANIZATION
OF AMERICAN
STATES

ANN VAN WYNEN THOMAS
A. J. THOMAS, JR.

1963
SOUTHERN METHODIST UNIVERSITY PRESS: DALLAS

A LAW INSTITUTE OF THE AMERICAS STUDY

PUBLISHED WITH THE ASSISTANCE OF A GRANT
FROM THE
SOUTHWESTERN LEGAL FOUNDATION

Library of Congress Catalog Card Number: 63-9754

To the memory of
HAZEL PORTER STOREY
and to
ROBERT GERALD STOREY

If we work marble, it will perish; if we work upon brass, time will efface it; if we rear temples, they will crumble into dust; but if we work upon immortal minds and instill into them just principles, we are then engraving upon tablets which no time will efface, but will brighten and brighten to all eternity.

Daniel Webster

PREFACE

It has been facetiously said that the Organization of American States can never be accused of subscribing to a "do or die" philosophy, for it seldom does yet it refuses to die. The authors of this study, while not in complete accord with this theory, are nevertheless well aware of the fact that survival of the Organization of American States in this tumultuous century depends to a considerable extent on its capacity to adapt itself to the important developments taking place in the relations among the nations of the Western Hemisphere.

Many of the problems now faced by the inter-American community are new; others have been with us for a long time. The solution of both old and new problems must take into account the interests not only of one country or one group of countries but of the whole inter-American community. The members of the OAS have devised effective weapons with which to tackle impediments standing in the way of hemispheric peace and well-being, but of late the organization instead of settling hemispheric problems has tended to make settlements more difficult. Until the members of the OAS accept both the need for making its broad and sometimes vague goals more explicit and the responsibility for backing them by a more purposeful program of action, the nations of the Western Hemisphere are failing to employ the instruments of the organization with maximum effectiveness to achieve desirable ends.

For the reader increasingly concerned with inter-American relations and the search for inter-American co-operation, this book attempts to chronicle the rise of the OAS and to offer a rounded survey of its legal forces and developments. The authors feel that today the Organization of American States is becoming more and more mechanical, and unless it reverses this trend, instead of developing a more secure and fruitful basis of international association it will continue its present process of stagnation and decay. It is therefore earnestly hoped that this study will be of aid to those who are seeking to revitalize the role played by the OAS in hemispheric affairs. The authors have attempted in this juridical-political study of the organization to provide a pragmatic basis for judgment on the value of the OAS to the Western Hemisphere, on the limitations on what can be expected from the organization under existing conditions, and on the kind of co-operation that each American state must be prepared to give to make it function effectively.

With the idea of bringing the investigation as nearly up to date as was practicable, we have tried to deal with relevant developments through February, 1963. We are indebted to a number of law journals for the opportunities which they have granted us to develop the views expressed in these pages and for having granted permission for the reappearance in this volume of materials based on studies originally prepared for them. The chapter on collective security appeared in Volume XIII of the *Southwestern Law Journal;* that on the province of the inter-American conference in Volume VI of the *St. Louis University Law Journal;* and that on democracy in Volume XLVI of the *Minnesota Law Journal.*

We are profoundly grateful for the permission granted by Southern Methodist University Press to reproduce herein certain pertinent excerpts from our previous book, *Non-Intervention: The Law and Its Import in the Americas*.

Our thanks are due to the staffs of Fondren Library and the Law Library of Southern Methodist University for their co-operation. The typing of the manuscript was done by Mrs. Margaret Seifert, Mrs. Mary Nelle Jeffers, and Mrs. Mary Grace Shuey. Their efficiency, patience, and cheerfulness at times of strain were greatly appreciated.

The writing and publication of this volume would not have been possible without the financial support of the Southwestern Legal Foundation of Dallas, Texas. It is our pleasant duty to express our deepest gratitude to that organization and its distinguished Board of Trustees.

A. J. THOMAS, JR.
ANN VAN WYNEN THOMAS

School of Law
Southern Methodist University
Dallas, Texas

CONTENTS

BOOK I

HISTORICAL BACKGROUND

BOOK II

LEGAL CHARACTERISTICS AND ORGANIZATIONAL STRUCTURE OF THE OAS

BOOK III

THE PRINCIPLES OF THE OAS

BOOK IV

FUNCTIONS OF THE OAS

BOOK I

Historical Background

CHAPTER I

INDEPENDENCE TO WORLD WAR I

ORIGINS OF AN AMERICAN COMMUNITY

The origins of an organized American community with a goal of mutual assistance for hemispheric welfare governed by homogeneous international principles can be traced to that historical era when the Spanish American nations fought their wars of liberation against the mother country, successfully acquiring their independence. Many factors of the time tended to give the people of the Americas a sense of community. A common denominator of political freedom and independence acquired by violent revolution against colonialism was present. Geographical propinquity existed as something of a unifying factor; and, in addition, the newly freed Hispanic American nations adopted, in theory at least, a democratic-republican form of government similar to that of the United States.[1]

The original basis of an American community was to a degree idealistic, founded upon the premise that the New World was to be dedicated to democracy, liberty, and peace in contrast to the monarchy, tyranny, and belligerency prevailing in the Old. It was only natural that an America dedicated to these ideals should seek to insulate itself and set itself apart from the historic disputes, accumulated passions, and political struggles of Europe. Possibly more important to the cause of continental solidarity at the time was fear of European reconquest. From 1816 to 1824, the security of the United States and the Spanish American nations, in the last stages of their struggles for independence, was threatened by a combination of European powers—the Holy Alliance—dedicated to the maintenance of the monarchial system of government and the divine right of kings at the expense of democracy and republicanism and inclined to aid the Spanish king in the recovery of his lost empire in the Western Hemisphere by crushing the new nations being constructed upon its ruins.[2] This menace confronting the Americas so early in their history created a lasting attitude of sink or swim together. National independence was emphasized. It was insisted that the hemisphere newly liberated or in process of liberation should not once again be absorbed by Europe. So seriously were the activities of the Holy Alliance viewed by President Monroe of the United States that he was prompted to proclaim the doctrine which bears his name to meet the threat of possible European intervention.[3] The Monroe Doctrine announced that the American continent was no longer open to European settlement, and, further, that the United States could not view with indifference an extension of the political system of the Holy Alliance to any portion of the hemisphere; nor could the United States view any interposition by any European power for the purpose of oppressing or controlling in any other manner the destiny of the new governments as anything other than a manifestation of an unfriendly disposition toward the United States.[4] Insofar as the United States was concerned, the doctrine was one of self-defense and self-preservation, vital to the peace and security of the nation and promulgated to prevent the establishment of strong European powers on this side of the Atlantic.[5] Nevertheless its terms produced a feeling of insularity or separation from the Old World by the demand that European nations were to seek no political or territorial gain or advantage in the Americas. Although the doctrine expressed a consciousness of continental solidarity, of an American community with similar political institutions and ideas antithetic to those of Europe,[6] no development of international co-operation among the American nations to maintain its principles followed. To the contrary, the United States made it clear that the doctrine was a unilateral pronouncement, not a proper subject for multilateral action.[7] Therefore, the United States lost, by its own default, the leadership in the movement for international co-operation and organization in the hemisphere, the mantle being assumed for a time by Latin America and her statesmen.

At the very beginning of the Wars of Independence various projects of political union of the different Spanish provinces of the Americas were advocated.[8] In 1810, for example, some of the earliest discussions for continental unity sprang from Chile and called for a federal union of the Spanish possessions in America.[9] Again, in a project entitled the Declaration of the Rights of the People of Chile, principles of political union were advanced for the following reasons:

First, that the main object of a people seeking self-government being to establish its liberty in such a manner as to insure internal and external peace, the States of America must unite for their external security against the aims of Europe, and to avoid wars between themselves which would annihilate these new-born States, each preserving, however, its own internal economic policy.

Secondly, that it is very difficult for each nation to maintain by itself in the face of constant danger an isolated sovereignty, which is not believed to be of great interest provided the internal happiness or welfare is secured.[10]

The declaration then called for a meeting of the nations of America in a congress so as to strengthen and organize themselves. It did not limit this union to Hispanic American peoples only but stated: ". . . the day when America assembled in congress, either of the nation or of its two continents or of the South, should speak to the rest of the world, her voice would command respect, and the resolutions of that congress will with difficulty be contradicted."[11]

The plans of Chile came to nothing. The divisive elements of nationalism had already appeared. Argentina, which had practically become independent from Spain in 1810 by the establishment of a provisional government, answered Chile in opposition through the secretary of its governing junta, Mariano Moreno:

How would the wills of men who inhabit a continent where distances are measured by the thousand leagues be harmonized: Where would the great congress hold its sessions, and how could it meet the urgent demands of peoples from whom it could receive news only after the lapse of three or four months? It is chimerical to pretend that the whole of Spanish America should constitute a single state. . . . Every effort that is aimed at preventing the provinces from establishing their own political systems is meant to paralyze the enthusiasm of the peoples until the occasion presents to give them a new master.[12]

In 1815 Simón Bolívar vaguely envisioned international union or co-operation, when in his famous Jamaica letter, written in poverty and exile, he stated:

How beautiful it would be if the Isthmus of Panama could be for us what the Isthmus of Corinth was for the Greeks! Would to God that some day we may have the good fortune to convene there an august assembly of representatives of republics, kingdoms, and empires to deliberate upon the high interests of peace and war with the nations of the other three-quarters of the globe. This type of organization may come to pass in some happier period of our regeneration.[13]

By 1822 his thinking had so far crystallized that the new nation of Colombia, at his instigation, concluded special conventions with certain of the other former Spanish colonies calling for a meeting of plenipotentiaries.[14] The objectives of such an assembly were, in the words of the treaty,

... to lay the most solid foundation for, and to establish the intimate relations which ought to subsist between all and each of them; and that may serve them as counsel in great emergencies, as a point of union in cases of common danger, as a faithful interpreter of their public Treaties should difficulties arise, and as a judicial reference and mediator in their disputes and differences.[15]

These treaties served as preparatory acts to Bolívar's great project of unification of the new Spanish American states by means of an international assembly made up of representatives of each: a confederation or a league to protect the American states against attack from outside the hemisphere and to maintain peace among themselves. By 1824, when victory over Spain seemed assured, Bolívar, as head of the Republic of Peru, issued an invitation to those American republics which were formerly colonies of Spain to take part in an Assembly of Plenipotentiaries at Panama. Brazil and the United States were later invited—Brazil by the government of Colombia and the United States by the governments of Colombia, Mexico, and Central America.[16]

Bolívar's ideas again become apparent in the first three paragraphs of his circular invitation:

After fifteen years of sacrifices devoted to the liberty of America to secure a system of guaranties that in peace and war shall be the shield of our new destiny, it is time the interests and relations uniting the American Republics, formerly Spanish colonies, should have a fundamental basis that shall perpetuate, if possible, those governments.

To initiate that system, and concentrate the power of this great political body implies the exercise of a sublime authority, capable of directing the policy of our Governments, whose influence should maintain uniformity of principles, and whose name alone should put an end to our quarrels.

Such a respectable authority can exist only in an assembly of plenipotentiaries, appointed by each of our Republics, and called together under the auspices of the victory obtained by our arms over the Spanish power.[17]

THE CONGRESS OF PANAMA

The nations reacted in various ways to Bolívar's invitation. Chile and Bolivia were friendly but delayed the appointment of delegates so that it was impossible for them to reach Panama in time. Paraguay was strongly isolationist and declined. The United Provinces of the Rio de la Plata also declined. The two non-Spanish American invitees, the Empire of Brazil and the United States, were not represented. The Brazilian Empire, recently independent of Portugal, did appoint a delegate, but failed to send him to Panama. The United States ordered two delegates to attend, but unfortunately they never reached Panama. One fell ill on the journey and died before arrival, and the other's departure was delayed too long. When the congress was inaugurated on June 22, 1826, the following states were represented: Gran Colombia, which included the present states of Colombia, Venezuela, Ecuador, and Panama; Mexico; Peru; and Central America, which was a unified republic including what is now the independent republics of Guatemala, Costa Rica, El Salvador, Nicaragua, and Honduras. Great Britain was represented by an observer, and the Netherlands had present a nonofficial representative.[18]

The congress held ten meetings, the last of which took place on July 15, 1826;[19] its main accomplishment was a Treaty of Perpetual Union, League and Confederation[20] which contained thirty-one articles and an additional supplementary article. The treaty was far-reaching in character. By its terms the parties sought to create a mutual alliance and confederation among themselves operative in peace as well as in war in order to maintain defensively and offensively, in case of necessity, the sovereignty and independence of all and each of the confederated powers against all foreign domination; to secure to the parties the enjoyment of peace; and to promote harmony and understanding between themselves, as well as with other nations.[21] To carry out the alliance, the contracting nations bound themselves to mutual defense against every attack endangering their political existence and pledged themselves to employ their influence, resources, and military forces against the enemies of any or all of them, the proportion each was to contribute to the common cause being set forth in a separate treaty.[22]

Recognizing the need for strengthening the fraternal bonds of the signatories, the parties agreed to meet every two years in time of peace, and every year while the war with Spain progressed, or during any future wars, in a general assembly composed of two ministers plenipotentiary of each party.[23] The principal objects of this general assembly were stated to be:

First. To negotiate and conclude between the powers it represents all such treaties, conventions and arrangements, as may place their reciprocal relations on a mutually agreeable and satisfactory footing.

Second. To contribute to the maintenance of a friendly and unalterable peace between the confederated powers, serving them as council in times of great conflicts, as a point of contact in common dangers, as a faithful interpreter of the public treaties and conventions concluded by them in the said assembly, when any doubt arises as to their construction, and as conciliator in their controversies and differences.

Third. To endeavor to secure conciliation, or mediation, in all questions which may arise between the allied powers, or between any of them and one or more foreign powers to the confederation, whenever threatened of a rupture, or engaged in war because of grievances, serious injuries, or other complaints.

Fourth. To adjust and conclude during the common wars of the contracting parties with one or many powers foreign to the confederation all those treaties of alliance, concern, subsidies, and contributions that shall hasten its termination.[24]

The parties pledged themselves to submit all differences to the assembly for the formulation of an amicable recommendation.[25] In cases of complaints or injuries they were prohibited not only from declaring war, but also from ordering acts of reprisal without first submitting the case to the conciliatory decision of the general assembly.[26] No party was to go to war with a nation foreign to the confederation without first soliciting the good offices, interposition, and mediation of all allies.[27] Sanctions were provided in that any one of the parties violating these stipulations by commencing hostilities against another, or by failing to comply with the decisions of the assembly having previously submitted to it, was to be excluded from the confederation. In such event restoration of the offender was impossible except by unanimous vote.[28] It was further stipulated that if any one of the parties substantially changed its present form of government it should by that act be excluded from the confederation and should not be recognized nor reinstated except by unanimous vote of all the parties.[29]

Articles concerning territorial integrity are also of interest. Article 21 seems an internationalization of the Monroe Doctrine, at least that portion relating to noncolonization by European powers, in that the parties bound themselves to uphold and defend the integrity of their respective territories and to oppose any attempt of colonial settlement within them. By Article 22 the parties mutually guaranteed the integrity of their territories, placing them under the protection of the confederation as soon as the respective boundaries had been marked and fixed in accordance with special conventions to be celebrated by the interested states. Thus a need was seen not only for conferences at regular intervals and machinery for settling disputes, but also for the elimination of difficulties among the members through the mutual guarantee of territorial boundaries on the basis of the status quo.

Other important articles prohibited any of the parties from making peace with the enemies of their independence without including all the other allies;[30] regulated the manner in which the parties should, in case of necessity, give their aid on land or sea;[31] permitted the admission of other American states into the confederation;[32] prohibited the slave trade;[33] regulated the status of citizens of one state residing in another;[34] and provided that commercial relations should be regulated at the next assembly.[35] In the additional article it was declared that after ratification of the treaty the parties should proceed to fix by common agreement all the points, rules, and principles that were to govern their conduct in peace and war.

Almost simultaneously with the establishment of the new nations of the Americas, Bolívar sought to give them an international organization and an international law for their mutual relations. From the point of view of modern international organization little was overlooked. A league or confederation of a politico-military character on a broad hemispheric scale was contemplated. Arbitration, conciliation, territorial integrity, and a system of guarantees were all encompassed, as well as the elimination of economic and political barriers, deterrents to effective peaceful co-operation. Even social problems were not overlooked, for the slave trade was to be abolished. Unfortunately the Bolivarian dream of common action for the peace and security of the hemisphere was in advance of the time. A system of collective security failed to be created because forces of disunity among the American states prevented its acceptance. One nation only, Gran Colombia, ratified the treaty, and then with reservation. Not only did the Panama agreements fail to obtain acceptance, but the follow-up conference scheduled to meet at Tacubaya, Mexico, the next year was never held. Nevertheless, Bolívar's inspiration was to persist as a precedent for future international conferences among the American states, and was to become the ancestor of today's Organization of American States. On a broader scale, it served as a precedent for modern world organization.

HISPANIC AMERICAN CONFERENCES

The unsuccessful conclusion of the Panama Congress, the subsidence of the threat from the Holy Alliance, the outbreak in Spanish America of civil war and despotism, and the attitude of the United States all contributed to the halting for a time of the hemispheric movement of international co-operation. As to the attitude of the United States, its failure to be represented at the Congress was most unfortunate, for it indicated in itself an unsympathetic position. As the years passed the United States tended to forget the Monroe Doctrine and directed certain action against its Latin American neighbors that did little to further the ideals expressed by Bolívar. For a combination of these reasons there was a tendency among the American states to revert to isolationism, or at best to view inter-American co-operation and organization as exclusively Spanish or Latin American.[36]

The idea of a league or confederation of American states did not completely pass away, for additional Hispanic American political conferences were held between 1846 and 1865, some devoted to organization on a hemispheric scale and some dedicated to a more limited co-operation of the Spanish American or Latin American nations only. These congresses were held in Lima in 1847, in Santiago in 1856, and again in Lima in 1864.[37] It is interesting to note that all of these conferences were called when new dangers threatened the independence of the Hispanic American nations from either within or without the hemisphere. In such instances Latin American leaders instinctively looked to some form of international co-operation or union to preserve their national sovereignty.

This is well exemplified by historical actions which menaced Latin America or certain parts thereof prior to the calling of these conferences. Mexico, for instance, proposed on several different occasions the convening of a Spanish American Congress in the early years following the Panama Congress, because of its apprehension of the designs of the United States upon Mexican territory following the revolt in Texas and the cry for annexation of that land which came from the United States. Mexico, faced with this danger, sought to alleviate it by means of a union and close alliance of the Spanish American republics for the purpose of common defense against foreign aggression and sought to foster the unity of these republics by arousing them against the United States at the expense of the solidarity of the hemisphere. The attempts by Mexico to assemble such a congress were unavailing for the congress so proposed never met.[38]

In 1846-47 certain of the Latin American states feared for their existence because of a military expedition which was being organized in Europe by an exiled Ecuadorian ex-President, General Juan José Flores, which was supported in Spain and elsewhere on the Continent for the expressed purpose of overthrowing the government of Ecuador. There was well-grounded evidence to further the belief that the real objective was to create a monarchy, over which a Spanish prince would be placed, which would embrace most of northern South America.[39] Since the threat to the existence of the Americas came from Europe, not from the United States, there was a revival of the idea of hemispheric solidarity. Peru took the lead in calling a meeting to consider the matter and to provide for collective defense. The invitation emphasized the continent-wide character of the proposed congress, and it was sent not only to the Spanish American states but also to Brazil and the United States. The invitees responded favorably with the exception of the United States, but when the congress convened at Lima in December, 1847, only Colombia, Ecuador, Peru, Bolivia, and Chile, the states most directly menaced by the machinations of Spain, were present.[40] In February of 1848 the parties signed a Treaty of Confederation which clearly attempted a resurrection of the entire hemispheric movement. It was expressly left open to adherence by all of the governments of the Americas, even those not represented at the conference, and, in addition, their adherence to it was solicited.[41]

The War of 1848 between the United States and Mexico, in which Mexico lost certain of her territories, and the filibustering expeditions in Central America organized in the United States by William Walker, once again awakened distrust and uneasiness among the Latin American nations, motivating a conference at Santiago, Chile, in 1856.[42] This conference resulted in the signing of the Continental Treaty by the representatives of Chile, Peru, and Ecuador. Only Latin American states were invited to adhere, inasmuch as the treaty was drawn in a spirit of hostility against the United States.[43]

The last of the congresses of this character was convoked in 1864, again in Lima, and this time to face serious new encroachments against the territorial integrity of the Americas emanating from Europe, as well as certain manifestations of expansionist and imperialistic policies of the United States which had aroused renewed fear. As to the European danger, Spain had reincorporated Santo Domingo in 1861, France had intervened in Mexico in 1862 to substitute for the republic a French-controlled empire under the Archduke Maximilian, and in 1864 Spain occupied the Peruvian Chinchas Islands.[44] The congress was attended by delegates from Chile,

El Salvador, Venezuela, Colombia, Ecuador, Peru, and Bolivia. Argentina was represented, but its delegate was not empowered to subscribe to agreements that might be drawn up at the conference.[45] Brazil failed to respond to its invitation. The United States was not invited, although Chile strongly urged the hemispheric idea, asserting that no congresses should be held unless all of the American nations were invited.[46] Once again a geographic division of the hemisphere ensued and solidarity was lacking.

It is interesting to note that in these Hispanic American treaties many of the organizational characteristics and most of the principles of the present-day Organization of American States are set forth. The treaties envisioned international co-operation of the member states for reciprocal defense against aggression by non-American powers. The second Lima Conference went farther and provided for an alliance against all aggressions, whether of foreign powers or of those signing the pact. The political union as advanced was somewhat vague, the word *confederation* being used to describe it. It is clear, however, that the parties had little idea of creating a superstate impinging on national sovereignty. On the contrary, there was contemplated an international organization, a league of nations, which would be composed of independent sovereign states, which would be restricted in its powers, but which, while respecting the autonomy of each nation, would protect all against foreign aggression and seek the peaceful settlement of disputes.

All of the treaties attempted to establish an assembly of plenipotentiaries composed of representatives from each state to meet at periodic intervals as the organ of the league or confederation, such assembly having powers for the restoration of harmony and the prevention or resolution of conflicts of the members.

Among other present-day principles of the Organization of American States making their appearance in these early treaties are the renunciation of war; reciprocal respect for the political independence and territorial integrity of the member states; conciliation, investigation, mediation, consultation, and arbitration as methods for dealing with disputes and preserving the peace; a system of sanctions to give obligatory force to the duties of the members of the league; and provisions to prevent the gathering of elements of war or the recruiting of men in the territory of one state for hostile operations against any of the member states.

Lack of ratification by the signatories prevented these treaties from becoming effective. The idea of a political league or confederation of the Americas failed to become a reality. It is easy to isolate the cause of disunity on the all-hemispheric scale. Not only did profound cultural differences exist between the United States and its Latin American neighbors which tended to obstruct an inter-American movement, but the policies of the United States were such as to preclude hemispheric co-operation. In the first place, the United States retreated to a position of extreme isolationism in this epoch, desiring no foreign entanglements. In the second place, manifest destiny and the expansionist tendencies of the United States created a division of the hemisphere; for this expansion took place in part at the expense of a Latin American neighbor, Mexico, and, in addition, the theme of manifest destiny often included the idea of further acquisition of territory in Central America and the Caribbean. Apprehension of such United States expansion divided the hemisphere, bringing forth proposals to read the United States out of the congregation; and at the same time it caused Latin America to seek unity and confederation to protect itself against the United States. This division effectively destroyed the fundamental geographical basis of hemispheric solidarity and also subverted the political basis by excluding a hemispheric nation with a republican form of government, while at the same time attempting to include Brazil with its monarchial form of government.[47]

It becomes somewhat more difficult to explain the failure of the confederation between the Hispanic American nations where cultural differences were not so marked and where there were present the unifying agents of fear of the designs of Europe as well as of the United States, of a presumptive devotion to democratic ideals, and of geographical propinquity. The lack of Hispanic American unity is demonstrated by the facts that never were all of the nations present at the various congresses and, even more important, that the nations failed to ratify the treaties which emerged. Actually the geographic factor proved to be a force of disunity because of the vast distances separating the states and because of the poor communications of the time. In view of easier sea communications with Europe some of the nations, notably Argentina, ridiculed the thought of an American unity and solidarity and objected to the anti-European bias of the inter-American idea. Thus an Argentine foreign minister remarked that it was foolish to speak of the American states as constituting a group of sister states set apart and in opposition to Europe, for the American states had more ties of common interest and sympathy with several of the European states than with each other.[48] Similar theories of democratic and republican government did not tend to unify, for the Latin American nations, although democratic in name, were ruled, by and large, by oligarchic and military dictatorship having little interest in any idea or ideal other than the maintenance of power.

Dr. Alejandro Alvarez states succinctly the difficulties which stood in the way of confederation of the Hispanic American nations. He questions:

How, indeed, were these states to overcome the obstacle of the enormous distances which separated them, the absolute lack of intercommunication, the highly developed spirit of national independence, the bad blood engendered by the boundary disputes, the conflicts over the navigation of rivers, the baneful influences of civil wars due to the personal ambitions of revolutionary leaders, the lack of preparation of the peoples for political life and the want of common traditions?[49]

An organization of American republics through a league or confederation for the maintenance of the peace proved unattainable in this era. Plans for the uniting of the hemisphere were overambitious. Nevertheless, these early congresses and pacts brought to the fore and kept alive the spirit of solidarity and served as models and guides for the inter-American principles and ideals of the future.

PAN-AMERICANISM

With the failure of the second Lima Congress the idea of a confederation of the Americas or even of the Latin Americas was largely abandoned as impracticable. The Bolivarian dream had faltered. The idea or ideal of a regional and international political organization through which the independent nations of North, Central, and South America could and would act together in working out their hemispheric destiny had waned by the middle half of the nineteenth century, but forces were culminating which would see a revival of inter-American co-operation.

This revival was made possible by changes of attitude in both the United States and Latin America. In Latin America the change was exemplified by the dynamism of certain intellectuals who no longer viewed the United States with apprehension as a menace, but on the contrary began to perceive the possibilities of inter-Americanism, and they demonstrated a willingness to accept the leadership of the United States to realize this aim. These leaders were politically impatient with a decadent Europe and tended to see in the United States the wave of the future. The United States was considered a model of Americanism, that is, a nation dedicated to political liberalism embodying value-concepts of liberty, progress, education, and material well-being for all classes. So that the other American nations could realize these elements of modernity, it was necessary for them to emulate the model and further to associate themselves closely with the United States in hemispheric solidarity.

This pro-United States view was strengthened by the fact that relations between the United States and Latin America were on the whole satisfactory during the middle and latter part of the nineteenth century. Expansion southward had ceased, slavery had been abolished, and Latin America had viewed favorably the United States reaction and protests against the French invasion of Mexico, the Spanish reoccupation of Santo Domingo, and the Spanish intervention against Peru. Too, an anti-European feeling had developed in some quarters, aroused by large-scale European economic penetration which was believed to be a form of imperialism — especially when certain European nations had shown inclination to use armed intervention to protect their economic interests in Latin America.[50]

This favorable climate of a renewed inter-American movement would have gone for naught, however, if the United States had continued its hard policy of isolationism; but in the last half of the nineteenth century this policy began to crumble insofar as Latin America was concerned. So true was this that the United States assumed the leadership in the new movement to be called Pan-Americanism. This change in the United States was brought about largely by the efforts of James G. Blaine, Secretary of State of the United States in 1881, who was imbued with the idea of bringing the American states closer together for the promotion of economic co-operation and for the establishment of methods for the peaceful settlement of their disputes.

In his efforts toward economic co-operation, Blaine was motivated by an alarm at the ever increasing European economic penetration in Latin

America and by a desire to increase the trade of the United States with this region at the expense of the old continent. Meanwhile, international conflict involving Brazil, Argentina, Uruguay, and Paraguay had occurred from 1865 to 1870, and in 1879 the War of the Pacific between Chile on the one side and Peru and Bolivia on the other had erupted. Blaine feared that continued conflict in Latin America would lead to European intervention. He sought to overcome these dangers by bringing the nations of the Americas together in a conference where treaties of friendship, arbitration, and trade could be concluded. The War of the Pacific furnished him with justification for issuing invitations in 1881 to the states of the Americas to participate in a congress in Washington the following year to consider and discuss methods of preventing war. The date of assembly was set so far in advance in the hope that the War of the Pacific would have ended by that time. Unfortunately, the congress was postponed. President Garfield was assassinated and was succeeded by President Arthur. Blaine himself was replaced by a new secretary of state who, as the War of the Pacific continued, recalled the invitation.

Nevertheless, Blaine's project was not abandoned. In 1884 the United States Congress authorized a commission of three men to ascertain means of fostering international and commercial relations between the United States and Latin America. The commissioners were to discover whether the nations to the south were disposed to enter into treaties of commerce with the United States and to meet with it in a conference where matters of common interest to the Americas could be discussed. The reports of the commissioners were favorable.[51] In 1888 the Congress of the United States passed an act which authorized the President to invite the American states to a conference to be held in Washington.[52] Secretary of State Bayard then issued invitations to all of the governments of the Americas proposing the following subjects for conference consideration: the promotion of peace upon the continent; the formation of an American customs union; the establishment of steamship lines between the ports of the American states; the establishment of a uniform system of customs regulations; the adoption of a uniform system of weights and measures; laws to protect patents, copyrights, and trademarks as well as for the extradition of criminals; the adoption of a common silver coin; and the formulation of a plan of arbitration of disputes and differences arising between the states.[53]

The conference opened on October 1, 1889, and ended April 18, 1890. Blaine, who was once again Secretary of State, was the presiding officer. All of the independent nations of Latin America, except the Dominican Republic, were represented. The actual results of the conference were somewhat disappointing. All of the items set forth in the invitation as well as others were subjects of discussion, and a series of recommendations were made which were not binding upon the nations represented.[54] The objectives of these recommendations have today been attained only in part. The customs union project was a complete failure, and an important plan for the arbitration of disputes between the American nations failed to be adopted as treaty.[55]

This first Pan American conference did achieve the formal establishment of an international organization under the name of the International Union of American Republics, composed of the nations represented at the conference. This union had as its limited purpose the prompt collection and distribution of commercial information. The organ of the union, called the Commercial Bureau of the American Republics, was to be located in the city of Washington under the supervision of the Secretary of State of the United States. The bureau was assigned the duty of publishing a bulletin containing information with respect to trade and commerce which the union was to seek to promote.[56]

Three additional international conferences of American states were held prior to World War I: at Mexico City in 1901-2, at Rio de Janeiro in 1906, and at Buenos Aires in 1910; but little more in the way of closer political, economic, or social co-operation was accomplished.[57]

In sum, not too much success can be attributed to the Pan American movement or to inter-American co-operation as they stood at the end of some thirty years, on the eve of World War I. On the affirmative side, an institutionalized international organization had come into being, a Union of American Republics having as its principal organ a system of periodic conferences. Moreover, certain special conferences on economic, sanitary, and scientific matters had been held. The Pan American Union as the agent of the Union of American Republics had had its original commercial responsibilities broadened to include cultural and archival matters, and its character as permanent secretariat had emerged. A few special institutions had been created, such as the Pan American Sanitary Bureau and the International Commission of Jurists. The organization had sought to develop ideas of inter-American solidarity and, to express this solidarity, treaties and resolutions had been drafted dealing with matters of commerce, health, finance, science, and a limited number of political matters such as international law and arbitration. By the expression of inter-American law through treaties an attempt had been made to meet one element of effective international organization, i.e., the formulation of law to govern by agreement the relationships of the member states.

Negatively it can be said that the organization which had emerged was extremely weak and restricted in its powers. The conferences had excluded from their agenda most questions of a political nature, that is, those problems concerning the juridical equality, the territorial integrity, the national independence, and the international obligations and rights of the American states. Only the less controversial political questions and questions of an economic and social nature had been permitted to come before these conferences. By the exclusion of many crucial areas from its counsels, the supreme policy-making body of the organization, the conference, was deliberately limited in its powers. Even acting within these restricted powers, the conferences were largely unsuccessful in the formulation of inter-American policy. Resolutions, even when signed by the delegations, were of dubious binding quality, and treaties adopted were all too often ratified by so few nations as to be of little import. Those that became binding as law between the ratifiers were remitted to the individual states for the carrying out of their terms. No judicial or executive power was created to apply and enforce the regional law of the Americas. The Pan American Union, being for the most part a mere informational agency, was not granted such power. In the absence of some central enforcement organ empowered to apply sanctions to transgressors of the law, each state remained free to take such action as it thought necessary to enforce its own rights.

Organization to preserve the peace is basic to community. Co-operation for the purpose of peace, as for other purposes, means organization and effective organization means the creation of institutions with sufficient power granted by the member states to carry out their purpose—to enforce the peace.[58] From this summary it can be readily seen that such an organization was not in existence at this time.

It must be noted that the vision had not been as broad in these years of the Pan American movement as it had been in the earlier era of the Hispanic American movement. One of the primary purposes of the earlier congresses had been to establish a political association of American nations for mutual defense and collective security, and by the Treaty of Perpetual Union of the Congress of Panama the organ, the assembly, was to be granted powers of a judicial and executive nature. Why was the second attempt at an inter-American movement so much more modest in its endeavors? Why was so little accomplished by these first conferences toward the creation of an effective inter-American organization? The answer is simple. Unfortunately, the Pan American movement had its beginning almost simultaneously with the adoption by the United States of an interventionist role in Latin America. This role earned the United States a reputation of seeking to impose its hegemony over the region to the south of it, of imperialism and dollar diplomacy.[59] Despite the Monroe Doctrine, it became clear to the Latin American nations that the United States did not consider itself bound by any non-intervention principle; for United States intervention in certain portions of Latin America, mainly the Caribbean and Central American area, became almost habitual and continued until the establishment of the Good Neighbor Policy in the 1930's. This interventionary policy came to be viewed with aversion by Latin America, and it was only natural that in such a climate Pan-Americanism could not prosper. The exercise of an international police power by a self-appointed policeman was the obstacle in the path of the inter-American movement. So true was this that a Mexican diplomat was prompted to say:

In the previous fifty years before 1933, the United States had intervened some sixty times in the affairs and territories of its Latin American neighbors—especially in the Caribbean . . . how could one speak of inter-American solidarity, Pan Americanism, or good neighborliness when the stumbling block in the path of the good relations was nothing less than the most powerful republic of the hemisphere? The situation could change only if and when the United States decided to abandon once and for all its imperialistic intervention.[60]

These interventions were taken for various purposes and reasons such as to protect the lives and properties of citizens of the United States and other foreigners; to secure the right to construct the Panama Canal; to safeguard and protect the canal after construction; to protect United States financial interests; to enforce the Roosevelt Corollary to the Monroe Doctrine; and, as an outgrowth of a missionary spirit, to right wrongs arising from chaotic revolutionary conditions, to end dictatorship, and to force democratic process.

At the time of these first conferences, however, the most disturbing factor in United States–Latin American relations was the statement of United States foreign policy as contained in the Roosevelt Corollary. As we have seen, economic pentration in Latin America had proceeded at a fast pace during the nineteenth century. Because of conditions of political instability in certain of the countries, the investments of European nationals therein had been placed in jeopardy, and there had followed interventions by the home countries of these nationals to protect their investments. In 1902, for example, a serious armed intervention against Venezuela had occurred when Germany, Great Britain, and Italy had blockaded its coast as a means of forcing Venezuela to settle outstanding claims of their respective citizens.[61] Arbitration as a means of settling the claims had in the end been adopted, but the incident had demonstrated how far European states would go to protect their claims. In view of this experience and because it was believed that unstable conditions of disorder in the Caribbean area were invitations to European intervention, Theodore Roosevelt announced in 1904:

Chronic wrongdoing, or an impotence which results in the general loosening of the ties of civilized society may in America, as elsewhere, ultimately require intervention by some civilized nation, and in the western hemisphere the adherence of the United States to the Monroe Doctrine may force the United States, however reluctantly, in flagrant cases of wrongdoing or impotence, to the exercise of an international police power.[62]

This corollary signified that the United States would intervene in an American state guilty of wrongdoing as judged unilaterally by the United States, to correct the wrongdoing so as to prevent forcible European interventions against that state which might lead to European or non-American territorial occupations in the Americas, which in turn would be a threat to the security of the United States and the hemisphere. In short, intervention to prevent intervention. This was an extension of the Monroe Doctrine, an assumption by the United States of a special unilateral police responsibility for order and stability in the hemisphere to forestall intervention by non-American powers.[63]

A different type of action to halt such European intervention in the Americas was proposed by Luis M. Drago, Foreign Minister of Argentina. As an immediate result of the armed intervention taken against Venezuela, Drago dispatched a note to Washington dated December 29, 1902, which stated in part:

But in very recent times there has been observed a marked tendency among the publicists and in the various expressions of European opinion to call attention to these [Latin American] countries as a suitable field for future territorial expansion. Thinkers of the highest order have pointed out the desirability of turning in this direction the great efforts which the principal powers of Europe have exerted for the conquest of sterile regions with trying climates and in remote regions of the earth. The European writers are already many who point to the territory of South America, with its great riches, its sunny sky, and its climate propitious for all products, as, of necessity, the stage on which the great powers, who have their arms and implements of conquest already prepared, are to struggle for the supremacy in the course of this century ... And it will not be denied that the simplest way to the setting aside and easy ejectment of the rightful authorities by European governments is just this way of financial intervention—as might be shown by many examples.[64]

Drago then concluded that the Americas should adopt as a corollary of the Monroe Doctrine the principle that a public debt cannot occasion armed intervention or the occupation of the territory of an American state by a European power. Here was the nucleus of a new regional policy of the Americas which all of the Americas were to share and to implement multi-laterally to make it effective.[65] The United States squelched Drago's idea, although not openly. Its course of opposition was not outright rebuff of the entire principle but an acceptance in a changed form.[66] At the Rio de Janeiro Conference it succeeded in having the question referred to the Hague Conference of 1907 so that the rule of non-intervention as espoused by Drago could through treaty be made a principle of universal international law. The convention which was proposed at the conference by the United States delegation prohibited the use of armed force for such recovery of contract debts, but not absolutely, for it was provided that such prohibition was not applicable when the debtor state refused to arbitrate or, after arbitrating, failed to submit to the award.[67]

A watered-down version of Drago's Doctrine became a rule of inter-national law as among the nations ratifying it, but no multilateral or collective action to enforce the principle between the Americas or between the nations of the world community was provided, and in the meantime the unilateral policy of the United States as announced by Theodore Roosevelt had been put into action.

The question arises of the reasons for the opposition of the United States to multilateral action by the American republics for the enforcement of Drago's Doctrine. A multilateralization of this proposed extension would surely have brought about demands for multilateralization of Monroe's original pronouncement. To this the United States at this time was unalterably opposed, desiring to go it alone. Conversion of the Monroe Doctrine into a common program to be defined, supported, and applied by all the republics would have had the effect of turning the Pan American movement into an organization with political powers of collective action. This would have created a league or union of nations similar to that desired by Bolívar, authorized to enforce the Monroe Doctrine through action taken by all of its members against transgressors. The power to enforce would have included the power of multi-lateral interpretation. This in turn could well have led to interpretations of the doctrine in a manner not desired by the United States. For example, the American republics might have decided that collective action should be taken against some non-American intervention in instances when the United States did not so desire. And it was not without the realm of possibility that the Latin American states might have interpreted the doctrine so as to add new corollaries, and extensions to the effect that it was also to apply to the interventions of the United States, limiting seriously its freedom of action. As a result the United States refused multilateralization and sought to eliminate consideration of most political matters from the conferences to avoid embarrassing and unpleasant discussions of such factors of United States foreign policy as its application of the Monroe Doctrine and its interventionary role.

In the years following, more formal references to the creation of a political association began to appear on the Pan American scene. For example, at the Third Conference, a delegate of Bolivia suggested the creation of an American superstate;[68] in 1907 José Battle y Ordoñez, a Uruguayan statesman, counseled that the American states should form a league to carry out their foreign policy and to settle their disputes by arbitration;[69] and at the Fourth Conference, the Dominican delegate suggested the creation of a society of American nations with its own executive, legislative, and judicial organs.[70]

When President Wilson came into office he began his administration by repudiating imperialism and dollar diplomacy, but following that, and throughout his tenure, his administration intervened in Latin America possibly more than preceding administrations. True, Wilson was prompted into taking these interventions for the idealistic reasons of encouraging constitutional government and discouraging revolution in the region; but to Latin America such intervention, no matter how good the motive or benevolent the intention, violated fundamental rights of independence and equality.[71] In view of these interventions it is somewhat surprising that Wilson came forth with a reversal of previous United States policy by proposing a treaty known as the Pan American Pact. The Pact provided that the contracting parties, the American republics, join one another in common and mutual guarantee of territorial integrity and of political independence under republican forms of government. It contained articles which related to the settlement of boundary disputes, control of the sale and manufacture of munitions of war, and the settlement of disputes by investigation and arbitration.[72] Had this pact been adopted, a true regional collective security system would have come into existence. A startling aspect of the Pact was that it was intended to multilateralize the Monroe Doctrine. The Pact, however, never got beyond the stage of proposal. The Latin American nations who were sounded out were hesitant to accept it, and later Wilson switched his attention to his global plan for collective security, the League of Nations.

At this era in the history of the Pan American movement it can be seen that little headway had been made in forging political bonds between the Americas. For that matter, little had been done to effectuate a real economic and social co-operation between the United States and the other American states. Continental solidarity was an ideal with little concrete action to back it up.

CHAPTER II

BETWEEN THE WARS

SCHISM

The date of the Fifth Conference of American republics had orginally been set for 1914, but the coming of World War I delayed its convocation until 1923. It was finally convened in Santiago, Chile, on March 25 of that year. Between the Fourth and Fifth Conferences, transformations had taken place in international relationships, chief among them being the creation of the League of Nations which counted among its members all of the American republics except the United States, Mexico, Ecuador, and the Dominican Republic.[1] Latin America was well represented on both the Council of the League and the World Court. The impact of the League and suspicions of United States foreign policy caused an acute situation at this conference, and, where past conferences had limited their discussions almost entirely to social and economic problems, the agenda of the Fifth included many controversial and delicate political questions.[2]

Dr. Baltasar Brum, President of Uruguay, had proposed that the Union of American Republics be reorganized into a regional League of Nations. He was of the belief that an American organization was a logical outgrowth of the Covenant of the League of Nations which by expressly recognizing the Monroe Doctrine seemed to limit the powers of the League in American affairs.[3] A proposal for the formation of a League was placed on the agenda of the conference.[4] It was supported mainly by the Central American and Caribbean nations.[5] The United States delegation was strongly opposed, for in 1923 the United States had reverted to extreme isolationism, and the phrase *League of Nations* whether used in conjunction with the Americas or otherwise, was anathema.[6] A weak resolution was adopted by the conference entrusting the Governing Board of the Pan American Union with the task of studying bases suggested by the various American governments to make their mutual association closer, to promote their common interests, and to make more effective the solidarity of the collective interests of the continent.[7] This innocuous resolution suppressed the conversion of the Union into a League, or the conversion of the Monroe Doctrine into a common program of the American states when encroachment by a non-American power on the rights of an American nation occurred. A Costa Rican proposal for the creation of a stronger inter-American organization by the founding of an Inter-American Court of Justice was also sidetracked by referral to the Congress of Jurists.[8] Other problems suffered a somewhat similar fate, such as that concerning the rights of aliens, which was also referred to the Congress of Jurists for consideration.[9] Compulsory arbitration between American states was rejected, as were proposals for disarmament.[10]

The Latin American nations did, however, obtain a slight reorganization in the Pan American Union. Satisfaction with the composition of the Governing

Board of this organ had been lacking, since its membership had been limited to diplomatic representatives of the American republics accredited to Washington. As a result, if diplomatic relations between Washington and another American republic were ruptured, the latter had no representation on the board.[11] This problem was solved by providing that normally the membership of the board would be composed of regularly accredited diplomatic representatives, but in those instances when a state had no diplomatic representative at Washington that state would be entitled to appoint a special representative.[12] Dissatisfaction with the privileged position of the secretary of state of the United States as permanent president of the board[13] also brought forth a resolution making the presidency and vice-presidency elective.[14] Some had thought that the Pan American Union might ultimately become the Council of the American League of Nations, but this, as we have seen, failed to become a reality.[15]

The conference did adopt the important Treaty to Avoid or Prevent Conflicts Between the American States—the Gondra Treaty.[16] This treaty provided that all controversies between the American republics, which diplomacy had failed to adjust, be submitted to a commission of inquiry for investigation and report. The parties bound themselves to refrain from hostilities or preparation therefor until the report by the commission was rendered. The reports of a commission, however, were not decisions or awards, but in the nature of findings leaving the disputants free to take such further actions as they desired. Here was the defect of the Gondra Treaty as considered in the light of collective organization for peace and the settlement of disputes.

The Fifth Conference interred the dream of Wilson and others for an American League of Nations, and with it defeated the multilateralization of the Monroe Doctrine. That the policy of the United States was one of continued unilateral interpretation and application of the Monroe Doctrine became completely clear when in 1923 Charles Evans Hughes, as secretary of state, declared: "As the policy embodied in the Monroe Doctrine is distinctly the policy of the United States, the Government of the United States reserves to itself its definition, interpretation and application."[17] To Latin America this meant continuation of United States hegemony, the adoption of an arbitrary right by the United States to act as the hemisphere's policeman, and, consequently, a continuation of United States interventionary policy.

Since the United States insisted upon the maintenance of this policy an inevitable reaction occurred. A clamor arose for an absolute doctrine of nonintervention to prevent intervention whether emanating from the United States or from non-American states, and it became a cardinal aim of Latin American diplomacy to formulate a code of public international law in the form of a multilateral treaty containing a renunciation of the right of intervention and binding all American states. It was thought that United States adherence to such a principle would tend to prevent the United States from intervening even to preclude the possibility of European intervention. The United States, if it desired further maintenance of the principles of the Monroe Doctrine under its own unilateral interpretation and application, would be forced to take action against the non-American state seeking to intervene in order to halt such action. It could not take action against the American state in the form of a protective intervention to prevent the non-American intervention. To achieve this purpose the jurists of Latin America made effective use of the inter-American system.[18] For example, renewed steps were taken by the Fifth Conference with respect to the codification of international law by the reorganization of the Commission of Jurists.[19] In 1927 the commission met at Rio de Janeiro and drafted projects of codification, the principles so incorporated to be submitted to the Sixth Conference to be held at Habana the following year. Some twelve important conventions were drafted in the field of public international law. Important as some of these principles contained in the conventions were, the primary interest of Latin America was centered upon the principle contained in project 2 of the commission's twelve projects, which proclaimed: "No state has a right to interfere in the internal affairs of another."[20] If such a principle were adopted it would mean the end of the police power exercised in Latin America by way of intervention.

With this non-intervention principle on the agenda, the atmosphere of the Sixth Conference when it met at Habana in 1928[21] was bound to be electric. In addition, however, and somewhat unfortunately for the success of the conference, the time of meeting came when the United States was being subjected to harsh criticism for its intervention in Nicaragua. These factors made of the Sixth Conference a diplomatic battleground. Political questions which hitherto had been cautiously skirted were brought up for frank discussion and much of the time was spent in a verbal tug of war between conflicting ideas. The result was a new low in Pan-American understanding.[22]

Despite the recommendation of the Commission of Jurists, the non-intervention principle was not adopted, although it was the subject of prolonged and critical dispute. It has been said that the principle would have been accepted had the United States not opposed it, but with actual United States intervention taking place, the time was not propitious for United States adherence. Still, the very fact of these interventions aroused certain Latin American delegates to cry for non-intervention in the Americas and to determine to obtain such a pledge from the United States.[23] The secretary of state of the United States, Charles Evans Hughes, during the course of the conference not only refused to adhere to a principle of non-intervention, but sought to justify temporary interposition where necessary to protect the lives and interests of United States citizens in a foreign nation when conditions of anarchy reigned therein.[24] The debate on the principle of non-intervention took on aspects of battle, with insults and denunciations filling the air. Nevertheless, Hughes managed to block the acceptance of the principle and the issue was postponed. It was resolved that the disputed projects should be subjected to further study by the Commission of Jurists under the auspices of the Pan American Union, the results to be considered at the Seventh Conference when it met in Montevideo.[25]

ACCORD

At the time of meeting of the Seventh Conference in 1933,[26] it was not at all clear that the principle of non-intervention would not meet the same fate accorded it at Habana. There had been a change in administration in the United States and the new President, Franklin D. Roosevelt, had declared:

In the field of world policy I would dedicate this nation to the policy of good neighbor—the neighbor who resolutely respects himself and, because he does so, respects the rights of others—the neighbor who respects his obligations and respects the sanctity of his agreements in and with a world of neighbors.[27]

This policy was to become known as that of the Good Neighbor, but at the time the words were uttered they were subject to the interpretation of being simple niceties binding the United States to no definite policy of non-intervention. Moreover, at conference time, Cuba was involved in political strife. Sumner Welles had been dispatched to that nation to attempt to resolve the controversy, and United States warships had been ordered to Cuban waters as a precautionary measure. In part because of non-recognition by the United States, the government of Dr. Grau San Martín was on the verge of falling. Many Cubans accused the United States of intervention in their affairs,[28] and the Cuban delegate at the conference bitterly denounced intervention in his country, a denunciation which was taken up by other Latin American delegations.[29] The actual interventions by the United States and its attitude as expressed at Habana in 1928 were considered the stumbling blocks to the codification of the principle of non-intervention as American international law and to American solidarity.

Such suspicion of the United States proved, however, to be ill-founded. The United States had changed its policy. Its delegation, headed by Secretary of State Cordell Hull, had been instructed to remove obstacles standing in the way of harmony and friendly relations with Latin America. When the Convention on Rights and Duties of States, which included the principle that no state has the right to intervene in the internal or external affairs of another,[30] was submitted to vote, it was found that the United States had now reversed itself and voted with the Latin American delegations in favor of the convention as a whole. It is true that when it signed the convention it attached a long reservation which in effect signified that the United States reserved its rights as generally recognized by international law,[31] but Secretary of State Hull promised that the government of President Roosevelt would observe the principle of non-intervention.[32]

The Latin American republics received the action of the United States with enthusiasm; still they would have preferred United States adherence with no reservation, for the reservation left the convention and the non-intervention article in doubt. Since rights were reserved under general international law, interventions could still be taken in those areas sanctioned by general international law. Events following the conference, however, proved that the United States intended a policy of non-intervention and removed lingering doubts. Prior to the conference the Army of Occupation had been withdrawn from Nicaragua,[33] and in 1934 Cuba was freed from the burden of the Platt Amendment.[34] United States forces were withdrawn from Haiti in 1934 and financial control in that country was terminated in 1941.[35] In 1936 a new treaty was signed with Panama whereby the United States government gave up the right of intervention, and in 1941[36] a treaty was ratified by which the United States government did away with its legal right to supervise the financial affairs of the Dominican Republic.[37]

Even though non-intervention seemed to be the determined policy of the United States, the Latin American nations were still of the opinion that the right to intervene should be legally abrogated by treaty. At the Inter-American Conference for the Maintenance of Peace, which met at Buenos Aires in 1936,[38] they won a complete victory for non-intervention. The United States adhered without reservation to the Additional Protocol to Non-Intervention:

The High Contracting Parties declare inadmissible the intervention of any one of them, directly or indirectly and for whatever reason, in the internal or external affairs of any other of the Parties.
The violation of the provisions of this article shall give rise to mutual consultation, with the object of exchanging views and seeking methods of peaceful adjustment.[39]

By adopting this protocol the American states restricted themselves to non-intervention. This represented a radical change in the policy of the United States, and prepared the groundwork for a true inter-American security system, the cornerstone of which was also laid at the Buenos Aires Conference. This step toward greater community responsibility came in the form of a treaty, known as the Convention for the Maintenance, Preservation and Reestablishment of Peace, which required the American republics to consult in the event of war in or threat to the peace of the Americas or in event of war or threat of war elsewhere which might affect the peace of the Americas, such consultation being had with respect to war between American states to seek a method of peaceful co-operation and as to international war outside America to co-operate, if the parties desired, in some action tending to preserve hemispheric peace.[40] The language of the treaty was vague. The form of collective security was feeble. Still, recognition of collective responsibility for the maintenance of peace when that peace was threatened by American or non-American sources—the latter provision a step toward the continentalization of the Monroe Doctrine—had come into existence.[41]

Non-American threats to the continent had decreased in the years following World War I. Europe was tired, and during this period the interventionary policy of the United States caused much of Latin America to view this nation as the principal menace to its existence. A geographical division of the continent prevented effective solidarity and hemispheric co-operation. By 1936 war clouds from abroad were once again hovering, causing the American states to react in the face of common danger from extra-hemispheric sources. As in the days of the Holy Alliance, dangers from abroad which might jeopardize the independence of the nations of America acted upon them as a catalyst and caused them instinctively to seek an increased inter-American co-operation to preserve themselves.

Thus, just prior to World War II at the Eighth Conference of Lima, in 1938,[42] the American republics were much preoccupied with hemispheric security in the face of threats from abroad. A Declaration of American Principles was here signed which gave further assurance to Latin America that the United States had accepted the principles of equality and independence and voluntary co-operation.[43] The way was clear for common action to meet the non-American dangers of the day. This came about through the Declaration of Lima which remedied a grave defect in consultative machinery by creating an organ of consultation, the Meeting of American Ministers for Foreign Affairs.[44] Through such meetings the procedure of consultation was to be made effective, and they were to be called when deemed desirable at the instance of any one of the American states.

It was soon necessary to make use of the new organ of consultation to meet the crises engendered by the coming of World War II. In 1939, after the outbreak of war, a Meeting of Foreign Ministers was held in Panama, a meeting which was primarily concerned with the maintenance of hemispheric neutrality in the face of the European conflagration.[45] A doctrine of neutrality was asserted.[46] It declared that the American republics would prevent the utilization of their territories as bases for belligerent operations and would prevent their nationals from engaging in unneutral acts. To keep the normal maritime routes of communications between the Americas free from the commission of hostile acts, a geographical zone of security with definite extent was created.[47] This zone surrounded the republics, extending far out to sea.[48] The governments then agreed to consult if necessary to determine measures to be taken to secure the observance of the Declaration.

The Declaration of Panama was to prove ineffective. The belligerents were officially informed of its terms, but they refused to recognize it.[49] Attempts at enforcement were vain, and the events of 1940, such as the German invasion of Western Europe, soon proved that organization for neutrality was a pipe dream. It became increasingly requisite to organize for defense.

The Habana meeting of 1940[50] witnessed a vastly extended inter-American co-operation to meet the emergency which affected the safety of the continent. It was feared that European territorial possessions in the Americas might fall into Nazi hands as a result of German invasions of the mother countries. It was, therefore, agreed that any transfer of sovereignty over non-American territories to another non-American state would not be in accord with American sentiments and principles and the rights of American states to maintain their security and political independence.[51] This no-transfer doctrine was an expression of United States policy antedating the Monroe Doctrine.[52] At Habana it was multilateralized through agreement of the American republics that in the event of a transfer such regions would be placed under the administration of those nations. Habana also established additional co-operation to prevent subversive activities,[53] as well as economic co-operation to meet the disruption of trade created by the European war.[54] Of great importance was the Declaration of Reciprocal Assistance and Cooperation which extended the principle of collective security in such a way as to create a mutual defense system just short of a defensive alliance. It was stated that an attack by a non-American state against the territory, sovereignty, or political independence of an American state should be considered an aggression against all. Such an attack would occasion consultation to agree upon advisable measures to be taken.[55] The principle was put to crucial test in something like a year and a half. Following the attack on Pearl Harbor the Third Meeting of Consultation was held at Rio to agree on bases for co-operation. Here was an attack upon an American state by a non-American state.[56] Would this be considered an attack against all in accordance with the Habana Declaration? Would there be acceptance of a common responsibility for hemispheric security? Even before the Rio meeting, following the attack on Pearl Harbor, the five Central American states, the three Caribbean states, and Panama had declared war on the Axis powers. Mexico, Venezuela, and Colombia had severed diplomatic relations.[57]

THE RIFT WITH ARGENTINA

The question of prime importance confronting the Third Meeting of Foreign Ministers was to decide on common action to be taken to meet the obligation of the Declaration of Reciprocal Assistance.[58] The United States was of the opinion that the minimum duty was a solidary rupture of diplomatic relations with the Axis powers, inasmuch as their diplomatic and consular posts in the Americas served as centers of propaganda, subversion, sabotage, and espionage which, if permitted to function, would endanger the effort of those neighbors at war.[59] Mexico, Venezuela, and Colombia were of the same strong opinion,[60] but Argentina and Chile, particularly the former, objected to a course of action violative of their neutrality. In the interests of solidarity Argentina finally retreated to a point which permitted the adoption of a weak resolution merely recommending that all the republics break diplomatic relations with Germany, Italy, and Japan.[61] Compliance with this resolution was promptly forthcoming, except for the two recalcitrants.[62]

Chile's defection from her pledge of hemispheric solidarity was occasioned largely by isolationist elements among her population and fear that the United States would be unable to defend her coastline in the event a severance of relations brought war or reprisals from Japan.[63]

These reasons also lay behind Argentina's refusal;[64] but her case was more complex, for throughout most of her history her sentiments toward a regional hemispheric system had been at best lukewarm and for the most part antipathetic.

Argentina had evinced little interest in closer union of the Hispanic American nations in the years subsequent to independence. Her representatives were notably absent from Hispanic American congresses attempting co-operation, except that meeting at Lima in 1864, where she was represented but her delegate had instructions from his government that he was not to vote. Rather early in her history Argentina emphasized that her ties were closer with Europe than with the Americas, a fact explainable partially by the fact of her isolated location at the extreme southern end of the hemisphere, but primarily because of her close economic and cultural affinity with Europe.[65]

This attitude, of course, precluded any idea of actively participating in a hemispheric community, especially one which was to be developed along hemispheric isolationist lines—a closed regional system. In 1902 Dr. Drago of Argentina had attempted a limited continentalization of the Monroe Doctrine,[66] but this advancement of a common regional policy was at variance with Argentina's customary course in relation to inter-American affairs; and after Drago's rebuff from Washington, Argentina reverted to her previous dislike of Monroeism, coolness for an inter-American system of co-operation, and disaffection for United States leadership of a Pan-American movement as well as for the Latin American policy of the United States.[67]

She did attempt to use Pan-Americanism as a forum to attack intervention, particularly that of the United States in Latin America, and as an agency to obtain multilateral acceptance of the Doctrine of Non-Intervention. At the Habana Conference of 1928, the Argentine delegate directly attacked the United States and denounced all forms of intervention.[68] As a result of the refusal of the United States to accept non-intervention, she failed to send representatives to the Washington Conference of 1929 on Conciliation and Arbitration.[69] Thereafter, she used her efforts to obstruct United States attempts to conciliate the Chaco War,[70] sought to postpone the Seventh Conference,[71] and attempted to take over the leadership of Pan America by the introduction in 1932 of a General Anti-War Treaty of Non-Aggression and Conciliation proposed by the Foreign Minister of Argentina, Saavedra Lamas, which was a peace pact offered for acceptance not only to the American republics, but to all nations of the world, and designed as a substitute for the Pan American peace treaties of 1923-29, none of which had been ratified by Argentina. In October, 1933, just prior to the Seventh Conference, Dr. Lamas, at Rio de Janeiro, obtained the signatures of six Latin American nations to this pact and thereafter the Treaty was placed upon the conference agenda.[72]

The change in the United States policy and the efforts of Secretary of State Cordell Hull brought a measure of co-operation between Argentina and the United States at the Seventh Conference. Hull agreed to United States adherence to the Anti-War Pact[73] in return for Argentine support for the United States Resolution on Adherence and Ratification of Inter-American Peace Treaties[74] a resolution, which if followed, would bring about a widespread ratification of such treaties. By this action Hull sought to co-ordinate the Anti-War Pact with previous peace instruments, so as to prevent the development of separate and rival American peace systems.[75] The United States then agreed to the Convention on Rights and Duties of States which contained the ban on intervention.[76]

Ratification by the United States of the Lamas Anti-War Treaty as well as the other conventions signed at Montevideo was prompt.[77] A year was to pass before the Argentines ratified the treaty of their own foreign minister, and Argentina never ratified the other treaties which Lamas had agreed to at the conference.[78]

Believing that the peace of the United States was inextricably linked with that of the continent and in view of the dangerous world situation which was already felt in 1935-36, the United States proposed in 1936 a special inter-American conference for the maintenance of peace (the Buenos Aires Conference), mainly for the creation of a program of continental solidarity and common action to confront extra-continental dangers. Here again divergence of United States and Argentine policy prevented full co-operation. Argentina adopted an attitude of opposition to any plan of solidarity and concerted continental effort directed against European dangers, for she did not care to offend any European power which might endanger Argentine markets in Europe upon which she was economically and financially dependent.

She also opposed a Pan-Americanized Monroe Doctrine because she believed that the United States, as the strongest American nation, would always predominate, and that through such United States domination Argentina might find herself obligated to a course of collective action against her wishes and against her European friends.[79]

Argentine obstructionist efforts were successful to the extent that a weak, loosely knit, voluntary inter-American collaboration was all that resulted from the conference, and she completely blocked the creation of consultative machinery. Although consultation was to occur whenever there was a threat to the peace of the Americas, a war between American states, or a non-American war threatening hemispheric peace, no binding obligation was placed upon the nations to take any action which might result from the consultation, particularly in the case of an extra-continental war, for consultation was provided "To determine the proper time and manner in which the signatory states, if they so desire, may eventually cooperate in some action tending to preserve the peace of the American continent."[80] The use of the words *if they so desire* destroyed obligation.

An interval of two years elapsed between the Buenos Aires Conference and the Eighth Conference of Lima, but the threat of war in Europe had increased and Axis penetration in Latin America had grown steadily.[81] The United States government was desirous of a stronger inter-American declaration of solidarity toward extra-continental threats to hemispheric peace, but again was met by Argentine opposition to any collective stand by the Americas which might be directed against Europe.[82] Secretary of State Hull was to prevail at Lima, however. With the support of many of the Latin American nations, and after a direct appeal to the President of Argentina,[83] unanimous adherence was obtained to the Declaration of Lima, under which the Americas, in case the peace, security, or territorial integrity of an American republic was threatened, proclaimed their common concern and their determination to make effective their solidarity by co-ordinating their respective wills through the procedure of consulation. The Declaration was weakened considerably by a concluding sentence to the effect that the governments would act independently in their individual capacity, recognizing fully their juridical equality as sovereign states.[84]

The Declaration also established that the procedure of consultation was to be carried out by the Meetings of Ministers of Foreign Affairs.[85] Though it was not in the form of a treaty, the United States was prone to interpret it as binding upon the signatory states. Argentina took no such view, as events were to prove.[86]

The Panama meeting was to find harmony between the United States and Argentina, for both nations favored a program of hemispheric neutrality at the time; but Argentina at the Habana Meeting balked at the plan for an inter-American trusteeship system for European colonies in the event of a transfer of such colonies.[87] This was a departure from strict neutrality. Nevertheless, the plan, with slight modifications prevailed, as did Resolution XV of the final act which made an attack against one American state by a non-American state an attack against all, calling for consultation to agree upon necessary common measures.

Despite Argentina's adherence, it was questionable that she, in reality, had changed her neutrality policy or regarded the commitment as binding. When World War II came, any doubt that might have existed was resolved, for

Argentina refused to break with the Axis nations. Total continental solidarity at the Rio meeting was not to be had.

One year after the Rio Conference, Chile did break diplomatic relations;[88] but it was not until 1944, and only after political and economic pressure had been applied, that Argentina finally ruptured relations, and even then she refused to follow up the severance with strong measures to counter Axis activities. The failure of a neutralist Argentina with Nazi-Fascist affiliations to honor her Pan-American commitments following her break with the Axis occasioned additional economic and political sanctions to force the Argentine government to change its foreign policy. Some of these sanctions were multilateral in nature, taken through the Inter-American Emergency Advisory Committee for Political Defense. Others were largely unilateral policy of the United States.[89]

Time was to prove that these coercive measures were for the most part ineffective. The impasse with Argentina was not broken, and as it continued the Latin American nations became restive and apprehensive. The ghost of United States unilateral intervention was raised again in Latin American minds even in face of aversion for Argentina's government, her Axis sympathies, and her breach of American solidarity. A Latin American sentiment developed for a Meeting of Foreign Ministers to resolve the Argentine situation.[90] To cap it all, in October, 1944, Argentina herself requested such a meeting.[91] To this Secretary of State Hull was opposed. He feared that the existing Argentine government which had been refused recognition by most of the other American governments, would, by means of a consultative meeting, gain such recognition without being required to change substantially her pro-Axis policy and that the meeting would be a sounding board for Latin American attacks on United States policy which many South American nations had stated they could no longer support.[92] Nevertheless, increasing pressure was placed upon the United States government from within the nation as well as from Latin American sources. It was believed urgent that a meeting be held to consider not only the Argentine question but other important problems confronting Pan-Americanism.[93]

A compromise was found in a Mexican proposal to call a meeting composed of only those republics co-operating in the war effort.[94] This would exclude Argentina. In early 1945 the Governing Board of the Pan American Union rejected the Argentine request for a Meeting of Foreign Ministers, claiming that "The American nations cooperating in the war effort have agreed through diplomatic channels to hold a conference within the near future to study urgent war and postwar problems, and that the said conference will offer an opportunity to the representatives of the said nations to consider the request presented by the Argentine Government."[95]

THE MEXICO CITY CONFERENCE

The Inter-American Conference on Problems of War and Peace met in Mexico City in February, 1945.[96] Although the problem of Argentina was placed last on the agenda, her absence was felt by the other delegations and sentiment existed for a move which would pave the way for her readmission to the hemispheric community. Resolution LIX, the last resolution of the final conference act, set forth a formula for her return as a member in good standing. The resolution, after deploring the fact that Argentina had not taken the steps which would permit her participation in the conference and after recognizing that the unity of the peoples of the Americas is indivisible and that Argentina was an integral part of the Union of American Republics, expressed the hope that Argentina would "cooperate with the other American nations, identifying itself with the common policy these nations are pursuing, and orient its own policy so that it might achieve its incorporation into the United Nations as a signatory to the joint Declaration entered into by them."[97] The final act of the conference was declared open to adherence by Argentina in accordance with the criteria of the resolution.[98]

This resolution was approved unanimously by the conference and Argentina accepted its terms by declaring war on Germany and Japan, by promising to take measures incident to the state of belligerency, and by preventing and repressing activities that might endanger the war effort of the United Nations or threaten the peace and security of the Americas.[99] On April 4, Argentina's representative in Mexico City signed the final act of the conference[100] and shortly thereafter the American republics, which had withheld recognition of the Argentine government, established, after consultation, diplomatic relations with that government.[101]

The absence of Argentina has raised some doubt as to just what classification the Mexico City Conference could legally be given. It could hardly be considered an Inter-American Conference since Argentina was not invited. Juridically speaking it was a conference of wartime allies. As such, it might be contended that it was not legally competent to effectuate the changes it sought to make in the inter-American system. It has been pointed out, however, that since Argentina did sign the final act the possible lack of legal competence was cured retroactively.[102]

The question of Argentina did occupy an important place at the conference, but the Americas were also confronted with other problems of significance. The primary purpose of the conference was to consider "the participation of America in the future world organization, and the further measures that should be taken to strengthen the inter-American system and the economic solidarity of the continent."[103] In accordance with this stated purpose, two of the most important resolutions adopted related to continental security and to the reorganization of the system.

Resolution VIII, the Act of Chapultepec,[104] was concerned with principles of continental security. It provided in part that *every* attack by a state against an American state should be considered as an attack against the other states which signed the declaration. This was an enlargement of the Habana Declaration, which had been limited to an attack by a *non-American* state against an American state. But the Act of Chapultepec went even farther. For the first time an inter-American instrument provided for collective sanctions to be taken by the consultative organ against an aggressor, sanctions of a political and economic nature as well as those involving the use of armed force. While the Act was adopted as a wartime measure only, it was contemplated that its provisions should be written into a permanent inter-American treaty at the close of the war.

The declaration represented a great advance in the inter-American security system and a tribute to and trust in the United States which, as the strongest nation of the continent, would be likely to dominate any system of sanctions which might be taken. The ready adoption of such provisions by the Latin American states can in part be attributed to the fear of some nations of what seemed to be an ambitious and possibly expanding Argentina, for the nationalistic government of that state was mysteriously talking of reuniting all the nations which in Spanish times had belonged to the Viceroyalty of the Rio de la Plata, and was embarking on a program of rearmament. To meet such a threat inter-American machinery was wanted to surpress or avert any attack upon an American state, whether that attack emanated from the hemisphere or from abroad. By agreement to this principle the strength of the United States would be pledged to the assistance of any attacked state.[105]

The Mexico City Conference also adopted a lengthy resolution dealing with the reorganization, consolidation, and strengthening of the regional system.[106] This had long been needed in order to make the system more effective, but the issue became imperative at Mexico: a new universal international organization then on the diplomatic drawing board constituted a threat to the existence of the regional hemispheric system. This was, of course, the project of world organization resulting from the Dumbarton Oaks discussions which had taken place shortly before the Mexico City Conference. Although Latin America had not been invited to the discussions, the proposals were at hand in Mexico City. To say the Latins took a dim view of these proposals is to understate the case, especially when they learned of the restricted role permitted to regional organizations.[107]

The Mexico City reorganization was, therefore, preparatory to a more drastic reorganization. It was agreed that a draft charter was to be prepared by the Governing Board of the Pan American Union to place Pan America under a permanent constitution.[108]

SAN FRANCISCO

In April, 1945, the Allied Nations met at San Francisco to establish a new organization for world peace and security. The Latin American nations united to make their wills prevail upon three major issues: the admittance of Argentina to United Nations membership, autonomy for regional systems which would include the Inter-American System, and the limitation of the proposed veto power.[109] The United States supported Argentina's bid for membership, and at an early stage of the conference she was admitted.[110] The question of Argentine membership caused a split in the unity of the sponsoring nations, inasmuch as Russia objected violently. Nor was there to be full collaboration of the United States with Latin America on the other two issues. The United States found itself in a difficult position. The interests of this country at the conclusion of World War II had become global, and this inevitably affected its attitude toward American regionalism. The United States had approved the Dumbarton Oaks Proposals which recognized the primacy of the Great Powers in the United Nations through the use of the veto and which subordinated regionalism to the world organization. Latin America was at odds with the United States, for Latin America distrusted and disapproved the Great Power veto in the Security Council, which violated the juridical equality of sovereign states, a principle which to Latin America was a traditional cornerstone of international law and relations. The Latin American republics were also determined to preserve a measure of autonomy and independence for regionalism.[111]

The Latin American stand can be attributed to various reasons. One factor was the realization that the nations to the south would need postwar economic aid; that only the United States would be in a position to furnish such aid on any scale; and that an Inter-American System was beneficial in the securing of such assistance. Moreover, the Latin American position reflected distrust and fear of Soviet Russia and her increased power and affluence. Consequently the nations of Latin America sought at this time to insulate themselves from the current of international communism emanating from Russia, and one way to achieve isolation from the menace was to create such an effective Inter-American System, even though dominated by the overwhelming power of the United States, that a world organization in which Russia would play an important part would have no reason to interfere in the political disputes of the continent. Latin America viewed with distrust a Security Council with supreme authority to intervene in any part of the world, including the Western Hemisphere, to maintain international peace and security, particularly in view of the fact that Soviet Russia was to be a permanent member of that body.[112]

Their fears of Russian domination of the Security Council and of possible attempts by Russia to extend her political system to the hemisphere through the auspices of this organ were probably largely groundless. The United States by use of its veto could preclude any such Security Council action in the Americas.[113]

The Latin Americans were on more solid ground when they argued that the Great Power veto or other obstacle might well prevent the Security Council from taking any action in a situation endangering the peace of the Americas and might also prevent regional action under the resolutions taken at Habana and Mexico City.[114]

Latin America lost the battle of the veto, but her will prevailed in large measure on regionalism. Two powerful members of the United States delegation, Senators Vandenberg and Connally, threw their weight behind a relatively independent regional system and persuaded the other United States delegates to their point of view.[115] As a result, a compromise between universalism and regionalism was written into the Charter in the form of Article 51, which authorized individual and collective self-defense against armed attack until action was taken by the Security Council. This relieved regional organizations of the obligation imposed by the Dumbarton Oaks Proposals, which had required Security Council authorization for action by a regional agency. It provided a legal basis for an inter-American security system contemplated by the Act of Chapultepec.[116]

This compromise was accepted by the Latin American republics only after President Truman promised that the provisions of the Act of Chapultepec would be written into a permanent treaty and that ratification by the United States would follow.[117] This treaty, the Inter-American Treaty of Reciprocal Assistance, was concluded in 1947. It was to be known as the Treaty of Rio de Janeiro.[118] In 1948 the reorganization and strengthening of the regional system of the American community was carried out at the Bogotá Conference. The system was placed on a definite juridical basis through the Charter of the Organization of American States, the Charter of Bogotá.[119] These two treaties and a third, the Pact of Bogotá,[120] also signed at the Bogotá Conference, were meant to be the basic constitutional instruments of the Organization of the of American States.

BOOK II

Legal Characteristics and
Organizational Structure of the OAS

CHAPTER III

BASIC CHARACTERISTICS

THE ESTABLISHMENT OF THE OAS

It is interesting to note that the Inter-American System, as opposed to other important international organizations, lacked a formal conventional or treaty basis prior to the Charter of Bogotá.[1] From 1890 to 1948 it had functioned in accordance with conference resolutions beginning with what may be described as the pre-Bogotá fundamental norm of the organization, the Resolution of April 14, 1890, which created the International Union and its organ, the Commercial Bureau (the Pan American Union).[2] Obviously mere resolutions of conferences are not on the same legal footing as a treaty, but prior to Bogotá the American republics did not see fit to produce a formalized basic instrument of organization. Proposals to establish the Union on a treaty basis had been made on several occasions. As early as 1910 the Director General of the Pan American Union sought, in a report to the Fourth Conference at Buenos Aires, to base the Union on an international convention,[3] a proposal which was repeated at the Fifth Conference held at Santiago, Chile, in 1923.[4] Both conferences continued the Union of American Republics and its organ the Pan American Union much the same as before.

A resolution of the Fifth Conference did authorize the Governing Board of the Pan American Union to present a draft resolution or convention on the Pan American Union to the Sixth Conference.[5] Finally at the Sixth Conference at Habana, in 1928, a Convention on the Pan American Union was signed,[6] but as it was recognized that there would probably be considerable delay in ratification, a resolution containing most of the important points of the convention was also passed.[7] The delegates were wise in the ways of Pan Americana, for the convention never received ratification by all members. Since it failed to become effective,[8] the system continued to proceed on the basis of resolutions.

Explanation and justification can be given for the failure to adopt a fundamental treaty. It was believed by some that a treaty would tend to freeze the organization into the rigid pattern of the written instrument's terms, to prevent flexibility and development step by step on the basis of experience. Resolutions permitted easier change and revision than a written constitution and were more nearly in accord with the empirical nature of the organization. The common law and constitutional forms of Great Britain were singled out to exemplify a system which permitted evolution of law through interpretation in accordance with the times. Similar elasticity was thought to be appropriate to the Inter-American System. There was also a practical reason for clinging to the resolution procedure. It had been amply demonstrated over the years that many inter-American treaties failed to become effective because of lack of ratification, a situation exemplified by the fate of the convention on organization signed at the Sixth Conference.[9]

It cannot be denied that the lack of a constitutional instrument permitted flexibility and promoted the growth of inter-American institutions as circumstances warranted; but that very flexibility had its drawbacks in that new agencies were established whenever the needs of co-operative endeavor demanded. As a consequence the development of agencies was haphazard, and the system became complex, confusing, and cumbersome. Agencies were created with uncertain competencies and insufficient funds. Duplications occurred. The resulting overall lack of integration, co-ordination, and centralization demanded a complete reorganization.

The need having made itself felt for a thorough overhauling of the Inter-American System that would streamline it into a machine adequate to meet the problems of the latter half of the twentieth century, it remained for the Americas to agree to strengthen their system. This agreement was reached at the Inter-American Conference on War and Peace (the Conference of Chapultepec) held in Mexico City in 1945.[10]

The influence upon the reorganization exerted by the Dumbarton Oaks Proposals, which were eventually molded into the Charter of the United Nations,[11] was of highest import. These proposals gave the necessary stimuli to the delegates at Chapultepec to produce the change.[12] Without the influence of the United Nations Charter, the Inter-American System would have probably continued its gradual evolutionary growth based on experience and necessity. But, in the light of the existence of a new overall international organization, it became urgent to give more definite legal form to the regional system of the Americas in order to define and limit the rights and duties of the member states; to define, integrate, and co-ordinate the activities of its organs; and to clarify its relations with the larger international community so that its survival would be guaranteed and it would not be absorbed by the United Nations.

The strengthening and reorganization of the whole Inter-American System as visualized at Mexico was to be based on three documents: (1) a treaty of reciprocal assistance in the event of an attack or threat of aggression from within or without the continent against an American state; (2) an overall charter or organic pact establishing the organizational elements of the system and defining its basic principles and purposes; and (3) a treaty co-ordinating all the inter-American procedures of pacific settlement.

The first basic instrument, the treaty of Reciprocal Assistance or the Rio Treaty, was concluded in 1947 at Petropolis, Brazil, on the occasion of the Inter-American Conference for the Maintenance of Continental Peace and Security. By this treaty a formal collective security system for the inter-American community came into existence. A mechanism was created for consultation and for the joint action necessary to maintain or restore the peace, inclusive of the possibility of the use of armed force.[13]

In accordance with Resolution IX on the Reorganization, Consolidation, and Strengthening of the Inter-American System approved at the 1945 Mexico City Conference, a comprehensive draft organic pact was prepared by the Pan American Union which in revised form was presented to the Ninth International Conference of American States as a basis of discussion. This program of reorganzation resulted in the adoption by the Ninth Conference of the second basic document, the Charter of the Organization of American States (the Charter of Bogotá).[14]

The third basic document, which was also approved at the Ninth Conference, is known as the American Treaty on Pacific Settlement or the Pact of Bogotá. This agreement was designed to meet the need for co-ordination of the hemispheric instruments for the prevention and peaceful solution of inter-American disputes. The Pact of Bogotá was thus designed to constitute the inter-American peace system.[15]

The Charter, the Pact of Bogotá, and the Rio Treaty are then the basic documents of the OAS. These and other agreements and resolutions which have established specialized agencies and have brought them into formal relationship with the organization make up the constitutional framework of the Organization of American States.

LEGAL FOUNDATION OF THE OAS

The instrument signed at Bogotá in 1948 as the organic pact of the inter-American juridical community is entitled "Charter of the Organization of American States."[16] These words constitute the title of the legal instrument and also designate the name of the organization which the American states have established by it. This Charter may be defined as a constitution of the OAS by which its powers and functions are granted and defined. As a constitution it is not a constituent act of the peoples of the American states. To the contrary, it is an agreement voluntarily entered into by the American governments. The contractual nature of the Charter is illustrated by the fact that the instrument itself declares it to be an agreement among the states represented. The preamble begins with the words "[In] the name of their peoples the States represented at the Ninth International Conference of American States" and ends with the declaration that these states "have agreed upon the following Charter of the Organization of American States."[17]

The American states have employed the customary legal technique, the multilateral treaty, to achieve their co-operative endeavor. The legal foundation of the organization is a treaty, the legal obligation being derived from the international law principle that states are bound by their agreements and must carry them out in good faith.[18]

The Charter, however, was not a legally binding obligation at the conclusion of the Bogotá Conference. Article 108 required ratification by the states in accordance with their respective constitutional processes. Legally binding validity was made dependent upon ratification. Moreover, Article 109 set forth the requisite that the Charter was not to enter into force among the ratifying states until two-thirds of the signatory states had deposited their ratifications. This condition was complied with on December 13, 1951, when the necessary two-thirds was obtained with the deposit of the instrument of ratification by Colombia.[19] As of this date the Charter had legal force among the states which had ratified. For states ratifying after this date, the Charter entered into force after the deposit of their ratification. The last ratification of an American republic was deposited in 1956;[20] therefore, the Charter is now in force for all of the states of the hemisphere except Canada, the new Caribbean nations which obtained their independence in 1962, and Castro's Cuba. When the OAS was placed on a treaty basis, it was presumed that changes or modifications in its structure could no longer be brought about by mere resolution as in the past. Any such changes in the future would have to be made by the much more complicated method of amendment of the charter, which can only occur at an Inter-American Conference called for that specific purpose. An amendment enters into force only after the same procedure that is required for ratification.[21]

The juridical foundation of the OAS does not rest on the Charter alone. The American states had provided not one treaty but three treaties of a constitutional nature to govern inter-American co-operation. This contrasts with the United Nations, which has but a single basic instrument, its Charter. In addition to the Charter of the OAS, the other two basic documents are, as we have seen, the Inter-American Treaty of Reciprocal Assistance (Rio Treaty)[22] and the American Treaty of Pacific Settlement (Pact of Bogotá).[23]

Although the Charter does contain sections on the rights and duties of states and certain principles which should govern the relations of the American states and their relations with the United Nations, its prime importance is related to the composition, competence, and functions of the organs of the OAS. The Charter incorporates the Rio Treaty only by reference,[24] not textually. As a result it becomes necessary to consult the latter treaty in the all-important field of collective security—i.e., as to the obligations placed upon the member states and the powers granted to the organization in relation to the maintenance and enforcement of the peace of the hemisphere. The Charter does set forth obligations for the pacific settlement of disputes,[25] but it then provides that a special treaty be drawn up to establish specific procedures for the settlement of disputes.[26] This was done, and the result was the Pact of Bogotá, the third pillar of the OAS.

This latter instrument was subjected to such vital reservations[27] by the signatory states and has received such a small number of ratifications[28] that it is of little importance at this time.[29] It provides, upon ratification, for supersedure of all the treaties pertaining to peaceful settlement formerly adopted.[30] Since ratification has been so scant, the preceding treaties of pacific settlement are still applicable among states which have accepted them and failed to ratify the pact. However, ratification of a number of these former treaties was also poor. Confusion therefore exists in this field, for it may well be difficult to find a treaty binding any two parties to a dispute.

It should also be pointed out that certain activities and agencies of the OAS are not covered by these instruments. The Inter-American Peace Commission, which was provided for by a resolution adopted at Habana in 1940, is not mentioned.[31] In addition, no attempt was made to bring semi-official agencies within the framework of the treaties, although agreements may be made with them by the OAS to establish bases of co-operative relations if such agencies are of recognized international standing.[32]

THE LEGAL NATURE OF THE OAS

Whenever an international organization comes into existence there arises the perplexing problem of what, in the eyes of the law, is the exact nature of the organization. When a treaty creating an international organization is ratified, the nations which have created the organization must determine what species of creature they have spawned. What manner of creature have the American states spawned in the creation of the OAS?

Article I of the Charter declares:

The American States establish by this Charter the international organization that they have developed to achieve an order of peace and justice, to promote their territorial integrity, and to defend their independence. Within the United Nations, the Organization of American States is a regional agency.

International Organization

Article I defines the inter-American juridical community as an international organization. This term refers to a voluntary association of separately organized nations for the achievement of a common purpose or purposes through their joint action or co-operation, and the body of institutions and procedures which they have brought into existence necessary to assure effective co-operation.

Co-operation of nations is, of course, a vital force of the international community, and although through the history of the community of nations the prevailing notion has too often been each state for itself and the devil take the hindmost, still in more modern times this basing of the relations of states upon rivalry and competition pure and simple has to some extent given away to co-operative action for the solution of common problems. Since collaboration of nations creates a need for the maintenance and development of the common interest, and since the pursuance of international relations solely through national instrumentalities has often been found wanting, states have found that an efficacious mode to assure collaboration is an appropriate international organization. Therefore, the growing interdependence of states and the need for carrying on general international business has given rise to the notion that the satisfaction of certain national interests and policies on an international scale requires active co-operation with other nations. This co-operation in turn demands international institutional mechanisms through which the members of the international community may act co-operatively.[33]

The basic instruments of the OAS form a constitution for a regional system of international organization. The Charter deals with the composition, competence, and functions of the organs or institutions of the organization. A constitutional agency is established with specified powers to perform certain designated functions. Although the power delegated is restricted, the range of functions is broad, covering the whole gamut of inter-American political, social, economic, and cultural co-operation.[34] The fact that the OAS is an institutionalized international organization possessing some power or authority signifies that such power has come from the nations which have created it. The voluntary act of combining into the international organization involves a partial surrender by each state of a measure of sovereignty, for power is granted to the OAS and the authority of the OAS within its proper and limited sphere automatically brings into being a mandatory element of power over its members subject to its ordering powers.[35]

In the field of municipal law, constitutional law controls the functions of the state and the rights, duties, and powers of its organs. The OAS is similarly conditioned by a body of rules that may be described as international constitutional law of the Americas or inter-American constitutional law. It has important duties to perform on behalf of the American community; its basic instruments provide that community with its constitutional framework. Although the constitutional structure by no means follows with exactitude the same pattern as in the constitution of a state, there are analogies, and the organs of the OAS do perform as organs of the society of American nations certain functions which can be roughly compared to the executive, legislative, and judicial functions of the state.

This is not to say that the OAS is endowed with power necessary to fulfil purposes which, in relation to the individuals of a state, are performed by the government of that state. Power for making, interpreting, and enforcing law in a complete, overriding, and coercive manner has not been granted to the organization. A surrender of a much larger amount of sovereignty than the American states have been willing to sacrifice would be necessary for the accomplishment of such a broad design.

Nevertheless, the states have united by the treaty method into an international organization to co-operate upon certain common problems which they feel can be more easily attained through united action, and some authority over the member states has been granted to the central agency to enable it to act to realize the group objectives. It would seem very definitely that in the OAS there exists an institution with certain governing power, albeit restricted or limited governing power, for the inter-American community. Possibly it is so restricted that the unsatisfactory *quasi* should be used before the term *governing;* but, to a degree, controlling authority has been granted.[36]

To speak of inter-American constitutional law, of a central agency composed of organs with governing or quasi-governing powers over the member states, conjures up the early Latin American dream of an American confederation of states, or in more modern parlance, a superstate or supra-national government.

The fact that the member states were called upon to delegate certain controlling power to the OAS, that they were to surrender some sovereignty by a formal treaty with legally binding validity upon ratification, caused apprehension at Bogotá. This is well illustrated by the sharp debate that developed at the conference over the issue of the organization's name—the third change of name for the inter-American organization. In 1890[37] the name International Union of American Republics was adopted. This title was changed in 1910 to the Union of American Republics.[38] The latter continued as the official designation until 1948, although the Ninth Resolution of the 1945 Mexico City Conference introduced an innovation in characterization when it spoke in terms of the "Inter-American System."[39] The same term was used in the draft organic pact drawn up by the Governing Board of the Pan American Union as a basis of discussion for the Ninth Conference.[40] This nomenclature was destined to be short-lived, for little support was forthcoming for "Inter-American System" at the conference. As an official designation it was claimed that the term "system" lacked juridical attributes.[41]

Strong opposition manifested itself to the use of any such name as union, association, or community, and, at first, even to organization on the ground that no implication should be made that the Americas were creating a superstate— i.e., an authority superior to its component parts, the member states, or an entity which might encroach upon the national sovereignty of the member states. Although the term *union* had long been in existence to designate the western hemispheric organization, still it was believed in some quarters that to use the same term in relation to a formal treaty-based organization would be to imply the establishment of a superstate—an implication not intended by the parties. Thus, the less certain term *organization* was used to signify the voluntary association of American states.[42]

Confederation of States

What, then, is the juridical nature or legal character of the OAS? Does it fall within any familiar type of legal relation between states? May it be described as a superstate? It all depends on how the term is defined. If the word *superstate* is meant to convey the thought that a federal state, which for international purposes is a single state, has come into existence, then the answer must be in the negative. A federal state in its most perfect form is generally thought of today as a union of several states, created either by treaty or by the mutual adoption of a constitution by which the states agree to surrender to a central government certain of their sovereign powers, and the central authority in exercising these powers acts directly not only over the member states, but also over their citizens. So far as concerns the residue of powers, generally of a local nature, not granted to the federal authority the competencies of the separate states remain unimpaired. With respect to the constitutional division of powers as between the states and the federal authority, international law has interest only to the extent that the control of external relations of all the member states has been transferred to the central government, so that the only state which exists for international purposes is the state formed by the union.[43]

From this brief and somewhat synthetic description of a federal state, it becomes clear that such a status has not been accorded the Organization of American States. There has been no such broad surrender of external sovereignty by the American republics to the central organization. Members have largely retained their individual capacity for action in the control of their external relations, i.e., in their power to make treaties and to send and receive diplomatic representatives. They have, of course, limited their power to make war. But an even more important fact prevents classification of the OAS as a federal state. The organs are not empowered to act directly or immediately upon the citizens of the member states. The organization can make legally binding decisions applicable only to the member states. The states of the OAS have not lost their international personality, and there has been no new composite personality created in the form of a federal state with all the rights and duties of such a sovereign state in international law.

But to say that a new federal state has not come into being is not to exhaust all types of legal relations between states. The member states have agreed to limit their sovereignty in certain ways and have, by their delegation of power within a framework of obligations and rights, brought into being an authority or power which in a limited way is superior to the autonomous and unilateral will of each of the member states, although the force emanating from this superior power acts only upon the member states and does not act upon the individual.[44]

As such it seems to fall within that type of relationship between states called a confederation, which is an association of a number of independent states bound together by an international treaty into a union with organs of its own for the purpose of maintaining the external and internal independence of all.[45] The essential difference between it and a federal state is that the central authority is vested with certain power over the member states, but not over the citizens of those states. Although the constituent states do consent to forego a part of their liberty of action for certain specific objects, they leave themselves in other respects sovereign and independent and thus maintain their international personality. They are not so combined under a common government that the latter appears to their exclusion as an international entity. Thus, a union of confederated states does not possess the full international personality of a state. For international purposes there exists not one state, but a number of states.[46]

The OAS may be described as a loose confederation of states with central organs of limited competence which are rudimentary governmental institutions. Although they possess some authority, there is no predominant or preponderate power of final decision. For the enforcement of its decisions the OAS must depend on the good faith of its members, for they retain control of their armed forces and their financial resouces. No allegiance can be claimed from the citizens of the member states, nor can direct contact be established with them. The essence of the sovereignty of the states is unaffected, remaining with each member; and the system, if it is to function in order to fulfil its ambitious objectives, rests on the good faith of the members, which may often falter when the primary national interest outweighs what the nation believes are the benefits it will gain from co-operative action.[47]

International Personality

The American states have relied upon the confederate pattern of political organization for their juridical community. Nevertheless, the OAS would not seem to be just an association of member states. It is the legal organization of the inter-American community and, as such, is a distinct entity possessing some measure of legal personality of its own apart from that of its members. Juridical personality signifies that an entity is a subject of legal rights and duties, capable of performing transactions and of participating in legal proceedings. An international organization possesses legal personality if the members, by the constituent treaty, confer upon its organs power to exercise certain functions in relation to the members, and particularly the competence to enter into treaties or agreements with other subjects of international law.[48]

In a sense the rights and duties of the organization are the rights and duties of its component parts, the members; but since they are to be exercised in a collective method by the organs of the organization, they become the rights and duties of the organization and are different from the rights and duties of the individual members.

There are two important possibilities with regard to the juridical nature of an international organization. First, the international organization may be likened to a corporation; that is, an entity with a personality and existence distinct from the legal personalities and existence of the individual states which are signatories to the treaty, with rights and duties distinct from those of any or all of its members. In other words, in the eyes of the law the organization is a sort of quasi-person, fictitious and non-physical. The second possibility is that the international organization may be likened to the common law idea of partnership; namely, an association in which each member has a dual legal personality—a personality with reference to group affairs which is distinct from its personality with reference to individual affairs. The assocation is then not a fictitious person or quasi-person or a legal entity in and of itself. The problem resolves itself into the question of whether the international organization is a thing of itself, or is merely a method, a *modus operandi*.

In either instance it is a question of what the parties drawing up the constituent treaty of the organization stipulated. All international organizations must operate on two levels — the level of international law and the level of municipal law.[49] To this rule the OAS is no exception. It functions primarily on an international level, to perform the duties of attaining hemispheric co-operation in the fields assigned to it. But in order to function it must also operate on the level of municipal law; for it must in its own name be able to acquire property, to hire employees and to make contracts, and to institute legal proceedings.

Although the preamble does declare that "juridical organization is a necessary condition for security and peace founded on moral order and on justice," nowhere in the Charter is the legal status of the OAS on the international level clearly defined. Nevertheless, it can be deduced that the OAS does have a legal personality distinct from the legal personalities of the individual states which comprise it, for legal powers and responsibilities are attributed to it. For example, the performance of almost all legally important functions of the OAS for the maintenance of peace and security of the hemisphere is conferred upon the Organ of Consultation or the Provisional Organ of Consultation, the Meeting of Consultation of Ministers of Foreign Affairs or the Council respectively.[50] Articles 3, 6, and 7 of the Rio Treaty empower these organs to take measures of enforcement in case of armed attacks against American states or in case of other aggressions or situations which endanger the peace of the hemisphere.

Article 8 sets forth the measures which these organs can take, while Articles 17 and 20 make the non-forceful measures, agreed upon by these organs by a two-thirds vote, binding upon all the members. In these instances do these organs act on behalf of a legal entity, i.e., the organization itself, or only on behalf of its members, as agents or representatives for the members? As has been noted, the members are obligated to carry out the decisions of these organs. If they act only as agents of the members this would bring about the anomalous position of the principal being subordinate to the decisions of the agent.

Furthermore, these organs may take enforcement action against the will of certain members of the OAS, and in such cases they cannot be acting on such members' behalf. It would seem more logical to conclude that these organs act on behalf of the organization and not on behalf of its members and that, therefore, the OAS must have juridical personality over and above the juridical personality of each of its members.

Other evidences of juridical personality of the OAS on the international level may be noted. The OAS has capacity to make agreements apart from its members. Paragraphs d and e of Article 53 of the Charter empower the Council of the OAS to conclude agreements with other inter-American organizations and with the United Nations. Moreover, Article 89 enjoins the employees of the Pan American Union in the performance of their duties not to seek or receive instructions from any government or any authority save the Pan American Union and requires them to refrain from action that might reflect upon their position as international officials responsible only to the Union.

From this summary it is apparent that there exists a centralized community in the form of the OAS, with competence to perform the duties and exercise the rights and competences of the community.[51] Not only can the conclusion be reached from an analysis of the basic instruments of the OAS that the OAS possesses legal personality on the international level, but also analogies in this respect can be made to the United Nations, which, in an advisory opinion on the subject of reparations for injuries suffered in its service, was held by the International Court of Justice to have a juridical personality separate from those of its members. The court stated:

In the opinion of the Court, the Organization was intended to exercise and enjoy, and is in fact exercising and enjoying, functions and rights which can only be explained on the basis of the possession of a large measure of international personality and the capacity to operate upon an international plane. It is at present the supreme type of international organization, and it could not carry out the intentions of its founders if it was devoid of international personality. It must be acknowledged that its Members, by entrusting certain functions to it, with the attendant duties and responsibilities, have clothed it with the competence required to enable those functions to be effectively discharged.

Accordingly, the Court has come to the conclusion that the Organization is an international person. That is not the same thing as saying that it is a State, which it certainly is not, or that its legal personality and rights and duties are the same as those of a State. Still less is it the same thing as saying that it is a "super-State," whatever that expression may mean. It does not even imply that all its rights and duties must be upon the international plane, any more than all the rights and duties of a State must be upon that plane. What it does mean is that it is a subject of international law and capable of possessing international rights and duties, and that it has capacity to maintain its rights by bringing international claims.[52]

In reaching a conclusion as to the legal personality of the United Nations the court resorted to standards in the United Nations Charter similar to those mentioned above which are accorded to the OAS under its constituent documents. Particularly was the court of the opinion that international legal personality was indispensable to the United Nations to carry out the ends of the organization; that it was a political body employing political means in dealing with its members and was charged with political tasks of an important character covering a wide field such as the maintenance of international peace and security, the development of friendly relations among nations, and the achievement of international co-operation in the solution of problems of an economic, social, cultural, or humanitarian character.[53] The OAS has been entrusted with similar political powers and political tasks covering similar fields. Therefore by analogy the OAS possesses the international legal personality necessary for the exercise of its functions and the accomplishment of its purposes on the regional level which the United Nations possesses on the world level.

Even though an international organization is admitted to have legal personality on the international level, it does not necessarily follow that it has such personality on the municipal law level. This would depend upon the internal law of each individual state.[54] When a new international organization is formed, provision can be made in two ways for its legal capacity in the territory of the member states. One method is to embody specific arrangements in the constitution of the organization. In that case, each member is obligated to take such steps by executive action or special legislation as may under its own constitution be necessary to grant the organization legal personality on the national level.

The other method is to state the principle of legal personality on the national level in general terms in the constitutive instrument of the organization, and leave the details to be added either by independent national action or by international conventions regulating national action. This method was chosen by the United Nations, the Charter of which states in Article 104: "The Organization shall enjoy in the territory of each of its members such legal capacity as may be necessary for the exercise of its functions and the fulfillment of its purposes."[55]

The same method was chosen for the OAS. Article 103 of the Charter of Bogotá reads much like Article 104 of the Charter of the United Nations: "The Organization of American States shall enjoy in the territory of each member such legal capacity, privileges and immunities as are necessary for the exercise of its functions and the accomplishment of its purposes." By this language there is imposed upon all the members the obligation to grant to the organization juridical personality in the field of national law to the extent necessary to perform legal transactions for the achievement of its purposes.

In 1948 the Council of the organization appointed a committee to study the most effective way to carry out the provisions of Article 103 as well as of Articles 104[56] and 105.[57] This study culminated in an Agreement on Privileges and Immunities of the Organization of American States[58] and a bilateral agreement to be signed by the organization and the government of the United States according additional privileges and immunities to be granted to representatives on the Council of the organization.[59] The multilateral agreement on privileges and immunities was opened for signature at the Pan American Union in 1949,[60] and is subjected to the approval of the appropriate authorities in each member state.[61] The privileges and immunities granted are similar to those granted to the United Nations.[62]

Since the organization functions by means of its organs, Article I of the agreement provides that the privileges and immunities of the organization shall be those which are granted to its organs and to the personnel thereof.[63] As a consequence, the organization and its organs, their property and assets enjoy immunity from legal process.[64] The premises of the organization and its organs and their archives are made inviolable. Their property and assets are also immune from search, requisition, confiscation, expropriation, and any other form of interference,[65] and are exempt from direct taxes, customs duties, and prohibitions and restrictions on exports and imports.[66] Power is granted to the organization and its organs to hold funds, and freedom is given to transfer these funds and to convert any currency held into another currency.[67] The Pan American Union is empowered to contract; to acquire and dispose of movable and immovable property; and to institute legal proceedings.[68]

Not only does the Charter impose an obligation upon the member states to grant legal personality to the organization, but Article 104 provides: "The Representatives of the Governments on the Council of the Organization, the Representatives on the Organs of the Council, the personnel of their Delegations, as well as the Secretary General and the Assistant Secretary General of the Organization shall enjoy the privileges and immunities necessary for the independent performance of their duties." In accordance with this provision and with Article 105 relative to the Pan American Union, certain privileges and immunities are granted to officials and personnel. Article 7 of the agreement provides that the representatives of the states which are members of the organs as well as the personnel of the delegations "shall, while exercising their functions and during their journey to and from the place of meeting, enjoy the following privileges and immunities:" immunity from personal arrest or detention and from seizure of their personal baggage; inviolability for all papers and documents; the right to use codes and the right of correspondence by courier in sealed bags; exemptions for themselves and their spouses from immigration restrictions, alien registration, or national service obligations in any state they visit or through which they pass in the exercise of their functions; the right to be accorded the same facilities respecting currency or exchange restrictions accorded to representatives of foreign governments on temporary official missions; the right to be accorded the same facilities as to their personal baggage which are granted to diplomatic envoys; and such other privileges, immunities, and facilities not inconsistent with the foregoing as diplomatic envoys enjoy, except that they shall have no right to claim exemption from customs duties on goods imported other than their personal baggage or from excise duties or sales taxes.

Article 8 grants to the secretary general and assistant secretary general as well as their spouses and minor children the same privileges and immunities as are granted to diplomatic envoys.

Officials and members of the staff of the Pan American Union are granted immunity from legal process for words spoken or written or acts performed in their official capacity, from national service obligations except as required by the state of which they are nationals, and together with their spouses and dependent relatives from immigration restrictions and alien registration. Their salaries from the Pan American Union are to be granted the same exemption that officials of the United Nations enjoy; they are to be accorded the same privileges concerning exchange facilities as are granted to officials of comparable rank forming part of a diplomatic mission to the government concerned; they are to have the same repatriation facilities in time of international crisis as diplomatic envoys; and they have the right to import free of duty furniture and household effects at the time of first taking up their post in a country.[69]

Unfortunately, this multilateral agreement on privileges and immunities has not received widespread approval from the member states, and the United States, which is the seat of much of the activities of the organization—for example, the Council and the Pan American Union—has not ratified it.[70] This failure of the United States to approve has been partially cured by the enactment by the Congress, in 1945, of the International Organizations Immunities Act.[71] To be eligible to receive the privileges set forth in this Act, the President of the United States must first designate by executive order those international organizations entitled to them, and each individual person must be notified to and accepted by the secretary of state as a representative or officer or employee of a designated organization.[72] In 1946 the President designated the Pan American Union along with the United Nations and other international organizations as entitled to the privileges and immunities enumerated in the Act.[73]

The Act grants to recognized public international organizations similar privileges and immunities in the United States as those accorded to foreign embassies and diplomatic officers and somewhat similar to those granted in the Agreement on Privileges and Immunities of the OAS. As to the status which the organization is to enjoy, Section 2 declares: "(a) International Organizations shall, to the extent consistent with the instrument creating them, possess the capacity—(i) to contract; (ii) to acquire and dispose of real and personal property; (iii) to institute legal proceedings."

It will be remembered that the Agreement on Privileges and Immunities of the OAS grants these competences to the Pan American Union. The Charter, however, does not in so many words set forth these competences as possessed by this organ; still it does grant legal capacity necessary for the exercise of the functions and the accomplishment of the purposes of the organization. As the central and permanent organ of the OAS with its seat in Washington, it can hardly be doubted, particularly in the United States, that the Pan American Union is possessed of legal personality to this extent as necessary for the performance of the functions entrusted to it.[74]

Certain defects of the International Organizations Immunities Act are apparent. It has been made applicable only to the Pan American Union and not to the organization as a whole. Moreover, it is an extension of privileges and immunities on a basis of unilateral comity by the United States. Consequently, the privileges and immunities do not rest on a treaty right under international law, although if the United States failed to give such legal capacity and privileges and immunities necessary for the functioning of the organization, there would be a violation of the Charter. It may further be noted that some derogation from the status of international organizations is accomplished by the act, as evidenced by the fact that the secretary of state is authorized to withhold the privileges and immunities concerned if an officer of an international organization is found unacceptable for entry into the United States.[75]

In addition to the drafting of the multilateral agreement on privileges and immunities, the Committee of the Council in 1948 also drafted a separate bilateral agreement between the organization and the government of the United States in order to grant privileges and immunities to the representatives on the Council over and above those granted in the multilateral agreement.[76] This agreement was necessary to correct certain inequities in the legal status of representatives of Latin American nations on the Council. The Charter in Article 48 states that the representatives on the Council are to have the rank of ambassador. Nevertheless their position at the seat of the Council in Washington was not clearly defined. As a consequence, an anomaly occurred. Certain Latin American representatives to the Council were also ambassadors of their respective countries accredited to Washington. As ambassadors, they enjoyed full diplomatic status, with the privileges and immunities conferred because of that status. Other Latin American nations named their ambassadors to Washington and in addition designated representatives or ambassadors to the OAS. Because of lack of legal authorization, these representatives to the OAS who, under the Charter, held the rank of ambassadors, could not be granted the consequent privileges and immunities. The bilateral agreement was meant to remedy this situation and to permit all representatives of a member state on the Council and the permanent members of any nation's delegation to enjoy the privileges and immunities enjoyed by all diplomatic envoys accredited to the United States.[77] This bilateral agreement was approved between the parties in 1952. Therefore, representatives of the Latin American states on the Council and members of their delegations receive in general the privileges and immunities which the government of the United States accords to diplomatic envoys accredited to it.

Regional Agency

Through the Charter of Bogotá the OAS becomes a regional agency of the United Nations. This is explicitly stated in Article I: "Within the United Nations, the Organization of American States is a regional agency." The fact that it is a regional agency in conformity to and in harmony with the United Nations Charter is brought out in several other places of the Charter of Bogotá. The preamble contains the resolve of the American states "to persevere in the noble undertaking that humanity has conferred upon the United Nations, whose principles and purposes they solemnly reaffirm." In Article 4, the essential purposes of the organization are proclaimed "in order to put into practice the principles on which it is founded and to fulfill its regional obligations under the Charter of the United Nations." Article 102, as a separate chapter of the Charter of Bogotá, declares: "None of the provisions of this Charter shall be construed as impairing the rights and obligations of the Member States under the Charter of the United Nations"; while Article 53e makes it a duty of the Council of the OAS "To promote and facilitate collaboration between the Organization of American States and the United Nations." The organs of the Council are also directed to co-operate with corresponding organs of the United Nations. Resolution XXXIX of the Bogotá Conference provides for the participation of the United Nations in the Inter-American Conferences and Meetings of Consultation.[78] Article 110 provides for the registration of the Charter with the Secretariat of the United Nations.

Despite these provisions, care is taken to preserve the relative autonomy or independence of the OAS in hemispheric affairs. Article 20 requires international disputes arising between American states to be submitted to inter-American procedures before being referred to the Security Council. The Charter incorporates the Rio Treaty and thus assures a hemispheric collective security system in many respects independent of the United Nations, although in conformity with it.[79] Moreover, Article 100 protects inter-American agencies from being absorbed by the corresponding agencies of the United Nations. Although collaboration is called for, stipulation is made that the inter-American agencies shall preserve their identity and status as integral parts of the OAS even when they perform regional functions of other international agencies.

In reality, to describe the OAS as a regional agency is somewhat charitable —that is, if one thinks of a regional agency as dependent and subordinate in character. Only in the very restricted area of Articles 34 and 35 and 51-54 of the United Nations Charter is it a regional agency; hence, for the most part it operates independently of the United Nations, and stands as an equal.[80] Although collaboration is required, it is not what would be considered as that of inferior to superior.

Chapter VIII, Articles 52-54 of the United Nations Charter deals with regional arrangements or agencies. Article 52 declares:

Nothing in the present Charter precludes the existence of regional arrangements or agencies for dealing with such matters relating to the maintenance of international peace and security as are appropriate for regional action, provided that such arrangements or agencies and their activities are consistent with the Purposes and Principles of the United Nations.

Although regional arrangements are permitted, no definition of the term "regional arrangements" is attempted. The Egyptian delegation at the San Francisco Conference proposed the following definition:

There shall be considered as regional arrangements organizations of a permanent nature grouping in a given geographic area several countries which, by reason of their proximity, community of interests or cultural, linguistic, historical, or spiritual affinities, make themselves jointly responsible for the peaceful settlement of any dispute which may arise between them and for the maintenance of peace and security in their region, as well as for the safeguarding of their interests and the development of their economic and cultural relations.[81]

The committee which considered this definition rejected it on the ground that while it clearly defined obvious, legitimate, and eligible factors for a regional arrangement it probably failed to cover all the situations which might be encompassed by the term.[82] A quest to probe and explore the outermost limits of the term "regional arrangement" for the purpose of fitting certain associations of states into a pattern of regional arrangement might confront the prober with some difficulty. No such difficulty is encountered in the case of the OAS, for it obviously fits easily into the above-mentioned and usual definition of "regional arrangement." The OAS is an organization of a permanent nature formed by the nations of the Western Hemisphere—a geographical area. Except for linguistic affinity, the reasons for the association set forth by the Egyptian delegation (proximity, community of interests, cultural, linguistic, historical, or spiritual affinities) are all met in varying degrees. The OAS fulfils the three purposes of a regional arrangement. It aims at the pacific settlement of all disputes among the member states, and through the Pact of Bogotá they have attempted to set forth the various methods to be employed to settle their disputes. The member states make themselves jointly responsible for the maintenance of peace and security within the region. The Rio Treaty, as a defensive alliance or mutual assistance agreement, obligates the parties to go to the defense of a hemispheric victim of an armed attack. Moreover, the organization can require the parties to take certain measures to enforce the peace in cases of aggressions and threats to the peace which are not armed attack.

Finally, the OAS is an instrument of inter-American co-operation in the economic, social, and cultural spheres as well as in the political sphere. The OAS is as highly systematized and institutionalized as the United Nations. It is in fact a regional United Nations. The United Nations is a universal agency whose principal purpose is to maintain and promote global peace and security. The OAS is an agency with a similar end in view confined to one region of the world — the Western Hemisphere. Within this region, therefore, the two international organizations operate with similar purposes, similar authorities, and similar functions. The possibility of discord caused by overlapping and conflicting jurisdiction is inevitably raised.[83]

The question naturally arises as to the need for a regional agency like the OAS when one considers that a global organization has been created for the accomplishment of the same ends and that the members of the OAS are also members of the United Nations. Arguments can be marshaled for and against[84] regionalism, but regional arrangements and organizations exist today mainly because a true world community does not exist. The nations of the globe have not yet arrived at the stage of unity to which they would be brought by the acceptance of certain common convictions and common standards as a mainstay of their own lives and of their relations with each other. This being the fact, no world organization capable of maintaining peace and security and of solving the economic and social problems of the world has emerged. As a result nations are forced to fall back on their own resources to endure; but in this era only a few, if any, individual nations are sufficiently prepared politically or economically to develop or even survive on a national basis alone. National power not being sufficient, some sort of group power must fill the vacuum; and those nations which share a great number of interests, or, as it is often put, among which aspects of political, economic, and social solidarity exist, organize themselves into regional agencies and thereby provide institutionalized means for the advancement and protection of the group.[85]

Speaking specifically as to collective maintenance of the peace, it would seem that in a perfect system of world collective security there should be no room for regional alliances and organizations with what in effect amount to police powers of their own. The fact that in the United Nations such a perfect system has not come into existence and the fact that even at the time of its formation there was prevalent a basic distrust in the ability of the United Nations to maintain international peace and security, are the principal reasons for regional organizations in the post-World War II world.

The crusade for regionalism was led largely by the Latin American statesmen, who were motivated by their lack of faith in the perfection of the United Nations and their suspicion of the Soviet Union. The fact that the inter-American system was already in being and the wish of the American republics to preserve it led to strengthening of regionalism in the United Nations Charter. The determination to make the system effective in the field of hemispheric security led to the inclusion of Article 51 of the Charter relating to the right of individual and collective self-defense.[86]

Upon learning of the Dumbarton Oaks Proposals of 1944, the Latin American nations made clear their belief that such proposals did not reserve a sufficient area of action for regionalism. The Dumbarton Oaks Proposals did permit the existence of regional organizations with purposes and principles similar to those of the global organization.[87] Moreover, they provided that the Security Council was to encourage the settlement of local disputes through regional agencies, either on the initiative of the states concerned or by reference from the Security Council.[88] The rub came, however, in a provision that in those cases requiring coercive or enforcement action, regional enforcement was to be permitted only on authorization of the Security Council.[89] This provision assured the primacy of the world organization and the primacy of those powers possessing the veto. Such a provision would have limited the application of those enforcement measures to maintain the peace of the Western Hemisphere which had been set forth by the Inter-American System in the Act of Chapultepec[90] as wartime measures and which were to be incorporated in the projected inter-American defense treaty, which became the Rio Treaty. The Latin American delegations made their opposition clear, for they feared that the use of the veto by any of the great powers would bring about complete paralysis in the application of coercive measures by the United Nations to maintain the peace of the hemisphere, since a veto in the Security Council could not only preclude action by the United Nations but could also defeat regional action.

Their opposition was successful. In order to preserve the relative independence of the Inter-American System and to quiet Latin American apprehension without jeopardizing too greatly the universality of the Security Council's jurisdiction in the field of collective security, the Dumbarton Oaks chapter on regionalism was incorporated into the Charter with some small changes, but in addition Article 51 was inserted:

Nothing in the present Charter shall impair the inherent right of individual or collective self-defense if an armed attack occurs against a Member of the United Nations, until the Security Council has taken the measures necessary to maintain international peace and security. Measures taken by Members in the exercise of this right of self-defense shall be immediately reported to the Security Council and shall not in any way affect the authority and responsibility of the Security Council under the present Charter to take at any time such action as it seems necessary in order to maintain or restore international peace and security.[91]

Article 53 of Chapter VIII of the United Nations Charter, which is concerned with regional arrangements, incorporates the similar provision of the Dumbarton Oaks Proposals and requires regional enforcement action to be taken only on the authorization of the Security Council. Article 51, however, reduces the scope of Article 53 and, in effect, creates an exception to it; for by Article 51 action even amounting to armed force may be taken by members of a regional security arrangement against a nation directing an armed attack against one of its members, whether that attack comes from within or without the region. And, according to Article 51, this action of collective self-defense may be taken independently by the regional union until the Security Council takes the necessary measures to restore international peace and security. By such a provision the states of a regional association are exempt from obtaining the authority of the Security Council when they take measures against an armed attack, and in such cases the veto of a member of the Security Council cannot prevent regional action. If an armed attack occurs, the regional agency may under Article 51 take action without waiting for authorization, and if a veto or other obstacle in the Security Council prevents that body from taking measures thereafter to maintain the peace, the regional organization can continue its own measures for the re-establishment of peace. Indeed under Article 51 a veto might possibly be used to defeat the necessary measures from being taken by the Security Council, thus permitting the regional organization continued liberty to pursue its local measures of collective self-defense.[92]

It was under the regional arrangement provisions of Chapter VIII and Article 51 of the United Nations Charter that the collective security system of the Western Hemisphere was constructed. The Rio Treaty is, therefore, based on these provisions; and it was drafted in such a manner that it qualifies both as a regional agreement under Chapter VIII and as a pact of collective self-defense under Article 51.[93]

Leaving aside the area of collective security or the use of collective measures for the maintenance of peace, the United Nations Charter would seem to create little or no difficulty for regional action.[94] As to the peaceful settlement of local disputes through a regional agency like the OAS, that charter makes no pretense to exclusive jurisdiction. To the contrary, the parties who are members of the United Nations are encouraged to settle their disputes peacefully, and the methods they use, whether of a bilateral nature or through a regional agency, are to be determined by them. The important fact is that the dispute be settled peacefully before it reaches such proportions as to threaten or bring about a breach of the peace. When the members of the OAS, through their basic instruments, provide procedures for the pacific settlement of disputes and agree that resort shall be had to these procedures before the members take the dispute to the United Nations, they must complement the aims and purposes of the latter organization.

This fact is recognized by Article 33 of the United Nations Charter, for it places the obligation upon members in the first instance to settle their disputes by resort to several methods of their own choosing, including regional agencies or arrangements. Article 52(2) goes even farther and requires members who have entered into regional arrangements or instituted regional agencies for the settlement of their disputes to make every effort to achieve peaceful settlement by such means before referring their disputes to the Security Council. Moreover, the Security Council is enjoined to encourage this.

Article 52(4), however, seeks to maintain the supremacy of the United Nations through the provision that resort to regional arrangements or agencies as permitted by Article 52 in no way impairs the application of Articles 34 and 35. Article 34 permits the Security Council to investigate any dispute, or any situation which might lead to international friction or give rise to a dispute, to determine whether its continuance is likely to endanger the maintenance of international peace and security. As to Article 35, any member of the United Nations is permitted to bring any such dispute or situation to the attention of the General Assembly or of the Security Council. Thus if a member of the OAS refers a dispute to the Security Council that body should limit its action to investigation in accordance with Article 34 and to the promotion of the regional settlement of the problem through the OAS. If, of course, the OAS fails to settle the matter peacefully, then the Security Council can obviously intervene.[95]

Some uncertainty seems to result from the fact that the Security Council is obligated to encourage settlement of the local dispute by reference to the regional agency. Under the terms of Chapter VI of the United Nations Charter dealing with "Pacific Settlement of Disputes," which precedes Article 52 and which covers all disputes in general, the Security Council has only the power to recommend a procedure of settlement to the parties. It would seem, therefore, that the Security Council could not refer parties to a regional means of settlement unless they agree. Nevertheless, it would appear that it is the duty of the Security Council to refer a local dispute of a regional nature to an existing and appropriate regional agency like the OAS, which the parties have by agreement established as permitted by Article 52(2), and which they have empowered to take the dispute.[96]

Co-operation by the members of the OAS in the economic, social, and cultural fields again seems to complement the United Nations. Some difficulty might arise from a possible duplication of functions in the hemisphere by various organs created by both organizations.[97] This danger would appear to be negligible, however, for the organs of the OAS are required to collaborate and co-operate with their respective world agencies. In drafting the United Nations Charter, the delegations of the nations directed little attention to the activities of regional agencies in the economic, social, and cultural areas. They considered only the relationship of such organizations to the United Nations in the security field. No provisions were inserted in the United Nations Charter for regional co-operation in the former areas. Nothing precludes such co-operation, however, and this type of activity forms an important aspect of the Charter of the OAS.[98]

CHAPTER IV

MEMBERSHIP IN THE OAS

ADMISSION TO MEMBERSHIP

The provisions of the Charter regulating membership are as follows:

Article 2

All American States that ratify the present Charter are Members of the Organization.

Article 3

Any new political entity that arises from the union of several Member States and that, as such, ratifies the present Charter, shall become a Member of the Organization. The entry of the new political entity into the Organization shall result in the loss of membership of each one of the States which constitute it.

These articles are in no sense detailed, for Article 2 sets forth only three conditions of membership: (1) that the member must be a state; (2) that it must be an American state; and (3) that it must ratify the Charter.

Prior to the Charter, the Union of American Republics or the Inter-American System granted entry to any American state as of right. An American state was not required to petition for admission, nor was a resolution of admission necessary. No conditions for admission existed beyond the requirement that the state be American.[1] At Bogotá geographic unity was maintained, in that the organization remains a regional hemispheric body composed of American states only. But the term *American state* might seem to be unclear. What are the limits of the Americas? What is the Western Hemisphere? These points are clarified by the delineation of the region in Article 4 of the Rio Treaty, which embraces both the North and South American continents including Canada and Alaska, together with Greenland, the Arctic and Antarctic regions adjacent to the continents, and all of the area lying between them. It seems apparent that any state within this zonal area is an American state.[2]

Juridically speaking the use of the term *state* would open membership to independent or sovereign states in the strict international law sense only, thus excluding colonies, states of a federation, protectorates, or any other community which is not completely self-governing.[3] The international law definition is the proper one for defining the term *state* when used without clarification in an international treaty. Such a characterization has been adopted by the American states in an earlier important agreement, the 1933 Convention on Rights and Duties of States, of the Seventh International Conference. Article 1 of that Convention declares: "The state as a person of international law should possess the following qualifications: (a) a permanent population; (b) a defined territory; (c) government; and (d) capacity to enter into relations with other states."[4]

Nevertheless, there is precedent of not fully sovereign states being admitted to international organization even where the charter of the organization uses the word *state* or *states* in reference to membership.[5] The United Nations is a notable example, for certain communities, such as India and the Philippines, that signed and ratified that Charter were not fully self-governing states at the time, and two members, the Byelorussian and Ukrainian Soviet Socialist Republics, were by no means sovereign and have not yet become so.[6] In the United Nations organization there is ample prerogative to decide whether a community is a state when it seeks admission. In view of such a precedent, it may well be that the OAS is possessed of a similar wide latitude and the possibility exists that it, too, could admit an entity with less than full self-government to membership.[7]

By use of the term *state* instead of *republic*, the Bogotá Charter clarifies a point. The choice of terms is evidence of an intent not to exclude from the organization any American state having a political structure other than that of a republic. The door is obviously opened for Canadian membership.[8] To date, however, only the traditional group of American republics are members.[9] Nevertheless, Article 3 provides for admission of new states that might at some future time come into being in the hemisphere. In actuality the right provided for here would seem already granted by Article 2 when it speaks of "all American States." Article 3 originated in a Salvadoran proposal and had as its basis a possible future federation by the Central American republics.[10] A new entity arising from a union of several member states will be entitled to membership, while the former states constituting the entity will lose their membership.[11] Article 2 also permits entrance into the organization of a former colony, located in the hemisphere, which acquires its independence.

Membership is no longer as of right, but requires ratification of the Charter. The Charter makes a change here from pre-Bogotá days. The Draft Organic Pact prepared by the Governing Board for consideration at the Ninth Conference had sought to continue the pre-existing formula declaring that the American states are as of right members of the organization.[12] It was believed that extending membership "as of right" would be somewhat compulsive in nature, an extension of membership *ipso facto* with no express act of accession being necessary. It was not felt desirable to set forth an inherent requirement of membership—to extend membership automatically to a state if it did not desire to assume the obligations of membership. To avoid any such interpretation a condition of accession was provided by ratification, and by this act the state voluntarily accepts the rights and duties of membership. An inherent right to become a member remains, this right being converted into membership by an exercise of will—ratification of the Charter.[13]

Article 108 of the Charter stipulates that it shall be ratified by the signatory states "in accordance with their respective constitutional procedures." This provision impliedly makes ratification conforming to internal constitutional requisites an essential conditional precedent of a valid membership, an unconstitutional ratification being invalid. The issue arises as to competence to decide the validity of a ratification. Under general international law the government of each state is competent to interpret its own constitution, and this would continue true concerning constitutional ratification of a treaty when no provision is made in the treaty requiring ratification in accordance with constitutional procedures of each state. When observance of respective constitutions is expressly required for ratification, the issue becomes more than an internal matter. It concerns the organization, and if it is of import to the organization, which organ is empowered to decide it? Kelsen, in relation to the United Nations, adopts the view that the agency called upon to apply the article would be competent to determine whether or not ratification is in accord with constitutional procedures.[14] Article 108 of the Bogotá Charter states: "The instruments of ratification shall be deposited with the Pan American Union." Following Kelsen, it can be deduced that when the Pan American Union is required to accept a ratification it would be justified in making a determination of whether such a ratification was in conformity with internal constitutional procedures in any doubtful case.[15]

In addition to the obvious variation in membership requirements arising from the fact that the OAS is a regional organization confining its membership to the hemisphere, membership provisions of the Charter of the OAS and the United Nations Charter differ somewhat drastically in other aspects. For example, the United Nations Charter distinguishes between original members and subsequent members.[16] The Charter of the OAS fails to make such a distinction. On the contrary, it indicates that possible future signatories will be in no different category from original members, by providing that the Charter is to remain open for signature by the American states.[17] This phrasing shows an intention to make no basic distinction between original and subsequent members, for the Charter remains permanently open not only for accession, but also for signature. For such a basic instrument of the Americas it was believed that no differentiation should be made.[18]

The United Nations Charter also conditions subsequent membership to "peace-loving" states which accept the obligations of the Charter and in the judgment of the organization are able and willing to carry out these obligations. No similar conditions expressly appear in the Bogotá Charter. The American states have bound themselves on many occasions not to use force and have condemned aggression.[19] It would seem somewhat superfluous to restrict membership to "peace-loving" states when those states have bound themselves to peace. There is also an element of superfluity in the requirement by the United Nations that membership be confined to states willing to accept the obligations of its Charter. Ratification of a treaty constitutes a pledge to fulfil its obligations.

At the conference some favor was shown for the idea that more detailed conditions of membership should be included. Brazil sought to make membership conditional not only upon ratification, but also upon a state's having a democratic form of government. Her representatives spelled out what they considered to be a form of government that would meet this requirement. It should, they said, be based on the following principles: plurality of political parties, freedom of the ballot, the opportunity of private enterprise, and the guarantee of the fundamental rights of man.[20] Nevertheless, the general desire prevailed that the organization should be hemisphere-wide in scope, and that location within the hemisphere was the essential requirement of membership, the only additional one being ratification to signify acceptance of membership.

Again there is a variation from the United Nations Charter in that no express act of admission is required by the OAS. Once the act of accession by ratification has been accomplished, admission is of right. The OAS has avoided the pitfall of the United Nations provision which places admission of a state to membership within the competence of the General Assembly and the Security Council,[21] whose judgment is to be based on the vague qualifications of the "peace-loving" character of a state, its acceptance of the obligations of the Charter, and its willingness and ability to carry out these obligations. This provision has permitted the improper exercise of power in admission of new members by the Security Council.[22] Within the OAS there is no provision requiring admission of any state to be effected by a decision of one of the organs. Admission is of right upon ratification, provided the entity is an American state.

The failure of the Bogotá Charter to stipulate an admitting agency does create the possibility of confusion, for a situation could arise compelling the organ to take action on admittance. If, for example, a new community comes into being which desires to ratify the Charter and become a member of the organization, or which does ratify the Charter, and doubt exists as to the statehood of the community, what then? It would seem that some organ of the OAS must resolve the issue and determine whether the community fulfils the requirements of statehood prior to becoming a member, inasmuch as statehood (construed either narrowly in the strict international law sense or more widely in the United Nations sense) is a condition of membership. There must then be in the organization power to recognize a community as a state, and until it is so recognized the entity would not be entitled to assume membership.[23] The issue then arises as to which organ is so empowered.

Since the Charter is silent on this point, it might be contended that the power is in the hands of the Pan American Union as the agency authorized to receive the ratification, and this may be true in the first instance when the new community seeks to deposit its ratification.[24] Such an issue, however, is fraught not only with juridical questions, as to the meaning of the word *state* in law, but also with political overtones. This would be particularly true in case a dispute arose among the members over the qualifications of the community as a state. With this in mind, the Inter-American Conference as the supreme organ of the OAS, with authority to determine the general action and policy of the organization and to consider any matter relating to friendly relations among the American nations, would have such power if it desired to exercise it. However, some difficulty remains with this interpretation. In reality the Conference should determine general action and policy, and not decide specific cases.[25] Moreover, the Conference meets ordinarily only every five years, and it could be necessary to obtain a more rapid decision. Therefore, it is logical to assume that the Meeting of Consultation of Ministers of Foreign Affairs, acting within its powers as bestowed by Article 39 of the Charter to consider problems of an urgent nature and of common interest to the American states,[26] is the body to resolve the issue as to whether a community is a state for purposes of admission.[27]

A somewhat similar situation could arise with reference to a state already a member, but with rival governments seeking to represent the state in the OAS.[28] Such a situation has not arisen in the inter-American system, for whenever a revolution was attempted it was either a success or a failure, and whichever faction obtained the reins of power, that faction established its representatives in the organization. If ever two rival governments should contend to represent a state in the OAS, probably Article 39 of the Charter of Bogotá would be applied; that is, a Meeting of Consultation of Ministers of Foreign Affairs would be held to consider the problem. In deciding which faction should represent the nation, the organization should be bound by the general rules of international law pertaining to recognition of *de facto* governments.[29]

EXPULSION AND SUSPENSION

The Charter of the OAS contains no provision on expulsion or suspension of members of the organization, an omission which is contrary to the constitutions of certain other international organizations.[30] The United Nations Charter, for example, provides that a member which has "persistently violated" the principles contained in the Charter may be expelled from the organization by the General Assembly upon recommendation of the Security Council.[31] The United Nations Charter also provides for the possibility of suspension from the exercise of the rights and privileges of membership of any member against which preventive or enforcement action has been taken by the Security Council. The suspension is to be effected by the General Assembly upon the recommendation of the Security Council.[32]

Expulsion of a member from an organization for violation of the principles of the organization's charter is a drastic measure in the nature of a penalty and has been called an enforcement action or sanction against the wrong-doing state.[33] The view prevailed in the United Nations that an expulsion provision should be included in the Charter, on the ground that an incorrigible member which violated the Charter's principles in a grave and serious manner would best be removed completely from the organization so that the evil effects of its persistent flaunting of the Charter would not spread and endure.[34]

On the other hand, expulsion of states flouting basic principles of an organization has been criticized primarily because it permits the state's release from its obligations under the basic instrument. Actually a state would thus succeed in effectively escaping from the very obligations it has violated. Such escape tends to weaken the organization and, in addition, reconciliation between the offending state and the organization becomes difficult if conditions later change.[35] Of course, those interested in universal membership for the world organization opposed the expulsion provision, for it permits the destruction of universality.[36]

The less harsh measure of suspension of rights of membership has generally received approbation as a method of showing disapproval. This has an effect somewhat similar to that of expulsion, and at the same time does not release the offender from its obligations.[37]

When the OAS Charter was drafted, some suggestion was made that a provision for either expulsion or suspension might be included, but this was quickly dropped. The Governing Board's Draft Organic Pact did contain an article to the effect that the American states shall fulfil in good faith the obligations inherent in their membership in the system in order to enjoy its rights and benefits. This projected article was rejected, however, because it was thought to be unnecessary. In ratifying the Charter each state promises to observe the obligations provided therein and is placed under such a duty.[38]

The fact that the Charter of the OAS contains no mechanism for the ouster of a nonconforming member caused difficulty at the Eighth Meeting of Consultation of Ministers of Foreign Affairs held at Punta del Este, Uruguay, in January, 1962, to consider problems created by the intervention of international communism in the hemisphere via Cuba. After failing to agree upon the imposition of effective and immediate sanctions against Cuba in conformity with the Rio Treaty, the ministers turned their efforts to other methods and emerged with a resolution excluding the present government of Cuba from participation in the OAS, thus ostracizing Cuba from the American community. Such exclusion had the effect of expelling Cuba from the organization, despite the absence of language in the Charter which would permit expulsion.

To support the validity of such exclusion, a resolution was first approved by the ministers, with only Cuba dissenting, which recognized that the continental unity and the democratic institutions of the Americas were in danger from the increased intensity of the subversive offensive of communist governments, the purpose of which is to destroy democratic institutions and to establish totalitarian dictatorships at the service of extracontinental powers. The principles of communism were declared to be incompatible with the principles of the inter-American system.

A second resolution was drafted setting forth certain of these objectives and principles of solidarity of inter-America such as respect for the freedom of man and preservation of his rights, the full exercise of representative democracy, non-intervention of one state in the internal or external affairs of another, and rejection of alliances and agreements that may lead to intervention in America by extracontinental powers. By identifying itself with the principles of Marxism-Leninism, by establishing a political, economic, and social system based on such a doctrine, and by accepting military assistance from extracontinental communist powers, including even the threat of military intervention in America on the part of the Soviet Union, the government of Cuba had acted contrary to inter-American principles and had thus violated the obligations inherent in OAS membership so as to be incompatible with it. It was further noted that no member of the OAS can claim the rights and privileges pertaining to its membership if it denies or fails to recognize the corresponding obligations.

It was therefore resolved that adherence by any member state to Marxism-Leninism is incompatible with the inter-American system, and the alignment of a government with the communist bloc breaks the unity and solidarity of the hemisphere; that the present government of Cuba, which has officially identified itself as a Marxist-Leninist government, is incompatible with the principles and objectives of the inter-American system; that this incompatibility excludes the present government of Cuba from participation therein; and that the Council of the OAS and the other organs and organizations of the inter-

American system should adopt without delay the measures necesssary to comply with the resolution. Acting in conformity with this resolution, the Council formally deposed the Castro regime from the OAS on February 14, 1962. It should be stressed that the words "expulsion" or "suspension" were not used in the resolution. There was no language in the resolution actually ordering the exclusion, for it was agreed that Cuba's deviation led automatically to exclusion.

However, this resolution, "Exclusion of the Present Government of Cuba from Participation in the Inter-American System," obtained only the bare two-thirds majority considered necessary for passage. Cuba, of course, voted in the negative. Argentina, Bolivia, Brazil, Chile, Ecuador, and Mexico abstained. Certain political considerations prompted the abstentions, but it was stated that there were also judicial misgivings. The abstainers as civil law jurists took the strict and inflexible juridical position that the inter-American codes (the Charter and other basic instruments) lack juridical procedures for expulsion or exclusion as a sanction, enforcement measure, or otherwise; therefore no legal basis existed for exclusion of a member. The exclusion worked by the Meeting of Consultation was considered as an act outside the powers of this organ, substantially modifying the fundamental OAS treaties without the consent of the members.

Those abstaining agreed that a member professing and practicing the theories of Marxism-Leninism is radically incompatible with the OAS, which requires of its components governmental systems with a character of representative democracy; but it was felt that such divergence did not and could not bring about automatic expulsion or exclusion of a communist member. The step of exclusion, according to the abstainers, could be taken only in conformity with a proper legal procedure. Since there was no procedure for exclusion, Charter amendment was requisite. In the absence of such an amendment, action by the Meeting of Foreign Ministers to exclude was viewed as an improvised illegal course.

The stand of the majority of American nations that incompatibility results in a member's automatic exclusion accords with an axiological concept of international law and inter-American law, for such law is conditioned upon the existence of a community of nations in agreement upon certain principles of behavior and fortified by agreement upon some fundamental values and beliefs. Nations unwilling to accept the underlying ethical concepts on which the law of the community is based cannot be considered to be members of the inter-national community and are dealt with on a political as distinguished from a legal basis. Consequently, Cuba cannot claim the rights and privileges pertaining to the inter-American system, for the Castro regime is no longer willing to govern its international conduct according to the community's basic rules and principles. It has denied its inter-American obligations. Cuba, under its present government, can therefore no longer be considered a member of the American juridical community.[39]

WITHDRAWAL

The Charter of Bogotá provides for withdrawal from the treaty by written notification to the Pan American Union. The Pan American Union shall then inform all other members of the notification of withdrawal, and two years from the date of the receipt of the notification the Charter ceases to be in force with respect to the denouncing state, which shall cease to belong to the organization after it has fulfilled the obligations arising from the Charter.[40] The conditions of withdrawal are an innovation in the inter-American system, for before the Charter's existence each member could withdraw from the organization when it so desired, subject only to payment of the quota for the current fiscal year, no other requirements such as previous denunciation or notification or cooling-off period being necessary.[41]

The first condition for denunciation, notification to the Pan American Union and communication of the denunciation by that body to other members, furnishes formal notice of the action. Two other restrictions on withdrawal are provided for: a two-year period of notice and a requirement that obligations arising from the Charter shall have been fulfilled at the time when the notice takes effect. A two-year minimum period of notice prior to an effective withdrawal is almost a necessity in a permanent organization like that created by the Charter. First, it is desirable to have a sufficient period of delayed action in order to permit the denouncing state to reconsider its action. Second, the withdrawal of a member may well involve difficulties in the financial situation of the organization resulting from loss of contributions. A period of notice prior to effectivity of the withdrawal is necessary to permit readjustments of the budgetary situation of the organization.[42]

The withdrawal provision in the Bogotá Charter makes it clear that a member cannot validly withdraw until it has fulfilled its obligations. Membership does not cease until all outstanding obligations have been met, even after the two-year notice period has passed. Thus, a defaulting state is prevented from terminating its membership.

In permitting withdrawal of members, the OAS Charter differs radically from the United Nations Charter, which makes no provision for withdrawal. The question of withdrawal from the United Nations was hotly debated at San Francisco.[43] On the other hand, at Bogotá the withdrawal article was unanimously adopted with little debate.[44] In all probability the Charter of Bogotá is superior in this respect. Certainly there is not the confusion on this point which exists in the United Nations. It may be admitted that in an international organization directed toward the maintenance of peace and designed to be permanent, it is desirable that there be universal membership within the society represented by the organization. In the present state of development of international politics and international law, however, the failure to provide for withdrawal from membership in the basic constitutional instrument does not remove the contingency of withdrawal. It simply produces a situation of legal perplexity as to the status of a member after a purported withdrawal, notwithstanding the non-existence of provisions permitting withdrawal or the failure to state methods to be followed in cases of withdrawal.[45] Moreover, the fact that states presently are still jealous of their sovereignty makes it difficult to obtain acceptance of a constituent instrument binding them together without specifications relating to withdrawal.

CHAPTER V

THE ORGANS OF THE OAS: THE CONFERENCES

THE CONFERENCES IN GENERAL

Over the years a system of conferences has become a basic characteristic of the Organization of American States. Through this method the nations of the Western Hemisphere have arrived at agreements on fundamental policies and have worked out ways and means for their execution. A conference of American states, like other international conferences, is a formal gathering of accredited representatives of the several nations, undertaken to discuss or review matters of inter-American interest with a view to obtaining agreement on or clarification of such matters. The conference is the primary form of international institutionalized co-operation. It is a technique which permits governments to meet together in representative assemblies to agree upon policies and programs of common endeavor. The Charter of Bogotá provides for three types of conferences: (1) the Inter-American Conference; (2) the Meeting of Consultation of Ministers of Foreign Affairs; and (3) the Specialized Conferences.[1]

THE INTER-AMERICAN CONFERENCE

The origin of the Inter-American Conference was in the convocation of the First International Conference of American States at Washington in 1889. Its forerunners, of course, were the various Hispanic-American conferences which began with the Congress of Panama in 1826.[2] These earlier conferences failed to become institutionalized as an organ of a union, but remained *ad hoc* in nature, meeting at irregular intervals for divergent purposes.

The First International Conference in 1889 gave little evidence that it would become a permanent organ of the Union of American Republics. It was not immediately apparent that a regular conference system for consideration of certain inter-American problems had come into being. It took three additional conferences—Mexico City, 1901; Rio de Janeiro, 1906; and Buenos Aires, 1910—to highlight the fact that the nations of the Western Hemisphere had developed an established pattern of periodic conferences. World War I forced a postponement of the normal meeting of the conferences, but following the war the meetings were again resumed with the Fifth Conference at Santiago in 1923. Thereafter, the Sixth was held at Habana in 1928, the Seventh at Montevideo in 1933, and the Eighth at Lima in 1938. Again war intervened to postpone the next regular gathering, and it was not until 1948 that the Ninth Conference was held in Bogotá.

The Ninth Conference was a truly constituent conference where a new charter for hemispheric organization was drafted and where the old name, the International Conference of American States, was changed to the Inter-

American Conference. The Tenth Conference, which met in Caracas in 1954, might well have been designated as the First Inter-American Conference, inasmuch as the preceding conferences were conferences of the Union of American Republics.[3] The OAS, however, is the legal successor to the Union of American Republics, and it was decided that the serial sequence of the conferences should not be interrupted but should continue as before.[4]

In addition to the periodic international conferences, certain special diplomatic conferences dealing with specific problems of a political nature were held prior to the Bogotá gathering. These conferences were deemed to be a distinct type of meeting which did not fall within the three categories of conferences. In reality, however, they were nothing more than extraordinary meetings of the International Conferences of American States. They were called to consider problems which because of their emergency character could not await the normal convening date of an international conference or to consider some specialized subject which could not be easily handled by a regular conference. Examples of these extraordinary conferences are the Washington Conference of 1929 on Conciliation and Arbitration,[5] the Inter-American Conference for the Maintenance of Peace, Buenos Aires, 1936;[6] the Inter-American Conference on the Problems of War and Peace, Mexico City, 1945;[7] and the Inter-American Conference for the Maintenance of Continental Peace and Security, held at Petropolis, Brazil, in 1947.[8] This fourth type of conference is now eliminated by the Charter of Bogotá and has simply become an extraordinary session of the Inter-American Conference in name as well as in fact.[9]

Not only is the Inter-American Conference a normal feature of the inter-American system, but since the adoption of the Charter of Bogotá it has become a constitutionally based organ of the OAS. Because it is the oldest of the inter-American assemblies and also because of the nature of the subject matter with which it deals, it is considered the parent body of the organization. Nevertheless, this oldest of institutions of the system had decreased in importance with the creation of new assemblies such as the Meeting of Consultation of Ministers of Foreign Affairs[10] and the Specialized Conferences, both of which had assumed, to some degree, the functions of the parent body. Recognizing this trend, the Charter of Bogotá attempted to restore the prestige of the Inter-American Conference by making it the supreme organ of the OAS.

SCOPE AND NATURE OF POWERS OF THE INTER-AMERICAN CONFERENCE

Article 33 of the Charter of Bogotá declares:

The Inter-American Conference is the supreme organ of the Organization of American States. It decides the general action and policy of the Organization and determines the structure and functions of its Organs, and has the authority to consider any matter relating to friendly relations among the American States. These functions shall be carried out in accordance with the provisions of this Charter and of other inter-American treaties.

This wording seems to confer a vast and almost unlimited power upon the Inter-American Conference. In the past the functions of the hemispheric international conferences were similar to those stated in Article 33, although they were not quite so broad. Nor, in reality, are they as broad as they would seem from the wording of Article 33, for the Charter itself sets out in some detail the policy of the organization as well as the structure and functions of all of its organs. Moreover, amendments to the Charter must be adopted at specially convened inter-American conferences and then ratified by two-thirds of the number of states of the organization.[11] Previous conferences had not been subject to such restrictions, for prior to the Ninth Conference the inter-American organization was not treaty based.[12]

Furthermore, despite the far-reaching competence set out in Article 33, limitations are placed upon the powers of this assembly by the fact that it is, after all, a diplomatic gathering and is thus limited by established rules governing such meetings. Actually, the Charter in describing the competence of the Inter-American Conference places emphasis on two principal functions. By its terminology the Inter-American Conference is the organ to decide or to formulate general policy for the organization and to act as its constituent body.[13]

Policy-Making

Under its power to decide the general action and policy of the organization and to consider any matter relating to friendly relations among the American states, the conference has the power to study any question within the scope of the Bogotá Charter or other inter-American treaties as well as any other inter-American problem.[14] Through discussion at a conference the delegates may exchange viewpoints on the interpretation of facts, on the interpretation of law, and on the best solution of problems. The powers of the conference are not limited solely to the realm of discussion, for the conference is not restricted to mere debate. Discussions and considerations are carried on in order to arrive at a choice or decision by which the conference sums up the debates or sets forth the consensus. The use of the word *decide* in Article 33 clearly indicates this to be true, and the decisions at which the deliberations of a conference arrive take the form of general treaties or conventions to be submitted to all member states for ratification, or of declarations, resolutions, or recommendations to member states or to the organs of the OAS. Moreover, in order to consider a matter or to arrive at a decision on policy, it is necessary to obtain the facts and other information relevant to the question at hand. Consequently studies may be initiated by the conference, and reports and information may be requested of the appropriate organs of the OAS.

The injunction in Article 33 to the effect that the conference must exercise its functions in accordance with the provisions of the Charter of Bogotá and other inter-American treaties creates no serious restriction upon the deliberative powers of the conference to discuss, study, and recommend, for the existing treaty provisions run the entire gamut of inter-American relations. Consequently the deliberations of a conference may range over an enormous area. Prior to the Charter, the treaties which were drafted at conferences and the resolutions, declarations, and recommendations which were passed by conferences had set forth the great purposes and principles now contained in the Charter and had defined the ends to be attained through individual or collective action of the American republics in all fields of inter-American co-operative endeavor. The continuation of this far-reaching competence is envisioned by Article 33, and thus the deliberative powers of a conference extend to the consideration of principles for the promotion of inter-American co-operation in the political, legal, economic, social, and cultural fields.

Is the conference empowered to consider and recommend measures for the maintenance of peace in a specific case of a dispute or situation in which an American state becomes involved, which endangers hemispheric peace or otherwise disrupts friendly relations? There would seem to be nothing to prevent a conference from so doing, in view of the authority granted to consider *any* matters relating to friendly relations among the American states. Prior to the adoption of the Charter of Bogotá, however, the International Conferences of American States seldom sought to settle an existing dispute, a notable exception being the Chaco controversy between Paraguay and Bolivia.[15] Nevertheless, the basic treaties of the OAS do not contemplate such action as a usual function of the conference. In the first place, the regular conference meets too seldom to exercise such a function efficiently, and, although an extraordinary inter-American conference might be called, any inter-American conference is in reality too unwieldy and time-consuming to be used as an organ for the settlement of disputes. Second, the power contemplated for the Inter-American Conferences seems to extend primarily to the establishment of general and permanent rules of inter-American cooperation, not to decisions upon the course of action or special policy for a specific emergency situation. Third, the American Treaty of Pacific Settlement (the Pact of Bogotá), also adopted at the Ninth International Conference of American States, provides the procedures for the settlement of any disputes, including recourse to the International Court of Justice,[16] that might arise among the American states before they reach such a serious stage as to create a possible danger to the peace. And finally, the conference is not granted power to take sanctions against states where a dispute reaches such proportions as to endanger the peace and security of the continent. By the terms of the Inter-American Treaty of Reciprocal Assistance (the Rio Treaty), adopted in 1947 and incorporated in the Charter of Bogotá by reference in Article 25, this power is specifically given to the Organ of Consultation or to the Provisional Organ of Consultation—the Meeting of Foreign Ministers or the Council.[17] Nevertheless, the conference can interpret and construe the instruments of the inter-American organization and can call the attention of the above mentioned organs to situations likely to endanger the peace and security of the Americas. This it did at the Tenth Conference when it declared the menace of international communism to be such a danger.[18]

Policy-Making as Legislation

Article 33 of the Charter of Bogotá empowers the Inter-American Conference to decide the general action and policy of the organization. The use of such words might suggest that the Inter-American Conference is a legislative body for the American community. It is not, however, a true legislative organ; it is a diplomatic assembly. Consequently, the delegates to the conference obtain and must follow the orders and instructions from their home governments; each delegation taking part in the conference is possessed of one vote; the conclusions of the conference are ordinarily not binding on any state whose delegation dissents therefrom, even in the face of approval by a majority vote; and, of high import, normally the labors of a conference require ratification according to internal constitutional processes of each state before they establish a legal obligation in the international sense. Thus, to equate such a body to a legislative assembly as known on the national level denies fact.

Nonetheless, it must be conceded that the Inter-American Conference is in some measure a rudimentary legislative organ which does bear a touch of resemblance to a national parliament or legislature. It is the highest forum for discussion of all matters within the scope of the OAS. It is a forum where problems of hemispheric importance are debated, and its composition is a guarantee that each member state shall have the opportunity to be heard. Furthermore, through the medium of the conference system, inter-American legislation has been developed.[19] Through the drawing up of multilateral law-making treaties and conventions which are signed by the delegates and submitted for ratification to the member states of the organization, the conference system has been and continues to be a device for international legislation among the American nations. The final conclusions of many of the Inter-American Conferences have taken the form of numerous law-making treaties by which the American community has sought to stipulate new rules for its future international conduct, has defined or abolished existing rules, and has created inter-American institutions. By this method the basic principles of the inter-American system have in large part evolved.[20] As a rule, there is no element of authoritative command in a treaty drafted by and signed at a conference.[21] Inter-American treaties become binding only between the powers which consent to them (assuming that a sufficient number of ratifications are received to fulfil the treaty's stated requisite to bring it into force), leaving the other nations free to remain outside the agreement and to be governed by existing law.[22] Consequently, the efficacy of the conference as a procedure for the advancement of the rule of law in inter-American relations is not found in the mere drafting and submission of treaties by the conference, but rather in their later ratification by member states.

The record on the completion of the law-making process by the obtaining of the requisite ratifications is not brilliant. Of some seventy-seven treaties and conventions submitted to member states by the regular or special conferences, only two have received unanimous ratification so as to be binding on all of the states.[23] Fortunately these are the two most important: the Charter of Bogotá[24] and the Inter-American Treaty of Reciprocal Assistance of 1947 (The Rio Treaty).[25] In addition to establishing the organizational elements of the system, these two instruments define basic and fundamental principles and incorporate obligatory rules of inter-American regional law. Almost one-half of the remaining treaties were ratified only by eleven or fewer than eleven nations. Many of the treaties ratified were later denounced by ratifying states, and a number of them were ratified with debilitating reservations to important provisions. Therefore, the American community of twenty-one republics of the Western Hemisphere can hardly be said to have created through the conference system a vast body of binding law. Still, it must be admitted that the record of the inter-American system on ratification of treaties compares favorably with that achieved by other international bodies.[26] And even though few treaties have been unanimously ratified, a number of treaties have been ratified by a sufficient group of states to bring the treaties into force and thus create a new body of law among the ratifying nations.

The conferences have also pursued inter-American objectives by passing several hundred resolutions, declarations, and recommendations many of which have defined the basic principles and policies of the inter-American system. The resolutions, declarations, and recommendations are included in the final conference documents and are often in a form similar to that of treaties, except that no provision is made in them for submission to the member states for ratification.[27] Often this failure to include provision for ratification appears to be the only difference between the resolutions and declarations of a conference and treaties or conventions. Many such conference resolutions and declarations are couched in terms of legally binding language and set forth specific norms of behavior. Through these instruments the conferences have attempted to modify rights as well as to provide for the assumption of new obligations. From the first inter-American conference, rules of inter-American conduct have been formulated by this process and a number of such rules have later been incorporated into more formal treaties or conventions.[28]

The early conferences sought to set forth the more important obligations in treaty form; but because of delays in ratification of such treaties or complete failure by some states to ratify them, fundamental principles were soon incorporated instead into conference declarations and resolutions, particularly in time of emergency. At the Lima Conference of 1938, for example, not a single treaty was included in the final conference documents. Rather the vital conclusions arrived at by the conference were set forth in resolutions and solemn declarations.[29] By this process the difficulties inherent in the treaty method were avoided, the resolutions and declarations apparently being intended to go into force and effect when signed by the conference delegation of the consenting states. There is little doubt that the delegates to the conference felt that all signing members would undertake to fulfil the commitments assumed in the resolutions and declarations.[30]

Still, the binding nature of resolutions or declarations has, from a juridical standpoint, been open to controversy and doubt. A number of authorities take the position that a mere conference resolution or declaration, no matter how strong the language used therein, does not have the force of law as would be the case if the same language were used in a ratified treaty.[31] It is claimed that resolutions and declarations at best create only moral obligations, not legal obligations. If this be true, then resolutions and declarations cannot be equated with international legislation. On the other hand, there is a strong body of authoritative opinion which declares that resolutions and declarations are juridical in nature and have an obligatory force upon signatory nations. This viewpoint is substantiated by the Act of Chapultepec signed at the Inter-American Conference on War and Peace in 1945, wherein it is stated that the American states had been incorporating in their international law since 1890 certain basic principles by means of conventions, *resolutions, and declarations*.[32] This statement would seem to place resolutions and declarations on the same level as formal treaties, for no distinction is made between the three. And, if true, it would mean that resolutions and declarations which incorporate basic principles are in the same category as treaties, and that, as a result, signatory states have obligated themselves to follow a prescribed line of conduct. Thus in the inter-American system resolutions and declarations of this sort are equivalent to international legislation.

Fenwick, noting the declaration of the Act of Chapultepec as well as the practices of the American states which have often demanded compliance with principles created by resolutions and declarations even to the extent of calling to account on occasion nations which violate such principles, concludes that certain conference resolutions and declarations are legally binding obligations upon signatory nations.[33] He therefore asserts that Inter-American Conference resolutions and declarations are sources of international law.[34]

United States Secretary of State Hughes was also of the opinion that resolutions of an international conference, depending upon their wording and character, may be considered as binding. As chairman of the Washington Conference on the Limitation of Armaments, he observed:

... certain of the resolutions adopted by the committee, and on its recommendation adopted by the Conference, are put in treaty form, and other resolutions are not put in that form. The distinction is that those engagements which it is deemed require the sanction of a treaty are put in the form of a treaty and proposed for execution by the Powers. In other cases, the resolutions are of a character not requiring such sanction in the form of a treaty, and *are deemed to be binding upon the Powers according to their tenor when adopted by the Conference.* [Italics supplied.][35]

If these opinions are correct and if resolutions and declarations of an Inter-American Conference when couched in legally binding terminology and when intended to set forth a rule for future conduct are juridical commitments, it must follow that to a limited extent the Inter-American Conference is a real international legislative organ. For, by the expression of its will in the form of a simple resolution or declaration, it can create norms automatically binding upon a state once that state's authorized conference delegation agrees to the terms of the resolution or declaration by signature. A formidable body of legal arguments can be marshaled for this viewpoint under present-day international practice and procedure.

An instrument which creates or modifies law applicable to the relations of states which are parties to it may go under many denominations. The classical title is that of treaty—an agreement between states or organizations of states creating legal rights and obligations between the parties. Treaties themselves, however, go under a variety of names which indicate a difference in procedure or a greater or lesser degree of formality. A conference resolution or declaration which is an agreement between signatory parties intended to create rights and obligations among them could be called a treaty. The label is unimportant from a legal point of view so long as a binding international agreement is intended.[36] However, those agreements designated by the formal name of treaty or convention by the conferences are always submitted to the member states of the OAS for ratification, while declarations and resolutions are not so submitted but seem to be considered as binding upon adoption. Does this difference of procedure prevent juridical effect? Although it is usual that legally binding international agreements are customarily concluded subject to ratification, this is not necessary under international law and an obligatory agreement may be brought into effect by mere signature.[37] Hudson is of the opinion that a state is bound by an agreement drawn up at an international conference when the agreement is signed by the duly authorized representative of the nation unless the instrument *expressly* states that ratification is required. In such cases, then, signature alone is the expression of a state's consent to adhere to the obligation.[38] Starke is in accord with Hudson, feeling that under modern international practice a treaty which is not subject to ratification or which is silent on the issue of ratification becomes binding upon signature.[39] Following the line of these authorities, it may be said that resolutions and declarations can impose an international legal duty when signed at the conclusion of a conference.

As opposed to these authorities, it must be admitted that strong reasons can be advanced and opinions of other international jurists set forth to bolster the conclusion that declarations and resolutions which seek to create, modify, or extinguish international rights and duties are not legally binding by signature alone and are not intended to be. The very fact that the declaration or resolution method is often utilized instead of resort to the more formal treaty method is indicative that declarations and resolutions are in lieu of or a second best substitute for a formal treaty agreement. Had there been a definite intent to bind, the delegates would have resorted to the more formalized instrument subject to ratification and, upon such ratification, the juridical nature of the obligation would be beyond dispute. This argument is further strengthened by the fact that certain principles which are of a contentious nature at the time of a conference are deliberately placed in the form of declarations or resolutions to avoid the possibility of a long delay in ratification or failure to receive any ratification at all.[40] By proceeding along the declaration or resolution route, the conferences indicate knowledge of a lack of juridical force as distinguished from moral or persuasive character.

The very manner in which the inter-American system has worked in the past demonstrates the lack of intention that these instruments should be tantamount to international legislation. Historically the desired rules of conduct have been formulated and reformulated in succeeding conference declarations. After much repetition through affirmation and reaffirmation in such resolutions or declarations, eventually many of the principles were incorporated into formal treaties or conventions and submitted for ratification.[41] Had the resolutions or declarations been regarded as binding in and of themselves, the final step into formal treaty would have been unnecessary. From this perspective, it may be said that the principles contained in inter-American conference declarations and resolutions are exemplary of what the law ought to be, as distinguished from the actual law itself which comes into being only through a properly ratified treaty.

The most serious drawback to the contention that conference resolutions and declarations are legally binding on signatory states is the fact that the ratification of these instruments has not taken place. Although, as stated above, one group of competent international authorities takes the position that an agreement which is silent concerning ratification becomes binding upon signature,[42] most publicists, while recognizing that ratification is not always essential to establish a legal obligation, hold that such an instance is the exception rather than the rule, and state that international law regularly requires ratification unless the instrument expressly provides that it will be binding upon signature alone.[43] In other words, ratification is a necessary prerequisite to legal responsibility unless expressly dispensed with.

Under the internal laws of most of the nations of the Americas, it is indeed difficult to escape this prerequisite of ratification, for the constitutions generally require that treaties can only be ratified by the executive after such ratification has been authorized by the legislative branch of the nation through consent and approval of one or both houses.[44] If formation of a state's consent must under general international law follow the constitutional requirements of its internal law, it becomes a matter of constitutional law within each state whether any legally binding agreement may be concluded without ratification by the executive and without the consent of the legislative body. Under such an approach, a treaty which has not fulfilled the constitutional law requirements of the signatory state, would be *ipso facto* invalid.[45]

In the United States, in spite of the fact that the constitution specifically refers to treaties as being made by the President, by and with the advice and consent of the Senate,[46] many international agreements are made by the President or by governmental departments without Senate advice or consent.[47] These agreements are known as executive agreements and have been recognized by the Supreme Court of the United States as having juridical force even though Senate approval was not obtained before they went into effect, and even though there often seems to be no substantial distinguishing feature between an executive agreement and a treaty.[48] Such an agreement, it has been declared, meets with the constitutional processes of the United States and is binding upon the nation. Nevertheless, if the view is taken that ratification is indispensable at international law unless expressly dispensed with in the instrument, such an executive agreement would not be binding until ratified unless it was made in person by the head of the state.[49] Therefore some doubt is cast upon the binding effect of conference resolutions and declarations even with respect to the United States, unless they are ratified in some manner by the executive.[50] Of course, no difficulty is encountered as to their immediate binding effect if the other position is accepted, namely, that an international agreement becomes a legal obligation upon signature alone unless the instrument specifically requires ratification.

In any event, the argument that executive agreements which create or modify rights are binding in the inter-American system becomes less persuasive when consideration is given to the fact that Latin American constitutional law does not seem to give the same weight to executive agreements without legislative consent as does that of the United States. To the contrary, it would seem that most Latin American constitutions expressly provide for an exclusive procedure of legislative approval to all international agreements. The term *executive agreement* is not used in any Latin American constitution except that of Haiti which, in Article 79, provides that not only treaties and conventions but also executive agreements are subject to the approval of the Haitian Congress. In all the Latin American nations with the exception of Venezuela, Colombia, and Nicaragua, treaties are required to be submitted to the approval of the legislative branch as a condition for their validity. In the Venezuelan Constitution of 1953 the broad and ambiguous terms of Article 81, paragraph 3, coupled with Article 108, paragraph 4, would seem to have given the Venezuelan president, in practice, the power to make all types of international treaties and agreements without the need of parliamentary approval. The 1961 Venezuelan Constitution, Article 128, places some limitations on this broad presidential power but still authorizes certain classes of executive agreements. The Colombian Constitution in Article 120, paragraph 9, and the Nicaraguan Constitution in Article 195, paragraph 8, do permit peace treaties to be made by the President of each of those nations without legislative approval. But all other treaties are subject to such approval in both nations. There is a possibility that executive agreements might be considered valid in many Latin American countries when they are promulgated by a presidential decree law by a *de facto* government or by such a decree law of a *de jure* government in cases where the nation has been declared to be under a state of siege. This has occurred, although not frequently.[51]

If the constitutional law of a nation determines whether a particular international agreement may be validly concluded, the proposition emerges that conference resolutions and declarations which attempt to be law-making in nature cannot be considered as legally binding unless the constitutional process of legislative approval is met. If this is a requisite, it is difficult to presume that the parties intend to create a binding international agreement upon mere delegate signature at a conference.

Acceptance of this latter statement may give rise to the conclusion that conference resolutions and declarations are entirely without legal significance. This would be erroneous. They are, in any event, an indirect fountain or source of inter-American law. To the extent that they are respected and followed by the American republics and that a continuous habit of compliance with their terms has grown up with the conviction that the action of compliance is obligatory—to that extent the rights and duties incorporated in such instruments translate themselves into customary international obligations. Even though not binding when adopted by the conference, they may become binding through custom.[52] This is probably what was meant by the statement of the Act of Chapultepec that American international law had been created by resolutions and declarations.

Although the obligatory force of certain resolutions or declarations may be subject to dispute, it is evident beyond cavil that prior to the Charter of Bogotá, conference resolutions or declarations which were concerned with the organization of the Union of American Republics and its organs were of a juridical character. The Union of American Republics was itself created by a resolution, the famous Resolution of 1890.[53] This resolution, which was actually a recommendation, was not legally binding by its adoption at the conference, for Point 14 of the resolution required the governments of the American states to present their adhesion or nonadhesion to the terms proposed. After a majority of the governments had adhered, the Commercial Bureau was formed; and finally consent through adherence was forthcoming from all the republics. No state was bound prior to its adherence, adherence in this instance being similar to the act of ratification. Consequently, the Union began its existence on the basis of a mere conference resolution, but such a resolution had to be ratified by an exchange of notes of foreign ministers and thereby closely resembled a formal treaty. If this resolution was ratified by a mere exchange of notes by the foreign ministers[54] of the republics only, with no submission to the legislative branches for approval (and apparently in most instances there was no such submission), it lends force to an argument that certain executive agreements are recognized in Latin America.

Point 16 of the Resolution of 1890 permitted amendments to and modifications of the plan of Union to be made by a majority vote of the members.[55] Accordingly, thereafter all resolutions of the organization were immediately binding on adhering members.

Resolutions by the conference are also clearly obligatory in character when they are made in accordance with a method agreed upon by the organic charter of the organization, for here the states have previously given consent through their ratification of the organic pact.[56] As supreme organ of the OAS it would seem that the Inter-American Conference is a legally constituted body to interpret inter-American treaties and the powers conferred by them upon the organization. Its resolutions of an interpretative nature may be said to be legally binding, even to the extent of what may be in effect an amendment to the treaty. For example, most treaties must be concluded in accordance with the internal constitutional methods established by the domestic law of each state. In order to overcome objections of the men composing the organ designated by the domestic law to assent to the treaty, a treaty establishing and empowering an international organization is often drawn up in vague and general terms. Once the ratification is *fait accompli,* and the international organization has come into existence, the organization may adopt interpretive resolutions which are far more specific than would appear from the general terms of the treaty. Although it has been said that resolutions are not legally binding, nevertheless in determining what is provided in a general provision of a treaty, a resolution interpreting the general provision would clearly establish the "intent" of the parties, and any state which had agreed to the resolution would be estopped from denying that the interpretive resolution was descriptive of the "intent" of the parties.

What then of a state which disapproved of the interpretive resolution? Disapproval can be signified by voting against a resolution or by abstaining from voting on the question. The effect of either of these actions would certainly permit the disapproving state to raise the issue of whether or not the resolution was truly interpretive of the intent of the parties at the time of the signing of the treaty, but would not of necessity mean that the interpretive resolution was not binding. The Charter of Bogotá contains no express norm with respect to conference voting on resolutions, but it would seem that resolutions can be taken with a simple majority vote unless otherwise provided.[57] As to an interpretive resolution, the will of the majority may govern disapproving states so that such disapproval would not operate to provide a loophole of escape from its general scope.

In addition to resolutions and declarations, the conclusions of the conferences have also taken the form of recommendations. These are directed to the governments and agencies of the system for execution and recommend the doing of or abstaining from some act. Unlike resolutions and declarations, they would not seem effective upon adoption. However, the legal character of and difference between resolutions and declarations on the one hand, and recommendations on the other, is by no means clear and the matter becomes especially confusing when a conference resolves and recommends in the same document. Recommendations by their very nature do not appear to constitute a legal obligation to behave in conformity with them. They are an invitation to act in a certain way and are legally non-binding. They are statements of policy which it is deemed desirable to follow. Although they may, on their face, carry no legal obligations, they may have far-reaching political consequences if they threaten the loss of certain values which a state, weighing all alternatives, is unwilling to sacrifice. The fact that states have banded together and formed an international organization places in that organization elements of power which single members of the international community can never possess in the same degree. Therefore, any action within the scope of authority of an international organization will tend to be of a mandatory nature if the values at issue are important to the member state involved, for a threat of loss of these values may compel it to act in accord with the will of the organization.[58]

Constituent Function

Another important function of the Inter-American Conference is the constituent function.[59] This type of conference has been the constituent assembly for the organization from the beginning, creating for it its constitutional law by defining its organization and indicating the power of its organs. The first conference brought into existence the organization under the name of International Union of American Republics as well as its permanent organ, the Pan American Union.[60] Later conferences modified the system and its organs,[61] while the Ninth brought about a complete reorganization thereof and gave Pan-America a constitution in the form of the Charter of Bogotá for acceptance by the American states. The Charter continues the constituent function of the Inter-American Conference by providing in Article III: "Amendments to the present Charter may be adopted only at an Inter-American Conference convened for that purpose. Amendments shall enter into force in accordance with the terms and procedure set forth in Article 109." Article 109 requires that an amendment be ratified by two-thirds of the signatory states before entry into force; and even then, of course, it would bind only those states which have ratified.

The fact that the organization is now treaty-based would seem to do away with the facility of modification and change of the organization by resolutions of the conference which previously existed.[62] Modification should only be brought about by amendment at a specially convened conference, the amendment itself being in the form of a multilateral treaty which must be ratified by the states to be binding upon them.

Article 33 makes the Inter-American Conference the supreme organ of the organization and declares that the conference determines the structure and function of its organs. The fact that it is the supreme organ does not mean that all the other organs derive their authority from the conference. On the contrary, they derive their authority from the Charter or from the instrument which created them. The fact that the conference determines the structure and function of the other organs does not mean that the conference in and of itself can create and empower new organs or change the powers of existing organs today, after the adoption of the new Charter. It can adopt an amendment to create a new organ or to alter or add to the powers of existing organs to be submitted to the states for ratification. Otherwise, in its determination of the structure and functions of the organs it would seem that it must act in conformity with the terms of the Charter which spell out with some particularity the composition and the powers of the organs created. As the supreme organ, probably the Inter-American Conference can, by a general directive embodied in a resolution, instruct an organ how to act within the powers conferred by the Charter; and it would seem certain that the final determination of an organ's competence within the terms of the Charter must necessarily reside with the conference.

REGULATIONS OF THE INTER-AMERICAN CONFERENCE

To carry out its work efficiently and effectively, an international conference must be subject to certain rules of procedure governing its composition, its organization, and its functioning. For the most part the Charter of Bogotá does not concern itself with these technicalities, contenting itself in this respect with the statement that "The program and regulations of the Inter-American Conference shall be prepared by the Council of the Organization and submitted to the Member States for consideration."[63]

Prior to the Tenth Conference, the regulations of each such assembly had been prepared specially for that meeting.[64] Between the Ninth and Tenth Conferences, however, Permanent Inter-American Conference Regulations were drafted by a Council Committee, and on April 1, 1953, after study by the Council and member governments, were approved.[65]

Composition

Both Article 34 of the Charter of Bogotá and Article 1 of the Regulations of the Inter-American Conference provide: "All Member States have the right to be represented at the Inter-American Conference." Article 1 of the

Regulations adds to this statement, ". . . by the delegates whom they appoint thereto." Thus, members of the conference are states, but states represented by individuals. The conference then consists of representatives of the member states of the OAS. All member states have the right to be represented at the Inter-American Conference, this right not being dependent on whether a *de facto* government of a member state is or is not recognized by the other states at the time in question. Proposals were advanced at Bogotá that participation in the conferences should be limited to governments which maintained diplomatic relations with at least two-thirds of the other American governments, but this suggestion failed to gain acceptance and the decision was in favor of regional universality of attendance as of right.[66]

The Charter makes no limitation on the number of delegates each member state may send to the conference. Governments may be represented by as many delegates as they wish to appoint. With each successive meeting of these assemblies, the number of participants has tended to increase. For example, at the Tenth Conference the total number of delegates and representatives participating, exclusive of advisers, counselors, and secretaries, was 216 as compared with 172 at the Ninth Conference.[67] Moreover, Article 4 of the Permanent Regulations provides that the delegations may be composed of alternate delegates, advisers, and secretaries who may represent delegates at plenary sessions and at committee meetings.

Chapter II of the Regulations permits participation in the deliberations of the conference, without vote, by the secretary general of the Organization of American States; provides that the secretary general of the United Nations or an alternate shall be invited to be represented; and declares further that representatives of Inter-American Specialized Organizations may take part as observers, as may representatives of other international agencies when existing agreements so provide.[68]

Time and Place of Meeting

The Inter-American Conference has never been a permanently functioning organ. The normal interval between conferences is five years, but longer times have elapsed between meetings when circumstances have made it impossible or undesirable to hold them at the usual time. Article 35 of the Charter seeks to establish the five year interval, stating: "The Conference shall convene every five years at the time fixed by the Council of the Organization, after consultation with the government of the country where the Conference is to be held." However, Article 36 of the Charter makes possible the changing of the date of the next regular conference meeting when special circumstances warrant and with the approval of two-thirds of the member states. Article 36 also authorizes the holding of a special Inter-American Conference in special circumstances and with the approval of two-thirds of the American governments. These special conferences must not be confused with the Specialized Conferences, which deal only with certain technical matters of co-operation.[69] The special conference is simply an extraordinary meeting of the Inter-American Conference.

The Charter continues the traditional practice of rotating the meeting place of the Conference. Article 37 determines that the place of meeting of each Conference shall be designated by the preceding one. If, for an unforeseen reason, the Conference cannot be held at the place designated, the Council is to choose a new place.

The Program or Agenda

Article 38 of the Charter grants authority to the Council to prepare the program and regulations of the Inter-American Conference, such program and regulations to be submitted to the member states for consideration.

The conferences have always worked through a prepared agenda. Chapter III of the regulations is concerned with this matter. The Council of the organization is given the duty of preparing the agenda. It is first charged to prepare a preliminary list of topics. In preparing this list the Council is called upon to consider pertinent provisions of the Charter, topics agreed upon by a former conference assembly or a former Meeting of Consultation, or those recommended by some other organ of the organization. This list of topics is then sent to the governments of the member states for study and comment.[70] These governments may also propose topics for the agenda.[71] The proposals and comments of the governments are to be considered by the Council in the preparation of the final agenda which is submitted, after preparation, to the governments for consideration.[72]

Article 11 of the Regulations prevents the agenda from being changed or amended after the Council has incorporated the results of the observations made by the governments and has approved it, unless unforeseen circumstances arise. If this does occur, new topics may be included by the Council only up to thirty days before the date of the conference, and for inclusion of such new topics an affirmative vote of two-thirds of the members of the Council is required.[73]

To provide ample time for preparation and study, the Regulations provide that governments wishing to submit drafts of treaties, conventions, declarations, resolutions, or recommendations relating to topics on the agenda must submit such drafts to the secretary general of the organization sixty days before the inaugural session of the conference in the case of treaties or conventions, and thirty days in the case of declarations, resolutions, or recommendations. The secretary general is required to distribute them to the other governments, the Council, and the secretary general of the conference.[74]

In case the drafts are not submitted within the time limit, draft treaties or conventions may be submitted at the preliminary session of the conference and the proposal admitted by a vote of two-thirds of the participating delegations.[75] Draft recommendations, resolutions, and declarations may be presented to the secretary general of the conference within twelve days[76] after the preliminary session, although this latter provision does not apply to proposals originating in the conference discussion.[77]

Reports, proposals, and studies on topics of the agenda are required to be distributed by the secretary general of the organization to the interested parties at least sixty days before the opening of the conference.[78]

Officers

The Regulations designate the officers of the conference as the temporary president, the president, and the secretary general.[79] The conference begins its work under the direction of a temporary president chosen by the government of the country where the conference convenes. The temporary president serves until the first plenary session of the conference, when the permanent president is elected[80] by an absolute majority of votes of the states represented.[81] It is customary to elect as president the first delegate of the state in which the conference is meeting. Article 22 sets forth the powers of the president and Article 23 makes the chairmen of the various delegations ex-officio vice-presidents, who, in the absence of the president, shall occupy the chair in the order of precedence established at the preliminary sessions.

The secretary general of the conference is appointed by the government of the host country.[82]

Committees

Since the conference is a body composed of delegations from each nation, it becomes too large and unwieldy to deal effectively with all matters under consideration. The plenary session is utilized for the formal organization of the conference as well as for the making of final decisions. For working purposes, however, the conference divides itself into smaller bodies, committees. Article 26 of the Regulations provides for a steering committtee, a committee on credentials, a style committee, and working committees.

The steering committee is composed of the chairmen of the various delegations and is presided over by the president of the conference. It meets when called by the chairman or at the request of any of its members, and it is charged with the task of assuring that the work of the conference proceeds satisfactorily. To this end it may make such recommendations to the plenary sessions and committees as it considers appropriate.[83]

The members of the committee on credentials are designated at the first plenary session. The duty of this committee, as the name implies, is to examine the credentials of the delegations and submit a report thereon to the general secretariat of the conference.[84]

The style committee is composed of four delegates appointed by the conference. Delegates representing the four official languages of the conference must be represented on this committee.[85] The committee receives all committee texts before they are submitted to the plenary session and is required to make any changes in form that it considers necessary. The style committee also co-ordinates the texts of the various diplomatic instruments in the four official languages.[86]

The working committees are composed of members of each delegation, and there are as many committees as there are chapters in the conference agenda. These committees study the topics assigned to them, formulate reports, and draft resolutions to be presented to the conference.[87] A chairman, vice-chairman, and rapporteur are elected by each committee.[88] As deemed advisable, subcommittees are designated by the chairman, who is charged to take into account the various opinions expressed.[89]

Sessions

The conference holds a Preliminary Session, an Inaugural Session, Plenary Sessions, and a Closing Session.[90] The Preliminary and Inaugural Sessions are held on the dates fixed by the host country. The others are held on dates determined by the conference.[91] For a session of the conference to be held, a majority of the participating delegations must be represented. For a committee meeting, a majority of the committee members constitutes a quorum. A vote is not to be taken unless at least two-thirds of the states participating in the conference or on a committtee are represented at the meeting at which the vote is taken.[92]

Conference sessions and committee meetings are public, although a delegation may request a closed session and in such a case the request is put to a vote.[93]

Voting

Although there exist no limits on the number of delegates which a state may send to an Inter-American Conference, the principle of equality of member states is strictly observed; for by Article 34 of the Charter of Bogotá each member, great or small, has only one vote and each vote has the same weight.[94]

The Charter contains no provisions concerning voting procedure in the Inter-American Conference. Under Article 38 this becomes a matter of regulation for the Council, to be fixed after submission to the member states for consideration.

Except as the Regulations otherwise provide, the decisions of the plenary sessions of the conference are taken with a majority vote of the participating delegations.[95] Although unanimity is always sought, it is not required. One or a few states may not prevent the adoption of conference decisions. On the other hand, the principle of equality of states prevents any state from being bound by a conference decision against its will. A conference decision attempting to create new obligations by resolution, declaration, or recommendation does not bind a dissenting state. But the refusal of assent by one or a few states does not prevent the majority from acting as they believe their interests demand.[96]

Minutes and "Diario" of the Conference

The Regulations contain detailed requirements as to the keeping of minutes of the conference sessions and the committee meetings, the minutes of the plenary sessions being required to be verbatim and those of the committee meetings in summary.[97] Article 60 requires the secretary general of the conference to publish a "Diario" of the conference, which is to contain the minutes and the summaries, proposals submitted by the delegations, reports of the rapporteurs and the subcommittees, and other material relating to the conference.

The Final Act

A final act is compiled which contains the declarations, resolutions, and recommendations approved by the conference.[98] Preparation of this act progresses with the conference, and after each plenary session the approved instruments are numbered and inserted into the draft of the final act.[99] The final act, which is drafted in the language of the host state, is then submitted to the conference for approval at a meeting called for this purpose on the day preceding the closing session.[100] This original document is afterward transmitted to the Pan American Union so that certified copies may be sent to the member states within ninety days following the conference.[101] After the conference ends, a committee of four, representing the four official languages, appointed by the Council of the organization, translates the act into the various languages. After council approval, these versions are considered official and authentic. They are published by the Pan American Union and certified copies are sent to the member states.[102]

Treaties and Conventions

Treaties and conventions are prepared in the four official languages[103] and submitted for approval of the conference at a special meeting on the day before the closing session. They are open for signature at the last session.[104] It is required that they contain any reservation made by the delegations.[105]

Publication and Deposit

The Pan American Union is called upon to publish the proceedings and documents of the conference and to send copies to the governments of the members, to the Council, to delegates, to the United Nations, to Inter-American Specialized Organizations, and to other international organizations represented at the conference.[106] The Pan American Union is made the custodian of the documents and receives them for deposit and safekeeping.[107]

THE MEETING OF CONSULTATION OF MINISTERS OF FOREIGN AFFAIRS

The second type of conference established by the Charter is the Meeting of Consultation of Ministers of Foreign Affairs. This organ is designed to provide on short notice, in time of emergency, a representative meeting of the ministers of the executive branch of the governments of the member states to which policy formulation in the field of foreign affairs is entrusted. Through this meeting discussion and resolution can be had to meet the circumstances calling for immediate action.[108] The Charter, in providing for this organ, again followed a traditional pattern, incorporating into the basic instrument an organ which had developed previously as a device by which consultation on matters of peace and security could be effected with celerity. The principle of consultation itself was agreed upon at the special Buenos Aires Conference of 1936. The threat of war in Europe lent urgency to a provision leading to common consultation by the American states to meet any impending threat to the peace of the continent. The Convention for the Maintenance, Preservation and Reestablishment of Peace established the principle of consultation by the states of the hemisphere with a view to co-operative action to maintain the peace of the continent, should that peace be threatened by any source either within or without the hemisphere. Here a principle of hemispheric collective security came into existence, but the convention failed to provide machinery for consultation.[109] Not until the Eighth Conference at Lima in 1936 was agreement reached that the consultations were to be effected by means of the Meetings of the Foreign Ministers. The Declaration of Lima stated:

Fourth. That in order to facilitate the consultations established in this and other American peace instruments, the Ministers for Foreign Affairs of the American Republics, when deemed desirable and at the initiative of any one of them, will meet in their several capitals by rotation and without protocolary character. Each government may, under special circumstances or for special reasons, designate a representative as a substitute for its Minister for Foreign Affairs.[110]

With modern modes of transportation available, this agency could be called when urgency required and assembled in a brief period so as to meet any pressing situation.

The conflict which menaced became actual in 1939, necessitating the calling of three wartime Meetings of Consultation at the crisis periods presented by the war to the peace and security of the American continent. The first meeting was held in Panama in 1939 after the German invasion of Poland;[111] the second was held at Habana in 1940 following the fall of France;[112] and the third at Rio de Janeiro in January, 1942, to cope with the situation created by Pearl Harbor and the entrance of several American nations into the war.[113] The fourth meeting was held in 1951, several years after the end of World War II, and was occasioned by a new danger to the peace and security of the hemisphere —the aggressive policy of international communism.[114] The fifth, held in Santiago, Chile, in August, 1951, was an emergency conference convened to consider Caribbean tensions brought about by political and military upheaval in that area. The sixth and seventh were held at San José, Costa Rica, in 1960, to consider charges of aggression by Venezuela against the Dominican Republic and the problem of communist penetration into the hemisphere; and the eighth was held in January, 1962, at Punta del Este, Uruguay, to give attention again to the intervention of international communism into the hemisphere by way of Castro's Cuba.[115]

Nature and Scope of Powers Prior to the Charter

It was mainly intended that the Meeting of Consultation should act as a special limited organ of consultation to meet emergency situations which threatened the peace and security of the Americas. Such competence was visualized by the Declaration of Lima, which called for consultation whenever the peace, security, or territorial integrity of any American republic is threatened.[116] Nevertheless, at the same Eighth Conference the door was thrown wide as to the scope of the Meeting of Foreign Ministers by Resolution CVII, *Improvement in the Procedure of Consultation*, which provided:

That the procedure of consultation, provided for in the conventions and resolutions adopted by the Inter-American Conference for the Maintenance of Peace, may also be applied, on the initiative of one or more Governments and with the previous agreement of the others, *to any economic, cultural or other question which, by reason of its importance,* justifies this procedure and in the examination or solution of which the American States may have a common interest. [Italics supplied.][117]

More specific competencies were added to the Meetings of Foreign Ministers by the meetings themselves as it became necessary to cope with some situation under consideration. The First Meeting called for consultation when necessary to determine measures to be undertaken to secure the observance of the neutrality zone fixed by the meeting, and in case a danger to the security of the Americas should result from a change of sovereignty of any geographic region of America subject to the jurisdiction of a non-American state.[118]

The Second Meeting agreed that in case of an act of aggression by a non-American state against an American state, or in case there was reason to believe that such an act of aggression was being prepared, the signatory states would consult as to what measures it would be advisable to take.[119] The Third Meeting declared that a treaty violation or contemplated violation which might disturb the peace or solidarity of the Americas would permit any American state to initiate consultation with the object of agreeing upon measures to be taken.[120]

The wide grant of power authorized by Resolution CVII of the Lima Conference and the power assumed by the Meetings of Consultation in effect brought into being a new form of conference with powers similar to or identical with those of the Inter-American Conference, and the anomaly resulted that the new conferences came to supersede the very organ which established them, the International Conference. It became apparent that the sphere of authority of the Meeting of Foreign Ministers encompassed any matter which the governments believed of sufficient import to justify the utilization of the consultative machinery. This pliable agency did in fact concern itself with matters formerly acted upon by the conferences, and although the three wartime meetings were called for emergency situations with limited agendas, the meetings refused to confine their deliberations to these situations, but introduced new subject matter which bore little relation to the principal matter for consideration. The Meeting of Foreign Ministers became a most influential policy-making organ acting not only in the political field, but in other fields of inter-American co-operation as well. Its importance as a policy-making organ can be seen by a review of some of the action taken at the meetings.

The First Consultative Meeting approved a General Declaration of Neutrality of the American Republics, which, in addition to stating that it was the unanimous determination of the American states to remain neutral in the European conflict, also set forth standards of neutral conduct to be followed and provided for the establishment of an Inter-American Neutrality Committee to study and formulate recommendations with respect to problems arising from the neutral attitude assumed. Resolutions and declarations on Contraband of War, on the Humanization of War, on Coordination of Police and Judicial Measures for the Maintenance of Neutrality, on the Transfer of Sovereignty of

Geographic Regions of the Americas held by Non-American States, on the Maintenance of International Activities in Accordance with Christian Morality, and on the Protection of the Inter-American Ideal against Subversive Activities were also adopted. Two other significant political declarations were approved: the Declaration of Panama, which established a security zone about the Americas in which no belligerent could commit a hostile act; and a Joint Declaration of Continental Solidarity which reaffirmed the Lima Declaration of Solidarity. The meeting also acted in the economic field by an all-embracing resolution on Economic Cooperation, the most important conclusions of which were the creation of an Inter-American Economic and Financial Advisory Committee, and recommendations to the governments as to the action to be taken to meet economic problems arising from the war and to promote closer economic relations between the republics.[121]

The Second Meeting approved one convention, twenty-one resolutions, one recommendation, and four declarations. Most significant was the Act of Habana, a declaration made to prevent European colonies in America from falling into German hands. It provided that such colonies might be taken under the protection, temporarily or permanently, of a group of American states should such colonies become the subject of a change of sovereignty. An Emergency Committee was created, empowered to meet at the request of any state and to assume administration of the region attacked or threatened. In addition to this provisional measure, a formal convention to the same effect was approved, called the Convention on the Provisional Administration of European Colonies and Possessions in the Americas. This meeting also passed resolutions and declarations on neutrality; on Norms Concerning Diplomatic and Consular Functions; on Coordination of Police and Judicial Measures for the Defense of Society and Institutions of Each American State; on subversive activities by foreign agents; on Codification of International Law; on Promotion of Continental Solidarity; on Hostile Acts in Territorial Waters and in the Security Zone; on the Peaceful Solution of Conflicts (recommending to the Governing Board of the Pan American Union the organization of an Inter-American Peace Committee); on Reciprocal Assistance and Cooperation for the Defense of the Nations of the Americas; on the Maintenance of Peace and Union among the American Republics; on Relations between the Governments of Chile and Spain; on the Question of Belize; and on various other subjects.[122]

The Third Consultative Meeting was assembled against a backdrop of war for most of the Americas. Many resolutions were approved, the most vital being those concerned with severing diplomatic and commercial relations with the Axis Powers. Economic problems raised by the war were considered, and measures were taken in the form of resolutions on Production of Strategic Materials; Maintenance of the Internal Economy of the American Countries; Mobilization of Transportation Facilities; etc. In the political field, the Meeting drew up resolutions on subversive activities; Inter-American Conference on Coordination of Police and Judicial Measures; Coordination of the Systems of Investigation; reiteration of the principle of non-intervention for the purpose of controlling the status or activities of aliens; Continental Solidarity in Observance of Treaties; the Good Neighbor Policy; Condemnation of Inter-American Conflicts; Condemnation of Japanese Aggression; Post War Problems; Penal Colonies of Non-American Nations on American Territory; Humanization of War; Support and Adherence to the Principles of the "Atlantic Charter"; Interests of Non-American Countries (diplomatic representation of the interests of the Axis Powers); Treatment of Non-Belligerents; Relations With the Governments of Occupied Countries; and establishment of the Inter-American Defense Board.[123]

These and other matters which were the concern of these meetings demonstrate their wide powers. It will be noted that their competence extended to any matter upon which the delegations desired to take action, and they made policy, established and empowered agencies, and called specialized conferences in the same manner as an International Conference of the American Republics. The results of their labors, like those of the conferences, were embodied in one convention for submission to the member states, and in numerous resolutions, declarations, and recommendations. This assumption of power was criticized by Dr. L. S. Rowe, who presented these comments in his conclusion to a Report on the Third Meeting:

In conclusion, it is desired to submit certain observations with reference to the Meetings of Foreign Ministers. As a result of attendance at three such conferences it is obvious that they have developed far beyond their original intent, and that they now partake more of the nature of International Conferences of American States than of Meetings of Consultation.

As originally conceived these Meetings were to be attended by a relatively small group consisting of the Ministers of Foreign Affairs of the respective countries or their personal representatives and a few technical advisers. They were intended to deal with a limited number of subjects of an emergency character and the sessions were to be conducted informally and without protocolary character. In contrast, with few exceptions the delegations have been as large as those attending the International Conferences of American States; the Meetings have undertaken to consider a wide variety of subjects, as witness the 81 projects submitted to the Rio conference and finally, the tendency has developed to organize and conduct the Meetings with all the elaborateness and formality of the International Conferences, overlooking their originally contemplated informal character.

It would seem to be of the utmost importance not to confuse the Meetings of Consultation with the International Conferences of American States. The former are for emergency purposes to consider problems of an urgent character; the latter are intended to establish broad principles of Pan American policy and to formulate programs of long-range activity. The one, therefore, should be called upon to consider a limited number of subjects; the programs of the International Conferences of American States might well be expected to be broad in scope, covering virtually the whole field of inter-American activity.[124]

Nature and Scope of Powers under the Charter

Article 39 of the Charter of the OAS declares: "The Meeting of Consultation of Ministers of Foreign Affairs shall be held in order to consider problems of an urgent nature and of common interest to the American States, and to serve as the Organ of Consultation." Thus, two broad functions are assigned to the meeting: to consider urgent problems the solution of which cannot await the utilization of the more cumbersome machinery of an Inter-American Conference, and to act as the Organ of Consultation under the Inter-American Treaty of Reciprocal Assistance in deciding upon the specific action to be taken in the field of security whenever a particular case arises.

Problems of an Urgent Nature

By stating that the Meeting of Consultation is to be held to consider common problems of an urgent nature, the Charter attempts to limit the broad competency conferred by Resolution CVII of the Lima Conference which did not require that an urgent or emergency situation exist before a meeting might be held. Article 39 does restrict the holding of a meeting unless an element of urgency is present, but it is doubtful if the scope of powers has been considerably reduced otherwise; for by the granting of competence to consider problems of common interest to the American states a whole Pandora's box of almost unlimited capacity is opened, restricted only by the necessity of urgency. In actual practice the meetings held prior to the Charter were always held to consider some urgency. It would seem that the word *urgency* as used here does not mean that there must always be some threat to the peace to warrant the calling of a meeting, but that other questions may be urgent and in need of prompt and immediate decision.

It has been said that the Meeting of Foreign Ministers does not have the power to alter the structure of the organization, and if it decides the policy of the organization it does so for a specific emergency and not as a general and permanent rule, as does the Inter-American Conference. Nevertheless, the results of the Fourth Meeting of Consultation indicate that this is still a body with broad policy-formulating competency.

This meeting was held "to consider a problem of an urgent nature and of common interest to the Americas." The emergency was the recently inaugurated Korean conflict and the growing threat of international communism. The "problem of common interest" was the need for the adoption of measures to insure the political, economic, and military defense of the hemisphere.[125]

The thirty-one declarations, resolutions, and recommendations covered a wide variety of topics but were primarily concerned with political and military co-operation, internal security measures, and emergency economic co-operation. The Declaration of Washington recognized the aggressive activities of international communism and announced the determination of the American republics to remain steadfastly united in the emergency, to maintain peace and security, and also to insure respect for the fundamental freedoms of man. It expressed strong support of the United Nations as the most effective means of maintaining peace, security, and well-being of the peoples of the world. Other decisions taken included the support of the United Nations "Uniting for Peace Resolutions"; Inter-American Military Cooperation, which placed emphasis on the role of the Inter-American Defense Board in this respect; the Importance of Maintaining Peaceful Relations among the States; provisions concerning military conscription of students (which recognized cultural advantages arising from the exchange of scholars and recommended that military conscription should not interfere with this exchange); Reaffirmation of Inter-American Principles Regarding European Colonies and Possessions in the Americas; the Strengthening and Effective Exercise of Democracy; strengthening of internal security through governmental action and technical studies directed by the Pan American Union; Improvement of the Social, Economic and Cultural Levels of the Peoples of the Americas (with special reference to participation by the Inter-American Economic and Social Council and the Inter-American Cultural Council); factors involved in economic development relating to strategic materials, scarce essential products, allocations and priorities, prices and transportation; and a draft resolution on the Statute of an Inter-American Court of Justice, transmitted to the Council of the organization for study.

Here again was broad policy-making, and although the conclusions were confined to what might be called "emergency" measures to meet the threat of international communism, still many of these resolutions were of a general and permanent nature, to deal with an emergency which seemed likely to continue for a long time.

The Fifth Meeting of Foreign Ministers, the second since the advent of the Charter of Bogotá, took place in Santiago from August 12 to 18, 1959. The emergency situation which necessitated that meeting was brought about by political unrest in the Caribbean, created in large measure by revolutionary fervor to overthrow dictatorships.[126]

Confronted with a deteriorating situation, the Fifth Meeting was proposed by the governments of the United States, Brazil, Chile, and Peru to consider the whole problem of current tensions of the Caribbean area with a view to the restoration of peace and security, confidence, and friendly relations among the republics of the region by co-operation through the OAS. Two principal problems—political unrest in the Caribbean and effective exercise of representative democracy in the Western Hemisphere—were considered. Issues emanating from these two problems were non-intervention, human rights, representative democracy, and the relation of economic development to political stability. The Declaration of Santiago and twelve political resolutions covering inter-American problems were formulated and signed at the conference. The two most important documents were the Declaration and the Resolution on the Inter-American Peace Committee.

The Declaration of Santiago expressed support for democratic institutions, condemned dictatorship, and stressed respect for human rights. It affirmed that the American governments should be the product of free elections and that perpetuation in power by force was incompatible with the effective exercise of democracy. The Declaration also reaffirmed the doctrine of non-intervention. By so doing, it condemned foreign-based invasions to help overthrow the hemisphere's dictatorships.

More specific and special powers were granted to the Inter-American Peace Committee, which was assigned to inquire into Caribbean tensions, to investigate foreign-based invasions and the reasons therefor, and to report to the Eleventh Inter-American Conference to be held in Quito. The committee was empowered to take action in the performance of its assigned duties at the request of governments or on its own initiative, although in either case its activity was made subject to the express consent of states involved if investigations had to be made in such states' territories.[127]

The Sixth Meeting of Foreign Ministers, held at San José, Costa Rica, in 1960, did not convene under the competency to consider urgent and common matters, but rather as Organ of Consultation under the Rio Treaty. Immediately following this Sixth Meeting, the Seventh Meeting was held at the same place, this one again under the powers to consider urgent and common problems. The agenda covered four topics, all related to the strengthening of continental solidarity in the face of extracontinental intervention by the international communist movement. Some thirteen resolutions were approved, the most important of which was Resolution I, which condemned intervention or threat thereof by an extracontinental power; declared that the acceptance of the threat of extracontinental intervention by any American state endangered American solidarity and security; and rejected the attempt of the Sino-Soviet powers to make use of any political, economic, or social situation in an American state, since such an attempt clearly endangered hemispheric unity and hemispheric peace.[128]

Outside the realm of policy-making, does the scope of the phrase "problems of an urgent nature and of common interest to the American States" permit the summoning of a Consultative Meeting to consider any dispute or controversy between states which would not fall within the terms of the Rio Treaty—i.e., one which would not threaten the inviolability or the integrity of the territory or the sovereignty or political independence of an American state? It seems clear that it was not the intention of the delegates to create under the urgency competency a body empowered to consider *all* disputes. It was not contemplated that the meeting should be a court of summary jurisdiction.[129] On the other hand, the term *urgency* is not limited to instances where there is a threat to the peace, and a Meeting of Foreign Ministers could be utilized in instances where a dispute took on an urgent character calling for prompt decision. Of course, the decision of the Meeting of Consultation in such a case would take the form only of a non-binding recommendation to the disputants.

Regulations of the Meeting of Consultation of Ministers of Foreign Affairs in the Conduct of Problems of an Urgent Nature

Just as procedures are necessary for the functioning of the Inter-American Conference, so are they necessary for the second type of conference or assembly, the Meeting of Foreign Ministers. However, since this assembly is not a general inter-American conference and since the characters of the delegations differ, the regulations have never been as detailed and formal as in the case of the Inter-American Conference. In 1951, just prior to the Fourth Meeting of Consultation, the Council, pursuant to Article 41 of the Charter of the OAS which provides that the regulations of the Meeting of Foreign Ministers were to be prepared by that body and submitted to the member states for consideration, approved a set of regulations intended to be of a permanent nature.[130] The approved regulations were to apply not only to the Fourth Meeting but to all future meetings.[131] Article 31 of the Regulations calls upon the Council to consider before each meeting the necessity of including temporary provisions relative to the special features of each meeting, and Article 32 permits amendment at any time, by the same procedures necessary for approval of the regulations in the first instance. Article 30 states that these regulations are not to be applied when a Meeting of Foreign Ministers is held to serve as Organ of Consultation under the Rio Treaty. They are applicable only when a meeting of consultation is called to consider problems of an urgent nature and of common interest to the American states.

Composition

The Charter of Bogotá is silent as to the right of member states to be represented at a Meeting of Foreign Ministers, but this right is assumed.[132] It is considered a Meeting of Foreign Ministers of *all* the member states, and Article 83 directs the Pan American Union to transmit to all member states the convocation to this assembly.

Unlike the Inter-American Conference, the Meeting of Foreign Ministers is relatively small. Article 5 of the Regulations makes the members of this meeting the Ministers of Foreign Affairs of the American states, although in the event the Foreign Minister of a particular state is prevented from attending, he may be represented by a special delegate. The delegations therefore are presumably limited, but Article 6 opens the door to wider attendance by declaring that the Foreign Ministers may be accompanied by counselors and technical advisers. The attendance at certain past Meetings of Foreign Ministers has tended to equal that of the Inter-American Conference, a situation that has been criticized.[133] Consequently, a recommendation has been made that the Foreign Ministers, or in their absence their special representatives, and *only* those technical advisers absolutely necessary for the consideration of the topics on the program should be designated to attend a meeting. Article 7 of the regulations permits the secretary general of the OAS to participate with voice, but not with vote. No provision is made concerning the attendance of United Nations officials or officials of other international agencies.

Time and Place of Meeting

No regular time of meeting is designated. A Meeting of Foreign Ministers is to be held when an urgent problem of common interest to the Americas demands. The meeting may be requested by any member state, the request being directed to the Council.[134] This latter body is then called upon to decide by a vote of an absolute majority whether circumstances warrant the meeting.[135] The Council then determines the date on which the meeting is to convene, and, by Article 1 of the Regulations, sets the place where the meeting is to be held.

The Program or Agenda

As in the case of an Inter-American Conference, the Council, under Article 41 of the Charter of Bogotá, is authorized to prepare the program of the Meeting of Foreign Ministers, which is then to be submitted to the member states for consideration. Articles 2, 3, and 4 of the Regulations are more specific concerning the drawing up of the program. The government that has proposed the meeting is requested to transmit to the Council the list of topics which it wishes to have discussed. The government making the request is directed to list topics in a detailed and concrete manner and to limit the topics to matters of an urgent nature and of common interest requiring prompt and immediate attention by the governments of the American states.

Other governments may present other suggestions for topics, or observations on those already presented, after the original topics have been transmitted to the Council. Taking into account all proposals made, the Council is then to draft the program and send it to the governments for consideration.

Once the Council definitely approves the program, new topics may not be included unless circumstances arise not foreseen at the time when the program was discussed. Moreover, any such new topic must concern a circumstance creating a problem of an urgent and common interest. To permit the inclusion of a program amendment, unanimous approval of the members of the meeting is required.[136]

Officers

The Regulations provide as officers of the meeting the provisional president, the permanent president, and the secretary general. The provisional president is named by the president of the republic where the meeting is held. He performs the duties of the office until the meeting elects the permanent president. Thereafter, in the absence of the permanent president, the sessions of the meeting are to be presided over by members of the meeting according to an order of precedence established by lot at the opening session.[137]

The secretary general of the meeting is appointed by the government of the state where the meeting is held. He is required to prepare the minutes of the session and to supervise the work of the staff of the secretariat.[138]

Committees of the Meeting

The committees of the Meeting of Consultation are the committee on credentials, a co-ordinating and drafting committee composed of representative members of the official languages, and such other committees as the meeting deems necessary.[139] The committees are to be installed by the president of the meeting, and each elects its chairman and rapporteur.[140] An absolute majority of the committee members is required to hold a committee session, and decisions of the committee must be approved by an absolute majority.[141] It is further provided that the members of the Meeting of Consultation may be represented on the committees by their counselors or technical advisers.[142] Committee reports are to be submitted to the secretary general at least twenty-four hours before the session of the Meeting of Consultation at which they are to be presented, so that copies of the report may be distributed in advance to the members.[143]

Sessions and Voting

As in the case of the Inter-American Conference, a preliminary session, an opening session, and a closing session are mentioned.[144] The opening and closing sessions are open to the public. The other sessions may also be public if the meeting so decides in advance.[145] Ministers or special delegates of two-thirds of the states represented must be present to hold a Meeting of Consultation.[146] If it is impossible for a Minister or a special delegate to attend a session, or if the Minister or special delegate is obliged to leave during the session, he may designate one of his counselors or technical advisers to represent him.[147]

All texts of decisions of the meeting, before being included in the final act, must go to the pertinent committee for purposes of co-ordination and style as well as for collation of the texts in the four official languages—English, French, Portuguese, and Spanish.[148] Any proposals that members wish to submit must be delivered to the secretary general within forty-eight hours after the preliminary session. This rule does not apply to proposals that may arise from the very nature of the discussions.[149]

As to voting in the meeting, each member has the right to one vote as is customary in inter-American assemblies.[150] However, a change is made here in that decisions are to be taken by a two-thirds majority vote of the countries represented at the meeting, except in amending the agenda or when procedural matters are under discussion.[151] In these latter cases decisions may be taken by a simple majority.[152]

Minutes and Publications of the Meeting

The secretary general is required to keep minutes of the sessions held, verbatim in the case of public sessions and brief minutes in the case of other sessions.[153] The decisions taken at the meeting are to be incorporated into a final act which is signed by the members at the closing session.[154] Reservations may be appended to the final act, but only when the reservation is stated at the time the decision was taken or else presented in writing to the secretary general and duly distributed by him to the other members for consideration at the session in which the final act is approved.[155] The government of the state where the meeting is held is called upon to send the documents to the Pan American Union. This body then issues certified copies of the final act and sends them to all the governments.[156]

Organ of Consultation

Not only does the Meeting of Foreign Ministers gather to consider urgent problems of common interest, but it also functions for the specific purpose of serving as Organ of Consultation under the Inter-American Treaty of Reciprocal Assistance to decide what action is to be taken in the field of security whenever a particular case arises. Article 11 of this treaty specifies: "The consultations to which this Treaty refers shall be carried out by means of the Meetings of Ministers of Foreign Affairs of the American Republics which have ratified the Treaty, or in the manner or by the organ which in the future may be agreed upon." The last clause of this provision was placed in the article so that it would not bind the forthcoming reorganization which took place at the Ninth Conference.[157] The Ninth Conference confirmed Article 11 by providing that the Meeting of Foreign Ministers should serve as the organ of consultation.[158]

There was some controversy at the Rio Conference as to what agency should be made the forum for consultation and decision under the treaty. It was suggested that consultation should be carried out through the Governing Board of the Pan American Union, or that a special organ should be created.[159] In view of the fact that the action contemplated by the treaty was most serious in character, the final decision was that the consultation should be carried out by the top spokesmen for foreign affairs of the American states,[160] although Article 12 granted to the Governing Board of the Pan American Union the power to act as Provisional Organ of Consultation until the Meeting of Foreign Ministers as Organ of Consultation could take place.

In its role as Organ of Consultation under the provisions of the Rio Treaty, the function of the Meeting of Ministers of Foreign Affairs becomes executive in nature, to the extent that it is charged with the enforcement of peace in the hemisphere.

Article 3 of the Rio Treaty requires that the Organ of Consultation shall meet without delay in the event of an armed attack by any state against an American state, in order to agree upon the measures of a collective character that should be taken by the American states. Article 6 of this treaty is broader in its requirement of consultation, for it requires a meeting of the Organ whenever the inviolability or the integrity of the territory or the sovereignty or political independence of any American state is affected by an aggression which is not an armed attack, or by an extracontinental or intra-continental conflict, or by any other fact or situation that might endanger the peace of America. The Organ of Consultation is called upon in case of aggression to agree on measures which must be taken to assist the victim of the aggression, or, in any case, the measures which should be taken for the common defense and for the maintenance of the peace and security of the continent.

Article 43 of the Charter of Bogotá, in line with the Rio Treaty, requires a Meeting of Consultation to be held in case of an armed attack within the territory of an American state or within the region of security delimited by treaties in force. This article refers only to situations arising under an armed attack. Article 25 of the Charter, however, is broader and includes all the situations which may arise under the Rio Treaty. The latter article incorporates the Rio Treaty, and thus the Meeting of Consultation acts as Organ of Consultation under all the circumstances set forth in the Rio Treaty and not merely in the event of an armed attack.[161]

This organ is then intended as the enforcement or police agency of the OAS, entrusted with the power to order the member states to take the collective measures or sanctions provided for in the Rio Treaty in the field of security whenever a particular case arises. It has the power to decide the collective coercive measures which are to be taken by the member states in any dispute or situation that reaches such a serious stage as to create a danger to the peace.[162] Its decisions in situations arising under Articles 3 and 6 of the Rio Treaty are legally binding upon the members. In consequence members may be called upon to participate in enforcement actions in the event of violations of or threats to the peace with the exception that a member state may not be compelled to use armed force. The obligatory effect of the decisions of the Consultative Organ is borne out by Article 20 of the treaty, which declares: "Decisions which require the application of the measures specified in Article 8 shall be binding upon all the Signatory States which have ratified this Treaty, with the sole exception that no State shall be required to use armed force without its consent." Therefore when two-thirds of the voting members at a Meeting of Consultation decide that the chiefs of diplomatic missions should be recalled from a country, or diplomatic or consular relations broken, or economic relations, transport, or communications interrupted, each of the parties is bound to carry out the decision even though it may have voted against it. The Organ of Consultation may also decide that the sanction necessary in the situation is the use of armed force. Although no state may be required to use armed force, this does not affect the validity of a decision by the organ to use armed force. It simply permits each state to decide of its own free will to employ this punitive measure in accordance with the decision. Any such use after a decision by the organ would, of course, be legal if in harmony with the United Nations Charter.[163]

Voting provisions in international bodies and the obligatory effect of decisions reached by such agencies on the participating states have long been troublesome problems. With the extension of international co-operation, nations have often assumed that the principle of equality of states required equality of representation and unanimity in reaching all important decisions. Such an assumption has made organized co-operation exceedingly difficult, if not well nigh impossible.

Prior to the Rio Treaty, the Meeting of Foreign Ministers proceeded for the most part in accordance with the assumptions springing from the state equality doctrine. Equality of representation was maintained. A slight departure was made in that decisions were as a rule taken by majority vote, but, in practice, unanimity was always sought and usually obtained, and, in any event, a decision of the Meeting was considered binding only upon concurring states.[164]

When the time came to create a system of collective security for the hemisphere based upon a definitive treaty, practical effectiveness of such a system demanded a change. Collective security would be but a myth if any sort of unanimity of voting were to be required before collective action could be taken to meet aggression. A rule of unanimity would permit one dissenting state to block the taking of enforcement measures by the others—a veto.

On the other hand, if something less than unanimity were to be adopted, for example a majority or two-thirds vote, and if the old rule were to remain, parties not concurring in the decisions of the Consultative Organ would not be bound by the measures agreed upon. This in turn would obstruct collective security, for sanctions, particularly of an economic or diplomatic nature, could hardly be effective if a leading state or two were not bound to take the measures agreed upon and decided not to do so. Concession was called for. Prior to the conference in 1947, the Governing Board of the Pan American Union initiated a consultation among the American governments. Point II was concerned with voting arrangements for agreeing on collective measures, i.e., whether the agreement should be by unanimous vote, by two-thirds of the parties, or by a majority. In addition the question was put as to whether the collective measures agreed upon should be binding for all of the contracting parties or only for those concurring.[165] Most of the nations favored the rule that collective measures be taken by a two-thirds majority.[166] Fourteen governments stated that the measures so agreed upon should be obligatory for all, and six were of the opinion that they should be obligatory only upon concurring states.[167]

The attitude of the substantial majority of American governments as to voting was incorporated into the Rio Treaty. Article 17 declares: "The Organ of Consultation shall take its decisions by a vote of two-thirds of the States which have ratified the treaty." Thus once consultation is initiated all decisions are taken by a two-thirds vote of the ratifying states. This represents a middle ground between a unanimity rule and a majority rule. It assures that the decisions calling for action are backed by a majority sufficiently high to represent the collective will of the Americas, and still avoids the possibility that a small minority can block the operation of the treaty.[168]

Issues which would require a two-thirds vote would be the existence of an armed attack under Article 3, the existence of an aggression and the determination of the aggressor under Article 6, the existence of other situations that endanger the peace of the Americas and affect the inviolability or the integrity of the territory or the sovereignty or political independence of an American state, matters connected with Article 7, and the collective measures to be taken under Article 8—their nature, timing, and extent.

As noted above, a state must have ratified the treaty in order to vote. In the case of a situation or dispute between American states, Article 18 also excludes from voting those states directly interested. States "directly interested" are those which are immediate and initial parties to the dispute.[169] This article embodies the principle that parties to a dispute should not judge their own case; but it should be noted that it is applicable to disputes between American states exclusively. If the situation or dispute occurs between an American state and a non-American state, the American state directly interested would not be deprived of the vote.[170]

The quorum necessary in the Organ of Consultation consists of the number of votes necessary for taking decisions—i.e., the number of two-thirds of the ratifying states.[171]

Despite the fact that the majority response to the consultation of the Governing Board indicated that the measures agreed upon by a two-thirds vote in the Organ of Consultation should be obligatory on all contracting parties, an adjustment was made under the terms of the treaty. The obligation was accepted to comply with decisions of two-thirds of the parties to put into effect the punitive measures enumerated in Article 8, with one exception —no state may be required to use armed force without its consent. This exception permits a state to exercise its individual judgment as to the necessity of the use of armed force in a particular case, and to hold back if it believes the use of such an extreme measure is not requisite even when the Consultative Organ so decides. Other states, however, are not so restrained and are free to use armed force as decided by the Organ, and all states, dissenting or not, are bound to take the punitive measures of a diplomatic or economic nature upon the decision of the Organ of Consultation.[172]

The idea of a permanent committee such as the Security Council of the United Nations through which the signatory governments would consult was rejected by the OAS. It was decreed by the Rio Treaty and the Charter of Bogotá that consultations would take place through the Meeting of Consultation of Ministers of Foreign Affairs, a non-permanent body. The Council of the OAS was empowered to act provisionally pending the convocation of the meeting.[173]

To date there have been only two convocations of the Meeting as Organ— the Sixth and the Eighth—although there have been several disputes involving threats to the peace in which prompt action has been needed. In these cases the Council, invoking Article 6 of the Rio Treaty, has called for a Meeting of Foreign Ministers but has set no date for such a meeting. In the meantime it has declared itself to be provisionally the Organ of Consultation. The prompt action by the Council as Provisional Organ made unnecessary the Meeting of Foreign Ministers and prevented these controversies from taking on a more dangerous character.[174]

It would appear from this action by the Council that this body has moved to some position similar to that of the United Nations Security Council in that the Council of the OAS, a permanent body like the Security Council, has, as Provisional Organ of Consultation, assumed duties of the Meeting of Foreign Ministers. It might be noted, however, that the final action of the Council in most cases has been a series of resolutions and recommendations to the states concerned in the dispute.[175] When sanctions or enforcement measures have been required, generally a Meeting of Foreign Ministers has been called.[176]

THE SPECIALIZED CONFERENCES

A third type of conference is stipulated in Article 93 of the Charter: the Specialized Conferences, which form another organ of the OAS. By the inclusion of these conferences, the Charter continues the many technical conferences which have figured as prominent components of the inter-American system. These technical or specialized conferences were convened to deal with a particular topic or topics too technical to be dealt with by the regular conferences.[177] Prior to the Charter, over two hundred such assemblies were held.[178] Little uniformity existed as to their organization and conduct. Some of them were called in accordance with resolutions of the International Conferences or the Meetings of Foreign Ministers; some were convened pursuant to resolutions of previous specialized conferences; others were called on the initiative of the Governing Board of the Pan American Union or by a government of a member state; and still others were unofficial, convened by private groups or organizations. The private or unofficial conferences were not considered agencies of the organizations. Some of these technical conferences convened only once, while others were given an enduring character and have continued to meet on varying occasions.

Article 93 of the Charter states that the Specialized Conferences shall meet to deal with special technical matters or to develop specific aspects of inter-American co-operation. By this wording a flexible competence is prescribed which permits this type of conference to deal with any complicated technical problem which may arise. This indefinite reference to the functions of Specialized Conferences makes it evident that their activities may cover an almost unlimited field of specialized inter-American co-operation, thus allowing experts to come together to work out technical problems and agree upon methods by which certain broad policies, often established by the other conferences, can be implemented by inter-American action. The conclusions of their deliberations take the form of conventions, declarations, resolutions, and recommendations similar to those of the other conferences. The broad field of endeavor of these conferences is indicated by the fact that prior to the Charter they were convened to deal with matters in the commercial, economic, and financial fields and related areas such as transportation, communications, and agriculture. In addition they have been held to solve inter-American social and cultural problems.

Co-operative action through these conferences has continued unabated since the establishment of the OAS. Conferences have been convened to deal with a wide variety of problems. For example, that of 1956, on the conservation of natural resources, concerned itself with the important problem of the continental shelf and marine waters. Inter-American Conferences on Agriculture; Travel and Highway Congresses; Statistical Congresses; and the important Economic Conferences of the OAS have been held. Others that may be mentioned are the conferences on public health, sanitary conferences, child conferences, and assemblies of the Pan American Institute of Geography.[179]

The Charter of Bogotá contains few norms pertaining to the Specialized Conferences. Its provisions, however, have been supplemented by certain Standards approved by the Council which set forth the characteristics of Specialized Conferences, and, in accord with provisions of the Charter, contain procedures and formalities to govern the convocation of Specialized Conferences, the preparation of their agenda and regulations, and the custody of their archives.[180]

The Standards describe a Specialized Conference as one which is intergovernmental, technical, and of common interest. "Intergovernmental" means that the membership with the right to vote at the conference is that of the governments of the member states of the OAS. "Technical" signifies that the conferences have it as their object to deal with special matters or to develop specific aspects of inter-American co-operation. The final requirement is that the conference be "of common interest"; i.e., it must deal with matters of general interest to the American community, open to the participation of all member states.[181] A conference possessed of these component elements is identified by the Council as a Specialized Conference and an organ of the OAS.

Other meetings of a technical character—official, semi-official, or private—not possessing all of these conditions are known as "Other International American Meetings," and are not considered Specialized Conferences.[182]

Article 93 of the Charter provides that Specialized Conferences are to be convened (1) when an Inter-American Conference or a Meeting of Foreign Ministers so decides; (2) when inter-American agreements so provide; or (3) when the Council so decides either on its own initiative or at the request of one of its organs or of one of the Specialized Organizations.

That section of Article 93 which declares that such conferences are to meet when decided by inter-American agreements is clarified by the Standards. "Inter-American agreements" are defined as treaties and conventions in force as well as resolutions duly approved at an Inter-American Conference, a Meeting of Consultation, or a Specialized Conference.[183]

The Standards also declare that, except as otherwise provided, the Council will fix the site of each Specialized Conference, will set the date of the meeting in consultation with the host country, and will convoke the conference.[184]

Article 94 of the Charter provides that the program and regulations of each of such conferences shall be prepared by the appropriate organs of the Council or by the Specialized Organization concerned, and that they shall be submitted to the member governments for consideration and transmitted to the Council for its information. In addition, Article 83 assigns to the Pan American Union the functions of advising the Council and its organs in the preparation of the programs and regulations; of transmitting to the member states the notices of convocation of Specialized Conferences; of placing at the disposal of the host governments, to the extent of its ability, the technical aid and personnel requested by them; and of serving, when possible, as the custodian of the documents and archives of such conferences.

The Standards recapitulate these Charter provisions and implement them by providing more detailed stipulations. In addition they require the study by the Council of the regulations of each Specialized Conference in order to formulate recommendations to avoid duplication of effort, overlapping of dates, and multiplicity of meetings, and, in general, to co-ordinate these meetings in the interests of the OAS.[185]

CHAPTER VI

THE OTHER ORGANS OF THE OAS

THE COUNCIL

The Council is the permanent executive organ of the OAS and is endowed by the Charter of Bogotá with important powers of a political, supervisory, and co-ordinating nature. It is the successor of the former Governing Board of the Pan American Union, which was created in 1902 to supervise the management of the International Bureau, later the Pan American Union, and which was joined together with the administrative offices of the Pan American Union as a single composite body. As the Governing Board of the Pan American Union, this body is one of the oldest organs of the organization. A principal change effected by the Charter was to separate the Governing Board from the Pan American Union and to change its name.[1]

Historical Evolution

As originally conceived by resolution of the Second International Conference, the Governing Board was to administer and control the Bureau of the American Republics. This resolution set forth the powers of management in some detail, providing that positions in the Bureau should be filled by appointments made by the Governing Board after examination of the applicants by an Examining Board; that the Governing Board should prepare the Bureau's budget and apportion the amount to be paid by each member government; and that it was privileged to appoint two of its members to examine the accounts of the Bureau at any time. The Governing Board was composed of the secretary of state of the United States as chairman and the diplomatic representatives of member states accredited to the government of the United States.[2]

The Third Conference, by resolution, provided again that the Bureau should be administered by a Governing Board, the composition of which would be the same. The immediate direction and administration of the Bureau was placed in the hands of a director appointed by the Governing Board. This resolution also created a Supervisory Committee to be composed of four members of the Governing Board, empowered among other things to recommend to the Governing Board improvements "regarding publications, the library and anything that it may deem advisable and beneficial to the Bureau, or to give greater efficiency to its work."[3]

The Fourth Conference changed the name of the Bureau to the Pan American Union and made a minor modification regarding the Governing Board by permitting any member having no representative in Washington to designate a member of the Governing Board to represent it.[4]

At the Fifth Conference in 1923 a proposal was made, supported by many Latin American nations, that the Governing Board should be composed of representatives of the American governments accredited to the Pan American Union rather than to Washington.[5] The reasons given for this proposal were that the diplomatic representatives accredited to any one government lacked freedom of attitude in the Governing Board, and that governments not enjoying diplomatic relations with the United States found themselves excluded from the Governing Board.[6] A compromise solution to the difficulty was found. By Article V of the resolution on organization of the Pan American Union, any American republic not having a diplomatic representative accredited to Washington was given the right to appoint a special representative on the Governing Board.[7] It was further provided that the governments of the American republics enjoy, as of right, representation at the conferences and in the Pan American Union. To meet other objections regarding the privileged position of the United States on the Governing Board through its monopoly of the chairmanship or presidency of that body, the office of president of the Governing Board was made elective.[8] By resolution the Governing Board was entrusted with the task of studying suggestions by the governments of the republics "in order to make their mutual association closer and in order to promote common interests";[9] and by another resolution the Governing Board was called upon to draft a resolution or convention to the Sixth Conference on the Pan American Union.[10]

An attempt was made at the Sixth Conference to give the Pan American Union a treaty or convention basis. A convention on the Pan American Union was adopted by the conference,[11] but as it was doubtful whether or not the convention would ever become effective through ratification, an *ad interim* resolution was also adopted by the conference containing the most important modifications set forth in the convention.[12] Inasmuch as the convention never did enter into force,[13] the members of the conference were wise to provide in this resolution that the Pan American Union should continue to be governed by previous resolutions in force subject to the changes set forth in the resolution.

The resolution modified the makeup of the Governing Board by providing that it should be composed of a special representative appointed by each American government, although a government could, if it so desired, designate its diplomatic representative in Washington. Both the resolution and the convention imposed an important restriction on the Board by providing that "Neither the Governing Board nor the Pan American Union shall exercise functions of a political character."[14]

Following conferences did little to expand the powers of the Governing Board until that at Mexico City in 1945. Thus, until that time its powers as provided by resolutions were limited mainly to the supervision and direction of the Pan American Union. As such, it appointed the Union's director general and assistant director; it was called upon to approve the appointments of the director general of other personnel necessary to the Union's work; it prepared the Union's regulations and fixed the status of the members of the staff, determining their salaries and conditions of retirement; it provided for the establishment of such administrative divisions of the Pan American Union as were deemed necessary; it approved the budget of the Union and assigned to the member states their quotas for the Union's maintenance; and it sought to bring about co-operation and co-ordination between the Union and other Pan American agencies. In addition to these duties in relation to the Pan American Union, the Board acted to fix the date and usually the place of meeting of the next conference and prepared its program and regulations. It also promoted the meeting of inter-American technical conferences. It acted to assure that the resolutions of the Pan American conferences were carried out, and maintained relations with the Pan American committees established in various member nations.

For the greater part of its first fifty years of existence, the Governing Board's growth in the political field was impeded. Various reasons have been ascribed for the prohibition against its exercise of political powers. The Board's location in Washington under the shadow of the United States Department of State undoubtedly led to suspicion and fear of its domination by the United States, and consequently made the Latin American members reluctant to part with any aspect of their sovereign power in the political field. Again, it has often been stated that controversial political issues would place too great a strain on the Board and the Union, and for this reason it was more advantageous to protect the central agency of the system by barring it from the exercise of such functions. If it became necessary to deal with such controversies it would be better to create an *ad hoc* body which could disappear when the problem was settled without permanently injuring the Pan American Union.

Possibly a more basic reason, however, can be found in the fact that the system as a whole did not assume political responsibilities of an executive nature until rather late in its history. For the most part the conferences were content to limit their political activities to the formulation of policies and procedures in the fields of inter-American peace and security and in the formulation of principles of inter-American conduct. The organization left the application of the principles and the use of the procedures in the hands of the member states. Enforcement or compliance machinery in case of breach did not materialize. Once agreement had been reached, the organization's work was done, and respect for the principle or the procedure depended on the good faith of the parties. Breach of the principle or failure to use the prescribed procedure perforce was dealt with on an *ad hoc* basis. This reluctance to create an effective agency with executive enforcement machinery persisted until the end of World War II, and evidenced a zealous desire on the part of the American republics to safeguard their sovereignty and freedom of action by a refusal to permit any invasion by a regional agency into the sphere of political decision of each republic. This refusal sprang in part from the fear of Latin America that an agency with executive political responsibilities might become an instrument of United States intervention. Moreover, United States policy was such as to discourage the creation of an international agency with political jurisdiction, for the United States was reluctant to hamper its own freedom of decision and policy in the political sphere.[15]

Although there was a determined effort to maintain the Governing Board primarily as an administrative agency, competing forces arose and, particularly following World War I and the advent of the League of Nations, proposals were made to transform the Board into a council similar to that of the world organization.[16] The various modifications in the representation of the Governing

Board to divorce it from domination by Washington by making its composition one of special representatives not dependent upon recognition of an American state by the United States furnish evidence of this position. The convention adopted at Habana in 1928 is somewhat schizophrenic in nature, for although it prohibited the exercise of political functions by the Board or the Pan American Union, at the same time it called upon the Union "to assist in the development of commercial, industrial, agricultural, social and cultural relations, . . . and the furtherance of more intimate mutual acquaintance between the American Republics."[17] It is difficult to see how the Union could carry out such a program without intruding into a political field. More confusing still was the provision of the convention declaring that a state which believed its vital interests to be involved in a question, or which believed that an obligation might thereby be imposed upon it, could require a resolution of the Governing Board to be adopted by unanimous vote.[18] Vital interests of a state must in some instances of necessity include political issues. And if the Governing Board could adopt a resolution thereon even though not obligatory in nature, surely at some point the Board would be exercising political functions. The treaty itself seems to illustrate the two opposing positions for and against the granting of political powers which existed within the system.

In the years following the Habana Conference the inter-American political climate began to change. Latin American fears of United States intervention faded with the good neighbor policy and non-intervention agreements to which the United States acquiesced. The reluctant attitude of the United States to the creation of an American League of Nations and the multilateralization of the Monroe Doctrine began to disappear, and the inter-American system began to assume collective responsibility for the peace and security of the hemisphere with the adoption of the principle and procedure of consultation at the Buenos Aires Conference of 1936.[19]

This conference, however, failed to create specific consultative machinery. It was not until the Conference of 1938 at Lima that such machinery came into being, where it was provided that the agency of consultation should be the foreign ministers of the American republics.[20] No definite method of convoking a Meeting of Foreign Ministers was provided, but this was cured by the Second Meeting of Foreign Ministers through a provision that any government wishing to initiate a consultative meeting should apply to the Governing Board of the Pan American Union, submitting the questions that government proposed for consideration. The Governing Board would then transmit the request to the other governments for observations and suggestions, and on the basis of these the Governing Board was authorized to fix a date for the meeting, prepare the agenda, and make any other necessary preparations.[21]

This same Meeting of Foreign Ministers also authorized the Governing Board to appoint a committee of five charged with the duty of "keeping constant vigilance to insure that States between which any dispute exists or may arise, of any nature whatsoever, may solve it as quickly as possible, and of suggesting, without detriment to the methods adopted by the parties or to the procedures which they may agree upon, the measures and steps which may be conducive to a settlement."[22]

With these two developments the Board was empowered to designate members of an organ for the settlement of disputes and to call the consultative meeting dealing with political issues. Despite the ban on political questions, the Board's powers here seemed to come close to an invasion of that field.

As the co-operative endeavors of the system increased, it became next to impossible to fix boundary lines between the political and the nonpolitical, for international co-operation in and of itself is bound to be political in character. Recognizing that the distinction between political and non-political was a shadowy one at best, and recognizing further that the inter-American system had assumed clear-cut political responsibility, the Mexico City Conference of 1945 provided by resolution that the Governing Board of the Pan American Union

shall take action, within the limitations imposed upon it by the International Conference of American States or pursuant to the specific direction of the Meetings of the Ministers of Foreign Affairs, on every matter that affects the effective functioning of the inter-American system and the solidarity and general welfare of the American Republics.[23]

It was the consensus that this language, although vague, conferred political functions on the Governing Board. The ambiguity of the language failed to settle the issue entirely, and there was evidence that some opposition to the exercise of political powers was still present at Mexico City.[24]

The Governing Board was also reorganized at this Conference by Resolution IX, point 3, of the Final Act, which required that it be composed of one *ad hoc* delegate designated by each of the American republics; those delegates were to have the rank of ambassador, and were to be no part of the diplomatic missions accredited to the United States. The chairman was not to be eligible for re-election during the period immediately following.[25] The latter language would prevent the constant re-election of the secretary of state of the United States, thereby opening the chairmanship to Latin American members.

The Inter-American Conference for the Maintenance of Continental Peace and Solidarity of 1947 would seem to have closed the issue, for by the Inter-American Treaty of Reciprocal Assistance (the Rio Treaty) the Governing Board was empowered to act provisionally as the Organ of Consultation and thus take decisions including imposition of sanctions under the treaty until the Meeting of Foreign Ministers could take place. Provisionally the Board was empowered to discharge the executive or compliance functions of the system in the field of collective responsibility for peace and security.[26] Nevertheless, opposition to the projection of the Governing Board into the field of political action continued. At the Bogotá Conference in 1948, certain nations took the position that the Council, as the Board's successor, should have no political authority whatsoever, and urged that the previous grant of power by the Rio Treaty should be abrogated.[27]

As finally adopted, however, the Charter of Bogotá, far from prohibiting to the Council a political authority, not only accepts the formula of the Rio Treaty, but assigns to it a somewhat wider competence by empowering it upon request of a member state and by a majority vote to call a Meeting of Foreign Ministers to consider problems of an urgent nature and of common interest to the American states.[28] Moreover, Article 50 contemplates the bestowal of additional functions which may or may not be political, for it authorizes the Council to take cognizance "within the limit of the present Charter and of Inter-American Treaties and Agreements of any matter referred to it by the Inter-American Conference or the Meeting of Consultation of Ministers of Foreign Affairs."

The competence of the Council today, then, comes primarily from two sources: the Treaty of Reciprocal Assistance and the Charter of the OAS. Power exists only if provided expressly or by implication in the basic constitutional documents of the organization, and thus the legal exercise of authority is dependent upon interpretation of their provisions.

Political Functions — as Provisional Organ of Consultation

The Rio Treaty obligates the states who are parties to the treaty to assist an American state subjected to an armed attack immediately in meeting the attack. Although each state is free to determine the immediate measures it will individually take, the obligation to assist in some way is clear. Article 3 of the treaty provides that in case of armed attack, *the Organ of Consultation is to meet without delay to examine the above-mentioned measures and to agree upon the measures of a collective character that should be taken.*

A second type of situation contemplated under the Rio Treaty which may bring into being collective security measures is concerned with an act or threat of aggression which is not an armed attack or in which there may be any other fact or situation that might endanger the peace of America and that affects the territorial integrity, sovereignty, or political independence of an American state. Article 6 commands that when *any such situation arises the Organ of Consultation shall meet* immediately in order to agree on measures which, in case of aggression, must be taken to assist the victim, or, in any case, measures which should be taken for the common defense, for the maintenance of the peace and security of the continent.

Article 11 makes the Meetings of Ministers of Foreign Affairs of the American Republics which have ratified the Treaty, the Organ of Consultation; but Article 12 declares that the Governing Board of the Pan American Union may act provisionally as Organ of Consultation until the meeting of the Organ of Consultation takes place.

The terms of Article 13 require the consultations to be initiated "at the request addressed to the Governing Board . . . by any of the signatory states which has ratified the Treaty." Article 15 makes the Board an organ of liaison among the American states and between these states and the United Nations in all matters concerning the treaty.

Although the Rio Treaty granted carte blanche authority for future change in the Organ of Consultation and the Provisional Organ,[29] the Charter of Bogotá in its reorganization of the inter-American system continued these two agencies in their respective positions as articulated by the former treaty, with the Governing Board of course becoming the Council. Article 52 of the Charter bears this out in part, in these words: "The Council shall serve provisionally as

Organ of Consultation when the circumstances contemplated in Article 43 of this Charter arise."

Article 43 refers to the case of an armed attack only, which is but one of the situations contemplated in the Rio Treaty — that set forth in Article 3. To find authorization for the Council to act provisionally in situations other than armed attack, i.e., those situations set forth in Article 6, it is necessary to direct attention to Article 25, which by its language incorporates the provisions of the Rio Treaty by reference.[30] Therefore, the Council is empowered to act provisionally in all of the situations contemplated in the Rio Treaty. The provisional competence granted is in recognition of the fact that in certain cases measures of collective security may be urgently necessary and cannot await the delay involved in the actual convocation of the non-permanent agency, the Meeting of Foreign Ministers.[31]

It may then be reasonably concluded that once the Council sets itself up as Provisional Organ of Consultation by the assumption of jurisdiction over a case arising under the Rio Treaty, its competence is identical to that of the Meeting of Foreign Ministers, although from a literal interpretation of the basic instruments this is an interim competence enduring until the foreign ministers can assemble.[32] In such instances its powers of settlement are the same. It may determine which of the states that are parties to the dispute is the aggressor; insofar as two contending American states are concerned, it can call upon them to suspend hostilities; it can call upon these states to take other necessary measures to re-establish and maintain inter-American peace and security and to solve their conflict by peaceful means; and it can call for the application of sanctions, including the use of armed force. Moreover, the Council as Provisional Organ can, in order to ascertain the facts in the case, request information or carry out its own investigations through the use of committees which may be sent to the scene of the conflict or aggression. That the Council has these broad powers is made clear by its actions in the actual cases which have arisen before it. In those cases it has requested additional information from the contending parties; has sent investigating commissions to the countries involved to obtain on-the-spot information; has ordered the disputants to abstain from further hostilities; has called on each government to eliminate conditions which led to the dispute; and has made other specific recommendations to them for settling the issue. The Council has requested the American governments to place at the disposal of the investigating committee aircraft to make pacific observation flights over the regions affected by the dispute, and in the Cuban missile crisis even recommended the use of armed force.[33]

Not only does the Council as Provisional Organ have the competence assigned to a Meeting of Foreign Ministers, but it can be asserted that the measures taken in that capacity are valid measures not subject to later ratification by the foreign ministers as a condition of their legality. This is brought out in the proceedings of the 1947 Conference for the Maintenance of Continental Peace and Security, where it was stated that the resolutions adopted by the Provisional Organ are not themselves provisional so as to require future ratification, although the Meeting of Foreign Ministers may revoke or modify resolutions of the Council when and if such a Meeting is convened.[34]

Neither the Council as Provisional Organ nor the Meeting of Foreign Ministers as Organ of Consultation is empowered to settle *every* dispute among the American nations. Read hastily, the terms of Article 6 might seem to confer an almost unlimited jurisdiction by permitting action whenever the peace of the Americas is threatened. It would follow, if this were true, that any dispute at almost any stage might threaten peace. Upon more careful scrutiny, however, it will be seen that Article 6 not only requires, prior to an assumption of jurisdiction, an aggression or situation that endangers the peace, but also requires that this aggression or situation affect in some way the inviolability or the integrity of the territory or the sovereignty or political independence of an American state. Such a literal interpretation was given to the article in the Haiti–Dominican Republic case of 1949 when Haiti charged an aggression of a moral order against the Dominican Republic. The Council decided not to convoke the Organ of Consultation in part on the ground that the dispute did not affect the inviolability or the integrity of the territory or the sovereignty or the political independence of Haiti.[35] The Council is not a court to decide each and every case which might be presented to it by the member states. At certain stages of a dispute it is incumbent upon the parties to resort to negotiation or some procedure of pacific settlement. Nevertheless, any dispute, even though it concerns a purely legal question such as a violation of a rule of international law or the breach of a treaty, might well reach a stage whereby a situation is presented which would fall within the terms of the Rio Treaty. At that point the Council may step in to take measures to maintain or restore peace.

Once the Council takes cognizance of a case and constitutes itself as Organ of Consultation, its competence, as discussed above, is plain; but there is an area where its competence is shadowy and not clearly set forth by the provisions of the applicable treaties. This clouded area concerns the Council's power when a case is presented to it but prior to its determination to convoke a consultative meeting; i.e., what are the Council's powers between the time of the presentation of a case to it and the issuing of a convocation? It is manifest that the Council has no power in this preliminary stage to take action as to the substance of the dispute.[36] Nevertheless, it would appear indisputable that doubtful cases can occur, so that the Council may have to establish certain facts in order to determine whether there actually exists one of the situations contemplated in the Rio Treaty, making convocation necessary. To determine these facts it must possess power to obtain information, even to the extent of undertaking an investigation of its own before calling the Organ of Consultation or constituting itself as such provisionally.[37]

The contention has been made that the Council is required to convoke automatically when a member state requests it to do so and invokes Article 3 or 6 of the Rio Treaty; that the Council is not required to determine whether the circumstances alleged by the complaining member come within the purview of the treaty. To support this view it is claimed that an assumption of power by the Council of an investigation and adjudication of the question as to whether a case is a proper one for the application of the treaty would extend its political authority in a manner not contemplated.[38] It cannot be denied that such an authority would extend the Council's power as a council, as distinguished from provisional organ, for despite the fact that it may be said that the Council would not be examining here with a view to fixing responsibility and settling the case, still discussion and investigation could not help but involve incidentally the question of responsibility and fault, and such an airing of the facts might well bring pressure upon the disputants to settle the dispute by voluntary agreement.[39] Still, it is evident that the treaty does imply the possession of such power by the Council. Under the Rio Treaty, the decision to convoke comes within the purview of Council action. No provision is made for convening a meeting automatically upon request of a member state only. Article 13 requires the consultations "provided for in Articles 3 and 6 ... to be initiated at a request addressed to the Governing Board [Council] by any signatory state which has ratified the Treaty," and Article 16 declares that the Council shall make its decision as to convocation by majority vote.

In the case of an armed attack this procedure is modified by Article 42 of the Charter of Bogotá. The language used in that article does create an almost automatic procedure for convoking a Meeting of Foreign Ministers immediately when an armed attack occurs and at the same time calling a meeting of the Council. Apparently dispensed with as prerequisite is a request by a member state or a vote of the Council. Doubtless the Council could overrule the chairman's action by vote, if, upon meeting, it found the circumstances did not warrant a convocation.

In cases arising in situations other than armed attack as set forth in Article 6 of the Rio Treaty, the procedures are by no means automatic. Here the original provisions of the Rio Treaty are still applicable, requiring consultation to be initiated by the request of a ratifying state to the Council and a majority vote by that body for decision.

Unlike the case of actual armed attack which unquestionably creates the need for a meeting, doubt may well be present as to whether the facts of a case warrant a meeting under Article 6. It is self-evident that a convocation should not be called without justification and unless there is some relatively serious situation. Moreover, Article 6 requires a judgment to be made. The Council must decide whether an aggression which is not an armed attack or some conflict or situation that might endanger the peace of the Americas has occurred. It must also be determined whether this aggression, conflict, or situation affects the inviolability or the integrity of the territory or the sovereignty or the political independence of an American state. To make other than a blind judgment as to Article 6 will usually require the possession of a great deal of information and a careful examination of the facts, for in many cases the question of contravention of this article will not be at all obvious.

Even in the case of an armed attack the chairman might not feel inclined to call a convocation without obtaining additional information unless the facts he had at hand demonstrated clearly, convincingly, and unequivocally that an armed attack had occurred.

The ability to obtain pertinent facts must then fall within the implied powers of the Council in this preliminary stage, and to obtain and clarify such facts the Council can indulge in extended discussion and debate; it can request information from the parties; and it can conduct its own investigations by appointment of investigating committees which may conduct their investigations at the scene of the alleged aggression. To take a contrary view could make for an unintelligent decision to convoke and could give rise to possible consultations unjustified and improper under the terms of the Rio Treaty.

Although an investigative power prior to convocation appears beyond dispute, the Council has been hesitant to use it. In no case arising before it has the Council conducted a thorough investigation of its own at this stage. In most of the cases the Council has proceeded to call a Meeting of Foreign Ministers *sine die,* and constituted itself as provisional organ after a rather summary presentation of the facts. Not until it had declared itself provisional organ did it actually send out investigation committees to obtain on-the-spot, accurate, and complete information. Its proceeding in this manner has been criticized on the grounds that it would have been more logical to investigate all the facts first to ascertain if they warranted consultation. The criticism is particularly apt in view of the fact that the Council accepted the charges of violation after a summary investigation which convinced it that the situation was of sufficient gravity to justify it in constituting itself as provisional organ, but at the same time the Council indicated that the situation was not of such seriousness to warrant an actual convocation of foreign ministers, for it did no more than provide a *pro forma* convocation; i.e., it called a Meeting of Foreign Ministers without setting a date or place. This procedure implies a belief on the part of the Council that it has no power of an investigative character until it has convened as provisional organ. It further indicates that the Council is not empowered to act provisionally until it has proceeded to call a Meeting of the Organ of Consultation, even in instances where the Council apparently is of the opinion that there is no necessity for an immediate convocation of the foreign ministers.

It is manifest that the Council *qua* Council possesses investigative competence in the preliminary state. But the answer to the second issue, that of convocation of the foreign ministers as prerequisite to Council provisional action, is not so clear. Article 12 of the Rio Treaty declares that the Council may act provisionally until the meeting of the Organ of Consultation takes place. If taken in conjunction with Articles 3 and 6, which require the Organ of Consultation to meet without delay or immediately, there may be an indication here that the Council must call a Meeting of Foreign Ministers before it can act provisionally. In addition, it is clear from the debates at the Rio Conference that the Meeting of Ministers is to be the normal organ of consultation. Because of the fear that the Council might supersede the Meeting, Article 43 was inserted in the Bogotá Charter, requiring a meeting to be held without delay upon the convocation of the chairman of the Council in case of armed attack.[40] Nevertheless, the fact that the Meeting of Foreign Ministers is the normal organ of consultation does not mean that it is to be the forum in all cases. This issue as to the essentiality of a Meeting in all situations was left in some confusion by the debates, but from an examination of the proceedings of the Rio Conference, the conclusion can be reached that a Meeting of Foreign Ministers would not always be warranted. For example, one delegate states:

... in practice it will happen that in ninety per cent of the cases the provisional character attributed to the intervention of the Governing Board of the Pan American Union will extend to the complete solution of the disputes, whenever the latter are not of the type to justify the Meeting of Foreign Ministers.[41]

The relator for the Third Committee, which recommended Articles 11 and 12, declared:

... as supreme organ of consultation we have established the Meeting of Foreign Ministers. The Committee is not unmindful of the excellence ... of the Governing Board ... but considers that the unleashing of active measures ought to be the direct responsibility of the Governments ... The Governing Board ... will have to assume the role of Organ of Consultation in cases of inevitable urgency, or in others in which the subject matter, without being insignificant, does not justify the Meeting of Ministers.[42]

This language makes it plain that a Meeting of the Organ of Consultation would not always be considered essential. Still, the Council has proceeded in actual cases as if it is always incumbent upon it to call a Meeting of Foreign Ministers before provisional action can be taken. It has, however, reached the same result in many of these cases as if it had never called the Meeting of Foreign Ministers, for it has only gone through the form of calling a meeting and then, acting provisionally, has dealt with the problems presented and solved the controversy by acting exactly as the Organ of Consultation. Because of the expense involved in an actual Meeting of Foreign Ministers and the inconvenience to the ministers themselves, the Council would seem justified in conducting itself in such a manner on the ground of expediency in a situation which is not so grave and urgent as to warrant a convocation and which can be settled by the provisional organ itself or in instances where the urgency is so immediate and vital that delay cannot be permitted. Nevertheless, by proceeding in this way, it would seem to contravene the language of the Rio Treaty which requires an *immediate* meeting.[43]

Since any agency necessarily must possess authority to pass upon the scope of its own competence in the first instance, the Council's interpretation which apparently requires a constituting of itself as provisional organ before it can act under the Rio Treaty, and, further, which requires at least a *pro forma* convocation of the Meeting of Foreign Ministers when it constitutes itself provisionally, will stand as correct until challenged and disavowed by a superior organ — the Inter-American Conference or a Meeting of Foreign Ministers.[44]

It must be emphasized that this interpretation by the Council of its powers is the most important event that has taken place in the field of collective security of the OAS. It often makes the Council the real political executive of the organization, for in most cases presented to it and accepted by it the Council, upon convening provisionally, has called a Meeting, but failed to fix a time and place of meeting. It has then proceeded to settle the dispute and to cancel the Meeting. In the case of the 1954 communist menace in Guatemala the Council did see fit to call a Meeting of Foreign Ministers and to set a time and date. In this instance the Council did not constitute itself as provisional organ. It never became necessary to hold the Meeting and it was postponed *sine die* because the danger to the peace and security of the continent by communist infiltration was allayed by the success of the revolutionary junta and its acquisition of power as provisional government of Guatemala.[45]

In the 1960 conflict between Venezuela and the Dominican Republic the Council once again saw fit to convoke a Meeting of Foreign Ministers, and again the convocation was not *pro forma*, for a time and place for the Meeting was set. At this Meeting of Foreign Ministers enforcement measures under Article 6 of the Rio Treaty were unleashed against the Dominican Republic on the grounds of that nation's aggression; while at the Eighth Meeting of Consultation in 1962, the Foreign Ministers were actually convened by the Council, and the Ministers saw fit to impose an arms embargo upon Cuba and to exclude Cuba from participation in the OAS — a sanction or measure not specifically provided for in inter-American instruments, but voted by a two-thirds majority on the ground of Cuban incompatibility with the inter-American system.[46]

The words of the relator of the Third Committee mentioned above in effect describe the Council's authority. In the light of that language coupled with the practices of the Council to date, the following conclusions can be drawn:

In a case "in which the subject matter, without being insignificant, does not justify the Meeting of Ministers," the Council will proceed as it has been doing by constituting itself provisionally and calling for a *pro forma* convocation only. In those situations of armed attack or of other extremely serious nature, particularly where "the unleashing of active measures" in the form of sanctions may be thought to be necessary, an actual Meeting of Consultation will be called, although in situations not admitting of delay the Council can clearly take all necessary measures to deal with the problem until the Meeting of Foreign Ministers can convene. This latter case was well exemplified by the Council's action during the Cuban missile crisis of October, 1962 (discussed in Chapter XVII), when, because of extreme urgency, the Council acting as provisional organ recommended individual and collective measures, including the use of armed force, to defend the Americas against the threat of nuclear attack.

Political Functions — Problems of an Urgent Nature and of Common Interest

Article 39 of the Charter of Bogotá provides that the Meeting of Consultation of Ministers of Foreign Affairs shall be held not only to serve as the Organ of Consultation, but also in order to consider problems of an urgent nature and of common interest to the American states. Moreover, Article 40 requires that for such a meeting to be convened a member state must request it. This request is to be addressed to the Council, which shall then decide by a majority vote whether such a meeting shall be held. What then is the power of the Council here? Obviously it has no authority until some member state requests that a Meeting of Foreign Ministers be held. When such a request is forthcoming the Council's authority is restricted to a determination by a majority vote as to whether the requested meeting will be held.

This, however, is not as simple as it would appear to be. Again the Council is faced with a decision as to whether the situation behind the request falls within the terms of Article 39. Does the situation involve a problem of an urgent nature and of common interest to the American states? Resolving this question is its sole competence here. But to resolve this question, to arrive at an intelligent decision, extended discussion, debate, and examination of the details and facts of the situation may be in order. It may even become necessary to conduct an investigation by the appointment of a special committee to gather the facts so as to determine whether the problem is urgent and of common interest. There seems to be no restriction on the competence of the Council to resolve the issue, for its implied power of inquiry and investigation appear to be broad.[47]

The Council has in fact been presented with a problem involving its competence here. In 1949 a note of the Chilean government was presented to the Council concerning the case of the ex-President of Venezuela, Romulo Betancourt, who had been granted asylum in the Colombian Embassy in Caracas. The note charged that the Venezuelan military junta had failed to grant a safe-conduct for the ex-President and that this failure contravened the principle of the right of asylum and the democratic tradition of America. The note then requested the Council to assemble to examine the matter and to take steps with the junta to obtain respect for the right of asylum. A similar note from the Guatemalan government was also presented to the Council.[48] This, then, was a presentation of a juridical question to the Council—that of a breach of international law right or treaty right of asylum. Venezuela immediately challenged the competence of the Council in this situation; charged that Chile's action constituted intervention in a matter which did not concern it; and asserted that the safe-conduct of the ex-President had been granted. Since the safe-conduct had been granted the Council resolved not to consider the matter "because the reason which determined the situation before it had disappeared."[49] Because of a dispute in the Council as to its competence, a special committee of seven Council members was appointed to study the Council's authority in this matter.[50] The committee then reported that "definitive interpretation of any matter involving the competence of the Council is, of course, the function of the governments themselves, to be executed either through the Inter-American Conference or in the manner that the governments considered fitting." It then drafted a resolution that the Inter-American Council of Jurists should prepare a study on the competence of the Council as set forth in the applicable instruments. Such a study, which would have no legal force, was to be used as a guide for the governments in formulating their opinions on the subject. This resolution was accepted and the views of the Council of Jurists were requested.[51] To date that body has been unable to complete its deliberations.[52]

A memorandum of the Mexican member of the Council accompanied the report of the special committee which sought to clarify the crux of the problem involved. The principle expounded was as follows:

...The Council is not invested by the Charter or by any other juridical instrument with power to take upon itself the study of questions arising in connection with the observance or interpretation of any international obligations, except when, under the circumstances envisaged in the Rio Treaty, such questions reach the stage where they represent a real threat to the peace of the continent.[53]

The memorandum of the United States proceeded in a different direction. It declared that questions concerning the Council's competence in any given case involve interpretations of basic inter-American agreements, and that such questions should be decided by the Council or by one of the two higher organs. The United States member also stated that it would be undesirable to draw up rigid rules concerning the Council's competence, for its competence depended not only on the subject matter of the case at hand, but also on the circumstances under which it was raised. Further, it was asserted that any government had the right to bring any question it desired to the Council, and any case presented merited a fair hearing as to whether Council action was authorized.[54]

The power of the Council to study questions arising in connection with the observance or interpretation of international obligations is limited to discussion and investigation to determine the justification for calling of a Meeting of Consultation. In the asylum case, the Council could clearly have discussed the problems involved even though such discussion would perforce have concerned an issue of international obligation—the right of asylum. The discussion, however, would have to be centered around the one question — whether the situation was of a nature of sufficient urgency and common interest to have justified a meeting.[55]

Here, as in those situations requiring discussion and investigation under the Rio Treaty, prior to the Council's constituting itself as provisional organ, a broad power of inquiry must exist, even though, incidentally, in the course of the inquiry, the Council may find a violation of customary or conventional international law, and even though the investigation, again incidentally, may have the effect of bringing about a withdrawal of the request for a Meeting of Consultation.

The Council may not under this power of inquiry, in this instance, decide the merits of the case and pass judgment in the form of a decision on the parties, nor can it recommend any action to be followed by the parties. The investigations are held only to determine if the meeting should be held under Article 39.[56] Any recommended action other than a decision as to the need for holding the meeting must come from the Meeting of Foreign Ministers. Only if the situation is one falling within the terms of the Rio Treaty, which threatens the peace of the Americas and which meets the other conditions required by the treaty, can the Council make decisions and order the parties to take measures to maintain or restore the peace.

Non-political Functions

Not only does the Council exercise political functions under the Rio Treaty and the Charter, but the latter instrument grants it diverse authority in non-political fields.[57] The Charter grants to the Council a wide supervisory function, i.e., the power of control and regulation of other organs and agencies of the OAS. Article 51 imposes upon it responsibility for the proper discharge by the Pan American Union of the duties assigned to that body. The Council also must approve the administrative structure of the Pan American Union, and it sets general personnel standards.[58] Moreover, the Council elects the secretary general of the organization[59] as well as the assistant secretary general,[60] and may, by a two-thirds majority vote, remove either officer.[61] It directs the Pan American Union in the promotion of economic, social, juridical, and cultural relations among all the member states.[62] The Council, then, like its predecessor the Governing Board, is charged with the surveillance of the Pan American Union.

Although the three organs of the Council—the Inter-American Economic and Social Council, the Cultural Council, and the Council of Jurists—are granted technical autonomy,[63] still they are subject to the general supervisory power of the Council. The Council formulates their statutes, but not their regulations.[64]

The Council also has important duties in relation to the Specialized Organizations. Article 53 directs the Council to draft and submit to the governments proposals for the creation of new specialized organizations or for the combination, adaptation, or elimination of existing ones; to draft recommendations for the co-ordination of their activities and programs after consultation with them; and to conclude agreements with such specialized organizations which will determine the relationship between them and the organization.

Not only does the Council have responsibility to co-ordinate the inter-American specialized organizations, but among its functions of co-ordination and collaboration are also the powers to draft recommendations to the governments for the co-ordination of the activities and programs of the Inter-American Conference and the Specialized Conferences; to conclude agreements for co-operation with other American organizations of international standing; and to promote and facilitate collaboration between the OAS and the United Nations and between the Inter-American Specialized Organizations and similar international agencies.[65]

The financial duties of the Council concern its responsibility for budgetary arrangements of the Pan American Union. Article 54 calls upon the Council to establish bases for fixing the quota which each member is to contribute toward the maintenance of the Pan American Union. In establishing these bases, it is required to take into account the ability of each nation to pay and the determination of each country to make a contribution in an equitable manner.[66]

The Council prepares its own regulations[67] and the program and regulations of the Inter-American Conference and the Meeting of Consultation.[68] It fixes the time for the Inter-American Conference,[69] and if such Conference cannot be held at the place designated, designates a new place.[70] The Council, along with certain other organs, may call for a meeting of a Specialized Conference.[71]

Finally, the Council has functions in the field of pacific settlement of disputes as provided in the Pact of Bogotá.[72]

Composition, Voting, and Council Procedures

Resolution IX, point 3, of the Final Act of the Mexico City Conference of 1945 provided that the Governing Board was to be composed of one *ad hoc* delegate from each of the American republics, each delegate to have the rank of ambassador, but not to be a part of the diplomatic missions accredited to the United States.[73] This provision was made to give the Board greater autonomy and independence and to quell any notions of subjection and domination by the Department of State of the United States, particularly in view of the fact that it was contemplated that the Board should have political authority. It sought to make obligatory the appointment of special representatives having no connections with the diplomatic missions.[74] Nevertheless, the matter was left pending until the Bogotá Conference.[75] After consultation with the governments, a majority agreed that the appointment of special representatives should be optional rather than obligatory.[76] Thus, although some governments did appoint special ambassadors to the Board, many others continued as before to be represented by their ambassadors to Washington.

At Bogotá the question was raised again. Mexico contended strongly that special representatives should be designated by each country, arguing that the increased authority granted to the Council demanded a full-time representative from each country. Smaller nations, on the other hand, opposed the appointment of special representatives on the grounds of expense and asserted that they were unnecessary.[77] The problem was finally resolved by a return to the practice which had previously existed. Article 48 of the Charter declares:

The Council of the Organization of American States is composed of one Representative of each Member State of the Organization, especially appointed by the respective Government, with the rank of Ambassador. The appointment may be given to the diplomatic representative accredited to the Government of the country in which the Council has its seat. During the absence of the titular Representative, the Government may appoint an interim Representative.

Under this provision the Council is democratic in its representation, for, unlike the Security Council of the United Nations, it is composed of one representative of each member state of the organization.[78] No general voting formula is set forth in the Bogotá Charter, but under Council Regulations the democratic spirit is again adhered to, with no special privileges given to any member or group of members, for each representative has the right of one vote only.[79]

Article 36 of the Council Regulations requires that decisions of the Council be taken "by an affirmative vote of the majority of the member states, except when otherwise expressly provided for." Article 27 fixes a quorum of an absolute majority of the members of the Council.

Under the Rio Treaty, when the Council acts on certain procedural and administrative questions, such as decisions to initiate consultation[80] and decision on matters connected with the Council's duties as organ of liaison among the ratifying states and among these states and the United Nations,[81] decisions are to be taken by an absolute majority of the members entitled to vote.[82] Members entitled to vote in all situations under the Rio Treaty are the ratifying states[83] not directly interested parties to an inter-American dispute.[84]

Matters to which the majority vote would be applicable would include: decisions as to the parties to a dispute or the parties involved in a situation; whether a dispute or situation concerns American states; whether the terms of the treaty are applicable to a situation making necessary a consultation; the time and the place of the consultation; and questions relating to the transmittal of information to the member states and to the United Nations.[85]

Once the consultation is initiated, the Rio Treaty requires that all decisions be taken by a vote of two-thirds of the states ratifying the treaty.[86] Accordingly, after the Council convokes itself as Provisional Organ of Consultation, decisions are to be taken by a vote of two-thirds of the ratifying states. A difference will be noted here from those situations requiring a majority vote, for there, only states eligible to vote are counted in determining the number needed for the absolute majority.[87] After consultation is initiated, a vote of two-thirds of the ratifying states is needed, and parties ineligible to vote because they are interested parties to an inter-American dispute are counted to determine the number necessary to obtain the requisite two-thirds majority.

The quorum required to permit the Council to take decisions under the Rio Treaty, either before or after initiation of consultation, is determined by the qualifications for voting and the type of majority required for decision. Thus, Article 19 provides: "To constitute a quorum in all the meetings referred to in the previous Articles, it shall be necessary that the number of States represented shall be at least equal to the number of votes necessary for the taking of decision."

A two-thirds vote is also required by the Charter of Bogotá in arriving at decisions on Pan American Union budgetary matters.[88] In the case of the election of certain officers—the chairman and vice-chairman of the Council[89] as well as the secretary-general of the organization and the assistant secretary-general[90]—the regulations require a vote by a two-thirds majority of the total membership. The Charter of Bogotá requires that to remove the last two mentioned officers the Council shall act by a two-thirds vote of its members.[91]

As to the officers of the Council, the Charter follows the resolution of the Mexico City Conference by providing for a chairman and vice-chairman, who shall serve for one year and shall not be eligible for re-election to either of these positions for the term immediately following.[92] In addition to these officials the Charter makes the assistant secretary-general the Council's secretary.[93]

The Council has its seat in Washington.[94] Under the regulations its regular meetings are held on the first and third Wednesdays of each month except during July and August, when special and protocolary meetings only may be held.[95]

The meetings of the Council are public, although it may go into executive session at the request of any representative and shall so continue if the Council decides this to be necessary.[96] Special meetings may be called by the chairman, and any representative may request a special meeting by stating its purpose in writing.[97]

Since the Council is a body composed of all members, the effective preparation of many matters it deals with must take place in smaller bodies. Article

43 of the Regulations states that any matter presented to the Council which requires prior study shall be referred to a committee which shall draft a report thereon. The Council's regulations provide for several permanent committees—the General Committee, the Finance Committee, the Committee on Inter-American Conferences, the Committee on Inter-American Organizations, and the Committee on Publications and Public Information.[98] Their functions are listed in some detail. The regulations permit the Council to set up special temporary committees when necessary.[99] The members of the committees are the representatives of member states appointed thereto.[100] This is true except as to the General Committee, which is to be composed of the chairman and vice-chairman of the Council and the chairmen of the permanent and special committees.[101] Ordinarily committees are to have no more than seven members.[102] Except in cases for which the Regulations provide otherwise, members may be appointed and their number fixed by the Council, or, if the Council shall fail to make any decision on these points, by the Council chairman.[103]

The Organs of the Council

The Charter of Bogotá provides for three separate organs of the Council: the Inter-American Economic and Social Council, the Inter-American Council of Jurists, and the Inter-American Cultural Council.[104] Each of these organs is possessed of full technical autonomy within the limits of the Charter, although an admonition is attached that their decisions are not to encroach upon the sphere of action of the Council.[105] Some confusion is thus engendered, for these organs are dependent organs of the Council, but at the same time are granted full technical autonomy. As organs of the Council they are in a sense subordinate to that body, for they must act through the Council as components of the OAS. Nevertheless, they possess technical autonomy, i.e., independence in the consideration of those matters falling within their specialized fields which are submitted to them, and capacity to act in those fields within the terms of the Charter.[106]

The Charter requires these organs to render technical services to the governments of the member states upon the request of the governments, and to advise the Council on matters within their jurisdiction.[107] They are authorized to establish co-operative relations with corresponding organs of the United Nations and other international agencies functioning in similar spheres.[108] The Council is empowered to draft the statutes of these organs with the advice of appropriate bodies and after consultation with the governments. The organs formulate their own regulations.[109]

The Inter-American Economic and Social Council

Historically the Inter-American Economic and Social Council had its inception as a wartime agency. Resolution III of the First Meeting of Ministers of Foreign Affairs, in 1939, created an Inter-American Financial and Economic Advisory Committee composed of one economic expert from each of the American republics. The committee was to function for the period of the emergency arising out of the European war and was entrusted with the study of problems affecting the economic situation of the American nations.[110]

Resolution IX, point 7, of the 1945 Mexico City Conference stipulated that there should be created, in place of this temporary agency, a permanent Inter-American Economic and Social Council as a subsidiary of the Governing Board of the Pan American Union and composed of representatives named by the respective governments. This body was to be the co-ordinating agency for all official inter-American economic and social activities. The Governing Board was authorized to organize this Council provisionally. The Charter of Bogotá provided for its organization on a permanent basis.[111]

The principal purpose of the Inter-American Economic and Social Council, according to Article 63 of the Charter, is "the promotion of the economic and social welfare of the American nations through effective co-operation for the better utilization of their natural resources, the development of their agriculture and industry and the raising of the standards of living of their peoples." The language of Article 63 is somewhat simplified by the Statutes, which declare the principal purpose to be the promotion of "the economic and social well-being of the American states, through effective cooperation among them."[112]

The Charter shows the functions of the Inter-American Economic and Social Council to be:

1. To serve as a deliberative body for discussion and consideration of hemispheric economic and social problems, thus providing for inter-American co-operation in this field for the solution of such problems and for the promotion of the economic and social development of the American nations.

2. To execute or carry out economic or social programs.

3. To act as a technical agency in the social and economic field and as such to advise the Council and the member governments.

4. To act as an agency of consultation for economic problems when the economy of an American state is so affected that the state is unable to solve them unaided.

5. To act as co-ordinator of all official inter-American economic and social activities.[113]

Thus this body is entrusted with many kinds of duties, the relative importance of each not being clearly delineated. This caused confusion and a loss of sense of direction, which was felt in the Council.[114] As a result, in 1953 the Inter-American Economic and Social Council requested its Executive Committee to recommend suitable measures to correct imperfections in this organ and to strengthen it in all aspects, especially in the matter of necessary financial resources.[115] The report of the committee, among other things, sought to clarify the scope and extent of the duties of the Economic and Social Council to relieve the sense of frustration which had developed. The report stressed that the primary and essential function of this organ was to serve as an "instrument of deliberation through which the American nations may discuss their regional economic and social problems and achieve such a degree of understanding and comprehension as will enable them to increase their cooperation in regard to these matters."[116] In this respect the Inter-American Economic and Social Council is to fulfil an essentially political purpose, confined to the solution of economic and social problems and the promotion of economic and social development of the hemisphere through its deliberations.[117]

The report went on to note that although the Inter-American Economic and Social Council is basically a political organ of a deliberative nature, still the Charter assigns technical-advisory functions to it, inasmuch as it is made an advisory body of the Council of the organization, is called upon to render technical services to the governments, and may undertake studies and prepare reports on economic and social matters for the use of the member states. This latter function creates confusion, for it is not realistic to assume that a body composed of representatives of all the American republics can act as a research agency to produce reports requested of it. Thus, according to the report, no attempt should be made to convert this body into an advisory agency or office of economic research; and as to the technical-advisory function, all that can be expected of the Council as a group of representatives specializing in various fields is that "it will be able to guide and define the scope of the various tasks entrusted to it, which would be performed by specialists."[118]

The new Statutes adopted in 1955 modified to some extent the wording of the Charter of Bogotá and the original Statutes as to the accomplishment of the purpose of the Inter-American Economic and Social Council.[119] The technical-advisory function was provided for in Article 4 of the Statutes; but it was declared that in rendering the technical services to the governments, the Inter-American Economic and Social Council should make the necessary arrangements therefor, and further, that the requests of the governments should be considered in relation to the work program that the organ was to develop and the facilities at its disposal. The function of advising the Council was continued unchanged. In this connection the standing committees of the body were required to undertake "such research as they consider appropriate or is entrusted to them by the Council, on its own initiative or at the request of a member state of the Organization or any organ or specialized agency thereof."[120]

Article 65 of the Charter of Bogotá declares that the Inter-American Economic and Social Council is to be composed of technical delegates appointed by each member state. The Regulations are more specific concerning the composition, in that this organ is composed of one representative of each member state, especially appointed by his government.[121] Each government is permitted to appoint alternate delegates, counselors, and advisers.[122] In the absence of a representative, the government of that representative may appoint an acting representative.[123]

A subject of some controversy within the Economic and Social Council concerns the quality of the delegates. It has been argued that a deficiency of this Council has been that the delegates appointed have not been sufficiently expert. The report of the Executive Committee commenting on this criticism set forth the opinion that the requirement that the delegate be "technical" is in reality a secondary consideration if the essential nature of the organ is deliberative and not technical-advisory. The report emphasizes that it would be almost an impossibility to find technicians with expert knowledge of the wide range of subjects that make up the social and economic field. It then concludes that in this respect the requirement of the Charter refers "to persons sufficiently versed in those subjects; otherwise it would be difficult to find any sense in the provision."[124]

The Charter of Bogotá makes the permanent seat of the Inter-American Economic and Social Council the same as that of the Pan American Union—Washington, D.C. It is permitted to hold meetings in any American city by a majority decision of the member states.[125] It meets on its own initiative or on that of the Council of the organization.[126] The Statutes and Regulations provide for regular meetings, special or extraordinary meetings, and a special annual meeting.[127] Regular meetings are held when the chairman or executive committee of the organ deems it advisable, when a committee of the organ requests the chairman so to call, or when any member state makes such a request.[128]

Special meetings are held when called by the Inter-American Conference, the Meeting of Ministers of Foreign Affairs, or the Council of the organization. In special circumstances the Inter-American Economic and Social Council may call a special meeting if requested by one or more governments and by an absolute majority vote. Attendance by the ministers of the economic or social branches of the governments is permissible if the governments wish. The organ is required to hold special meetings periodically, attended by the ministers of finance or economy, pursuant to the wishes of the governments, to give preferential consideration to the results obtained through the programs of economic development.[129]

There is also a special annual meeting; the period in which it is held is set by the executive committee. This meeting is devoted mainly to review of the work accomplished, examination of future plans and action, election of certain officers, and decisions as to membership of the standing committees, as well as any other matters of interest.[130]

A consultative meeting may also be held to aid a state suffering from serious economic problems when such a state wishes to utilize the consultation procedures and addresses a request to the chairman of the body. The chairman is then called upon to notify the governments through their representatives on the Economic and Social Council. He shall then proceed to convoke the organ in order to determine the most effective form the consultation should take.[131]

The decisions of the Economic and Social Council taken at the meetings are usually in the form of resolutions.[132] An absolute majority of the representatives constitutes a quorum.[133] Each member of the body has one vote, and the decisions are adopted for the most part by an absolute majority of the members.[134] The decisions are not binding on the member states; at best they are recommendatory only.

The nerve centers of this body are its committees, it being provided that the work of the Council shall be distributed among standing committees through which continued action is taken on all economic and social matters within the purview of jurisdiction.[135] It is these committees which maintain economic and social information on a current basis for periodic transmittal to the member governments; which undertake appropriate research entrusted to them by the organ on its own initiative or at the request of the members of other organs or agencies; which analyze economic and social phenomena and present studies, observations, and recommendations to the Inter-American Economic and Social

Council; and which suggest to it measures tending to improve the economic and social well-being of the American nations.[136]

In addition to the standing committees, the Economic and Social Council may establish special committees when it is so decided by the Inter-American Conference, the Meeting of Foreign Ministers, or the Council of the organization. It may establish committees it considers necessary on its own initiative, as well as special committees recommended by the Specialized Conferences in agreement with the Council of the organization.[137]

Provision is made for a permanent executive committee composed exclusively of the chairman and vice-chairman, the chairmen and rapporteurs of the standing committees, and one member designated by the organ. The Department of Economic and Social Affairs of the Pan American Union is the secretariat of the Inter-American Economic and Social Council, and its director is its executive secretary.[138]

In 1960 a special meeting of senior government representatives met in Washington to consider ways and means of strengthening the Inter-American Economic and Social Council. This special meeting approved eight recommendations. It was recommended that except when called upon to meet an emergency situation under the terms of Article 27 of the Charter, the Inter-American Economic and Social Council should hold only two short and consecutive meetings each year. The first, to be attended by technicians, would carry out preparatory work on the topics to be submitted to the second for consideration. This second meeting, which would preferably be attended by delegates of cabinet rank, would review the social and economic progress of the member countries, analyze and discuss the achievements and problems in each country, exchange opinions on measures that might be adopted to further social and economic progress, and prepare reports on the outlook for the future.

The special meeting also recommended that both the OAS Council and the Inter-American Economic and Social Council reorganize their committees and subcommittees to avoid duplication of tasks and multiplicity of meetings. It specifically called for the creation of a single Special Committee on Basic Products to replace the Economic and Social Council's Committee on Basic Products, Committee on Coffee, and Committee on Bananas.

The General Secretariat was advised to formulate and carry out plans and programs relating to the economic and social development of member states and technical co-operation projects, and it was suggested that the Secretariat give greater flexibility in the allotting of funds for the work program; make better use of the services of private or public organizations and individuals to prepare special studies; and broaden the technical training program for the Secretariat personnel. The secretary general was advised to intensify efforts to strengthen the relations between the OAS and other international agencies and organizations operating in the economic and social fields.

In order to comply with these recommendations, the Committee on Regulations and Procedure of the OAS Council revised the Economic and Social Council's Statutes and Regulations; these revisions were approved by the Council of the OAS in November, 1961.[139]

The Inter-American Council of Jurists

The second organ of the Council is the Inter-American Council of Jurists. Article 67 of the Charter of Bogotá assigns to this agency the authority "to serve as an advisory body on juridical matters; to promote the development and codification of public and private international law; and to study the possibility of attaining uniformity in the legislation of the various American countries, insofar as it may appear desirable."

This, then, is the body primarily designed to deal with juridical matters of the Americas, and, as such, it is a deliberative body in that it may study and discuss ways and means to promote the development and codification of international law, as well as ways and means to attain uniformity among the national laws. The term "development of international law" would seem to mean the preparation of studies and draft conventions on subjects not yet regulated by international law or in regard to subjects to which the law has not been sufficiently developed in the practice of states. The expression "codification" is generally accepted to mean the more precise formulation and systematization of existing rules of international law, i.e., in areas where state practice, precedent, and doctrine have crystallized as rules.

The Charter permits this agency to go beyond the mere promotion of public international law. It also permits action in the area of private law of the member states, for it may promote the development and codification of private international law and study the possibility of attaining uniformity in national legislation.

In carrying out its functions, the Inter-American Council of Jurists is directed "to seek the co-operation of national committees for the codification of international law, of institutes of international and comparative law, and of other specialized agencies."[140]

If such co-operation implies permanent relations with United Nations organs or with other international or national agencies functioning within the field, agreement must be forthcoming from the Council of the organization before the Council of Jurists may act.[141]

The Council of Jurists also acts in a technical-advisory manner, for it is called upon to render the governments of the member states technical services upon their request and to advise the organization on juridical matters.

Unlike the Inter-American Economic and Social Council, which meets in regular session at permanent headquarters, the Inter-American Council of Jurists meets only as required and with no fixed seat. In this it is more like a specialized conference. Article 72 of the Charter grants responsibility to the Council for the convocation of the Council of Jurists at the place determined by the latter Council at its previous meeting. Article 16 of the Statutes of the Council of Jurists requires the intervals between meetings not to exceed two years unless the Council of the organization, for special reasons, finds a longer interval expedient. If a government of a member state desires a special meeting, it may request the Council of the organization to call one and the Council shall then decide on the request by an absolute majority vote.[142]

Decisions taken at a meeting require an absolute majority vote of the member states, although this Council may decide, in exceptional cases, to require a two-thirds majority.[143] Each representative has the right to one vote,[144] the Council being composed of twenty-one jurists, representatives of all the respective member states.[145]

The Council of Jurists is considered a permanent organ of the OAS with continuous functions. However, the fact that it meets only periodically, with its representatives appointed at the sole discretion of the member states, can handicap the organ to considerable degree. If representatives are not appointed long enough before a meeting of the Council of Jurists, they cannot be sufficiently prepared to deal with the difficult juridical problems presented for their examination. Moreover, if their tour of duty ends with the meeting of this Council, no continuity of functioning can be maintained. It has been recognized that it would be ideal if the governments would appoint their representatives on a permanent basis, not simply for an occasional conference. But the final decision as to appointment and replacement of delegates rests with the governments and cannot be limited.[146]

This Council has attempted to deal with this problem to the best of its ability. A declaration has been made that the delegations do not dissolve after every meeting, but are maintained with such changes as the governments may make in them.[147] The Statutes of the Council of Jurists require the governments to inform the secretary general of the organization and the permanent committee of the body of the manner in which they have decided to constitute their delegations.[148] The Pan American Union is required to maintain an up-to-date list of the members of the Council of Jurists and, in order to do so, is to request reports from the member governments. Any changes are to be noted by the Union, and the list is to be placed at the disposal of the Council of the organization, the Council of Jurists, and its permanent committee.[149]

The Council of Jurists may establish at its meetings such committees as it considers necessary to study the topics on the agenda.[150] The Charter of Bogotá, however, provides for a permanent committee of the Council of Jurists—the Inter-American Juridical Committee of Rio de Janeiro—which undertakes preparatory studies and provides continuity in the work of the Council during the intervals between its meetings.[151] This committee is composed of jurists of nine countries which are selected by the Inter-American Conference. The selection of the jurists themselves is made by the Council of Jurists from a panel submitted by each of the nine countries chosen by the Conference. Although not every member state sends representatives to the Committee, the Charter states that the nine members of this committee represent all of the member states.[152]

By the terms of the Charter, this organ is called upon to undertake such studies and preparatory work as may be assigned to it by the Council of Jurists, the Inter-American Conference, the Meeting of Consultation, or the Council of the organization. It may also undertake studies it considers advisable.[153]

Following the assignment to this committee by the Charter of Bogotá of duties as permanent committee to the Council of Jurists, some confusion arose as to whether or not the committee was possessed of a dual personality: the one arising from the assignment set forth by the earlier resolution of the 1942

Meeting of Foreign Ministers, and the other resulting from the provisions of the Charter. The Council of the organization decided that it had only one personality, and that was the personality given to it by the Charter. In other words, despite its earlier faculties, this agency now serves in the sole capacity of permanent committee of the Council of Jurists.[154]

In the years after the inception of the OAS under the Charter of Bogotá, the Inter-American Juridical Committee was hampered in its work because of the lack of a quorum which prevented its effective functioning. This situation occurred for two reasons: some of the governments responsible for appointing members to the committee failed to do so, and certain jurists appointed were unable to occupy their positions through some confusion as to their qualifications.[155] This can be explained by a brief look at the background of the committee.[156]

This agency was first created in 1939 by the First Meeting of Foreign Ministers under the name of the Inter-American Neutrality Committee.[157] It was composed of experts in international law appointed by the governments. In some cases the diplomatic representatives of certain countries at the seat of the committee were appointed as members.[158] These members, of course, had dual functions. The Third Meeting of Foreign Ministers of 1942 changed the name of this agency to Inter-American Juridical Committee and expanded the scope of its activity.[159] It was also provided that the committee should be composed of jurists especially appointed by their respective governments, and that they were to have no other duties than those pertaining to the committee.[160]

At the time of its creation in 1939, the committee was composed of seven members.[161] The membership was later increased to ten.[162] The Charter decreased the number to jurists of nine countries. Since the designation of the nine countries is entrusted to the Inter-American Conference, the provision for organization on that numerical basis could not be carried out until the Tenth Conference. Resolution II of the Bogotá Conference therefore provided that the committee should continue as organized until the time when the provisions of the Charter could be carried out.[163]

The problem then was whether the provision of the 1942 resolution which prevented members of the juridical committee from exercising functions other than those pertaining to the committee itself was still applicable, despite the fact that the Charter of Bogotá contains no such restriction. If the resolution was still in force, diplomatic agents at the headquarters of the committee appointed by their governments to serve on it were unable to occupy the position. A need was felt to clear up the doubt and regularize the situation. The Council finally decided to suspend the "no other duties" requirement until the Tenth Conference, and also made repeated requests to the states on the committee to appoint their members;[164] but the situation remained unchanged. A leading cause was thought to be the fact that the committee was called to meet regularly in Rio de Janeiro throughout most of the year, which in effect would make a member especially appointed to the committee devote all his time to it. This the members were often reluctant to do, because it would force them to neglect other duties at home. Therefore it was believed to be more advantageous to set a fixed period of continuous work for the committee during which the members would take up permanent residence in Rio de Janeiro. This solution would make it easier for the governments which had encountered difficulty in insuring the presence of their members to fulfil their obligations.[165]

The Tenth Inter-American Conference adopted a resolution, the provisions of which were designed to correct the malfunctioning of the Juridical Committee so that it might better fulfil its aims.[166] It was provided that, beginning in 1955, the committee should function on a permanent basis during three consecutive months of each year, without prejudice to the convocation of a special meeting whenever any important and urgent matter might require it.

Considerable debate arose as to whether the members were to have no duties other than those pertaining to the committee. Brazil favored a reaffirmation of the "no other duties" principle. The United States favored revocation of the principle. Upon motion, the reaffirmation of the principle failed of adoption.[167] A formula was then advocated and accepted which recognized that "it is essential that the jurists selected to be members thereof devote themselves exclusively to the work of the Committee during the period of its meeting."[168]

The number for a quorum required for a meeting was set at five—i.e., an absolute majority, since the number of members was, as of the Tenth Conference, reduced from ten to nine in accordance with Article 69 of the Charter of Bogotá.[169] The number of votes for decision was also stipulated to be five.[170] At the same time the resolution called upon the Council to examine the Statutes of the Council of Jurists, incorporate the changes made therein, and also amend the regulations of the Juridical Committee.[171]

The Inter-American Cultural Council

The Charter of Bogotá includes the Inter-American Cultural Council as the third organ of the Council of the organization.[172] As such, it is an integral part of the OAS. The basic objective of this organ is to serve as a center for promoting educational, scientific, and cultural exchange and friendly relations and mutual understanding among the American peoples.[173] To carry out this objective the functions of the Cultural Council are outlined in some detail:

a) To sponsor inter-American cultural activities;

b) To collect and supply information on cultural activities carried on in and among the American States by private and official agencies both national and international in character;

c) To promote the adoption of basic educational programs adapted to the needs of all population groups in the American countries;

d) To promote, in addition, the adoption of special programs of training, education and culture for the indigenous groups of the American countries;

e) To cooperate in the protection, preservation and increase of the cultural heritage of the continent;

f) To promote cooperation among the American nations in the fields of education, science and culture, by means of the exchange of materials for research and study, as well as the exchange of teachers, students, specialists and, in general, such other persons and materials as are useful for the realization of these ends;

g) To encourage the education of the peoples for harmonious international relations;

h) To carry on such other activities as may be assigned to it by the Inter-

American Conference, the Meeting of Consultation of Ministers of Foreign Affairs, or the Council of the Organization.[174]

This Cultural Council functions much like the Inter-American Juridical Council. It is composed of one representative from each member state, especially appointed by the respective governments.[175] According to this organ's Statutes, the governments are to inform the secretary general of the organization and the executive secretary of the Cultural Council of the manner in which they decide to constitute or change their delegations.[176] The Pan American Union is directed to maintain an up-to-date list of the representatives.[177] The Cultural Council does not meet in regular sessions at permanent headquarters. The Charter provides that its meetings are to be convoked by the Council of the organization, the place having been determined by the Cultural Council itself.[178] Article 17 of the Statutes declares that the intervals between meetings may exceed two years only when the Council of the organization so decides. Decisions at a meeting of the Cultural Council require an absolute majority of the votes of the member states except in exceptional cases, when a two-thirds majority is required.[179] Each member state has one vote.[180]

This body is empowered to establish co-operative relations with the corresponding organs of the United Nations and other international agencies with related functions. Agreement of the Council of the organization must be obtained for such co-operative establishment.[181] The Cultural Council is also called upon to render technical services to the governments as they request and to advise the Council of the organization.[182]

As in the case of the Council of Jurists, the Cultural Council is assigned a permanent committee to undertake preparatory studies in the intervals between Council meetings. This agency is designated the Committee for Cultural Action.[183] Its members are five states chosen at each Inter-American Conference; the individuals composing the committee are selected by the Cultural Council from a panel submitted by each country chosen by the Conference. These individual members are to be specialists in educational or cultural matters.[184] The Charter of Bogotá does not designate the seat of the committee, but the Statutes of the Cultural Council establish the committee's headquarters at Mexico City.[185]

The Regulations of the committee stipulate that it shall hold ordinary sessions each year for the length of time necessary to complete its studies in accordance with its plan of work.[186] Each representative is entitled to one vote,[187] and decisions are taken by a three-vote majority of the representatives of the member states on the committee.[188]

The Cultural Council was delayed in coming into being for a longer time than the other two Councils. Actually, the Economic and Social Council was functioning prior to the Bogotá Charter. The Council of Jurists, although created by the Charter, possessed in its permanent committee, the Juridical Committee, an existing and operating organ. But no structural basis had been laid in the field of cultural co-operation.

The Council of the organization began its deliberations respecting the Cultural Council in April, 1949. On this date it received the first report prepared on the subject along with the draft statutes of the Cultural Council, and directed that the draft be submitted to the consideration of the governments of the member states. At a meeting in November, 1949, the Council adopted a resolution approving the Provisional Statutes of the Cultural Council and designated Mexico City as the seat of its first meeting. It then approved an agenda for the first meeting, and approved a motion for the provisional formation of the Committee for Cultural Action by the Cultural Council during the sessions in Mexico City pending definite action by the Tenth Inter-American Conference. The selected five members of the provisional committee were Brazil, Haiti, Mexico, the United States, and Uruguay.[189]

At the first meeting, the Inter-American Cultural Council constituted the committee provisionally, electing the individual members from the panels presented by the governments of the five states that the Council had chosen.[190]

The Committee for Cultural Action has been faced with difficulties similar to those which faced the Juridical Committee—e.g., the problem of a quorum, With an insufficient number of members, the committee has been hampered in the effective performance of its functions. Furthermore, it was recognized that a closer relationship needed to be established between the committee and the Department for Cultural Affairs of the Pan American Union.[191] Resolution LIII of the Tenth Conference requested the Council to study, in consultation with the Cultural Council, and to recommend measures advisable for improving the organ and the work program of the committee. In addition, the Council was specifically requested to consider as part of its study the possibility of ensuring the presence of a quorum, the co-ordination of the work of the committee with that of the Department of Cultural Affairs, and the methods by which the committee might contribute more effectively to the work of the Cultural Council.[192]

As a result of the Council's deliberations, the Statutes of the Cultural Council were amended, and a section was added entitled "Principles and Standards to Govern the Committee for Cultural Action." These amendments and standards were designed to establish in clearer and more precise terms the functions assigned to the committee, the position it occupies with respect to the Cultural Council, and the relations that should exist between the committee and its secretariat, which is the Department of Cultural Affairs of the Pan American Union.[193]

THE ADVISORY DEFENSE COMMITTEE

The Charter of Bogotá creates an Advisory Defense Committee, composed of the highest military authorities of the American states, to advise the Organ of Consultation on problems of military co-operation that may arise in connection with the application of existing special treaties on collective security.[194] The Charter of Bogotá further stipulates that the Advisory Defense Committee shall be convoked under the same conditions as the Organ of Consultation, when the latter deals with matters relating to defense against aggression.[195]

The committee is not a continuously functioning organ, for it serves as advisory agency to the Organ of Consultation, the Meeting of Foreign Ministers, on matters of military operations and meets concurrently with that organ. As the Council is designated Provisional Organ of Consultation, the Advisory

Defense Committee may also serve as advisor to the Council when it acts in its provisional capacity in matters of collective security involving defense against aggression.[196]

The Charter also calls upon this body to meet when the Inter-American Conference, the Meeting of Consultation, or the governments, by a two-thirds majority, assign to it technical studies or reports on specific subjects.[197] To date no situation has arisen that has made it necessary to convene a meeting of the Advisory Defense Committee.

The Mexico City Conference of 1945 recommended the establishment of a permanent military organization,[198] and it was originally planned that such a body should be created as the fourth organ of the Council to advise on all matters of military collaboration.[199] However, disagreement arose, some Latin American nations believing that a permanently functioning military organ would be inconsistent with the essentially civilian character and the pacific traditions of the inter-American system.[200] A compromise was in order, so the Advisory Defense Committee was established, not as a permanent council, but as a mere appendage of the emergency meetings of the Organ of Consultation. To meet the need for a continuously functioning military body, the existing Inter-American Defense Board, although not mentioned in the Charter, was continued by Resolution XXXIV of the Final Act of the Ninth Conference until such time as the American governments should decide by a two-thirds majority to consider its labor terminated. This Board was first organized pursuant to a recommendation of the Third Meeting of Ministers of Foreign Affairs (1942) to consider questions relating to the military defense of the continent.[201]

The resolution of the Ninth Conference stipulated that the Board continue to act as the organ of preparation for collective self-defense against aggression, to perform any similar functions ascribed to it by the Advisory Defense Committee, and to serve as the secretariat of that committee. The Board was empowered to draw up its own regulations as to organization. This it did in 1949.[202]

Under the regulations, the Board consists of three organs: the Council of Delegates, the Staff, and the Secretariat. These organs are headed respectively by a chairman, a director of the staff, and a secretary.

The Council of Delegates is a governing body making recommendations to the governments for the measures of preparation necessary for the collective self-defense of the American continent against aggression, as well as for the security of the hemisphere. The staff is the technical working body and, as such, studies, plans, and recommends measures for collective defense against aggression and other measures conducive to close military collaboration for hemispheric security. It is organized with a director, a vice-director, an advisory group, and three permanent committees. As of 1958, the staff was composed of twenty-two officers representing twelve nations. The secretariat is the administrative body, performing administrative and secretarial duties for the organs of the Board and for the Advisory Defense Committee.[203]

In 1950, the Council of the organization conducted a survey of the status of the Inter-American Defense Board. It was concluded that the Council had competence to consider the status and activities of this agency by the terms of Resolution III of the Ninth Conference, which recommended that the Council make a survey of all existing inter-American organizations; that the Board is not a political body and has no such powers, its functions being of a technical-military character; that the continuance of the Board depends upon the actions of the American governments which can terminate its labors by a two-thirds vote in accordance with Resolution XXXIV of the Ninth Conference; and that the Board, although it has essentially the consultative functions specified in the above-mentioned Resolution, has also the right of initiative necessary for the fulfilment of its duties as a technical-military agency.[204]

Resolution III of the Fourth Meeting of Consultation of Ministers of Foreign Affairs included certain recommendations directed to the Board. It sets forth the positive measures of inter-American military co-operation to be undertaken by the American republics, and urged the governments to maintain adequate and permanent representation on the Council and staff of the Board; to support its work; to give prompt consideration to its projects, plans and recommendations; and to co-operate in organizing a co-ordinated system of exchange of appropriate information within this organ. The Board was also charged with the preparation of military plans for the common defense, to be submitted to the governments for their consideration and decision.[205] As a result, the agency has prepared the "General Military Plan for the Defense of the American Continent."[206]

With these developments it can be said that the Inter-American Defense Board has developed into a sort of permanent military organ of the OAS.

THE INTER-AMERICAN PEACE COMMITTEE

A resolution, "The Peaceful Solution of Conflicts," of the Meeting of Foreign Ministers in Habana in 1940 recommended to the Governing Board of the Pan American Union the organization of a committee composed of five countries which should have the duty of "keeping constant vigilance to insure that states between which any dispute exists or may arise, of any nature whatsoever, may solve it as quickly as possible." To that end the committee was further authorized to suggest measures and steps which might be conducive to a settlement—without prejudice, however, to methods adopted by the parties or procedures they might agree upon.[207] From this language it can be seen that there is a complete absence of any element of legal obligation in the relations of the committee with the parties to the controversy; it was authorized to suggest measures but no nation legally bound itself to accept these suggestions. This committee, now known as the Inter-American Peace Committee, was conceived of as an agency to promote the pacific settlement of controversies among the American republics.

At Bogotá in 1948, the Pact of Bogotá or Treaty on Pacific Settlement was adopted. One of its purposes was to co-ordinate and replace existing machinery of pacific settlement, and Article 58 of the Pact specifically lists the treaties, conventions, and protocols which it would supplant upon ratification. But by some oversight it failed to include the Inter-American Peace Committee.

Strangely enough this committee was not formally constituted until 1948, although in 1940 the Governing Board had decided that the committee should have its seat in Washington and should be composed of representatives of two North American nations, two South American nations, and one located in Central America or the Antilles. Later it was decided that the countries to be represented on the committee were to be Argentina, Brazil, Cuba, Mexico, and the United States.[208]

Events and disputes occurring in the Caribbean area occasioned the actual formation of the committee. In July 1948, the Dominican Republic requested the Council to request the member states to appoint their representatives to the committee so that it could consider and assist in the settlement of a controversy between the Dominican Republic and Cuba.[209] The installation of the committee took place on July 31, 1948, in Washington after the member nations had appointed their delegates.[210] The committee quickly demonstrated its usefulness in this first case, as well as in a second one arising a short time later between Haiti and the Dominican Republic,[211] by bringing the parties to a dispute together and by getting them to agree on a solution of their controversies.

The name initially given to this agency was the Inter-American Committee of Methods for the Peaceful Solution of Conflicts. In July, 1949, it was given a simpler name, the Inter-American Peace Committee.[212]

As its status was overlooked at Bogotá, a question was raised as to the relationship of the Inter-American Peace Committee to the OAS.[213] It was assumed that the committee was an agency of the organization, but that it did not come under the control of the Council because the functions of the Council were set forth in detail in the Charter of Bogotá, and this list did not include the supervision of agencies of the OAS other than those mentioned in the Charter. The Committee proved to be a highly practical body, for it demonstrated that there was need of supplementing the Pact of Bogotá, which many nations have refused to ratify, by some informal procedure which would facilitate the pacific settlement of disputes among American states.

Since the Council believed that the Inter-American Conference was the organ charged with deciding upon the general action and policy of the organization and with determining the structure and functions of its various organs, a decision was approved to include the study of the Inter-American Peace Committee as a topic on the agenda of the Tenth Inter-American Conference.[214]

At the Tenth Conference of American States, held in Caracas in 1954, no attempt was made to integrate the committee with other procedures set forth in the Pact of Bogotá, although there was certain discussion centering around the need for the rotation of membership of the committee and the desirability that the committee should be authorized to act only with the consent of all the parties to the dispute.[215] The conference passed a resolution commending the work of the committee and continuing it as a body of the OAS. The Council was called upon to draw up a new statute for the committee based upon the draft prepared by the committee itself and submitted to the conference.[216]

The Statutes were approved by the Council on May 9, 1956, after submission to the governments.[217] The competence of the committee was set out much as before, to "keep constant vigilance, within the scope of its authority, to ensure that states between which any dispute or controversy exists will solve it as quickly as possible, to which end it shall suggest measures and steps conducive to a settlement, and it shall at all times respect the methods or procedures agreed upon by the Parties."[218]

Article 2 of the Statutes permits any state directly concerned in a dispute or controversy to request the committee to take action. Prior to so doing, the committee must first consult the other party or parties to the dispute as to whether they consent to committee action in the case,[219] and thereafter offer the committee's services pursuant to its mandate and the nature of its functions.[220] If consent of the parties is forthcoming, the committee shall take up the case immediately, if no other procedure for pacific settlement is in progress.[221] If consent is not given, the committee must refrain from acting on the case.[222] All it is empowered to do in such an event is to transmit the replies received to the governments of the members of the OAS through their respective members on the Council,[223] to inform the Council, the Meeting of Consultation of Ministers of Foreign Affairs, and the Inter-American Conference.[224] It is also called upon to keep the Security Council of the United Nations informed of its action.[225] These duties of transmission of replies and information are also required if the committee becomes seized of the case by consent of the parties.

The membership of five states is continued, the states to be designated by the governments through the Council. The chosen states are to serve for a five-year period.[226] Rotation of membership is made possible. No provision requires the member states to be chosen from a geographical area,[227] and Article 4 prohibits re-election to membership on the committee at the conclusion of a term; nor is a state permitted to serve again until at least one year has elapsed. One member state is to be replaced each year, and the governments are called upon to designate each year, through the Council, the state that is going to replace the outgoing member.[228] A transitory article, placed in the Statutes to determine the initial membership, required the governments through the Council to designate five states to serve for terms of one, two, three, four, and five years respectively. In case a term of a member expires while the committee is engaged on a specific case, the term of that member is automatically extended, but only for that particular case.[229]

The representatives of the member states are designated by their governments and may be the same representatives accredited to the Council.[230] Alternate representatives are to be designated to replace the representative in his absence or when he is otherwise prevented from serving.[231]

Article 10 sets forth the principle that a state shall not be a judge in its own case by prohibiting a state which is a member of the committee from acting when it is an interested party in a dispute or controversy in which the committee has been requested to take action. In such an instance, the committee shall, without prejudice to its taking action with a legal quorum, request the Council to name as a substitute another state whose representative shall act solely with respect to the dispute or controversy under consideration.[232]

The chairmanship of the committee is a rotating one, a new chairman being elected each year.[233] The seat of the committee continues to be in Washington, but it may meet in other places when it deems it necessary.[234] Article 20 requires a quorum of at least three committee members, and decisions are taken by a vote of at least three members.[235] Parties appearing before the committee are represented by delegates especially accredited for that purpose. Such delegates may be accompanied by advisers.[236] The General Secretariat of the OAS provides secretariat services and working facilities for the functioning of the committee.[237]

The Fifth Meeting of Consultation of Ministers of Foreign Affairs, held in Santiago in 1959, was called to study the international tension in the Caribbean. As a result of the meeting, the Inter-American Peace Committee was fortified with additional powers. It was called upon to go into the details of the problems confronting the hemisphere in the Caribbean. The committee was assigned three topics: methods and procedures for preventing activities designed to overthrow established governments or to provoke intervention or aggression; the relationship between violations of human rights or non-democratic governments on the one hand and the political tensions affecting hemispheric peace on the other; and the relationship between economic under-development and political stability. In studying these matters, the committee is empowered to act on its own initiative without the consent of the parties, although a government's consent is necessary for an actual investigation within the territory of that government. This temporary broadening of the committee's power is to remain in effect until the Eleventh Inter-American Conference. At that time the committee must report.[238]

Under the committee's original Statute, this agency could take action at the request of any American state. Such a request did not need to come from a directly interested party, and the consent of the parties was not required.[239] But the 1956 Statute stipulated that only a state directly concerned can request committee action and that the consent of all parties is required. After this change was made the committee was not called upon to deal with any controversy, although before that it had worked successfully to relieve certain situations or controversies in the Caribbean and Central America.

The new Santiago interim rule has helped to restore the committee's effectiveness. Since the Santiago Meeting the committee has met frequently to study and deal with the matters entrusted to it.

THE PAN AMERICAN UNION

The Pan American Union came into being in 1890 as a result of a resolution adopted at the First International Conference of American States.[240] This resolution recommended the formation of an association of the nations present at the Conference which was to be called the International Union of American Republics and was to be represented by an organ in the City of Washington, D.C., named the Commercial Bureau of the American Republics. At the Second Conference a reorganization changed the name of the Commercial Bureau to the International Bureau of the American Republics.[241] The Fourth Conference was to see another change of name. Here the Bureau was given the name which it presently bears, the Pan American Union.[242]

Over the years there have been many modifications of the organization and functions of the Pan American Union. Until the Charter of Bogotá it operated under resolutions of the conferences, the attempt made at the Sixth Conference to place it on a treaty basis having failed through lack of subsequent ratifications by the member states of the convention drafted there. Resolutions changed the management of the Pan American Union from the hands of the secretary of state of the United States, where it was originally placed, to those of a Governing Board of diplomatic representatives of the American republics.[243]

The International Union of American Republics was originally organized by the First Conference "for the prompt collection and distribution of commercial data and information." The Commercial Bureau was charged with "the care of all translations and publications and with all correspondence pertaining to the International Union." In addition it was also to publish a bulletin containing information concerning trade and commerce which it was the purpose of the Union to promote.[244]

From this humble beginning as an organ with extremely restricted authority, the Pan American Union's duties were broadened and expanded so that just prior to Bogotá it served principally in two non-political capacities primarily administrative in nature: (1) as a permanent international secretariat, and (2) as a center for the exchange of information and the promotion of inter-American co-operation.

The Charter of Bogotá separated the Pan American Union from the Governing Board (now the Council); but the separation was not complete, for many links between the two bodies remain.[245] The duties of the Pan American Union were continued much as before, with some expansion of activities. The Charter outlines the functions of this organ and defines more precisely its relations to the other organs of the organization. The regulations of the Pan American Union repeat these functions, adding details and instructions as to the manner in which the duties shall be performed.[246]

Article 78 of the Charter makes the Pan American Union the central and permanent organ of the OAS and its general secretariat. Its seat is in the City of Washington, D.C.[247] As central and permanent organ, the Pan American Union, under the direction of the Council and through its technical and informational offices, is called upon to promote economic, social, juridical, and cultural relations among all the members of the organization.[248] The secretariat functions of the Union are listed in Article 83 of the Charter, under which it is called upon to perform services for the other organs as well as for the member states. Thus, the Pan American Union transmits to the member states the convocation to the various conferences; it advises the Council and its organs in the preparation of programs and regulations of the conferences; when a conference is to be held, it places at the disposal of the host government the technical aid and the personnel which that government may request; it serves as custodian of the documents and archives of the conferences and as a depository of the instruments of ratifications of inter-American agreements; it performs the duties entrusted to it by the Inter-American Conference and the Meeting of Consultation; and it submits annual reports on the activities of the organization and also reports to each Inter-American Conference on the work accomplished by the inter-American organs since the previous conference.

The Pan American Union provides secretariat services to the Council and its three organs[249] and in addition finances out of its budget the special secretariats in Rio de Janeiro and Mexico City respectively for the Juridical Committee and the Committee for Cultural Action. It also performs certain functions for other inter-American agencies.

The organization of the Pan American Union is as follows:

The secretary general directs the Pan American Union and is its legal representative.[250] He is designated as the highest international administrative officer of the OAS.[251] He is elected by the Council for a ten-year term.[252] Formerly the secretary general was known as the director general, and the person filling the office was always a citizen of the United States.[253] The Charter not only changed the name of the office, but also provided that this official may not be re-elected or be succeeded by a person of the same nationality.[254] The secretary general is responsible for establishing and abolishing technical and administrative offices of the Pan American Union with the approval of the Council; for redistributing the functions of existing offices for greater efficiency provided no budget increase is involved; for determining the number and classification of the staff members of the union; for appointing and regulating their powers and duties; for fixing their compensation and providing them with necessary training in accordance with policies fixed by the Council; for contracting special or technical services; for issuing and applying administrative provisions concerning the staff; for carrying out decisions of the Council relating to the functions of the Pan American Union; for seeing that the regulations are faithfully complied with; and for furnishing reports requested of him by the Inter-American Conference, the Meeting of Foreign Ministers, or the Council. He is responsible to the Council for the proper performance of the Pan American Union's duties. He participates with voice, but without vote, in the various conferences, and in the Council and its organs. His participation in other organizations is governed by provisions of agreements entered into by the Council.[255]

The secretary general is assisted by the assistant secretary general, also elected by the Council for a term of ten years. Unlike the secretary, he is eligible for re-election.[256] He serves as advisory officer to the secretary general, who may delegate authority to him. He also exercises the powers of the secretary general in case of the latter's temporary absence or disability, or in the event of a vacancy until the new secretary general takes office. The assistant secretary general is designated the secretary of the Council.[257]

The secretary general and the assistant secretary general may be removed by a two-thirds vote of the members of the Council when the proper functioning of the organization so demands.[258]

The 1957 Pan American Union Regulations set forth four departments of the Pan American Union: the Department of Economic and Social Affairs,[259] the Department of International Law, the Department of Cultural Affairs,[260] and the Department of Administrative Affairs. In 1958 a reorganization took place and the Department of Administrative Affairs was abolished. The name of the Department of International Law was changed to the Department of Legal Affairs,[261] and three new departments were added: the Department of

Technical Co-operation,[262] the Department of Statistics,[263] and the Department of Public Information.[264] All departments are units of the Pan American Union with functions of a technical nature aimed at carrying out substantive programs. In addition there are three units designated as offices, the functions of which are essentially in the nature of administrative services:[265] the Office of Conference and Secretariat Services, the Office of Financial Services, and the Office of Publication Services.[266]

The staff members of the Pan American Union are described as international civil servants.[267] As of 1960 the staff numbered 553.[268] The Charter of Bogotá requires that in the selection of such personnel the first consideration shall be efficiency, competence, and integrity, but it also requires that importance be given to the necessity of recruiting personnel on as broad a geographical basis as possible.[269] Article 89 of the Charter declares that such employees are not to seek or receive instructions from any government or authority other than the Pan American Union. They are also commanded to refrain from any action that might reflect upon their positions as international officials responsible only to the union. The member states also pledge themselves to respect the international character of the secretary general and the personnel and not to seek to influence them in their duties.[270] The duties, obligations, and privileges of the personnel of the Pan American Union are set forth in detail in the regulations.

SPECIALIZED ORGANIZATIONS

Prior to 1948 the Inter-American System had spawned a host of specialized organizations. These agencies had been created by the conferences to promote co-operation in certain technical fields through studies, exchange of information, and recommendations to the governments and to the conferences. Some of them were of a permanent nature. Others were brought into existence to meet the special needs of an emergency situation. For the most part they were established in a sporadic haphazard fashion with no planned development pattern and not always in accord with sound organizational structure. This multiplicity of agencies, some with overlapping functions and with no overall direction or central control office to maintain contact and co-ordinate their activities, created confusion, caused inefficiency, and became financially burdensome to the governments.[271]

A need to eliminate or adapt existing inter-American agencies and to co-ordinate their functions as among themselves and other international agencies was recognized, and, as early as 1945, at the Chapultepec Conference, a mandate was given to rectify the situation.[272] Although some attention was given to the elimination and integration of certain existing entities at the Ninth Conference, time did not permit a complete fulfilment of the task.[273] Thus the Council was given certain standards and directions regarding the creation, adaptation, or elimination of Specialized Organizations; the co-ordination of their activities; and the power to conclude agreements with them to determine their relations with the OAS.[274] Resolution III of the Ninth Conference charged the Council with the duty of making, as soon as possible, a complete survey of the status and activities of existing organizations in order to discontinue, with the authorization of the governments, certain agencies whose maintenance no longer served a useful purpose, and in order to strengthen, adapt, or merge the others as would be appropriate.[275]

The Charter of Bogotá does not contain specific details as to the organization and functioning of the specialized agencies. It only provides general norms and outlines their position within the whole system. Inter-American Specialized Organizations are defined by Article 59 as "the intergovernmental organizations established by multilateral agreements and having specific functions with respect to technical matters of common interest to the American States." An agency which fulfils these criteria qualifies as an official specialized organization.[276] The Council is required to maintain a register of such organizations.[277]

These agencies are accorded full technical autonomy, but it is specified that they are to take into account the recommendations of the Council in conformity with the provisions of the Charter.[278] They are also required to submit to the Council periodic reports on the progress of their work and on their annual budgets and expenses, with an additional stipulation that the agreements between them and the Council may provide for transmittal of these budgets to the Council for approval.[279] The Pan American Union is authorized to receive and distribute the quotas of countries contributing to the support of such organizations.[280] Although the Council is called upon to promote co-operative relationships between the Inter-American Specialized Organizations and analogous world agencies, the Charter cautions that the inter-American agencies "shall preserve the identity of their status as integral parts of the Organization of American States, even when they perform regional functions of international agencies."[281]

Article 101 of the Charter is concerned with the geographical location of the Specialized Organizations, which is determined in each case with a view to the interests of all the American states. The juridical status of these agencies is mentioned in Article 105, which provides that the question of their privileges and immunities shall be resolved in each instance through agreements between the organization and the government concerned.

Acting to perform the tasks placed upon it by the Charter and Resolution III of the Ninth Conference, the Council created a Committee of Inter-American Organizations[282] and gave it the duty of drawing up standards to serve as a guide in the classification of specific agencies as Specialized Organizations and in the precise definition of the powers and duties of the Council with respect to these organizations.[283] An initial step in this process was to establish a distinction between entities of two types: the Specialized Organizations and other inter-American organizations. In accord with these standards, as prescribed by the Charter, an agency to be regarded as specialized and an organ of the OAS must meet the following conditions:

1. It must be inter-govermental, that is, an official entity formed by the governments themselves.

2. It must be established by a multilateral agreement, i.e., by an agreement among more than two governments.

3. It must have a specific function in that its purpose must be clearly specified.

4. Its function must be of a technical character. That which is technical matter includes functions corresponding to all the fields of international collaboration with the exception of the political.

5. The subject matter of its activities must be of common interest to the American States. Organizations constituted by a group of states to serve a regional purpose, or to meet any other given restricted need are not included within this definition.[284]

After establishing these standards, the committee began a survey of all existing inter-American organizations, official or nonofficial, with a view to classifying them in accordance with the required criteria. As of 1960, a group of six inter-American agencies has been designated Specialized Organizations. They are: the Pan-American Institute of Geography and History, the Inter-American Institute of Agricultural Sciences, the Inter-American Children's Institute, the Inter-American Commission of Women, the Pan-American Health Organization, and the Inter-American Indian Institute.[285]

The Charter of Bogotá also directs the Council under the terms of Article 53(d) to conclude agreements or special arrangements for co-operation with those inter-American organizations which are not official Specialized Organizations, but which enjoy recognized international standing. Resolution III of the Ninth Conference directs that a special register for them is to be maintained. On April 4, 1952, the Council approved the standards and procedures to be applied by the Council and its organs in concluding agreements or special co-operative agreements with nongovernmental organizations.[286] These standards were designed to be applied primarily to dealings with nongovernmental organizations; however, they have, in practice, served as a guide in the consideration of requests made by semiofficial organizations, i.e., where there is both governmental and private participation. These standards provide for two types of relations — general and special. Special arrangements are those established "to carry out projects of common interest within the competence of such organizations and to which they can make a special contribution."[287] Examples of such relations are those that have been established with two semiofficial organizations: the Inter-American Statistical Institute and the Pan-American Railway Congress Association.[288]

Certain privileges are established by the standards for nongovernmental organizations entering into general relations. These organizations have the right to receive regularly the publications of the OAS and to address communications to it on any matter in which they are interested.[289]

Three other special agencies or commissions associated with the OAS are the Inter-American Commission on Human Rights, which was created by the Fifth Meeting of Consultation of Ministers of Foreign Affairs in 1959, whose task is to promote respect for human rights; the Inter-American Nuclear Energy Commission, founded in 1959 as an outgrowth of a recommendation made by the Inter-American Committee of Presidential Representatives in 1957, whose task is to facilitate co-operation among the American states in matters relating to the peaceful application of nuclear energy; and the Inter-American Development Bank, established in 1959, to provide financing for development projects, thereby aiding economic growth in the hemisphere.[290]

BOOK III

The Principles of the OAS

CHAPTER VII

PURPOSES, FUNCTIONS, AND PRINCIPLES

PURPOSES

The fourth Article of the Charter of Bogotá proclaims that the Organization of American States, in order to put into practice the principles upon which it is founded and in order to fulfil its regional obligations under the Charter of the United Nations, has five purposes:

a) to strengthen the peace and security of the continent;
b) to prevent possible causes of difficulties and to ensure the pacific settlement of disputes that may arise among the Member States;
c) to provide for common action on the part of those States in the event of aggression;
d) to seek the solution of political, juridical and economic problems that may arise among them;
e) and to promote, by cooperative action their economic, social and cultural development.

These purposes express ideas of co-operation which had been recognized as the objectives of the system long before the Charter of Bogotá. From an examination of this statement and of other relevant parts of the Charter and other inter-American instruments, the conclusion may be reached that the fundamental purposes of the organization can be reduced to two broad areas of action: ensuring the peace of the hemisphere, and promoting human welfare. These may be said to be the actual ends sought: the ultimate results or the final objects which are desired from the activity of the organization.[1]

When the Charter speaks of strengthening peace and security, its language implies that the task of the organization is one of developing conditions of international intercourse of the states of the continent in a manner that will afford the greatest assurance that the peace will not be broken. This signifies action to be taken by the organization in an attempt to abolish or to minimize cancerous conditions existing among states, often long-standing in nature, which may bring about a breach of the peace.

More, however, is meant. Obviously peace is not strengthened if it is broken or imminently threatened. Therefore, the organization also has as its object the maintenance of peace on a day-to-day or immediate basis, for it must at all times be ready to seek to prevent an immediate breach of the peace and to restore peace if it is broken. This is well borne out by purposes 4(b) and (c) and by the existence of the Rio Treaty, the preamble of which speaks of matters relating to the maintenance of peace and security as appropriate for regional action and indicates as a purpose of the treaty the assurance of peace.[2]

Thus an ultimate goal of the organization is to insure peace by its maintenance in case it is immediately threatened, by its restoration in case it is broken, and by the long-run promotion of conditions of peace.

The peace and security with which the organization, as a regional agency of the Western Hemisphere, is concerned are continental peace and security. It is not its purpose, except incidentally because of international hemispheric implications, to insure internal peace within the individual states or to intervene in an internal revolutionary situation.[3] Although the peace and security of the continent are primary ends, it is not to be thought that the activities of the organization to keep this peace need always be limited to the continent, for extracontinental aggressions and situations may well endanger hemispheric peace or hemispheric security.[4]

Possibly even more fundamental as an ultimate end of the OAS is the purpose of providing for human welfare. This aim can be deduced from Article 4(d) and (e). It is recognized that peace cannot be thought of as a political good to be obtained by means of political co-operation only. It must be buttressed by international co-operation in the economic, social, cultural, and humanitarian spheres. As a consequence it might be contended that co-operation of nations to solve and promote issues of an economic, social, and cultural nature is designed only to create conditions favorable to the existence of peace. As to the objectives of the United Nations this line of reasoning is correct, for the prime goal of that organization is the maintenance of international peace and security among the nation-states of the world; all other aims are conceived as being merely auxiliary, subsidiary, or necessary concomitants of this main purpose.[5]

But this is not the whole story in the case of the Charter of the OAS. The Bogotá Charter clearly acknowledges that security and peace are beneficial to mankind and that it is essential to remove the causes of strife and war. But at least equal or possibly greater stress is placed on human welfare, and it has been declared that the prime purpose of co-operation in the Americas[6] is to establish in the hemisphere a system of liberty and social justice for the individual based on respect for the fundamental rights of man.

FUNCTIONS

Not only do relevant portions of the Charter give the ultimate ends of the organization, but the statement of purposes reveals in broad outline the functions of the organization, i.e., the type of activity to be carried on and the ways and means by which the essential ends may be realized. In accordance with Article 4, the functions of the organization fall within two general groups: those dealing with the maintenance of peace and security and those dealing with the achievement of inter-American co-operation in the political, economic, cultural, social, and legal spheres. By the carrying on of co-operative activities in these fields the ultimate ends of the organization are to be attained.

The maintenance of peace in the immediate sense is outlined by Article 4(b) and (c). The latter, 4(c), sets forth the co-operative principle of collective responsibility through common action of the American states for the peace and security of the hemisphere. This can be called the police function of the organization, to take measures of an enforcement nature against a nation or nations which breach or threaten to breach the peace. This responsibility is one which attempts, through the application of coercive measures by the organization and its members, to prevent a threat to the peace or to remove or suppress an actual breach thereof.[7]

Less drastic than the police function but of equal importance for the maintenance of peace are arrangements for settling disputes that arise among nations, for unsettled disputes can be immediate causes of international strife. Hence, Article 4(b) relates to the pacific settlement of disputes among the American states.[8]

Since it was realized that peace and human welfare can only be obtained by reducing or removing from the life of nations those conditions of a deeprooted nature which hamper and yoke the spirit and progress of mankind, a third province, which may be called the co-operative function, has been included among the activities of the OAS. Through continuing co-operative endeavor carried on under the aegis of the OAS, the American states attempt to advance the well-being of the peoples of the hemisphere in all areas of social life. This co-operative function is set forth in Article 4(d) and (e), where the OAS is called upon to seek the solution of inter-American political, juridical, and economic problems and to promote through co-operation the economic, social, and cultural development of the American states.

Article 4(d), unlike 4(e), does not expressly state that co-operative action is to be carried out, but this is implied; for within an organization made up of member states the solution of the problems mentioned in that paragraph can come about only through joint co-operation.

The scope of activity of the OAS, by the terms of Article 4 (d), extends to seeking for a solution not only of juridical and economic problems but also of political problems among the American states. The Pan-American movement has always, to a greater or lesser extent, been involved in inter-American co-operation in the political field, even though, until recent times, the term *political* was either anathema or ignored. Belated recognition of the fact that effective hemispheric co-operation must include some political areas culminated in the formulation of fundamental standards to harmonize the divergent interests of the American states and to guide them in their "political" relationships. Through the creation of these principles or norms, an attempt has been made to regulate and restrict the political action of the nations of the hemisphere.

Sections (d) and (e) of Article 4 make a distinction between co-operation in the political field and co-operation in the juridical, economic, social, and cultural fields, apparently on the basis that the latter four areas can be nonpolitical in nature. Such a distinction is difficult to justify, for as has been pointed out above it is almost impossible to mark out an absolute boundary line between political and nonpolitical activity in any field of inter-American effort. All such fields are fraught with political implications, and almost any effort of collaboration to achieve a common policy may be designated "political." Even a decision to co-operate would, in the first instance, be a political one.[9]

Unfortunately the Charter gives no explanation of the meaning of "political," but sets it off from the other areas of co-operation. Thus it would seem that the juridical function, for example, is not to be regarded as "political," since it is mentioned in addition to that category. To solve juridical problems places upon the organization an obligation relating not only to the codification of international law, *i.e.*, the establishment of a more precise definition of existing law, but also to the development of international law by creating and extending it into new areas to regulate the various conflicts of interest which have not yet been presented for decision under the rules of law.[10] The creation of new areas wherein law shall govern state action is clearly political in nature, and if codification extends beyond the definition of existing law to the modification of such law by adaptation of the law in being to changing conditions, then it is no longer purely juridical but tends toward the political.[11]

The same difficulty is encountered when an attempt is made to separate the political from the economic, social, and cultural fields of inter-American endeavor. The principal problems in these areas are fundamentally political. Their solution certainly bears on the maintenance of peace. If the maintenance of peace is "political," as it is admitted to be, then any type of co-operation for this purpose is political in nature.

Kelsen, in discussing the meaning of political co-operation in contra-distinction to co-operation in the economic, social, and cultural fields under the United Nations Charter, concludes that political co-operation for purposes of that instrument was intended to refer to co-operation in the field of international politics. Other matters which could be characterized as objects of co-operation in the field of national politics would not be considered political. Matters of an economic, social, cultural, or humanitarian character are not primarily international questions but national questions, since, in the first instance, they are the concern of national policy. They become international only when dealt with through international co-operation. According to Kelsen, states may co-operate in the field of international politics and in the field of national politics, and it is the former which, by his interpretation of the United Nations Charter, is characterized as "political."[12]

Such an interpretation might be maintained as to the Charter of Bogotá by an isolated consideration of 4(e), which requires co-operative action to promote the economic, social, and cultural development of the American states. It can be argued that such development is basically internal development of each state in these areas, and that matters falling within them such as improved standards of living, human rights, and educational development basically fall within the field of national policy; hence, following Kelsen, they are nonpolitical.

But a glance at Article 4(d) explodes this interpretation as far as the OAS is concerned, for here it is asserted that one of the purposes of the OAS is to seek the solution of political, juridical, and economic problems that may arise *among* the American states. To speak of the solution of these problems arising *among them* is to refer to co-operation in the field of international politics, and, since co-operation to solve economic problems is mentioned here, the conclusion may be reached that the economic co-operation contemplated for purposes of 4(d) is co-operation in the field of international politics, which is, according to Kelsen, political. Reasoning technically, this could not be political co-operation for purposes of 4(d), for the section speaks of the solution of economic problems in addition to the solution of political problems and by so doing differentiates them.

Dr. Ricardo J. Alfaro, writing in 1938, distinguished political problems from economic and social problems by placing in the category of "political" those questions concerning the codification of international law, the organization of an American League of Nations, the creation of an inter-American Court of Justice, the pacific settlement of international conflicts, the definition of the aggressor, the exercise of neutrality, and the maintenance of peace in the continent. Nonetheless he still described that which is "political" very broadly as "all those problems which concern the juridical equality, the territorial integrity, the national independence, the international obligations, and the rights of American states . . ."[13]

He too, like Kelsen, was apparently thinking mainly of co-operation in the field of international politics — in matters primarily of an international character among states. However, when he speaks of matters concerned with the international obligations, the national independence, and the rights of states as being political, he opens wide the Pandora's box of troubles of an economic and social character which affect the relations among states. An attempt to exclude from the field of international politics that which is economic, social, or cultural, thereby seeking to differentiate from that which is political, does not jibe with fact.

Insofar as inter-American co-operation is directed to the economic, cultural, and social development of a state or states in the internal sense through technical aid, improvement of an educational system, development of the social legislation of each state, and the like, such co-operation may possibly be called nonpolitical functional inter-American co-operation if one makes the extremely dubious assumption that divergent state interests do not exist with respect to it.[14] But when economic, social, or cultural conflicts of interest arise among the states of the Americas requiring inter-American co-operation through the OAS to seek their solution and harmonization through the synthesizing of the national or international policy of the states by restriction upon them or by a call for action on their part, then such co-operation is political, whether or not the matter can be thought to be in the main national.

Political matters cannot in reality be distinguished from other types of matters, for the others may well fall within the political category. Article 4(d), when it speaks of the solution of political problems, simply reinforces the function of the OAS to secure co-operation among the American states to seek the solution of all problems which are or which may be the source of conflicts of interest among them, so that inter-American peace and security can better be maintained.

PRINCIPLES, RIGHTS, AND DUTIES OF STATES

It has been said that the purposes of an international organization are inclusive of the end or ends aimed at by the organization, its ultimate goals; the ways and means by which the ends are to be reached, which may be called the functions; and finally, the principles or values of the community in accordance with which the organization and its members are to act in performing the functions to achieve the desired ends.[15] Even though a specific measure under contemplation might be regarded as a means to a desired end of the OAS, such a measure could not be consummated if it would run counter to some competing value of the inter-American community. Hence, for a complete understanding of the purposes of the OAS, account must also be taken of these other values or guiding principles which may limit freedom of action in the performance of the functions of the OAS.

Chapter II of the Charter of Bogotá contains the Principles of the OAS and Chapter III the Fundamental Rights and Duties of States.[16] Subsequent chapters present norms for the pacific settlement of disputes,[17] principles of collective security,[18] and economic, social, and cultural standards.[19]

The principles expressed in Chapter II, Article 5, were taken largely from previous inter-American agreements, declarations, and resolutions, and are thus merely reaffirmations in the Charter. In summary, they relate to international law as the standard of conduct of states; respect for the sovereignty of states; faithful fulfilment of international obligations; good faith in inter-American relations; effective exercise of representative democracy; condemnation of wars of aggression; the concept that aggression against one is aggression against all; peaceful settlement of disputes; social justice; economic co-operation; fundamental human rights without discrimination; respect for cultural values of the American countries; and the directing of education toward justice, freedom, and peace.

The Fundamental Rights and Duties of States as given in Chapter III, Articles 6-19, cover juridical equality of states; respect for international legal rights; norms relating to the recognition of states; the precept that sovereignty does not authorize the commission of unjust acts; jurisdiction of the state over citizens and aliens; respect for the rights of the individual and principles of morality in the pursuance of the right of the state to develop its own life; respect for treaties coupled with the mandate that they are to be made public; non-intervention; inviolability of territory; prohibition of the use of force except in self-defense; and the exemption of collective measures from the principle of non-intervention.

These Principles and Rights and Duties of States may be regarded as basic values of the inter-American community. Upon them inter-American solidarity is founded, and they are to be respected and applied to attain the declared ends.

From a legal point of view the distinction between the Principles and the Rights and Duties of States is not clear. It has been said that the Principles merely proclaim general aspects of inter-American conduct and are not to be considered as legally binding norms. They are broad policy expressions upon which legal norms may be constructed in the future. On the other hand, it is declared, the Rights and Duties of States are concerned with specific juridical relations. They are to be regarded as legal norms.[20]

No issue can be taken with the latter contention, for it is clear that the Rights and Duties of States are considered as obligatory upon the American states. But certain statements included in the declarations contained in the Principles are couched in legally binding language. The Charter is a legal instrument, and, to the extent that it creates obligations, these obligations are intended to have legal force. The creation of such obligations is largely dependent upon the wording. Statements in a treaty are binding if they are declared in terms of legal obligation. Statements not so formulated are to be used as evidence in interpreting the provisions of the legally operative portions of the treaty.[21] The Charter of Bogotá compounds confusion by the fact that while certain ideas contained in the Principles are not stated in language which may be said to produce juridical norms, such ideas are repeated or stated elsewhere in legally binding language.

Analysis makes it clear that the members of the OAS do seek to establish standards of conduct, principles, and rules, some of which they accept as binding upon them. Their assent to these prescriptions provides a common basis for their relations in the pursuance of their common objectives. Still, certain of these principles appear to be nothing more than a program of aims and consequently must be viewed as a gantry from which to erect a larger structure of inter-American accord. These declarations are not, therefore, all of the same force, as is evident from the differing ways chosen to give them expression.

Another puzzle difficult of solution when one is confronted with the standards of inter-American conduct as contained in the Principles as well as in the Rights and Duties of States concerns their applicability. To what entities are they meant to apply? Upon whom are they obligatory? These stipulations are drawn up in such a manner as to appear to be addressed to the states. To the extent that right-duty relationships are created by the normative provisions, each state of the inter-American community has certain duties imposed upon it, and by such impositions rights are conferred upon the others.

Since the language used in the Principles and Rights and Duties is primarily directed to states, and not to the OAS as a separate entity, the question arises as to whether the Charter herein imposes obligations upon the organization as such. These principles, insofar as they are binding, do obligate the members. The organization is composed of members. Therefore it is manifest that the members in their organizational activity are required to respect the standards. Thus to designate specifically that the organization as well as the member states is to respect these principles would appear to be superfluous and unnecessary. If the OAS is merely an associated group of states, each member having a dual personality—that is, each state having a legal personality in its private affairs, but one distinct from the personality it has in its group affairs—then the organization cannot exist apart from its members.[22] Any restrictive principle applicable to the states, its members, would apply to the OAS, for the association of states would have no legal standing per se in the eyes of the law even though the associated states have acquired rights and duties different from those in their individual transactions.

It would seem, however, that the OAS has a legal personality apart from the legal personalities of the individual states of which it is composed. It has rights and duties distinct from those of any or all of its members.[23] As it is an entity with a legal personality of its own, any principle restricting the freedom of action in the exercise of its functions should be stated — otherwise confusion results. Can it be assumed that because no mention of the OAS is made in these guiding principles the juridical person may ignore them in the exercise of its functions as an entity? Such assumption would be risky, for the principles are said to be foundation stones of inter-American solidarity, binding to the extent that they create obligations on the members and the juridical entity they have produced, the OAS, alike; and Article 4 proclaims that the OAS is to put into practice the principles on which it is founded.

The basic juridical political principles of the hemispheric community are scattered through many inter-American instruments concluded at dates earlier than the Charter of Bogotá. They have been restated in the Charter and in other constitutional instruments of the OAS, but unfortunately clarity does not result from a reading of these documents, for the various stipulations overlap and tend to be prolix. A study of their wording permits classification, and the following propositions may be set forth as guiding principles:[24] (1) respect for sovereignty, (2) equality of states, (3) non-intervention, (4) jurisdiction over aliens, (5) principles of recognition and nonrecognition, (6) conformity with international obligations, (7) repudiation of the use of force, (8) pacific settlement of disputes, (9) reciprocal assistance, (10) recognition of the fundamental rights of man, and (11) representative democracy.

These so-called basic rules and others are often spoken of as American international law.[25]

CHAPTER VIII

SOVEREIGNTY AND EQUALITY

RESPECT FOR SOVEREIGNTY

Respect for the sovereignty and independence of each state has been called the essence of the international order arising from the solidarity of the American republics, and if one judges its importance from the number of times it has been expressed in declarations and treaties this would be an understatement. To mention but a few, the Declaration of Principles of Inter-American Solidarity and Cooperation of 1936 proclaims "the unqualified respect of every American nation for the sovereignty of every other American nation";[1] The Act of Chapultepec, 1945, declares that every state has the right to the respect of its individuality and independence by the other members of the international community,[2] while the Declaration of Mexico, 1945, proclaims as an essential principle that each state is free and sovereign.[3] Many such allusions are made in the Charter of Bogotá. Article I affirms that a reason for the establishment of the organization is to defend the sovereignty, territorial integrity, and independence of the American states; Article 5(b) of the Principles declares that respect for the personality, sovereignty, and independence of states is an essential element of the international order. A resolution of the Bogotá Conference on the Preservation and Defense of Democracy declares that one of the two undeniable postulates of American freedom is the sovereignty of the nation as a state;[4] and the Declaration of Solidarity for the Preservation of the Political Integrity of the American States against the Intervention of International Communism proclaims that American policy is designed to protect the sovereign rights of the American states.[5]

Although sovereignty is not defined in these instruments, the traditional international law definition is obviously intended: self-determination by each state as to its external and internal affairs. From this premise is derived a cornerstone of international law and of inter-American law—the right of independence.[6] This right has two aspects, the freedom of action possessed by each state to conduct its relations with other states as it deems fit—external independence —and the right of self-government by the state or the supreme authority to control all persons and things within its boundaries—internal independence.[7] Within these spheres of state independence or sovereignty it follows that each state is, as of right, permitted liberty of action, free from the interference from other states or outside authority, and that other states are duty bound to respect this sovereignty.

This right of independence has been a battle cry of the statesmen and jurists of the Americas from the beginning of American liberation from the mother countries. The Monroe Doctrine was in part proclaimed to protect the independence of the new states of Spanish America. The Congress of Panama and other early conferences were called to protect this sovereignty. The strict

145

non-intervention principle of the Americas was a result of the policy of intervention into the affairs of certain Latin American nations by other nations which, it was claimed, violated the independence of the state so intervened.[8] Not only this principle of non-intervention, but many of the other American principles which have been adopted are corollaries of or complementary to the principle of sovereignty and were set forth for the protection of the right of independence: for example, the principle of state equality, the repudiation of the use of force, the nonrecognition of territorial acquisitions by force, and principles relating to the status of aliens. Indeed it is probably true that the entire collective security system of the Americas is designed primarily to protect the sovereignty of the American states from aggression or threats thereof and to guarantee insofar as possible the right of independence.

There can be no doubt that respect for sovereignty is a fundamental postulate of the OAS and that the American states have bound themselves to the principle. But the principle of sovereignty in the Americas is affected with schizophrenia; it is janus-faced. It and its related principles would lead one to believe that each American state has unrestricted self-determination, and that the rights and duties of the states flowing therefrom are guarded as prerogatives subject to no encroachment. This is not the case, for no American state, nor any other state, is in effect sovereign to the extent that it possesses unlimited freedom of action or independence.[9] The right of independence is always subject to the restrictions imposed by international law.[10] The freedom envisaged by the right connotes freedom from the control of other states; not freedom from the restrictions of international law which binds all states. To elevate sovereignty above international law would not be in accord with the existence of international law.[11] Thus states are bound by that part of international law which has evolved from the practices and customs of civilized states in their mutual relationships. This principle that international law is a standard of conduct of states is itself an expressly recognized principle of the Americas. By general international law and by the particular international law of the Americas, there is established a conflicting principle which subordinates sovereignty to the limitations imposed by international law and to that extent restricts the complete right of self-determination.

States are bound not only by rules of general international law but also by those rules which they have expressly accepted in treaties, and every treaty creating rights and duties between states limits the exercise of state sovereignty. Again, the American states have expressly recognized the general international law requirement of the faithful fulfilment of obligations derived from treaties. It may be pointed out, however, that by agreeing to international obligations as contained in a treaty or convention a state does not in reality violate its sovereignty. It is a prerogative of the state at international law to assume such obligations. The conclusion of a treaty by which the state restricts the exercise of its sovereignty is a corroboration of its sovereignty.[12]

Through the Charter of Bogotá and other treaties of the OAS, the American states have bound themselves to certain principles which limit their freedom of action — their sovereignty — to a greater degree than that existing at general international law.

Although the repudiation of force and the nonrecognition of territorial acquisition by force protect the sovereignty of the state against which force is used or which has its territory taken by force, these principles restrict the external independence of the state against whom they are directed. General international law recognizes the use of force at least on certain occasions,[13] and also recognizes certain territorial acquisitions by force.[14] Moreover, the duty to settle disputes peacefully[15] and the duty of solidarity in resisting aggression[16] limit the external independence of the American states in a manner not required by general international law. If the American states have adopted the principle that representative democracy is the form of government which shall be maintained in each American nation and have recognized that each American nation must accord its citizens certain basic human rights, they have again drastically curtailed their internal sovereignty from that established by general international law.[17]

The principle of co-operation or inter-American organization itself is at odds with state sovereignty as generally recognized. The Charter of Bogotá calls for political, economic, social, and cultural co-operation by American states, and organs have been created to further this co-operation. There exists an international co-operative pattern, an international organization, by which the American states seek to further reciprocally shared interests of a political, economic, social, and cultural nature which they feel can be better or more easily attained through united than through separate action.

In providing for such co-operation the sovereignty of each state suffers some devaluation, for by combining into an international organization each state has surrendered some of its powers to the various organs of the organization and has obligated itself to a certain pattern of conduct which results in limitations on its internal and external sovcrignty. By conclusion of the basic treaties of the OAS, the American states have delegated to the OAS powers which they previously held without restrictions other than those following from previous treaty obligations or from the customary rules of international law, and the grant of this authority to the organization has automatically brought into being a mandatory element of outside power over its members subject to its ordering powers within its proper sphere. Any action taken or inaction permitted by an international organization will have a certain amount of influence on the action of its members. This can be called the rule of anticipated reaction; that is, member states will be inclined to determine their policies by the expectation of the resulting conduct of the international organization.[18] This also tends to bring about a reduction in each member's unrestricted self-determination.

The OAS has been granted powers of direct action in the field of collective security, for under the Rio Treaty not only are the states bound to act upon the commands of the Organ of Consultation by which they can be required to take enforcement measures, but under certain circumstances they must also tolerate the application of coercive measures against themselves. Through this power of direct action the OAS has the right to prescribe certain behavior by providing coercive measures to be taken in case of contrary behavior. These measures are forcible interference in the sphere of interests of states normally protected by law, and as such diminish state sovereignty to the extent that they are authorized.[19]

In addition, the OAS has powers of indirect action over its members. It has the powers to consider, discuss, and recommend concerning matters of broad scope. The power to consider and discuss implies that there can be a hearing, an inquiry into the issues in which the parties involved may participate. But the power to consider may well be broader than mere inquiry. It can include calling for a report, hearing witnesses, and even appointing a commission of investigation. It has been amply demonstrated in the past that investigation is a reality with an automatism of its own. Both consideration and discussion may include the power to obtain information against the wishes of the state or states being investigated, as well as information voluntarily given. Furthermore, consideration and discussion, even without any threat of other action, may have the effect of compelling a state or states to act in accord with the will of the international organization if the values at stake (for example, international respect or loss of prestige, or some other deference value) are important to the state or states.[20]

Recommendations may, on their face, carry no legal obligation, but they too may have far-reaching political consequences if they threaten the loss of certain values which a state, weighing all alternatives, is unwilling to sacrifice.[21]

The fact that states have banded together and formed an international organization places in that organization elements of power. Therefore, any action within the scope of authority of an international organization will tend to be of a mandatory nature if the values at issue are important to a member state involved, for a threat of loss of these values may compel it to act in accord with the will of the organization.[22] Therefore, the surrender of elements of power to the organization is incompatible with that liberty of conduct which in the general view accrues to sovereign states for, insofar as the organization, an outside authority, takes direct or indirect action against member states and thus influences their internal and external policy, a diminution of sovereignty occurs.

Nevertheless, the substance of state sovereignty remains undisturbed in each American state. In the first place, the OAS is created on the confederate pattern so that the authority of the organization is directed only to the member states, not to citizens of those states.[23] And in the long run this authority is effective only to the extent that the states accept it. Moreover, since a state may withdraw from the organization after two years from date of notice, it can for the most part escape that authority. Again, the authority granted is extremely limited. It is largely authority for indirect action only. Power of direct authority is limited to aggressions and threats thereof or other threats to the peace. In the last analysis, the principles or values of the Americas set forth to bind the states are binding only to the extent that treaties in general are binding, for no clear-cut measures to enforce them are created except as the states act on order of the organization in case of breach of or threats to the peace. Even here there are no enforcement measures against a state that fails to come to the aid of a victim of an armed attack or aggression or which fails to carry out the enforcement measures adopted by the organization to maintain the peace.

THE PRINCIPLE OF EQUALITY

The principle of state equality is a basic concept of inter-American relations and a foundation stone of the inter-American system. The concept is derived logically from sovereignty or the right of independence. For if it is admitted that sovereign states are independent among themselves, that no state recognizes or is subject to the authority of any other state, and that there are neither inferior nor superior sovereign states, then it follows that within the community of nations all states are equal.[24]

The strongest clamor for equality has in fact come from the Western Hemisphere. This can be ascribed to the psychological attitudes of the Latin American nations, determined to be free from the domination or hegemony of other nations. Dr. Carlos Calvo, the Argentine jurist, whose treatise on international law first appeared in 1868, rested his work largely on the principle of the equality of the sovereign state, having in mind European interventions in Latin America such as the French-English incident in the Rio de la Plata region and the French intervention in Mexico.[25] He was of the opinion that the European nations during the nineteenth century had followed a different rule or principle of intervention in their relations with American states from that which controlled their relations with each other. According to him, interventions in Europe had rested upon some important principle, while in the New World they had rested upon no legitimate principle but were based solely on force, the strong over the weak. This was a refusal to recognize the parity of the freedom and independence of the American states, for the Latin American nations were not granted rights equal to those of the nations of Europe. To Dr. Calvo the Latin American nations were therefore placed in a position of inferiority. He set forth the principle of equality as follows:

> Equality is one of the natural and primitive rights of nations. It is the right by virtue of which every sovereign State may demand that another State shall not assume more extensive rights, in their mutual relations, than it enjoys itself, and shall not free itself from any of the obligations imposed upon all.
>
> The equality of sovereign States is a generally recognized principle of public law. It has a twofold consequence in that it attributes to all States the same rights and imposes upon them reciprocally the same duties.
>
> The right of equality is the necessary consequence of their sovereignty and of their independence. All States enjoy an independent personality; each may assert all rights which are derived from that personality; consequently, their rights are equal.[26]

Another Latin American jurist, Dr. Luis M. Drago, Minister of Foreign Relations of the Argentine, has also had a profound effect on Latin American thinking in this field. The coercive and forcible intervention taken by Great Britain, Germany, and Italy against Venezuela in 1902 in order to collect public loans, was denounced by Dr. Drago as violative of the principle of equality of states:

> Among the fundamental principles of public international law which humanity has consecrated, one of the most precious is that which decrees that all states, whatever be the force at their disposal, are entities in law, perfectly equal one to another, and mutually entitled by virtue thereof to the same consideration and respect.

The acknowledgment of the debt, the payment of it in its entirety, can and must be made by the nation without diminution of its inherent rights as a sovereign entity, but the summary and immediate collection at a given moment, by means of force, would occasion nothing less than the ruin of the weakest nations, and the absorption of their governments, together with all the functions inherent in them, by the mighty of the earth. The principles proclaimed on this continent of America are otherwise.[27]

The actions of the United States prior to 1933, which, with respect to some Latin American states, were interventionary in character, caused the nations of Latin America to insist with even added vehemence upon the concept of equality. As a result the principle has been written into many inter-American instruments, notably the Convention on Rights and Duties of States, Montevideo 1933,[28] and the Rights and Duties of States of the Charter of Bogotá.

Article 4 of the Montevideo Convention declares:

States are juridically equal, enjoy the same rights, and have equal capacity in their exercise. The rights of each one do not depend upon the power which it possesses to assure its exercise, but upon the simple fact of its existence as a person under international law.

Article 6 of the Charter of Bogotá proclaims the principle in similar words, inserting language pertaining to the equal duties of states:

States are juridically equal, enjoy equal rights and equal capacity to exercise these rights, and have equal duties. The rights of each State depend not upon its power to ensure the exercise thereof, but upon the mere fact of its existence as a person under international law.

From these words set forth in legally binding treaties it can be seen that the American states recognize the principle of juridical equality as governing their relations *inter se*. However, the principle of juridical equality has differing connotations. One such connotation is "equality before the law." Reasoning from municipal law, the common meaning to be ascribed to the term "equality before the law" is simply that all persons shall have equal consideration of the law for the maintenance and security of the rights to which they are legally entitled. Or in different terminology — with the same connotation — equality before the law means that everyone is entitled to stand before the law on equal terms with others in a like state, to enjoy the same rights as belong to the others, and to bear the same burdens as are imposed upon them. When this concept is transposed into the law of nations, it does not mean that all states have the same rights and duties, but simply sets forth the proposition that when a rule of international law confers rights and duties upon international persons, i.e., states, it confers them upon all states legally entitled to them. Hence all states are equally entitled to receive such protection as the law of nations offers for the rights they have, and all states are equally compelled to fulfil the obligations which international law imposes upon them.[29]

Another aspect of state equality is often expressed as equal capacity for rights. Dickinson, who probably offers the most complete exposé of the concept of equality,[30] points out that some jurists have misunderstood or confused the attributes of equality. He declares that the only element of equality is equality before the law, which can also be termed the equal protection of the law. Equality before the law is essential to stable societies but it does not, as some writers have claimed, include equality of rights of states, for any such assertion is something more than equality before the law. It is equivalent to saying that general international law recognizes an equal *capacity* for rights by each state,[31] which is inaccurate and absurd. Dickinson points out that all states do not have the same legal status and consequently to claim that all states have equal capacity to acquire rights, to enter into transactions, or to perform acts is not in accord with reality but is only the expression of an unattainable ideal.[32]

Legal capacity, reasoning from municipal law, is the attribute of a person who can acquire a right or rights (i.e., exact certain acts or forbearances or benefits with the aid and assent of the law) and enter into transactions (conclude juristic acts) without restraint or hindrance because of his status or legal conditions. This definition in itself signifies that some persons are restrained in their legal capacity because of status, while others are not so hindered. Differences in legal status or condition, therefore, create unequal legal capacity. A subnormal legal status such as infancy, idiocy, or coverture restricts the scope of rights which persons in that status may acquire. Although such persons are equal before the law—that is, they are equally protected in the enjoyment of such rights as they have—still they are unequal insofar as capacity for rights is concerned.[33]

In the international community there are also international persons, i.e., states, whose status is subnormal. It follows then, according to Dickinson, that states with subnormal legal status do not have the same capability of acquiring rights, entering into transactions, and performing rights as do states with normal legal status. As a result a legal inequality ensues.

Despite Dickinson's assumption that equality of capacity of rights is not in accord with reality, it is quite clear from the American Declaration of Rights and Duties of States that the nations of this hemisphere have adopted both connotations as inter-American law; for it is clearly enunciated in these conventions that states have equal capacity to exercise their rights. This, then, assumes that all American states are of equal legal status—fully sovereign, with no limitations which restrain their equality. All states of the American community are equal before the law in the sense that they are equally entitled to protection in the enjoyment of their rights and equally compelled to fulfil their obligations. Moreover, between states of equal status there should be an equal capacity for the acquisition and exercise of rights. Since physical capacity supposedly has no relation to status, it should follow that the weakest American state and the most powerful American state fall within the same legal status, and should be accorded equal capacity for rights. Before the law there are no great or small powers, so that, assuming equal status, states each have the same rights or the same capacity for rights.

This can be said to be true legally and theoretically in international law and in the private law of states. In human society equality of individuals is a basic tenet of democracy, but individuals are in reality unequal at birth, in education, in wealth, and in ability, and even before the law the individual's position, wealth, personality, and intellect affect the administration of justice. Such inequality of physical capacity is manifest, and it is also obvious that a poor man may be precluded from exercising his right to enjoy property or restricted in his liberty to contract. The same can be said of the international person. Factually a weak state does not have the ability to exercise all its rights to the same extent as a great state. As Fenwick points out, for example, ". . . a state with poor material resources may not be able to offer inducement for reciprocal trade favors in a commercial treaty."[34] Yet such a state, being presumed to be a normal "equal" state, has the right by law to enter into reciprocal trade treaties. Nevertheless, unequal physical capacity does not invalidate the principle of legal equality, although it is clear that it affects vitally the exercise of rights conferred by law, whether municipal, inter-American, or international.

Legal equality is met if no restriction is placed by the law upon the exercise of the rights granted to all persons, natural or international; legal equality is thus consistent with unequal physical capacities or potentialities which may cause unequal exercise of rights. In this light, any legal equality of substantive rights of states or equality before the law becomes relatively unimportant.

There is nothing amiss, however, with the doctrine of equality before the law. Indeed, to the contrary, equal treatment of nations similarly situated with respect to an issue at hand is a deep implicit expectation of a just international legal order; but equality can never be absolute, for there are always extant certain natural inequalities which bear on international issues. The Aristotelian theory of justice demands only equal treatment of those equal before the law, and it remains for each political order to determine whom to treat as equals or otherwise.[35] But any classification by such a political order which results in inequalities in treatment must make sense, for the sense of injustice of the community is revolted by whatever is unequal by caprice.[36] Why does the "sense of injustice" call actively for equality? One explanation is that equal treatment of all within a recognized class is a necessary attribute of any legal order; the very concept of law requires that minimal regularity.[37] Such a statement may be considered a truism, but equality before the law as synonymous with equal protection of the law becomes a specialized problem in the international community. In municipal law it is taken for granted that when equality before the law is mentioned those rights to which individuals are entitled will be protected legally and equally by the judicial and executive machinery of the state.

Equality of substantive rights loses what little import it may have and becomes merely theoretical if no equal protection is afforded. It is all very well to say that what one state may claim, another may claim, or that states of equal status have identical legal rights to enter into juridical acts; but unless equal protection is given, some states may claim and some states may attempt to exercise their rights and little more. If a small state has no remedy to enforce its rights there is no equal protection or, bluntly, no protection at all. The international order has not yet reached that stage of development wherein agencies function adequately to protect all rights and to assure equal protection of all rights, and this is also true of the inter-American order. The remedial processes of international law have not always proved sufficient against encroachment on the rights of small states by powerful states, and have failed to function even at times when the national existence of a small state was at issue. Indeed, the independence of states has been violated so repeatedly that to some legal realists the entire principle of equal protection before the law seems an abstraction—a phantasmagoria of the law. In fact the final, the ultimate remedial process of international law is inconsistent with the principle of equality, since the law of nations recognizes self-help as a remedial process, and in most instances where self-help has been utilized it has been used by a powerful state against a weak state.[38]

Although the remedial process of self-help is stated to be legitimate at international law when taken in the form of a sanction to secure redress against a state guilty of a breach of the law or to uphold or vindicate the law, still dangerous tendencies for arbitrary action develop. In the absence of proper international organization each state acts as law enforcer and judge in its own case if it resorts to self-help against another state.[39] In order to give import to the ideal of equal protection of the law, a truly effective international organization must come into existence capable of enforcing the rules of international law.

The establishment of the OAS is a step forward in this direction for the American states; but as presently constituted the OAS is primarily an agency for the enforcement of peace rather than of law. It does seek to restrict the international law right of individual nation self-help. The Charter condemns the use of armed force—except in case of self-defense—as well as other measures of self-help which amount to intervention.[40] But the enforcement agency created is not given power to enforce the law in all instances of breach thereof. It may act as an enforcement agency only in case of armed attack or other threats to the peace of the Americas.[41]

Of course the Charter does obligate the American states to settle their disputes peacefully, and certain procedures are set forth in the Pact of Bogotá which may, under certain circumstances, bring the dispute before the International Court of Justice if the matter is justiciable.[42] In cases where judicial settlement is possible through an appeal to international law, the law is the same for all nations of equal status, and equality before the law is present. Moreover, the Meeting of Consultation of Foreign Ministers is given power to ensure the fulfilment of the judicial decision.[43]

Nevertheless, there are many obstacles to be encountered on the road to equal protection of the laws under the Pact of Bogotá. In the first place many matters which may give rise to dispute are exempted from the court's jurisdiction, and indeed from the jurisdiction of any procedure of pacific settlement.[44] In such cases, each party to a dispute can advance its own notions of the law and, if it has sufficient power, it can seek its own redress with impunity through the application of reprisals so long as a situation does not come about which threatens the peace.[45] To some extent, therefore, the supremacy of power can assert itself.

Another difficulty in the Pact of Bogotá is that it is so elastic as to pacific procedures to be utilized by the states in the settlement of their disputes that it is almost impossible for a state ever to force another state to judicial settlement or arbitration, the only procedures which can lead to binding results. Further-more, the pact has had such a small number of ratifications that its obligatory effect on the American states is extremely limited.[46] As a consequence of these factors, the machinery in the OAS for enforcement of rights and duties of states is still defective; and until that defect is remedied, equal protection of the law cannot be fully realized.

Another aspect of the concept of state equality at general international law is that no state can be legally bound without or against its will and no decisions to which it has not agreed can be enforced against it. This has had a profound effect on the lawmaking process of international law, for it is said that all the laws of nations rest upon common consent of the members of the family of nations; thus a rule is not considered a rule of international conduct binding upon a state unless it has been assented to by each state. Since this common consent can be an implied or tacit consent as evidenced by custom or an express consent as evidenced by treaties, custom and treaties are the principal sources of international law. Oppenheim deduces from this principle of com-mon consent the inference that states are equal to each other as subjects of international law.[47]

As a consequence of this traditional rule, international agreements bind only the contracting states, and the decisions of international agencies are not obligatory on a state which has not agreed to be bound by them.[48] In an inter-national organization, therefore, a majority vote is not sufficient to bind a non-assenting state. In attempting to overcome this effect, many international organi-zations have had to work under the principle of unanimity, and unanimity is usually difficult to obtain on any controversial issue. When a member state is insistent that it will not be bound without its assent, organized international co-operation becomes exceedingly difficult. This characteristic of the doctrine of state equality has, therefore, led to the strange anomaly that it creates a serious obstacle to effective international organization, whether that organization has been concerned with international legislation or the administration of inter-national affairs.[49]

In international organization, equality of states, according to some jurists, is no longer a principle of juridical equality, but becomes one of political equality concerned with political action of states. To Dickinson the political capacity of the state is something quite different from legal capacity. He states:

Legal rights and transactions constitute the principal subject matter of legal capacity, while political capacity is concerned with such matters as representation, voting, and contributions in international conferences and congresses, administrative union, and arbitral or judicial tribunals. Laws in regard to legal capacity affect the relations between the states as individual entities, while laws in regard to political capacity affect their participation in the privileges and responsibilities of collective inter-national activity.[50]

Dickinson reaches the conclusion that equality before the law is essential to any legal society, while equality of capacity of rights and duties as a second aspect of juridical equality is not an essential, but an ideal toward which any system of law should develop. That is, legal inequalities of status should be removed from any legal system insofar as this is possible. Political equality, to the contrary, is not thought to be essential nor is it an ideal, inasmuch as equal participation in governmental organization, whether national or international, by all has never been regarded as realistic or practical. To insist on complete equality in the functioning of international organization will preclude effective international organization.[51]

The American states have accepted the principle of juridical equality as governing their mutual relations. In the inter-American system, the OAS is also seemingly bound to respect the principle in dealings with its members under the Charter. Article 6 of the Charter, which sets forth the principle of equality, is not directed specifically to the member states, but is phrased in general language declaring states to be juridically equal. From this it can be deduced that the principle is basic both to the states and to their organization. This is reinforced by the fact that the principle of equality has always been declared as an essential principle of the system. In the last analysis the organization is one of independent states created to facilitate voluntary co-operation among them and established in part to defend their sovereignty and independence. Since the concept of equality is said to be derived from sovereignty or is a corollary of it, an obligation of respect for this principle is placed upon the organization as an entity.

As a consequence, the OAS, insofar as it is empowered to do so, must make certain that each state receives the equal protection of the law, that each state exercises its equal capacity for rights, and that each is bound to the same duties, inasmuch as all American states in their legal community are possessed of equal status. This means that an infringement of the rights of the smallest must be given the same consideration by the OAS as an infringement of the rights of the most powerful; that all states, whether weak or strong, must be subjected to the same international and inter-American obligations by the OAS to the extent that its ordering authority permits; and that all states should be accorded equal access to the remedies provided under the constitutional documents of the OAS. In short, the OAS should act impartially, unmoved by considerations of power, for all American states, irrespective of power and influence, are equally entitled to the protection guaranteed by the Charter.

The American states have carefully guarded juridical equality. Political equality within their quasi-constitutional structure, the OAS, also remains largely intact, although some inroads have been made on it by agreement, as set forth in the Charter and other inter-American treaties.

In the policy-making and decisional organs of the OAS, such as the Inter-American Conferences, the Meetings of Consultation, and the Council, equality of representation and voting is assured.[52] Each state has representation, each state has one vote, and each vote is of equal weight. Departure from the principle of equality has come about, however, in that unanimity to reach decision has been abolished. Unanimity in the conferences is the goal for all important action; still, in general, decisions may be taken by an absolute majority, and the principle of state equality will protect a dissenting state from a majority decision. To this extent equality is preserved as to the creation of new obligations which require voluntary acceptance. An important exception to this is to be found in the power of the Organ of Consultation and the Provisional Organ acting under the Rio Treaty to take substantive decisions which create obligations for members that have not concurred in the decision. Under that treaty, the members obligate themselves to comply with decisions of two-thirds of them to put into effect the enforcement measures enumerated in Article 8 in instances of armed attack against an American state or other aggressions or threats to the peace in the Americas, with the sole exception that a state is not required to use armed force without its consent.[53] Here no isolated state may block the action which the other states believe should be taken under the circumstances. In this connection, the primacy of certain nations is not recognized. No state or group of states is placed above or beyond the law as in the case of the United Nations where, on the Security Council, the permanent members are possessed of the veto. The hope that the same law may be applicable to all nations large and small is dispelled by this power of the permanent members of the United Nations, for enforcement measures cannot be used against such a member without its consent or, more broadly, in any case unless the permanent members unanimously consent.

A further departure from strict state equality may be noted in the OAS. It is generally assumed that the principle of equality in the field of capacity for rights signifies also equality of duties or obligations. This is not always true, for there are instances within the OAS where the larger, wealthier states are subject to greater obligations than the smaller. For example, with respect to the financial contributions to the maintenance of the Pan American Union, the Charter itself calls for unequal obligation, for the bases for fixing each state's financial quota are the ability of each country to pay and the determination of the members to contribute in an equitable manner.[54]

Chapter IX

THE PRINCIPLE OF NON-INTERVENTION

BACKGROUND AND DEFINITION

With a long historical background involving a checkered pattern of foreign intermeddling in the internal affairs of the American republics,[1] the statesmen and jurists of Latin America waged a persistent campaign to codify the principle of non-intervention as an integral part of American international law.[2] Most Latin American publicists who support the doctrine of non-intervention and deny the right of intervention defend their position on the theoretical ground that a right cannot violate a right. The absolute right of state independence which they claim is the cornerstone of the modern law of nations is violated when a right of intervention is acknowledged. If the right of independence calls for full liberty of action by a state within its jurisdiction, it follows that another nation can have no right to interfere in this sphere, without detracting from the right of independence. Non-intervention is then a corollary of the doctrine of the independence of sovereign states and as such becomes a duty of the states.[3]

Latin American jurists reasoned juridically in an effort to establish the illegality of intervention and to proclaim what to them was the correct principle of international law—not intervention, but non-intervention.[4] Protest was registered against what was termed a dual standard of international treatment followed by world powers, whereby the nations of Latin America were regarded as inferior and therefore proper subjects of intervention.[5]

The policy of the United States also contributed to the doctrine both positively and negatively. In the first place, the outright affirmative proscription of intervention by European nations in the Americas via the Monroe Doctrine was a clear statement of a doctrine of non-intervention, though limited in scope to certain nations only—those outside the Americas. Negatively, when the United States itself began to pursue a policy of intervention, the reaction in Latin America was so strong that it became an obsession to proclaim an absolute doctrine of non-intervention and to bind the United States to it.[6]

The first attempt by the Latin American nations to adopt a principle of non-intervention into their public law was made in 1826, at the Congress of Panama, called by Bolívar.[7] Bolívar, who was acquainted with the designs of the Spanish king to reacquire his lost dominions and with the interventionary policy adopted by the members of the Holy Alliance, sought an understanding among the American governments looking toward common resistance to the right of intervention adopted by certain of the European powers, and toward adherence to the principles set forth by Monroe.[8] The Treaty of Perpetual Union, League and Confederation signed at the congress contained only a germ of the concept of non-intervention, however, in a statement that the object of the compact was to maintain the sovereignty and independence of all the American states against foreign subjection.[9]

Non-intervention was stated more clearly as an American rule at the Hispanic American Congress of 1848. By a Treaty of Confederation, the parties agreed to regard as *casus foederis:*

When any foreign government intervenes or tries to intervene by force.... to alert the institutions of one or more of the confederated Republics, to require them to do what is not lawful by the law of nations, or is not permitted by their own laws, or to prevent the execution of those laws, or of the orders, resolutions or judgments dictated in accordance therewith.[10]

A much deeper impression was made by the treatise on international law written by Dr. Carlos Calvo.[11] Calvo was of the opinion that armed or diplomatic intervention for the purpose of enforcing private claims of a pecuniary nature was illegal. To him the independence of a sovereign nation should not be subjected to such intervention, which abridges the independence of its governmental agencies such as its legislature and its courts.

Later Dr. Luis M. Drago of Argentina also contributed to the doctrine. In a note sent to the government of the United States on the occasion of the attempt by Great Britain, Germany, and Italy to collect claims against Venezuela by forcible means, he sought to prohibit forceful intervention in order to coerce a state to pay its public debt.[12]

Both Calvo and Drago, although stating their principles as universal rules of international law, still were concerned, as was Monroe, primarily with non-American interventions in the Western Hemisphere. With the advent of the Theodore Roosevelt corollary to the Monroe Doctrine and United States interventions, there arose from Latin America a clamor for an absolute doctrine of non-intervention to prevent the practice whether emanating from the United States or from non-American states, and it became a cardinal aim of Latin American diplomacy to formulate a code of public international law in the form of a multilateral treaty containing a renunciation of the right of intervention and binding all American states. Adherence to such a principle by the United States would prevent its intervening even to preclude the possibility of European intervention. The United States, if it desired further maintenance of the principles of the Monroe Doctrine, would be forced to take action against the non-American state seeking to intervene in order to stop such action. It could not take action against the American state in the form of a protective intervention to prevent the non-American intervention.[13] To achieve this purpose the jurists of Latin America made effective use of the inter-American system.

Through the Commission of Jurists established by the American states a project of codification of American international law was carried out. Among these principles as finally formulated was that of non-intervention,[14] which was presented in 1928 to the Sixth Conference in Habana, where it failed to be adopted, although it was the subject of prolonged and critical dispute.[15] The United States managed to block the acceptance of the principle and the issue was postponed.

When the project was once again brought up at the Seventh Conference in Montevideo in 1933, it was not at all clear that the principle of non-intervention would not meet the same fate accorded it at Habana. The United States, however, had changed its policy. Its delegation, headed by Secretary of State Cordell Hull, had been instructed to remove obstacles standing in the way of harmony and friendly relations with Latin America. When the Convention on Rights and Duties of States, which included the principle that "no state has the right to intervene in the internal or external affairs of another,"[16] was submitted to vote it was found that the United States had now reversed itself and voted with the Latin American delegations in favor of the convention as a whole. It is true that when it signed the convention it attached a long reservation which in effect signified that the United States reserved its rights as generally recognized by international law.[17]

The Latin American republics received the action of the United States with enthusiasm; still, they would have preferred United States adherence with no reservations, for the reservation left the scope of non-intervention in doubt as long as the United States adhered to its stand that intervention could still take place in those areas sanctioned by general international law.

At the Inter-American Conference for the Maintenance of Peace which met at Buenos Aires in 1936, the Latin American nations finally won a complete victory, for the United States adhered without reservation to the Additional Protocol Relative to Non-Intervention:

The High Contracting Parties declare inadmissible the intervention of any one of them, directly or indirectly, and for whatever reason in the internal or external affairs of any other of the Parties.
The violation of the provisions of this Article shall give rise to mutual consultation, with the object of exchanging views and seeking methods of peaceful adjustment.[18]

By signing this treaty the United States bound itself to an unrestricted course of non-intervention—a rather radical change of policy, brought about, at least in part, by the approval at the same conference of a convention which provided for consultation by all the American republics in the event the peace is threatened. It was reasoned that when such situations occurred as had prompted past interventions, a threat to the peace would arise which would bring about collective consultation of all the American republics in the effort to seek a solution.

At the Ninth International Conference of American States at Bogotá, at the insistence of the Latin American states, the Fundamental Rights and Duties of States incorporated the non-intervention principle. Here a more sweeping statement on non-intervention was made than in previous agreements: Article 15 prohibited intervention by one state and also by a group of states. In conformity with the previous doctrine, intervention in the internal or external affairs of another state, directly or indirectly, was proscribed. A more detailed definition was given in the statement that the principle applied not only to armed force but to any other form of interference or attempted threat against the personality of the state or its political, economic, and cultural elements. In addition, Article 16 went still further by forbidding a state the use of coercive measures of an economic or political character to force the sovereign will of another state and obtain from it advantages of any kind.

Not only in the particular international law of the Americas but also at general international law there has evolved, among other duties placed upon those subjects of international law called states or nations, a duty of non-intervention. Nevertheless, the majority of publicists do not refer to non-intervention, the negative form, but discuss the doctrine of intervention and its juridical or political nature. Non-intervention is a restriction or limitation on intervention; and actually the interest in non-intervention arises from or has as its source those interventions which are carried on by states against other states. Intervention and non-intervention are inextricably bound together, and it is obviously impossible to discuss non-intervention without marking out what is meant by intervention.

Reasoning from principles and sources of the law of nations and evaluating acts and declarations of states, one may say that intervention occurs when a state or group of states interferes in order to impose its will, in the internal or external affairs of another state, sovereign and independent, with which peaceful relations exist and without its consent, for the purpose of maintaining or altering the condition of things.[19]

To meet the terms of this definition there must be an interference by which one state encroaches upon the sovereign prerogatives of another state; but ordinarily interference is not synomymous with intervention, although intervention includes within its meaning interference or intermeddling. The clearest example of intervention contains a second element; that is, interference which is meant or intended to compel certain action or inaction by which the intervening state imposes or seeks to impose its will. An interference to compel another state to do an act which if not so compelled it would not do, or to refrain from doing any act which if not so compelled it would do, would, of course, effectively alter or maintain the condition of things as to the state intervened.

It is then the constraining nature of the act of interference which undoubtedly constitutes intervention, whether the act is one involving the use of force or one involving a lesser type of compulsion, i.e., political or economic.[20] A mere friendly interference such as a tender of advice or an official communication requesting a state to take or refrain from taking certain measures, or the offer of good offices or mediation wherein there is no element of compulsion, is not intervention.[21] International law presupposes friendly relations among states. A fact of importance which is often forgotten is that there must be in the interference a factor to force compliance with the will of the interfering state. The interference must take place as action or inaction or threat thereof of an adverse nature or one thought to be adverse in case the state should fail to conform to the will of the intervening state. Mere interference by which a state seeks by lengthy persuasion and arduous negotiations to induce another state to act or refrain from acting constitutes no intervention, unless pressure is brought in the form of armed force, economic or political ill consequences, or threat thereof to be applied by the interfering state if the other fails to comply. The essence of intervention is the attempt to compel, for if a state interfering is not disposed to support the interference with some form of pressure, it is evident that it is not imposing its will; such pressure would consist in placing the state in a position where it must submit or face certain consequences if it refuses.[22]

This does not, however, imply that to be an intervention the interference must actually compel. Even though the state subjected to the interference pays it no heed, refuses to be constrained or frightened by the threats of ill consequences, an intervention has occurred if by the interference and threats the intervening state attempted to compel or coerce the sovereign will of the other state.

The above definition and analysis of intervention is inescapable under the American doctrine of non-intervention accepted by the American republics at Bogotá in 1948. By the language used in Articles 15 and 16 of the Charter, a multilateral treaty which has been ratified by the American states, a broad form of non-intervention is accepted as a principle of American international law, binding the ratifying states legally and applying to any form of compulsion exerted by a state which seeks to coerce the sovereign will of another.

The basis for the principle of non-intervention in international law is, as stated above, the theory of the independence of the sovereign state. Postulating from this theory it can be deduced that it is incumbent upon states not to intervene in the affairs of sister states, for intervention is an act which usurps the sovereign attributes of the state against which it is invoked, which is an infringement of the independence of the state intervened. Nevertheless—and this continues true at the present time—publicists maintain that there are exceptions to the rule of non-intervention in international law, and in those instances intervention becomes legal or permissible.

Even though the right of independence be clearly recognized and though it be agreed that non-intervention in external as well as internal affairs is the correct rule of states, intervention can still be justified as legal in certain instances where the intervening state can show that its action is sanctioned by some principle that takes precedence over the right of independence.[23] Under international law no state can expect to retain the right of sovereign decision called independence when by its conduct it makes clear that it cannot or will not fulfil the international law obligations of an independent and sovereign state; for it is obvious that state sovereignty is subject to limitations and that states are not above the law of nations but are subjected to it.[24] Thus the right of independence is subjected to the restrictions imposed by international law. The freedom envisaged by the right of independence is freedom from control of other states, not freedom from the restrictions of international law, which binds all states. When a state violates its obligations under international law, for example, it is liable to encounter intervention by the state against whom it has committed the delict or by other states which are of the opinion that such wrongful conduct is an attack upon principles necessary to international society.

It can then be said that there are special circumstances in which intervention may be legitimate under general international law, even though intervention by one state in the sphere of interests of another is normally illegitimate. Intervention is legal at general international law when exercised in pursuance of the right of self-defense, as a sanction, and by consent. In reality we need not concern ourselves with the last of these, for this type of interference cannot be called an intervention, inasmuch as intervention signifies an act or threat of compulsion or coercion of the will of a state by another, an imposition of the will of the intervenor. If consent is given freely, there is no imposition of will.[25]

SELF-DEFENSE

An intervention by a state is legitimate under international law when the intervention is occasioned by an exercise of the right of self-defense. This right has never been seriously questioned. From a circumscribed point of view, a state, like an individual, may protect itself against an illegitimate attack, commenced or imminently impending. From a wider point of view, a state may exercise a right of self-defense not only against an illegitimate attack but also against any serious delictual conduct when there is an absence of other means of protection for the essential rights of the state subjected to the wrongs.[26] Therefore, since there is a right of self-defense, intervention by one state in the affairs of another by which the former protects itself constitutes a legal intervention, even when carried to the extent of invading the territory of the wrongdoing state and there performing acts of a compulsive nature.[27]

Can intervention in pursuance of the right of self-defense be considered consistent with the seemingly absolute principle of non-intervention incorporated by treaty into the law of the Americas? Some jurists take the position that the acts practiced in the exercise of the right of legitimate self-defense are not intervention.[28] Such a proposition can hardly maintain itself as compatible with the definition of intervention stated in the Charter of Bogotá, i.e., any form of interference or attempted threat against the personality of the state or against its political, economic, and cultural elements.

If it be conceded that intervention for the purpose of self-defense is intervention proper, it can still be legally justified in the Americas, for under conventions in force between the American nations the right of self-defense is recognized. Article 3 of the Rio Treaty specifically recognizes the right of individual and collective self-defense in case of an armed attack against an American state. Article 18 of the Charter of Bogotá binds the American states in their international relations not to have recourse to force "except in the case of self-defense in accordance with existing treaties or in fulfillment thereof."

These articles make out an exception to the non-intervention principle and make intervention, at the least for the purposes of self-defense to meet an armed attack, legitimate.

SANCTIONS

Although general international law has been classified as a primitive law with no central organ to enforce the rights and duties of sovereign states, still certain enforcement procedures have been recognized. In the absence of proper international organization, self-help by a state itself has been accepted as a means of obtaining redress, reparation, or conformity with legality. If a state defied international law to commit an international wrong, the state upon which the blow fell was driven to self-help to secure the fulfilment of the duties which the law-breaking state owed to it. Self-help has been universally recognized as a means of enforcement,[29] as a sanction; two types of sanctions, both forms of self-help, are authorized by international law as reactions against a state guilty by commission or omission of an international wrong.

These two specific sanctions are war and reprisals; and, as Kelsen shows, they differ only in degree—war being an unlimited interference in the affairs of a state derelict in its duties with the aim of bringing about the delinquent state's subjection or destruction, and reprisals being a limited violation of certain rights, a restricted interference in the affairs of the wrongdoing state.[30] In war as a sanction against an international wrong we are not here interested, inasmuch as intervention may not be classified as war—although of course it may, when force is used, approach war, and any intervention may lead to war. Measures short of war whereby a state attempts to secure satisfaction from another for a wrong which has been committed against it, i.e., reprisals which are a limited interference by the wronged state in the sphere of interests of the wrong-doing state to coerce the latter to fulfil its obligations and duties to the former, may be classified as intervention.

Reprisals have been subjected to varying classifications and have taken many forms. Some classify them as negative and positive. A negative reprisal is said to be the denial of an obligation which the injured state owes to the delinquent state. For instance, the injured state may, as a means of obtaining redress, refuse payment of its national debt owed to the state committing the delict.[31] Positive reprisals issue when the offended state takes affirmative acts through the use of armed force or economic or political sanctions against the offending state or its persons or goods.[32] This indicates that reprisals may be classified as those which are armed and those which take place without the force of arms: economic or political measures. No matter what the form, they are intervention, although at general international law they are considered legal.[33]

Sanctions by an injured state in the form of reprisals to secure redress are then permitted against a state guilty of a breach of the law; but the broader issue arises as to whether international law justifies intervention to uphold or vindicate the law by a state not directly concerned, not directly injured in cases where there has been a breach. Here there is a split of authority and a conflict. But the better view recognizes intervention for such purposes as legitimate and views breaches of fundamental law as something akin to a crime giving rise to a public action—not a mere action for reparation or redress at the behest of the injured, but a punitive action to vindicate and enforce the law.[34]

This doctrine, of course, should be limited to a breach of a universally accepted legal duty and a gross and patent violation in a matter of serious importance which threatens the peace and order of the community of nations. In such an instance, it would become the business of every member of the community, for it would be a legal injury to all—a violation of each nation's right to have the law maintained.[35]

Since sanctions in the form of reprisals taken by the injured state to obtain redress or to vindicate international law are subject to criticism as coercion by powerful states of weaker states, and since there is a dangerous tendency toward the development of arbitrary action by the intervening state, such methods have been circumscribed by particular international law through treaties.

The members of the OAS have condemned resort to the threat or use of force and have obligated themselves to settle all disputes peacefully. Thus under the OAS armed sanctions, whether pursued as reprisals or to vindicate international law, are prohibited unless taken collectively under the authority of the OAS. But what of sanctions not involving armed force, which in some instances may be permitted under the United Nations Charter?[36]

The non-intervention principle of the Charter of Bogotá proscribes all intervention, not only by armed force but also by other form of interference or attempted threat against the personality of the state or against its political, economic, and cultural elements. While under general international law measures to uphold the law as a reaction against a state guilty of a breach of the law are permitted, under the Charter of Bogotá that general right has been abrogated: "No state has the right to intervene for any reason whatever."[37]

The right is denied and, therefore, under the OAS there is no longer a legal right to apply unilateral sanctions. This language also seems to prohibit acts such as retorsion, which are not classified as sanctions, but which can in some instances fall within the definition of intervention.[38]

Although the use of self-help in the form of sanctions to uphold the law against a nation which has breached the law, whether armed or otherwise, is prohibited by the Charter, the question might arise as to whether a plea of justification for self-help would be legal under certain unusual circumstances.

The plea of justification could be based on one of two arguments. The first of these would be that in spite of the Charter of the OAS, a general right of intervention by self-help must exist in cases where a breach of international law (general or particular) has created an immediate, very serious, and common danger to the international regional community of the American states. In this event, general international law justifies intervention even by states not directly concerned.

The Provisional Organ of Consultation is in permanent session, and, under both the Charter and the Rio Treaty, it would seem that the Organ of Consultation is under a duty to meet "immediately" whenever a fact or situation arises which might endanger the peace of the Americas. Therefore the plea for the necessity of immediate action which might stand up under the Charter of the United Nations[39] might fall under the OAS, for there is at hand an instrumentality of immediate action which can be used to avert a common danger. But it might be asked, what if the OAS fails, because of political reasons, to take necessary action to avert an immediate, very serious, and common danger?

The second reason for a plea of justification for self-help arises when a norm of particular international law established by an international treaty fails to function. Then the corresponding norm of general international law reappears, for no treaty has power to abolish completely and eternally laws of general international law.

If the regional procedures for settling an issue endangering the peace of the

Americas should completely break down, the OAS is required by both the Rio Treaty and the United Nations Charter to submit that issue to the Security Council or the General Assembly of the United Nations. If the plea of justification on this ground is valid, it can be so only after the norms of the inter-American system have broken down and the norms of the United Nations have failed to function. The plea of justification would have to run the gauntlet of both treaties before it would be valid, for only then could general international law be reinstated in place of particular international law. But this would not imply that in every conceivable situation the case must be formally submitted to both organizations. When it is obvious that no action will be taken by either, no jeopardized nation is required by general international law to engage in futility to justify its legitimate actions.

The question remains whether the OAS as a jural personality is obligated to respect the principle in exercising its powers in relation to the member states.

If the OAS is a jural personality, that is if it has a legal personality distinct from the legal personalities of the individual states of which it is composed, then it has rights and duties distinct from the legal personalities of individual states of which it is composed.[40] It can be argued that if this be the case, Article 15 has no application to the organization because the OAS is more than a "group" of states; it is a juridical entity in its own right and as no mention of this juridical entity is made in Article 15, the non-intervention principles do not apply to the OAS.

If the OAS is merely an associated group of states, each member having a dual personality—that is, each state having a legal personality in its private affairs, but this being distinct from the personality it has in its group affairs—then the organization cannot exist apart from its members. Consequently Article 15 when speaking of a "group" of states would apply to the OAS, for the association of the states, even though the associated states have acquired rights and duties different from those in their individual transactions, has no legal standing per se in the eyes of the law. The only legal basis for collective action or intervention by the OAS would then be Article 19 of the Charter, which declares that measures adopted for the maintenance of peace and security in accordance with existing treaties do not constitute a violation of the non-intervention principle.

The OAS is in some degree possessed of jural personality. The conclusion can, therefore, be reached that it is not obligated to non-intervention, since such a course is not expressly indicated for it by the Charter. This rationalization, while sound from a standpoint of logic, fails to take into account the importance attributed to non-intervention within the American community. It is so basal that it is extremely unlikely that the American states in creating their juridical community would grant to it an unlimited right of collective intervention in their internal and external affairs while at the same time binding each state in its relation to other states to strictest non-intervention.

That such a grant was not intended is apparent from the fact that the drafters of the Charter carefully excepted from the principle of non-intervention those collective enforcement measures permitted under existing treaties—the Rio Treaty and the United Nations Charter.[41]

The enforcement measures permitted by the Rio Treaty are in effect the only true enforcement measures granted to the OAS. They are the police powers of the organization to be used against a nation which breaches or threatens the peace of the Americas and as such are repressive in nature. They are coercive, for they are meant to compel an aggressor state to cease its threats to the peace or to return to a state of peace by a collective interference if conformity to the will of the OAS does not ensue. Although these collective enforcement measures are interventionary in character, they are permitted through the consent of the American states based on their agreement to the Rio Treaty and the Charter of Bogotá, the latter specifically excepting these measures from the doctrine of non-intervention.[42]

The power of the OAS under the Rio Treaty is a power of direct action— a power to prescribe a certain course of behavior by providing coercive measures to be taken in case of contrary behavior. But the OAS has also broad power to discuss, study, investigate, and recommend, and it has been contended that the exercise of such power in certain cases by an international organization may amount to intervention.

On this issue divergent views have been expressed. With respect to Article 2, Paragraph 7 of the United Nations Charter, which prohibits United Nations intervention in matters essentially within the domestic jurisdiction of a state, it has been asserted that the word "intervene" as used here was aimed only at stopping any direct enforcement action which might be taken by an organ of the United Nations if the subject matter was essentially within the domestic jurisdiction of a state, and thus the article would permit, with reference to purely domestic issues, discussion, study, inquiry, and even recommendation, so long as that recommendation was not backed by the threat of enforcement action. None of these activities, so it has been contended, can be termed intervention.[43]

Other jurists contend that collective intervention must be distinguished from collective action. Any action taken by an international organization is taken in the general interest of states or for the collective enforcement of international law and is not then intervention. The type of intervention referred to in Article 2, Paragraph 7 of the United Nations Charter must then be modified by the word "arbitrary."[44] To adopt either thesis with reference to the OAS would permit that organization the broadest latitude of discussion, investigation, and recommendation without reference to the non-intervention principle, inasmuch as such action would not be termed intervention.

However, there are writers who take the position that Article 2, Paragraph 7 of the United Nations Charter was meant to exclude discussion, study, and investigation; formal action by way of recommendation to a state within whose domestic jurisdiction the subject matter lies; and certainly all enforcement action.[45] These writers feel that such action is intervention which is precluded by the Article when it also involves domestic jurisdiction of a state. To take such a position as to the OAS would seriously curtail the organization's power of discussion, investigation, and recommendation; for then the organization would be bound by Article 15 which proscribes intervention, with no exception granted here as is the case with enforcement measures under the Rio Treaty.

None of these contentions seems completely accurate. Intervention is a technical legal word involving interference with the internal or external affairs of a state without its consent, in an attempt to make the will of the interfering agent prevail. Whether discussion, investigation, or recommendations are to be considered acts of intervention by the OAS would depend on whether they were coercive attempts to maintain or alter existing conditions against the state's will.

Ordinarily discussion or investigation by organs of the OAS would not amount to intervention. Discussion and investigation are traditional methods of diplomacy and cannot be considered intervention so long as such discussion or investigation permits presentation of both sides of an issue and does not involve coercion. The fact that such discussion or investigation might mobilize against a nation whatever power may exist in the nebulous force of inter-American public opinion is insufficient to equate it with intervention, for to prohibit such discussion or investigation in all instances would be to close virtually all channels of communication between the organization and states or among states themselves.

Nevertheless, there is a possibility that discussion and investigation could fall within the aegis of intervention. Since a state might lose international prestige through the mobilization of public opinion against it, a discussion and investigation may have the effect of compelling a state to act in accord with the will of the organization, even though no threat of other action is made by the organization.[46] In such instances, if the organization entered into a consideration, discussion, or investigation directed against a specific state with the purpose of coercing that state to act in conformity with the will of the organization, then certainly this would seem to be equated with intervention.

The same might be said as to a recommendation. Ordinarily a recommendation is of a general nature, recommending a course or policy which all the states of the organization should follow and made within the authority of the particular organ. But again a specific censorious recommendation made against a state for the purpose of forcing that state's will would seem to be intervention.

Granting that discussion, investigation, and recommendation might in some instances be interventionary in character, would such action always be violative of the non-intervention principles of the Americas? They would, of course, be permissible when taken in case of a breach or threat to the peace under the Rio Treaty by the Meeting of Foreign Ministers as Organ of Consultation or by the Council as Provisional Organ.

The position has been taken that this type of action by the organization may be legal in another instance, inasmuch as the OAS, as a legal entity, has been made a protector of international law in the Americas, although it has very limited powers in this respect.[47] It has been contended that since a fundamental purpose behind the establishment of the inter-American juridical community was to bring about security and peace founded on moral order and justice, and hence on international law, such a basic purpose should not be defeated or nullified by the non-intervention limitation of Article 15.[48] Therefore, even if discussion, investigation, and recommendation are interventionary in character, they would be permissible so long as the matter dealt with was a question of international law, although it goes without saying that no direct enforcement action could be taken unless a case falls within the terms of the Rio Treaty as constituting a breach of or threat to the peace.

It must be recognized that any discussion involving the contention that security and peace based on moral order, justice, and international law overrides the non-intervention principle is extremely arguable. The non-intervention principle governing the OAS and the American states is exceedingly broad, prohibiting intervention in the internal or external affairs of a state, directly or indirectly, *for any reason whatever.*

If one does conclude that the OAS may take such action—discussion, investigation, and recommendation—of an interventionary nature in a matter of international law, the implication exists that there are certain areas in which international law does not impose any restriction on the liberty of action of the states. Within this sphere of national jurisdiction wherein the state is permitted by international law an unlimited liberty of action, the OAS would not be authorized to carry on discussions and investigations or make recommendations which could be classified as intervention, inasmuch as the plea of protecting or enforcing international law could hardly be justified. This area wherein the state is not restricted by international law is the "domestic jurisdiction" of the state set forth and protected in some degree by the United Nations Charter against certain interventionary action by the United Nations.

The borderline between domestic jurisdiction and international law is, however, fluid and relative. If there is international regulation restricting a state's freedom of action in the area, the subject is no longer a question of domestic jurisdiction, and this international regulation may be a rule of general international law or of particular international law—i.e., international agreements.[49] Hence, in these areas—including, of course, matters regulated by the Charter of Bogotá and other inter-American agreements which impose obligations on the members—a plea of domestic jurisdiction can never be raised as an excuse for denying the competence of the OAS.

CHAPTER X

JURISDICTION OVER ALIENS

Sovereignty of states as a fundamental principle of international law signifies independence, and one of its two aspects is internal independence, the so-called supreme authority of each state to control all persons and things within its territory. This internal independence, this supreme authority within the national domain, is jurisdiction. In general, it is taken to mean that a state has an *exclusive* right to exercise jurisdiction over all persons and things within its territory. This right reflects the duty of other states to refrain from the exercise of jurisdiction within a state, and if this duty is breached the territorial integrity, the sovereignty or independence, of the state subjected to the transgression is violated.

As has been noted, the right of independence is not absolute, for it is subject to the limitations imposed by international law. The extent of the right of a state to exercise jurisdiction within its domain is fixed by the law of nations. Broad authority over internal administration is left to each individual state by the community of nations, but some restrictions have been placed on it by international law, particularly with reference to obligations imposed for the protection of aliens.[1]

The jurisdiction of a state over persons within its territory includes both nationals and aliens. An alien resident in a state owes temporary allegiance to the state in which he resides and is, therefore, normally governed by local laws.[2]

On the other hand, there seems to be little if any question at international law that a state has a right as well as a duty[3] to protect its own nationals whether at home or in a foreign country. Yet it may well be asked whether a state is under a corresponding duty to protect the rights of aliens in its territory. The responsibility in relation to the protection of life and liberty which a state owes to aliens who are resident within its territory, that which it owes to aliens who own property within the country, and that to aliens with whom it has entered into certain contractual relations for the loan of money or for the performance of certain services have been subjects of controversy. In general it can be asserted that a state is under no responsibility to grant greater protection to foreigners than to its own citizens. An alien can claim no greater concessions or favors than the state establishes for its own citizens, and a foreigner voluntarily entering within a state's territory must accept that state's institutions as they exist. The alien's personal rights and property rights are ordinarily not entitled to any greater degree of protection or greater guarantees of justice than the nation affords to its own citizens.[4]

Although this rule is the accepted standard of general international law, there has been engrafted on it a limitation that in some instances aliens are permitted a privileged position by rules of international law, for if a state's standard of justice with respect to its own nationals is so low that it fails to measure up to a general norm governing members of the family of nations, the alien is granted the right to appeal to the average norm rather than to the lower norm ruling within the state. Two rules are accepted as starting points in the approach to the determination of a state's responsibility to an alien. The first of these is that the alien by entering the foreign country subjects himself to local law. The second is that the state is not an insurer of the safety, lives, and property of aliens. Offsetting the first rule is the concept of the international standard which qualifies the supremacy of local law, including the administration of law, by asserting that the local law is not the last resort if it falls below an international average standard in its general application or in its application to a particular case.[5] The second rule is qualified by a set of subsidiary rules stating the conditions under which the state is liable for an injury to an alien. For the most part, liability is predicated on fault, and the fault may be one of commission or omission.

The international standard of justice which a state is called upon to follow in the treatment of aliens is not a technical or precise one.[6] It merely states that aliens must be treated in such a way as to accord with ordinary standards of civilization. If an alien suffers injury to his person because the state in its treatment of him falls below this standard, or has his property confiscated, or if the state breaches governmental contracts with the alien or refuses to pay public bonds held by aliens and provides no redress for its own default, then the state becomes delinquent at international law, having violated an established duty of states. After an injured alien has exhausted all local remedies available to him and sustained a denial of justice, then the state of citizenship has the right of intervention in the form of reprisals as a sanction in order to protect its citizens.[7]

The denial of justice concept and the right of a state to intervene to take measures of self-help to enforce reparation and prevent future repetition were declared legitimate by Grotius, who alleged that a state in the event of injuries to its citizens was authorized to exercise a right of reprisal with respect to the delinquent state.[8] Vattel later adopted this concept, limiting it to instances where the *courts* denied justice.[9] As time passed, the concept was extended to instances wherein the state denied justice to aliens by legislative act, judicial decision, or administrative action—in short, the denial of justice standard applies to all internal governmental actions with reference to aliens.[10] Such a broad interpretation permits a denial of justice plea where the propriety of any governmental act falls below an international standard recognized and approved by reasonable men, whether the failure to meet the standard is a result of deficient execution of the nation's laws with respect to the alien, or of the fact that the laws do not permit the authorities to measure up to international standards.

Intervention by a state on behalf of its citizens for the protection of their lives, liberty, and property abroad was often directed at certain Latin American nations during the nineteenth century and the early part of the twentieth, because the unsettled social and economic conditions in those countries often placed the lives and property of aliens in jeopardy. Loud protests were made by certain Latin American statesmen and jurists at these interventions, which were declared to be violations of sovereignty.

It was claimed by Latin Americans that there is no higher international standard applying to the treatment to be accorded to aliens than the national standard applying to the treatment accorded to citizens. If a state grants equality of treatment to nationals and non-nationals, it fulfils its international obligations.[11] Reasoning from this premise, then, a state does not breach any international obligation when it treats both groups equally; and if no breach of international law occurs, the alien's home state can have no right to intervene for the protection of the alien.[12]

The equality of treatment doctrine was proclaimed by various states at the First International Conference of American States, where the following recommendation was made:

(1) Foreigners are entitled to enjoy all the civil rights enjoyed by natives, and they shall be accorded all the benefits of said rights in all that is essential as well as in the form of procedure, and the legal remedies incident thereto, absolutely in like manner as said natives. (2) A nation has not, nor recognizes in favor of foreigners, any other obligations or responsibilities than those which in favor of the natives are established, in like cases, by the constitution and the laws.[13]

The United States voted against the recommendation, pointing out that a state's concern with the affairs of its citizens abroad is a far older concept of international law than that of territorial sovereignty, and that, furthermore, aliens are entitled to special protection under international law because they have no political right to take part in the shaping of the social and economic policies of the country involved. This divergence of views has continued to be a source of discussion and friction in most of the subsequent inter-American conferences.

At the Seventh Conference, the United States did sign the Convention on the Rights and Duties of States, which established by Article 9 the principle: "Nationals and Foreigners are under the protection of the law and the national authorities and the foreigners may not claim rights other or more extensive than those of the nationals."[14] Although the United States signed the Convention, still a reservation was made to the effect that it reserved all rights of international law. This took the teeth out of the article insofar as the United States was concerned.[15]

The issue was again raised at Bogotá in 1948 with respect to the rights and duties of states established by the Charter of Bogotá. It was first suggested that the following provision should be included in the Charter: "The jurisdiction of states within the limits of national territory applies to all inhabitants. Nationals and aliens are under the same protection and owe the same obedience to the laws and authorities of the country." Such a stipulation would tend to create an absolute right to the exercise of jurisdiction over nationals and aliens alike, unrestricted by international law at least as regards the protection of aliens by the state of nationality.

The United States delegation refused to accept this proposition, affirming that it recognized as a rule of international law that nationals and aliens are subject to the jurisdiction of the state in which they reside, but denying that it was a correct statement of general international law that they should both necessarily be entitled to the same protection. The United States thereby reaffirmed its adherence to the rule that if the treatment of an alien, whether with reference to his life, his liberty, or his property, falls below certain international standards, the government of the state of which the alien is a citizen may bring the matter to the attention of the authorities of the other state. In order that accord might be reached on this issue, the wording of the article was changed to read: "The jurisdiction of States within the limits of their national territory, is exercised equally over all the inhabitants, whether nationals or aliens."[16] In practice, therefore, the equality of treatment approach has not been successful in overthrowing the rule of general international law that a state has a right to protect its citizens abroad.[17]

Dr. Carlos Calvo was probably the first eminent Latin American jurist to condemn financial interventions, armed or diplomatic, on behalf of citizens abroad as violative of the principle of the equality of states, in that such action is usually taken by strong states against weaker nations. He stated:

Aside from political motives these interventions have nearly always had as apparent pretexts, injuries to private interests, claims and demands for pecuniary indemnities in behalf of subjects or even foreigners, the protection of whom was for the most part in no wise justified in strict law. According to strict international right, the recovery of debts and the pursuit of private claims does not justify *de plano* the armed intervention of governments, and, since European states invariably follow this rule in their reciprocal relations, there is no reason why they should not also impose it upon themselves in their relations with nations in the new world.[18]

Calvo speaks in the main of injuries suffered by aliens from civil wars or mob violence, but from the general tenor of his text his doctrine may be said to be that private claims, whether arising in tort or contract, should not be made the basis of intervention, at least until the injured alien has exhausted his local remedies and has suffered a denial of justice. Only then would the alien be justified in seeking the protection of the state of which he is a national. Moreover, it would seem that even after its national had exhausted all remedies and suffered a denial of justice, a state should not resort to armed intervention in order to collect the claim until other means had been tried and had failed.[19] This Calvo Doctrine was carried a step farther by some publicists and writers, so that it has come to mean a final jurisdiction of local courts over claims of aliens with a complete denial of diplomatic and other type of intervention even when a denial of justice has been sustained.[20]

Another restraint against interventions to collect financial claims was attempted by Dr. Drago, who specifically excluded from his doctrine claims arising from damages suffered during civil wars or revolutions, and confined himself solely to the forcible collection of a public debt.[21] He proclaimed that the capitalist who lends money to a foreign state always considers the resources of the country with which he negotiates, and because of the risks involved he may place onerous conditions to the granting of the loan. One lending money takes into account before entering into the bargain the value of the security, the stability of the debtor government, the credit of the debtor government, and many other factors. The lender is fully cognizant of the fact that the entity with whom he contracts the loan is sovereign and that the payment may be refused or the debt reduced by sovereign act; that the usual civil remedies open to lenders are barred as against a sovereign; and that the state is the sole judge of its ability to pay.

Drago thought it unfair to the people of the debtor government as well as to the people of the government of the alien creditor to make such a voluntary contract, which the alien entered into with his eyes wide open, the subject of armed political action involving whole nations, and in effect making the government of the alien speculator the guarantor of its citizens' bonded investments. To Drago such intervention violated the fundamental principle of international law that states are equal and thus have a right to equal consideration and equal respect. Drago stated that he did not intend to make his doctrine a defense for bad faith, disorder, and deliberate, voluntary bankruptcy. However, compulsory collection by means of force could cause the ruin of the weaker nations and the absorption of their governments by the more powerful. Drago concluded that the Argentine government desired recognition of the principle that a public debt cannot occasion armed intervention or the occupation of the soil of the American nations by a European power. Thus Drago sought to align his thesis with that of the Monroe Doctrine.

It can be seen that the Drago Doctrine is narrower in its scope than the Calvo Doctrine.[22] Drago denounces armed intervention as a legitimate means of collecting a public debt, whereas the Calvo Doctrine denies the right, prima facie, to employ force in the pursuit of all private claims of a pecuniary nature. The Calvo Doctrine does not even admit that diplomatic interposition can be made to collect such claims, except possibly after a denial of justice. The Drago Doctrine protests only against the use of armed force and not directly against diplomatic interposition.

It has been pointed out, however, that the Drago Doctrine is more comprehensive and radical than that of Calvo, for Drago denounces armed intervention as a means of enforcing payment in a more decisive manner than does Calvo. Calvo, in denouncing intervention for recovery of debts or private claims, stated that recovery did not justify armed intervention *de plano*. From this it is deduced that by using the expression *de plano* Calvo implied that intervention could not proceed prima facie — that it could not be undertaken except as a last resort. When all other methods have been tried and failed, then apparently Calvo would admit that compulsory collection by intervention could proceed. Drago, on the other hand, denounces categorically all intervention by force to collect debts.

The issue raised by Drago was placed on the agenda of the Third International Conference of American States held in 1906, and the following resolution was adopted: "To recommend to the Governments represented therein the point of inviting the Second Peace Conference, at the Hague, to examine the question of the compulsory collection of public debts, and, in general, means tending to diminish between nations conflicts having an exclusively pecuniary origin."[23]

At the Hague Conference the next year,[24] Horace Porter, the United States delegate, offered a formula which was adopted in convention form:

The Contracting Powers agree not to have recourse to armed force for the recovery of contract debts claimed from the government of one country by the government of another country as being due to its nationals.

This undertaking is, however, not applicable when the debtor state refuses or neglects to accept an offer of arbitration, or after accepting the offer, prevents any *compromis* from being agreed on, or after the arbitration, fails to submit to the award.[25]

The Porter Doctrine is somewhat less broad than the Drago Doctrine, for it recognizes the use of armed force and the legality of such use in the last instance, However, it is broader than the Drago Doctrine in that it applies to all contractual debts, whereas the Drago Doctrine was restricted to public debts. The United States ratified this convention with certain reservations; but, on the whole, it was not popular with the Latin American nations, because of their opposition to admitting an obligation to arbitrate and their opposition, also, to the right of intervention in the event arbitration was refused.[26]

Both the Drago Doctrine and the Calvo Doctrine have been largely incorporated as treaty law by the inter-American system, first by the Seventh Conference Convention on Rights and Duties of States, in which all intervention was proscribed,[27] and later by the Additional Protocol Relative to Non-intervention of the Buenos Aires Conference of 1936[28] and the non-intervention principle incorporated in the Bogotá Charter. Thus, it can be said that intervention by a state, whether by force or otherwise, for protection of the property or the lives or liberty of its citizens in another state has been made generally illegal under the particular international law of the Americas, unless the approach is taken that the right of self-defense, which is excepted from the non-intervention doctrine, may be exercised by a state as a last resort to prevent illegal, irreparable injury to its citizens by another state.[29]

However, the Calvo Doctrine condemns not only armed force, but also diplomatic protection in such instances, at least where there has been no denial of justice. And the tendency of Latin American nations has been to deny such right of diplomatic protection in all cases, whether or not a denial of justice has occurred, so long as there has been equality of treatment as between aliens and citizens. At the Ninth Conference this was the subject of much debate, and a proposition to this effect was placed in the Pact of Bogotá:

The High Contracting Parties bind themselves not to make diplomatic representations in order to protect their nationals, or to refer a controversy to a court of international jurisdiction for that purpose, when said nationals have had available the means to place their case before competent domestic courts of the respective state.[30]

This wording abolishes the right of protection of nationals by the home state even in instances of denials of justice, so long as the person has had opportunity to place his case before a competent domestic tribunal.

As opposed to this doctrine, the United States adheres to a theory that there is an international standard with respect to the treatment of aliens; that a state which is a member of the family of nations is required by international law to maintain a minimum standard in its treatment of aliens; and that, therefore, the state of origin may interpose diplomatically on behalf of its nationals when the treatment falls below that standard, after the aliens have exhausted their local remedies and have sustained a denial of justice.[31] Consequently, the United States interposed a reservation to Article 7 of the Pact of Bogotá.[32]

No agreement has yet been reached on the question of whether diplomatic protection of citizens falls within the term "intervention" so as to be prohibited by the principle of non-intervention. It has been stated that diplomatic representations cannot be classified as intervention, as they are merely interpositions without threats of coercion.[33] But if the diplomatic protection goes farther than requests to arbitrate or settle judicially, and threatens the use of economic or political coercive measures to force the sovereign will of the other state, then diplomatic interference by a state advancing a claim on behalf of its citizens because of treatment accorded them or their property by another state would fall within the limits of the non-intervention principle.

It can be seen from this discussion that no clear-cut binding principle or norm relative to the status and protection of aliens has yet come into being in inter-American law. Two doctrines are at present competing for acceptance as legal principle — the minimum standard theory, of which the United States is a proponent, and the Latin American theory of equality of treatment. Latin American members of the Inter-American Juridical Committee have recently gone so far as to state that "Acts by which it is attempted to impose or there is imposed upon a state the recognition of a privileged status for aliens beyond the rights, remedies, and guarantees granted to its nationals under local law"[34] are to be characterized as violations of the principle of non-intervention.

The United States member of the Juridical Committee dissented to this, maintaining once again that the international legal rights and remedies of aliens may differ from those which nationals enjoy under local law and that to characterize diplomatic protection of citizens abroad under international law as intervention was an abuse of the term.[35]

CHAPTER XI

RECOGNITION AND NONRECOGNITION

RECOGNITION OF STATES AND OF DE FACTO GOVERNMENTS

Recognition of states is dealt with in Articles 9 and 10 of the Chapter on Fundamental Rights and Duties of States of the Bogotá Charter. The fundamental norm is contained in Article 9: "The political existence of the State is independent of recognition by other States."

The nascence of a state may come about in differing ways. It may occur by the separation of part of the territory of an existing state, as exemplified by the breaking away of a colony from the mother state or by the secession of a portion of the territory of a state. It may also take place by the joinder of two or more states into a whole.[1]

When such a new entity is born, the issue arises of the legal status of the new formation as a member of the international community. As defined at international law, a state is said to be composed of a people occupying a well-defined territory, possessing external independence, and organized under a government exercising effective internal authority.[2] When a new entity meets this definition, is it a state? The answer to this question is a subject of controversy.

One group of jurists would reply in the negative. They admit that in order to exist in fact a state must attain the likeness of a state by acquisition of the essential characteristics stated in the above definition, but they deny legal existence until the state is recognized by other states. Since recognition is a prerequisite to membership in the society of nations and to the attainment of international personality, it is constitutive in character.

A contrary point of view takes the position that a new state becomes a member of the family of nations automatically by coming into existence upon acquisition of the essential characteristics of a state. The legal existence is therefore a pure question of fact. Recognition is not constitutive, but declarative only. The act of recognition merely declares that the new entity exists as a state, and the declaration is without legal effect, for even in its absence the state exists legally.[3]

The long struggle of the Spanish American states for independence has caused them to insist that the political independence of the state is not dependent upon recognition.[4] Language to this effect was incorporated in both Article 3 of the Montevideo Convention on Rights and Duties of States and Article 9 of the Bogotá Charter. As a result it is thought that the inter-American principle is the declaratory theory. This theory does underlie the terminology used, but the language speaks of "political existence" as independent of recognition, and thus does not necessarily deny a constitutive theory. Exponents of the constitutive theory admit that a state may be in existence prior to recognition, but that international law takes no notice of it before recognition, for it is not a member of the family of nations. In other words, "political existence" of the state does not depend upon recognition, but "legal existence" does.[5]

This argument is negated by those who adopt the declaratory theory, who consider that the word "state" and the word "existence" must be used in an international law sense, and a state if it exists in fact or has political existence must exist also in law. Use of the word "state" in the international law sense, it is said, can only mean a sovereign state independent of other states. If a state as a sovereign state exists, then international law must take notice of it. It is contradictory to say that a state exists but is not a subject of international law or a member of the family of nations. Following this line of reasoning the terminology of Article 9 is said to express a declaratory theory as to recognition, and political existence must also be legal existence prior to recognition. Under a true constitutive theory the words "existence as a state" cannot be used, for until recognition is forthcoming, the new formation at international law is not a state; it is only an entity possessing the likeness of a state.[6]

A refutation that recognition has constitutive effect in the inter-American system is also borne out by the language of Article 9 of the Charter, which declares:

Even before being recognized, the State has the right to defend its integrity and independence, to provide for its preservation and prosperity, and consequently to organize itself as it sees fit, to legislate concerning its interests, to administer its services, and to determine the jurisdiction and competence of its courts. The exercise of these rights is limited only by the exercise of the rights of other States in accordance with international law.

A strict constitutive theory includes the idea that an unrecognized state has neither rights nor duties at international law.[7] Article 9 establishes the contrary, declaring the state to have these rights "even before recognition." To say that an unrecognized state has some rights and duties is in accord with a declaratory effect of recognition.

Since, under the declaratory view, a state exists independently from recognition, does recognition have any real significance? The answer must be in the affirmative, for even according to the declaratory view participation in relations with other states must await recognition, and the bulk of rights and duties between states results from active international relations. Moreover, the recognizing state admits the fact of existence, thus dispelling some uncertainty as to this fact which might have existed prior to recognition, and the recognized state is assured that it is permitted to hold its place and rank as a sovereign nation. The recognizing state, by its act of recognition, then declares that it is ready to accept the consequences of the fact of existence by according the recognized state the courtesies of international intercourse.[8]

It is believed that the Charter of Bogotá means to ascribe such effects to recognition in Article 10: "Recognition implies that the State granting it accepts the personality of the new State, with all the rights and duties that international law prescribes for the two States."

The Montevideo Convention on Rights and Duties contained statements that recognition of a state may be express or tacit, and further that it is unconditional and irrevocable.[9] These principles were not repeated in the Charter of Bogotá, probably because it was not necessary. It is fully accepted at international law that recognition may be expressly stated or may take place by implication through acts which leave no doubt as to intention.[10]

The probable adoption of the declaratory theory as an inter-American principle makes superfluous a declaration that recognition is irrevocable or not subject to withdrawal.[11] Since a state exists without recognition, it continues to exist independently of a withdrawal of recognition. Its existence is ended only when the essential requirements of statehood disappear. An acknowledgment that the entity no longer exists as a state once it ceases to fulfil these requirements is not the withdrawal or revocation of a prior recognition, it is merely an admission that new facts exist.

Moreover, it is the consensus that a conditional *de jure* recognition is not legally possible.[12] If a conditional recognition is attempted and if the recognized state fails to fulfil the obligation, such failure cannot annul that state's existence as a state, which under the declaratory view is quite independent of recognition.

The Charter of the OAS does not set forth norms pertaining to the recognition of new governments, which is not to be confused with the recognition of new states,[13] the personality of which is not affected by a change in the form of government. Nevertheless, similar problems are created; and this problem is more acute in the Americas than recognition of a new state, inasmuch as revolutionary changes or changes by coup d'état in government which break legal continuity can be said by way of understatement to have been prevalent in the hemisphere. Here again there are the two conflicting theories. The constitutive theory would say that recognition is an act which vests the new government with international status or authority, while the declaratory theory states that the authority of a new government exists as such prior to and independently of recognition.

As to recognition of states, the Charter sets forth only general norms to the effect that the state exists independently of recognition and that recognition implies certain consequences. The really important issue as to when and whether a new American state or government is to be recognized is not provided for.

Jurists taking the constituent view maintain that certain conditions of fact impose a duty of and confer a right to recognition. The declaratory view would say that recognition is a mere formal act, of political significance only; hence each state may recognize in its discretion and as its own policy dictates. But even under a declaratory view, recognition through the establishment of diplomatic relations does have important political, economic, and even legal consequences for a new state or government, and an arbitrary grant of diplomatic relations or refusal to establish diplomatic relations for political considerations only becomes intervention and is illegal under the OAS Charter by virtue of the non-intervention principle.

Premature recognition of a revolted portion of a country as a new state, prior to the time when the parent government's efforts to maintain its rule have become hopeless, is of course a violation of the rights of the legitimate government.[14] It is clearly intervention, being an unwarranted interference in the internal affairs of the mother country aimed at altering the conditions of things within the nation.[15] Premature recognition of a new government coming to power by rebellion is also an intervention in the affairs of the state subjected to civil strife, for the interfering state by its recognition shows a sympathy for and confers advantages on the rebel government and consequently affects the right of a state to govern internally as it sees fit.

Again intervention may result if recognition is delayed too long, for it is of importance to the new state or government. The withholding of international relations after certain conditions are met by the new state or government is easily equated with intervention; for such delay would deny advantages of recognition in an effort to attempt to coerce the state to return to the old order or to obtain political concessions as a price for recognition, and thus would constitute coercion to alter the condition of things within the state.

This much can be said, but clarity ends here; for the conditions which should bring about recognition are subjects of controversy. As to recognition of a new state, the Montevideo Convention, in Article 1, sets forth the essential requirements of statehood and declares that when they are met the state is a person at international law. That convention therefore seems also to adopt the declaratory view, as the entity becomes a state automatically upon the existence of these essential facts. But no clue is given as to the according of recognition by other American states in the sense of entering into diplomatic relations.

One approach at international law is that the new state should be recognized when it meets the essential requirements of statehood—when it has external independence and effective internal government.[16] If this were the true rule of general international law, then whenever a community fulfilled these requirements, any nations which withheld recognition for any reason whatsoever would be committing an international wrong. By refusal to recognize, the nonrecognizing state is refusing to acknowledge that the community is a state and is denying it an equal rank and place with other nations. The consequence of such nonrecognition is clearly an interference in the internal and external affairs of the nonrecognized community, an attempt to alter or maintain its status without its consent.

A contrary view, on the other hand, is that the mere fact that a community is actually a state would not automatically require establishment of international relations with it. Those who take this position maintain that the community must have not only external independence and effective internal government, but also an ability and willingness to fulfil international obligations established by international law.[17] Until it demonstrates such ability and willingness, nonrecognition by another state based on evidence indicative of its unwillingness or inability would be neither an international wrong nor an act of intervention. As a matter of fact, recognition by another state in spite of evidence indicative of unwillingness or inability to abide by international law would be premature recognition and an international wrong affecting all other members of the international community of nations and would be an intervention in their external affairs, for the act of recognition would thereby acknowledge as an equal member of the family of nations a state which has not fulfilled the necessary prerequisites of membership.

The controversy also exists in regard to recognition of a new government. One view is that the individual or body of individuals seeking recognition as a new government of a state must be competent to act on behalf of the state in its relations with other states through effective control of the machinery of government. When this requirement has been fulfilled, the refusal of a state to recognize an established government for any reason whatsoever is a violation of the principle of internal autonomy and an act of intervention. Under this line of reasoning, facts are law, and a refusal to recognize facts constitutes an intervention.

The other view accepts the fact that the new government seeking recognition must be competent to act on behalf of the state in its relations with other states, but adds a further condition precedent—it must show in some manner a willingness to accept the legal rights and duties imposed on all governments by rules of general international law. Until these requirements are fulfilled, nonrecognition is not an illegal interference in the affairs of the state.

The whole field of recognition as intervention is thus divided into two camps: the side which might be characterized as positivist, which declares that facts are law; and the opposite side, which is axiological in character. It does not refuse to recognize facts, but rather in addition to these facts requires an area of agreement upon certain principles of behavior, for without such agreement there can be no appeal to law between states but merely an appeal to power. It would seem elementary that there can be no international community based on international law unless there are general principles which states recognize as obligatory in their relations and dealings with each other, and therefore the axiological approach must be the proper approach to this whole field of recognition and nonrecognition.[18]

Nevertheless, to say that nations adopt one viewpoint or the other would be to deny historical reality. Confusion, misinterpretation, misunderstanding, contradiction between words and deeds dot the landscape of recognition. The American republics have at various times based their recognition policies on both approaches, and particularly with respect to the recognition of new governments they have even required additional conditions.[19] It has been stipulated that governments coming into power by revolutions contrary to the constitution of the country should not be recognized, or at least should not be recognized until the freely elected representatives of the people have constitutionally reorganized the country.[20] In recent time the proposition has been advanced that anti-democratic American regimes or an American government guilty of grave violations of fundamental human rights should not be recognized.[21]

Though the American states are by no means unanimous, there is nevertheless a strong indication that they accept as correct the axiological approach, that recognition must be granted a state when there is external independence, effective internal government,[22] and a willingness and capability to abide by principles of international law.[23] As to recognition of a new government, the latter two conditions would be the test. But notwithstanding the acceptance of this approach, the contents of each of these concepts give rise to much contradiction.

External independence causes the least trouble. If the national legal order is inferior only to the international legal order, a state has external independence. But effective internal government is another matter. It is usually said that the government must exercise effective authority over national territory, based upon the acquiescence of the population manifested in an adequate form. This of course would demonstrate stability; but sometimes it has been interpreted to mean a superficial appearance of stability, while at other times it has been contended that it requires further inquiry to see in what manner and by what means the apparent stability has been obtained and the probability of its continuance. The Jeffersonian principle, for example, indicates that effective internal government is possible only if the government is based on the will of the nation, substantially declared.[24]

Others would base the test of effective internal control on whether the commands of the government are obeyed by the majority; whether there is no widespread active resistance to the government; whether the new authority has control over the administrative machinery of the state and apparent general acquiescence of the people.[25]

The general rule is that recognition granted prior to effective internal government is an act of intervention; yet the scale of interpretations given to effective internal government is so flexible as to allow wide leeway. A government which suppressed all opposition by widespread terroristic methods might by some be called effective internal government, and by others declared not to be effective internal government because it did not represent the will of the people substantially declared. Or again, a totalitarian type of election offering the people but one choice, with serious consequences to the individual daring to vote against that choice, might by some be called the will of the people substantially declared, but this might be denied by others on the ground that an element of the will of a nation is what is consented to and how that consent is obtained. Can the issue be resolved?

The act of recognition is an acknowledgment that the state or government is entitled to *all* the rights and courtesies and subject to all the duties of the international community. If it be admitted that the international community is based on a concept of ethical values common to all members, then the internal form of government of any state is of importance to the international community as a whole. International law recognizes that each nation has a right to a government of its own choosing; but if this government contravenes those broad ethical values common to members of the community of nations, it cannot claim all of the rights and privileges in that community. Under this reasoning effective internal government must mean more than control of the machinery of state. Control based on widespread terrorism, for example, is not consonant with the ethical values upon which the community of nations or the inter-American community rests.

It might be argued that these values, being ethical in nature, are so nebulous as to be impossible of legal definition. Yet there is in the inter-American system a core of common reaction to any sweeping activity which tends to destroy inter-American values.

The extent of the concept of willingness and ability to abide by principles of international law also provides a stumbling block. At times it has been held that a mere general statement to this effect was sufficient, while at other times further inquiry has taken place to ascertain whether the state's action was in accordance with its words, and proof of its words has often revolved about a government's willingness to agree to observe international legal obligations created by former governments.

Here again, there exists no obligation to accept the statements of a government at face value if there is substantial evidence indicating that the government is merely seeking recognition and is in fact not desirous of abiding by the rules of general international law. If a new government renounces all commitments made by prior governments, there is strong evidence that it is unwilling to abide by international law. On the other hand, for another state to insist that before it grants recognition to a new government pledges be given by that government of its intention to carry out the obligations of a specific treaty signed by its predecessor—unless such treaty were in the nature of a constitutional instrument for the community such as the Charter of Bogotá—would be to use recognition as a means of obtaining special advantages and would be an act of intervention counter to the non-intervention principle.

The spirit of the inter-American system and its actions, if not always its words, seem to support the conclusion that the axiological approach is the standard of that system. If this is true, then in the absence of a collective determination by the inter-American community, each state must decide for itself whether or not the new community has effective external control. Each state must also decide for itself whether there is effective internal government, as viewed axiologically, and a willingness to abide by international law. And its decisions must be based on substantial evidence. Decisions based on other grounds than these can be viewed as political, not legal, decisions, and hence must be acts of illegal interference.

Collective action in recognizing or not recognizing a new authority has long been a goal of the inter-American system, but it must be admitted that the American governments have not succeeded in adopting a uniform rule which it would be obligatory for all nations to follow.[26] On the other hand, the OAS as an entity has been given powers in the field of inter-American relations. Can the organization recognize a community as a state?

Article 2 of the Bogotá Charter says that all American states ratifying the Charter are members of the organization. If a new community comes into being and ratifies the charter, and some question exists as to whether or not it is a state, it would seem that the OAS must determine whether or not that community fulfils the requirements of statehood prior to accepting such a ratification.[27] There must then be in the organization the power to recognize a community as a state for purposes of membership.[28]

This gives rise to the question of what the effect of such recognition should be on other member states. The Montevideo Convention sets forth the essential requirements of statehood and existence of international personality: permanent population, defined territory, government, and capacity to enter into relations with the other states.[29] Membership in the OAS is conditioned, therefore, on these facts of statehood. Thus after ratification of the Charter if the OAS is called upon to make a decision for purposes of membership, its decision would be limited to these requirements of existence of a state. But by ratification of the Charter the new state agrees that its government is in accord with the values of the inter-American system and also agrees to abide by international law.[30] In such a case it would seem that a new community has shown by substantial evidence that it has external independence, that its government is in accord with the values of the inter-American system, and that it has the willingness and ability to abide by international law. If this be true, then admission of the new state to membership, being a collective determination of the legal requisites, would make it the duty of all other members to recognize it, and failure to do so would be an act of intervention.

It has been argued that membership in an international organization and recognition by other member states are two different concepts and are unrelated.[31] But in the inter-American system, in the case of a new state seeking membership, the necessity for the OAS to determine that the new state fulfils the requirements and the necessity that the new state agree by ratification to fulfil the requirements laid down by the Charter would seem to make it inescapable that nonrecognition by another member must be based on other than legal grounds, and hence must be an intervention.

This does not follow with respect to the recognition of a new government, for once a state is admitted to membership in the OAS a coup d'état does not affect that membership, even though the new government does not fulfil the legal requisites laid down for recognition. The question of whether or not a government which was not recognized by the majority of American states may be invited to an inter-American conference without implying recognition by all other participants of that conference was extensively debated by the Governing Board of the Pan American Union in 1947.[32] No decision could be reached. But with the ratification of the Charter of Bogotá, the question appears to be settled. Article 34 provides that all member states of the OAS have the right to be present and vote at an inter-American conference, which is the supreme organ of the OAS. This right is granted to each member state as such, and is not diminished by the fact that the government of the member does not fulfil legal requirements for recognition. Consequently the question of recognition of governments is unimportant for participation; participation does not imply recognition, nor does participation imply the right to be recognized by other members. Thus, even though it has a right to act for the state in the OAS, a new government does not *ipso facto* have a right to be recognized by other members.

What if rival governments should seek to represent a state in the OAS? Such a situation has not arisen in the inter-American system, for whenever a revolution was attempted it was either a success or a failure and the faction which obtained the reins of power then established its representatives in the inter-American system. If ever two rival governments should contend to represent a state in the OAS, probably Article 39 of the Charter of Bogotá would be applied; that is, a Meeting of Consultation of Ministers of Foreign Affairs would be held to consider the problem. It would probably be largely a political decision, for the Charter lays down no rules for such recognition. Nevertheless, the OAS should be bound by the general rule of international law which declares that there is a presumption in favor of the established, legitimate government, and that, until that government has in fact finally and permanently been divested of its sovereignty in a portion of the state's territory, any acts which favor an insurgent faction would be acts of intervention contrary to international law.[33]

The OAS can in certain instances bind the members to a severance of diplomatic relations, although it is questionable whether such severance is collective nonrecognition.[34] In case of aggression which is an armed attack, or any other type of aggression committed against an American state, the OAS is empowered to call upon the members to take measures to aid the victim and to assure the peace and security of the continent. One such measure upon which the OAS can agree is the breaking of diplomatic relations. When it decides that this specific measure should be taken, the members are legally bound to follow this decision.

REPUDIATION AND NONRECOGNITION OF THE FORCIBLE ACQUISITION OF TERRITORY

The term "conquest" is often used to signify the forcible acquisition of the territory of one state by another. But conquest and even military occupation do not in themselves create a title by conquest. Legal change of sovereignty must await at least the formal annexation or subjugation of the occupied territory by the conqueror,[35] and to some jurists a legal title by conquest must, in addition, become effective by recognition by other states when the conquest was the outcome of an illegal use of force.[36]

Distinguished from title by conquest is title by cession, even though the latter may also come into being by the use of force and duress. If a conqueror forces a conquered state to cede a portion of its territory by treaty, then the territory is acquired by cession and not by subjugation.[37]

In either instance traditional international law seems to recognize the transfer of sovereignty over the territory to be legal. As to subjugation some take the position that conquest is never the result of an illegal act, inasmuch as the use of force, or more particularly war, is permitted by international law as a legitimate means of altering rights. Resort to war and a resulting acquisition of territory are legitimate and title by conquest becomes effective after the conqueror establishes its dominion over the conquered territory and annexes it.[38]

Other jurists, while recognizing that the use of force by one state against another may be illegal as a violation of international law unless taken in self-defense or as a sanction against a delict, still maintain that the invalidity of the results of unlawful conduct may be cured by recognition or acquiescence on the part of other states acting as organs of the international community in the general interest, although such recognition may be carried out by states acting individually as well as collectively. Thus illegal acts, if they give rise to effective situations, are to be considered as law-creating acts. This is known as the principle of effectiveness: namely that the creation of new legal rights and obligations may be brought about by illegal acts, if the illegal acts are effective. In order that a change may be effective, it is said that there must be acquiescence either express or implied, by other states. Therefore as applied to title by conquest when a state by the illegal use of force subjugates territory of another state, the illegality of the acquisition is validated by subsequent recognition on the part of third states.[39]

In instances of title by cession resulting from conquest, the transfer of sovereignty is valid by reason of the treaty of cession. Even those recognizing the fact that the use of force may be illegal recognize also that the defect of illegality may be cured and the acquisition of territory validated by consent of the injured party. The conquered state through the treaty of transfer consents to the cession, notwithstanding the fact that the consent is obtained by duress. Traditional international law has permitted coercion or duress in the making of treaties, and the fact that they were so made has not been considered a legitimate reason for their nonobservance.[40] At general international law a consent obtained by duress or coercion would be a legal consent.

The inter-American system has searched for a formula to overcome these principles of general international law, and today it can be stated unequivocally that in the particular international law of the Americas the acquisition of territory by force is illegal and recognition thereof by other states is forbidden.

As far back as 1890, at the First Conference,[41] the governments were urged to adopt the principle that the right of conquest should not be recognized as admissible under inter-American law during the validity of the treaty of arbitration recommended by the conference, and that all cessions of territory taking place during this period should be void if made under threat of war or in the presence of armed force.[42] All the countries present but Chile voted in favor of the recommendation.[43] Chile refrained because the recommendation directly affected certain pending territorial questions in which she was interested.[44] The treaty of arbitration to which this recommendation was tied was never ratified.[45] Nevertheless, the wide agreement with the principles set forth was an indication of community sentiment.[46]

In the early part of 1932 United States Secretary of State Stimson had occasion to bring this Pan American formula to the fore, but not in relation to the Americas. In protesting Japan's invasion of Manchuria, he denounced acquisition of territory by force, whether by treaty or by subjugation, and notified the two governments that the United States would not recognize such an acquisition.[47]

Later in the same year the principle was to be declared by the representatives of nineteen American republics to the warring governments of Bolivia and Paraguay. After the two contestants were invited to arbitration or conciliation it was stated: "The American nations . . . declare that they will not recognize any territorial arrangement of this controversy which has not been obtained by peaceful means nor the validity of territorial acquisitions which may be obtained through occupation or conquest by force of arms."[48]

During the boundary dispute between Colombia and Peru over Leticia in 1932-33, the United States called the attention of Peru to the Resolution of the Sixth Conference in opposition to aggression, and also to the above-mentioned Chaco declaration, in which Peru had joined.[49] In this case non-recognition was never invoked, for through the efforts of the League of Nations the issue was settled before it became necessary to deny collectively the validity of Peru's title.[50]

The year 1933 was to see a denial of the validity of territorial acquisition by force incorporated into treaties. The first, the Anti-War Treaty of Non-Aggression and Conciliation, condemned wars of aggression; declared that territorial questions must not be settled by violence; and bound the contracting parties not to recognize territorial arrangements effected by other than pacific means, or the validity of occupation or acquisition of territories that may be brought about by force of arms.[51]

The second such treaty was the Convention on Rights and Duties of States of 1933. Article 11 of this Convention obligated the parties not to recognize territorial acquisitions or special advantages obtained by force, whether in the employment of arms, in threatening diplomatic representations, or in any other effective coercive measure; and declared that the territory of a state is inviolable and may not be the object of military occupation or of other forcible measures imposed by another state directly or indirectly or for any motive whatever, even temporarily.[52]

In 1940, in the face of conquests by the Axis nations, the Convention on the Provisional Administration of European Colonies and Possessions in the Americas proclaimed: "That the American Republics consider that force cannot constitute the basis of rights, and they condemn all violence whether under the form of conquest, of stipulations which may have been imposed by the belligerents in the clauses of a treaty, or by any other process."[53]

Similar declarations were made in other conferences such as those at Buenos Aires in 1936,[54] Lima in 1938,[55] and Mexico in 1945.[56] The Rio Treaty of 1947 contained a reaffirmation of the renunciation of the use of force,[57] and the Charter of the OAS in Article 17 contains a restatement of the terminology used in Article 11 of the Convention of Rights and Duties of States of 1933. Moreover, Article 5(e) reaffirms the principle that the American States condemn wars of aggression and that victory does not give rights.

By creating these norms, the American republics have abrogated principles of general international law which do recognize the legality of the acquisition of territory by force. To overcome the position taken by some jurists that war and conquest constitute normal legal powers of a state, the American states not only have outlawed war, but have declared the use of all force or threat thereof or other methods of intervention to be illegal in their individual relations, except for force used in the exercise of self-defense. To lay added stress here, the territory of a state is declared to be inviolable and not to be made the object of military occupation or other measures of force.

With regard to the viewpoint that recognition of title by conquest can cure the illegal use of force, the members of the OAS have bound themselves not to recognize an acquisition of territory or any special advantage obtained by force of arms or by any other effective coercive measures.

Title by cession when gained by force is also abolished by the Habana Convention of 1940, to the effect that force cannot constitute the basis of rights whether by conquest or by stipulations imposed in treaties, and the above wording relative to the principle of nonrecognition precludes recognition of cessions of territory obtained by force or by any coercive measure.

Not only have the American states made the forcible acquisition of territory a delict and obligated themselves not to engage in such conduct, but they have also bound themselves to affirmative individual measures and collective measures through the OAS to preserve the territorial integrity of any member. Thus, in case of armed attack against the territory of an American state each member is obligated upon request of the attacked to take some action to aid the victim until the Organ of Consultation can meet and decide upon collective action.[58] The OAS, as an entity, is called upon to enforce this principle, for in case of aggression affecting the inviolability or the territorial integrity of an American state, whether that aggression involves armed force or not, the OAS must meet to agree on collective measures to be taken by all of the American states to aid the victim, and each state is bound to apply any measure so ordered except a measure calling for the use of armed force.[59]

The competency of the OAS to enforce the principle of nonrecognition of illegal territorial acquisitions is not so clear. Each state is duty bound to refrain from recognition in such a case, but it is not beyond the realm of possibility for a state to fail to carry out an international obligation.

To assure such fulfilment some organ should be empowered to decide in the specific case that due to the facts the duty of nonrecognition is at hand, and thus to order collective nonrecognition and to enforce its order.

Any decisional organ of the OAS would seem to be competent to decide the question and to recommend nonrecognition. Such a recommendation for collective nonrecognition would obviously be legal, for the organ would simply be recommending that which the states are duty bound to do in the event of a forcible acquisition of territory. But to enforce the recommendation against a recalcitrant state would be another matter. Only if the state in its failure to adopt nonrecognition endangered the peace of the Americas could the enforcement of the Rio Treaty be taken against it.

CHAPTER XII

CONFORMITY WITH INTERNATIONAL OBLIGATIONS

THE AMERICAN STATES AND INTERNATIONAL LAW

Obligations are imposed upon states by the norms of international law and by international treaties to which they have manifested assent.[1] Since the binding force of treaties springs from a customary rule or maxim of international law—*pacta sunt servanda*—it can be said that all international obligations are prescriptions of international law.[2] The OAS is based on the assumption that the American republics are members of a hemispheric community which has definitely adopted international law as a basis for interstate relationships.[3] This does not mean that all American states are in absolute agreement as to the content and meaning of every rule of international law, for it is inherent in all law that when it comes to the concrete application of a particular rule there is often a wide diversity of opinion.[4] Moreover, in no system of law does every rule enjoy an equal degree of legal or social force. The utility of a rule may wane with changing conditions, but the repudiation of a particular rule does not indicate the discarding of the orderliness or underlying philosophy of a system of law which has been built up by custom, practice, and juristic efforts.[5]

The American states have reiterated on many occasions that international law is the code of conduct binding on states and that respect for and faithful observance of treaties constitute the indispensable rule for the development of peaceful relations among states.[6] The Principles of the OAS as set forth in the Bogotá Charter declare in Article 5(a) and (b):

> International law is the standard of conduct of states in their reciprocal relations;
> International order consists essentially of respect for the personality, sovereignty and independence of states, and the faithful fulfillment of obligations derived from treaties and other sources of international law.

The chapter on the Fundamental Rights and Duties of States stipulates that every American state has the duty to respect the rights enjoyed by every other state in accordance with international law, and that the exercise of rights by a state is limited only by the exercise of the rights of other states in accordance with international law.[7] Article 14 repeats: "Respect for and the faithful observance of treaties constitute standards for the development of peaceful relations among States."

These declarations make it manifest that the American states consider themselves bound by principles of general international law and by treaties and obligated to fulfil faithfully the duties imposed thereby. These reiterations of the binding force of international law are admissions by the American states of the limitation of their sovereignty. The principles discussed in previous chapters are primarily assertions by the American nations designed to protect their sovereignty to the utmost. Here they acknowledge that rights of internal and external independence are subject to the limitations imposed by international law. The principle of sovereignty in its extreme form implies the complete freedom of the state from the control of any higher authority claiming to regulate its acts. Such unlimited sovereignty, which connotes complete freedom of action by a state subject to no restraint other than that imposed by its own will, would mean a negation of international law. Although this extreme theory has had adherents, the better view today recognizes that state sovereignty is subject to restrictions and that the American states are not above the law of nations but subjected to it. As a result complete freedom of action of the state is limited by the body of customary international law and by treaties whereby states renounce their liberty of action in respect to certain matters.[8] A community in order to be a sovereign state must, it is true, be independent of other states. But sovereignty insofar as the international legal order is concerned does not connote freedom from control of international law, nor is there incompatibility with sovereignty of states and the conclusion of treaties by states. It is rather the reverse. It is one of the prerogatives of sovereign states to conclude treaties under international law, and the act of concluding a treaty, even though limiting the exercise of sovereignty, is a confirmation of a nation's status as a subject of international law and as a sovereign state. Treaties are one of the means by which states as subjects of international law acquire rights from, and undertake obligations toward, other subjects of international law.[9]

AMERICAN INTERNATIONAL LAW—THE THESIS OF JUDGE ALVAREZ

The American republics are governed in their interstate relationships by two normative orders, general international law and American international law. Being members of the community of nations and subscribing to the fundamental values underlying international law, they are bound by rules of general international law; and, furthermore, insofar as they have added to these rights and obligations or modified them by particular international law, they are bound by their express or implied agreements of this nature.

Since the turn of the century there has been an unending controversy among leading Latin American jurists over the question of whether or not there exists an American international law peculiar to the interstate relationships of the Western Hemisphere. The principle proponent of the theory that a characteristically American international law prevails has been Judge Alejandro Alvarez of Chile,[10] while its leading rejectors were Manoel Alvaro de Souza Sá Vianna of Brazil[11] and more recently Daniel Antokoletz of Argentina.[12]

The conception of an American international law was not created by Judge Alvarez, for, as Jacobini points out in an excellent study[13] on the question, a number of Latin American foreign offices had made use of the expression long before Alvarez appeared on the scene; and in 1883 a heated dispute arose between two Argentine international jurists, Amancio Alcorta and Carlos Calvo,[14] in which Alcorta defended and Calvo disputed the validity of the theory of recognizing the existence of an American international law.

In spite of earlier writings on the subject, it can be said without fear of dispute that Judge Alvarez has been the principal factor in bringing the theory to present day world-wide attention. Judge Alvarez would define this American international law in the following manner:

By American international law one ought to understand the aggregate of institutions, principles, rules, doctrines, conventions, customs and practices which are characteristic of the American republics in the domain of international relations. The existence of this law is due to the geographic, economic, and political conditions of the American continent, to the way in which the new republics were formed and entered into the international community, as well as to the solidarity which exists among them.[15]

He goes on to say that American international law is not subordinate to traditional international law but is "correlated to it."[16] Furthermore, he contends that American international law can also be subdivided, for instance into Latin American international law or the law of the Latin American Republics of the New World, which law is not binding upon the United States.[17]

In his writings, Judge Alvarez lists what he considers to be the five principal characteristics of this American international law:[18] (1) pacifism, idealism, and optimism; (2) respect for law and international morality condemning all violation of their precepts; (3) an American moral conscience; (4) an American juridical conscience; and (5) a sentiment or spirit of continental solidarity.

It is not to be questioned that there are in existence problems of international law peculiar to America or of American origin, but is Judge Alvarez' view of an American international law as regarded in a more extended sense theoretically sound?

Before this question can be answered, one must analyze what Judge Alvarez considers to be the five principal characteristics of American international law.

As to the first, pacifism, idealism, and optimism, it can be said that the position which Christianity had occupied as a formative element in international law was replaced, as international law became more secularized, by eighteenth- and nineteenth-century ideological standards which began under a philosophy of enlightenment and were expressed politically in various forms of liberalism, humanitarianism, and democracy. As the dignity and freedom of men, the power of human reason over social and political conditions, and the unity of civilized nations became the dominant tendencies of Western political thought, the original Christian source of international law receded into the background, and modern international law was transformed into a system of legal and moral norms common to all civilized states.[19]

Among these norms, pacifism, idealism, and optimism are inherent. Any international society based on international law must depend in the final analysis on a willingness of nations to live together in harmony, and this harmony in turn depends upon peaceful relations and a certain amount of idealism and mutual optimism among the cojurors. Where these elements are not present, each individual state can only be dedicated to everything for the state, nothing against the state, nothing outside of the state, and all international law must then be viewed as a mere fiction; for under such circumstances there could be no concept of mutual rights and duties in the international field, as each individual state would have the right to destroy the rights of all other states in pursuit of what it deemed to be to its individual best interest. But if it be conceded that it is the function of international law to adjust relationships between state and state and between states and men on an international level, indicating that there are international rights and international duties, then pacifism, idealism, and optimism are fundamental to traditional international law, and no support can be given to the contention that these qualities are intrinsic traits peculiar to American international law.

Furthermore, if the existence of international law be admitted, respect for this law and its ethical precepts and condemnation of violations of the law must also exist. Law, by its very nature, cannot exist without the respect of those it governs.[20] This respect may be based on a recognition that all are benefited when relationships are regulated by law, or it may be based on a fear of punishment for breach of the law, or it may be permeated by both elements. As there is not as yet a strong enforcement agency in the international field able to secure obedience to international law, international law must rely heavily upon the recognition by nations of the benefits accruing from the law, plus a widespread antipathy against nations which violate the law and the ethical precepts underlying the law. Even the international positivists contending that in the main international law is made up only of treaties and acts of sovereigns must concede to some minimum of ethical precepts, for the whole concept of treaty law is based on the rule *pacta sunt servanda* (treaties are to be kept), which is based on a moral obligation that states must carry out their legal treaty obligations in full good faith. If one concludes that states have no moral obligations toward each other, it must follow that treaties have no binding force, and the international positivist would then be forced to conclude that international law does not exist. That there may be a greater number of ethical precepts recognized by the Western Hemisphere, that there may be a greater respect for law in the Western Hemisphere, plus a concomitant greater fear of punishment by an American nation which violates the law, may or may not be true, but in any event respect for law and international morality condemning all violations of their precepts are essential qualities fundamental to traditional international law and cannot be described as being elements unique to American international law.

In his assertion that the third characteristic of American international law is an American moral conscience, Judge Alvarez is apparently contending that in the Western Hemisphere the positivist philosophies of law have never gained the widespread acceptance granted them by other portions of the globe. Few Latin American or North American authorities on international law have ever completely denied the legal significance of the moral or ideal element in the field of international law or relegated it entirely to a position of minimum importance. The axiological approach to international law has always played a dominant role in the underlying legal philosophy of the Western Hemisphere, but that is not a peculiarly American stand. Many non-American nations and non-American international jurists have fought unceasingly any and all encroachments on the abstract ideas of right and justice upon which international law was founded. The theory that there is an American moral conscience distinct from the moral conscience of all other civilized states would therefore seem to be untenable.

In support of his allegation that the Americas have a distinct juridical conscience, Judge Alvarez points out that the American nations are traditionally dedicated to democracy and to the equality and independence of nations.[21] As to the first, democracy, it can be readily demonstrated that traditional international law assumes that all members of the family of nations are democratic. This does not refer to parliamentary democracy, for democracy does not exhaust itself in political techniques. It is, above all, a fundamental attitude, a scale of values, a definite conception of man and his place in society. There can really be no official definition of democracy, for it is neither a system, nor a set of institutions, nor a code of law, nor a combination of policies. It is rather a belief in human nature and a code of behavior which translates that belief into thought and action. It is therefore a type of social philosophy in which the form of government is incidental, a means and not an end in itself. The only end of democratic government is to minister to the community life of society, to remove the disharmonies that trouble it; consequently it becomes a reality only through the sum total of the personal lives of individual citizens. Democracy is therefore the antithesis of totalitarianism, for the former is based on concepts of human values directed by individual freedom, while the latter is unconcerned with human values, placing the state as the sole element to which mankind owes respect, permitting no divergence of opinion from that officially proclaimed. Totalitarianism is the direct outcome of positivist teachings, and totalitarian nations do not admit the existence of international law. International law, therefore, can be effective only between those states which subscribe to some theory of democracy.

The ethical goals of democracy are a continuation in secular form of the traditional doctrines of Christianity. One of the foundation stones of Christianity was equality, for the ethics of Christianity denied any difference between high and low, between race and race, between freeman and slave. With the secularization of the doctrine of equality, democratic equality at first laid stress on the importance of each individual; during the period of the French Revolution the concept of equality broadened and the issue of the rights of man became a demand for equality between individuals; as the impact of the industrial revolution impressed itself on the Western world, this demand was expanded in the next century from a demand for equality between individuals to a demand for equality between social groups. With the birth of the twentieth century, the issue again became enlarged and extended beyond social groups and classes to equality between nations. By equality of states is not, of course, meant the absolute equality of size, resources, possessions, or even rights, but rather the equality of states before the law; that is, that there shall be equal treatment of nations equally situated with respect to the issue at hand. Equality of states is unquestionably an ethical goal of international law. Alvarez, nevertheless, contends[22] that the balance of power concept which so long dominated European politics is sufficient proof that equality of states is purely an American phenomenon. But this confuses the ideal with the actual. Perfect equality of either individuals or states is unobtainable, and the assertion that the American nations have more nearly approached equality in their intracontinental legal relationships would still not refute the fact that equality of states is a fundamental principle of international law.

The independence of states which Alvarez establishes as a basic quality of the American juridical conscience is also a vital principle of general international law. Clearly Alvarez is not speaking of absolute independence, for if each state were absolutely independent, as is contended by the positivist philosophies of law, there could be no international law. The whole concept of international law, whether traditional or American, is based on a theory of social interaction giving rise to a more intensive and more extensive attitude and practice of interdependence, co-operation, collaboration, and unification. To proclaim the absolute independence of each state would be to deny in advance the possibility of any international law. Although there are important local considerations which each state must be permitted to adjust without external interference, yet this precept of state independence cannot be absolute. Since the object of international law is the preservation and prosperity of the society of states, it follows that the rights which it has recognized for the protection of each state are subject always to the restriction or proviso that they be not used to the detriment of others. Each state is obligated not to insist on is own right when it will thereby cause a disproportionate injury to the interests and prosperity of the whole community of nations. In international law, then, there are no perfect, no absolute rights, for rights which have been given for the common good of all the states may not be perverted to menace international society.[23] The right of independence is a right of international law, but in some instances there are other principles which take precedence over this right of independence. Any democratic concept of government recognizes the fact that state sovereignty is subject to limitations, and that states are not above the law of nations but are subject to it. Therefore the right of independence inherent in the American juridical conscience cannot be more absolute than the right of independence underlying the juridical conscience of other nations which are members of the international community.

It can then be concluded that the first four characteristics upon which Judge Alvarez attempts to establish American international law must be fundamental qualities essential to traditional international law. To assert, as apparently Judge Alvarez would do, that the American states have advanced farther than other nations along the road toward these ideal goals is not to say that any nation has ever realized, or probably ever can realize, in perfection all these fundamental concepts which are the underlying foundation of international law. Furthermore, the fact that all civilized nations, as members of the international community of states, are bound by international law to chart their course by these fundamental concepts would negate any claim that the essential values of American international law vary from those of international law as a whole. Consequently, it can be stated that as the first four characteristics which Alvarez establishes as the bases of an American international law are in truth descriptive of the ideal goals of traditional international law, there is no substantial ground for the assertion that there can be a variation in international law between the hemispheres.

Nevertheless, it must be recognized that a serious challenge of these fundamental values exists in the world today, and there is merit to the assertion that
as between the two concepts of international law struggling for dominance, most
of the nations of the Western Hemisphere have been dedicated to the axiological
rather than the positivist view. The values of traditional general international
law are the values by which the nations of the Americas desire to govern their
international conduct. But these values cannot be described as purely American,
for all nations not yet dedicated to the totalitarian theories of law are committed
to strengthening these values.

What then of Judge Alvarez' fifth characteristic, the sentiment or spirit of
continental solidarity? Clearly continental solidarity is not an element in the
value scale which generally applies between all civilized states. Traditional
international law is governed rather by the sentiment or spirit of solidarity
among the members of the family of nations. We have here, therefore, something peculiar to the international law of the Western Hemisphere.

A sentiment or spirit of continental solidarity assumes action in some manner
indicative of that tendency. It might be well to reiterate that traditional international law is customarily subdivided into two classifications: general international law and particular international law. General international law consists
of those norms which are considered binding on all members of the international community, while particular international law applies to such norms
as are binding on a group of members of the international community but
not on the whole community.[24] The fact that the sentiment or spirit of continental solidarity has been translated into legally binding international instruments and agreements governing the American republics is of highest importance.
These instruments and agreements definitely establish an American international law in the sense that they change, or reaffirm more strongly through
particular international law, rules of general international law. Certainly to this
extent there is merit in the stand that there is an American international law.

What then of those phases of the sentiment of continental solidarity which
do not as yet fall within the scope of international treaties or written agreements, but which have resulted in customs and practices that are not characteristic of general international law but are none the less characteristic of the
American republics in the domain of their relations among themselves? Two
points of view are possible. The first holds that as general international law can
be established by custom, particular international law can also be established by
custom, for there is nothing in the nature of particular international law that
requires absolutely that it be reduced to a treaty form.[25] The second asserts
that the mere fact that a custom exists in a physical sense has no legal significance until it has been given juridical consideration either by some manner
of codification, or at least by sanction through the dominant juridical opinion
of each nation.[26] Under this approach those customs and practices which have
not achieved express juridical reality cannot be said to be a part of American
international law. This viewpoint is of course a direct consequence of the
positivist stand that law can only be those rules clearly sanctioned by the
sovereign.

This latter attitude has received a measure of affirmation by the majority opinion of the International Court of Justice in the first Haya de la Torre Asylum Case.[27] In that case the Colombian government invoked "American International Law,"[28] relying among other things on an alleged regional or local custom of asylum peculiar to the Latin American states. The majority opinion evidently recognized that particular international law would permit the establishment of a regional international law based on treaties or written agreements, but evaded the issue of whether or not there was in fact a particular international law for the Americas which could be based on local custom. The Court declared:

> The party which relies on a custom of this kind must prove that this custom is established in such a manner that it has become binding on the other party....
> The court cannot ... find that the Colombian Government has proved the existence of such a custom. But even if it could be supposed that such a custom existed between certain Latin-American States only, it could not be invoked against Peru which, far from having by its attitude adhered to it, has, on the contrary, repudiated it by refraining from ratifying the Montevideo Conventions of 1933 and 1939....[29]

Now undoubtedly the granting of asylum has long been practiced by Latin American states. There is no Latin American nation that has not at some time been both on the granting end and on the receiving end of the institution of asylum. All authorities would agree that custom in its legal sense means something more than mere habit or usage. It is a usage felt by those who follow it to be an obligatory one. There must be present a feeling that if the usage is departed from some sort of evil consequence will probably fall, or at any rate ought to fall, upon the transgressor.[30] But can customary regional international law be created by the general consent of the Latin American nations independent of any express treaty or other public act? Sir John Fischer Williams declares: "The Rubicon which divides custom from law is crossed silently, unconsciously, and without proclamation."[31] But the International Court is here implying that the transition from custom to law can be consummated only by treaties or written agreements or else by enunciation through the dominant juridical opinion of each nation.

Custom is the generalized practice which proves the existence of the rule; custom proves the achievement of general consent to the rule. Treaties, written agreements, and jural acts of states are also, unquestionably, either acts of consent or evidence of consent. But to declare that these latter can be the only evidence of custom would amount to a negation of customary law, for it is of the essence of custom that the binding force of its rules is based on implied, not express, consent.

Strangely enough, it was Judge Alvarez, among the dissenters from the majority opinion, who accepted the court's reasoning that although asylum might be a usage of Latin American states, it had no legal significance, since it was not a part of customary American international law:

> In view of the fact that asylum is utilized when the political order within a country is disturbed, and inasmuch as the situation resulting from this disorder may vary considerably, there is no customary American international law of asylum properly speaking; the existence of such a law would suppose that the action taken by the

Latin American States of the New World was uniform, which is not at all the case: governments change their attitudes according to circumstances and political convenience.[32]

It was left to Judge Azevedo of Brazil and Judge Caicedo Castilla, the *ad hoc* judge from Colombia, to take issue with the majority, as well as with Judge Alvarez, on this point. Judge Azevedo, in his dissenting opinion, mentions the antiquity, the extent, and particularly the continuity of the practice of asylum among the Latin American nations, indicating that he felt law could emanate from continuous usage implying general consent without the necessity of its being reduced to express consent through treaty or other public act. Furthermore, he declared that every state has a right to presume the continuance of a customary law which had long subsisted between nations, ". . . a State cannot oppose a custom previously accepted."[33]

In his dissent Judge Caicedo Castilla declares:

Diplomatic asylum is an international custom of Latin America. . . . We are dealing with a custom one century old and consequently much earlier in date than any treaties that exist on the matter . . . by recognizing the practice of asylum, the American Republics accepted it as obligatory.[34]

Judge Caicedo Castilla flatly denies the theory that the transition from custom to law can be consummated only by express juridical action; and he answers Judge Alvarez' statement that the practice is not uniform because governments change their attitudes by declaring that although states are entitled to change their minds as far as purely political questions are concerned, with regard to legal questions a change of opinion is scarcely admissible except for the future. Furthermore, he demonstrates that uniformity of practice does exist between all Latin American nations, whether or not they are signatories of express conventions on asylum.

Judge Read of Canada, also dissenting from the majority, indicates that he too believes that custom is a part of the particular law of the Americas: "With regard to 'American International law,' it is unnecessary to do more than confirm its existence—a body of conventional and customary law complementary to universal international law, and governing inter-state relations in the Pan American world."[35]

If one recognizes that law can emanate from continuous usage implying general consent, then it would seem that the particular international law governing the Americas is not limited to rules accepted by express consent, but can also include customary regional law. In other words, such an approach would recognize that particular international law is to be distinguished from general international law only by spatial validity, not by the procedure of the creation of norms. But if one accepts the concept of law imposed by a superior authority, then it would seem that custom can have no role in particular American international law until it has been reduced by some juridical action to an instrumentality evidencing express consent. This viewpoint amounts to a denial of customary law on a regional level and would distinguish particular international law from general international law by the procedure of the creation of norms.

The controversy regarding the existence or nonexistence of an American international law can be resolved by recognizing that traditional international law includes the concept of particular international law, namely, a clearly constituted system of particularist norms applying only to a group of states and not to all members of the international community. Such norms as are established by treaty or other form of express agreement are clearly within this category, but the issue of whether such norms can be established by regional custom is in dispute. Nevertheless, as to this latter point, the better approach in view of the purposes and history of international law would seem to be that regional custom can also establish rules of particular international law. Alvarez' analysis of a sentiment or spirit of continental solidarity as the basis of the particular international law of the Americas can be substantiated in view of the many regional pacts and agreements in force between the American states. But it would seem safe to say that the other elements which he claims are characteristic of American international law are in fact fundamental to traditional international law, and consequently no American international law distinct from traditional international law can be predicated upon them. Nevertheless, they are of utmost importance in that they indicate that in the contemporary state of division of thought on the fundamentals of international law, the American states are without doubt in the camp of those nations which accept the traditional values as a basis for international law, as opposed to those nations which claim they are establishing a fresh foundation of international law upon standards incompatible with the standards of traditional international law.

GENERAL INTERNATIONAL LAW AND AMERICAN INTERNATIONAL LAW

Since the American republics are governed by two normative orders, it is important to determine the relationship between them—that is, the relationship between general international law and American international law. Kelsen has pointed out that three different relationships are possible between two normative orders: either normative order A is derived from normative order B, or normative order B is derived from normative order A, or both are based on a higher normative order.[36]

Without question, particular international law is derived from general international law, whether that particular international law be based on express or implied agreement. The rule of general international law, *pacta sunt servanda*, underlies all particular international law emanating from express agreement.[37] Particular international law of a customary nature also derives its validity from general international law, namely *ubi societas ibi ius*, and consequently whenever a portion of the family of nations follows a customary usage, it is to be inferred that the custom is derived from a fundamental principle which must be regarded as correct for that social division by the fact of being generally accepted by it.[38]

Thus it can be determined that American international law, being a type of particular international law, derives its validity from general international law and must be based on the presupposition of the continued validity of general international law. American international law, nevertheless, has created for its society some new rights and duties; therefore it is a *lex specialis* having priority over the dispensable norms of general international law.[39] It is a general principle of international law that as to those parties governed by rules of particular international law, the particular international law rule will take precedence over the rule of general international law. This principle is limited by two major exceptions. Where the norm of particular international law fails to function, the corresponding norm of general international law must reappear, for particular international law suspends but does not abrogate or abolish general international law.[40] And where the rule of particular international law violates what may be termed the public policy of the international community as a whole, it is illegal and will not be recognized as a valid norm of law.[41]

Those rules of general international law not covered by particular international law are still binding on the American states in their relations with each other, and it is generally stated that in relationships with states not parties to particular international law, the rules of general international law must govern. Nevertheless, it must be recognized that particular international law may relate to nations not parties to agreed norms of this law in one of the following ways: (1) a particular norm may have no effect upon nonacquiescing states; (2) a particular norm may benefit a nonacquiescing state; (3) a particular norm may injure a nonacquiescing state; or (4) a particular norm may codify a norm of general international law. Where a particular norm has no effect upon nonacquiescing states and is not in violation of what may be termed the public policy of the international community as a whole, then the nonacquiescing state obtains neither rights nor duties under the particular international law norm, and the nonacquiescing state is free to base its relationship with the states bound by particular international law upon rules of general international law.

In some instances a particular norm may benefit parties not bound by it. Ordinarily states acquiescing to a particular law norm are free to pursue their own policy and to alter this policy among themselves as they deem fit. But if this policy should benefit a nation not a party to the agreement, there arises a duty, in the event the agreeing states determine to change this policy, that the third state must be informed of the change.[42] The principle of good faith in general international law requires that protection extend to the confidence and reliance that can reasonably be placed in conclusive acts of other states.

Some norms of particular international law which voluntarily confer privileges but no obligations upon third states not parties to the agreement may develop into a customary right under general international law. Fenwick points out that a self-imposed obligation may, after a sufficient lapse of time, obtain the character of an inchoate legal obligation, and consequently can no longer be changed without the acquiescence of the third state.[43]

When a norm of particular international law incidentally injures a **third** state, the rights of the third state will depend upon whether the injury **was a** result of a violation of a legal right or was merely a loss which involved **no** legal wrong.[44] As to the first, particular international law cannot take away a just right of a nonacquiescing state established by general international law, for general international law supersedes particular international law where the rights of third states are concerned. But where the norm of particular international law is merely injurious to the interests of another state, but does not invade the sphere of legally protected areas under international law, then no legal wrong has been committed. For example, a commercial treaty between States A and B by which A agrees to import certain products from State B duty-free may be injurious to State C with which no commercial treaty exists. Still, this would give rise to no international duty of redress, for each state has the right to pursue its own commercial policy. Nevertheless, this rule is limited by the abuse of right theory,[45] which states that the exercise of a right for the sole purpose of causing injury to another is prohibited. Every right is the legal protection of a legitimate interest. An alleged exercise of a right not in the furtherance of such interest, but with the malicious purpose of injuring others, can no longer claim the protection of the law. *Malitiis non est indugendum.*

Finally, a particular law norm may codify a norm of general international law. In that case, it can be said that the particular international law norm furnishes evidence of the norm of general international law by which third powers not party to the agreement may be bound. There the obligation flows from general international law, not from particular international law.

Particular international law is also correlated to general international law in that the former has contributed to the growth of the latter. Numerous standards of international conduct which were developed originally by particular international law have become so widely accepted by all the members of the community of nations that they have been transformed from particular international law into general international law.

The legal relationships of Western Hemisphere nations with non-American nations are therefore predicated primarily upon general international law, except where these relationships have been transformed by bilateral or multilateral treaties with such nations. The legal relationships of the nations of the Western Hemisphere among themselves are also primarily predicated upon general international law; but where they have been transformed by American international law, that law takes precedence over, but does not abolish, general international law. American international law is a *lex specialis,* a branch of particular international law standing under the impact of general international law, and consisting of a body of specific rules established by express and implied agreements which are based on a sentiment or spirit of continental solidarity.

THE OAS AND INTERNATIONAL LAW

The deficiencies of international law can be cured only through an international organization endowed with power to create, ascertain, and enforce the law.[46] It has been seen that the OAS contributes to the creation of international law.[47] The hemispheric community has long concerned itself with the formulation of principles of inter-American conduct, but after formulation the application of these and other principles has been left largely in the hands of the member states. Whether or not the American states conformed to a rule of international or inter-American conduct was dependent upon their good will and good faith. The functions of the organization as it existed prior to World War II did not extend to the enforcement of standards of international law, and although principles of pacific settlement of disputes and procedures of pacific settlement had been worked out, they were primarily bilateral in character, the system itself having little or no continuing responsibility for assuring their application.

A historical idea and ideal has been that the rule of law should reign in the international sphere.[48] This means that the international relations of states should be subordinated to the body of rules known as international law as a substitute for force and unadulterated power politics. One would expect to find in an international organization like the OAS, composed of the republics of the hemisphere with the purpose of insuring the peace and the pacific settlement of its members' disputes, a close relationship between the organization and the rule of law. It might be thought that the establishment and maintenance of international law would be a primary aim of the OAS and that it was possessed of the necessary organs for the achievement of this aim in the Americas. The basic documents of the OAS, however, show that such a state of affairs has by no means come into being, although the organization has been given a limited role to play as protector of international law. The Charter of the OAS, in the Preamble, declares juridical organization to be a necessary condition for security and peace founded on moral order and justice, and Article 1 speaks to the point that the organization is established to achieve an order of peace and justice. The capacity of the OAS as a protector of international law can hardly be deduced from references to its role of promoting justice. Justice and law are not identical,[49] although justice is possibly the highest aim or goal of any system of law including international law.[50]

More specific evidence of the faculties devolving upon the OAS in the field of international law may be found in the principles, where international law is proclaimed as the standard of conduct of states in their reciprocal relations and it is stated that international order consists in the faithful fulfilment of international obligations.[51] These principles are not made applicable in so many words to the organization as an entity, but since they are principles of the OAS and since the OAS is founded to put them into practice,[52] it can reasonably be concluded that the OAS is to attempt to establish conditions permitting justice and respect for international obligations.

Nevertheless, the fact is that the organization has been given little power to enforce international law. Where a violation of legal right occurs, general international law authorizes the individual members of the international community to take sanctions to uphold the law against the state which is responsible for the violation. Such sanctions may be peaceful or nonpeaceful, and may even amount to war.[53] But the power of the individual members of the hemispheric community to take such action has been abrogated by the principle of nonintervention,[54] and thus a method of enforcing international law has been removed. So that a delinquent state would not be permitted to benefit by its breach of international law, the American states have sought to substitute for individual action collective action through the OAS. As a result of the Rio Treaty, compliance machinery came into being and the OAS acquired certain executive or enforcement functions.[55] The enforcement measures permitted by this treaty are the only true enforcement measures granted to the OAS. Nevertheless, this collective action is by no means a complete replacement of the individual action permitted by general international law as a sanction to uphold the law; and the question as to whether the collective enforcement action permitted can even be placed in the category of sanctions to uphold the law has been a subject of dispute.[56] In any event, the OAS as presently constituted is not primarily a law enforcement agency, and even though the collective measures are considered as sanctions, under the Rio Treaty the Organ of Consultation is not given power to enforce the law in all instances of its breach. The Organ may order collective action only in case of armed attack against an American state or in case of other aggressions or situations which endanger the peace of the continent and affect the inviolability or the integrity of the territory or the sovereignty or political independence of an American state.[57]

Over and above the powers of the OAS to enforce the law, the question remains as to whether the OAS as an entity is bound to respect principles of international law and govern its actions in all relevant instances in conformity therewith. Indisputably, respect for principles of international law is imposed by the terms of the Bogotá Charter upon the ratifying states.[58]

According to Article 1(1) of the United Nations Charter, that organization is enjoined to observe justice and international law in the special function of the "adjustment or settlement of international disputes or situations which might lead to a breach of the peace." As a result of this wording the deduction has been made that conformity with international law is not required by the world organization in the pursuance of its other functions, particularly in the performance of its police functions—enforcement action of a collective nature "for the prevention and removal of threats to the peace, and for the suppression of acts of aggression or other breaches of the peace."

This distinction in the United Nations Charter springs from belief in the principle that order comes before law, that in the face of an imminent threat to the peace or breach of the peace the United Nations must be permitted to act as a policeman by separating the culprits and restoring peace, free from consideration of which of the contending parties is legally in the right. After the threat to the peace has been averted or the breach of the peace has been stopped, there is to be conformity to international law in the efforts made for a peaceful settlement or adjustment of the dispute.[59]

As has been noted, no express requirement of conformity to international law is directed against the OAS as a juridical order by the Charter of Bogotá. Still, respect for these principles may be implied by the stress placed upon international law as a standard of conduct and by the fact that faithful fulfilment of international obligations is declared to be an essential for international order.

The same considerations which created in the United Nations Charter the distinction between the exercise of the police function and the pacific settlement function and the requirement of conformity with international law as to the latter only are, of course, applicable to the OAS in the performance of its functions. However, it is doubtful that the Organ of Consultation is completely untrammeled by considerations of international law in the application of coercive measures under the Rio Treaty.

The collective measures authorized by the Rio Treaty are primarily to be taken against illegal situations, such as illegal armed attack or aggression, which would seem to call for determination of international legal rights before a decision could be taken to apply such measures.[60] The Organ of Consultation is authorized to take measures in other situations endangering the peace of the Americas.[61] It might be contended here that the Organ would be free to ignore rules of international conduct and could direct its attention solely to action which would be effective to maintain the peace and security of the continent. Such reasoning can be refuted by the fact that the collective measures are not to be taken in any event unless the inviolability or the integrity of the territory or the sovereignty or political independence of an American state is affected. To determine whether the sovereignty or independence is threatened, a determination of international legal rules would be necessary; for the meaning and content of sovereignty are determined by these concepts.

In one instance under the Rio Treaty the Organ of Consultation is unhampered by consideration of international law. In case of a conflict between two American states, Article 7 of that treaty requires the Consultative Organ to call upon the contending states to suspend hostilities and restore matters to the status quo and to take, in addition, all other measures to re-establish or maintain international peace and security and to resolve the conflict by peaceful means. At this stage the Organ is not required to consider which party is in the right. Here pacifying action is called for. If, however, a party rejects the call, then the Organ is to consider this rejection in its determination of the aggressor and in the application of coercive measures. This language would appear to make it incumbent upon the Organ to consider which party is in the right.

CHAPTER XIII

PACIFIC SETTLEMENT OF DISPUTES
AND RECIPROCAL ASSISTANCE

REPUDIATION OF THE USE OF FORCE, PACIFIC SETTLEMENT OF DISPUTES

Requisite to the effectiveness of any system designed to maintain the peace of the Americas is acceptance by the American nations of the proposition that the maintenance of peace is essential to their welfare. All should be of a mind to forego the use of violence and force in the settlement of controversies arising among them, and there must be an obligation to do so, to which each and every nation must be required to conform.

A cardinal purpose of the OAS is the maintenance of the peace of the hemisphere, and consequently the Charter and the Rio Treaty place an obligation upon the contracting parties to maintain peaceful relations among themselves in both a negative and positive manner. Negatively, the parties condemn war and bind themselves to abstain from the threat and use of force. In addition, they agree positively that they will settle their international disputes by peaceful procedures.[1]

The principle that only peaceful means are to be employed to settle inter-American conflicts can be traced to the Congress of Panama and early Hispanic American conferences, but unfortunately the conventions emanating from these conferences were never accepted.[2] Early Pan American conferences tussled with the problem of extracting agreement against the use of force, mainly by attempting to obtain acceptance of the principle of the arbitration of disputes.[3] The results were meager.

The Gondra Treaty of the Fifth Conference created certain procedures of pacific settlement, and a resolution of that conference expressed hope that the progress of the peaceful settlement of disputes would continue;[4] it was not until the Habana Conference in 1928 that clear-cut wording was used to outlaw aggression and to obligate the American republics to the use of peaceful means in the settlement of their disputes.[5]

The Anti-War Treaty of Non-Aggression and Conciliation of 1933 also condemned wars of aggression and stipulated that no dispute should be settled by other than peaceful means;[6] while the Convention on Rights and Duties of States of the Seventh Conference went even farther, moving from a mere condemnation of "wars of aggression" to a proscription of the use of force against the territory of a state.[7] Article 10 of this same Convention proclaimed the principle of pacific settlement but used words of a nonobligatory nature, simply stating that differences arising between states *should* be settled by pacific methods.

Later conferences proclaimed these principles over and over again, and the present fundamental documents of the OAS,[8] the Rio Treaty and the

Charter, bind the parties to these concepts. The Rio Treaty condemns war and obligates the parties not to resort to the threat or use of force in any manner inconsistent with the United Nations Charter or of the provisions of the treaty.[9] The Charter of the OAS censures all intervention including, of course, that carried out by armed force;[10] declares that force may not be used against the territory of a state;[11] and binds the American states not to have recourse to force except in the case of self-defense in accordance with existing treaties or in fulfilment thereof.[12] Moreover, both treaties[13] state that disputes between the contracting parties are to be settled by peaceful means.

While the United Nations makes no attempt to settle all international disputes, the OAS does.[14] It does not guarantee to settle them all, but the members are under obligation to submit every controversy to methods of peaceful settlement and to endeavor to settle all of them peacefully.

This obligation has one limitation. Article 5(g) of the Charter of Bogotá requires controversies of an *international character* only to be settled by peaceful procedures. This wording makes it clear that the obligation does not refer to domestic disputes.

Article 21 of the Charter, like the Pact of Bogotá, enumerates peaceful procedures that may be used, although the list is not exhaustive, as the parties are permitted to use other methods. Since force or threat of force is abolished, any settlement method involving force could not be considered a peaceful procedure, even though it might not be classified at international law as war—as for example would be the case with armed interventions or reprisals.

In requiring the parties to refrain from the threat or use of force, the Charter gains in clarity over certain earlier international agreements which forbade "resort to war." To prohibit war is not necessarily to prohibit force—or so it is often contended, inasmuch as it is possible to quibble that force short of a legal state of war is not included in an outlawry of war. The prohibition of force and the threat of force settles the matter unequivocally.

The force proscribed is generally understood to mean physical or armed force. Its actual use or the threat of its use is thus abolished. The Charter of the OAS does not lose sight of the fact that the threat or use of economic, political, or diplomatic weapons may also effectively coerce; it prohibits all unilateral coercive measures to force the sovereign will of a state.[15]

The parties undertake to abolish force in their *international relations*. Therefore, the obligation is restricted and the principle does not apply to prevent the use of force by a state in its own domestic affairs and within its own borders to put down a local disturbance or revolution.

Even with respect to international relations, the threat or use of force is not completely eliminated. Under the Rio Treaty and the Charter of Bogotá resort to force may be had if it is not inconsistent with the Charter of the United Nations or the Rio Treaty. Thus it is the *unilateral* use of force, whether it be lawful or unlawful under general international law, which is banned. Here too there is exception created by the United Nations Charter and the Rio Treaty. An American state is permitted to react in an exercise of self-defense with the use of armed force. And in such an instance, by assent to the Rio Treaty the other American republics have obligated themselves in the exercise of collective self-defense to take measures to aid the victim upon its request. Ostensibly these individual measures could include the use of armed force.[16]

Moreover, the members may, if they so desire, legitimately use force in the participation in collective sanctions if such a sanction is recommended by the Organ of Consultation in accordance with the Rio Treaty.[17] In view of certain deficiencies in human nature, which unfortunately are transposed to the behavior of nations, the power and right to use force must of necessity reside somewhere so as to deter temptation to disturb the peace, and must be subject to utilization to compel a disturber to return to peace. Mere pledges by nations against the use of force and promises to settle their disputes peacefully are not enough. In any organized community the force monopoly to compel obedience to law and to prevent violations of the public peace is placed in the hands of the community. As a result, the unilateral use of force becomes in most instances illegal, the members of the community relying for their security not upon their own individual action, but upon the concerted or joint action by all the members of the community which, if carried out in practice, means protection of any victim against a law-breaker and peace-disturber.

THE PRINCIPLE OF COLLECTIVE ACTION AND RECIPROCAL ASSISTANCE

Recognizing that war, aggression, and threats to the peace cannot be banned by the adoption of pledges against such anomalies alone, the Charter of Bogotá provides for a system of collective security. The principle of collective action or security is simply a projection of the principle of one for all and all for one into the field of international relations. It is an agreement of reciprocal assistance entered into by a group of states whereby each member of the participating group contracts to protect the security of every other member.[18] As a system of collective security, the Charter and the Rio Treaty do require reciprocal assistance by the member states against any state guilty of aggression or guilty of threatening the peace of the hemisphere.[19] By pooling their strength and by obligating themselves to take collective action against a disturber of the peace— American or non-American—the American states seek to assure peace and security, upon the theory that the group power of all the member nations will generate sufficient strength to repel actual aggression and discourage any breaches of international obligations which disrupt or threaten the peace of the continent.

Ross speaks of three types or stages of co-operative action to combat breaches of the peace and remove imminent threats to it.[20] The first type he calls "automatic." Here each nation of a community may by agreement pledge itself to take certain action when peace is disturbed. This type of action is called automatic because it is to come into operation of itself. No organ is empowered to determine when and how each member of the community is to act. The members are simply to react on their own initiative, to do what they have agreed to do when certain conditions become realities.

The second type of co-operation is called "organized" co-operation, in that an organ is empowered by the members of the community to make the decision as to the action to be taken by the members to maintain or restore peace.

The execution of the measures is left to the members, but each member has previously agreed to obey the commands of the authorized body.

The highest type of co-operation is "institutionalized joint action," whereby a police force is established and placed directly under authority of the organ.

Following this classification, the system of collective security of the OAS falls under the first and second types. In cases of armed attack against an American state, all the other states are pledged to assist in meeting the attack; and, in the first instance, each state may determine the measures it will use to meet its obligation, although each state is duty bound to act in some way. At this point the members are directly bound to use coercive measures against the attacker.[21] The co-operation is automatic, for it comes into operation by the action of the members in accordance with the conditions of Article 3 of the Rio Treaty without the intervention of the Organ of Consultation.

After the initial stage, when the Organ of Consultation can meet in cases of armed attack[22] as well as in all cases of aggressions which are not armed attacks and other situations endangering the peace of America, the system becomes "organized" co-operation, for in these instances the Organ makes the decisions as to what is to be done and by whom.[23]

The third type of co-operation, "institutionalized joint action," does not exist, for no inter-American army or police force to execute the orders of the OAS through the Organ of Consultation has as yet been established for the maintenance of the peace of the continent.

Agreements by the American states binding themselves not to use force, to settle disputes peacefully, and to assist one another reciprocally are again deviations from the principle of strict sovereignty, and even from those sovereign rights recognized by general international law; for in the past general international law permitted sovereign states in various cases to use force,[24] did not command the peaceful settlement of disputes at least in those instances where the use of force was authorized, and placed no duty upon states to come to the aid of others.[25] Moreover, by agreement to the principle of collective security the American states gave up rights to remain neutral or to claim neutrality from others. Neutrality and collective security are incompatible, for under the latter each state agrees in advance to dispense with neutrality when aggression or other threats to the peace of the hemisphere occur.[26]

These agreements against the use of force, for peaceful settlement, and for collective security not only restrict sovereignty, but at the same time protect it. By binding themselves to these duties, the American states have sought to maintain the status quo of the hemisphere against any change but peaceful noncoercive change. By the outlawing of the use of force, the independence of each state is protected against its use by other states. And if forceful measures or coercive measures which threaten hemispheric peace are used by one state against another, the power of the member states is to be directed against the state acting illegally so as to deter it and preserve the status quo.[27]

The collective action envisaged by the Charter of the OAS and the Rio Treaty consists of certain enforcement measures, including the use of armed force, which are to be taken against nations disrupting peace and security. These measures are, of course, interventionary in character.

Collective intervention is collective enforcement action to protect the rights of states as a reaction against a violation of international law. The legality of such intervention by a body of states acting together has been the subject of controversy among international jurists, but it would appear that the mere fact that an intervention is a joint action of a number of nations rather than the action of a single nation would not make such action legal if it were otherwise illegal under rules of general international law.[28] The force of number does not give a group of states a greater right of intervention than is given an individual state; consequently, the test for the legality of collective action is the same as that applied to an intervention by a single state.[29]

However, when a group or body of states organizes into an international juridical community by multilateral treaty, and in that treaty each state grants rights of intervention, in certain circumstances and for certain purposes, on behalf of the juridical community, any intervention taken in pursuance of the treaty must be legal.[30] The legality of collective intervention under these circumstances is based on the prior acknowledgment by each signatory of the rights of all other signatories, acting collectively, to interfere with such conduct by any party to the treaty as may be contemptuous of the general agreement. Collective intervention under such a treaty stands completely separate, and does not resemble intervention by a single nation or by a body of states not so bound together. Actually it is taken out of the category of intervention proper by the element of previous consent.[31]

The desirability of collective intervention to bring about enforcement of the principles of international law and to maintain a just and peaceful international order quickly becomes apparent when it is realized that under general international law the protection of the legal interests of a state against violation on the part of another state is left, for the most part, to the state whose right has been violated. Where a violation of legal rights occurs, general international law authorizes the individual members of the international community to take sanctions to uphold the law against the state which is responsible for the violation. Such sanctions may be peaceful or nonpeaceful, and may even amount to war.[32]

The primary criticism of permitting each state to take individual sanctions is not that such actions are without justification, but rather that even when a particular sanction is undertaken in the interest of law and justice, the action of the interfering power is of necessity arbitrary, for action is always arbitrary when the intervening state is the sole judge of the type of sanction it wishes to apply. Even where the end results are good, leaving the individual state the sole judge of the type of action it shall take must inevitably weaken the general structure of order and justice in the community.[33]

That a community as a whole must be the ultimate repository of the practical rules upon which the conflicting claims of states must be decided would not seem to be open to question. In the final analysis, if nations subscribe to the theory of the supremacy of law, community action is the only alternative to individual action. If a state might with impunity violate all rules of international law and all other states were required to maintain an attitude of indifference, it would obviously be impossible for international society to exist.

Whenever a state violates a rule of international law in its relations with another state, the immediate damage arising from the wrongful act violates not only the rights of the injured state, but also those of all states jointly and severally interested in the legal basis of the society of nations. Consequently, all measures and institutions designed to assure the authority of international law must be considered within the collective protection of all states.

Even prior to the Congress of Panama, the principle of common action for the peace and security of the hemisphere was advanced, and such a scheme of collective security continued to be promoted from time to time throughout the following years.[34] But it was not until the American states adopted an almost absolute prohibition against unilateral intervention as a method of enforcing general international law that collective action became feasible. The doctrine of non-intervention removed a very important sanction of general international law and, if nothing was substituted for it, would have the effect on many occasions of permitting a delinquent state to benefit by its breach of general international law. Law, like nature, abhors a vacuum, and in a vital system of law no hiatus can exist.[35] For this reason the inter-American system has developed a series of multilateral treaties which permit collective action to uphold international law. But this collective action is not a complete substitution for the individual action permitted by general international law as a sanction to uphold the law.[36]

The first step, though an exceedingly hesitant one, toward greater community responsibility was taken at the Montevideo Conference in 1933 — the same conference that saw agreement to the non-intervention principle. It was recommended there that the American states should adhere to the Anti-War Treaty of Nonaggression and Conciliation which had been signed at Rio de Janeiro in the same year.[37] This treaty condemned wars of aggression, required disputes to be settled by pacific means, and provided for the nonrecognition of territorial acquisitions secured by force. It then bound the parties, in the event of violation of these commitments, to adopt in their character as neutrals a common and solidary attitude; to exercise the political, juridical, or economic means authorized by international law; and to bring the influence of public opinion to bear without resorting to intervention—diplomatic or armed.[38]

There is a bare suggestion of collective action here, in the requirement of the adoption of a solidary attitude in the face of aggression. No provision was made for methods by which this solidary attitude could assume any fixed and definite form, and the action relied on to maintain the peace through this solidary attitude was apparently the pressure of public opinion only — a nebulous sanction at best — for the prohibition upon the participating states against intervention effectively precluded any type of collective enforcement action against a delinquent, despite the fact that certain measures of a political, juridical, or economic nature were authorized. There is an anomaly here, of course, for any exercise of these methods would tend to be interventionary. Nevertheless, a beginning had been made, for here was an instrument setting forth collective responsibility to keep the peace.

At the Buenos Aires Conference of 1936[39] further steps toward greater community responsibility were taken. There a treaty was signed known as the Convention for the Maintenance, Preservation and Reestablishment of Peace.[40] As a vehicle for collective action it was extremely vague in its provisions. Article I of the treaty required consultation by the signatories for the purpose of finding and adopting methods of peaceful co-operation in the event the peace of the Americas was threatened, whether the menace that brought about that threat was intracontinental or extracontinental.

The first part of Article II required consultation without delay in the event of war or a virtual war between American states—i. e., inter-American war or intracontinental war—to seek a method of peaceful collaboration.

The last part of Article II spoke in terms of international war outside the Americas which might threaten the peace of the hemisphere. In such an event, consultation was called for "to determine the proper time and manner in which the signatory states, if they so desire, may eventually cooperate in some action tending to preserve the peace of the American Continent."

The treaty spells out no obligation other than an obligation to consult, for nowhere are the participants bound to carry out the methods of peaceful co-operation or peaceful collaboration which might be adopted by the consultation. This is strikingly manifest in the last part of Article II in case of non-American war, for there any action is expressly left to the desires of each individual state.

Moreover, what was meant by methods of peaceful co-operation or peaceful collaboration, as these terms were used in the treaty to describe the action to be taken by the consultation, was unclear. The use of the term "peaceful," however, ruled out any collective action taking the form of armed force.

The Convention to Coordinate, Extend and Assure the Fulfillment of the Existing Treaties Between the American States was also signed at the Buenos Aires Conference.[41] It was limited to intracontinental controversies only, and set forth again the obligation of consultation. Here consultation was defined with somewhat more precision, its primary objective being to assist disputing American parties to fulfil the obligations assumed in treaties of pacific settlement through the tender of good offices and mediation. Little was added to the principle of collective action other than a statement that should mediation efforts fail and hostilities break out or threaten to break out between two or more American states, the other states, through consultation, should immediately adopt in their character as neutrals a common and solidary attitude. They might then, in their individual capacity, consider the imposition of embargoes on arms, munitions, and implements of war and on loans and financial help to the states in conflict, as the municipal legislation of each state authorized. In effect, collective action or methods of peaceful collaboration as to conflicts between American states seemed to be confined to collective neutrality.

Buenos Aires had stressed primarily measures for the settlement of intra-American conflicts and disputes; but in the years following, with war impending and then becoming a reality, the inter-American system became much concerned with strengthening the organization to permit it to take measures of common defense against extracontinental dangers to the hemisphere. Although the Lima Conference of 1938 contributed little to the principle of collective action, still machinery was established there for a procedure of consultation by Meetings of the Ministers of Foreign Affairs.[42]

Confronted with actual European war and its danger to the hemisphere and with a background of the German triumph over much of the continent of Europe, the American states met in the Second Consultative Meeting at Habana in 1940, and among other things sought to strengthen their collective responsibility for the security of the Americas against external dangers. The Declaration of Reciprocal Assistance and Cooperation for the Defense of the Nations of the Americas recognized "That any attempt on the part of a non-American State against the integrity or inviolability of the territory, the sovereignty or the political independence of an American State shall be considered as an act of aggression against the States which sign this declaration."[43] It was further agreed that in case of aggression or threatened aggression by a non-American state against an American state, the signatory states would consult among themselves in order to agree upon the measures it was advisable for them to take.[44]

The only obligation mentioned here directly is to consult, and again no specific measures of collective defense to be taken by the consultation are incorporated. There is controversy as to the binding effect of a declaration such as this which was not submitted to ratification as a treaty, but assuming it to be binding, it does seem that the words set forth an obligation upon the signatories to take some measures of collective defense upon which agreement had been reached through consultation. The declaration stated that consultation was to take place *to agree* upon measures to be taken and went on to provide for the negotiation of complementary agreements by the signatories so as to organize co-operation for defense and the assistance they should lend each other in the event of aggression.

The declaration did for the first time create a more definite basis of collective responsibility for the hemisphere, and it made the defense of the Americas a common concern of all of the republics. The principle of reciprocal assistance established here served as a basis for collective action by the Americas against the Axis Powers following the attack upon Pearl Harbor. At Rio de Janeiro in 1942, for example, resolutions were taken by the Third Consultative Meeting recommending the breaking of diplomatic relations with the Axis nations and providing for control of subversive activities of alien Axis sympathizers.[45]

The Inter-American Conference on Problems of War and Peace held at Mexico City in 1945 was to see a most important advancement in the development of collective action for the preservation of the peace and security of the Western Hemisphere. The Act of Chapultepec provided that for the duration of the war every attack against an American state was to be considered as an attack against all the other states which signed this act.[46] This was an extension of the Habana principle, which was limited to attacks by non-American states.

Prior to the Mexico City Conference, a distinction had grown up between intracontinental and extracontinental situations. As a result of the Habana Act and the practices which Pan America followed during the war years, the principle of reciprocal assistance had come into being as to non-American aggressions against an American state and, through consultation, measures of collective action had been taken against non-American aggression.

A different theory had been developed as to procedures to be followed in case of aggression against an American state from an American source. In such instances of intra-American aggression consultation was provided for, but primarily for pacific settlement purposes and to deprive the parties to a conflict of the means of continuing hostilities. No real collective coercive measures were provided.

At Mexico City the parties took the final step by pledging themselves to take collective action against aggression from any source directed against the Americas. For the first time specific provision was made for the application of coercive enforcement measures in case of aggression against an American state.

The Act of Chapultepec was adopted as a wartime measure. It was recommended in this act that a formal treaty which would incorporate the obligations undertaken should be forthcoming. This recommended treaty came to be the Rio Treaty of 1947, which gave permanent form to the principle of collective action. By the terms of this treaty the inter-American juridical community finally evolved a system of collective security through the principle of collective action to assure the peace of the hemisphere. The parties to the treaty agreed to the principle of reciprocal assistance to meet armed attack against any of the American states and to deal with threats of aggression against any of them, and assumed obligations to fulfil this purpose.

Chapter XIV

DEMOCRACY AND HUMAN RIGHTS

DEFINITION

The crisis in Western civilization manifested by wars and revolutions has made our century one of the most turbulent in the long and unending struggle between democracy and authoritarianism. With the explosion of scientific and technical progress has come a perfection of the leviathan state far beyond any Machiavellian dream. On the one side the democrats proclaim that the life, the mind, the heart, the soul of each individual is important for itself and that any economic system, socialist or private, is tested by its usefulness in preserving and liberating the individual. On the other side totalitarianism, whether it be of the extreme right or the extreme left, proclaims that the highest development of civilization is the state; that this alone is important; and that all individual development is tested by its utility in promoting the interest of the state. Between these two philosophies, one maintaining the value of the individual and his development and the other proclaiming the value of the state to which everything must be sacrificed, there is an unbridgeable abyss.

In recent years the tempo of the struggle has quickened in the Western Hemisphere to such an extent as to threaten the very solidarity of the American community of nations. From the beginning of the inter-American movement,[1] democracy was proclaimed as a common denominator among North America, Central America, and South America, although admittedly many nations of the hemisphere have often had periods of dictatorships. The inter-American system slowly developed over the years on the premise that all its members maintained at least an ideological fidelity to the ethical conceptions of democratic society in spite of widely different physical conditions and differences of religion, of social background, of economic interest, of cultural background. But the forces which have led a great number of Europeans and Asians to accept the disciplined submission to the authoritarian state as an escape from the responsibilities and isolation of freedom have continued their work in the nations of the Americas, and again there has been cast over the hemisphere the dark shadow of the establishment in the Americas of a non-American totalitarian government — international communism. With it have come a serious challenge in the stated fundamental values of the inter-American system, a corrosion of mutual trust, and a threat to the stability of the Organization of American States.

That such a situation has come about may seem an anomaly when one considers that ever since the Wars of Independence, the republican form of government and the democratic political ideal have been proclaimed for each of the nations of the Americas.[2] So true is this that the people of the Western Hemisphere are firm in the belief that this area of the world is the hemisphere of freedom. They have adopted similar internal democratic constitutions, and their political leaders, even the most dictatorial and absolutist, have all worked against a background in which the democratic ideals are persistently repeated. Their diplomats have signed international treaties extolling democratic republican institutions and proclaiming that the defense of democracy is a guiding principle for the American family of nations. With this background, it might then be supposed that democracy has not only become a form of government and a way of life within the confines of each national boundary, but has also developed into a legal norm of the inter-American system or international law of or in the Americas, binding each of the American republics. If this were true, it would follow that any American nation which departed from the principles of democracy not only would be committing a violation of its own internal constitutional norm, but at the same time would be breaching international law and in so doing could invite upon itself sanctions from the other members of the hemispheric community to uphold the law.[3]

Before it can be determined whether or not inter-American commitments which have solemnly proclaimed the existence of a "common democracy throughout the Americas" have developed into enforceable legal norms, there must be an examination of the fundamental meaning of democracy, for democracy is one of the magic words of the twentieth century with a wide range of different uses in different parts of the world.[4] Because of its misuse and distortion by communist nations, the term can be used in international life only with the utmost caution. Yet democracy in the Western sense cannot be precisely defined, as it is neither a system nor a set of institutions nor a code of law nor a combination of policies. It is rather a belief in human nature and a code of behavior which translates that belief into thought and action.

To say that the classical Western concept of democracy cannot be precisely defined does not mean that one cannot delineate its central theme or its primary elements. Western democracy has a central theme relating to form, content, and aspirations. First and foremost, it is a designation of a certain form of government—that is, of the manner in which a state is organized, and in this sense democracy is a legal and formal concept. It indicates how political decisions are made, not what these decisions are in substance. It designates a method for the establishment of the political will, not its object, end, or means. Political democracy is a form of government by persons who are freely chosen by and responsible to the governed. The population as a whole must be able to exercise a choice as to who is to govern them under minimum conditions of pressure and force, and even more vital, they must have the opportunity of peacefully revising or reversing their choice, of changing the government.[5] Western political democracy rests upon the right of a people to make their own mistakes, plus the opportunity to correct those mistakes.

The tale of democracy does not end with political democracy. In the words of Quincy Wright:

Democracy is a theory, policy, procedure and art, emphasizing human welfare, individual freedom, popular participation, and general tolerance. It can adapt itself to many conditions, but it thrives in an atmosphere of education, toleration, peace and prosperity. Ignorance, dogma, war and poverty are its enemies. They breed absolute and arbitrary government, uncritical and lethargic people, which are the reverse of democracy.[6]

Thus the overtones of democracy are ethical in nature, concerning that inter-related complex of ideas which centers around the notions of right and wrong, justice and humanity, liberty and peace. These ethical aspirations of democracy are attitudes or ways of life which appear not only in the political sphere, not only in public life, but also in the realm of economics, in family life, community life, in social relations, and in international affairs—in other words, in all contacts between man and man. Democracy must include these ethical aspirations even though they are but dimly grasped and at best imperfectly realized; for whenever these ethical elements are repudiated, there is no authority to limit the power of the state, the political and economic liberty of the citizen is lost, human dignity vanishes, mutual fears replace mutual confidence as the basis of all human contacts, and, in the international sphere, power politics—naked and avowed—takes the place of the rule of law.

These then are the form, content, and aspirations of democracy; they blend and merge confusingly one into the other in the historical evolution of Western democracy and have become inseparably connected in men's minds. While democracy does not evolve in precisely the same manner in any two countries, since each people has its characteristic institutions and traditions and each epoch its peculiar problems, nonetheless, in the twentieth century, no nation can claim it is a democracy in the Western or classical sense of the word unless it contains at least some rudimentary elements of political democracy and some understanding of the humanistic goals of democracy which can be called human rights and fundamental freedoms. The two elements of democracy, popular constitutional governments and human rights and fundamental freedoms, are therefore complementary aspects of the way in which political communities seek to resolve the problems of power, welfare, freedom, and creativeness. They are parts of each other, and each of them is fruitless unless set in the context of the other.

POLITICAL DEMOCRACY

The American republics have historically proclaimed that their governments were dedicated to the theories and practices of political democracy. This common democratic ideal, even if not always practiced, has been the foundation on which the new world community was slowly but patiently constructed. The Monroe Doctrine was decreed in part because of North America's opposition to any intervention by the Holy Alliance which might be taken to re-establish divine-right dynasties at the expense of the hard-won battles fought to establish republican, democratic governments in Latin America.[7] The Latin Americans, three years later, meeting in the Congress of Panama of 1826,[8] reaffirmed Monroe's stand, and, under the inspiration of Bolívar, attempted to secure the goals of political democracy throughout the hemisphere by drawing up the Treaty of Union, League and Perpetual Confederation which included expulsion from the proposed federation as a sanction against any state which deserted the democratic form of government.[9] This treaty failed to become effective for lack of ratification by the signatory nations,[10] but it stands as a monument to Bolívar's farsighted political percipience.

Through the years that followed, however, the principle of political democracy as a cornerstone of the Pan American movement received scant attention, the leaders of the nations showing little enthusiasm for establishing a legal norm for the community which would obligate the members to maintain political democracy internally or for a system of sanctions which could be directed against any state departing from a democratic form of government. The majority of Latin American writers and statesmen, while voicing their basic and common devotion to political democracy, were far more vociferous in proclaiming that no nation or group of nations had the legal right to interfere in the domestic or internal affairs of another state, and they gave this principle of non-intervention far higher precedence than the goal of political democracy. They emphasized a basic tenet of international law, the right of independence — that is, a state must be free to manage its internal affairs as it sees fit, subject to no interference from other states except to the extent that it is bound by international law. A state is thus free to choose any form of government or political institutions it desires. As a corollary of this right of independence, each state is subjected by international law to a duty of non-intervention in the internal affairs of another state, and consequently any intervention to hinder or prevent a state from exercising its right to choose its own government, even by means of a violent revolution and even though the government which emerges is totalitarian, is an illicit act under rules of international law.[11]

This doctrine of the right of a people to establish any form of government they desired made great strides about the time of the French Revolution, for that was a time of optismism when liberalists assumed unquestioningly that democratic constitutionalism would in due course become everywhere the paramount form of government, and that logically the ultimate beneficiaries of a doctrine of non-intervention in the internal form of government would be the people of a state asserting their natural rights against oppressive rulers.[12] Consequently, Kant, who has been called the father of the doctrine of non-intervention, laid down the prohibition against intervention in absolute terms, yet qualified it by his statement that the civil constitution in every state shall be republican.[13] To Kant, the purpose of international law was to maintain world peace, and he felt that world peace would be maintained only if and when the republican form of government had become universal. Accordingly, Kant's conception of international law was based upon a community of nations having similar political ideas and hopes; and his prohibition against intervention was absolute only as to the members of that community of nations, and was not relevant to nations which did not accept certain principles of behavior fortified by agreement upon some fundamental values and beliefs.[14]

The late nineteenth century and early twentieth century saw a shift away from ethical values as part of the concept of the community of nations, and the geographical ambit of international law was extended to all states, whatever their internal form of government. This resulted in a modification of Kant's original thesis, leaving nothing but the absolute imperative — namely, that the internal form of government of any state was unimportant to the world community or to the peace of the world and therefore no right of intervention in any internal form of government existed.[15]

Because of historical circumstances,[16] Latin American jurists have been insistent in codifying non-intervention;[17] but a vociferous minority has always kept alive the issue of democracy as it relates to the American community, claiming that where political democracy and human rights and freedoms are denied, a nation has no right to feel that the sacred curtain of national sovereignty should be permitted to shield domestic policy from outside interference. In 1837, for example, Pedro Felix Vicuña of Chile published a widely read pamphlet urging the establishment of an international organization, which he called the General Congress of America, in which he would vest the power to support popular revolutions against tyrannical governments.[18] In 1844, Juan Bautista Alberdi, while a refugee in Chile from the tyranny of the Argentine dictatorship of Rosas, maintained that intervention should be used to promote democratic governments in the American states.[19] In December, 1847, at the Congress of Lima, a Bolivian proposal that collective intervention should be used as a method of establishing and supporting constitutional governments was thoroughly discussed, though it was finally rejected.[20]

In 1907 an Ecuadorian diplomat, Carlos R. Tobar, advocated the adoption of the legal rule that the American republics should not grant recognition to governments which came into power by revolutions contrary to the constitution of a state.[21] He felt that if nonrecognition was used as a sanction in this manner, greater respect for constitutional order and political democracy would naturally follow. While a majority of the nations viewed this doctrine with some scepticism, the Central American republics decided to experiment with it; thus they incorporated the Tobar Doctrine, with some clarification and addition, into two treaties.[22] It was agreed by these nations that none of the signatories would recognize a government coming to power as a result of a coup d'état or revolution so long as the freely elected representatives of the people of the country had not constitutionally reorganized it. Moreover, it was agreed that even after subsequent legitimation by the will of the people substantially declared, the states would not grant recognition if the government was to continue to be headed by or made up of the leaders of the revolution.

Here was the first attempt in the Americas to create by treaty an international law norm supporting political democracy and sanctioning through collective nonrecognition a state having a revolutionary government which refused to hold democratic elections. Although the United States was not a party to these treaties, it followed in relation to the signatories the principles laid down in the treaties for granting or withholding recognition, until the treaties were repudiated by the Central American nations.[23]

In 1914 President Wilson attempted to bring into being a multilateral treaty guarantee of democracy by all the American nations. While his proposed Pan American Pact was primarily concerned with the establishment of a system of hemispheric collective security, it also sought some means of securing representative democracy throughout the hemisphere. The first article of the pact provided that "the high contracting parties . . . hereby join one another in a common and mutual guarantee of territorial integrity and of political independence under republican form of government." In other words, if an American state departed from the republican form of government, it apparently would be excluded from the mutual guarantee of territorial integrity or political independence. This pact died in the proposal stage. The Latin American statesmen who were sounded out as to its feasibility were hesitant to endorse it.[24]

It was not until there began to occur a rapid spread of totalitarianism, both of the right and of the left, after World War I, that the inter-American system began to concern itself seriously with the principles of political democracy. By 1936 threats of world conquest emanating from fascist and communist dictatorships were having repercussions in the Western Hemisphere, and at the Inter-American Conference for the Maintenance of Peace which met at Buenos Aires the nations of the Americas signed a declaration which stressed "the existence of a common democracy throughout America" as a basis of inter-American solidarity and co-operation. The conferences and meetings held during and following World War II contained scattered references to democracy in their final acts, most of them as resolutions or recommendations to the governments to prevent the spread of subversive doctrines and activities inimical to democracy in the continent.[25] None of the resolutions or recommendations were so imperatively worded as to permit them to be interpreted as laying down a legal norm binding upon the member states to maintain a system of political democracy within their national borders.

Nevertheless, certain wartime actions taken by the American nations did have a bearing upon the form of government to be maintained in each American state. Although collective nonrecognition of regimes coming to power by revolutionary or unconstitutional methods had not been adopted as an inter-American rule of law, and had even been abandoned by those few Central American states which had adopted it for a short period, the Emergency Advisory Committee for the Political Defense of the Continent, created in 1942 for the purpose of studying and co-ordinating measures for preventing subversive activities by individuals or groups of individuals that might be harmful to the security of the American republics, brought again to the fore collective nonrecognition of certain governments — this time on a hemispheric scale. In 1943 a resolution was adopted recommending to all American governments that for the duration of the war they should not recognize a new government constituted by force before consulting with one another in order to determine, among other things, the circumstances which led to the establishment of the new government.[26]

In 1943 the government of Bolivia was seized through a coup d'état by a revolutionary junta which gave indications of antidemocratic and pro-fascist leanings. After consultation initiated by the Emergency Advisory Committee, nineteen American states agreed to withhold recognition.[27] The effect of this collective action forced Bolivia to purge its government of some of its pro-totalitarian elements.[28] The inter-American system was less successful when it later applied the same procedure to Argentina.[29] This wartime action was a definite recognition of the fact that the foreign policy of any state is based upon its internal type of government, and that in time of emergency such as a world war, the form of internal government of each and every state must become the concern of all of the states of the inter-American community.

When the war ended, the question of using collective nonrecognition as a sanction against new regimes suspect of being antidemocratic was aired at the February, 1945, Conference on War and Peace held in Mexico City. Some American states were violently opposed to such a procedure on the grounds that it again opened wide the door to intervention. These states proposed that the whole institution of recognition should be abolished and suggested that whenever a new government was established, either legitimately or by revolution, the pre-existing diplomatic relations should not be disturbed.[30] Those nations which felt that the American states would continue to evade internal political democracy no matter how strongly they extolled its virtues backed a resolution by Guatemala which recommended that the American republics refrain from "granting recognition to and maintaining relations with antidemocratic regimes which, in the future, may establish themselves in any of the countries of the continent; and in particular with regimes which may result from a *coup d'état* against legitimately established governments of a democratic structure." The Guatemalan resolution likewise recommended a special test whereby such regimes could be adjudged, namely the extent to which the popular will in a particular country may have contributed to their establishment according to the free judgment of each state.[31]

In proposing the use of the weapon of nonrecognition against antidemocratic regimes, Guatemala pointed out that such regimes constituted a serious danger to the unity, solidarity, peace, and defense of the continent, since it was impossible to expect from such regimes full, sincere, or effective co-operation in the democratic advancement of Pan-Americanism in time of war or in time of peace.

Guatemala declared that World War II had created a worldwide demand that the rights of man should be recognized and protected on the international level, and that the inter-American movement should therefore support this universal yearning by recognizing that antidemocratic regimes were the primary cause of denial of human rights and freedoms.[32]

The nations attending the Mexico City Conference were not yet ready to take even such a tentative step toward advancing the inter-American ideal of political democracy, and neatly sidestepped the issue by referring Guatemala's proposal to the Inter-American Juridical Committee for study and consideration, the results of which were to be reported at the Ninth Conference of American States in 1948.[33] At that time the Inter-American Juridical Committee declared that its study had shown that the Guatemalan proposal would again subject the American states to intervention in internal matters, and this would have deplorable consequences; hence the Juridical Committee could not support the proposal.[34]

The governments which supported the Guatemalan position in Mexico were not easily brushed aside, and continued to seek ways and means of assuring internal democracy in all the nations of the Americas. In November, 1945, Eduardo Rodriguez Larreta, the Uruguayan Minister of Foreign Affairs, handed a sensational note to the Ambassador to Uruguay of each of the American republics.[35] In this note he accepted Kant's thesis equating peace with the democratic form of government, highlighting what he termed the "parallelism between peace and democracy." Rodriguez Larreta listed the numerous resolutions taken at Inter-American Conferences which affirmed adherence to democratic ideals and in which the twenty-one republics had agreed that it was advisable to protect the integrity of these ideals. He then emphasized that the need in the Americas was to transform these oft-repeated principles and standards into realities. Therefore, he suggested that within the inter-American system there should be established the definite responsibility for collective intervention to assure democracy whenever circumstances required:

Peace is safe only where democratic principles of government prevail. The basic rights of man are part of these principles. Thus, though once exclusively domestic concerns, they now affect international interests and require international protection. In case of their violation in any American republic, the community of nations should take collective multilateral action to restore full democracy there. Such action is really nothing more than the fulfillment of obligations freely assumed by the American republics, all of whom have proclaimed at inter-American conferences their devotion to democracy and the rights of man.[36]

All of the nations replied to the note, eight expressing approval and thirteen disapproval.[37] Those disapproving declared that it would be difficult to discover whether a particular government was democratic, for it might be fulfilling the ideals of democracy in some of its actions but not in others. Furthermore, it was observed that since democracy in all its aspects was such a utopian state, it was doubtful if any nation now in existence or ever having existed had lived up to all the true ideals encompassed in the term. Some replies alleged that while democracy would of necessity include "representative democracy," a government that came into power through a revolution might well represent the desires and the will of the people of a nation, even though not elected democratically. On the other hand, it had not been unknown in Latin America that a state had a totalitarian government which denied many of the liberties conceived to be inherent in a democratic system and which, nevertheless, came into power by constitutional means and maintained itself with popular support and democratic elections. And finally it was alleged that it was impossible to equate democracy with peace in all instances, for some governments that were democratic in nature had nevertheless constituted on occasion a major threat to the peace.

The fact that the Larreta Doctrine was rejected by the majority of the American republics is not as important as the fact that over one-third of the republics, even in face of all apparent obstacles, were willing to accept it as a principle of the international law governing the Americas. This was a strong indication that in the Western Hemisphere the quest to make internal democracy an international legal norm was by no means dead.

At the Ninth International Conference of American States held in Bogotá in 1948, the whole inter-American system was revamped and a basic Charter for the organization, known as the Charter of Bogotá, was adopted. But prior to the adoption of this instrument, long hours of debate took place over the issue of the establishment of democratic regimes in the hemisphere. The Brazilian delegation sought to make membership in the reconstituted inter-American system conditional not only upon ratification of the new Charter but also upon the adoption of a democratic form of government. Requirements for such a government were listed as follows: freedom of the ballot, the opportunity or possibility of private enterprise, a government founded upon more than one political party, and a guarantee of the fundamental rights of man.[38] Although Brazil's stand received some support, it was finally rejected.

In spite of an unwillingness to adopt the views of Guatemala set forth at the Mexico City Conference, or the doctrine of Rodriguez Larreta, or the position of Brazil, when completed the Charter of the Organization of American States[39] contained many proclamations affirming belief in the aims and aspirations of democracy. The Preamble of the Charter declares that its signatories are "confident that the true significance of American solidarity and good neighborliness can only mean the consolidation on this continent, within the framework of democratic institutions, of a system of individual liberty and social justice based on respect for the essential rights of man . . ." Article 5(d) of the Charter "reaffirms" that the "solidarity of the American States and the high aims which are sought through it require the political organization of those states on the basis of the effective exercise of representative democracy."

There has been some discussion among authorities on international law as to the legal effect of a preamble to an international instrument. Some writers declare that it is not a binding portion of the treaty,[40] while other authorities argue that a preamble has the same legal validity and the same binding force as the other sections of the treaty, and that if it is couched in terms of legal obligation, a legal obligation arises.[41] Whichever stand is accepted as to the Preamble of the Charter of Bogotá, the conclusion arrived at must be the same. It is of ideological rather than legal significance, for it sets forth certain political ideals without guaranteeing their realization by establishing a legal obligation to behave in a certain manner. The statement that the signatory nations are confident that American solidarity means the consolidation in the Americas of a system of individual liberty and social justice within a framework of democratic institutions does not set forth a basic obligation of the members of the organization.

What then of Article 5(d), in which the states "reaffirm" that the solidarity of the Americas requires the political organization of American states on the basis of representative democracy? Does the reaffirmation of a requirement have any legal effect at all? Does it constitute an obligation on the part of each and every ratifying state to have a government based on representative democracy? To reaffirm is to affirm again in order to strengthen. To affirm means to maintain as true. "We maintain as true that continental solidarity requires each state to have representative democracy" obviously spells out no legal obligations,[42] and does not place either on each state or on the OAS the duty to see that this condition is brought about.

These considerations indicate that under the Charter of Bogotá there is no right of collective intervention by the Organization of American States to secure a democratic form of government in each of the American republics, nor is there an international treaty duty for each of the republics to establish a democratic form of government. This interpretation is given added weight in view of Article 13 of the Charter of Bogotá, which declares that "each state has the right to develop its political life freely and naturally," that is, according to its nature, without outside interference. As this is couched in terms of a legal right, there would appear to be a duty of noninterference on the part of the organization.

But the Charter of Bogotá is not the sole instrument governing the inter-American system.[43] The Inter-American Treaty of Reciprocal Assistance, signed at Rio in 1947 and ratified by all of the American states, is also an integral part of the OAS.[44]

In the Preamble to the Rio Treaty there appears this statement:

Considering:
That the obligation of mutual assistance and common defense of the American Republics is essentially related to their democratic ideals and to their will to cooperate permanently in the fulfillment of the principles and purposes of a policy of peace;
That the American regional community affirms as a manifest truth that juridical organization is a necessary prerequisite of security and peace, and that peace is founded on justice and moral order and, consequently on the international recognition and protection of human rights and freedoms, on the indispensable well being of the people, and on the effectiveness of democracy for the international realization of justice and security . . .

If there is no importance to be attached to the location of a statement in a treaty, the sole fact of importance being whether or not the words used are legally obligatory, one arrives at the same conclusion arrived at under the Charter of Bogotá. "Considering that the obligation of mutual assistance is related to democratic ideals" and "considering that peace is founded on the effectiveness of democracy" are merely clauses indicating that the signatories have taken these things into account, and are actually less forceful than the reaffirmations and confidence expressed in the Charter of Bogotá. They certainly define no legal duty of either the members of the organization or the organization itself, and their sole legal validity consists in their use as evidences of the basic motivating ideas which the framers had in view.

Thus we see that the two fundamental documents of the inter-American system, while giving florid recognition to the ideals of political democracy, do not back their high phrases by making internal democracy a legal enforceable rule of inter-American law. Both of these documents stress the fact that it is not the internal government of a nation, but rather the international situation created by the acts of a government (whatever type that government might be) that is important to the peaceful development of the inter-American community. In other words, there exists in these treaties no right of collective intervention for democracy per se; but should a nation have an internal government which creates an international problem threatening the independence, the sovereignty, or the inviolability or the integrity of the territory of any American state,

methods have been established by treaties to take care of this. A paramount
and primary purpose of the OAS is the maintenance of hemispheric peace,
and the realization of political democracy within each nation is apparently left
up to the people of that nation.

HUMAN RIGHTS

As we have mentioned earlier, political democracy is but one aspect of
democracy; and one can, to some extent, distinguish between democracy in a
political sense and democracy in a human sense, although it must be admitted
that these different aspects of the word are mutually connective by a derivative
relation. True political democracy is the result of political maturity, which is
the outgrowth of long development of aspirations and hopes of human betterment. Advancing human rights and fundamental freedoms are part of the
process of growth toward political maturity.

In the long slow development of international law, human rights have
traditionally been the concern of the individual state. Each state recognized
rights for or withheld rights from its citizens according to its own concepts,
and no state could justifiably criticize the internal behavior of its neighbors.[45]
But in the inter-American system, there was an early recognition that a minimum
of human rights should be of international concern. Bolívar's proposed Treaty
of Union, League and Perpetual Confederation, discussed at the Congress of
Panama in 1826, sought to establish a continental, international citizenship and
in addition called upon all signatories to abolish slavery.[46] This was a far cry
from any extensive concept of individual human rights in all the countries of
the hemisphere as a problem deserving international legal protection, and even
this minimum failed to be adopted. In the years that followed, while political
democracy or the more nebulous idealisms of democracy were vocally stressed
at inter-American gatherings, human rights as such were virtually ignored.

Only since World War II has there been an admission in the Western
Hemisphere that human rights are a subject of international concern, "that
governments which systematically disregard the rights of their own people are
not likely to respect the rights of other nations and other people and are likely
to seek their objectives by coercion and force in the international field."[47]
Several resolutions of the 1945 Conference held in Mexico City dealt with
human rights, notably Resolution XL on International Protection for the Rights
of Man, which proclaimed the adherence of the American republics to the
principles established by international law for safeguarding the essential rights
of man and declared support of a system of international protection of these
rights.[48] Apparently the resolution was not intended to indicate that violation
of human rights was to be accepted as a breach of international law or even that
such violation might constitute a threat to hemispheric peace, but rather was
adopted "to eliminate the misuse of diplomatic protection of citizens abroad."[49]
The inalienable rights of man were still considered subordinate to principles of
state sovereignty and non-intervention.

At the Rio Conference of 1947, partisans of human rights introduced into
the preamble of the Inter-American Treaty of Reciprocal Assistance an idealistic
(but nonlegal) statement that "The American regional community affirms as a

manifest truth ... that peace is founded on justice and moral order, and consequently, on the international recognition and protection of human rights and freedom. ..." And when the Ninth International Conference of American States met the following year in Bogotá, there was a strong movement to incorporate into the Charter of the Organization of American States a legal obligation binding each nation to respect human rights and fundamental freedoms, with a concomitant duty placed on the OAS to see that each nation lived up to its obligations in this respect.[50] Those opposing argued[51] that the Charter was to be in the nature of a constitutional instrument and should be confined to provisions establishing the OAS and defining the nature, function, and relationship of its organs, and that all other policies of the inter-American system should be set up in separate agreements. For the most part this viewpoint prevailed, and the Charter generalizes about the legal duty to respect human rights and fundamental freedoms.

The preamble declares "the true significance of American solidarity and good neighborliness can only mean the consolidation on this continent ... of a system of individual liberty and social justice based on respect for the essential rights of man." It also incorporates statements relating to the encouragement and promotion of respect for human rights and fundamental freedoms appearing in the Charter of the United Nations, by a declaration that the signatories solemnly reaffirm the principles and purposes of the United Nations. And Article 5(j) of the Charter of the OAS states: "The American States proclaim the fundamental rights of the individual without distinction as to race, nationality, creed or sex." As none of these declarations were expressed in terms of a binding legal obligation, their sole utility was to leave open the way for further inter-American legislation by treaty in this field. However, Article 13 of the Charter of Bogotá observes: "Each state has the right to develop its cultural, political and economic life freely and naturally. In this free development, the state shall respect the rights of the individual and the principles of universal morality." It can be demonstrated that the final sentence of Article 13 establishes a legal duty on the part of states. Grammatically speaking, "shall" when used in the third person expresses an obligation, a command. If the authors of Article 13 had desired to express simple futurity, the article would have read "the state will ..." The word "shall" is here equivalent to the word "must." It is imperative, not merely directory. Consequently Article 13 can be interpreted to declare that each state has a legal right to develop its own way of existence, but in so doing it has the legal duty to respect the rights of individuals. But even if this interpretation is granted, neither individual states nor the Organization of American States is given the right to take enforcement action to establish human rights in a state which fails in its obligation. Only if a violation of these values results in a threat to the peace of the hemisphere could collective intervention be undertaken under the terms of the Rio Treaty.[52]

But those nations seeking to give human rights international protection in the Western Hemisphere were not satisfied with these statements and demanded more. So a further action was taken at the Ninth Conference, the adoption of a resolution known as the American Declaration of the Rights and Duties of Man.[53] This Declaration constitutes the first comprehensive intergovernmental statement of human rights in the history of the hemisphere. While it was nothing more than a statement of aims and hopes and was not intended to be legally binding, it had educational and inspirational value. It has been a source of new hope to those people throughout the continent who were working to assure international legal protection of human rights. It symbolized the deep concern of many statesmen over the defining of these rights and the establishing of an acknowledgment of the fact that there was a connection between their denial and acts of aggression against other nations, so that such denial constituted a continual threat to hemispheric peace.

The rights to which the inter-American system would seek to give international protection are of a great variety, and among them are differences of kind. First, there are certain rights which may be described as inalienable and fundamental; inalienable because there are no circumstances in which a nation could justify a denial of them, and fundamental because a persistent denial of them will undermine and finally destroy any community based on democratic precepts.[54] An ordered society, dedicated to the goals which democracy has set, really should not confer such rights on the individual, but should rather presuppose them. Into this class would fall:

The right to life, liberty and personal security (Art. 1).

The right to equality before the law (Art. 2).

The right to religious freedom and worship (Art. 3).

The right to freedom of investigation, opinion, expression and dissemination (Art. 4).

The right to the inviolability and transmission of correspondence (Art. 10).

The right to recognition of juridical personality and of basic civil rights (Art. 17).

The right to a fair trial (Art. 18).

The right to nationality (Art. 19).

The right to vote and to participate in government (Art. 20).

The right of assembly (Art. 21).

The right of association (Art. 22).

The right of petition (Art. 24).

The right of protection from arbitrary arrest (Art. 25).

The right to due process of law (Art. 26).

These rights can all be classified as the basic political rights which underlie the political aspects of democracy. They are the important personal and civil rights of citizens which make it clear that in a democratic state the people are the masters and the sovereign is the servant. They set the bounds of political authority and reserve to the individual those areas of individual differences necessary for the operation of popular government and political democracy. One other political right is listed, namely the right of every person in the case of pursuit not resulting from ordinary crimes to seek and receive asylum in foreign territory (Art. 27). If all the other political rights listed were fully realized in every nation of the Western Hemisphere, the necessity for such an inter-American right would fall by the wayside. Under present conditions in Latin America, its inclusion is a good indication of the hardheaded realism which is as much a part of the Latin American character as idealism.

The second group of rights listed in the declaration are derived from the general economic objectives of a democratic community:

The right to education and equality of opportunity (Art. 12).

The right to work and to fair remuneration (Art. 14).

The right to leisure time and to the use thereof (Art. 15).

The right to social security (Art. 16).

The right to private property (Art. 23).

In the nineteenth century the emphasis of Western democracy was placed on the political aspects of democracy, but in the twentieth this emphasis has shifted to the economics of democracy. While many nations of the Western Hemisphere have achieved some measure of political democracy, many of them are in dire need of a far fuller measure of economic democracy. Economic democracy implies something in the nature of an economic order which has in view a leveling of economic privilege and economic inequalities to the advantage of the underprivileged sections of the population.[55] The ideal of economic equality is a matter of approximation and not of absolutes, but democracy cannot survive unless political democracy demonstrably yields economic betterment for the majority of the population. All historical experience shows that a people without hope of prosperity or a rough equality of opportunity will fall into the pit of tyranny. In a society with deep-seated sources of economic discontent, extremism cannot be overcome simply by invoking the superior values of political democracy. Nevertheless, economic equality is no panacea in itself. It is void of democratic content, apart from its coefficient of political democracy or the ethical aspirations of democracy. Thus the American Declaration of the Rights and Duties of Man places important emphasis on the economic objectives, which in most nations are as yet merely goals to be achieved and not legally enforceable rights which have been actually attained internally.

The final group of rights listed in the declaration can roughly be classified as some of the ethical aspirations underlying any democratic system. These include:

The right to protection of honor, personal reputation, and private family life (Art. 5).

The right to a family and to the protection thereof (Art. 6).

The right to protection for mothers and children (Art. 7).

The right to residence and movement (Art. 8).

The right to the preservation of health and to well being (Art. 11).

The right to the benefits of culture (Art. 13).

These ethical aspirations indicate the belief that democracy as a political legal technique is not enough. If the leading ideas of mankind are not to languish they must show their power to realize the masses' obscure urge for a better ordained social order, greater happiness, and a fuller life for the common man. The immediate importance of these rights is less of achievement than of intent. Particularly in Latin America, their ideal has force. Citizens of the United States tend to pay less attention to theory than to practice, but to Latin Americans, no matter how far practice at any moment in history falls short of high aims, these aims remain a living standard and no less a living reproach to those who violate them. Thus the American Declaration of the Rights and Duties of Man indicates an inter-American recognition of the fact that democracy must exist not only on the legal or political field, but also in the economic and ethical fields. The struggle must advance on all fronts at one and the same time, for all these areas are intimately interconnected.

The chapter on rights is closed by an article of general limitation: "The rights of man are limited by the rights of others, by the security of all, and by the just demands of the general welfare and the advancement of democracy."

This statement is a recognition of the fact that while the rights of man arise because individuals live in communities—and in an ordered society they are protected by that society—their rights are subject to qualifications and even restrictions where the interests of the community so require. The principle underlying such restrictions seems to be that each individual shall, so far as it is practicable, have an equal enjoyment of his rights and freedoms with every other individual in the community. This equality can perhaps never be fully attained, but it is the measure by which the rights and freedoms of each are limited for the benefit of all.

As its title indicates, the Declaration also concerns itself with the "duties" of man. The preamble states: "The fulfillment of duty by each individual is a prerequisite to the rights of all. Rights and duties are interrelated in every social and political activity of man."

The duties of the Declaration can be classified roughly into social duties, political duties, and economic duties. Under the social duties fall the duties to society (Art. 29); duties toward children and parents (Art. 30); duty to acquire an education (Art. 31); duty to serve the community and the nation (Art. 34); duty to co-operate with the state with respect to social security and welfare (Art. 35). The two economic duties set forth are the duty to pay taxes (Art. 36) and the duty to work (Art. 37). The political duties listed are the duty to vote (Art. 32); the duty to obey the law (Art. 33); and the duty to refrain from political activities in a foreign country (Art. 38).

The idea underlying the inclusion of these duties is that each individual should recognize that he has certain responsibilities to the society in which he lives, and that therefore the stress should not be placed solely upon the responsibility of the state to secure human rights. Nevertheless, one may question the utility of including such a concept in an international document, for the whole basic theory of the protection of human rights on the international level is that the individual can be easily overwhelmed before the aggregate collection of power lodged in a state. A sovereign state, on the other hand, still retains its power to exact from all individuals the duties which are owed to it.

Furthermore, as the human rights and the duties of man are placed on equal footing in the Declaration, a state denying human rights might well plead that the denial was brought about by failure of the individual or individuals to fulfil the duties which are set forth in the Declaration, and consequently if the Organization of American States ever attempted to protect the rights of man on an international level it could well be frustrated.[56] The inclusion of the duties of man in the Declaration can be labeled a confusion of values; without doubt the duties listed are some of the major social, political, and economic obligations owed by the citizen to his political community, but each nation is still capable of exacting such duties from its citizens without invoking the authority of the whole international legal community.

There was one further action taken at Bogotá with relation to human rights— a resolution recommending that the Inter-American Juridical Committee prepare a draft statute providing for the creation and functioning of an Inter-American Court to guarantee the rights of man.[57] This draft was to be presented at the Tenth Conference of American States "if it felt that the moment had arrived for comment thereon."

The Inter-American Juridical Committee, which is the permanent committee of the Inter-American Council of Jurists, presented to the Council of Jurists, at their first meeting in May, 1950, their unanimous opinion that it would be impossible to create a statute of this nature at that time.[58] The committee suggested, therefore, that the Council inform the Tenth Conference that until such time as a formal convention on human rights had come into being governing the American system, it would be premature to establish enforcement procedures. Hence, the Tenth Conference merely adopted a resolution[59] reaffirming that each nation should strengthen its system for the protection of human rights and another resolution requesting the Council of the OAS to continue its studies on the juridical aspects of protection of human rights, in order that the matter might be considered at the Eleventh Inter-American Conference.

While the inter-American system has not as yet constituted legal norms from which human rights can be derived under positive law, it certainly must be acknowledged that the Rio Treaty, the Charter of Bogotá, and the American Declaration of the Rights and Duties of Man have expanded the problem of human rights from the national to the international level by the assertions in all of these instruments that the observance of human rights is now a matter of international concern. Thus there is here a partial recognition that some aspects of democracy are of hemispheric rather than purely national import and significance.

DEMOCRACY VERSUS NON-INTERVENTION

Even though there has been an apparent unwillingness to adopt binding legal obligations that each nation in the hemisphere shall become a democracy both in the sense of political democracy and in that of human democracy, the inter-American community has, nevertheless, been faced with concrete issues where certain of the American states have sought to impose democracy on neighboring states.

Under Article 6 of the Inter-American Treaty of Reciprocal Assistance of 1947, signed at Rio, when there is an act or threat of aggression which is not an armed attack on a nation or nations of the hemisphere or in which there may be "any other fact or situation that might endanger the peace of the Americas" and that affects the inviolability, territorial integrity, sovereignty, or political independence of an American state, the Organ of Consultation of the inter-American system is required to meet immediately to agree on measures which, in case of aggression, must be taken to assist the victim, or in any case, measures which should be taken for the common defense for the maintenance of the peace and security of the continent. The Meeting of Consultation of Ministers of Foreign Affairs was designated as the Organ of Consultation under the Rio Treaty, with powers to decide upon the measures to be taken in the field of security whenever a particular case should arise, and the Council of the OAS was named as Provisional Organ of Consultation.[60]

Hardly had the ink dried on this document before the OAS was called upon to use the powers granted under it to resolve problems relating to freedom and order in the Caribbean–Central American area. In 1948 the Council of the OAS, as Provisional Organ of Consultation, was faced with a case involving Costa Rica pitted against Nicaragua, and in 1949 and 1950 two additional cases, which were in reality the same case, arose involving Haiti, the Dominican Republic, Cuba, and Guatemala.[61] The agitations which gave rise to these cases were concerned with political antagonisms between authoritarian governments on the one hand and democratic regimes (or regimes with some democratic tendencies) on the other, and involved the shadowy organization known as the Caribbean Legion, dedicated to the overthrow of dictatorships. First targets were the dictatorships of Somoza of Nicaragua and Trujillo of the Dominican Republic.[62] The Caribbean Legion was composed of a strange assortment of mercenaries, adventurers, and patriots in political exile. The latter were "battling for their ideals" and hoping to restore democratic government in their various countries, while the former were "taking advantage of that struggle for selfish purposes."[63] The Legion was more or less sponsored by Costa Rica, Guatemala, and Cuba, which permitted their territories to be used for revolutionary activities such as Legion efforts to organize expeditions and fighting forces for invasion, and also permitted illegal activities as regards traffic in arms and passage of planes. In retaliation, the Nicaraguan and Dominican governments aided and abetted revolutionary movements and subversive activities aimed at overthrowing the governments of Costa Rica, Guatemala, and Cuba. The result was turmoil and discord in the relations of these contending governments, which were to erupt in armed invasions by revolutionary groups bent on the overthrow of existing regimes; and conspiratorial plots fomented trouble in democracies as well as in dictatorships.

The OAS pointed out that the right of a people to maintain within their own territory a government of their own choosing so long as such action does not endanger other states or the peace of the Americas has long been an established principle of inter-American relations, and the OAS has no power to intervene either on behalf of a government or on behalf of internal forces seeking to overthrow that government. But when a foreign nation goes to the aid of rebel forces seeking such an overthrow, the issue is no longer an internal domestic question, but a controversy between two states which falls under Article 6 of the Rio Treaty.[64] In each of the cases, the prompt action of the OAS averted further activities and resulted in the signing of Pacts of Amity by the contending governments. The Council was adamant in condemning both the democracies and the dictatorships for their intervention. While the OAS acknowledged that representative democracy and participation in government were fundamental to the inter-American system, it nevertheless declared that endorsement of such principles did not in any way or under any concept authorize any government or group of governments to violate the inter-American commitments relative to the principle of non-intervention. Therefore, the Council of the OAS tacitly admitted that in concrete tests of democracy and human rights versus non-intervention, the latter duty rules supreme.[65]

These initial cases confronting the OAS concerned a conflict between democracy and home-grown American dictatorships. But soon a different type of situation arose. International communism, which breeds on chaos and discontent, was not long delayed in taking advantage of the situations in Central America. By 1954, Guatemala had become of concern to the inter-American community as it became apparent that there was an increasing intervention in its government by the international communist movement.[66]

At the Tenth Inter-American Conference held at Caracas in 1954, the United States was particularly perturbed and called the attention of the other nations of the continent to the fact that should any nation fall completely into the hands of the Communists, such a nation would of necessity be a satellite of the U.S.S.R. and would constitute a serious menace to the peace of the Americas. The Tenth Conference adopted a Declaration of Solidarity for the Preservation of the Political Integrity of the American States against the Intervention of International Communism which stated that domination or control of the political institutions of any American state by the international communist movement would constitute a threat to the sovereignty and political independence of the American states, endangering the peace of America, and would require a Meeting of Consultation to consider the adoption of appropriate action in accordance with existing treaties.[67] This language in effect interprets Article 6 of the Rio Treaty in such a way that domination of the government of an American state by international communism requires the application of collective measures for the common defense and the maintenance of the peace and security of the hemisphere. In other words, in the conflict between non-hemispheric totalitarianism and democracy, there is a possibility that collective intervention could be taken to protect the inter-American ideals of democracy and human rights against the recognized dangers of the international communist movement which neither acknowledges nor accepts such principles.

From 1954 to 1959, the tide of democracy began to swell in Latin America, and dictator after dictator was overthrown. However, the struggle between dictatorial and antidictatorial factions again spilled outside national borders and into the international arena and again created situations of extreme danger to hemispheric peace. This became very apparent after the dictator Batista departed from Cuba and left the state to the revolutionary movement of Fidel Castro. Castro, picturing himself as another Bolívar, announced that this revolution, *Fidelismo*, was not only a fight to liberate Cuba from the tyranny of Batista, but a product for export to help overthrow tyrants wherever they could be found.

This determination of Castro to export his revolution to other American republics soon manifested itself in attempts to overthrow certain of such governments, democracies as well as dictatorships.[68] His activities took various interventionary forms, from aiding and supporting armed invasions by revolutionary exiles, as in three cases[69] arising before the OAS in 1959 involving Panama,

Nicaragua, and the Dominican Republic, to incitement, to political and propaganda activities of Cuban diplomats in Cuban embassies in the hemisphere.

The Council of the OAS attempted to solve the Panamanian and Nicaraguan cases,[70] but the Dominican case led to a convocation of a Meeting of Foreign Ministers at Santiago, Chile, in 1959 acting not as consultative organ under the Rio Treaty, but under its Charter of Bogotá powers as set forth in Article 39 to consider hemispheric problems of an urgent and common nature.[71] Two main problems, political unrest in the Caribbean and effective exercise of representative democracy in the hemisphere, were considered. Issues emanating from these two problems were non-intervention, political democracy, human rights, and the relation of economic development to political stability. Actually the essential problem of the Fifth Meeting of Consultation when it convened in Santiago on August 12, 1959, was to reconcile the growing demand for democratic progress and social change in Latin America, and particularly in the Caribbean, with the traditional inter-American principles of non-intervention in internal affairs and peaceful relations. Opinions as to how these two requirements should be reconciled differed widely.[72]

Cuba and Venezuela called upon the hemispheric democracies to band together in condemnation of all dictatorships and specifically that of the Dominican government. The Venezuelan foreign minister took the position that only democratic governments should be admitted to the OAS. A democratic country was defined as one with freedom of the press, periodic changes of government by peaceful means, and effective suffrage. The argument that democracy could not be imposed on a nation by outside forces was refuted, and a demand for collective action was made to end dictatorial abuse of democracy and human rights. It was stated that such collective action could not be equated with intervention.[73]

The overwhelming majority of American governments rejected the Cuban and Venezuelan thesis, re-endorsed the principle of non-intervention, and rejected the notion that collective action should be permitted to overthrow Latin American dictatorships. Again the Latin Americans indicated that dictatorships, no matter how deplorable they might be, were to be preferred over any action which might lessen the effectiveness of internal sovereignty. Nevertheless, the meeting at Santiago again went on to give extensive expressions of support for democracy and respect for human rights. A declaration was adopted, known as the Declaration of Santiago, which announced in its preamble that it was "the general aspiration of the American peoples to live in peace under the protection of democratic institutions, free from all intervention and all totalitarian influence."[74] The Declaration reaffirmed that there was a relationship between respect for human rights, fundamental freedoms, and the effective exercise of representative democracy on the one hand and inter-American peace and harmony on the other, noting that failure to adhere to the principles of democracy is "a source of widespread disturbance and gives rise to emigration that causes frequent and grave political tensions between the state the emigres leave and the state that receives them."[75]

The Declaration went beyond former inter-American pronouncements in favor of democracy in that it listed in detail the usual attributes of a democratic system, to permit national and international public opinion to judge whether or not a particular regime measures up to democratic standards. Such an announcement, it was stated, would help to eradicate "forms of dictatorship, despotism, or tyranny" but this statement was cautiously amended by concluding, "without weakening respect for the rights of peoples freely to choose their own form of government."

The attributes of a democratic regime were set forth as follows:

1. The principle of the rule of law should be assumed by the separation of powers, and by the control of the legality of governmental acts by competent organs of the state.

2. The governments of the American Republics should be derived from free elections.

3. Perpetuation in power, or the exercise of power without a fixed term and with the manifest intent of perpetuation, is incompatible with the effective exercise of democracy.

4. The governments of the American states should ensure a system of freedom for the individual and social justice based on respect for fundamental human rights.

5. The human rights incorporated into the legislation of the various American states should be protected by effective judicial procedures.

6. The systematic use of political proscription is contrary to American democratic order.

7. Freedom of the press, of radio and television, and, in general freedom of information and expression are essential conditions for the existence of a democratic regime.

8. The American states, in order to strengthen democratic institutions, should cooperate among themselves within the limits of their resources and the framework of their laws so as to strengthen and develop their economic structure, and achieve just and humane living conditions for their people.[76]

This Declaration of Santiago was an admission by the inter-American system that the hitherto vague statements of principles relating to democracy did little to provide a means for distinguishing democracy clearly from alternative political schemes. The moment had arrived, intellectually as well as practically, when the statesmen of the Americas were willing to take one more step— possibly small and faltering—toward their professed goal, by establishing a more definite description of the nature of that goal. At the Santiago meeting the Foreign Ministers also expanded the powers of the Inter-American Peace Committee, an agency composed of representatives of five American nations which had previously been granted the duty of keeping vigilance to insure the prompt settlement of disputes between American republics and to that end to suggest measures for the peaceful settlement of such disputes, although such suggested measures were in no wise legally binding on the disputants or on the OAS.[77] Under its new mandate the Peace Committee was entrusted with the examination of:

1. Methods and procedures to prevent any activities from abroad designed to overthrow the established governments or to provoke instances of intervention or acts of aggression;

2. The relationship between violation of human rights or the non-exercise of representative democracy, on the one hand, and the political tensions that affect the peace of the hemisphere, on the other, and

3. The relationship between economic underdevelopment and political instability.[78]

In examining these issues the Peace Committee could take action at the request of governments or on its own initiative, although in either case its activity remained subject to the consent of a state in the event an investigation had to be carried on within the territorial boundaries of that state. Broad studies were to be initiated immediately and a preliminary report was to be prepared so that the American governments might formulate their observations on it. After these observations had been taken into account, a definite report was to be presented at the Eleventh Inter-American Conference scheduled to meet at Quito, Ecuador.

At the Fifth Meeting of the Ministers of Foreign Affairs the issue of safeguarding human rights to protect the political stability of the continent was given serious consideration. So that the human rights activities of the OAS would not remain compromised at the lowest level of controversial principles— mere statements of rights without legal effect or effective means of implementation—the Inter-American Council of Jurists was ordered to prepare, in time for consideration by the Eleventh Conference, a draft convention which would define substantive human rights and which would create a supranational mechanism to guarantee those rights.

The initial draft convention drawn up by the Council of Jurists includes the whole range of human rights discussed earlier by the various organs of the inter-American system—civil rights, political rights, economic rights, and social rights.[79] The enforcement procedure involves a commission on human rights and a court on human rights. When there is a claim that a ratifying member state has violated an obligation assumed under the treaty, the initial step will be the submission of a petition to the commission, which is to investigate the claim and attempt to achieve a friendly settlement of the dispute. If this cannot be done, the commission shall draw up a confidential report on the facts and state its conclusions, and submit this report to the nation concerned. If the nation concerned has not accepted the jurisdiction of the court on human rights, and has not altered the situation in accordance with the commission's confidential report within a stipulated period of time, then the commission may make the report public, thereby invoking continental public opinion against the state accused of denying human rights. If the state has accepted the jurisdiction of the court, after the original decision of the commission and failure of the state to agree thereto, then the case is turned over for final decision by the court, and the treaty provides that the "contracting parties undertake to abide by the decision of the Court in any case to which they are parties."[80]

Two classes of complaints are provided for by the draft convention. The first relates to a complaint by another state of an alleged breach of the treaty. The second permits the commission to receive petitions addressed to it by any person or group of persons or associations or corporations claiming a violation by a signatory state. This latter is a departure from the classical principles of international law, which restrict standing before international tribunals to states only. The right of petition of an individual is limited by the fact that the commission can consider it only after all domestic remedies have been exhausted according to the generally recognized principles of international law, except for those cases in which justice has been denied.

The United States delegation to the Fifth Meeting pointed out that while it supported the promotion of respect for human rights in the inter-American system, because of the structure of its federal government it would not be possible for the United States to enter into a multilateral convention with respect to human rights or with respect to an inter-American court of human rights; "it, of course, raises no objection to other states' entering into conventions on these subjects should they find it possible to do so."[81] Mexico declared it felt that the preparation of the Draft Convention on Human Rights "was not carried with the thought and consideration required for the preparation of an instrument that so widely restricts domestic jurisdiction and seriously compromises the international responsibility of the State."[82] Consequently she abstained from voting for the draft.

Argentina, while voting for the draft, did so with the reservation that she considered it but a preliminary document designed to serve as the basis for subsequent studies.[83]

The Fifth Meeting of Consultation of Ministers of Foreign Affairs also created an Inter-American Commission on Human Rights, composed of seven members elected by the Council of the Organization.[84] The Human Rights Commission is therefore an autonomous entity of the OAS whose function is to promote respect for human rights by preparing studies and recommendations on progressive measures in favor of human rights, and generally to serve the OAS as an advisory body in respect of human rights.[85]

After the Human Rights Commission was constituted it held a number of meetings and began the preparation of studies on such matters as methods for making the promotion of respect for human rights and their defense effective; the relation between promotion and protection of human rights, on the one hand, and the effective exercise of representative democracy, on the other; improvement of electoral procedures and measures for assuring the right to vote; the most effective legal measures for the protection of rights; and measures to assure freedom of inquiry, opinion, and expression. The Human Rights Commission concluded that its scope of action, as defined by the Fifth Meeting and by the Council of the OAS, was too narrowly limited for it to perform the task expected of it by the people of the Americas. It felt that its functions should not be confined to the mere promotion of respect for human rights, but rather its duty should be to see that these rights are not violated. Therefore it drew up a series of requests to the Council suggesting that it be given the additional power to examine complaints about rights violations and prepare confidential reports on them, including recommendations to the government accused of violating human rights. If that government should not adopt the recommended measures in a reasonable time, the Commission would then publish the report. The Council has referred these requests to the Eleventh Conference for decision.[86]

Without waiting for the Eleventh Conference, in two instances at least the Commission decided that it was empowered to make some recommendations to a specific government with respect to complaints submitted to it. Under Article 9 of the Statute of the Inter-American Commission on Human Rights approved by the Council of the OAS, the Commission was given the power

b) To make recommendations to the governments of member states in general, if it considers such action advisable, for the adoption of progressive measures in favor of human rights within the framework of their domestic legislation and, in accordance with their constitutional precepts, appropriate measures to further the faithful observance of those rights . . .[87]

At its meetings in April, 1961, the Commission pointed out that it had received forty-five communications relative to the grave situation in Cuba, requesting the Commission to act immediately to avoid irreparable violations of human rights in that nation. The Commission felt that under the above authorization it was justified in calling the attention of the government of Cuba to the accusations against it, suggesting that it live up to the American Declaration of the Rights and Duties of Man, and that under its broad power to ask member states to supply it with information, the Commission on Human Rights could request from Cuba a report on measures it was taking in the field of human rights.

At the beginning of its third session, held in October and November, 1961, the Commission requested of the Dominican government permission to visit that nation to investigate complaints it had received of violations of human rights. The Dominican government granted this permission on the understanding that the Commission would limit its investigations to violations which had taken place since the departure of the Trujillo family from the island. The Commission accepted this stipulation. On its visit it gathered information on the arrests and disappearances of persons in the Dominican Republic, on the limitation of freedom of expression, and on the problems of conflicts between governmental authorities and students and governmental authorities and labor unions. Upon the basis of this information, the Commission submitted a report to the Dominican government urging it to take immediate steps to advance human rights.[88]

Resolution IX of the Fifth Meeting of Consultation called upon the Council of the OAS to prepare, in co-operation with the technical organs of the organization and taking into the consideration the views of the American governments, a draft convention on the effective exercise of representative democracy and the establishment of procedures and measures applicable thereto.[89] The Council set up a special committee to prepare this draft, and as a result of its endeavors a Draft Convention on the Effective Exercise of Democracy has been transmitted to the American governments for observation, for eventual submission to the consideration of the Eleventh Inter-American Conference.[90]

This project characterizes democracy and its requirements in language similar to that of the Santiago Declaration. The overthrow of a democratic government by force would require collective nonrecognition of the new regime by the other American governments, and, further, the new regime would be denied the right of representation in the Council of the OAS.[91] An unlawful dissolution of the national legislature of an American state would call for a Meeting of Foreign Ministers at the request of any American government.[92]

Other departures by an American state from the requirements of democracy as delineated by the treaty demand an investigation and report by a special committee of the Council of the OAS. The Council may bring this report to the attention of the delinquent government, and if the latter fails to reply within three months the report may be published.[93] If, after three months of the Council's decision to publish the report, there is still no satisfactory reply, the Council may debate the issue in public session. Moreover, a Meeting of Foreign Ministers of states ratifying the convention may be convoked if the examination of the reported violation demands it in the interests of inter-American solidarity and peaceful relationships.[94] This Meeting may by a two-thirds vote of the ratifying states call upon the guilty state to cease and desist from its violation, and may recommend withdrawal of chiefs of diplomatic missions or rupture of all diplomatic relations.[95]

It should be stressed that this project at the present time is only a working paper and it is extremely doubtful if the American states can be persuaded to accept its provisions. If they did, inter-American enforcement of the democratic norm would become possible. Sanctions in the form of an appeal to public opinion and diplomatic measures are authorized, although the treaty does not go so far as to authorize economic coercive measures or the use of armed force.

In spite of the strong reaffirmations of democracy as an inter-American principle, the results of the Santiago conference did little to alleviate tensions in the Caribbean and the situation continued to vex the OAS. In February, 1960, the Council was faced with the problem of the conflict between the principle of non-intervention and the principle of maintenance of respect for human rights, the crux of the problem being how to conduct, without intervening in the affairs of the Dominican Republic, an investigation into an allegation by Venezuela that the Trujillo government was flagrantly violating human rights by mass political arrests and imprisonment. The Council decided to investigate and called upon the Inter-American Peace Committee to do so in accord with this committee's competence as granted by the Santiago Meeting.[96]

The committee's investigation found the Dominican Republic guilty of the denial of freedom of speech and assembly, arbitrary arrest, cruel and inhuman treatment of prisoners, and the use of intimidation and terror as political weapons. The committee's report stressed the fact that international tensions in the Caribbean area would continue to increase as long as the Dominican Republic remained a dictatorship and did not live up to the ideals of democracy.[97] No immediate action was taken by the OAS. Caribbean tensions did not abate.[98]

By August a Foreign Ministers Meeting at San José, Costa Rica, became necessary to consider Venezuelan charges against the Dominican Republic resting upon Dominican acts directed against the former government, including an attempt to assassinate the Venezuelan President,[99] as well as charges of aggressive acts by Cuba against the United States which had been referred to the OAS by the Security Council of the United Nations.[100] In considering the Venezuelan–Dominican Republic case, the Meeting of Foreign Ministers acted for the first time as organ of consultation under the Rio Treaty. Finding that Dominican governmental officials had been engaged in a plot to overthrow the government of Venezuela which included the attempt on the life of the

President of that country as well as the providing of arms for the coup and other actions,[101] the Sixth Meeting condemned the Dominican Republic as having committed acts of intervention and aggression. Thus in accord with Articles 6 and 8 of the Rio Treaty the Meeting took enforcement measures against the Dominican Republic in the form of a collective rupture of diplomatic relations and a partial interruption of economic relations.[102] This action was taken because the Dominican Republic had engaged in acts of aggression, and not because of the nondemocratic aspects of the regime.

The United States, however, feeling strongly that the two were connected, proposed that more should be done—that the OAS action should be linked with the establishment of democracy in the Dominican Republic. The United States suggested that in place of the sanctions proposed by Latin America, the Organization should call upon the Dominican Republic to accept inter-American supervision of free elections in that nation after a period of free expression and free assembly. If the Dominican government refused to receive such supervision, then strong sanctions should be imposed, not as punitive measures for aggression only, but as measures to force the Dominican government to accede to the international organization.[103] This, then, was a major effort to enforce the principles of political democracy and human rights against a member of the inter-American community violating these avowed community principles.

This proposal of the United States met with cool reception from the Latin American nations. It was tantamount to setting up a provisional inter-American political trusteeship over the Dominican Republic, and most Latin American nations felt this was outside the power of the OAS. It smacked of collective intervention.[104] The Latin American democracies had for years been demanding an ouster of the Trujillo regime, but when faced with a legitimate manner of accomplishing this under inter-American treaties, they could not bring themselves to the point where they would concede that democracy was more important than non-intervention. Their attitude was naturally colored by the hope that the moral impact of the rupture of relations, the condemnation of the Trujillo government, and the partial rupture of economic relations would be sufficient to topple the Trujillo regime. Therefore the United States proposal was rejected and sanctions for aggressive acts were imposed, the United States agreeing to accept the Latin American views. Only after this move had been taken did some concern arise in the minds of Latin American statesmen lest if Trujillo were thus toppled a power vacuum might rise in the Dominican Republic, which could then immediately be taken over by a Castro-Communist government.[105]

Adjourning for twenty-four hours, the Meeting reconvened to consider the problem of Cuba, this time as the Seventh Meeting of Foreign Ministers acting under its Charter powers to consider problems of urgent and common interest to the American states.[106] From the outset it was clear that many of the ministers present, although disturbed by the communist penetration of a hemispheric nation and by Cuba's unending war of propaganda attempting to promote unrest and revolutions throughout the Americas, were prevented from taking a strong stand because of the widespread sympathy with *Fidelismo* among their own peoples. Many Latin Americans are in deep sympathy with the Castro revolution, for they see in its drastic economic reforms efforts to correct evils which are a part of most of the Latin American scene—concentration of ownership of land and other forms of wealth in the hands of a few, poverty of the masses, lack of opportunity, lack of industrialization. As anti-Americanism has long been a favorite rallying cry for all of Latin America, Castro's tweaking of the eagle's beak has not been unrelished, and very few Latin American governments were willing, in face of a widespread internal sympathy for Castro, to risk political overturn by pro-Castro masses.[107]

The foreign minister of Colombia was a most cogent speaker for the Latin American viewpoint. He expressed support for the aims of the Cuban revolution, and openly declared that if the controversy were between the United States and Cuba solely, the Latin Americans would all be on the side of Cuba; but in a conflict between America and Russia, or between democracy and international communism, no nation in the hemisphere could remain neutral.[108] The United States Secretary of State Christian Herter pointed out that Sino-Soviet imperialism was exploiting the situation in Cuba as a means of installing a communist regime there, which meant not only the loss of that country's independence but also the establishment of an excellent operational base for communist infiltration and subversion against all other American nations. He pointed out that resistance to such extracontinental intervention was the cornerstone of the inter-American system, and to permit communist intervention in this hemisphere was to negate the basic political objectives of the American people—namely, the establishment of political democracy and the recognition of human rights and freedoms.

Taking the Declaration of Santiago as the instrument setting forth the inter-American concept of what democracy entailed, Herter listed one by one the violations by Cuba of the principles enunciated in that document. Cuban suppression of these democratic freedoms to serve the purposes of an extracontinental power was no longer a local and internal matter, but should be a matter of deepest concern to all members of the OAS. The United States therefore called upon the members of the organization to condemn communist intervention in inter-American affairs and to indicate grave concern over Cuba's toleration and encouragement of such intervention. Herter did not seek sanctions against Cuba; rather he sought merely a censure of that nation's government as a warning.[109]

Most Latin American delegates were unwilling to go along with such a strong denunciation of Cuba, again using the doctrine of non-intervention to thwart any possible actions to aid in the spread of political democracy and thus indirectly aiding an alien ideology which was seeking to extend its dictatorial system to all of Latin America. The declaration which did come out of this, the Seventh Meeting of Ministers of Foreign Affairs, placed the OAS on record against communist intervention in the Americas without specifically naming Cuba, and condemned the attempts by Russia and Communist China to make use of the political or social situation of any American state for their own purposes. The document reasserted the axiom that the inter-American system was incompatible with any form of totalitarianism.[110]

While the United States delegates attempted to read into the resolution a rebuke of Cuba, most Latin American delegates did not agree, seeing in the resolution a mere appeal to Cuba to seek protection within the inter-American system rather than within the communist orbit. The Mexican delegate went so far as to issue a special statement to the effect that the declaration was general in character and did not constitute a condemnation or threat against Cuba.[111]

One significant statement in favor of democracy was sent to the Seventh Meeting of Ministers of Foreign Affairs by President Betancourt of Venezuela.[112] He called for a declaration or a treaty to be drawn up at the Eleventh Inter-American Conference which would oust from the OAS governments not freely elected by the people of the country. This instrument, he stated, should also stipulate that the member states were under a duty to respect the fundamental rights of man, guarantee freedom of the press and information, and recognize the rights of minorities to organize political parties. This plan would involve sanctions against any state violating such principles by isolation and exclusion from the inter-American community, which Betancourt deemed would be a protection against dictatorships of the right or of the left.

Aspects of President Betancourt's proposal were adopted at the Eighth Meeting of Foreign Ministers which convened at Punta del Este, Uruguay, in January, 1962, as Organ of Consultation under the Rio Treaty to seek ways of facing hemispheric dangers subversive in nature emanating from Cuba as a consequence of the Castro government's alliance with the communist bloc. Here communism was declared incompatible with the inter-American system, and because the present government of Cuba had accepted the principles of Marxism-Leninism, it was excluded from participation in the OAS on the ground of incompatibility. Principles basic to the inter-American system are democracy and respect for human rights. In fact Article 5(d) of the Charter proclaims that the solidarity of the American states and the high aims of the OAS rest on a foundation of representative democracy as the political organization of OAS members. Thus, the conclusion might be reached from this action of the Foreign Ministers that the OAS does recognize adherence to the democratic principle and respect for human rights as norms of inter-American law to be observed by the member states and to be backed by the sanction of exclusion from the organization of those members not effectively observing such norms. If this be true, Pan America has finally adopted the Bolivarian thesis as included in the Treaty of Union, League and Perpetual Confederation which provided for expulsion from the proposed federation of any state which deserted the republican-democratic form of government. However, one cannot be sure. In the first place, the action of exclusion was not apparently regarded as a sanction or enforcement measure. Stipulation for exclusion is not made in OAS instruments. In the absence of any provision of exclusion or expulsion as a sanction, the ministers supporting Cuba's exclusion took the view that Cuba's incompatibility with the principles of the OAS led automatically to the exclusion. In other words, since the solidarity of the OAS rests on a community of nations committed to representative democracy, any American state departing from such ideology breaks the ties of unity and volunteers out of the community—a principle of self-exclusion. If Cuba automatically excluded itself, such exclusion could hardly be considered a sanction taken by the OAS for violation of the democratic norm. Cuba's incompatibility, which led automatically to exclusion, was stressed. In fact, the ministers did not actually order the exclusion. Nevertheless, this action had much the effect of a sanction, for when the resolution of exclusion was voted by the Meeting, it would work and apparently was intended to work a punishment of Cuba for violation of inter-American norms by bringing about Cuban isolation from the community and according that nation a future treatment by her neighboring states on a political basis, unfettered by inter-American law.

Also militating against a judgment that the members of the OAS have at long last come to regard democracy and its concomitant human rights as inter-American norms subject to sanction is the fact that the exclusionary vote barely mustered a two-thirds majority for passage. Six nations—Argentina, Bolivia, Brazil, Chile, Ecuador, and Mexico—abstained from the vote, while Cuba voted in the negative. The six abstainers were to a degree moved by the juridical consideration that in the absence of provision for expelling or excluding a member, such a procedure by the Organ of Consultation would be an illegal extension of the Charter and an illegal collective intervention in Cuban internal affairs as relating to her form of government. The abstainers all recognized the incompatibility of a communist form of government in an American nation with the principles of inter-America, primarily because of its hostility to the principle of representative democracy. By the proclamation of such variance through resolution, democracy was recognized as a guiding principle of the OAS, a basis of solidarity of the American community; but through failure to vote any sanction against a nation departing therefrom, democracy seems relegated to an "ought," not an "is."

The only sanction or enforcement measure in accord with the Rio Treaty which was taken against Cuba was one suspending trade with Cuba in arms and implements of war. But here again there were four abstentions—Brazil, Ecuador, Mexico, and Chile—as well as a Cuban negative vote. Moreover, it is doubtful if this can be considered a measure in support of the democratic norm per se. To the contrary, it was an action taken to alleviate in some degree the danger to the peace of the hemisphere emanating from a communist Cuba intent on expanding its ideology by direct or indirect subversion to other American nations, and thus threatening the inviolability or the integrity of their territory or their sovereignty or political independence.[113]

In summation, what conclusions can be drawn from the pronouncements and practices of the OAS concerning collective efforts to advance democracy in the Western Hemisphere? It should be apparent that Pan-Americanism has placed its major stress upon the principle that a state must be free to choose any form of government or political institution it desires, must be free to treat its own citizens as it wishes, and no other nation or group of nations may interfere in this protected sphere. Since the first stirrings of the movement democracy has been stressed as an inter-American goal, and in recent years many resolutions and declarations have pledged the American nations to political democracy and to the protection of human rights; nevertheless, no firm legal obligations backed by adequate sanctions have been agreed upon to assure the growth of democracy throughout the region.

In actual situations involving contests between democracy and indigenous dictatorships arising before the organization since World War II, little comfort can be found in the actions of the Council of the OAS for those seeking to foster democratic governments and observance of human rights in the Americas. The Council has clearly indicated that whatever collective measures were prescribed, they were taken only for the prevention of the use of force or threats thereof as international instruments of political change and were not related to the characteristics of any internal regime. Collective measures under the Rio Treaty were to be taken against any nation menacing or breaching the peace, without taking into consideration the question of whether the delinquent nation was attempting to foster democracy or totalitarianism. Judging from the Council's action, non-intervention was to be upheld in every circumstance under the assumption that the internal form of government of any state was relatively unimportant to inter-American peace and security; or at least, it was not of sufficient significance to justify collective measures to assure internal democracy.

This staunch maintenance of the absolute right of internal self-determination resulted in the immunity of totalitarian dictatorships from outside pressures for democratic purposes. Yet once the totalitarian government obtained a stranglehold upon the people of a nation, it often embarked upon external aggressive policies that brought with them international conflict, not peace, and immunity from collective intervention became a tool of those who used democratic rights to destroy democracy and international law rights to destroy international law.

While the inter-American system was unwilling to authorize measures to overthrow indigenous dictatorships, in face of the cold war, it did to a limited extent recognize the aggressive nature of international communism as a threat to the peace of the Americas. By the declaration of Caracas it cleared the way for collective measures under the Rio Treaty against an American state dominated by this type of totalitarianism. It should be noted, however, that the loss of democratic values in an American state absorbed by the international communist movement was not the primary motivating force behind the declaration of Caracas. In sponsoring the declaration, the United States stressed that its concern over communist penetration in the hemisphere was based on the requirement of hemispheric security, not on the political color of a national government.

At the behest of the Latin American nations, still too much concerned with non-intervention and too little concerned with the goals of democracy, the declaration of Caracas carefully stated: "This declaration of foreign policy made by the American republics in relation to dangers originating outside this hemisphere, is designated to protect and not to impair the inalienable right of each American state freely to choose its own form of government and economic system and to live its own social and cultural life."[114]

It was maintained that this clause stipulated that each Latin American nation is to continue free from the threat of intervention in the event a local political party should succeed in imposing upon the people a "national" (as distinguished from an "international") brand of communism.[115] This view completely ignores international reality, for a national brand of communism is indeed uncommon.

At the San José Meeting in 1960, it was re-emphasized that international communism was contrary to the democratic principles espoused by the Americas and was a threat to hemispheric peace and security; but even so no sanctions were proposed against the American nation which was linked to the international communist movement. Even the condemnation by those gathered at San José of Sino-Soviet intervention was said by some of the delegates not to be a condemnation of the particular American nation which had invited such intervention. Notwithstanding this attitude, the American nations in the declaration of Caracas did go on record that collective enforcement machinery did exist for action against a regime dominated by international communism. That the American republics did not have the political fortitude to make use of it is another matter. A somewhat greater degree of fortitude was demonstrated at the Punta del Este Meeting; but even here the nations could not agree to bring to bear against Cuba the full collective enforcement measures of the Rio Treaty, but instead resorted to exclusion of the Cuban government from participation in the OAS. Even this measure barely passed. It was subjected to cries of "nay" from many of the important American nations on grounds that it was illegal and not wise politically. Moreover, the action appeared to be taken because a communist government by its subversive activities is a threat to peace, and not necessarily because it is also dictatorial. If action is to be taken to enforce representative democracy in the Americas, there are dictatorships in addition to that of Cuba against which measures should also be directed. Thus, the Punta del Este Meeting sets forth an OAS position of condemnation of dictatorship not because it is dictatorship, but because it is communist dictatorship which endangers the democratic governments of the other republics by spearheading its subversive efforts against them.

But aside from the nondemocratic international communist movement, which due to its subversive and aggressive nature constitutes a special threat to the security of the hemisphere and becomes taboo because it would impose an extracontinental and hostile ideology in violation of the Monroe Doctrine and the treaties governing the inter-American system, in reality the collective advancement of democracy has fared poorly at the hands of the OAS.

A sharp division between the ideal and the real, between official platitudes and official policy, has thus characterized the relationship between democracy and hemispheric unity. The nations of the Americas have proclaimed the lofty goals of democracy, but they have remained for the most part unwilling or unable to implement them. Consequently it would seem that all the inter-American declarations and avowals on democracy are but exercises in futility, frustration, and self-deception.

It is easy to condemn such inconsistency as undesirable, unwholesome, and even immoral. But to do so overlooks the Latin American feeling that the importance of such proclamations lies in the fact that they are anticipatory; that is, they represent the "ought to be" rather than present reality. In this respect the pronouncements must not be underestimated. A group of nations

which has a vision, however hazy, of the path which they wish to travel together
has developed the first essential of a true international community. When the
total inter-American world thus subscribes unhesitatingly to democratic ideals,
the prompt achievement may not be forthcoming, but the dream has some
validity.

Man is, after all, an ideological animal; he acts in accordance with his
innermost convictions. Thus when the nations of the Americas establish, as
they did at Santiago in 1959, an excellent outline of democratic policy which
epitomizes the philosophical and political creed of all the peoples of the Americas, they set forth a goal toward which governments and people should strive.
While the Santiago meeting stopped short of the creation of any new procedures
to secure democracy in nations with despotic governments, and even re-emphasized absolute non-intervention, it did nevertheless set up a standard which
public opinion can use to measure violations of democracy and alert the people
of a nation and the people of the hemisphere to the dangers inherent in those
governments which fail to measure up. This appeal to public opinion, even
without any threat of other action, may at some times and under some circumstances have a compelling effect on governments, either internally by arousing
the people to rise up against the regime, or externally by threatening the loss
of international respect and prestige or some other deference value which may
be of importance.

The Inter-American Peace Committee in effect appealed to the censure of
public opinion when it investigated and condemned the flagrant denial of human
rights by the Trujillo government. The Dominican government complained
bitterly that such investigation and censure were interventionary in character
and in contradiction to the non-intervention principle, even though no enforcement measures followed at the time. While in this case the power to study,
investigate, recommend, and condemn did not have the coercive effect of
compelling the Dominican government to act in accord with the will of the
OAS it was sufficiently disturbing to elicit protests from that government.

Of greater significance was the equating by the Inter-American Peace Committee in the Dominican case of a flagrant denial of human rights and lack
of representative democracy by a local despot with hemispheric tensions and
threats to the peace. The germ of this idea is to be found in the Declaration of
Santiago, where it was said:

That harmony among the American Republics can be effective only insofar as human
rights and fundamental freedoms and the exercise of representative democracy are
a reality within every one of them, since experience has demonstrated that failure
to adhere to such principles is a source of widespread disturbance and gives rise to
emigration that causes frequent and grave political tensions between the state the
emigres leave and the states that receive them;

That the existence of anti-democratic regimes constitutes a violation of principles
on which the Organization of American States is founded, and endangers the living
together in peaceful solidarity in the hemisphere.[116]

It was United States Secretary of State Herter who attempted to bring
the idea to full fruition at the San José meeting in 1960 by showing that

hemispheric tensions and threats to the peace created by denial of human rights and political democracy would permit the application of coercive measures under the Rio Treaty against nations such as the Dominican Republic. To sustain his argument he harked back to the Peace Committee's report which blamed the aggravation of Caribbean tensions upon the widespread violations of human rights in the Dominican Republic and which declared that these tensions would continue and increase so long as such violations persisted. Herter, following the lead of Kant and Rodriguez Larreta, declared that collective measures to obtain respect for human rights and the assurance of democracy were called for to remove threats of aggression and threats to the peace.

Latin America again shied away from this theory, preferring to deal only with the symptoms of the disease and not the disease itself. The states were willing to apply diplomatic and economic sanctions under the Rio Treaty against the Dominican Republic for its international aggressions, but were unwilling to force the Dominican Republic to hold free democratic elections under the control of the OAS. Presumably some nations believed that such sanctions for aggressive action would topple the Dominican dictator without forcing direct action to attain the inter-American goal of democracy. Whether or not the measures had this effect is hard to say. But after Generalissimo Trujillo's assassination the regime did finally fall.

In any event, in recent times a path has been dimly lighted showing that inter-American machinery does exist under the Rio Treaty for multilateral measures to assure democracy inasmuch as hemispheric peace and security have been linked to democracy not only when the democratic principles are violated by international communism, but also when they are violated by an American dictatorship unaffected by extracontinental ideology.

There is great controversy over the issue of whether collective measures should be taken for democracy and over the issue as to whether such measures will always be effective for such a purpose. As of now, the OAS can act only under the Rio Treaty when totalitarianism becomes a threat to hemispheric peace. It may be that this would be too late a moment to take effective action to ensure democracy, for once a dictator is firmly ensconced in power, with all the modern informational facilities at his control, he can force his people to uphold their dictatorial regime in a fit of patriotic and nationalistic fervor against interventionary measures from outside. Another problem is the extent and kind of collective action that should be taken. Diplomatic and economic isolation in themselves alone may not be sufficient. Nations outside the hemisphere, and even some within it, have demonstrated that they are quite willing to fill such a vacuum. Herter's suggestion of requiring the Dominican government to hold free democratic elections under the supervision of the OAS could possibly not have come about without the use of force. Thus it would seem that reliance on coercion in an area such as this would mean in practice a choice between tacit appeasement so that the international situation will not be further aggravated, or collective use of force in order to enforce a principle. By the use of collective force probably a dictator could be removed, a country pacified, human rights secured, and free elections held. But the legal problem which arises here is that the American nations, either individually or through collective action under their regional organization, are prohibited from using armed force by the United Nations Charter except in cases of individual or collective self-defense.[117]

A further criticism of the use of sanctions or collective measures to promote or re-establish democracy is the suffering that may be brought upon the heads of innocent people. This, of course, must be balanced against the suffering they endure under the dictatorship. It is axiomatic that once freedom is lost, tyrants are not to be shaken off again without endless pain.

It is argued that no international organization ought to step in to redress antidemocratic situations because there is no absolute definition of democracy which would enable an organization at all times to judge accurately whether a particular government is or is not democratic, democracy being such an ideal state that even the most democratically inclined nations fail to live up to all of its goals. If the inter-American system were to use all of the high aims expressed in the American Declaration of the Rights and Duties of Man as its standard, this argument might be valid; but the Declaration of Santiago, being more limited and more realistic, established a reasonable standard against which governments can be measured. The inter-American system cannot seek perfection. In trying to secure democracy it cannot demand the realization of the sum total of the democratic ideal or nothing, but must try to introduce into reality as much of the ideal as is possible at any given time. It would be manifestly impossible to correct every deviation from the goals of democracy in the Americas. Under present treaties, the OAS is limited to maintaining continental peace and could take action only in situations where totalitarianism has created international political tensions. The Dominican case has shown that such a situation is readily recognizable.

An entirely separate problem is the feasibility or the possibility of imposing democracy upon a people from without. If democracy is foisted upon a people, foreign and unassimiliated, as a panacea, political penicillin, warranted to cure all social ills, and if it manifestly does not promote stability and public order, then it will fail, leaving the way open for a more compulsive creed such as communism. Democracy grows from decent and capable rulers, a sense of historical achievement, some geographical security from external aggression, a sense of social responsibility, a minimum of mutual confidence between the citizens of the state, and reasonable prosperity. In Latin America, this latter is particularly important, for without prosperity or hope of prosperity democracy cannot function. Therefore in Latin America the fate of democratic institutions is bound up with the continuation of land reform, the integration of the agricultural classes into the state, and economic and social progress. In a society with deep-seated sources of social discontent, extremism cannot be overcome simply by invoking the superior values, moral and political, of democratic government. They have to be demonstrated by action. History teaches that ultimate stability is achieved not by attempting to suppress changes in the established order, but by understanding the underlying forces and imprinting upon the process itself the outlines of the desirable outcome. The task of the OAS, therefore, must be more than just overthrowing a dictator and holding free elections; it must give purposeful direction to the process of change in a newly freed nation instead of leaving it to random fortune or attempting to prevent it. New creative solutions must be found if democratic ideas are effectively to shape the life of this hemisphere. They must become dynamic ideas which are given substance. A more stable continental environment calls for finding ways of influencing the course of social revolution sweeping Latin America, so that when it has run its course the nations will not emerge as totalitarian but rather as nations where democratic values can flourish and society prosper. The task for those who cherish freedom is to develop the capabilities of the Latin American countries for democracy and to see that the possibility of enjoying their economic progress in freedom is left open to them.

But in the immediate sense, when outrageous denials of democratic freedom lead to threats and breaches of inter-American peace, the OAS has a mandate to act. It must utilize all collective measures to remove the threat to the peace caused by antidemocratic regimes, always bearing in mind that care will be required to steer a proper course between excessive zeal and unjustified caution. It is to be hoped that the nations of Latin America will awaken to the fact that the dogma of absolute sovereignty, of non-intervention, is maintained at an incalculable cost to the well-being of the whole hemisphere. No community can be held together for long unless it has some more positive ideal than the maximum of noninterference in the affairs of its members. There must be a minimum of mutual confidence between the nations of the Americas so that they can co-operate freely in seeking democratic goals. The things that unite the American nations are far greater than those that divide them. They can also be far more potent, but the things that unite must become dynamic; the unity must be translated into action.

There is no solution or set of solutions that will effectively and permanently eliminate all oppressive governments from the hemisphere. But if the nations of the Americas are motivated by good will and guided by reason, they can work out piecemeal solutions to the problems of oppressive power as these manifest themselves. Through collective action under the OAS they may be able to enforce a democratic regime in one country, if not in another. Eventually, if the Americas retain both courage and respect for democratic rights, democracy may become secure in all of the nations of the Western Hemisphere. There is no patented solution to the problem. The OAS can seek only to effect running adjustments to work out tentative and even imperfect—because experimental—solutions.

It is impossible to predict with certainty whether the immediate future of the Western Hemisphere lies with democracy or tyranny, but the fundamental cleavages in the world today cannot be compromised or eliminated merely by renewed avowals of dedication to the goals and ideals of democracy and human rights. The American nations must bear in mind that proclamations and declarations alone do not create democracy. Democracy is at the crossroads, and to survive it must be defended by all the potentials of the inter-American community. The lofty but unimplemented statements laid down as hemispheric goals must be backed by the organized power of the inter-American system or they should no longer be considered as inter-American principles. By failing to promote democracy and respect for human rights, by failing to take definitive action for their defense, by creating a wide discrepancy between professed ideals and a willingness to work for those ideals, the inter-American system is merely smoothing the way for antidemocratic alternatives. If democracy is worth defending, it is worth defending now; for the time has come to "suit the action to the word, the word to the action."[118]

BOOK IV

Functions of the OAS

THE INTER-AMERICAN SYSTEM OF PEACE AND SECURITY: HEMISPHERIC COLLECTIVE SECURITY

To aid in the maintenance of the peace of the Western Hemisphere, there has been conferred upon the OAS a power aimed at preventing or removing actual or threatened breaches of the peace through the application of effective measures. This function is nothing more nor less than organized collective security, by which each member of the inter-American community pledges to take certain action against any nation which commits or threatens to commit a breach of the peace. If all member nations fulfil this pledge it should mean protection for a victim of aggression and probable defeat to the aggressor.[1]

The inter-American system took a long time to erect this function, for it was not until the Act of Chapultepec in 1945 that a system of collective security similar to that now in being was fashioned. The Act of Chapultepec, binding only for the remaining months of World War II, contemplated its own replacement by means of a permanent inter-American treaty.[2]

In 1947 such a treaty was concluded with the signing of the Inter-American Treaty of Reciprocal Assistance, more commonly known as the Rio Treaty, at the end of the Inter-American Conference for the Maintenance of Continental Peace and Security.[3] It is this treaty that is the heart of the Western Hemispheric system of collective security. The Charter of Bogotá incorporates it by reference in Article 25 and perhaps modifies it slightly, but does not repeat its detailed provisions.[4] The treaty has as its legal basis certain provisions of the United Nations Charter which grant a limited competence for the maintenance of peace and security to regional organizations such as the OAS. It is therefore subject to the regional arrangement stipulations of Articles 52-54 of the Charter of the United Nations, and its provisions also fall within the scope of the right of individual and collective self-defense under Article 51 of that Charter.[5]

ACTION IN THE EVENT OF AN ARMED ATTACK

The Rio Treaty distinguishes the obligations to be undertaken and the procedures to be followed in the event of an armed attack and the obligations to be undertaken and the procedures to be followed in the event of other acts of aggression or potential threats to continental peace.[6] Article 3 of the treaty is concerned with action in the event of an armed attack. After reiterating the principle that an armed attack against an American state constitutes an attack against all the American states, it declares that each of the contracting parties undertakes to assist in meeting the attack in the exercise of the inherent right of individual or collective self-defense recognized by Article 51 of the Charter of the United Nations. If the attack occurs within a security zone outlined in Article 4, or within the territory of an American state, each signatory is bound to take, at the specific request of the state attacked, such individual measures as it may deem appropriate to fulfil its obligations to help meet the attack until collective measures have been agreed upon. An Organ of Consultation is to meet as quickly as possible to determine the collective measures to be taken.[7] The concluding paragraph of Article 3 recognizes that the defensive measures to be employed in the case of armed attack within the region or within the territory of an American state are limited by Article 51 of the United Nations Charter; that is to say, they may operate only until the Security Council has acted to maintain or re-establish peace, and all measures resorted to by the OAS under the Rio Treaty must be reported to the Security Council.

While Article 3 of the Rio Treaty is highly significant, in certain of its aspects it is obscure and its meaning unclear.

The Right of Self-Defense

Article 3 is an outcropping of the concept of an inherent right of self-defense which is mentioned by Article 51 of the United Nations Charter and which has always been recognized at general international law as a special and necessary form of self-help. Neither the Rio Treaty nor the United Nations Charter illuminates the exact contours of this inherent right of self-defense, and at general international law there have been conflicting opinions as to when the right arises.

Some authorities would limit the exercise of this right to a situation of protection against an actual illegitimate attack or when such an attack is apparently imminently impending.[8] Following this line of authority self-defense is self-help against a specific violation of the law, against the illegal use of force, not against other violations of the law. It is the use of force by a person (in municipal law) or by a state (in international law) illegally attacked by another. The attack against which self-defense is permitted must have been made or must be intended to be made by force. As such, self-defense is that minimum of self-help which, even within a system of collective security based on a centralized force monopoly of the community, must be permitted. It is recognized by national law as applicable to individuals and by international law as applicable to nations. It is impossible for any system, national or international, to prevent all illegal attacks upon its subjects, and in case of such an attack if the attacked subject were always required to wait for the enforcement authorities to take action, he would be doomed.

This restricted viewpoint outlines the prerequisites of legitimate self-defense as follows: the armed attack, actual or impending, must be objectively illegal; the state exercising the right of self-defense must show a direct and immediate danger; the act of self-defense must not be excessive, going no farther than to avert or suppress the attack; and it must not be continued after the needs of defense have been met.[9]

It is possible, however, to view self-defense at international law as wider in its scope, and some authorities do not restrict the right as against illegal use of force only, but extend it to other delinquencies where it is exercised in a preventive and nonretributive manner. It is claimed that a state may legitimately resort to the right of self-defense for its protection when its essential rights are endangered by delictual conduct of another state. The danger to these rights must be unlawful; it must be serious and actual or so imminent that the necessity to resort to self-defense is instant and overwhelming. In additon the exercise of the right is conditioned upon an absence of other lawful means of protection, and the measures used must be reasonable, limited to averting the illegal danger to the safety of the wronged state and proportionate to that danger.[10]

This broader approach leans heavily upon the conception that international law is at present an immature law lacking a centralized law enforcement machinery, and consequently such a legal system must permit a large measure of unilateral action for the protection against illegal violation of those legal rights which are necessary for the security of the state. For if the international enforcement machinery cannot safeguard such rights, either at all or in an expeditious and prompt manner, the subject of the legal system must be empowered to protect them by its own action. When international society matures to a point where centralized machinery is available and efficacious for securing the rights of its subjects, then the right of self-defense should be circumscribed to a point where it can be considered as legitimate only to avert and to protect against an illegal use of force which is permitted as of necessity by the most developed legal systems.[11]

The United Nations Charter imposes the obligation on the members of that organization "to refrain in their international relations from the threat or use of force against the territorial integrity or political independence of any state, or in any other manner inconsistent with the Purposes of the United Nations."[12] The Rio Treaty reiterates the obligation of the American states "not to resort to the threat or use of force in any manner inconsistent with the provision of the Charter of the United Nations or of this treaty."[13] Both instruments, however, do permit the use of force with reference to the inherent right of individual and collective self-defense at least until the Security Council takes the necessary steps to re-establish international peace, but both of these instruments, while speaking in terms of "inherent right of self-defense," also refer to it only in terms of action against armed attack. This gives rise to the question of whether these treaties seek to define the inherent right of self-defense narrowly by limiting it to instances of armed attack.

It can be maintained that if self-defense is "inherent" it is inalienable, incapable of being surrendered—a natural right. If it is incapable of being surrendered in whole, it can be reasoned that it is incapable of being surrendered in part; therefore in spite of the seeming limitation imposed by these two treaties, if it is truly inherent the right of self-defense can still be resorted to wherever it is permitted under general international law.

Nevertheless, some jurists are of the opinion that the right of self-defense under the United Nations Charter is limited to action after an armed attack has occurred.[14] It has been pointed out that the use of the word "inherent" is unfortunate, for it equates self-defense with an unalterable natural right. The answer to this may be that the word "inherent" as used is of little significance legally speaking, for after using the word the United Nations Charter is not reverent of its legal meaning but apparently seeks to alter and change the general international law significance of self-defense. Moreover, it is contended that in municipal law self-defense is also spoken of as a natural and thus unalterable right, but at the same time the positive law often does alter and change its meanings.[15] These jurists conclude that the United Nations Charter does alter the right of self-defense as it existed at general international law, restricting it to instances where there has actually been an armed attack by an aggressor, and neither an imminent armed attack nor other violation of a state's legally protected interests is thought sufficient to invoke the right under Article 51.

Issue has been taken with this severely limited view of the right of self-defense on the grounds that Charter interpretation does not necessarily warrant such a circumscribed conclusion.[16] To the contrary, it is contended that the United Nations Charter does not change the right of self-defense as it existed at international law; hence, until the Security Council takes measures to maintain international peace and security, a member state is still free to take action, inclusive of the use of force, for its own security and protection on its own volition not only against an armed attack, but also against an imminent attack, as well as against violations of a state's other essential legal interests.[17]

It is reasoned that Article 51 is only a declaratory article designed to preserve the right of self-defense, not to limit it, and containing no additional obligations.[18] It is then maintained that Article 2(4), the relevant article of obligation here, is not inconsistent with the traditional right of self-defense, for interim measures taken by a state to protect and defend its vital legal rights cannot be considered—even when involving a threat or use of force—as being taken against the territorial integrity or political independence of the state committing the delict or inconsistent with the purposes of the United Nations.[19] From a more practical point of view, it is pointed out that the political necessities of modern international life force a recognition by general international law, as well as the international law of the United Nations Charter, of a right of self-defense of broader scope, for to limit such right to armed attack in the absence of a truly effective collective security system could well circumscribe the legal right of a state to protect against its own destruction. A state can hardly be expected to wait for this actual attack in the face of imminent threat thereof, for if it did so the state might be so paralyzed by the attack that it could no longer render resistance. Nor can it be expected to sit idly by in the face of other types of aggression and illegal acts which jeopardize its security with no legal right to resort to self-defense.[20]

Actually the best that can be said about the right of self-defense under Article 51 is that it is susceptible of varying interpretations; the wording of the United Nations Charter pertaining to this right is both ambiguous and confusing. Armed self-defense is definitely permitted against an armed attack, but the picture is hazy as to whether self-defense is permitted against other illegal acts.

The Rio Treaty sheds no other clarifying light on the meaning of the "inherent" right of self-defense. Article 3 merely acknowledges that such a right exists. It can be asserted that the restrictive viewpoint governs in the OAS, in which case it would be hard to establish legal justification for any action taken by an American state on the broader general international law theory of self-defense. For example, the Report of the Investigating Committee of the Organ of Consultation concerned with the Haiti–Dominican Republic Affair stated:

Furthermore, the Committee is convinced that the treaties and agreements in force among the American States, in assuring the integrity of these States and their defense in case of any aggression, have established the measures and the organs required to meet the needs of collective self-defense; and it is evident that the American States have formally condemned war and have undertaken to submit every controversy which may arise between them to methods of peaceful settlement. The Committee holds, therefore, that the attitude of any *American Government resorting to the threat or the use of force, even on grounds of self-defense,* in any manner inconsistent with the provisions of the Charter of the United Nations, the Rio de Janeiro Treaty, and the Charter of the Organization of American States, and without having made every reasonable attempt at peaceful settlement, constitutes a violation of the essential norms of inter-American relationships.[21] [Italics supplied.]

In the face of an impending or imminent attack or other illegal acts, there would in many instances be opportunity for further attempts at peaceful settlement; and certainly the right of self-defense under this interpretation cannot be utilized as a provocation. Moreover, in cases where there is not an actual armed attack, even where the danger is direct and immediate, Article 6 of the Rio Treaty permits a state to request the Organ of Consultation to meet to take action to assist it where the inviolability or integrity of its territory, its sovereignty, or its political independence is affected by an act of agression other than an armed attack, any extracontinental or intracontinental conflict, or any other fact or situation that might endanger the peace of the Americas.

The Report of the Investigating Committee presupposes that an inter-American collective security system able to protect the rights of the member states has come into existence, thus permitting curtailment of the traditional right of self-defense. If such an effective organization is in being it can hardly be reasoned that a state would be justified in taking matters into its own hands, using armed force to precipitate conflict for the protection of its essential legal rights. But it must be remembered that the right of self-defense is conditioned upon an absence of alternative means for the protection of vital rights of the state which are endangered. If the organized security system is capable of protecting those rights, self-defense may not be legally exercised. It would, however, be indeed optimistic to believe that given today's hemispheric conditions the inter-American community is capable of defending all such rights in every circumstance. It is legally empowered to act in cases of armed attack, and where the inviolability or the integrity of the territory or the sovereignty or political independence of an American state is affected by any aggression or by other situations that endanger the peace of the Americas. Whether it will always act so as to defend a victim state is problematical, and whether it can always act quickly enough, particularly in the face of an imminent armed attack or even an insidious form of subversive intervention, is even more problematical. There is even some question whether the OAS is legally empowered to protect all rights of a state essential to its security. Confronted with such a situation it would be a dubious conclusion to say that the member states of the OAS have accepted an interpretation of the right of self-defense under the Rio Treaty which restricts their right to protect themselves to protection solely against an armed attack.

The Right of Collective Self-Defense

Article 3, paragraph 1, grants a right of individual self-defense to a state or states subjected to an armed attack,[22] and also confers a right of collective self-defense upon the states which have ratified the Rio Treaty. At the same time it imposes upon such states an obligation, under certain conditions, to take measures to assist the injured party in the exercise of the inherent right of collective self-defense.

An obligation of collective self-defense comes into being in two stages under the Rio Treaty. When an armed attack is launched within the territory of an American state or within the security zone established by the treaty, the contracting parties have not only a right but also a duty to take measures to assist in meeting the attack upon request for aid by the victim. The requirement that aid must be requested by the injured party was included in the treaty to prevent possible simulated aggression which might occur under the guise of conferring aid upon a victim of a supposed attack.[23]

In this preliminary stage following attack and a request for aid, each state is free to determine the immediate action which it will individually take, although the obligation to assist in some way is entirely clear. In the selection of measures to be taken at this time, the states are limited to those listed in Article 8, that is, diplomatic or economic measures or the use of armed force.[24] The nature, time, and extent of the immediate measures is left to the complete discretion of each party.

The second stage of collective self-defense begins with the convening of the Organ of Consultation, which is enjoined to meet without delay to examine the immediate measures of assistance which have been taken by the individual states and to agree upon collective measures to be taken. Under the Rio Treaty the consultation was originally to be initiated by a request of a ratifying state to the Governing Board (now the Council).[25] This procedure has been modified by the Charter of Bogotá, which requires a meeting to be called immediately by the Chairman of the Council in the event of armed attack within the territory of an American state or within the security zone.[26] In this more advanced stage, the obligation is placed upon the member states to consult in order to agree upon collective measures. Thus, the Rio Treaty places a double obligation upon the signatories, that of individual assistance and that of consultation. After the Organ of Consultation agrees upon collective measures, the parties are obligated to comply with its decision,[27] although the measures which each state is required to take need not be of the same type and nature for all the American states.[28] This decision on the collective measures ends the duty of the parties to take individual measures, but it would not terminate the right of the victim state or the member states to continue to take such measures in the exercise of the right of individual and collective self-defense—the right to continuing collective self-defense actions, of course, being dependent upon a continued request for assistance from the victim. Such measures would be in addition to those measures ordered by the consultative organ.[29]

In this consultation on collective measures, decisions are to be taken by a two-thirds vote[30] which is binding on all parties including those not concurring, except that no state is required to use armed force without its consent.[31] In other words, a party to the Rio Treaty may be required to take part in a number of specific steps, such as complete interruption of economic relations with the aggressor, even though it did not originally favor such action. It may not, however, be required under the treaty to use armed force without its consent. Nevertheless, if the Organ of Consultation decides that the situation necessitates the use of armed force as a measure of collective self-defense, each member state has the legal right, although not the duty, to use armed force.

Collective self-defense as sanctioned by Article 51 of the United Nations Charter is a term which has caused considerable controversy. By some it is considered a new term of international law; it is thought that it is not collective self-defense but collective defense—that is, that the Charter recognizes that a state subjected to attack has a right of self-defense and that other states have a right to come to its assistance.[32] If it is a new principle the right can hardly be called "inherent." It would only be considered inherent because the Charter bestows upon it the characteristics and requisites of being inherent.

But it can be reasoned that collective self-defense means no more than it means at general international law, i.e., that two or more states can take collective action in the right of self-defense when each has an individual right of self-defense.[33] For example, if state A has illegally attacked or otherwise invaded legally protected interests of states B and C, both could react in self-defense and the reaction could be in concert—collective self-defense. This of course presumes that both states have been direct victims of the delictual conduct. If only state B has been directly subjected, can state C ever aid state B in a right of self-defense, or would this be merely collective defense? To act in accord with self-defense, state C would have to show some legal interest of its own invaded by the action of state A. Within the concept of self-defense at municipal law there is recognized a limited right and a duty to protect others where a close relationship or kinship exists between certain parties, for example the members of one's household, or where some special family relationship exists with the person defended. Extending this concept into the field of international law by analogy,[34] the conclusion can be drawn that a state would be acting in self-defense when it defended another state having a legal right of self-defense where there existed a close relationship based on solidarity, for the legal interests of both would be violated. If the security of a group of states is dependent in fact upon the security of each and every one of them, a violation of the rights of any one of the group would be a violation of the rights of all, permitting joint effort for protection. Thus, it can be reasoned that the United Nations Charter takes notice of the close integration and solidarity between certain nations and simply incorporates the concept of international law that each state has a legal right in the security of the actual victim; therefore, an aggression against one is equivalent to an aggression on the other nations integrated with it.

Since Article 51 of the United Nations Charter speaks of the right of individual and collective self-defense in the same context and without defining either, it could be presumed that the legal meaning of collective self-defense would be similar to the meaning of individual self-defense under general international law, but the collective concept has created certain problems of its own.

It is often assumed that the exercise of the right of self-defense involves the use of physical force to repel an illegal attack.[35] Does collective self-defense connote the use of armed force only? If so, measures taken against the delict which do not involve the use of armed force should not properly be labeled self-defense. If this is so, under the Rio Treaty it becomes erroneous to speak of an obligation of collective self-defense either at the preliminary stage when resort is to be had to individual measures or at the secondary stage when the Organ of Consultation decides on collective measures, for in neither stage are the American republics bound to use armed force. The Rio Treaty would then only establish a right, as distinguished from a duty, of collective self-defense.

An interpretation which equates collective self-defense only with the retaliatory use of armed force creates difficulties and confusion, for the possibility exists that such construction would prevent the OAS and its members from using measures of a nature less than armed force, e.g., economic or diplomatic measures, inasmuch as the United Nations Charter declares that only measures of collective self-defense and no other collective enforcement measures may be taken by members of the United Nations and regional organizations without Security Council approval. The requirement of such prior approval might well rule out all unarmed collective measures if those other measures are considered to be enforcement measures.[36]

Although the classic example of self-defense is a meeting of force with force, still there would appear to be no reason why the defending state cannot react with lesser measures not involving force if the state is acting to protect its rights and is not taking punitive or retributive action in the form of sanctions or reprisals.[37] Although the meaning of collective self-defense is not clear under the United Nations Charter, under the Rio Treaty collective self-defense includes not only armed force but also other measures of an economic and diplomatic character as set forth in Article 8 of that treaty. Article 3 declares that in the preliminary stage the parties may determine the *immediate measures* to be taken in fulfilment of the obligation of collective self-defense. Thereafter the Organ of Consultation shall meet to agree on *measures of a collective character* that should be taken. Article 8 lists the collective measures which the Organ of Consultation may use, including the recall of chiefs of diplomatic missions; breaking of diplomatic relations; breaking of consular relations; partial or complete interruption of economic relations or of rail, sea, air, postal, telegraphic, telephonic, and radiotelephonic or radiotelegraphic communications; and the use of armed force. Therefore, it is apparent that the measures other than the use of armed force are considered by the Rio Treaty as measures of collective self-defense.

When the prerequisites for the application of collective self-defense arise all collective measures, whether by armed force or otherwise, must be considered measures of collective self-defense, and their use must be legitimate under Article 51 of the Charter of the United Nations and Article 3 of the Rio Treaty until the Security Council acts by taking measures necessary to maintain or restore international peace and security. Thus, under the Rio Treaty there is an obligatory duty of collective self-defense at both stages, for the parties are immediately required to take some measures and thereafter the Organ of Consultation must agree upon the measures of a collective character to be taken, this decision being binding upon the parties with the sole exception that no state shall be required to use armed force without its consent.

Article 51 of the United Nations Charter and Article 3 of the Rio Treaty speak in terms of armed attack for an exercise of the right of individual and collective self-defense. General international law adds a further qualification— self-defense is to be exercised against an illegal act or omission attributable to a state. Hence, the adjective "illegal" must be added before "armed attack," i.e., self-defense is justified against illegal use of force. This element of illegality, although not specifically stated in either the United Nations Charter or the Rio Treaty, must nevertheless be applied in those documents. The right of individual or collective self-defense cannot be exercised against a *legal* use of force.[38] From the very purposes of the United Nations, a right of self-defense cannot exist against a legal enforcement action by that organization.[39] Should that body be forced to resort to armed force against a recalcitrant nation, such action is the action of the international community against which self-defense is not allowed. The same is equally true of a legitimate use of force as a measure of collective self-defense or enforcement by the members of the OAS upon a valid decision of the consultative organ or, in the first stage of collective self-defense, when one American state comes to the aid of another which is the victim of the armed attack.

Article 9 of the Rio Treaty declares that an unprovoked armed attack by a state against the territory, the people, or the land, sea, or air forces of another state may be characterized as an aggression. The use of the term "unprovoked" is unfortunate, for by reading Article 9 in conjunction with Article 3 one might come to the conclusion that no right of self-defense exists if one state provokes another state to the point of armed attack, for in that case the provoked state would not be an aggressor. This is not the fact. The United Nations Charter prohibits the use of force except under Article 51. Neither a provoked nor an unprovoked state has a right to use force unless the state is provoked to such use in the right of self-defense by the delictual conduct of another state. The use of force except in pursuance of a right of self-defense is illegal.[40]

Article 9 of the Rio Treaty, in setting out acts which in addition to others may be characterized as aggressions, lists the following:

a. Unprovoked armed attack by a state against the territory, the people, or the land, sea, or air forces of another state.

b. Invasion, by the armed forces of a state, of the territory of an American state, through the trespassing of boundaries demarcated in accordance with a treaty, judicial decision, or arbitral award, or, in the absence of frontiers thus demarcated, invasion affecting a region which is under the effective jurisdiction of another state.

This language indicates that the attack must be made by a state directed against the territory, people, or armed forces of another state.[41] This might raise a question of whether or not an attack on a merchant vessel or a civil aircraft could be equated to aggression, since Article 9 mentions various branches of the armed services. But such attacks could clearly be armed attacks or aggression; for Article 9 does not claim to be exclusive, as it states that these listed acts "in addition to other acts" may be characterized as aggression.[42]

As in the case of individual self-defense, Article 51 of the United Nations Charter and Article 3 of the Rio Treaty would appear to limit the exercise of collective self-defense to instances of armed attack.[43] And it can be maintained that collective self-defense under the Charter is so limited; that collective self-defense did not exist at general international law; that it is created and made inherent by the Charter; and that therefore the agency which created the right can restrict it and has restricted it to armed attack only.

As has been noted in the discussion of individual self-defense, this viewpoint has been questioned. It is argued that Article 51 does not restrict the right of self-defense as known at general international law, and that Article 2(4) does not prohibit the use of force or threat thereof when used properly in self-defense, i.e., to defend or protect the vital legal interests of a state. If the term collective self-defense does no more than recognize that the parties may exercise collectively that which is their individual right, that it does not create new rights, then it, like individual self-defense, is not limited, but may be exercised jointly by the community when each of the members thereof is subjected directly to a violation of its rights, or when the members have a legal right in the security of the actual victim because of a proximate relationship.[44] Such a thesis may be justified under the Rio Treaty, for that treaty permits the use of force to be ordered by the consultative agencies not only in cases of armed attack, but also in situations not involving armed attack— for example, in instances of aggressions which are not armed attack and in other situations affecting the peace of the Americas.[45] Since force is presumed to be a monopoly of the United Nations, except in the case of self-defense, it would appear that self-defense may be broader in concept and not confined solely to armed attack. Moreover, a wider scope for collective self-defense is recognized by the later juridical instrument, the Charter of Bogotá. The Charter of Bogotá returns to the language of the Act of Chapultepec of 1945 and declares in Article 5(f): "An act of aggression against one American State is an act of aggression against all the other American States." Again in Article 24 it is stated: "Every act of aggression by a State against the territorial integrity or the inviolability of the territory or against the sovereignty or political independence of an American State shall be considered an act of aggression against the other American States." And further, Article 25 calls for the application of measures and procedures established in special treaties in case of such aggression or in other facts or situations that endanger the peace of America and affect the inviolability or the integrity of the territory or the sovereignty or political independence of an American state. Such language sounds like collective self-defense and is certainly more extensive than "armed attack." Hence, it can be argued that when the members through the OAS are acting collectively to defend their legal rights vital to their continental solidarity and security, they are exercising the right of self-defense.

Self-defense in municipal law, as well as in international law, is not designed to enforce or vindicate the law. It is not meant to be a form of self-help to punish the aggressor or obtain reparation. It is not remedial in character. It serves to repel an attack or to protect certain essential legal rights—to avert or repel an unlawful danger to those rights. As such, general international law requires that it not go beyond the necessity to avert the danger or suppress the attack and that it must cease after the needs of defense have been met. There is no reason why these requirements of proportionality and the restrictions against unreasonableness and excessiveness should not apply to the right of self-defense under the United Nations Charter and the Rio Treaty.[46] But the wording of these instruments is vague on this point.

As self-defense is permitted against any illegal armed attack, the right could be claimed and exercised against a frontier incident of small import.[47] Furthermore, since no limitation is presented in either treaty, the force used as a repellant in the exercise of the right of self-defense might well be excessive in relation to the attack or delict which acted as the catalyst, and this excessiveness might of itself bring about serious hostilities. It may also be possible for self-defense to go beyond a repulse of the attack. Article 3 of the Rio Treaty not only permits but also requires measures to be taken upon the occasion of an armed attack until the Consultative Organ agrees upon collective measures. These measures may in each instance include the use of armed force. Even after the Consultative Organ agrees to the collective measures, each state may continue taking measures of individual and collective self-defense including the use of armed force, for the right of self-defense is not terminated by the decision of the Organ of Consultation. Furthermore, the Organ of Consultation may decide that armed force is the collective measure that must be taken. Then each American state has a right, although not a duty, to use armed force until the Security Council of the United Nations has taken measures to maintain or restore international peace and security. If the action of the Security Council is paralyzed, as by use of the veto power, for example, then it would seem that the measures of self-defense may continue indefinitely. If requirements of reasonableness, proportionality, and nonexcessiveness are removed, the right of individual and collective self-defense may degenerate into a major war.

Despite these possible defects surrounding the exercise of the right of self-defense, some improvement has been made in the right established by the United Nations Charter and the Rio Treaty over the right as it existed at general international law, for at general international law the final decision as to whether self-defense is exercised legally within principles surrounding its legitimate exercise often rests with the unilateral will of the individual state. Under the Charter and the Rio Treaty, a state resorting to self-defense does not possess the legal faculty of remaining the ultimate judge of the justification of its actions. Individual states as well as fellow treaty signers have the right, upon request of the victim, to decide in the first instance whether they are in the presence of a situation calling for armed resistance, but this right is subject to some control and their actions are accountable to a higher authority. Without doubt the Organ of Consultation of the OAS may determine whether or not there has been a legitimate use of the right of self-defense, and if it decides in the negative it could issue a call for a cessation of hostilities. If this is disobeyed, the Organ of Consultation could order measures to be taken against the state or states acting illegally under color of the right of self-defense. Even if the Organ of Consultation should find that there has been a legitimate use of the right of self-defense, the Security Council of the United Nations can also pass judgment on whether recourse to the right of self-defense was justified by the circumstances and whether the extent of the action was warranted. Nevertheless, its judgment, even if handed down by a majority of members, could be valueless if one of the veto-bearing nations chose to overrule the decision of the majority. Under such circumstances the regional organization and the member states thereof could continue to exercise the right of self-defense.

Geographical Limitations

Article 3 of the Rio Treaty makes no distinction in principle between an armed attack from inside the Western Hemisphere and an armed attack from without the Hemisphere.[48] Article 3 refers to all cases of armed attack against an American state, without differentiating between an American and a non-American aggressor. Nevertheless, Article 3 does require that when resort is to be had to its procedures and obligations the armed attack must occur within certain geographical limits, no matter whether it originated from an American or a non-American source. The first paragraph of this article is generous in stating that an armed attack by any state against an American state shall be considered as an attack against all the American states which will bring into being the right of individual and collective self-defense. Paragraph 3 of this article declares that the provisions of Article 3 are to be applied in case of any armed attack which takes place within the region described in Article 4 or within the territory of an American state, but when the attack takes place outside these areas, the provisions of Article 6 shall be applied.

The language employed leads to the conclusion that the provisions of Article 3 are applicable when an armed attack by any state occurs against the territory, the people, the armed forces, etc., of an American state within the region described in Article 4. This region may be said to correspond with what the contracting parties believe to be the Western Hemisphere. However, an attack by any state against the territory of an American state outside the hemispheric security zone also brings into operation the procedures, the rights, and the duties of Article 3. An attack against Hawaii, for example, which lies outside the security zone but which is the territory of an American state, would come under the provisions of Article 3. It should be stressed that under this latter type of situation, where the attack takes place outside the described region, it must be directed against the *territory* of an American state. An attack of another nature outside the security zone will not come under Article 3, but will fall under Article 6.

When speaking of an attack against an American state, Article 3 makes no distinction between American states which are members of the Organization of American States and those which are not members. In all instances, measures of collective self-defense are to be taken by the ratifying states. An American state such as Canada receives certain benefits under this Article even though it is not a member of the OAS and even though it has not signed the Rio Treaty. If Canada were subjected to armed attack arising against its territory or within the security zone, it could request the other American states as ratifiers of the Rio Treaty to come to its aid. And there is an obligation on the part of the other American states immediately to take measures to aid this nonmember victim and to consult and agree on further collective measures to be taken against the aggressor.[49]

The region described in Article 4 covers the territory of some non-American states and vast stretches of the seas surrounding the Western Hemisphere. As paragraph 3 of Article 3 declares that the provisions of that article are to be applied in the case of *any* armed attack which takes place within the delineated security zone, there has arisen the question of whether the obligation of collective self-defense by the contracting parties to the Rio Treaty arises when a non-American state is subjected to an armed attack within this region; e.g., would an armed attack against a European colony in the Western Hemisphere call Article 3 of the Rio Treaty into play?

There can be little dispute that an armed attack within the described region creates a special hazard to the peace and security of the continent and to all the American states which are members of the OAS, whether that attack occurs against an American or a non-American state. Consequently, the position has been taken that an armed attack within the region against a nonmember or a non-American state brings into operation the obligations and procedures of Article 3.[50] Little difficulty is realized in reconciling this view with general international law or with Article 51 of the United Nations Charter. Under general international law, it has long been recognized that parties to a treaty can confer benefits upon third states not signatory to the document. Moreover, under Article 51, there is no requirement that collective self-defense be based upon a treaty arrangement. If collective self-defense is equated with collective defense, then under Article 51 whenever a state is illegally attacked by an armed force it has a right of self-defense, and other states have a right to come to its assistance. Such an interpretation would obviously permit the contracting American states to come legally to the assistance of a non-American state under illegal armed attack. On the other hand, if collective self-defense means that there is a close integration between certain nations so that an attack on one amounts to an attack on others integrated with it, then, under Article 51, the integrated nations can come to the assistance of the attacked state to preserve their own integrity and to exercise their own right of self-defense. Under this interpretation of collective self-defense, the American states could act to aid a non-American state attacked within the region even if they had not previously provided by treaty that an attack against all states, American or non-American, within the region would be equivalent to an attack against all of the contracting parties. All that would be required would be an integration or interdependence between the nations, and the fact that a non-American state had territory within the designated security zone would seem to be sufficient proof of such integration, permitting assistance by the American states.[51]

Although such a line of reasoning seems to remove any possible obstacle to American collective self-defense to aid a non-American victim of an illegal act of aggression within the region, difficulties are still encountered with the terminology of Article 3, which in some respects fails to make clear the intention of the contracting parties.

In the first place, paragraph 1 of Article 3 declares that an armed attack by any state against an American state is an attack against all the American states, and in such event the parties to the Rio Treaty agree to assist in meeting the attack in the exercise of the right of individual or collective self-defense. This language would seem to limit the right of self-defense insofar as the Rio Treaty is concerned to an attack against an *American* state. It can be argued that the broad language of paragraph 3 of Article 3 which covers *any armed attack* which takes place within the region must be read in conjunction with paragraph 1; that is, that *any* armed attack refers only to an armed attack against the territory of an American state within the region or against the people or the land, sea, or air forces of an American state. Such an interpretation would lead to a construction that Article 3 is not applicable in case of an attack against a non-American state unless the attack took place against the people or the forces of an American state within the territory of a non-American state, e.g., if it were an attack against the United States forces in Greenland. Under this approach an attack against the territory of a non-American state within the region, or an attack against the people or forces of a non-American state within the region (e.g., upon a British battleship within the region) would not bring the provisions of Article 3 into operation.

Another semantic difficulty encountered here is that paragraph 2 of Article 3 requires that the preliminary measures of collective self-defense be subject to a request from the state or states directly attacked. If the words "State or States" relate back to paragraph 1, then it must mean only American state or states, and it is questionable if a non-American state could under such interpretation request and obligate American states to take immediate collective measures.

Of course the language of the treaty permits a meeting of the Organ of Consultation in the case of an armed attack against a non-American state within the region, for paragraph 2 calls for such a meeting without delay to agree upon measures of a collective character, and Article 43 of the Charter of Bogotá (the primary constitutional instrument of the OAS) specifically requires the chairman of the Council to call such a meeting immediately in the case of an armed attack within the territory of an American state or within the region of security. The calling of such a meeting is not contingent upon the request of an American state.

In view of these obstacles raised by the wording of the Rio Treaty, it would seem that for measures of collective self-defense to be taken on behalf of a non-American state under the treaty, paragraph 3 of Article 3, referring to *any* armed attack within the region, materially modifies the first two paragraphs of the article to the extent that an armed attack against any state within the region, be it American or non-American, must be considered as an attack against all. This would support the conclusion that the phrase "on the request of the State or States directly attacked" signifies either an American or a non-American state.

Jurists have reached the conclusion that Article 3 is applicable in the event of an attack against a non-American state within the region;[52] nevertheless, it must be admitted that the intention of the parties was imperfectly expressed and argument can be made pro or con either view. The best that can be said is that Article 3 is subject to varying interpretations in this respect, and no definite answer can be forthcoming until the consultative organ clearly defines its powers upon presentation of an actual case.

Article 3 does create a limitation, geographical in nature, on its operation, for it does not apply to armed attack outside the security zone and outside the territory of an American state. This limitation was based upon the idea that an armed attack outside the region and not on the territory of an American state would not create such an immediate and direct danger to the hemisphere as to require individual assistance by all the American nations prior to consultation. As has been stated in this connection:

Outside the zone armed attack, which would necessarily be upon the land, air, or sea forces of an American state, would allow time for consultation, as would be true in cases that are not armed attack, but other types of aggression or threat of aggression, and consequently for agreement upon measures *that should be taken to assist the victim of the aggression.* There is a practical reason for this conclusion: the American states may have, and in fact some do have, international military obligations in zones far distant from their own mainland or island possessions, and may find themselves involved in incidents whose gravity cannot be determined at first, even by the state that has apparently suffered the aggression. There it could happen that a mistaken interpretation of the facts would lead the other American states to offer assistance that would be out of proportion to the gravity of the incident, and that might even be greater than the state directly attacked would expect. Or it might happen that an incident initially thought to be of minor importance, even by the state attacked, would become a much more serious threat, which could not be evaluated except by a formal explanation of the facts to the other states bound by solidarity. Prior consultation is obligatory in that case, and the Treaty made it so. Armed attack within the geographical security zone, on the other hand, does not present that uncertainty, in the first place; in the second place, it is so great a threat to collective security that, without prejudice to the procedures later outlined in consultation, it would be necessary to take individual measures immediately in defense of the victim.[53] [Emphasis added.]

The geographical limitation is not of great moment. It does relieve the contracting parties of the obligation of collective self-defense in the preliminary stage, i.e., of the duty to take immediate individual measures to aid the victim upon the victim's request. The right of individual self-defense still exists for the state subjected to the attack outside the zone; the right of collective self-defense in the preliminary stage would still exist if other American nations chose to take action to aid the victim of armed aggression; and both a right and a duty of collective self-defense arise at the next stage of collective activity, for Article 6 of the Rio Treaty requires an immediate meeting of the Organ of Consultation to agree on measures which must be taken to assist the victim of an aggression. These measures may legally include the use of armed force or measures of an economic or diplomatic nature, and the signatory states are bound to take the measures so prescribed, except that no state can be required to use armed force against its will.

ACTION IN THE EVENT OF OTHER SITUATIONS WHICH MAY ENDANGER THE PEACE

The second type of situation contemplated by the Rio Treaty is concerned with an act of aggression which is not an armed attack, an extracontinental or intracontinental conflict, or other fact or situation that might endanger the peace of America, provided that such aggression, conflict, fact, or situation affects the inviolability, or the integrity of the territory, or the sovereignty or political independence of any American state. When such situation arises, under Article 6, the Organ of Consultation shall meet immediately in order to agree upon the measures which must be taken in the case of aggression to assist the victim of the aggression, or, in any case, the measures which should be taken for the common defense and for the maintenance of the peace and security of the continent.

Under the Charter of the United Nations, collective self-defense is not limited to regional arrangements for it stands by itself in Article 51, which stipulates that "nothing ... shall impair the inherent right of ... collective self-defense if an armed attack occurs ...." Although the Rio Treaty was drawn up mainly with reference to Article 51, it must be remembered that it is also an integral part of a regional arrangement and must conform with provisions of Articles 52-54 of the United Nations Charter.[54] Article 51 permits collective and individual self-defense in the case of armed attack, but the Rio Treaty also provides for measures against aggressions which are not armed attack. If the restrictive viewpoint is taken that self-defense is limited to armed attack, then in case of aggression which is not an armed attack, the Organization of American States is not free to take those measures in the exercise of collective self-defense which it would be free to take in cases of aggression that constitute an armed attack. The use of force in the event of an aggression would be a prerogative of the United Nations and not of the inter-American system except with respect to the right of self-defense against armed aggression.

Take the following hypothetical case as an example. American state A complains to the Council of the Organization of American States that American state B is in the process of committing an aggression against A which does not consist of an armed attack but which threatens the inviolability or the integrity of the territory or sovereignty or political independence of A. Under the Rio Treaty all signatories are duty-bound to meet in consultation in order to agree on the measures which must be taken to assist the victim. The Rio Treaty makes no reference to obtaining Security Council approval in this instance.

Article 52, paragraph 2, of the United Nations Charter commits the members of the United Nations to make every effort to achieve pacific settlement of local disputes through regional arrangements or agencies, but Article 53 declares that "no enforcement action shall be taken under regional arrangements or by regional agencies without the authorization of the Security Council."

If, in the hypothetical case set out above, after having explored all peaceful methods of settlement such as conciliation or arbitration and having failed, the consultative organ determines to take action against state B under Article 8 of the Rio Treaty which sets forth the coercive measures such as economic and diplomatic measures and the use of armed force, can the OAS take action under the Rio Treaty without violating the United Nations Charter?

If the Organ of Consultation orders only measures relating to economic or diplomatic relations, in other words "peaceful" measures, and if the term "enforcement action" mentioned in Article 53 of the Charter refers only to the use of armed or physical force, then probably the OAS need not request authorization of the Security Council to take such measures, for Article 52, paragraph 3, of the Charter permits "pacific settlement of local disputes through such regional arrangements or by such regional agencies either on the initiative of the States concerned or by reference from the Security Council."[55] But should the Organ of Consultation of the OAS decide that the unarmed aggression of American state B against American state A can be stopped only by force of arms, it is then clear that authorization of the Security Council of the United Nations is required. Such authorization can come about only when all the permanent members of the Security Council refrain from using the veto. This means that a permanent member of the Security Council from outside the area where the regional arrangement applies, and one not party to the regional agreement, is able to prevent such action from being taken even though a two-thirds majority of the members of the OAS is in favor of such action and even though all other members of the Security Council may favor it.

But Article 6 suggests a recognition of the broader theory of self-defense when it requires in case of aggression which is not an armed attack that the Organ of Consultation meet to take measures to assist the victim for the common defense and for the maintenance of the peace and security of the continent; and, hence, this too would be considered self-defense if taken for and limited to the protection of rights against aggression which by its very connotation is illegal. Following this line, action even involving the use of force can be taken in case of such aggression or in the case of other facts or situations endangering the peace and affecting the inviolability or the integrity of territory or political independence of an American state, provided also essential legal rights are violated; for this would be self-defense and permitted until the United Nations takes measures to maintain the peace if the action is taken for a preventive, nonretributive purpose and there are no alternative means for protection.[56] Thus it would seem that the OAS may act in two ways. First, it may act in the right of collective self-defense when the requisites of this are present; and in such instances the right may be exercised without prior authorization of the Security Council. But when the OAS, for the peace of the Americas, acts to take enforcement measures or sanctions of a punitive nature to compel an offending state to cease its breach or threatened breach of the peace, to return to legality, and to avoid further offenses, then it is bound by the regional arrangement provisions of the Charter, particularly Article 53 which prohibits enforcement action by regional agencies without Security Council authorization.[57]

Although the United Nations Charter is specific in saying that no regional arrangement or agency may take "enforcement action" without the authority of the Security Council, it would appear logical to assume that in the light of the Uniting for the Peace Resolutions passed in 1950,[58] the General Assembly of the United Nations may call upon disputing states to settle their disagreements through the use of a regional agency or arrangement if the Security Council, because of the barrier of the veto, is unable to act when a threat to the peace or an act of aggression occurs. The Uniting for the Peace Resolutions are broad enough to permit the General Assembly to authorize the members of regional pacts or agencies to undertake "action" at its request. These resolutions stated that in the event of a threat to the peace, a breach of the peace, or an act of aggression which the Security Council, because of lack of unanimity among its permanent members, failed to stop by taking necessary action, the General Assembly would consider the matter immediately with a view to making appropriate recommendations to members for collective measures, including measures of force. The issue of the legality of these resolutions was resolved with the reasoning that the whole United Nations organization, and not the Security Council alone, was responsible for the maintenance of the peace of the world; that the resolutions were legal under the provisions for collective self-defense; and that although the Charter does limit the powers of the General Assembly, it does not limit its competence, for it is given competence in the whole field which the Charter covers. The General Assembly is limited to discussion and recommendation, but it is not limited as to the extent of its discussion or as to the type of recommendation it may make.

Article 6 of the Rio Treaty also covers extracontinental or intracontinental conflicts or any other fact or situation that might endanger the peace of America, and requires the signatories to meet in consultation in order to agree upon measures which should be taken for the common defense and for the maintenance of the peace and security of the continent when such situations arise. Here again, the Rio Treaty makes no reference to obtaining approval from the Security Council for the measures upon which it decides. But where in instances of aggression (either armed or unarmed) the Rio Treaty establishes a legal obligation to assist the victim, in the case of situations or conflicts which might endanger continental peace but are other than actual aggressions, only the duty to consult arises, and the taking of other measures appears to be optional with the Organ of Consultation of the OAS. Nevertheless, all signatory states are under the obligation to accept decisions of the Organ of Consultation[59] with respect to the application of measures in cases of situations other than aggressions, with two exceptions: the Organ of Consultation cannot require the use of armed force, unless elements of self-defense are present, without authorization from the Security Council, except perhaps under the Uniting for the Peace Resolutions, and even with such authorization, no state is required to use armed force without its consent.[60]

In summation, the provisions of Article 6 of the Rio Treaty become operative in the following hypothetical cases:

1. Armed attack by any state against an American state outside the delineated security zone and not within the territory of an American state.

2. Aggression which is not an armed attack, whether inside or outside the hemispheric zone, provided such aggression affects the "inviolability or the integrity of the territory or the sovereignty or political independence of any American State."

3. An extracontinental or intracontinental conflict or any other fact or situation that might endanger the peace of the Americas, whether within or without the security zone, and again provided that the inviolability or the territorial integrity or the sovereignty or political independence of any American state is affected.

Under hypothesis 1, an obligation to consult is placed upon the parties followed by an obligation to agree upon measures to aid the victim, for the Organ of Consultation is required to meet immediately and it *must* take collective measures if it finds an armed aggression affecting the sovereignty, etc., of any American state. Under hypothesis 2, there also arises the duty to consult immediately and to agree upon measures which *must* be taken to aid the victim. But under hypothesis 3, only a duty to consult arises, and the taking of other measures appears to be optional with the Organ of Consultation.

The meaning of the word "aggression" becomes a matter of prime importance in cases involving hypothesis 2. Although great controversy exists as to its meaning at international law, the Rio Treaty tries to avoid a dispute over this issue by Article 9, which sets forth two unquestionable examples of aggression and declares that the Organ of Consultation is empowered to characterize *other acts* as aggression. The two examples set forth by Article 9 are unprovoked armed attack against the people, or the land, sea, or air forces of a state, and invasion of the territory of a state by the armed forces of another state. Even though there is confusion in international legal terminology as to the exact extent of "aggression," there is agreement that its definition would include at least the illegal use of or threat to use armed force by one state against another.[61] It is evident from the terms of Article 9 that the Rio Treaty recognizes that the actual illegal use of armed force is an aggression. Moreover, since the Rio Treaty condemns not only the actual use of armed force but also the threat to use it, and since general international law recognizes that aggression includes the threat to use force, it can reasonably be assumed that a threat of force is an aggression which is not an armed attack and falls under hypothesis 2.

To limit aggression only to these instances, however, is too narrow an approach. There have been great refinements in the techniques of aggression in the first half of the twentieth century, and the trend appears to be to wipe out the territorial integrity or political independence of a state by means far more subtle than armed force or even a threat of force.[62] Thus, use of or threat of armed force cannot be said to exhaust acts which the consultative organ may characterize as aggression. Except for the examples given, the treaty provides no rules or criteria as to what constitutes aggression, inasmuch as its drafters felt that the Organ should be left free to characterize acts as aggressions when confronted with the facts of a particular case. Hence there is nothing to prevent the Organ of Consultation from extending the concept to acts of states which are often called "indirect aggression," such as the fomenting of civil strife in other nations through the use of hostile propaganda; fifth columns; infiltration of the political parties of the nation sought to be destroyed; or the organization, encouragement, or toleration of armed bands operating against another state; as well as interventions by means of economic or political coercion in order to obtain advantages.[63]

Indeed, it seems that the Organ of Consultation has equated aggression to intervention, which has been vigorously condemned by inter-American treaties (see, for example, Articles 15 and 16 of the Charter of Bogotá), for in the second case involving a dispute between Haiti and the Dominican Republic, the Council of the OAS, acting as Provisional Organ of Consultation, faced with facts involving intervention by certain Caribbean states in domestic revolutionary situations in other states, declared:

Even though the said facts fortunately did not result in the violation of international peace they did very seriously weaken American solidarity; and if they were to persist or recur, they would give occasion for application of the procedures of the Inter-American Treaty of Reciprocal Assistance [the Rio Treaty] in order to protect the *principle of non-intervention* and to ensure the inviolability or the integrity of the territory or the sovereignty or the political independence of any American state against *aggression* on the part of any state or group of states.[64] (Emphasis added.)

The secretary general of the Organization of American States, in his Annual Report for 1949-1950, stated in this connection:

Actually, this affirmation creates nothing more nor less than the teeth that were lacking in the inter-American treaties and conventions which, in the Committee's judgment, were violated in the cases it investigated. It is almost the same as saying that intervention, as condemned in those treaties and conventions, is one of the acts of aggression that give occasion for applying the measures contemplated by the Treaty of Reciprocal Assistance. No future meeting of the Organ of Consultation, in similar cases, could fail to be guided by this criterion if there should be any doubt as to the application of the Rio de Janeiro Treaty, or if it should be necessary to define the aggressor in the circumstances covered by Articles 6, 7 and 9 of that Treaty. Indeed, the Council was acting under the power of Article 9, which authorizes it to characterize acts other than armed attack and invasion as acts of aggression.[65]

Situations which fall under the third type of hypothetical case give rise only to the duty to consult on the part of the signatories of the treaty. No duty is created by which the parties are required to take collective measures prior to consultation. As the consultative organ is required to meet and agree upon measures which *should* be taken for the common defense and for the maintenance of hemispheric peace, if the Organ agrees that the situation warrants the taking of measures, the parties to the treaty are required to carry out the Organ's decisions—unless, of course, that decision involved the use of armed force. The Organ of Consultation could not legally request measures involving the use of armed force without United Nations authorization, except where the right of collective self-defense arises.

SPECIFIC MEASURES TO BE TAKEN

Article 8 of the Rio Treaty enumerates measures which are to be taken by the member states individually or on which the Organ of Consultation may agree in cases of aggression or threats thereof. These measures are quite similar to those listed in Article 41 of the Charter of the United Nations, except that Article 8 adds as a measure the use of armed force, which under the United Nations Charter was dealt with separately in Article 42. The measures applicable for purposes of the Rio Treaty are: the recall of chiefs of diplomatic missions; the breaking of diplomatic and consular relations; the partial or complete interruption of economic relations or of rail, sea, air, postal, telegraphic, telephonic, and radiotelephonic or radiotelegraphic communications; and the use of armed force. When the Organ of Consultation decides by a two-thirds vote[66] to employ any or all of these punitive measures, each of the contracting parties is required to carry out the decision even though it may have voted against the measure, with the exception that no state is required to use armed force without its consent.[67] The Organ of Consultation is confined in all instances but one to agree upon these specified measures.[68]

However, in the case of a conflict among American states, without prejudice to the right of self-defense in conformity with Article 51 of the Charter of the United Nations, the consultative organ is required by Article 7 of the Rio Treaty to call upon the contending states to suspend hostilities and restore matters to the *status quo ante bellum*. Although the Rio Treaty makes no fundamental distinction between an American and a non-American aggression, a special procedure is provided in Article 7 in case of such an inter-American conflict. The reason for this distinction is simple; in case of a non-American attack launched against a nation of this hemisphere, an order by the Organization of American states to suspend hostilities and restore matters to the *status quo ante bellum* would in all probability prove completely unsuccessful. There is little that can be done other than to meet the attack in the exercise of individual and collective self-defense. On the other hand, when conflict occurs between American states so closely bound together, it is within the realm of possibility that an order from the Organ of Consultation would induce a cessation of hostilities even after a resort to armed force.[69]

This order to suspend hostilities and restore matters to their former position is called by Article 7 a pacifying action. If it fails, the Organ of Consultation may, of course, apply collective measures. Moreover, the rejection of the pacifying action "will be considered in determining the aggressor and in the application of the measures which the consultative meeting may agree upon." This language of the article engenders some confusion. If, for example, hostilities occur between American state A and American state B and it is clear beyond all doubt that state A was the original aggressor, obviously a rejection of the pacifying action by A would bring about determination that A was the aggressor all along. But suppose B rejects the pacifying action, would it be branded as the aggressor? The language of Article 7 in this respect only makes sense in a situation where there is doubt as to just which state, A or B, is the aggressor. In an equivocal situation the Organ in its consideration would, naturally, be influenced by a rejection of the pacifying action, and that rejection could well tip the scales toward consideration of the rejector as the aggressor. Nevertheless, it cannot be conclusively presumed that in all instances an American state (engaged in hostilities with another American state) which rejects the pacifying action, the order to suspend hostilities, will automatically be named the aggressor.[70]

Article 7 also requires the consultative organ, after calling for a suspension of hostilities, to "take in addition all other necessary measures to re-establish or maintain inter-American peace and security and for the solution of the conflict by peaceful means." Here wide authority is given to the Organ as to the peaceful measures it may take. If the situation so warrants, particularly in the event both parties heed its orders to cease hostilities, the Organ of Consultation could seek to induce the parties to resort to methods of peaceful settlement such as negotiation, arbitration, or conciliation.

It is obvious that for purposes of the Rio Treaty, the measures listed in Article 8, when taken as collective coercive measures to maintain the peace of the Western Hemisphere, are enforcement in nature. The measures involving the use of armed force, as well as those of diplomatic or economic nature, are measures necessary to make effective the decisions of the Organ.[71] These are measures by which the Organ, through commands to the contracting parties, seeks to enforce its decisions upon states breaching or threatening to breach the peace of the Americas. In reality, these measures are nothing more or less than coercive measures of a system of hemispheric collective security as well as measures of collective self-defense.

Measures taken in pursuance of the right of collective self-defense might be considered from a practical viewpoint as regional collective enforcement action against a state committing the attack, but technically speaking they are not taken to enforce the law as sanctions, but are limited to defense of legal rights of the states of the community. No real difficulty as to the nature of these measures is, however, encountered, for Article 51 of the United Nations Charter permits measures to be taken in the exercise of the right of collective self-defense until the Security Council takes the necessary steps to maintain peace and security.

Difficulty does exist, however, as to whether measures can ever be taken by the Organization of American States without approval of the Security Council in cases where the requisites of self-defense are not present. Article 53 of the United Nations Charter declares that "no enforcement action shall be taken under regional arrangements or by regional agencies without the authorization of the Security Council." Clearly this would prohibit the use of armed force in the face of a situation which is not one of self-defense, unless the Security Council authorized it. But could the OAS call on its members to use measures of diplomatic or economic coercion in this situation? This would depend, to a great extent, upon the exact definition given to "enforcement action" as used in Article 53 of the United Nations Charter.[72] In this connection, the report of the director general of the OAS on the Rio Conference stated:

In the Charter of the United Nations there are two types of measures, closely coordinated with the procedure to be followed in the Security Council when faced with threats of aggression, with the refusal of the states to comply with the recommendations of the Council, or with a breach of the peace. The first type is that of Article 41, according to which the Security Council is empowered to decide what *measures not involving the use of armed force* are to be employed to give effect to its decisions, and it is empowered to call upon the members of the United Nations to apply such measures. But if these measures are or have proved to be inadequate, coercive measures will next be applied, with the use of air, sea, or land forces. There is a clear distinction for the reader of the Charter between the measures of Article 41 (enforcement action) which are not coercive, in the sense that they lack the element of physical violence that is closely identified with military action, and those of Article 42. Enforcement action, with the use of physical force, is obviously the prerogative of the Security Council, with a single exception: individual or collective self-defense. But the other measures, those of Article 41 are not; it may even be said that it is within the power of any state — without necessarily violating the purposes, principles, or provisions to the Charter — to break diplomatic, consular, and economic relations or to interrupt its communications with another state.[73]

Therefore the director general of the Organization of American States concluded that measures not involving physical violence can at any time be legally employed by the OAS without violating the provision of the United Nations Charter requiring that all "enforcement action" by a regional organization or agency be taken only under the authorization of the Security Council.[74]

MEASURES AS SANCTIONS

Can the measures which are to be taken under Article 6 of the Rio Treaty be regarded as sanctions—actions on the part of the inter-American community taken against a delinquent state which has violated the law? It is a generally accepted principle of general international law that sanctions are permitted only to uphold or enforce the law as a reaction against a state guilty of a breach of the law.[75] This qualification must, of necessity, refer to the application of sanctions by a single nation as well as to collective sanctions by an organization under an international treaty. That being the case, any treaty providing for enforcement measures in the nature of sanctions, if it is to be interpreted as being in conformity with general international law, can only stipulate that the enforcement measures to be taken must be taken against conduct by a nation or nations which constitutes a breach of international law. Otherwise the treaty cannot be held to be in conformity with general international law.[76] This does not mean to imply that only conduct which is prohibited or proscribed by general international law can be the object of legal sanctions, for a breach of international law may occur when a nation does not fulfil its obligations which are set forth in a treaty; that is, there may be a breach of particular international law (treaty law) as well as of general international law.

Article 1, paragraph 1, of the United Nations Charter clearly stipulates that one of the purposes of the United Nations is to "take collective measures ... in conformity with the principles ... of international law." Consequently, any enforcement measures, whether by armed force or by other means, when taken by the United Nations must comply with the requirements set up for sanctions under general international law. The actions must be taken as measures to uphold the law, as a reaction against a state guilty of a breach of law. Yet it can be questioned if all the collective enforcement actions permitted under the Charter can fulfil the requirements of true sanctions, for the Charter makes no clear stipulation that enforcement action is permitted only against a state or states guilty of a breach of the law. Since the Charter appears to contain no rule that the Security Council must definitely take action against the nation which is legally wrong, it has been deduced that the Security Council is free to decide against whom the enforcement action shall be directed, and it may take into consideration all surrounding factors, e.g., the legal rights of the parties involved, the deeper substantial rights of those parties, and the most practical means of ending the situation speedily. It is conceivable that coercive measures may be directed against both contending parties at once. As a result it is often thought that the enforcement measures taken by the Security Council under the authority of the United Nations Charter may not fulfil the requirements of true sanctions.[77]

While this issue presents some problem under the United Nations Charter, it would seem that the measures of the inter-American community are sanctions, although of course they may not be taken against all violations of law, but only against certain ones. It should be remembered that the particular treaty law of the Americas prohibits the use of sanctions (interventions) by individual states, but it does not prohibit their use by the OAS acting within the terms of the Rio Treaty.[78]

The Rio Treaty was drafted in such a manner that it qualifies both as a regional arrangement under Chapter 8 of the United Nations Charter and as a pact of collective self-defense under Article 51.[79] Measures taken in an exercise of individual or collective self-defense can hardly be considered sanctions, inasmuch as self-defense is self-help against the illegal use of force, or certain other violations of the law, and is exercised only to avert or suppress the danger. On the other hand, the object of sanctions is to obtain redress or reparation from the wrongdoing state, to force a return to legality, to avoid new offenses, and to uphold or vindicate international law.

Technically, the measures exercised in the right of collective self-defense seem similar to sanctions, particularly if they are considered as measures to uphold or vindicate the law. However, such a view does not appear to be the correct view of collective self-defense under either the United Nations Charter or the Rio Treaty. Collective self-defense is not a right to intervene to uphold or vindicate the law as such. Like individual self-defense, it may not be exercised in instances of all violations of legally protected interests of a victim state. Too, the Rio Treaty declares that an attack against one American state is an attack against all; thus, those states coming to the aid of the attacked state apparently are to be considered as repelling an attack against themselves or otherwise acting in defense of their interests. Self-defense, whether individual or collective, must, as in municipal law, stand alone both under the Charter of the United Nations and under Article 3 of the Rio Treaty. Self-defense cannot be termed a sanction to uphold the law; it is merely that minimum of self-help by a victim permitted by any legally organized community for protection until the lawful authorities can take over; it is up to the lawful authorities to sanction the attacker.

Under the Rio Treaty, therefore, sanctions must relate to enforcement measures taken in pursuance of situations not involving self-defense. Moreover, since armed force may not be used in such situations by the Organization of American States without the consent of the United Nations, armed force as a sanction is for the most part ruled out.

Article 6 envisions certain types of situations—aggressions which are not armed attack, extracontinental or intracontinental conflicts, and other facts or situations that might endanger the peace of the Americas. In the case of aggressions which are not armed attack, the OAS is to take measures to assist the victim of aggression if that aggression affects the inviolability or the integrity of the territory or the sovereignty or political independence of an American state. Although, as has been pointed out, the term "aggressor" has many disputed definitions in international law, whatever definition is chosen, an aggression is still an unlawful act under general international law, and consequently any measures taken by the OAS which go beyond assistance of the victim of aggression, i.e., purely protective action, and are of a punitive character would automatically be measures against the nation breaching international law and would qualify as true sanctions.

Under the other types of situations foreseen by Article 6, the Organ of Consultation shall meet in order to agree on measures which should be taken for the common defense and for the maintenance of the peace and security of the continent. In instances of this nature, the Organ of Consultation need not take action against the nation legally in the wrong. It might be claimed that whatever measures are employed here would not be sanctions, for they would seem to be not measures to uphold the law, but rather measures of common defense and to maintain the peace and security of the continent. But under Article 2 of the Rio Treaty, the signatories undertake to submit every controversy which may arise between them to methods of peaceful settlement. Hence, if a fact or situation arises between two American states, they are under a legal duty to settle the issue peacefully, and if they fail to do so with the result that their failure or refusal brings about a threat to the peace of the Americas, any measure which the Organ of Consultation decides upon, even though applicable to both nations, would be in the nature of true sanctions applied against nations violating the particular international law established in the Rio Treaty.

If one of the nations agrees to settle the dispute or controversy by peaceful means, and the other nation refuses, then the final portion of Article 7 comes into play, to the effect that the rejection of the pacifying action will be considered in the determination of the aggressor. And here too, any measures applied by the Organ of Consultation would then be in the nature of sanctions. Moreover, if both states refused the pacifying action, it would be possible to label both states as aggressors and to take collective action in the nature of sanctions against both.

If such an intra-American conflict occurs between an American state and a non-American state, or between two non-American states within the hemispheric zone, the matter is not so clear. It can well be argued that in a situation where it becomes necessary to utilize measures against nonmembers threatening to breach the peace within the region, such measures could not be called sanctions to enforce the law, but must be measures for the maintenance of hemispheric peace and security. On the other hand, the Charter of the United Nations definitely creates a legal duty for all its members—among which are most of the nations of the world—to settle their disputes by peaceful means in a manner which does not endanger international peace and security.[80] If a member state of the United Nations violated this duty, then the whole international community would have a right to act jointly against the state breaking the law, and it would seem that the whole international community could be represented by a smaller unit, such as a regional organization like the Organization of American states, permitting it to sanction the law-breaking nation.[81]

As to an extracontinental conflict which is an aggression or other situation between two non-American states outside the security zone but disturbing the peace so as to affect the territorial integrity or political independence of an American state, it can be contended that measures taken by the consultative organ are simply measures to defend the continent and maintain its peace and security and not measures to enforce the law, for in the case of an aggression, the right to repel such an aggression would be within the exclusive jurisdiction of the United Nations.[82] But again, the extracontinental aggression or threatened breach of the peace would be a violation of the treaty law laid down in the United Nations Charter; and here as well as in the situation above, the regional organization could represent the larger organization so its measures might be equated to sanctions against a violation of the law if that violation affected the members of the regional organization.

If the measures of the Rio Treaty can under the outlined situations be regarded as sanctions, it must be emphasized that they are sanctions of an extremely limited scope applicable against only certain violations of the law. They are to be applied only where there is involved an aggression or other situation bringing about a breach of the obligation to settle disputes peacefully or a breach of the obligation to refrain from breaking or threatening to break international peace.

THE RIO TREATY AND NONMEMBERS

The Rio Treaty was drafted in such a manner as to affect third states not parties to the agreement. As mentioned before, Article 3 confers benefits or rights on all American states, whether such states ratified the treaty or not, whenever an armed attack occurs against an American state.[83] Moreover, Article 3 probably confers benefits on non-American, nonmember states when an armed attack occurs against such states within the security zone, for the contracting parties felt that any armed attack within the region creates such a danger to all the American states that it warrants defensive action.[84] Under Article 6, if any American state is subjected to an aggression which is not an armed attack, the other American states are obligated to consult and agree on measures to aid the victim. No distinction is created between contracting and noncontracting parties. The sole requirement is that the victim be an American state.

A customary rule of general international law is found in the adage *pacta tertiis nec nocent nec prosunt*—treaties do neither harm nor good to third parties.[85] According to this principle, a treaty concerns only the contracting parties, and, as a rule, imposes no rights or duties upon third states not parties to it, inasmuch as it would be incompatible with the equality of sovereign states that parties to a treaty should be able to bind third states in any manner without their consent. Nevertheless, international law has slowly come to the realization that many treaties do affect relations of third states, although courts and writers cautiously warn that the practice is so unusal that "such results cannot be lightly presumed."[86]

Today, it is generally accepted that it is legally possible for contracting states to create rights in favor of third states if the intention of the contracting parties to do so is very clear. Controversy does exist, however, as to the exact nature of the right so conferred and the obligations of the contracting parties. Although Kelsen declares that a treaty cannot impose obligations upon a noncontracting or nonconsenting state because this would do violence to the principle of sovereignty or equality of states,[87] this rule would not apply to a treaty which only conferred rights upon a third state without exacting obligations from that state.[88] Signatories of a treaty may by the terms of that treaty be legally bound to live up to the rights which the treaty conferred upon the third state, and such is the case as to Articles 3 and 6 of the Rio Treaty, where the contracting parties conferred stipulated benefits upon nonsignatory states.

Nothing in the United Nations Charter prevents this, for measures of collective self-defense under Article 51 need not be based upon a treaty arrangement, and the benefits of such collective self-defense may be bestowed upon a noncontracting American state or upon any noncontracting state within the delineated security zone. Outside the realm of self-defense, the measures of the Organ of Consultation are not taken under the collective self-defense provisions of Article 51 of the United Nations Charter, but under the regional arrangement provisions, which give the regional agency the power to act within the region and do not confine the grant of power to action only within the regional agency or arrangement.[89] Of course, measures involving the use of armed force are not conferred by these provisions without the consent of the United Nations.

In a certain sense, the Rio Treaty imposes obligations upon noncontracting parties—that is, a duty seems to be incumbent upon all states not to commit armed attack against any American state, or in fact against any state within the security zone, nor to commit aggressions which are not armed attacks or other acts which endanger the peace of the Americas and which affect the territorial integrity, sovereignty, or political independence of an American state. If such situations occur, collective measures will be taken by the OAS under the right of collective self-defense to aid the victim of aggression and repel the aggressor or to provide for the common defense and for the maintenance of the peace and security of the continent.[90] Under the Rio Treaty, no distinction is made as to whether the delinquent state, the disturber of the peace, against whom the measures may be taken is a ratifying or nonratifying state. Even though benefits may be conferred upon third states, it can be questioned whether a treaty can impose obligations upon noncontracting parties; and it might well be questioned whether measures can be taken against nonratifying parties.

If the Rio Treaty stood alone, difficulties might well be encountered when the attempt is made to justify the legality of measures taken by the OAS under the fact situations it was designed to cover. But these difficulties vanish in view of the fact that the Rio Treaty is buttressed by the United Nations Charter, signed by most of the nations of the world. That Charter makes the use of force illegal and places a duty upon its signatories to settle their disputes peacefully and not to breach or threaten to breach the peace.[91] As Article 51 of the Charter establishes the right of collective self-defense, recognizing the principle that an attack against one state is an attack against all other states closely integrated with it, any action taken by a regional agency or arrangement against a noncontracting nation guilty of an attack in the described region is legal under the rules of the United Nations Charter. A nation which is a signatory of the United Nations Charter has bound itself to obey the injunctions of the Charter and consented to be subjected to the exercise of collective self-defense on the part of other nations should the nation breach the treaty.

Under the Rio Treaty, the right to take measures against nonratifying states does not stop with measures relating to collective self-defense, for under Article 6 measures can also be taken against noncontracting states disturbing the peace of the continent. The right to enforce this section of the Rio Treaty against nonsignatories is derived directly from Article 52 of the United Nations Charter:

Nothing in the present Charter precludes the existence of regional arrangements or agencies for dealing with such matters relating to the maintenance of international peace and security as are appropriate for regional action, provided that such arrangements or agencies and their activities are consistent with the purposes and principles of the United Nations.

All ratifiers of the United Nations Charter thereby agree to the possibility that they may become subject to regional arrangements or agencies dealing with matters within the region relating to the maintenance of international peace. The United Nations Charter establishes no prerequisite that a nation within a particular region must be signatory to the pact establishing the regional arrangement or agency. The only prerequisites are that the matter must be appropriate for regional action, and the action taken must be consistent with the purposes and principles of the United Nations. By ratification of the United Nations Charter, a nation falling within a region in which there is a regional arrangement or agency has indirectly given its consent to intervention by that agency in matters in its region relating to the maintenance of peace.

CHAPTER XVI

THE INTER-AMERICAN SYSTEM OF PEACE AND SECURITY: THE PACIFIC SETTLEMENT OF DISPUTES

HISTORICAL BACKGROUND

Under the Rio Treaty, the OAS to some extent exercises a police function by which, through organized co-operation and joint decision of the member states, coercive measures are to be taken against a breach or threatened breach of the peace. The system as conceived can be said to create a primitive executive function aimed at repressing lawless and violent attempts to overthrow existing inter-American order. But in legally organized communities something more than a police function is requisite. Policing becomes necessary at a point of time when law and order are broken or are in imminent danger of being broken. Conflicts between parties of a community are in most instances the result of an unsettled dispute which eventually erupts. If peace is to be kept in a community, the peaceful settlement or adjustment of such disputes becomes imperative, and must take place before the dispute reaches a stage where police measures become necessary. In a national society this function of settling disputes peacefully is placed within the hands of judicial or quasi-judicial organs, through which machinery is provided for the compulsory and pacific adjustment of disputes between antagonistic persons and groups.

A major goal of Pan-Americanism has been to provide ways and means for the pacific settlement of disputes. At the first International Conference in Washington, in 1890, attempts were made to establish the principle of compulsory arbitration of all controversies not involving the independence of any one of the nations. A formal treaty evolved which was based upon the conference Plan of Arbitration, but lack of ratifications prevented it from becoming operative.[1]

The results in this field of three succeeding conferences were meager. A general arbitration agreement was signed at the Second Conference,[2] but it was ratified by only a few states.[3] This conference also brought forth a Protocol on Adherence to the Conventions of The Hague of 1899,[4] as well as a Treaty of Arbitration for Pecuniary Claims, which provided that disputes over such claims were to be submitted under the Hague Convention.[5] This agreement was ratified by nine states.[6] It was changed slightly and extended at the Third Conference[7] and was replaced by another convention at the Fourth.[8] This later Convention on Pecuniary Claims obligated the parties to submit to arbitration all "claims for pecuniary loss or damage . . . which cannot be amicably adjusted through diplomatic channels, when said claims are of sufficient importance to warrant the expense of arbitration." Again the tribunal of arbitration was the Permanent Court of Arbitration at The Hague, unless both parties agreed to a special jurisdiction. The treaty was to remain in force indefinitely unless denounced. It was ratified by twelve nations.[9] The scope of its arbitration, however, did not extend to all inter-American disputes, but only to those involving claims for pecuniary loss.

These early conferences created a trend which, between 1923 and 1936, resulted in a series of nine treaties covering almost all procedures of pacific settlement such as good offices and mediation, investigation and conciliation, arbitration, and prevention of controversies.[10] The first of these was the Treaty to Avoid or Prevent Conflicts between the American States—the Gondra Treaty —signed at Santiago in 1923.[11] Here provision was made for the settlement of disputes through an impartial investigation of the facts by a commission of inquiry. All controversies which were not settled through diplomatic channels or arbitration and which did not affect constitutional provisions or questions already settled by other treaties were to be submitted to the commission. The reports of the commission were not to be conceived of as decisions or awards, but were to be regarded as in the nature of findings to assist the parties in their negotiations to bring about a settlement of the dispute. If the findings were unacceptable to the disputing parties, they recovered entire liberty of action to proceed as they believed their interests required, although they were pledged to refrain from hostile acts or preparations for hostilities during the inquiry and the following period of negotiation.

This treaty also created two permanent diplomatic commissions located at Washington and Montevideo and composed of the three diplomatic representatives longest accredited to those two capitals. The sole function of these commissions was to receive from one party to a dispute the request for convocation of the special commission of inquiry and to transmit it to the other party involved in the dispute. The commission of inquiry was composed of five members, all nationals of the American republics. Four were chosen by the parties to the dispute (each party appointing two, only one of whom could be a national of the appointing country). The fifth was to be chosen by common accord of those already appointed, subject to the qualification that a citizen of a nation one of whose nationals had already been appointed could not be chosen. If the fifth member thus selected was not agreeable to the disputants, a different person was to be appointed to this position by the president of a neutral American republic, who was to be chosen by a complicated procedure.

The General Convention of Inter-American Conciliation signed at the Conference of Arbitration and Conciliation, Washington, 1929, created the inter-American conciliation procedure.[12] This Convention was based on the Gondra Treaty, retaining the commissions of this treaty, but extending the functions of the special commissions into the field of conciliation and, in addition, permitting the permanent diplomatic commissions to exercise conciliatory functions in certain circumstances while the special commissions were being constituted. The parties agreed to submit to the procedure of conciliation all controversies of any kind arising between them which it had not been possible to settle through diplomatic channels. The commission as organ of conciliation was called upon to procure the conciliation of differences by endeavoring to effect a settlement between the parties. As under the Gondra

Treaty, the reports and recommendations of the commission were not considered binding.

This conference also produced the General Treaty of Inter-American Arbitration,[13] which provided for settlement of all justiciable questions by arbitration. Excepted from the obligations were controversies involving domestic jurisdiction and not controlled by international law, and those affecting the interest or referring to the action of a state not a party to the treaty.

The treaty permitted the parties to designate the arbitrator or arbitral tribunal by agreement, but in the absence of agreement a procedure was set forth. The disputants were called upon to organize an arbitral tribunal of five members, each party to nominate two arbitrators of whom only one could be its own national, or in the alternative to select from the party's delegates to the Permanent Court of Arbitration at The Hague. The other arbiter could be of any other American nationality. These four arbitrators were to choose a fifth. If they were unable to reach agreement on an American, they could choose a non-American. If no agreement was possible among the four arbitrators, the parties to the dispute were each called upon to designate a non-American member of the Court of Arbitration, and the two members so designated were to select the fifth arbitrator, who could be of any nationality other than that of a party to the dispute.

The award handed down by the tribunal was made binding on the parties and was declared to settle the dispute definitely and without appeal.

The Anti-War Treaty of Non-Aggression and Conciliation, signed at Rio de Janeiro in 1933,[14] provided for an alternative procedure of conciliation. Disputes could be submitted to conciliation, but unlike the Convention of 1929 this treaty permitted the exclusion of four categories of controversies.[15] It omitted the permanent diplomatic commissions and set forth a differing method for constituting the commissions of inquiry.[16] The findings of the commissions were not binding upon the parties, but the commissions could include recommendations regarding the best solutions of the differences.

In 1933 an Additional Protocol to the General Convention of Inter-American Conciliation was signed at the Montevideo Conference.[17] This protocol was designed to give a permanent character to the Commissions of Investigation and Conciliation established by the Gondra and Conciliation Treaties. Under these previous instruments the commissions were *ad hoc* in nature. They were not formed until after the dispute had arisen, and the procedures for their formation were somewhat complicated, particularly if controversy developed as to the fifth member. To permit the commissions to be constituted and ready for action in advance of conflict, each contracting party was called upon to name its members to the commission by means of a bilateral agreement, which was recorded in an exchange of notes. The Governing Board of the Pan American Union was authorized to initiate the choice of the fifth member.

Three other conventions in the field of pacific settlement were signed in 1936 at Buenos Aires. The Inter-American Treaty on Good Offices and Mediation[18] provided for recourse to the mediation of an eminent citizen of the American states in case of controversy between the contracting parties.

Mediators were preferably to be chosen from a list communicated to the Pan American Union by the ratifying states, each government naming two citizens. From this list the parties to a dispute could select as mediator the eminent citizen with whom representatives of the disputants could negotiate a peaceful and equitable solution of their differences.

The Treaty on the Prevention of Controversies of 1936[19] stated that its purpose was to bring into being a preventive system for the consideration of possible causes of future controversies and their settlement by pacific means. It obligated the parties to establish permanent bilateral mixed commissions composed of representatives of the signatories, which should in fact be constituted at the request of any of them. The duty of these commissions was to study the causes of future difficulties or controversies and to propose measures which might be taken to promote the due and regular application of treaties in force between the respective parties and in each connection to promote the development of increasingly good relations. The functions of the commissions seem unclear; about the best that can be said from the language used is that they were to undertake to study situations and to submit recommendations to the governments as to the proper way to deal with certain conditions before they led to a dispute.

The final treaty was the Convention to Coordinate, Extend and Assure the Fulfillment of the Existing Treaties Between the American States.[20] This treaty, however, left much to be desired and did little as to pacific settlement other than to reaffirm previous obligations.

The inter-American peace system as attempted by these various treaties was a delusion. Although inter-American disputes and conflicts occurred during this period, the treaties were seldom if ever applied.[21] The peace machinery was ineffective for a variety of reasons. One great drawback was that none of these treaties was ratified by all of the American republics. Moreover, many of the instruments were made the subject of extensive reservation by the ratifying parties. Such a situation was ready made for conflict and confusion, creating a problem of "if" and "how." Upon the occurrence of a dispute, it would be necessary to determine whether all parties to a dispute were bound through ratification to a particular treaty and its procedures. Extensive reservations to the treaty would further complicate the matter, raising the question of just how the disputants were bound, even though they had all ratified.

But even had the treaties been ratified without reservation, no effective inter-American system for the settlement of disputes would have materialized, for under the terms of most of these treaties no compulsory and binding procedures for settlement existed. The parties bound themselves to have recourse to the procedure of investigation and conciliation in case of controversy, but the Gondra Treaty and the Anti-War Treaty exempted a large area of controversy from the obligation. As to conciliation, the Conciliation Convention did seek to remedy the matter by requiring all controversies not settled by diplomatic means to be submitted. Moreover, the agreements relied on *ad hoc* commissions of investigation and conciliation, which was a drawback, for in general the commissions were to be organized after the disputes and the complicated method by which the parties were to choose the members could well bring about delay so as to cause, for all practical purposes, disruption of the system of investigation and conciliation. The Additional Protocol to the Conciliation Commission attempted to remedy this fault so as to permit the constitution of the commissions in advance, but few of the states ever named their members to the commissions, and only two such commissions were ever organized.

By the terms of the General Treaty of Arbitration the ratifying parties obligated themselves to submit certain of their differences to arbitration, and further to accept the award of the arbitrators. But in effect the parties only agreed to agree to arbitration. The parties were called upon to submit all international juridical questions to arbitration, but they were not required to arbitrate political questions or domestic questions. Since the treaty failed to grant to the arbitral tribunal the right to resolve its jurisdiction, the decision as to whether the matter was arbitral was apparently left in the discretion of the disputants. This situation weakened drastically the binding quality of the agreement, for it would permit the interpretation by a party to the dispute that the matter was not arbitral, thus precluding arbitration. Moreover, even if the dispute did reach the stage of arbitration further difficulties could arise in such matters as the forming of the tribunal and agreement upon the particular subject matter of the controversy. If all these hurdles were surmounted, the many reservations to the treaty could still prevent successful arbitration.

The unsatisfactory state of the inter-American system for the pacific settlement of disputes led to attempts to improve the procedures for pacific settlement and to co-ordinate the various treaties on the subject into an organized and harmonious instrument. With the reorganization of the inter-American system at Bogotá in 1948, consideration was also given to the improvement and simplification of the peace structure.[22]

The Charter of Bogotá proclaims an essential purpose of the OAS to be "to ensure the pacific settlement of disputes that may arise among the Member States,"[23] and Article 5(g) obligates the parties to settle their international controversies by peaceful procedures. Other guiding principles of pacific settlement are set out in Chapter IV of the Charter, which requires that the parties resort to certain named peaceful procedures before referring their disputes to the Security Council of the United Nations and which obligates the parties, in the event of a controversy which in the opinion of one of them cannot be settled through diplomatic channels, to agree on some other peaceful procedure for the finding of a solution. However, this chapter declares that a special treaty will establish procedures for the pacific settlement of disputes and will determine appropriate means for their application, so that it will not be possible for a dispute among the American states to fail of definite settlement within a reasonable time.

THE PACT OF BOGOTA

This special treaty, the American Treaty of Pacific Settlement—the Pact of Bogotá—was also signed at Bogotá in 1948.[24] It attempts to formulate effective methods for the pacific settlement of inter-American disputes. Thus the peace and security system of the hemisphere was intended to rest upon two basic documents, the Rio Treaty and the Pact of Bogotá, the latter being concerned with mechanisms for pacific settlement of disputes, the former with enforcement measures by the organized community to be applied for the maintenance or restoration of peace in the event the pacific settlement procedures prove unsuccessful and the unsettled dispute reaches such serious proportions as to endanger the peace.

The Pact is subject to ratification and is to have force between the parties upon their respective ratifications.[25] It is intended as a replacement of all of the earlier treaties in this field of pacific settlement, which are to cease to have force upon the parties as they ratify.[26] It was the aim of the framers of the pact to codify inter-American peace machinery in one instrument.

General Obligation of Pacific Settlement

Chapter I of the treaty contains several provisions having to do with the general obligation of the parties to settle their disputes by peaceful means. By Article I they renounce the use of force or threat thereof or any other means of coercion for the settlement of their controversies. They further pledge themselves to have recourse to pacific procedures only. This language and similar language used in the Charter of Bogotá and the Rio Treaty clearly stipulate an inter-American obligation of peaceful settlement and an undertaking by the contracting parties to submit every controversy of an international character arising between them to methods of pacific settlement. Moreover, the obligation is present to make use of inter-American pacific procedures for the settlement of inter-American controversies before referring them to the Security Council of the United Nations.[27]

There are few requirements as to the specific peaceful procedures which are to be used or the order in which they are to be used, the parties being given the greatest freedom of choice, although if one procedure is initiated another cannot be commenced until the first is concluded.[28] Article II does bind the parties to resort to the pacific procedures established in the treaty, but continues quickly with the words "or, alternatively, such special procedures as, in their opinion, will permit them to arrive at a solution." Moreover, the parties need not resort to any procedures (either those of the treaty or others of their choice) until in their own opinion the controversy cannot be settled by direct negotiations through diplomatic channels. This proviso would seem to permit a party great latitude in refusing to submit to pacific procedures, since it could simply fail to agree that the controversy could not be settled through diplomatic channels. Even if a party were acting in good faith, undue delay could occur before agreement was reached to the effect that the dispute could not be settled by diplomacy.

Four important exceptions were made to the obligation to submit disputes to pacific procedures for settlement. Excepted were matters within the domestic jurisdiction of a state; matters already settled by agreement or arbitral award or judgment of an international tribunal; matters involving protection of nationals when recourse to competent domestic tribunals is open to the persons who are concerned; and instances where the right of self-defense may be legally exercised.

Domestic Jurisdiction

Resort to the pacific procedures of the Pact of Bogotá or to any pacific procedures is excepted by Article V, which makes the procedures of the treaty not applicable "to matters which, by their nature, are within the domestic jurisdiction of the state." Exclusion of matters within the domestic jurisdiction has been common in treaties for the pacific settlement of disputes. For example, the 1929 General Treaty of Inter-American Arbitration excluded from the obligation of arbitration those differences "which are within the domestic jurisdiction of any of the Parties to the dispute and are not controlled by international law."[29] The words "not controlled by international law" should not signify that matters within the domestic jurisdiction are above and beyond the realm of international law—that no international law rule exists in relation to domestic jurisdiction questions. What it does or should signify is that international law regulates here in a negative rather than a positive way; i.e., the law as to certain matters may, rather than imposing an obligation on its subject to behave in a certain manner, abstain from so doing. Within this sphere where no obligation is stipulated, the subjects of the law are left legally free to act as they please. In effect they would have a right so to act conferred by law, for since the law does not legally forbid, it legally permits. Thus, that area where norms of international law refrain from stipulating obligations for its subjects, states, leaving them free to behave as they choose, is the domestic jurisdiction of a state. Within this sphere international law gives unlimited liberty of action to the state; the state is sole judge, having exclusive jurisdiction.[30] Matters falling in this sphere are thought of as exclusively national or internal matters. A listing of them would encompass a study of the entire field of international law, but generally speaking they are usually thought to include the form of government of a state and its political system, the scope of its armaments, the composition and treatment of its citizenry and laws regulating the admission of aliens, its social and economic policy including policies relating to labor and religious problems, tariff and trade problems, and its internal legal system.

The language of Article V of the Pact of Bogotá when it speaks of matters "which, by their nature, are within the domestic jurisdiction of a state" is unfortunate. This would seem to imply that certain matters are by their very nature not susceptible of regulation by international law, but only by national law. This would be fallacious reasoning, for there are no matters which are inherently or by their very nature outside the realm of international law, and which may be thought of as reserved for all time to the exclusive jurisdiction of the state. Future international obligations may be created by the formation of new customary rules of international law applicable to the whole international community or as between two or more states by treaty. When such general or particular norms come into being as to matters usually relegated to the domestic jurisdiction, the liberty of action of the state is curbed; obligation to behave in accordance with the new norm is established, and the matter is removed from the reserved domain by international law. All of the matters listed above may become matters of international obligation.[31] Indeed, all or most of them have become the subjects of international treaty obligation as to some of their phases as between certain states and at one time or another.

Thus the limits of the reserved domain of a state or its domestic jurisdiction are fluid. Matters which today may still be within those limits may tomorrow be lifted from the sphere of domestic jurisdiction by the progressive development of international law which creates new international obligations, or by the assumption of treaty obligations by a state which would infringe upon the otherwise reserved sphere.

The drafters of the Pact apparently, and perhaps naïvely, concluded that a matter falling within the domestic jurisdiction can never be (or perhaps should never be) an object of an inter-American dispute, for such a matter is an internal affair which by definition refers to the area in which international law permits each state complete freedom of action. Hence, any objections by a state to the way in which another state conducts itself within the prescribed area would not have the character of an international dispute, and, therefore, under the Pact of Bogotá need not be submitted to peaceful procedures. Indeed, if the matter in controversy were truly within the domestic jurisdiction of a state, a state subjected to such objection could legitimately complain of interference from the outside, and the objecting state would itself appear to violate international law by its intereference or intervention, thus creating dispute and subjecting the objecting state to whatever obligations exist as to submission to peaceful procedures.

In any event, the exercise of domestic power by a state may and often does give rise to conflicts of interests between states which may in turn lead to controversy. If the matter is under international law one where a state is given unlimited liberty of action, a contending state has no right legally to press the issue and would appear to be under a legal duty to refrain from doing so. Nevertheless, the question as to whether a matter is within the domestic jurisdiction is not a simple one. It is a legal question and may well be extremely difficult to determine, involving a consideration of international law in general and the obligations it prescribes as well as other obligations which a state may have assumed by treaty. It is a question which an involved state should not be permittd to self-judge.

The problem of who shall decide whether of not an issue is one of domestic jurisdiction and whether it shall be decided on the standards established by international law presents no issue under the Pact of Bogotá if the dispute reaches the International Court of Justice. Under Article XXXIII if there is controversy over the question as to whether or not the matter falls within the domestic jurisdiction limitation, this preliminary question is to be submitted to decision by the International Court of Justice. Once before the court it will or should be interpreted by standards of international law. The issue is then settled one way or another. If the court finds the question one of domestic jurisdiction the controversy is declared ended.[32]

Considerable progress over earlier inter-American agreements has been made by the Pact in providing for submission of this preliminary question to the International Court of Justice in case of disagreement with regard to it. However, the advance made in the provisions of the treaty was largely obliterated by reservations entered against Article V at the time of signing. For example, the United States, as it had done when adhering to the Statute of the International Court of Justice, reserved in such a way as to permit the United States rather than the court to determine whether a disputed matter falls within the domestic jurisdiction of the United States.[33] Such a self-judging limitation leaves the United States itself free to decide what is and what is not within the domestic jurisdiction of the United States and permits it to block the court from passing on the suit. The reservations of Argentina and Peru were similar in nature.[34]

Matters Already Settled

Article VI excepts from the obligations of the Pact of Bogotá "matters already settled by arrangement between the parties, or by arbitral award or by decision of an international court, or which are governed by agreements or treaties in force on the date of the conclusion of the present Treaty." As a result such matters are excluded from the general obligation to submit international disputes to pacific procedures. By eliminating such conflicts from the application of the treaty, an attempt is made to bring the principle of *res judicata* within the terms of the Pact. A matter once decided or settled should not be subject to continuing dispute or continuing litigation. Once again, however, the initial question as to whether a conflict between the parties has been so settled is not left to the parties to decide within their unlimited discretion. If circumstances prevail so that the dispute is submitted to the International Court of Justice, the court is permitted to decide this question. If it finds the conflict to fall within one of the exceptions, the court is called upon to declare itself to be without jurisdiction and to declare the controversy ended.[35]

Matters Involving Protection of Nationals

Article VII binds the contracting parties "not to make diplomatic representations in order to protect their nationals, or to refer a controversy to a court of international jurisdiction for that purpose, when the said nationals have had available means to place their case before competent domestic courts of the respective state." At first glance the language of this article might be interpreted as creating only a limited exception to the obligation to settle disputes by pacific procedures, for it only seems to except the type of controversy referred to from submission to a court of international jurisdiction, i.e., judicial procedures. If a state is prevented from making diplomatic representations as to such matters, however, it would in effect be precluded from mentioning such a matter to another state; and if this cannot be done, it would be impossible ever to arrive at, say, an agreement to mediate or to conciliate or some other procedure of a lesser nature than international court proceedings. The provision then creates an exception which excludes controversies involving protection of certain treatment of citizens abroad from pacific settlement.

Contention has long been prevalent in the Americas concerning the protection of nationals. One view recognizes that a state has jurisdiction over all persons, foreigners and nationals, within its territory and that aliens are bound by the laws of any state in whose jurisdiction they find themselves; but there is still a legal requirement set up by general international law that states must maintain certain minimum standards in their treatment of aliens. If an alien suffers injury because the state in its treatment of him falls below this standard, the state becomes delinquent at international law, having violated an established duty of states. After the injured alien has exhausted all legal remedies available to him and has still sustained a denial of justice, the state of citizenship has at general international law a right of intervention in the form of reprisals as a sanction in order to protect its citizens, or in inter-American law a right of diplomatic intercession.

The other view, adhered to by many Latin American nations, denies that there is a higher international law standard applying to the treatment of aliens than the national standard applying to the treatment accorded to citizens. If a state grants equality of treatment to citizen and foreigner alike it fulfils its international obligations.[36]

Article VII would seem to incorporate the latter theory. It clearly seeks to do away with the minimum standard rule and makes the treatment of aliens in a state a matter subject to the exclusive jurisdiction of that state alone, a matter within the domestic jurisdiction of that state which should not be a subject of international controversy between that state and the state of citizenship as long as the alien has recourse to the domestic courts. On the face of it Article VII may appear reasonable. Even under the minimum standard rule there must be a denial of justice to the alien before his state of citizenship can complain. Such denial of justice could not be said to have occurred until all remedies had been exhausted, which would require resort to the courts. The article, however, becomes unreasonable at least if the minimum standard rule is to obtain, for it is quite within the realm of possibility in any society that the alien may still be denied justice after resort to the courts of the nation. Hence, what Article VII does in reality is to destroy the international responsibility of states for injuries to foreigners. And as to inter-American controversies between adherents to the Pact of Bogotá, it provides that the International Court of Justice may not hear such cases, for it must declare itself to be without jurisdiction when such a controversy is presented to it and further must declare the controversy ended.[37]

As might be expected, the United States reserved to this article, which was believed to do away with the international law requirement that states maintain minimum standards in the treatment of aliens and their property.[38]

Questions Where the Right of Self-Defense May Be Exercised

Article VIII stipulates that the invocation of procedures of peaceful settlement shall not have the effect of delaying the exercise of the right of self-defense in cases involving armed attack. The right of individual and collective self-defense is specifically recognized by the United Nations Charter and by the Rio Treaty. Thus, in effect, an American state subjected to an armed attack by another American state is excused from the obligation of the Pact to submit its controversies to pacific procedures and can take measures, including the use of armed force, immediately in order to meet the illegal armed attack as permitted by Article 3 of the Rio Treaty. By the same provision the other American states would be not only permitted but obligated to take measures to assist the victim.[39] It should be noted that in case of such a conflict between two or more American states the Organ of Consultation is required to call upon the contending parties to suspend hostilities and, after such suspension, is called upon to take measures to re-establish or maintain peace and to bring about the solution of the conflict by peaceful means. At this point, the Organ could recommend submission of the controversy to pacific procedures.[40]

Procedures of Good Offices and Mediation

Chapter II of the Pact provides for the two pacific procedures: good offices and mediation. The procedure of good offices is the attempt by the government of an American state not a party to the controversy or by one or more eminent citizens of an American state not a party to the controversy to bring the disputants together for the purpose of reaching a solution.[41] Once the disputing parties have been brought together and have resumed direct negotiation, the state or citizens engaging in good offices have no other function, although they may, if the disputants agree, be present at the negotiations.[42]

The function of mediators is not so limited. The procedure of mediation is defined as the submission of the controversy to an American government not a party thereto or one or more eminent citizens of an American state not a party to the controversy, to assist the disputants in the settlement of the controversy in the simplest and most direct manner, avoiding formalities. The mediator or mediators must be chosen by mutual agreement of the disputants.[43] If the parties have agreed to the procedure of mediation, but cannot agree on the choice of mediators within two months or cannot reach a solution of the controversy within five months after mediation has begun, they are required to have recourse to another procedure of pacific settlement established in the Pact.[44]

Any of the contracting parties may offer their services as mediators, but not if the controversy is in the process of settlement by another procedure established in the treaty.[45]

The Pact of Bogotá follows conventional international law ideas concerning the procedures of good offices and mediations, i.e., that those offering good offices or acting as mediators do not attempt to decide the controversy for the parties, but seek to prevail upon them to decide it themselves—good offices being the attempt to induce the parties to negotiate, while mediation goes a step farther in that the mediators take a part in the negotiations themselves, assisting the parties in their settlement.[46]

Procedure of Investigation and Conciliation

In many international disputes the facts may be elusive. If both sides will agree to an impartial and conscientious investigation of the facts, fuller evidence may be obtained and a more accurate appraisal of rights involved becomes possible. The process of inquiry or investigation is designed to facilitate the settlement of disputes arising from differences of opinion on points of fact by the establishment or elucidation of the facts through an investigation and report by a commission.

In the procedure of investigation combined with conciliation, not only is the dispute referred to a commission whose task is to find the facts and report on them, but the commission in its report also makes recommendation for settlement. Such a recommendation may take into account any rules of international law or may be based solely upon considerations of international policy. Each party to the dispute may accept or reject the recommendations of the commission, as it chooses.[47]

The Pact of Bogotá combines investigation and conciliation into one procedure, declaring that this "consists in the submission of the controversy to a Commission of Investigation and Conciliation."[48] It attempts to assure that the formation of the commission shall not be hindered by providing two methods for its establishment. The first method is simple and envisages the establishment by bilateral agreement of any two contracting parties of a commission which will be available for any controversy that may come about between those parties. By this agreement each party appoints two members, only one of whom may be of its nationality. The fifth member, who also acts as chairman, is then appointed by common agreement of the members already designated.[49]

The second method is used when no such permanent conciliation commission has been established, and requires each party to the dispute to designate two members to an *ad hoc* commission from the permanent panel of American conciliators. The members are not to be of the nationality of the appointing party. The completion of the commission is then provided. The four members appointed are required to choose a fifth member from the panel, not of the nationality of either party. If within thirty days the four members have not been able to agree on a fifth, these members "shall each list the conciliators composing the permanent panel, in order of their preference, and upon comparison of the lists so prepared, the one who receives a majority of the votes shall be elected." The fifth member is the chairman of the commission.[50]

The Permanent Panel of American Conciliators is drawn up by the Pan American Union and consists of two nationals of each of the contracting parties with highest reputation for fairness, competence, and integrity. These two nationals are appointed by the parties for three-year periods.[51]

Article XXI permits an increase of the number of conciliators when more than two states are involved in the dispute and all have different interests. Such an increase does not take place, however, if two or more states hold similar points of view, for in that instance they are considered as a single party.

The function of the commission is "to clarify the points in dispute between the parties and to endeavor to bring about an agreement between them upon mutually acceptable terms."[52] Its duties may be confined to investigation or inquiry only if in the opinion of the parties the controversy relates solely to a question of fact.[53] Its work should be concluded within a six-month period, although this may be extended by mutual agreement of the parties.[54] If agreement is reached by conciliation, the final report is limited to the text of the agreement.[55] If no agreement is reached, the final report contains a summary of the commission's work. In either case, the report is adopted by majority vote.[56] It is made clear that the report and conclusions of the commission are not binding upon the parties as to either fact or law. They have "no other character than that of recommendations submitted for the consideration of the parties in order to facilitate a friendly settlement of the controversy."[57]

The Council of the OAS is given certain responsibility with respect to this procedure. For example, the Council is called upon to take immediate steps to convoke the commission, regardless of the method used in its formation, when the party initiating the procedures requests the Council to do so.[58] After the Council has received the request, the controversy between the parties is immediately suspended, and the parties are called upon to refrain from any act that might make conciliation more difficult. To this end, at the request of one of the parties, the Council may, pending the convocation of the commission, make appropriate recommendations to the parties.[59] The Council also determines when the commission shall originally meet, but the commission decides where it shall finally carry out its duties.[60]

Judicial Settlement

A permanent court to which inter-American disputes can be submitted for the adjudication of the legal rights of the disputant states and with power to hand down a binding award has long been advocated. The first real international court—the Central American Court of Justice—was established in 1907 by the five states of that area. Jurisdiction over all disputes which might arise among the five states was granted to this body, and even individuals were permitted to bring suit against a state. The court could determine its own jurisdiction and might even hand down a judgment in the face of a refusal of one party to appear. The court existed some ten years and rendered eight decisions. Unfortunately the court was inclined to proceed too fast; difficulties were encountered which brought about its demise, and it has never been re-created.[61] It did, however, inspire efforts to establish an all-American court of justice. In 1923 Costa Rica made such a proposal;[62] and five years later, at the Habana Conference, Colombia made a similar one.[63] Mexico in its Peace Code submitted a project for an American Court of International Justice at the 1933 Montevideo Conference. According to the plan such a court would be composed of one member from each member American state and a Canadian member as well. It would have compulsory jurisdiction over legal or justiciable disputes and general jurisdiction over others.[64] The subject was again broached at the 1936 Buenos Aires Conference. As usual it was submitted for further study and report at the Eighth Conference.[65] The report was duly presented there, but no agreement on it was reached.[66] At Bogotá in 1948 an inter-American court again failed of establishment, although an Inter-American Court to Protect the Rights of Man was discussed and the Inter-American Juridical Committee was called upon to prepare a draft statute for its creation to be submitted to the Tenth Conference.[67] Instead of an Inter-American Court, the Pact of Bogotá places its reliance upon the International Court of Justice as the judicial institution for the settlement of controversies between the

American states; for when the Pact was drafted it was believed that this body was completely competent to decide American disputes and to interpret American law, and further that the establishment of an American court might weaken the World Court.[68]

Thus, the Pact of Bogotá recognizes judicial settlement as a procedure for pacific settlement of inter-American controversies and makes the International Court of Justice the agency for such judicial settlement. Article XXI incorporates acceptance of the jurisdiction of the International Court as compulsory *ipso facto* and without special agreement in juridical matters concerning the questions listed in Article 38, Paragraph 2 of the court's statute, namely, the interpretation of a treaty; any question of international law; the existence of any fact which if established would constitute the breach of an international obligation; the nature or extent of the reparation to be made for the breach of an international obligation.

This article and following articles attempt to place the American states under some legal compulsion to submit their international legal disputes to the court for binding decision, and in this the treaty marks some advance. However, it must be remembered that in the first instance resort to adjudication by the court is just another procedure of peaceful settlement. The parties are bound to submit their international disputes to some pacific procedure, but they are given complete discretion as to what procedure they shall agree upon. They may agree to arbitration, good offices and mediation, investigation and conciliation, or some other pacific procedure of their choice rather than judicial procedure. They may agree on the latter, but there is nothing to bind them to do so.[69]

However, if the disputants submit to the procedure of conciliation, and if this procedure does not lead to a solution and if the parties have not agreed upon an arbitral procedure, then either party is entitled to have recourse to the International Court of Justice.[70] In the event that this particular pattern becomes reality, the court's jurisdiction is compulsory in accordance with Article 36, Paragraph 1 of the statute of the court, and one party to the dispute unilaterally may require the other to submit to judicial procedure.

The International Court of Justice is granted power by the Pact to determine its own jurisdiction if the parties fail to agree upon this preliminary question.[71] If the court determines that the controversy falls within Articles V, VI, or VII of the Pact—that is, if it concerns a matter of domestic jurisdiction, matters already settled by arbitral or judicial decision or governed by agreements in force, or matters involving the protection of nationals abroad—the court declares itself without jurisdiction, and the controversy shall be declared ended, for these are the exceptions to the obligation to resort to any pacific procedures inclusive of judicial procedures.[72]

Article XXXV then declares: "If the Court for other reasons declares itself to be without jurisdiction to hear and adjudge the controversy, the High Contracting Parties obligate themselves to submit it to arbitration, in accordance with the provisions of Chapter Five of this Treaty." This article is something of a Chinese puzzle as it relates to the jurisdiction of the court. This jurisdiction as set out above extends to disputes of a *juridical nature* or, in the synonymous language of the statute of the court, to "all legal disputes" concerning the interpretation of a treaty, questions of international law, the existence of facts which constitute a breach of an international obligation, and reparation to be made for such breach. Excluded from that jurisdiction under the Pact are matters falling within Articles V, VI, and VII. The language of Article XXXV implies that other matters are also without the jurisdiction, for the court may *for other reasons* declare itself to be without jurisdiction. Since the compulsory jurisdiction of the court under its statute and under the Pact extends to disputes of a juridical nature only, it belabors the obvious to say that disputes of a nonjuridical character are excluded. If the court finds that the dispute is nonjuridical in nature, then for this reason it is without jurisdiction.

To speak in these terms is to bring up the dubious distinction between legal, justiciable, or juridical disputes on the one hand and nonjusticiable, nonjuridical, nonlegal, or political disputes on the other.[73] Such a distinction is ensconced in international practice and much discussion has centered around the problem in an endeavor to determine what is legal and what is nonlegal or political. A widely held view is that there are disputes which cannot be settled by an international tribunal applying existing rules of international law. It is often stated that a justiciable dispute is one governed by international law, that there is a rule of international law existing and applicable to govern the dispute at hand. It would follow that a nonjusticiable dispute is one where a court of law could not be called to deal with the dispute and give a decision because no applicable norm of international law exists, or at least no clear norm exists for the solution of the conflict.[74]

To reason in this fashion is to assume that there are gaps in international law, but in reality lacunae do not exist.[75] There are areas where norms of international law refrain from stipulating obligations, and within this sphere of domestic jurisdiction the state is unrestricted. International law still governs in the sense that since it does not legally prohibit, it permits, and if the contentions of a complainant state fall within the sphere where the defendant is free from obligation it behooves the court to decide in favor of the freedom of the defendant state, not because there exists no international law norm to control the action of the defendant, but because the norm of international law leaves the defendant its liberty of action in the dispute at hand. Consequently all international disputes can be given a legal formulation. A court may always give a decision on the basis of international law—on the legal rights of the parties to the dispute—and no valid distinction exists between legal and nonlegal disputes insofar as the contents or inherent characteristics of the dispute are concerned.[76]

Taking either of the above-mentioned viewpoints, one ends up with a question of domestic jurisdiction, i.e., an area where the state is given complete liberty of action either because there is thought to be no controlling rule of international law to proscribe such freedom or because international law itself permits such freedom by a failure to obligate.[77] Since domestic jurisdictional matters are excluded by Article V of the Pact of Bogotá, something more must be signified when the court's jurisdiction is limited to legal or juridical disputes. If the issue of a justiciable or nonjusticiable dispute does not depend on the inherent characteristics of the dispute, then there must be another distinction as to what is a legal and what is a political dispute, for it is clear that the court is only competent to deal with juridical disputes under the compulsory jurisdiction. It may not treat of political problems except to give a judgment *ex aequo et bono* when requested to do so by the parties to the dispute.[78]

Whether a dispute is legal or political, justiciable or nonjusticiable, depends on the approach or attitude of the parties to it. If the parties in an endeavor to settle their dispute seek a determination of their rights on the basis of international law, the dispute is a legal and justiciable one. If at least one of the parties regards international law as unsatisfactory insofar as the particular dispute is concerned and is not content to have the dispute decided on the basis of legal rights, demanding satisfaction of its own interest even though this may require a revision of the existing law, then the dispute is nonjusticiable or political, for if such a party has its way the dispute will be settled on nonlegal or political grounds.[79] It is possibly this distinction which the United States delegation may have had in mind in taking its position, which was stated as follows:

The other principal point of the United States position was to draw a distinct line between controversies which depend for their solution upon the interpretation of existing rules of law and those which, in effect, seek changes in legal relationships. Cases of this latter category, wherein the complaint does not rest upon a claim of legal right, were variously referred to as "non-legal" or "political" controversies.[80]

Article XXXIII of the Pact of Bogotá and Article 36, Paragraph 6, of the statute of the court grant to the court the power to determine its jurisdiction in the event the parties are in dispute over the issue or fail to agree upon it. If both parties agree to the jurisdiction and it is not agreed that the dispute may be settled *ex aequo et bono,* the dispute is a legal one, for the court in such instance under its Statute may only apply international law. The question of whether a dispute is legal or nonlegal becomes important only when the parties disagree as to jurisdiction. In such a case, what standard shall be used to determine whether the dispute is legal or nonlegal, whether the court has or has not jurisdiction? Inasmuch as there is nothing in the inherent nature of any dispute which deprives it of a juridical character—i.e., which precludes the possibility of a decision by existing international legal principles—the International Court may declare any dispute to be a legal one where one of the parties submits it to the court under Article XXXI of the Pact and Article 36, Paragraph 2, of the statute.[81] This would seem to do some violence to the language of the statute and the Pact, both of which recognize a distinction between juridical and nonjuridical, even though the dispute falls within one of the enumerated subjects such as the interpretation of a treaty, any question of international law, etc. If the approach to the dispute determines its legal or nonlegal character, it would seem that the court would be justified in designating a dispute as legal only if both parties are willing to have their controversy settled on the basis of international law; for if one party justifies its claims or counterclaims on other than existing international legal principles, i.e., on morality or on justice or on a change in international law—then as to that party the dispute is not legal but political, and the language of Article 36, Paragraph 2, of the statute and Article XXXI of the Pact would not exclude such an interpretation of its jurisdiction by the court. This interpretation, of course, would permit one party to the dispute to block compulsory settlement by the court if said party declares the dispute to be a political one, i.e., one to be governed not by norms of international law but by nonlegal norms.[82]

Apparently in recognition of the possibility that the court can give this interpretation which would allow a party to escape its jurisdiction, and so as not to permit the dispute to go undecided because of its nonjuridical character, Article XXXV of the Pact obligates the parties to submit the dispute to arbitration. Thus, under the Pact it is possible for a party to the treaty to institute proceedings which will result in a legally binding decision either by the International Court or by an arbitral tribunal, for if resort to conciliation is had and this does not lead to a solution and the parties have not agreed to an arbitral procedure, then either of the parties may have recourse to the court. If the court decides that the dispute is nonjuridical and without its jurisdiction, then the parties are obligated to submit to arbitration.

Arbitration

Closely allied to judicial settlement is arbitration, a method for the pacific settlement of disputes which historically has been the most efficacious procedure.[83] The Hague Convention for the Pacific Settlement of International Disputes defined this procedure as follows: "International arbitration has for its object the settlement of disputes between States by Judges of their own choice and on the basis of respect for law. Recourse to arbitration implies an engagement to submit in good faith to the award."[84]

According to this statement arbitration is regarded as a legal procedure in that it involves an impartial proceeding based on legal rules, the decisions of the tribunal being regarded as final and binding upon the parties. It differs from judicial settlement only in slight degree, in that the members of the arbitral tribunal are chosen by the parties; the judicial functions for these members end when the case for which they have been nominated is decided; and finally, a somewhat greater control over the arbitration rests in the parties to the dispute.[85]

The Pact of Bogotá makes arbitration one of the procedures for the settlement of inter-American disputes. As with the other pacific procedures, the parties are given almost complete latitude with respect to resort to this method. As we have said, obligation to resort to arbitration exists only when the International Court of Justice has declined jurisdiction in a case for reasons other than those given in Articles V, VI, and VII. In such an instance, where the court declines jurisdiction because the dispute is nonjuridical, the parties obligate themselves to submit to arbitration, and if a party fails to meet this obligation, automatic procedures provide for the creation of the arbitral tribunal and for a final decision of the case.

Over and above this obligation of arbitration, the parties may, if they so agree, submit pre-existing differences as well as those arising in the future, whether juridical or not, to arbitration.[86] In permitting, and in certain instances requiring, nonjuridical disputes to be submitted to arbitration, the Pact of Bogotá departs from the concept of arbitration as a legal procedure, for if nonjuridical disputes are subject to arbitration the adjudication will not be based on international law. Such a broadening of the procedure of arbitration was pressed by various Latin American governments in the belief that the time had come to make of arbitration a procedure of deciding all disputes, whether political or legal, by a binding award.[87] This aspect of the Pact did not escape criticism, for states have been hesitant to agree in advance by treaty to submit to arbitration, particularly in view of the fact that the award is final, when they do not know what rules the arbiters will follow in deciding the controversy. This hesitancy has only been partly cured by making of arbitration a legal procedure; that is, by limiting the discretion of the arbiters to international law. To open the door to the submission of political or nonjuridical disputes to arbitration would clearly be to permit decision on a nonlegal basis, and this would appear to leave the basis of decision to the discretion of the arbiter. The Pact contains no language as to what shall be the basis of an arbitral award, nor does it make provisions that this is to be settled by the *compromis* between the parties. Conceivably the arbitrators could even decide a judicial dispute on a political basis.[88]

Since the arbitrators are not necessarily bound to law as a basis of decision, a further difficulty may be considered. The Pact requires the arbiters to be jurists. Jurists are trained to deal primarily with legal conflicts, and they may not be the most competent persons to perform political tasks.[89]

The parties may by agreement establish the arbitral tribunal they deem most appropriate; if they desire they may even select a single arbiter.[90] However, if no previous agreement exists, provisions set forth the manner in which the tribunal shall be constituted. Article XL requires each party to designate one arbiter of recognized competence in questions of international law and of highest integrity, and to transmit these designations to the Council of the OAS together with a list of ten jurists of different nationality from their own, selected from the panel of members of the Permanent Court of Arbitration of The Hague. The Council shall then proceed to select the three additional members of the tribunal as follows: if the two lists contain three names in common, they will be chosen as the neutral members; if there are more than three in common, the three arbiters needed to complete the formation are to be selected by lot. In either of these instances the five shall choose one of their number to preside. If the list contains only two names in common, these and the members designated by the parties shall choose the fifth, who is to be presiding officer. This fifth member must be on the Panel of the Hague Court of Arbitration, but not included on the lists of the parties. If the list contains only one name in common, he shall be a member and another name shall be chosen by lot from the remaining names on the list. The four shall then elect the fifth member as above. If the list contains no names in common, one arbiter is to be chosen from each list and the fifth again is to be chosen as above. If agreement cannot be had by the four arbiters as to the fifth within a month's time, the four are called upon to arrange the list of jurists according to preference, and after comparison the person who first obtains a majority vote is to be elected as the fifth member.

Article XLV contains additional provisions as to the formation of the tribunal. These have to do with the automatic creation of the tribunal in instances in which the parties are obligated to submit to jurisdiction. By the terms of this article and of Article XL, if a party fails to designate its arbiter and submit its list within a two-month period after notification of the decision of the court, the other party may request the Council to establish the tribunal. The Council, after calling upon the delinquent party to fulfill its obligation within a period of fifteen days, may then act as follows: it shall select one member by lot from the list presented by the petitioning party; it shall choose by majority vote two jurists, not nationals of either party, from the panel of the Hague Arbitration Court. The three so chosen, together with the one directly chosen by the petitioning party, shall select the fifth, who will act as presiding officer.

Article XLII is concerned with the problem that arises when two or more states are involved in the same controversy. In this instance two states defending the same interests are considered as a single party. If, on the other hand, they have opposing interests, the number of arbiters may be increased so that all parties have equal representation.

In addition to these provisions relating to the establishment of the arbitral tribunal and the selection of its members, the Pact includes provisos regarding the *compromis,* an agreement between the parties whereby, according to Article XLIII, the parties define specifically the subject matter of the controversy, the seat of the tribunal, the rules of procedure, and the period within which the award is to be handed down. Note that nothing is said about the parties' agreement as to the basis of the award. To obviate difficulties which in the past often precluded arbitration because of the parties' failure to agree on the terms of the *compromis,* this article requires the parties to draw up the special agreement within three months after the installation of the tribunal; but if they do not do so within that period, then the International Court of Justice is empowered to draw up the agreement through summary procedure which is binding upon the parties.

The award is rendered by a majority vote of the arbiters and, once handed down and made known to the parties, settles the dispute definitively.[91] Review may be had within a year if a previously existing unknown fact is discovered.[92] Differences concerning interpretation of the award are to be decided by the arbitration tribunal.[93]

The Pact of Bogotá makes the arbitration award definitively binding, and of course the decision of the International Court is regarded as binding. But the matter of obligation is not left solely to the good faith of the parties, for if one of them fails to carry out obligations imposed by the decision of the court or of an arbitral award, the other party before resorting to the Security Council may propose a Meeting of Consultation of Ministers of Foreign Affairs to agree upon measures to be taken to assure fulfilment of the decision or award.[94] The type of measures to be taken are not set forth, but it is conceivable that as a last resort the measures of the Rio Treaty (except possibly the use of armed force) could be ordered to persuade the recalcitrant.[95] If measures taken by the foreign ministers fail to enforce the decision or award, then the case may be taken to the Security Council of the United Nations.[96]

An unusual feature of pacific settlement is contained in Article LI. According to this article, parties to a dispute by agreement may petition the General Assembly or the Security Council to request of the International Court of Justice an advisory opinion on any juridical question. This petition is to be made through the Council of the OAS.

EFFECTIVENESS OF THE PACT

The Pact of Bogotá does seek to improve inter-American peace machinery so as to give a system which will guarantee definitive settlment of inter-American disputes within a reasonable time. In this it has been only partially successful, although improvement has been made. The codifying and co-ordinating of the maze of previous procedures of pacific settlement is in itself an advance, and there has been some betterment in the procedures. New and simplified methods for the creation of the commission used in the procedure of conciliation and investigation lessen the chances of failure of its formation. The arbitration stipulations to insure the establishment of the tribunal, and the drawing up of the *compromis* in case the parties fail to agree, attempt to cure the principal defects of the Arbitration Convention of 1929. Resort to the International Court for judicial settlement is a procedure which was formerly ignored, and the Pact does attempt at some stage to obligate the parties to settlement by binding award or decision of both juridical and nonjuridical disputes.

Nevertheless, compulsory peaceful settlement is largely an illusion, for the compulsory jurisdiction of the court at the unilateral submission by one party comes into being only when conciliation has failed and the parties have not agreed on arbitration. If one party obstructs resort to conciliation, the other cannot unilaterally come before the court. Since obligatory resort to arbitration is required only when the dispute has been submitted to the court and it has declared itself without jurisdiction, resort to arbitration can also be frustrated. In reality, if a party refuses to agree that the dispute cannot be settled by diplomatic negotiation, it would seem that all other procedures can be effectively sidestepped.

Apart from the effectiveness of the Pact *qua* pact, obligation of compulsory submission to pacific procedures is further reduced by reservations. As has been seen, the United States reserved to that part of Article V which in cases of controversy between the parties as to whether or not a matter is within the domestic jurisdiction permits referral of the question to the International Court of Justice for preliminary jurisdictional decision. The United States utilized its reservation to the court's statute which excepted from the compulsory jurisdiction of the court "disputes with regard to matters which are essentially within the domestic jurisdiction of the United States as determined by the United States."[97] Additional protection for this United States right is declared by way of specific reservation: "The United States does not undertake as complainant State to submit to the International Court of Justice any controversy which is not considered to be properly within the jurisdiction of the Court."[98]

This latter language also constitutes a reservation to Article XXXII, the heart of the compulsory jurisdiction of the court, which permits unilateral submission to the court after conciliation has been tried and failed. Since this article does not limit the scope of disputes to those of a juridical nature but includes all disputes, the United States was of the opinion that this was a grant of power to the court in excess of that granted in its statute, which embraces juridical disputes only.[99] Hence, the United States reservation in effect refuses to submit to the court disputes it considers nonjuridical. Since the court has no jurisdiction over nonjuridical disputes and would be obligated to dismiss such a dispute submitted to it, this reservation might seem specious. But not so. What this accomplishes is to prevent the court from deciding its own jurisdiction and permit the United States to self-judge.[100]

Under the Pact, if the court considers the matter as nonjuridical and without its jurisdiction, then the parties are obligated to submit to arbitration. To this compulsory feature the United States also reserved, stipulating: "The submission on the part of the United States of any controversy to arbitration, as distinguished from judicial settlement shall be dependent upon the conclusion of special agreement between the parties to the case."[101]

This language, of course, removes the element of compulsion from arbitration insofar as the United States is concerned. Again the United States was disturbed at making an advance commitment to forced submission of nonjuridical controversies, i.e., controversies not based on a claim of legal right and not to be decided by the guides of international law.

Argentina, Peru, and to a lesser extent Paraguay also made far-reaching reservations to the compulsory features of the Pact,[102] and it should be realized that these restrictive reservations do not apply solely to the parties who made them. If a dispute occurs between a state not so reserving and a state which has so reserved, the former may take advantage of the latter's reservation on the basis of reciprocity. Article LV reads: "Should any of the High Contracting Parties make reservations concerning the present Treaty, such reservations shall with respect to the state that makes them, apply to all signatory states on the basis of reciprocity."

The Pact of Bogotá is unlike the Rio Treaty and the Charter, which did not become effective until two-thirds of the signatory states ratified, for it comes into effect between the parties ratifying when they ratify.[103] However, as of March, 1961, it had been ratified by only nine states, and by only one of the larger states—Mexico.[104] This lack of ratification renders the Pact almost a nullity, and as a result the juridical arm of the inter-American system of peace and security can hardly be considered effective. Attempts have been made to revise it so as to bring its provisions more in accord with viewpoints of some of its signatories and thus obtain more widespread ratification.[105] To date such attempts at revision have been unsuccessful, and if they were to succeed the more rigid systems of compulsory judicial or arbitral settlement would in all probability have to be deleted in favor of greater flexibility, which in turn would cripple obligatory procedures designed to result in final decisions.

CHAPTER XVII

MAINTAINING THE PEACE OF THE AMERICAS

To insure or maintain inter-American peace in the immediate sense the instruments signed at Bogotá placed reliance upon the obligation adhered to by the parties to settle their controversies by peaceful procedures, and the Pact of Bogotá details these procedures and sets forth ways and means for their use. If, however, these procedures are unsuccessful and a threat or breach of the peace occurs, then the Rio Treaty provides machinery in the form of joint measures for the maintenance or restoration of peace. To deal with dangers to hemispheric peace the Charter relies primarily upon the Meeting of Consultation of Ministers of Foreign Affairs, acting either in its capacity "to consider problems of an urgent nature and common interest" or as Organ of Consultation under the Rio Treaty.

The OAS was called upon to use the powers granted under the Rio Treaty to resolve threats to the peace immediately following its coming into effect by the necessary ratification by two-thirds of its signatories and, since that time, a series of cases have confronted the consultative organs of the regional system.

COSTA RICAN–NICARAGUAN AFFAIR

On December 11, 1948, the Costa Rican representative on the Council of the OAS charged that an armed force had invaded Costa Rica's territory from the neighboring state of Nicaragua.[1] Costa Rica specifically requested that the provision of Article 6 of the Rio Treaty be invoked, i.e., the provision which does not require all nations to come to the immediate assistance of the victim, but which does require immediate consultation among the parties to the treaty.[2]

The chairman of the Council of the OAS called for a meeting on the following day, December 12, and, as there was a lack of complete and accurate information, permitted each nation forty-eight hours to obtain the necessary facts to present its case. With this information in hand, the Council invoked the Rio Treaty, calling for a Meeting of Consultation of Foreign Ministers, although not setting any date for that meeting, and in the meantime declaring itself to be provisionally the Organ of Consultation under the treaty. Then it immediately sent an investigating commission to San José and Managua to obtain on-the-spot accurate and complete information. At both places the commission met with the utmost co-operation. The actual crossing of the border of Costa Rica had not developed into a serious threat to the stability of that government, and there was evidence that both Costa Rica and Nicaragua had been remiss in discouraging revolutionary groups whose aim in each country was to overthrow the government of the other.

On December 24, 1948, the special commission reported back to the Council,[3] which, on the basis of the commission's findings, ordered both governments, in the name of the principles of non-intervention and continental solidarity, to abstain from further hostilities; called on each government to eliminate those conditions which led to the dispute; and made other specific recommendations to both for settling the issue. In order to guarantee the fulfilment of these obligations by the two nations, a commission of military experts was dispatched to the scene of the conflict. After much negotiation, all of which was undertaken by the Council itself, the controversy was brought to an end on February 21, 1949, when a Pact of Amity and Friendship was signed between the two nations.[4] The Council then informed all the governments of the OAS of the termination of the incident and of the fact that the circumstances giving rise to the calling of the Meeting of Consultation of the Ministers of Foreign Affairs no longer existed.

The Council appears to have taken the position that the formality of convoking the Meeting of Consultation of the Ministers of Foreign Affairs must be complied with, but that if the affair could be handled by the Council as Provisional Organ of Consultation and the peace maintained without actual resort to the meeting, the procedure for settlement would be simplified and that this method was therefore more desirable.[5] Furthermore, the prompt action by the Council as Provisional Organ of Consultation prevented the controversy from taking on a more dangerous character.

THE HAITI–DOMINICAN REPUBLIC CASES

In a letter to the Council dated February 15, 1949, the Haitian Government charged the Dominican Republic with "moral" aggression and petitioned for immediate convocation of the Council as the Provisional Organ of Consultation.[6] The note alleged that the Dominican government had given asylum to and was supporting the activities of Astrel Roland, a former colonel in the Haitian army, who was charged with plotting the overthrow of the Haitian government. Specifically, Roland had used the Dominican radio to propagandize against the Haitian government.

In a special session held on February 23, 1949, the Council heard statements from the representatives of both governments and came to the conclusion that the dispute did not affect the inviolability or the integrity of the territory or the sovereignty or political independence of Haiti, and hence Haiti and the Dominican Republic were under a duty to settle the dispute by peaceful measures as provided for in existing inter-American treaties. The Council decided not to convoke the Organ of Consultation. The two governments then placed the matter for settlement before the Inter-American Peace Committee, which suggested that the nations pledge not to tolerate in their respective territories activities which had as their object the disturbance of the domestic peace of either of the two nations. The pledge was signed by both in June, 1949.[7]

In spite of this pledge, the Dominican government permitted the continuation of the activities, and the Haitian police in November and December, 1949, suppressed an armed conspiracy against the Haitian government. As a result of this abortive plot, the Haitian government on January 3, 1950, again invoked the Rio Treaty against the Dominican Republic,[8] declaring that officials of the Dominican Republic had been involved in the plot and that now the territorial integrity, sovereignty, and political independence of Haiti were threatened and the peace of the Americas was endangered.

On January 6, 1950, the Council of the OAS met in special session to consider the new complaint. The Dominican representative denied all Haiti's accusations, and requested the Council to apply the Rio Treaty against Haiti and other Caribbean nations because of their toleration and support, over a considerable period of time, of activities hostile to the Dominican government.

Acting under the precedents which had been established by the Costa Rican–Nicaraguan Case, the Council took the following actions; it constituted itself as Provisional Organ of Consultation; it called for a Meeting of the Ministers of Foreign Affairs without setting a date; it authorized the chairman to appoint an investigating committee to determine the facts upon which subsequent decisions of the consultative organ would be based.

The Organ of Consultation met on January 11, 1950, and decided it should take up the Haitian and Dominican charges as separate cases. The investigating committee heard evidence in Washington, then visited the Dominican Republic, Haiti, Cuba, Guatemala, and Mexico. It divided its report into two parts, one dealing with Haiti's charges and the other with the charges of the Dominican Republic.

In support of Haiti's complaint it found that the failure of the Dominican Republic to prevent the activities was in violation of the joint declaration of June, 1949, and that there was substantial evidence to prove that the Dominican government had encouraged and aided the abortive attempt to overthrow Haiti's government.

In support of the complaint of the Dominican Republic, it was found that the governments of Cuba and Guatemala had tolerated, and in some instances supported, activities within their territories which were aimed at the overthrow of the Dominican government. The committee also found that various groups of political exiles were engaged in revolutionary activities and were receiving encouragement and support from governmental authorities, and that the existence of such activities constantly endangered the peace of the Americas.

The Organ of Consultation delivered its decisions in a series of resolutions on April 8, 1950:

1. It requested the Dominican Republic to take immediate and effective steps to prevent its government officials from tolerating, instigating, or encouraging seditious movements against other governments.

2. It requested the governments of both Haiti and the Dominican Republic to comply strictly with the declarations of June, 1949.

3. It asked the governments of Cuba and Guatemala to take measures that would prevent conspiracy in their territories against the security of other countries, and to prevent the acquisition of war materials by conspiring groups.

4. It requested Cuba, Guatemala, Haiti, and the Dominican Republic to adhere strictly to the principle of non-intervention, and requested each of these countries to make every effort to avoid systematic and hostile propaganda against the others.

5. It provided for the appointment of a special provisional committee of five members which would place itself at the service of the parties to facilitate compliance with these resolutions.

6. It recommended that the Council of the OAS, through its organs, undertake studies on the possibilities of stimulating and developing effective exercise of representative democracy; on the strengthening and perfecting of the Habana Convention of 1928 on the Duties and Rights of States in the Event of Civil Strife; and on rules for political exiles and refugees.

7. It canceled the convocation of the Meeting of the Ministers of Foreign Affairs and terminated the provisional action of the Council as Organ of Consultation.[9]

It was again significant here, as in the Costa Rican–Nicaraguan Case, that all parties to the dispute agreed to co-operate with the Council in its investigations and accepted the decisions reached. None of the nations questioned the precedent established in the Costa Rican–Nicaraguan Case of convoking a Meeting of Consultation of Ministers of Foreign Affairs without specifying date or place, and then going ahead as Provisional Organ of Consultation and handling the dispute itself.

Over and above this, other precedents were set by these early cases with respect to OAS peace and security machinery. In effect two agencies, the Council and the Inter-American Peace Committee, emerged as the most important for the peaceful settlement of disputes — rather surprisingly, in view of the fact that neither was really intended by the framers of the Rio Treaty or of the Charter and Pact of Bogotá to play such a part, or at least not to the extent to which this has developed. The Council as Provisional Organ of Consultation under the Rio Treaty did not in reality exercise a police function in these cases, for no coercive measures were applied. To the contrary, the Council acted to settle the disputes, thus assuming a role in pacific settlement. In effect, as has been pointed out, it has become "a sort of court of summary jurisdiction."[10] Its actions, partaking of something akin to investigation and conciliation, have resulted in resolutions and recommendations to the states in conflict for peaceful settlement — recommendations ostensibly nonbinding, but at the same time backed with an implied threat that if the disputants did not comply therewith, the more stringent coercive measures of the Rio Treaty would be brought to bear. That is, there would be a call for collective action either by the Council acting provisionally or, more probably, by a Meeting of Foreign Ministers as Organ of Consultation, since an ordering of such measures would be so serious as to warrant a meeting of the latter group.[11]

It is not clear from the Council's action in these cases whether it was, in making its recommendations to the parties for peaceful solution, acting under Article 7 of the Rio Treaty which, in conflicts between two or more American states, permits it to order a suspension of hostilities, a return to the status quo, and the taking of all other necessary measures to re-establish and maintain inter-American peace; or whether it was merely acting through implied powers to recommend ways and means to the parties for a peaceful solution, such recommendations possibly not being considered measures of the Council at all. In either event it is apparent that the Council considers itself empowered to act in this manner.

In the second Haitian–Dominican Republic Case the Council not only set forth its resolutions aimed at settling the controversies and terminated its status as provisional consultative organ, but set up a special committee for the Caribbean to supervise the terms of settlement so as to insure that the resolutions and recommendations to the parties were carried out. This shows the elasticity of the term "provisional," for actually the Council's action, despite the fact that it officially terminated its action as provisional organ, was extended and continued until its special committee reported and was discharged.[12]

When the Inter-American Peace Committee was brought into the picture in the first Haitian–Dominican Republic Case, an agency for the settlement of disputes not even contemplated at Bogotá was added. This committee is possessed of characteristics similar to those of a commission of inquiry and conciliation, and the Council in making use of the committee felt that it would be useful for the settlement of disputes that did not fall within the terms of the Rio Treaty so as to permit Council action—the committee being able to take cognizance of any dispute, while the Council as provisional organ was limited in its powers by the Rio Treaty.[13] Thus in disputes of a less dangerous character the committee could investigate and conciliate and is empowered to suggest to the disputants how the dispute should be settled. In a more dangerous situation where the dispute threatens hemispheric peace by affecting the inviolability or the integrity of the territory or the sovereignty or political independence of an American state, then the Council can also suggest ways and means for the settlement of the dispute, but at the same time the threat is present of Rio Treaty enforcement measures in case compliance is not forthcoming.

These cases indicate further evolution of the inter-American peace and security system—and, it may be noted, evolution away from the complicated pacific procedures of the Pact of Bogotá. This change was probably necessitated by the fact that the Pact was and is not now widely ratified, as well as by the further fact that a more prompt settlement than its complicated procedures would allow was advisable in cases where the parties found it inconvenient to resort to them or were too impatient to do so—or, as in the cases at hand, where the subject matter was so political and so involved with ideology that a political settlement in the interests of maintenance of peace was all that could be hoped for.

THE 1954 COMMUNIST MENACE IN GUATEMALA

In June, 1954, a series of incidents led to an invasion of Guatemala, launched from neighboring Honduras, by an anticommunist force of exiled Guatemalan military men under the leadership of Guatemalan Lieutenant Colonel Carlos Castillo Armas.[14] This group was bent on overthrowing the Communist-infected government of President Jacobo Arbenz. On June 19, 1954, a cable from the Guatemalan minister of foreign affairs to the president of the Security Council of the United Nations reported the invasion and charged that aircraft coming from the direction of Honduras and Nicaragua had bombed and machine-gunned various locations in Guatemala. The cable charged that open aggression had been perpetrated against Guatemala by the governments of Honduras and Nicaragua, at the instigation of certain foreign monopolies whose interests had been affected by the progressive policies of Guatemala. To stop this aggression, the president of the Security Council was requested to convene a meeting in accordance with Articles 34, 35, and 39 of the United Nations Charter.[15]

These accusations were elaborated upon at the Security Council[16] meeting the following day by the Guatemalan representative, who, together with the representatives of Honduras and Nicaragua, had been invited to participate. Guatemala alleged that it had been invaded by expeditionary forces which were elements of an unlawful international conspiracy that was masked as a rising of Guatemalan exiles, and that the way for such a campaign had been paved by the United Fruit Company and other monopolies encouraged by the United States Department of State, which was seeking to represent Guatemala as an outpost of Soviet communism on the American continent, a tool of Moscow, a spearhead of the Soviet Union against the United States, and a disturber of and a threat to hemispheric peace. Denying all these imputations, Guatemala demanded that the Security Council call upon Honduras and Nicaragua to apprehend the exiles and mercenaries who were allegedly invading Guatemala, and requested the Council to verify the facts by setting up an observation commission to establish Nicaraguan and Honduran connivance in the invasion.

The Nicaraguan and Honduran representatives denied the Guatemalan allegations and supported a draft resolution, sponsored by Brazil and Colombia, referring the dispute to the Organization of American States. The Brazilian representative declared that there had "long been a tradition among the American states that all disputes and situations which could threaten or endanger the friendly relations among American republics should be dealt with by the organization which those republics themselves have set up for that purpose."[17] He pointed out that the Charter of the OAS empowered the regional organization to deal with such disputes or situations, and that the Security Council was called upon under the United Nations Charter to encourage the development of pacific settlement of local disputes through regional agencies, either on the initiative of the states concerned or by reference from the Security Council. The Colombian representative argued that Article 33 and Article 52, paragraph 2, of the Charter of the United Nations imposed an obligation upon all members to apply first to the regional organization before referring a dispute to the Security Council. The Guatemalan representative disagreed with these contentions, arguing that Articles 33 and 52 were inapplicable because they spoke in terms of settlement of *disputes* by regional organizations before reference to the Security Council. He maintained that the issue was simply *aggression* and did not involve a *dispute* with any state. Therefore Guatemala had the unchallenged right to appeal directly to the Security Council under Article 34, which permits the Security Council to investigate any dispute or any *situation* which might lead to international friction or give rise to a dispute; under Article 35, which permits any member to bring any such dispute or *situation* to the attention of the Security Council; and under Article 39, which calls upon the Security Council to determine the existence of threats to or breaches of the peace as well as acts of aggression and to take action to maintain or restore international peace and security. In other words, Guatemala was asserting that no *dispute* existed, but rather that there had arisen a *situation* in the form of an aggression which endangered the peace, thus bringing the conflict within the meaning of these articles of the United Nations Charter and excluding it from the articles on regional arrangement which are semantically limited to a *dispute* only.

The technical argument of Guatemala appears to have little merit for, although debates have arisen in the United Nations as to the distinction between disputes and situations, no clear-cut differentiation has ever been agreed upon. In practice, the Council has seldom sought to draw the line but has dealt with matters coming before it, whether labeled *dispute* or *situation,* in a flexible and expedient manner.[18]

Logically speaking, there is a dissimilarity between the two: a situation is somewhat broader than a dispute. Every dispute occurs because of some situation and may bring about other situations, but every situation does not necessarily result in a dispute. A dispute can be characterized as "disagreement on a point of law or fact, a conflict of legal views or interests between two or more states."[19] Under this definition, in view of the facts of the case, the weakness of the Guatemalan position can be illustrated, for the Guatemalan accusation contained the words "aggressor governments" and charged that open aggression had been perpetrated by the governments of Honduras and Nicaragua—charges which were rejected by Honduras and Nicaragua as false, thus establishing that there was a matter of law or fact asserted on one side and denied on the other.

Guatemala contended that the act of aggression was not a dispute. Clearly all disputes are not aggressions, but it hardly appears possible to have an aggression which does not involve a dispute. By some stretch of imagination, one state might illegally attack another or support an illegal attack on another where there was no underlying dispute, but this in reality would be extremely unlikely. In the present case, it should be noted that the parties had been engaged in contentious argument or dispute even before the submission to the Security Council, for Guatemala had charged a policy of hostility and aggressiveness by Nicaragua and Honduras and had further charged that Nicaragua had unilaterally broken off relations with Guatemala, giving false explanations for its action; and Guatemala admitted making representations to Honduras to restrain and control armed groups operating from Honduran territory, a request which Guatemala declared Honduras had ignored. By her own admissions, Guatemala indicated that a dispute existed.

In fact, on June 19 the government of Guatemala was not quite so sure that a dispute did not exist as it was the following day at the Security Council hearing, for on the 19th, when it cabled the Security Council, Guatemala also appealed to the Inter-American Peace Committee to take steps to preserve the peace. At this point Guatemala apparently believed a dispute existed, for the Inter-American Peace Committee is confined in its considerations, again semantically, to a consideration of disputes. On June 20, Guatemala changed its position and officially declined to allow the Peace Committee to concern itself with the situation, declaring before the Security Council, "We cannot go to a regional organization to discuss a dispute which does not exist. . . . We are faced with an outright act of aggression."[20]

Tsarapkin of the Soviet Union voiced his opposition to the proposal to refer the issue to the OAS, maintaining that when aggression had actually taken place, the Security Council could not refuse to accept responsibility for ending it, and adding that there was no obligation to refer such a matter to regional agencies. He asserted there was insufficient time for regional action, for Guatemala would be overcome while the question was still under discussion in the OAS, and taxed the OAS with being dominated by the United States, which had demonstrated its hostility to the government of Guatemala.

Other representatives emphasized that the draft resolution was in no way intended to relieve the Security Council of its responsibility, but sought to employ the Charter machinery providing for the use of regional arrangements. The United States representative, Lodge, felt that a dispute of this nature could be dealt with most expeditiously and most effectively by the OAS, to which Guatemala had already presented a request for action. He denied that the United States had in any way connived in an invasion of Guatemala or that it dominated the OAS, and expressed gratification that the Guatemalan representative had made it clear that he was making no charges whatever against the United States government. Directing his remarks to Russia, he continued, "I say to the representative of the Soviet Union, 'Stay out of this hemisphere and do not try to start your plans and your conspiracies over here!' " Mr. Lodge also said that from the information so far received by his government it appeared that the situation "does not involve aggression but is a revolt of Guatemalans against Guatemalans."[21]

The Brazilian-Colombian draft resolution proposed that the Security Council, bearing in mind the provisions of Chapter 8 of the Charter dealing with regional arrangements and being conscious of the availability of inter-American machinery which could deal effectively with problems concerning the maintenance of peace and security in the Americas, should refer the complaint to the OAS for urgent consideration. The OAS would be asked to inform the Security Council as soon as possible of whatever measures were taken.

To this resolution France submitted an amendment, accepted by Brazil and Colombia, which added the stipulation that the Security Council, without prejudice to such measures as the OAS might take, should call for the immediate termination of any action likely to cause bloodshed and should request all members of the United Nations to abstain, in the spirit of the Charter, from giving assistance to any such action.

The joint draft resolution as thus amended was put to the vote and received ten votes in favor. Since the one vote against referral was that of the permanent member of the Council, the Soviet Union, it acted as a veto and the draft resolution was not adopted. Subsequently, France introduced its amendment as a separate proposal which was unanimously adopted. This omitted any reference to the OAS.

Five days later, on June 25, 1954,[22] the Security Council met again at Guatemala's request. Among various communications from the government of Guatemala there was one, dated June 22, stating that the resolution, although absolutely binding under the Charter, had not been complied with by those members of the United Nations who had acquiesced in or assisted from their territories the acts of aggression suffered by Guatemala. "During the last 48 hours," the letter stated, "aggressive acts against my country have continued by land, sea and air and have undoubtedly been committed from airfields and centers of operation situated outside Guatemalan territory while the Guatemalan National Army has confined its operation to the defense of the national territory and to repelling the aggressors."[23]

Guatemala therefore requested another emergency meeting of the Security Council so that the Council could use its authority with Honduras and Nicaragua to secure the cessation of all assistance to or acquiescence in the aggressive acts being committed by the "mercenary" forces.

Honduras and Nicaragua, meanwhile, reiterated that they had not participated in the violations of territorial integrity complained of by Guatemala. They had, furthermore, expressed their views at a meeting of the Inter-American Peace Committee of the OAS on June 23 when the committee, at the request of Honduras and Nicaragua, endorsed the setting up of a commission of inquiry to proceed to Guatemala, Honduras, and Nicaragua to obtain the necessary information to enable the committee to establish the facts and to suggest effective methods of achieving a speedy settlement. The committee had expressed the hope that Guatemala would see fit to co-operate. Guatemala refused to receive such a commission on the ground that it could not consent to having this matter brought before the committee before the earlier resolution of the Security Council was fully complied with.

After a long discussion, the Security Council voted against adopting the provisional agenda listing the Guatemalan complaint. The vote was four in favor (Denmark, Lebanon, New Zealand, and the U.S.S.R.) and five against (Brazil, China, Colombia, Turkey, and the U.S.A.), with two abstentions (the United Kingdom and France). Those opposed to resuming consideration of Guatemala's charges emphasized their belief that the Security Council should await the outcome of the machinery set in motion by the Inter-American Peace Committee. The Security Council was informed by Brazil and Colombia that whether or not Guatemala decided to receive the commission established by the committee, the commission could perform a useful task by visiting Honduras and Nicaragua. The position of Denmark, Lebanon, and New Zealand was substantially that the correct procedure would be to place the matter on the agenda, hear what Guatemala had to say, and then, if nothing new emerged, adjourn to leave the examination, with full confidence, in the hands of the Inter-American Peace Committee.

In its letter of June 22 to the Secretary General of the United Nations, Guatemala again contended that it was within its rights to refuse to submit this aggression to the OAS, and that, in the event of conflict between the obligations of Guatemala as a member of the United Nations and its obligations as a member of the OAS, its obligations toward the United Nations prevailed. Guatemala stated that the OAS, under international law, could not take action because

although Guatemala might be considered to belong to the Organization, which is the case, as far as this specific instance is concerned, it has not completed the ratifications of the Organization's fundamental agreements of Rio de Janeiro and Bogotá. It follows that neither the Organization of American States itself, nor the Inter-American Peace Committee, which forms part of it, may deal with the aggression against Guatemala; the former for the reason already noted, and the latter because it is only competent to deal with disputes between Member States, and certainly Guatemala has no dispute of any kind with the neighboring States of Honduras and Nicaragua.[24]

This language is obfuscatory and probably deliberately so. It sounds like "yes, yes—no, no" all uttered in the same breath, for Guatemala admits and then denies membership in the OAS. In denying membership, Guatemala was saying that she had not consented to be bound by OAS obligations. Without a doubt these justifications for seeking Security Council intervention in the matter in preference to OAS intervention were illegal, both under the Charter of the United Nations and under the treaties governing the inter-American system.

Guatemala could hardly deny the competency of the Inter-American Peace Committee on the ground of lack of consent, for this committee was not created by the Rio Treaty or the Bogotá Charter but by a resolution at Habana in 1940. This committee's competence and existence had been continued by a resolution of the Tenth Conference. To these resolutions Guatemala had acceded.[25] Recognizing this, Guatemala asserted that the committee was only competent to deal with disputes, and then fell back to its previous position that no dispute existed.

As to the OAS in general, the Guatemalan representative admitted that Guatemala was a member but then asserted in effect that it could not be required to submit to OAS agencies created and empowered to deal with hemispheric disputes, situations, and threats to the peace by the Rio Treaty and the Charter of Bogotá because it had not completed the ratification of the Bogotá Charter or the Rio Treaty. This was true in that Guatemala's ratification of these instruments contained reservations. A treaty ratified with reservations is held to be in force between the reserving state and those states which accept the reservations, but is not in force between a state ratifying with reservations and another state which had already ratified but which does not accept the reservations.[26] The Eighth International Conference of American States, seeking to discourage the introduction of reservations, adopted a resolution[27] providing that if a state proposed to adhere to or ratify a treaty with a reservation, it should first transmit the text of the reservation to the Pan American Union so that this agency could inform the signatory states and ascertain whether they accept it or not. According to this procedure the ratifying state still has the right to proceed to ratify with the reservation, in spite of the fact that the effect will be to bring the treaty into operation as to the states accepting the reservation and leave it inoperative as to other states. Not all the nations of the OAS had come to a decision on Guatemala's reservations, hence her status as to those nations which had not indicated whether or not the reservations were acceptable was debatable. But the fact that Guatemala had participated in the meetings and work of the organs of the OAS, fully and at all times, including the Tenth International Conference of American States held in Caracas in March, 1954, would certainly indicate that most American nations considered Guatemala subject to the Charter of Bogotá.[28] And having accepted the right to participate in the affairs of the OAS, Guatemala was estopped from denying that she had accepted the fundamental duties attached to the right.[29]

One of the fundamental duties established by the Charter of Bogotá is set forth in Article 20: "All international disputes that may arise between American States shall be submitted to the peaceful procedures set forth in this Charter before being referred to the Security Council of the United Nations." Furthermore, under Chapter 8 of the United Nations Charter, members of the United Nations entering into regional arrangements are under an obligation to try to settle local disputes through regional agencies before referring them to the Security Council; and alternatively, if regional facilities for the settlement of a regional dispute exist, the Security Council is under a duty to "encourage" the parties to try local methods of settlement before asking aid from the Security Council. Failure of the Security Council to refer the issue to an agency of the OAS was at least a sin of omission if not of commission. Guatemala's plea in the alternative that, if it did have an obligation toward the OAS, that obligation would be overridden by its obligation to the United Nations in the event of conflict between the obligations was untenable because there is no conflict between the two. Article 52, paragraph 2, places an imperative duty on members of regional arrangements to achieve pacific settlement of local disputes through the regional agency.

Had the Security Council lived up to the spirit and letter of the United Nations Charter when Guatemala requested Security Council action, the Council should have encouraged the regional settlement of the problem. An attempt was made to do so, but this was defeated by Soviet veto. If and when inter-American agencies failed in settlement then, obviously, the Security Council could intervene. Had the Security Council desired it could have investigated to determine whether a situation existed likely to disturb international peace and security,[30] but even here there was nothing to prevent it from relying upon the Inter-American Peace Committee or other agency of the OAS for such investigation.

Legal criticism might be directed at the Council decision on June 25 not to adopt the agenda permitting consideration of the Guatemalan complaint, for, to a degree, Guatemala was denied a hearing which seems accorded by Article 35. A more correct position was that of those states who urged a hearing and, if nothing new emerged, leaving the matter in the hands of the OAS, although, as a matter of fact, there is nothing uncommon in the failure of the United Nations to adopt an agenda. Aside from legal niceties, the adamant stand of the United States determined to prevent United Nations discussion at this point resulted in a loss of prestige, tended to confirm some suspicions that the United States was implicated in the revolutionary activities, and left wide open the door to propaganda exploitation by Russia.[31]

The universalists or antiregionalists who direct criticisms at the United States and at the American states which demanded regional action should in reality direct their barbs at the United Nations Charter, for the antiregionalists lost the day at San Francisco in 1945 when regional autonomy was recognized by the Charter, at the behest of Latin America, to permit the inter-American system to deal with just such hemispheric situations.[32] It is then doubly disturbing to see one of those selfsame Latin American nations violating its United Nations and inter-American commitments by seeking to avert regional action and by seeking interference with such action through the Russian veto.

As a result of the June 25 decision of the Security Council to the effect that the Council would take no direct action until it received a report from the Inter-American Peace Committee, Guatemala reversed its stand and on June 26 invited the committee to send the fact-finding commission to Guatemala. The committee, noting this changed attitude, determined that it would send a five-member team to Guatemala, Honduras, and Nicaragua on the 28th. But the government of Guatemala changed hands during the night of the 27th and by the time the committee arrived at Mexico City it was informed that mediation had been initiated by the United States and El Salvador between the new government and the revolutionary forces, and that the committee should not interfere in these negotiations. On July 2 the three governments thanked the committee for its good offices and informed it that the controversy between them, which was the occasion for the journey of the mission, had ceased to exist.[33] Guatemala's new minister for external relations informed the Security Council that, as the occurrences which had prompted the previous government to appeal to the Council had completely ceased and as peace and order had been restored, the new *Junta de Gobierno* of Guatemala considered that there was no reason why the question should remain on the Council's agenda.[34]

Following the Security Council's action on June 25 in refusing to reconsider the Guatemalan complaint, on June 26 the representatives of ten of the American states on the Council of the OAS addressed a note to the chairman of the Council which stated in part:

Our Governments view with increasing concern the demonstrated intervention of the international communist movement in the Republic of Guatemala and the danger which this involves for the peace and security of the Continent ... the undersigned members propose that a Meeting of Ministers of Foreign Affairs be convoked, in accordance with Article 6 and Article 11 of the Inter-American Treaty of Reciprocal Assistance, to act as Organ of Consultation for the purpose of considering the danger to the peace and security of the Continent and to agree upon the measures which it is desirable to take ...[35]

Despite the fact that the government of Guatemala had changed on June 27, the Council of the OAS took cognizance of this note at a special meeting held on June 28, 1954, and adopted a resolution convoking a Meeting of Ministers of Foreign Affairs to serve as the Organ of Consultation for the purpose of considering all aspects of the danger to the peace and security of the continent resulting from the penetration of the political institutions of Guatemala by the international communist movement. In this case, the Council did not rely on a pure *pro forma* convocation of the Meeting of Ministers of Foreign Affairs, for it established both a date and a place for the meeting: July 7, 1954, in Rio de Janeiro.[36] Furthermore, in view of the fact that Guatemala had denied the jurisdiction of the regional organization, taking its case directly to the United Nations, the Council did not constitute itself as Provisional Organ of Consultation.

The following day another special meeting of the Council was called at the behest of the representatives of El Salvador and the United States. These nations informed the Council that their respective ambassadors to Guatemala had been requested to lend their good offices to bring about a cessation of the violence taking place in Guatemala. The representatives of both nations indicated the willingness of their governments to respond favorably to the Guatemalan request, but before taking definite action they wished to inform the Council so that any steps taken in the process of good offices would be done with the full knowledge and approval of the members of the OAS, in recognition of that organization's responsibility concerning the problems affecting Guatemala.[37]

At a third special meeting of the Council held on July 2, the chairman reported that the peace negotiations in Guatemala had terminated successfully with the formation of a junta of military officers which would act as the provisional government of Guatemala. The new junta, it was declared, had affirmed its opposition to communist penetration and had given evidence of its determination to see that the penetration was terminated. Consequently the Council decided that the danger to the peace and security of the continent which had been created by the penetration of the political institutions of Guatemala by the international communist movement had, for the time being at least, ceased to be a matter requiring the urgent attention of the Ministers of Foreign Affairs. It was thereupon resolved to postpone *sine die* the Meeting which had been convoked, with the understanding that the American governments would watch developments in Guatemala and if necessary later set a new date for the meeting.[38]

In all fairness it must be admitted that the OAS did present a sorry spectacle in coping with this case, one which lends credence to the contention that its agencies were incompetent to deal with the situation at hand. A situation or dispute should not be referred to a regional agency unless adequate machinery exists for a fair and impartial proceeding and a quick settlement.

It cannot be denied that the OAS possesses, at least on paper, adequate machinery for the settlement of inter-American disputes and for the maintenance of hemispheric peace. There is the Inter-American Peace Committee empowered to investigate and conciliate. The Meeting of Foreign Ministers and Council have coercive power to maintain peace under the Rio Treaty. In previous cases, the Council had been successful in stopping hostilities and in smoothing the way for peaceful relations by detailed fact-finding and conciliation, dissuading the antagonistic parties from making more trouble. Moreover, the Meeting of Foreign Ministers and the Council, provisionally, may order collective enforcement measures to stop hemispheric aggression, and, at least according to OAS interpretation, they can order coercive measures not involving use of armed force even against aggressions which are not armed attack, without Security Council authorization.[39] This would give the lie to Guatemala's contention that the OAS could not put a stop to aggression in progress.

With this battery of inter-American agencies action should have been forthcoming to maintain the peace either before resort to the Security Council or immediately thereafter. From the facts of this case it can easily be seen that the OAS was neither speedy nor effective. Guatemala, of course, blocked the intervention of the Inter-American Peace Committee, which was unfortunate; for had it been permitted to investigate, some clarification of the facts would have resulted. Guatemala also refused to exercise her right to take the case to the consultative organs as Costa Rica and Haiti had done previously. She apparently wanted nothing to do with the OAS, claiming that the United States domination of inter-American agencies would preclude her receiving a fair hearing. Guatemala wanted a wider international review which could be provided by the Security Council. As far as the Soviet Union was concerned, Guatemala's presentation to the Security Council permitted that nation to invade the realm of activity reserved to the regional organization of this hemisphere. But beyond this reality of communist support, it is difficult to see what Guatemala expected to gain by presentation to the Security Council. Her leaders must have been aware that the United States and other American nations would fight any attempt to have the Security Council deal with the matter, even to the extent of employing the United States veto power if necessary. Had Guatemala proceeded through OAS channels, it is not without the realm of possibility that the Latin American members would have forced the OAS condemnation of the interventionary actions of Honduras and Nicaragua as similar actions in previous OAS cases had been condemned. Some authorities believe that this might well have happened and also that the United States, in seeking to condemn the interventionary activities of the international communist movement in Guatemala, would have failed to gain the necessary two-thirds votes required to take action.[40]

Guatemala could not have forestalled consideration of the whole problem by the Meeting of Foreign Ministers or by the Council of the OAS under the Rio Treaty, for any member state may request consultation and this can then come about by a majority vote. Why did not other members make such a request until after June 28, when the matter was absolutely settled by the fall of the Arbenz government? The OAS was caught in a quandary because of the conflicting political views of its members which would have made impossible any true collective action. The Guatemalan case was not a simple, rather insignificant dispute among small Central American republics, with which the OAS could, as past experience had proved, successfully deal. It involved the whole sphere of cold war pressures as Russia attempted to extend her imperial colonialist system to the Western Hemisphere, an attempt which the United States was bound to resist. Coupled with this was the inability of many Latin Americans to recognize that a local communist movement was deeply enmeshed with the international communist movement. There was also involved the rising tide of Latin American nationalism, Latin American pique at the postwar policies of the United States toward the nations of this hemisphere, and an unforgivable inability on the part of American leaders to comprehend and judge the feeling of Latin Americans.

Since the United States had been concerned, with justification, over the communist infiltration in Guatemala, it would have seemed logical, particularly after the Tenth Conference resolution equating domination of an American state by the international communist movement with a threat to the peace of the hemisphere in accord with the Rio Treaty,[41] that a call for consultation would have been immediately forthcoming to consider whether Guatemala was in fact so dominated. If so, collective measures could have been taken against her. By failing so to act, it would seem that the American nations violated their obligations under the treaty.[42] Unfortunately basic misunderstandings existed between much of Latin America and the United States, the Latin Americans fearing intervention, even though collective, more than they feared the spread of international communism. And certain Latin American opinion, at least, viewed the difficulties as having little to do with communist penetration, but as merely being caused by the pursuance by the United States of a policy of Yankee imperialism and dollar diplomacy toward Guatemala.[43]

A shift in Latin American attitude came about when it was announced on May 17 that arms had been shipped surreptitiously from the Soviets to Guatemala, a fact which showed Guatemala's intimate connection with Russia and which further worried Guatemala's neighbors since the quantity of arms was greater than Guatemala's legitimate defense need.[44] On May 19, when Nicaragua broke off diplomatic relations with Guatemala, the Nicaraguan government indicated that it desired a Meeting of Foreign Ministers, but the United States demurred, arguing that the time was not yet ripe.[45] However, the United States did begin to act by strengthening the armed forces of Nicaragua and Honduras, by attempting to prevent additional communist war materials from reaching Guatemala, and by seeking to obtain strong Latin American support for a consultative meeting. By the middle of June such support had been obtained on the understanding that the United States would not demand drastic sanctions against Guatemala beyond an embargo on foreign arms. The United States stressed that it was mainly interested in a reaffirmation of the anticommunist resolution and in the creation of a commission to keep close watch on Guatemala. The meeting was tentatively scheduled for July 1, later changed to July 5, and actually never took place, for the revolutionary invasion occurred and Guatemala turned from the OAS to the Security Council of the United Nations.[46] Insofar as the OAS was concerned, its hesitancy in calling a meeting is to be deplored, for a Meeting of the Ministers of Foreign Affairs could well have established the fact of communist infiltration of the institutions of a hemispheric nation, a fact which obviously could never be established by the Security Council.

The note of the sponsoring governments in mid-June to the Council of the OAS requesting a Meeting of Foreign Ministers emphasized that the nations requesting the meeting were primarily concerned over "the demonstrated intervention of the international communist movement in the Republic of Guatemala." At the Council meeting itself, the discussion indicated some disagreement with the stand of the representative of the United States that the Guatemalan affair could be interpreted *only* as an attack on the hemisphere by the international communist movement.[47] And although approval was obtained for a Meeting of Foreign Ministers, with the fall of the Arbenz government the meeting was later called off.

In any event, the inaction of the international organizations combined with the success of the invasion led by Castillo Armas, a success which to a great part can be attributed to the unwillingness of the regular Guatemalan army to defend the government of Arbenz, brought an end to the communist conspiracy in Guatemala.[48] Insofar as international organization was concerned, the case highlights a complete failure, for neither the United Nations nor the OAS was able to act effectively. Here again was a tangible demonstration of the failure of a mechanical solution to assure a peaceful settlement of disputes by international institutions such as the Organization of American States or the United Nations, when they are involved in cold war conflicts between Western nations and Russian imperialism. Neither international law nor international organization can function harmoniously unless trust, good faith, and responsibility are acknowledged and living attributes of all members of international society.

THE 1955 COSTA RICAN–NICARAGUAN DISPUTE

On January 8, 1955, Costa Rica requested a Meeting of Consultation of Foreign Ministers, claiming its independence was seriously threatened by acts of the government of Nicaragua.[49] Upon learning of an invasion of Costa Rica, the Council met on January 11 in emergency session, issued a call for a Meeting of Consultation, without setting a date therefor, and in its capacity as Provisional Organ of Consultation appointed a Committee of Investigation to proceed to the two countries to report upon the facts. The Council requested the two governments to pledge themselves to refrain from the commission of any act which might aggravate the situation.

On January 12, the Council met again at the request of Costa Rica to consider the bombing by the insurgents of various cities in Costa Rica. At that time, the Council requested the other American governments who were in a position to do so to place at the disposal of the Investigating Committee aircraft which, in the name of the committee and under its supervision, might make pacific observation flights over the regions affected, after receiving the consent of the governments whose territories were traversed.

This was ostensibly no more than a measure to make the work of the Investigating Committee more effective, and as the flights were called "pacific" observation flights they did not fall under the ban against "enforcement action" which would possibly have required consent by the Security Council of the United Nations under the United Nations Charter, Article 53.

On January 16, at the request of the Council directed to the governments of the other American states, the United States sold four airplanes to Costa Rica to assist it in its efforts to defend itself. If the armed attack was an attack attributable to the Government of Nicaragua this might have been done by the United States under its own initiative as permitted by Article 3 of the Rio Treaty requiring the parties to the treaty to assist immediately in meeting an armed attack launched against the American state by any state.[50] However, if this case is considered as falling outside of collective self-defense, and if this uprising was a case of insurgency, such a sale would still have been permitted by general international law rules governing intervention in civil strife and by the particular international law of the Habana Convention on Civil Strife.[51]

On February 18, 1955, the Investigating Committee presented its report to the Council. The report stated that there had been foreign intervention in respect to equipment and transportation of the invading forces; that a substantial number of troops had entered Costa Rica across the Nicaraguan border; that aircraft proceeding from abroad had dropped arms and ammunition at predetermined points and had made flights in which they had bombed and machine-gunned Costa Rican towns; that in consequence there had been violation of the territorial integrity, sovereignty, and political independence of Costa Rica; and that while a large majority of the attacking forces were of Costa Rican nationality, nevertheless this did not alter the fact that Costa Rica had been a victim of acts of intervention.

The Investigating Committee recommended that the Pact of Amity signed by Costa Rica and Nicaragua in 1949 be improved and strengthened; that a special bilateral treaty be signed looking to the more effective application of the Habana Convention on the Duties and Rights of States in the Event of Civil Strife; and that a bilateral Commission of Investigation and Conciliation under the terms of the Pact of Bogotá (which both Nicaragua and Costa Rica had ratified) be appointed to serve as a permanent guarantee of the settlement of any future difficulties. The Ecuadorian member of the committee entered a reservation stating that while he was in general agreement with the report, he considered that it was incomplete in that it failed to identify the author or authors of the "foreign intervention," and stating further that a permanent inter-American police force should be established and there should be an early Meeting of Ministers of Foreign Affairs to consider the possibility of improving the system for the control of the traffic in arms and the limitation of armaments within the requirements of hemispheric defense.

On February 24 the Council, still acting as Provisional Organ of Consultation, adopted the following resolutions:

1. It pointed out that its resolution of January 14 had condemned the acts of intervention of which Costa Rica had been the victim and that the favorable outcome of the situation had rendered unnecessary the additional measures provided in the Rio Treaty, and expressed its deep concern over the acts in question and the Council's earnest desire that they should not be repeated, and in addition announced the Council's satisfaction that the sovereignty and independence of Costa Rica had been preserved in consequence of the measures taken by the OAS.

2. It called upon the governments of the two nations to implement the provisions of the Pact of Bogotá by creating the Commission of Investigation and Conciliation provided for in the treaty and at the same time to enter into the bilateral agreement contemplated in the Pact of Amity of 1949 for the better supervision and control of their respective frontiers in respect to the illegal activities of exiles and the traffic in arms.

3. It proclaimed the termination of the activities of the Investigating Committee, but at the same time created a Special Commission of the Council to co-operate with the representatives of Costa Rica and Nicaragua in carrying out the provisions of the second resolution and to continue the functions of the military observers as long as would appear to be necessary.

THE 1955 ECUADORIAN-PERUVIAN CONTROVERSY

A dispute which had its origin in the uncertain boundaries of Ecuador and Peru at the time of independence of these neighboring states,[52] which had been the subject matter of several efforts of settlement, and which was thought to have been settled by the Protocol of Peace, Friendship and Boundaries signed by the parties at Rio de Janeiro in 1942[53] erupted once again in 1955. On September 8, 1955, the government of Ecuador requested of the Council an immediate Meeting of Ministers of Foreign Affairs to act as consultative organ in accordance with the Rio Treaty, charging that Ecuador was faced with a serious situation created by Peru which affected and placed in danger Ecuador's territorial integrity, its sovereignty, and its political independence. More specifically Ecuador charged Peru with a heavy concentration of armed forces along the border and in the vicinity of Ecuador's coastline. Such military deployment, it was claimed, seriously menaced Ecuador and endangered hemispheric peace and security.

The Council took no action to convoke a Meeting of Consultation, but in effect turned the matter over to the representatives of the four states which had been named guarantors and mediators by the terms of the Rio de Janeiro Protocol of 1942.[54] Ecuador had also submitted the matter to this group and the Council had received information that its representatives had been requested to appoint a commission of military observers to investigate the scene to determine the facts. The military attachés of the guarantor states stationed in Lima and Quito then conducted an on-the-spot investigation, air and land reconnaissance, and observed nothing abnormal. Thereafter, at a Council Meeting of September 26, Ecuador withdrew its request for convocation of a consultative meeting, stating that this was no longer necessary because of the action of the guarantor governments in relieving tensions. Thus, in this case it was not necessary to utilize the machinery provided by the Rio Treaty. But the boundary question still plagues the two countries and is a potential trouble spot in inter-American relations.

THE HONDURAN-NICARAGUAN CASE OF 1957

In 1957 a conflict arose between Honduras and Nicaragua, growing out of a half-century-old boundary dispute between the two nations, which led to some military action in the disputed area.[55] On May 1, the Council met to consider a complaint from Honduras stating that Nicaragua had invaded Honduras with military forces. The Council was requested to convoke a Meeting of Consultation.

On May 2 the Council met again to consider a note of the Nicaraguan government which stated that Honduras had no right to say that the disputed territory was Honduran, for Nicaragua had rejected for good reasons the 1906 arbitral award of the King of Spain which had granted the territory to Honduras.[56] Nicaragua then charged Honduras with being an aggressor. On this day the Council convoked the Organ of Consultation in accord with the Rio Treaty. It did not name a place or time for the Meeting of Foreign Ministers. It constituted itself as Provisional Organ, authorized the naming of an investigating committee, and requested the two governments to refrain from action which would aggravate the situation.

On May 16 the Investigating Committee submitted to the Council its report of the facts, which concluded that because of the uncertain state of the boundary lines, the dispute existing with respect thereto, and the reservations of Honduras and Nicaragua to the Rio Treaty which, on the part of Honduras, maintained the line as established by the King of Spain, and, on the part of Nicaragua, refused the award as null and void, it could not place responsibility for the aggression.

The Council then terminated the activities of the Investigating Committee and created an *ad hoc* committee of five members (Argentina, Bolivia, the United States, Mexico, and Panama) to assume the responsibilities of the Investigating Committee and to seek to procure a pacific solution to the controversy. Thereafter this *ad hoc* committee presented its report to the Council together with agreements subscribed to by the parties to accept the compulsory jurisdiction of the International Court of Justice in accord with the provisions of the Pact of Bogotá for the pacific settlement of the boundary controversy. The case was decided by the International Court in 1960 in favor of Honduras, the court holding that Nicaragua was obligated to accept the 1906 award of arbitration.[57]

On June 27 the Council canceled the Meeting of Foreign Ministers and ended its provisional status as Organ of Consultation.

CARIBBEAN TENSIONS SINCE 1959

The final action of the Council of the OAS in the above-mentioned cases where it acted as Provisional Organ of Consultation was a series of resolutions and recommendations, none of which hinted at or threatened sanctions or other measures of enforcement to be taken by the inter-American community as a whole. With the exception of the Guatemalan case, where the OAS failed to function, the organization was reasonably effective. The manner in which the losers as well as those who were successful accepted resolution of the hotly debated issues and the views of the impartial investigating board, together with the willingness of the nations to co-operate in the investigation and to abide by the resolutions of the Provisional Organ of Consultation, indicated that mere resolutions and recommendations could be very effective cogs in the machinery for peace and security.[58] The OAS proved itself to be an important factor in the maintenance of hemispheric peace and security, as a stabilizing influence. A drastic change was to occur, however—a change which has in large degree rendered the OAS impotent.

After the success of the Cuban movement of July 26 and the ascent of Fidel Castro to power in 1959, Cuba became headquarters for the preparation and launching of revolutionary expeditions by political exiles aided by Cuban authorities and directed against several states. At the outset the Venezuelan government associated itself with Cuba for the purpose of liquidating dictatorships, especially that of Trujillo in the Dominican Republic. With the ever increasing orientation of the Cuban revolution toward the Moscow-Peiping Axis, such activities were alarming not only because they breached the inter-American international agreements on non-intervention, but also because they were abetted and encouraged by a foreign nonhemispheric power. With *Fidelismo* as the front, anti-yankeeism as the rallying cry, and communism as the directing force, an increasing and continued threat has come to exist for many established governments of Latin America.[59] As a result the Caribbean area in particular has been in the throes of political and military upheaval. Within the space of the first six months of 1959 the governments of Panama, Nicaragua, and the Dominican Republic appeared before the Council of the OAS officially charging invasions by exiles and others attempting to overthrow their governments. In each case Cuba was implicated, and in the Dominican Republic case, Venezuela was also accused of aiding the conspirators. In this latter instance Cuba and Venezuela expressed views that Cuba was suffering from a threat of attack from the Dominican Republic and that the Venezuelan government was concerned over Dominican propaganda attacks against it.[60]

In the Panamanian and Nicaraguan cases the Council followed its usual procedure of invoking itself as Provisional Organ under the Rio Treaty, sending out investigating committees, and attempting to settle the matter.[61] In the Dominican case, however, the pressures were such that the Council was unable to act under the Rio Treaty, for the governments of Cuba and Venezuela opposed its application and announced that they would permit no OAS investigation to be carried out in their territory.[62] Other governments of Latin America were also uneasy at any manifestation of support for the dictatorial regime of the Dominican Republic or at any suggestion of censure of attempts to overthrow that government, for most of the democracies of Latin America longed for the downfall of the repressive and long-lasting Trujillo regime.

Action was, however, required. A compromise was therefore found. Instead of convening the Foreign Ministers as Organ of Consultation or the Council as Provisional Organ of Consultation, which might have necessitated enforcement measures against the aggressors under the Rio Treaty, the Council resorted to Articles 39 and 40 of the Charter of Bogotá which permit a Meeting of Foreign Ministers to consider problems of urgent and common interest to the American states. Under these provisions the Foreign Ministers have only power to consider, not to take sanctions. Thus, a Meeting of Foreign Ministers was called at Santiago, Chile, to consider the whole problem of tensions in the Caribbean area with a view to the restoration of peace and security, confidence, and friendly relations among the republics of the region by co-operation through the OAS.[63]

The Meeting of Foreign Ministers increased in small measure the powers of the Inter-American Peace Committee and set forth strong declarations for democracy and denunciations of dictatorship, but adhered to the principle of non-intervention.[64] It did little to alleviate tensions in the Caribbean. The situation continued to harass the OAS.

In February, 1960, Venezuela charged before the Council that the Trujillo government was flagrantly violating human rights by mass political arrests and imprisonment. The Council agreed to give the function of investigation to the Inter-American Peace Committee under the Santiago mandate.[65] The committee's investigation verified Venezuela's charges, finding the Dominican Republic guilty of the denial of freedom of speech and assembly, arbitrary arrest, cruel and inhuman treatment of prisoners, and the use of intimidation and terror as political weapons.[66] No other action was taken by the OAS and the Caribbean continued to seethe. Castro's Cuba, aligning itself ever closer with the communist bloc, shouted daily vituperations at the United States and at many Latin American regimes, including the democracies of Venezuela, Argentina, and

Costa Rica, rattled Russia's missiles, and continued an unceasing campaign of expropriation of the property of American citizens in Cuba. Castro, who when he first came to power had been one of the greatest enemies of the Trujillo regime, gradually ceased his tirades against that government, and in turn the Trujillo regime stopped beaming anti-Castro radio programs to Cuba. It was soon reliably reported that these two dictators had arrived at some sort of rapprochement, leaving Trujillo free to concentrate on their now mutual enemy, President Betancourt of Venezuela.[67]

The month of July, 1960, was filled with charges and countercharges, with Venezuela requesting the OAS Council to call a Meeting of Foreign Ministers to consider acts of intervention and aggression by the Dominican government against that of Venezuela, which had culminated in June in an attempt to assassinate President Betancourt.[68] Meanwhile the United States, heartily sick of Castro's unending vilification and unceasing animosity against American citizens and property, cut the Cuban sugar quota.[69] In retaliation, Castro immediately nationalized the remaining property of Americans in Cuba. Russia threatened attack on the United States if Cuba were faced with armed aggression and in addition offered to purchase at world market prices all Cuban sugar refused by the United States, assured Cuba of vast Soviet economic and moral support, and declared the Monroe Doctrine to be dead.[70] President Eisenhower then retorted that the United States would not stand idly by and permit the establishment in the Western Hemisphere of any regime dominated by international communism.[71] Cuba sought and obtained an emergency hearing of the Security Council of the United Nations, charging that the United States was guilty of aggressive acts toward Cuba. At the urging of Ecuador and Argentina a motion was approved by the Security Council referring the issue of Cuban–United States relations to the OAS.[72]

An emergency session of the Council of the OAS, reviewing the Caribbean problems, decided to call a Foreign Ministers Meeting at San José, Costa Rica, and this, the Sixth Meeting of Foreign Ministers, was convened on August 16, 1960.[73] This was the first Meeting of Foreign Ministers, ever convened as Organ of Consultation acting under the Rio Treaty, and it was so convened to take up the Venezuelan charges of aggression by the Dominican Republic. An investigating committee, which had probed into Venezuela's charges, indicted the Trujillo regime for complicity in the attempt against the life of President Betancourt.[74] The preponderant feeling of the ministers was that punitive action should be taken against the Dominican Republic; hence, for the first time, the collective measures of the Rio Treaty, as authorized by Articles 6 and 8, were applied, the Organ of Consultation calling for an immediate break in diplomatic relations and for a partial interruption of economic relations by all the member states, such measures to continue until the Council by a two-thirds vote should decide that the Dominican government had ceased to constitute a danger to the peace and security of the hemisphere.[75] This action was taken because the Dominican Republic had engaged in acts of aggression.

After a delay of twenty-four hours following its deliberation and action in the Venezuelan-Dominican controversy, the Meeting of Foreign Ministers at San José turned to the problem of Cuba–United States relations. The meeting at this point was called the Seventh Meeting of Ministers of Foreign Affairs, and was not held under the Rio Treaty but was called "to consider problems of an urgent nature and of common interest."[76] A weak declaration was the result of this Seventh Meeting of Ministers of Foreign Affairs, which placed the OAS on record against communist intervention in the Americas, without specifically naming Cuba, and condemned the attempts by Russia and Communist China to make use of the political or social situation of any American state for their own purposes.[77]

By January, 1961, it had become apparent that the break in diplomatic relations which followed the San José meeting and the almost universal hostility to the Dominican Republic's dictatorship of Trujillo had little effect in weakening Trujillo, who continued to cling to power by ruthless elimination of any possible rivals and by denials of fundamental rights to his people. In an effort to bring further pressure on Trujillo, the Council of the Organization of American States voted to cut off exports of oil and trucks to the Dominican Republic, although a number of Latin American nations abstained from voting on this issue, either on the ground of non-intervention or because they had come to believe such measures were not effective in view of the cold war realities.[78]

An assassin's bullet ended the life of Generalissimo Trujillo on May 30, 1961, but the regime was not immediately toppled and the collective measures of the OAS were not lifted, although the Dominican government attempted to give some evidence of modification of its ways and gave pledges of reform.[79] Shortly after the death of the dictator, an OAS four-nation subcommittee of the seven-nation Sanctions Committee, which was established by the Council on instructions from the San José meeting, was ordered by the OAS to the Dominican Republic on a fact-finding mission to ascertain whether the government had ceased repressive measures, for after the assassination reports of torture and mass arrests were rife. The Dominican government consented to receive the subcommittee, which spent a seven-day period of investigation and inquiry in the nation, and continued to concern itself with this problem until Trujillo's heirs were finally ousted.[80]

The OAS condemnation of Sino-Soviet intervention in the Americas, the Declaration of San José, did not remedy the difficulties with Cuba or prevent a continuation of such penetration. Indeed, in the months following, the situation worsened. In October, 1960, the United States placed an embargo on Cuba which prohibited the export to that nation of all United States products except medical supplies and some foodstuffs. In taking this course the United States cited the subjection of the United States by the Castro regime to an increasing campaign of hostility and slander as well as a series of arbitrary, illegal, and discriminatory economic measures which injured American citizens and drastically altered previous mutually beneficial patterns of trade between the two countries. The Department of State declared that because of these discriminatory, aggressive, and injurious economic policies of the Castro government, the embargo was necessary to defend the legitimate economic interests of the people of the United States.[81]

Cuba then charged before the United Nations that the United States was waging economic aggression against Cuba and planning military intervention.

The United States denied the charges, but accused Cuba of flagrant disregard and defiance of the appropriate organs of the OAS, and, further, charged that it was Cuba, aided and abetted by the Soviet Union, which had created the present tension. Cuba hoped for an airing of her charges in the plenary session of the General Assembly, but that body, on November 1, adopted the recommendation of the General Committee to allocate the complaint to the First Committee.[82]

November also witnessed a new eruption of violence in the Central American area, with accusations directed against Castro's Cuba as the behind-the-scenes troublemaker. The three nations involved were Costa Rica, Nicaragua, and Guatemala. The Somoza government of Nicaragua was threatened when rebel groups invaded Nicaragua from Costa Rica, an action which brought about fighting along the Costa Rican border between this group of Nicaraguan insurgents and the Costa Rican civil guard. Timed to coincide with this invasion was an uprising in Nicaragua itself. In Guatemala the government was faced by a rebellion within the armed forces. Allegations were made by Nicaragua that the rebels from Costa Rica were "mercenaries aided by the communist government of Cuba," and Guatemala charged that the rebels there had received aid, including planes, from Cuba. Costa Rican officials reported that they had found communist documents and Cuban arms among the effects of the captured rebels. The president of Guatemala talked of invoking the Rio Treaty so that collective police action could be taken against Cuba to prevent communist agitation in Central America. No formal complaint was made to the Council, however, although the Inter-American Peace Committee did agree to consider Guatemala's charges against Cuba. Failing specific proof to substantiate the Guatemalan charges, judgment was withheld.[83]

The Guatemalan and Nicaraguan governments did request a United States Navy patrol in the Caribbean to block a possible Cuban invasion. Washington complied with a task force, stating that this action was taken to seek out and prevent any intervention by communist-directed elements in the internal affairs of the two requesting nations through the landing of armed forces or supplies from abroad. The United States forces were to carry out a regular search of the Caribbean so that invasion parties could not move against Central America undetected, but the forces would not act to intercept suspicious vessels unless the ships were within the three-mile territorial limits of Nicaragua and Guatemala and those countries requested interception. The United States government acted here without consultation with the other American governments, considering its action legal as it was done at the request of and in response to legitimate governments of sovereign nations. The action was compared to the landing of United States marines in Lebanon in 1958.[84] Although this action may be regarded as legal when taken at the requests of the governments involved, still the OAS avoided its responsibility of an immediate meeting of consultation to decide on collective measures if necessary to meet an armed attack if such had occurred, or to meet an aggression other than an armed attack if such had occurred. The American governments were not, however, anxious to bring the case before the OAS and no action was taken.

The revolts were quickly crushed by the concerned governments and by

December 7, 1960, the naval patrol was withdrawn after Guatemala and Nicaragua declared that the emergency had passed.

Relations between Cuba on the one hand and the United States and other American countries on the other continued to deteriorate. On December 31, 1960, the Security Council of the United Nations was requested to adopt the necessary measures to prevent a United States military aggression against Cuba which was to be perpetrated within a few hours.[85] Specifically the Cuban note alleged in part:

The Cuban Government has in its possession evidence of the sinister plan conceived by the Central Intelligence Agency, in close collaboration with the Pentagon and the United States monopolies adversely affected by the public welfare legislation promulgated by the Cuban revolution, and with the open cooperation of Cuban war criminals who have sought refuge in the United States — including mercenaries, adventurers, spies, saboteurs and terrorists of every kind — and of various puppet governments of the Western Hemisphere.[86]

The complaint went on to allege that the contemplated intervention was the culmination of a policy of "vexation, pressure, coercion, subversion and aggression on all fronts" carried out by the United States government against Cuba in consequence of the Castro movement of popular liberation which had overthrown the corrupt tyranny of Batista.[87] The United States was accused of engaging in psychological warfare in the form of deception and confusion through the dissemination of rumors, false news, and threats, and of attempting to isolate Cuba from the other Latin American states by diplomatic maneuvering. As evidence of such maneuvering news dispatches from Montevideo were cited which claimed that a confidential document had been circulated to the foreign ministries of the American republics declaring that the United States was preparing to invade Cuba to prevent the installation on that island of sites for the launching of Soviet rockets, and that although the construction of the launching pads had been suspended, still intervention would be ordered if construction were resumed. The construction of such rocket launching sites in Cuba was characterized by the Cuban Foreign Minister as absurd.[88]

When the Security Council met on January 4 it had another note from the Cuban Minister referring to new and alarming developments which consisted of the rupture of diplomatic and consular relations between the United States government and that of Cuba.

The break in relations by the United States was taken following a request from Cuba to the United States to reduce the staff of its embassy in Havana within forty-eight hours to eleven, to equal the number of Cuban officials at the Cuban Embassy in Washington. In terminating the relations President Eisenhower stated:

This unusual action on the part of the Castro government can have no other purpose than to render impossible the conduct of normal diplomatic relations with that government. . . . This calculated action on the part of the Castro government is only the latest of a long series of harassments, baseless accusations, and vilification. There is a limit to what the United States in self-respect can endure. That limit has now been reached . . . Our friendship for the Cuban people is not affected . . . Meanwhile our sympathy goes out to the people of Cuba now suffering under the yoke of a dictator.[89]

At the Security Council meeting for the adoption of the agenda the United States representative pointed out the many times that Cuba had charged the United States with aggressive intentions and actions against Cuba and that Cuba was making itself ridiculous with such charges, which were false and spurious. He went on to outline the Castro government's attempts to extend its ideology to other American nations; its subversive and military activity against such nations; and its thirst for power and domination and the fanatical intolerance of all dissent which had isolated Cuba from the hemisphere. From this Cuban state of mind, he stated, had flowed many tragic results such as:

The imposition of censorship and thought control;

The banning of all political parties except the communists;

Summary justice by drumhead courts, which have arbitrarily caused hundreds to be put to death;

The consequent flight of many thousands of refugees, including many of Cuba's ablest citizens;

Economic troubles arising from irresponsible policies and a constant defection of political and economic leaders;

The official creation of a "Yankee Devil," whom the unfortunate Cuban people, including the smallest school children, are taught to fear and despise as being ready to invade their beloved fatherland;

An open advocacy of subversion and violent revolution throughout Latin America;

The mortgaging of Cuba's economic future for the purchase of large quantities of arms from the Soviet Union and Czechoslovakia;

The military mobilization of hundreds of thousands of Cubans;

And, finally, the gradual transformation of an increasingly insolvent Cuba into a political and economic dependency of the Soviet Union and a springboard for Soviet ambitions in the Western Hemisphere.[90]

As to the charge that the United States was trying to isolate Cuba from the continent and that the United States had exercised pressure on the other American republics to break relations with Cuba, it was pointed out that such ruptures were understandable, for Cuban diplomatic missions in the hemisphere were used for subversive and hostile propaganda. It was admitted that thousands of Cuban refugees were in the United States, having fled from the suppression of freedom in Cuba, and that it was natural that some of them should want to engage in activities against the government which had harmed them. But it was denied that the United States had supported military incursion by Cuban refugees into Cuba and had associated with such activities. The United States then opposed any resolution before the Security Council taking cognizance of these Cuban charges.

A draft resolution was put before the Security Council by the Chilean and Ecuadorian delegates calling upon Cuba and the United States to make every effort to resolve their differences by peaceful means provided for in the United Nations Charter. The delegate of Ecuador spoke of the non-intervention cornerstone of the inter-American juridical community and stated:

If more powerful states, whatever their ideologies, tried to use an underdeveloped country as a platform for propaganda in ideological struggles or as an instrument of penetration of ideas that would endanger the security of other states, that would be veiled intervention, as also would be the case if one state tried subversively to extend a political experiment from one people to another.[91]

He went on to suggest that Cuba's fears appeared to be largely baseless, but that the Security Council was competent to deal with the matter and that it should allay Cuba's fears by attempting to reach a solution. Since all of the permanent members of the Council except Russia were against taking action, the Chilean-Ecuadorian resolution was not pressed to a vote. The French delegate seemed to sum up the opposing members' viewpoint by a statement that the Cubans had not shown any complicity or connivance by the United States and that Cuba had made the request mainly for propaganda reasons. He concluded that the resolution would establish some parity between the attitudes of the United States and Cuba and that France would hesitate to adopt a text that would express recognition of the Cuban complaint.[92]

The president of the Security Council at this meeting declared that "he was confident that the debate would contribute to a reduction of tension between the United States and Cuba."[93] Such did not prove to be the case. The ways of Castro did not change, counterrevolutionaries in and out of Cuba stepped up their activities, forming a Revolutionary Council with the avowed purpose of overthrowing Castro, and the United States issued a white paper which proved to be a prelude to invasion, and which set forth United States charges against the Castro regime and at the same time called upon that government to sever its ties with international communism and return to the original aims and purposes of the Cuban revolution upon pain of continued striving by the Cuban people for their liberty.[94]

Thereafter, on the morning of April 15, 1961, an ill-starred attempt against Castro's government began with a surprise attack by light bombers on Cuban airports. On April 17 the invasion of Cuba by United States trained and supported Cuban refugee counterrevolutionaries began—an invasion that was doomed to bloody defeat, for after three days of fighting Castro was able to announce that the invasionary forces had been crushed.[95]

At the time of the first air raids the Cuban government demanded United Nations action, and on April 15 the General Assembly's Political Committee (Committee I) heard Cuban charges holding the United States responsible for such raids and declaring that they were a prologue to a large-scale invasion planned by the United States and certain nations of Latin America.[96] The United States representative claimed the charges were without foundation. The debate was continued on April 17, when the Cuban foreign minister charged that Cuba had been invaded by a force of mercenaries, organized, financed, and armed by the United States, and that the attack had been launched from Florida and Guatemala under the direction of the Central Intelligence Agency. As a result of this United States complicity, Cuba charged, Articles 15 and 16 of the OAS Charter had been violated.[97]

The United States representative rejected the charges, stating that the United States had committed no aggression against Cuba and that no offensive had been launched from territory of the United States. He did not deny that Cuban rebels had been allowed to operate on United States territory, but he pointed out that the United States had previously allowed supporters of Castro to do the same thing during their campaign to overthrow Batista. He expressed sympathy for the rebels and the hope that they would be successful in restoring democratic processes to Cuba. He then noted the statement previously made by the President of the United States to the effect that there would be no intervention in Cuba by American armed forces. However, he did not reply to a series of questions posed by the Cuban representative as to whether the United States had supplied to the Cuban rebels certain military equipment which had been captured by the Cuban government.[98]

At the April 15 meeting, prior to the invasion, some twelve Latin American nations had proposed a mild resolution which would call upon members of the OAS to help settle the Cuban–United States dispute by peaceful means according to the purposes and principles of the OAS Charter and which would also call upon all states to refrain from any action that might make the situation worse.[99]

However, after the rebel landings in Cuba several of the Latin American sponsors withdrew their support for this resolution, fearing that its language would be interpreted as condoning the United States position in the crisis, for the United States admission that it had permitted Cuban rebels to operate in its territory had caused strong anti-United States sentiment in their countries.[100] Therefore, Mexico introduced a draft resolution which would have the General Assembly express belief in the principle of non-intervention as imposing an obligation on members to refrain from encouraging or promoting civil strife in other states; urgently appeal to all states to make certain that their territories and resources were not used to promote a civil war in Cuba; urge states to put an immediate end to any activity that might result in further bloodshed; and request them to co-operate in the search for a peaceful solution to the present situation.[101]

The United States opposed this resolution, since it contained an implied endorsement of the Cuban charges and also omitted reference to the OAS. The milder proposal sponsored by seven Latin American nations was also presented as a draft resolution. Both resolutions were adopted by the Political Committee for presentation to the General Assembly. In plenary session the Mexican resolution failed to be adopted. The other resolution was adopted but with the deletion of the paragraph exhorting members of the OAS to aid in achieving a settlement. As adopted, the resolution expressed concern over the situation which disturbed world public opinion and which if continued could endanger world peace; pointed out that the members of the United Nations are obligated to settle their disputes by peaceful means so that international peace and security and justice are not endangered; and exhorted all member states to take such peaceful action as is open to them to remove existing tensions.[102] Although the resolution was not too strong in its language, its passage was considered a defeat for the United States, which had maintained the view that the situation was a hemispheric matter for the OAS to handle.

The Cuban invasion caused the Soviet Union to sound again its rocket warning, to which the President of the United States replied that the United States would honor its inter-American obligations to protect the hemisphere against external aggression.[103] On April 20 the President of the United States, in a speech on the Cuban debacle, although disclaiming unilateral United States intervention in Cuba unless the United States were subjected to attack, still declared that United States restraint was not inexhaustible and continued:

Should it ever appear that the inter-American doctrine of non-interference merely conceals or excuses a policy of non-action; if the nations of this Hemisphere should fail to meet their commitment against outside Communist penetration, then I want it clearly understood that this Government will not hesitate in meeting its primary obligations, which are the security of our nation.[104]

This speech showed an intent not to abandon Cuba to communism. Nevertheless, Cuba became even more firmly entrenched in the communist orbit and little was done by the American nations either collectively or unilaterally. As we have said, some of the American republics ruptured diplomatic and consular relations with the Castro government, and Cuba was barred from secret sessions and from access to classified data of the Inter American Defense Board.[105] In December, 1961, Castro removed all doubt about his political commitment by proclaiming openly that he was and had been from the beginning a Marxist-Leninist. He announced that he was determined to make Cuba a communist state in every sense of the word. With such evidence and with fresh efforts by the Castro regime to export its creed in a revolutionary manner to other parts of the hemisphere, the United States and some other nations, particularly the small Central American nations and certain nations of northern South America which had come to regard Castroist subversion as a danger to their security, favored calling a Meeting of Foreign Ministers in order to bring about the imposition of diplomatic and economic sanctions against Cuba. Finally, the Council of the OAS voted to convene a Meeting of Ministers of Foreign Affairs in accordance with Articles 6 and 11 of the Inter-American Treaty of Reciprocal Assistance to consider the threats to the peace and to the political independence of the American states that might arise from the intervention of extra-continental powers directed toward breaking American solidarity, and particularly to point out the various types of threats to the peace or certain acts that, in the event they occur, justify the application of measures for the maintenance of the peace and security, pursuant to Chapter V of the Charter of the OAS and the provisions of the Inter-American Treaty of Reciprocal Assistance, and to determine the measures that it is advisable to take for the maintenance of the peace and security of the continent.[106]

The very vote in the Council on calling a Meeting showed a deep division among the hemispheric nations as to what measures could or should be taken against Cuba. At this time, Argentina, Bolivia, Brazil, Chile, and Ecuador abstained, while Cuba and Mexico voted in the negative. In explaining the Mexican "nay," a Mexican spokesman said that the proposal to call the Meeting lacked proper juridical basis because it dealt only with possible threats to the peace and not with present threats. Therefore, it was stated that the Council had no legal right under the Rio Treaty to call a Meeting, and that Mexico could not vote in the affirmative to what the Mexican representative claimed would be a treaty change unless the matter were first submitted to the Mexican Senate for approval in accord with the Mexican Constitution.

There is little legal merit in this Mexican contention, despite the fact that the representatives of that country were so careful to appeal to law. The Council is called upon to initiate the consultation at the request of any signatory state, by majority vote, in accordance with the treaty. Although the wording of the Council in calling a Meeting was unfortunate and obtuse in the desire to please all members, and even though its language was directed to threats to the peace that *might arise* from the intervention of extracontinental powers toward breaking inter-American solidarity, the terminology of Article 6 of the Rio Treaty is broad enough to cover such possibilities.

Article 6 does not speak in terms of aggression, threats thereof, or actual and specific threats to the peace only. Article 6 requires the American states to meet in consultation immediately to assist a victim of aggression, and, further, requires a Meeting of Consultation to agree upon measures to be taken for the common defense and for the maintenance of the peace and security of the continent if the inviolability or the integrity of the territory or the sovereignty or political independence of any state should be affected by an extracontinental or intracontinental conflict, or by any other fact or situation that *might* endanger the peace of America. The words "any fact or situation that might endanger the peace," render Article 6 most extensive, so that it covers present and actual as well as possible situations that might threaten the peace. To say that the communist subversion emanating from Cuba and directed against other American republics is not a possible as well as present threat to the peace and security of the continent is to blind oneself to reality. Such subversive activities are a continuing threat and danger.

Moreover, Mexico would apparently concede no power to the Council to interpret the Rio Treaty and its own authority thereunder. Certainly an organ of an international body like the OAS may, at least in the first instance, interpret its own powers, and such interpretation should stand until overruled by a higher organ. In the OAS such a higher organ would be an Inter-American Conference or a Meeting of Foreign Ministers.[107]

The lack of unity that prevailed at the Council meeting was a harbinger of a similar disunity that was to prevail at the Meeting of Consultation of Foreign Ministers which was convened at Punta del Este, Uruguay, on January 22, 1962.[108] Several nations refused to support strict sanctions in the form of severance of diplomatic and trade relations with Cuba—measures provided by Article 8 of the Rio Treaty. Apart from the question of whether such measures would be legally justifiable and politically effective, there was considerable concern in some of the nations about pro-Castro sentiments among their own populations. Faced with such intransigence, the Meeting found compromise inevitable.

A declaration was adopted which stated that the principles of communism were incompatible with the principles of the inter-American political system. This declaration warned of the intensification of the communist subversive offensive and affirmed faith in social progress and representative democracy through free elections and respect for human rights as countermeasures to communism.

It is noteworthy that all of the members except Cuba voted for this declaration, but when it came time to do something about this incompatibility—specifically in the case of Castro's Cuba—divergence became evident.

A second resolution which called Cuba's Marxism-Leninism incompatible with the principles and objectives of the inter-American system, which declared that this incompetence excluded Cuba from the OAS, and which called upon the Council of the OAS and its commissions to adopt without delay the necessary measures to carry out the resolution was carried by the slimmest two-thirds majority. Abstainers were Argentina, Bolivia, Brazil, Chile, Ecuador, and Mexico. Cuba voted in the negative. As noted earlier, the abstaining parties here questioned the legality of the exclusion on the ground that inter-American instruments make no provision for the exclusion of a member.[109]

A resolution to exclude Cuba completely from the Inter-American Defense Board fared much better, with a vote of twenty to one.

The only action taken in accord with the measures of Article 8 of the Rio Treaty was the resolution suspending immediately trade with Cuba in arms and implements of war and instructing the OAS Council to study the feasibility and desirability of extending the suspension to other items, with special attentions to items of strategic importance. Here the vote was sixteen to one, with Brazil, Ecuador, Mexico, and Chile abstaining.

These declarations and resolutions were the only ones that could be considered as direct action against Cuba. The other resolutions were in general a call for action by the American republics to counter the aggressive nature of international communism in the hemisphere. Thus a declaration in favor of the Alliance for Progress program to promote Latin American economic and social development as essential to the security of the hemisphere was adopted with only Cuba in the negative. This declaration demonstrated that the OAS was concentrating on indirect action to answer the Castro-communist challenges, i.e., economic and social reform and foreign aid. Resolutions on holding elections in all American countries and on amplifying and strengthening the Inter-American Commission on Human Rights attempted to give service to hemispheric representative democracy. A resolution directed the Council to establish a committee of experts to recommend security measures against communist subversion,[110] and, as always, another resolution reiterated the principles of non-intervention and self-determination.

Following this Meeting of Foreign Ministers, Cuba was, on February 14, 1962, officially ousted from the OAS by the Council. Moreover, the United States placed a near-absolute embargo on United States trade with Cuba. In taking this action it announced that the loss of this dollar income to Cuba would reduce the capacity of the Castro regime to engage in acts of aggression, subversion, or other activities endangering the security of the hemisphere. The United States trade embargo was followed by a United States effort to persuade its NATO allies to cut down their trade with Cuba—an attempt to call in the Old World to redress the New. The United States trade embargo was taken under the existing laws of the United States, but the government of the United States sought to present it within a hemispheric framework, stating that the embargo was imposed in accordance with the decisions of the recent Meeting of Foreign Ministers of the inter-American system at Punta del Este, Uruguay.

Despite these words, the embargo seemed to be a unilateral action of the United States, for there were no measures taken at Punta del Este ordering a general trade embargo. Only an embargo on arms was ordered, and the Council was called upon to study the feasibility and desirability of extending the suspension in arms to other items.

On February 15, 1962, the Political Committee of the United Nations General Assembly overwhelmingly rejected a Cuban charge that the United States was planning aggression against Cuba, and on February 27, 1962, the Security Council refused to consider a new Cuban charge against the United States to the effect that the United States had induced the OAS to take illegal action against Cuba by the vote at Punta del Este to expel her.[111]

In the months following the Punta del Este meeting, events in Cuba became even more ominous and Russian communist domination even more clearly apparent as the Soviet Union moved to bolster the military power on the island by an accelerated buildup of Soviet military and technical personnel as well as of arms and military equipment. Early in September 1962, the flood of Soviet weapons and personnel into Cuba was described by United States authorities as defensive in nature and not of such significant offensive power as to constitute a threat to other parts of the hemisphere.[112] However, the President of the United States announced that should the communist buildup in Cuba endanger the security of the United States, or should Cuba attempt to export its aggressive purposes by force or the threat of force against any nation in the hemisphere, or should Cuba become an offensive military base of significant capacity for the Soviet Union, then the United States "will do whatever must be done to protect its own security and that of its allies."[113] At that time the President stated that the increased military activity would remain under careful surveillance, and he requested from Congress the authority to call up reserve forces if a crisis made such action necessary. In the days following, the Congress of the United States adopted a resolution declaring that the United States was determined to prevent, by whatever means necessary including the use of arms, the spread by force or threat thereof of the aggressive or subversive activities of the Marxist-Leninist regime to any part of the hemisphere; to prevent in Cuba the creation or use of any externally supported military capability endangering the security of the United States; and to work with the OAS and the freedom-loving Cubans to support the aspirations of the Cuban people for self-determination.[114]

On September 25, 1962, Castro announced that Russia would construct a fishing port in Cuba to facilitate the operation of the Soviet fishing fleet in the Atlantic. Concern was expressed in many quarters of the hemisphere lest such a port should in reality be turned into a naval base for the Soviet fleet.[115]

During these days of crisis, the officials of the United States never gave serious thought to the possibility that Cuba might become a military threat to the United States, but viewed the activities on the island as in the nature of a launching area for the spread of communist subversive conduct to other parts of the hemisphere. Consequently United States policy was aimed at isolating Cuba as a source of infection, and at the same time at making it very costly for the Soviet Union to maintain its communist beachhead in the Americas.[116]

To carry out this policy the United States urged its fellow American republics to take all actions needed to contain the expansion of communism from Cuba and to take steps which might lead to the eventual liberation of Cuba, and introduced an innovation in inter-American consultative procedures by calling an informal meeting of the foreign ministers of the American republics at Washington on October 2 and 3, 1962.[117] The meeting was designated as being outside the framework of the OAS; nevertheless the secretary general of the organization was requested to attend. The principal purpose of the meeting was to obtain an exchange of views regarding the Cuban situation. The meeting was held without formal agenda, voting, official minutes, or resolutions, and the sessions were closed to the public. It was reliably reported that the United States reviewed for the ministers the mounting Soviet power in Cuba and urged the ministers to recommend to their governments the need to curb all remaining trade with Cuba, the need to take stronger internal measures to combat communist infiltration, the need to restrict travel of the many Latin Americans who were going to Cuba for sabotage and indoctrination courses, and the need to encourage the formation of Cuban liberation groups throughout the area.[118]

A final communiqué was issued at the conclusion of the meeting, but it made no mention of concrete decisions or of formal recommendations.[119] It did state explicitly that there was unanimous agreement that the "Sino-Soviet intervention in Cuba was an attempt to convert the island into an armed base for communist penetration of the Americas and subversion of the democratic institutions of the hemisphere." But less clear and explicit were the actions which were to be taken to deal with the problem. Apparently the majority of the ministers did not deem military intervention in Cuba justified at that time; only if the Soviet Union or Cuba engaged in open aggression, as opposed to indirect aggression or subversion, would they be willing to consider the need for collective military steps. In the words of the communiqué, the OAS "should stand in readiness to consider the matter promptly if the situation requires measures beyond those already authorized." Increased economic pressures against Cuba were suggested, including the prohibition of the use of ships of American nations in the Cuban trade plus a request to other nations to cease providing their ships to Soviet bloc countries for trade with the Castro regime. It was agreed that each republic would intensify its efforts to prevent the agents of international communism from continuing their subversive operations, that there should be close individual and collective surveillance of arms shipments to Cuba, and that studies should be made concerning the need to transfer funds to the Latin American nations to help them combat propaganda emanating from Cuba.

By implication this communiqué gave the United States government a greater degree of flexibility in taking unilateral measures within a collective framework regarding the Cuban situation. Also by implication, it recognized the Washington position that the Castro regime must eventually be ousted. Almost immediately the United States sought to force a disruption of maritime traffic from the Soviet bloc to Cuba by announcing on October 4, 1962, a four-point program which it planned to set in motion within two weeks which would penalize world shipping engaged in the Cuban trade. It was planned to withhold from any shipowner cargoes owned or financed by the United States government, if his ships engaged in carrying goods from communist nations to Cuba; to close all United States ports to all ships of any country if any ship flying that country's flag was engaged in transporting war materiel to Cuba; to bar from United States ports any ship which on the same voyage delivered nonmilitary cargoes to Cuba; and to forbid all United States ships to carry goods to or from Cuba.[120]

Before this order could enter into force, a climax was reached when on October 22, 1962, the President of the United States announced to the world that surveillance of Cuba gave incontrovertible evidence that the Soviet Union, "under a cloak of secrecy and deception," was converting the island into a potentially offensive nuclear base against the United States and the whole of the Western Hemisphere by rushing to completion offensive missile sites capable of launching both medium range and intermediate range ballistic missiles capable of carrying nuclear warheads, as well as by basing in Cuba jet bombers also capable of carrying nuclear weapons.[121]

These actions of the Soviet Union were viewed as "an explicit threat to the peace and security of all the Americas, in flagrant and deliberate defiance of the Rio Pact of 1947, the traditions of this nation and hemisphere . . . [and] the Charter of the United Nations." The President directed a strict naval quarantine on all shipping carrying offensive military equipment to Cuba, which would be extended if necessary, and announced that the United States would continue and increase its surveillance of the island in face of this threat to the defense and security both of the United States and of the rest of the hemisphere. It was made clear that the United States would regard "any nuclear missile launched from Cuba against any nation in the Western Hemisphere as an attack by the Soviet Union on the United States requiring a full retaliatory response upon the Soviet Union." The President called for an immediate meeting of the Organ of Consultation of the OAS to consider this threat to hemispheric security and to invoke Articles 6 and 8 of the Rio Treaty in support of all necessary action, and he requested an emergency meeting of the United Nations Security Council to take action against the Soviet's threat to the peace.

On the following day the Council of the OAS convoked the Organ of Consultation, but without setting a time or fixing a place for the meeting. It then constituted itself as Provisional Organ of Consultation in accordance with Article 12 of the Rio Treaty.[122] Acting provisionally, the Council found that unquestionably it "has appeared that the government of Cuba, despite repeated warnings, has secretly endangered the peace of the continent by permitting the Sino-Soviet powers to have intermediate and middle range missiles on its territory capable of carrying nuclear warheads." The Provisional Organ then resolved:

1. To call for the immediate dismantling and withdrawal from Cuba of all missiles and other weapons with any offensive capability;
2. To *recommend* that the member states, in accordance with Articles 6 and 8 of the Inter-American Treaty of Reciprocal Assistance, take all measures, individually

and collectively, including the use of armed force, which they may deem necessary to insure that the Government of Cuba cannot continue to receive from the Sino-Soviet powers military material and related supplies which may threaten the peace and security of the Continent and to prevent the missiles in Cuba with offensive capability from ever becoming an active threat to the peace and security of the Continent;

3. To inform the Security Council of the United Nations of this resolution in accordance with Article 54 of the Charter of the United Nations and to express the hope that the Security Council will, in accordance with the draft resolution introduced by the United States, dispatch UN observers to Cuba at the earliest moment;

4. To continue to serve provisionally as Organ of Consultation and to request the Member States to keep the Organ of Consultation duly informed of measures taken by them in accordance with paragraph 2 of this resolution. [Italics supplied][123]

The vote on this resolution was 19 to 0 (Uruguay abstained at the time for lack of instructions from its government, but approval came later, hence the vote was unanimous).[124] This crisis over Cuba produced the clearest showing of unity since World War II, although it was reported that Brazil, Mexico, and Bolivia had certain reservations and had abstained on the second portion of paragraph 2 of the resolution, which authorized measures including the use of armed force to prevent the missiles from becoming operational. They feared that such wording might be construed as an endorsement of an invasion of Cuba if the United States deemed it necessary.[125]

The President of the United States then issued a proclamation entitled "Interdiction of the Delivery of Offensive Weapons to Cuba."[126] Citing that he was acting under the Constitution and laws of the United States, the Joint Resolution of Congress of October 3, 1962, and the resolution of the OAS of October 23, 1962, he ordered interdicted the delivery of offensive weapons and associated materials to Cuba. The land, sea, and air forces of the United States, in co-operation with forces made available from other American nations, were authorized to enforce the interdiction by interupting any vessel or craft proceeding to Cuba, directing it "to identify itself, its cargo, equipment and stores and its ports of call, to stop, to lie to, to submit to visit and search, or to proceed as directed." If any vessel refused to stop, it was to be taken into custody. Those found to be carrying forbidden cargoes to Cuba were to be directed to proceed to another destination of their own choice, and if they refused, they were to be taken into custody. Force was not to be used except in case of the failure or refusal of a vessel to comply with directions after reasonable efforts had been made to communicate such directions to the officers aboard, or in the case of self-defense. In any event, no more force than was necessary was to be employed. This blockade (or quarantine as it was called) of Cuba went into effect at 10 A.M. on October 24, 1962.

At the emergency meeting of the Security Council requested by the President, the United States presented a resolution calling for the immediate dismantling and withdrawal from Cuba of all missiles and other offensive weapons as a provisional measure under Article 40 of the United Nations Charter, suggesting that this be carried out under the supervision of the United Nations, promising to end the quarantine upon compliance with the resolution, and recommending that the United States and the Soviet Union promptly confer on measures which would remove all of these threats to hemispheric and world peace.[127]

After a few nervous days and a great deal of diplomatic maneuvering at the United Nations level and between Kennedy and Khrushchev, the latter agreed to end the construction of the Soviet bases, to dismantle and return to Russia under United Nations supervision the offensive arms in Cuba, and to halt the further introduction of such weapons there. In return, the United States promised that once adequate United Nations arrangements had been established to assure that Russia carried out its commitments, the United States would lift the Cuban quarantine and would give assurances against an invasion of Cuba.[128]

The fly in the ointment of this plan proved to be the refusal of the Castro regime to permit on-site inspection in Cuba unless the United States met Castro's demands, which included cessation of the United States economic blockade of Cuba, cessation of subversive activities by exiled Cubans against Castro from United States territory, cessation of piratical attacks by exiled groups, cessation of violations of Cuban airspace and territorial waters, and the return of Guantanamo Naval Base to Cuba.[129] The United States announced that all of these were unacceptable. Another difficulty arose over the removal of the Russian jet bombers from Cuba, Castro claiming they belonged to the Cuban government. Pressure from the Soviet forced Castro to back down, and at a press conference on November 20, 1962, Kennedy announced that Khrushchev had given assurances that the bombers would be removed within thirty days.[130] On the strength of this assurance, the United States called off the naval quarantine, but in the absence of an adequate inspection system inside Cuba, it continued air reconnaissance activities to ascertain what military activities were taking place on the island. As to the no-invasion pledge which had been given by the President of the United States if United States demands were met, including dismantling and removal of offensive weapons and satisfactory on-site inspection, the President declared: "As for our part, if all offensive weapons systems are removed from Cuba and kept out of the hemisphere in the future under adequate verification and safeguards, and if Cuba is not used for the export of aggressive communist purposes, there will be peace in the Caribbean."[131]

This language indicated that the United States intended to keep the Castro regime under careful surveillance, with an implicit threat of military action if the Cubans showed signs of aggressive intent.

Interesting problems of inter-American law were raised by the actions and words of the United States and the OAS in this Cuban crisis. It will be noted that the Council acted, as it had acted in many previous cases, by convoking the Organ of Consultation at some future unstated time and place, and then constituting itself as Provisional Organ of Consultation. But in previous cases where the Council had seen fit to handle the difficulties itself the situations were not so serious and the final action of the Council resulted in mere resolutions or recommendations which contained no hint or threat of enforcement measures. Cases in which such measures were deemed requisite had been referred to the Meeting of Foreign Ministers acting in their capacity as Organ of Consultation under the Rio Treaty.[132] Because of the urgency of the situation, the

Council, acting as Provisional Organ, saw fit to take those steps necessary to meet the crisis immediately.[133] It should be noted, however, that the Provisional Organ did not actually make any decision in terms of the Rio Treaty which would have compelled or obligated the members to take specific measures. To the contrary, the Council called for the dismantling of the weapons, and then simply *recommended* that the member states take all measures individually and collectively, including the use of armed force, to meet this threat to hemispheric peace and security. As such a recommendation would not bind the members to a course of action, it was politically more expedient. The only specific measure mentioned was the use of armed force, a measure which is provided for under Article 8 of the Rio Treaty. Article 20 of that treaty, while recognizing the decisions which require the application of Article 8 measures to be binding, specifically excepts therefrom the use of armed force as obligatory, declaring that "no state shall be required to use armed force without its consent." Hence the Council could not order or compel the use of armed force; it could only recommend such use. Moreover, a recommendatory action would be less prone to an accusation that it fell under the term "enforcement action" of Article 53 of the Charter of the United Nations, which would then require Security Council authorization, for the International Court of Justice has held (although admittedly in another context) that recommendatory action by the General Assembly of the United Nations to organize peace-keeping operations does not fall within the term *enforcement action*. While the OAS has never considered its measures not involving the use of armed force as "enforcement measures" requiring United Nations authorization, there has been indication in the OAS that the use of armed force, except in the case of individual or collective self-defense, might be considered as enforcement action and thereby fall under the prerogatives of the Security Council.[134]

Although this was not expressly stated and although the OAS acted under Article 6 of the Rio Treaty rather than Article 3 which deals with self-defense, it is clear from all the statements issued at the time that the organization felt it was confronted with a situation requiring self-defense measures, and consequently all measures taken were defensive measures.[135] Nevertheless, the OAS was apparently somewhat confused, for the Provisional Organ decided to inform the Security Council of the United Nations of the resolution which was adopted "in accordance with Article 54 of the United Nations Charter." Article 54 is set out in the United Nations Charter's Chapter VIII, which is concerned with regional arrangements. Article 53 of this same chapter prohibits enforcement action without authorization of the Security Council. Article 54 requires that the Security Council be kept fully informed of the activities of regional arrangements for the maintenance of international peace and security. A legal case could be made that Article 53 and Article 54 should be read together as far as the quarantine measures recommended were concerned, and consequently the action of the OAS was illegal without Security Council authorization. It would have been wiser for the organization to report to the United Nations under Article 51 of that Charter, which recognizes the right of nations to take measures of individual and collective self-defense. While Article 51 also requires self-defense measures to be reported to the Security Council, parties acting under the right of self-defense need no prior authorization from the Security Council, but are empowered to act until that body takes adequate measures to enforce the peace. That the nations of the Western Hemisphere were acting in self-defense can be deduced from the fact that the OAS never requested Security Council authorization for the action taken, but only petitioned the United Nations to bring about a dismantling and removal of the missiles from Cuba and to establish an adequate inspection system under Article 40 of the United Nations Charter, which permits the Security Council in the face of aggression or threats to or breaches of the peace to require the parties to take provisional measures so that the situation will not be further aggravated.

That measures of self-defense are not limited to situations where an armed attack has actually occurred and that they may be resorted to not only under Article 3 of the Rio Treaty but also under Article 6 was well exemplified by the actions of the OAS.[136] The individual and collective measures taken were aimed at preventing an armed attack, not at stopping one which had occurred. Acting under a broad interpretation of the right of self-defense as set forth in Article 51 of the United Nations Charter, the OAS acknowledged that this right could legally be exercised when, in Daniel Webster's words, "the necessity of that self-defense is instant, overwhelming, and leaving no choice of means and no moment for deliberation."[137] Obviously there was no other alternative, for in view of its past history the Security Council could not have been relied upon to assure an effective and rapid removal of the threat to the hemispheric peace. The words of United States Secretary of State Rusk were indicative of the urgency of the situation:

These facts demonstrate that the U.S.S.R. is making a major military investment in Cuba with advanced weapons systems with substantial offensive capability. What do these facts mean to the independent nations of this hemisphere? Their significance is immediate, direct, and perhaps fateful to the maintenance of that independence. . . . This offensive capability is of such a nature that it can reach into the far corners of our hemisphere with its destructive force. . . . The new sites for intermediate-range ballistic missiles in Cuba will be able to carry mass destruction to most of the major cities in the Western Hemisphere. In the face of this rapid buildup, no country in this hemisphere can feel secure, either from direct attack or from persistent blackmail.[138]

Although the preamble of the resolution of the Provisional Organ recognizes the obligation of the members of the OAS to meet armed attacks, still the resolution invoked Article 6 of the Rio Treaty rather than Article 3, which deals with the right of individual and collective self-defense. While the organization might have proceeded under a broad interpretation of Article 3, the members preferred to base their action on the more extensive language of Article 6, invoking the right of self-defense against an aggression which is not an armed attack or against a situation which endangered the peace and security of the hemisphere and which affected the inviolability or the integrity of the territory or the sovereignty or political independence of any American state. As the threat to use armed force illegally is an aggression, the broad view of self-defense under both the United Nations Charter and the Rio Treaty gives rise to the right of individual and collective self-defense when an imminent threat of such aggression occurs. It therefore follows that the protective measures taken by the OAS under Article 6 were legally permissible.

The actions taken pursuant to the OAS resolution were limited to a naval quarantine to prevent the further introduction of offensive weapons into Cuba and an air surveillance of the island to ascertain what military activities were taking place. These actions were taken mainly by United States Naval and Air Force units, although other nations offered their services to the OAS if needed.[139] The quarantine ordered by the United States President did not become effective until the Provisional Organ had agreed to take collective measures; consequently the United States acted under authority of the OAS resolution. However, as there was clearly a right of individual self-defense, the United States could have acted on its own had it so desired.

The quarantine comes closest in analogy to a pacific blockade, that is a blockade during peace resorted to by a state or a group of states against another nation as a compulsive measure to bring the latter to terms for its delinquency and its violation of the international legal rights of the blockading state or states. While some international jurists question the legality of a pacific blockade, it is generally accepted that such action is legal if taken as a reprisal against a violation of international law to obtain redress or reparation against an offending state. If taken for any other purpose, it would, of course, be an illegal intervention. Unanimity does exist on the point that there is no right to seize or sequester ships of third states who attempt to violate the blockade, but these ships may be stopped and ordered to alter their destination, since they are under a duty to respect a legal blockade.[140]

A pacific blockade generally seeks to interrupt all maritime commerce with the delinquent state; but the quarantine instituted in the Cuban affair sought only to interrupt the flow of offensive weapons to the island, although it was stressed that if the necessity arose it would become more sweeping. It applied to the vessels of any nation proceeding toward Cuba, including those of third states. Vessels were to be subjected to visit and search, and any vessel carrying prohibited material was to be directed to proceed to another port. Although seizure and sequestration of ships were not ordered, if a vessel failed to stop and submit to visit or search, or if it was found to carry prohibited items and it refused or failed to proceed to another port, then it was to be taken into custody and sent to the United States for appropriate action.

A case for the legality of this action as an enforcement action under international law might have been made out. But as a reprisal involving the use of force (if the resort to naval forces in and of itself can be considered force) or the threat of the use of force (which was present if a ship refused to honor the blockade) would have made it illegal as individual or collective enforcement action under the United Nations Charter without prior Security Council authorization. Consequently the legality of the quarantine was predicated on the basis of individual and collective self-defense. The quarantine was not an enforcement action or a reprisal taken to obtain redress and reparation. It was taken as a protective measure, a partial interruption of economic relations as provided for in Article 8 of the Rio Treaty, backed by the threat of the use of force also as provided for in Article 8, to assure that the imminent threat of nuclear holocaust would not succeed in destroying the independent nations of this hemisphere.

The air surveillance of Cuba cannot properly be spoken of as a measure taken under Article 8. It was a procedure collectively authorized by the American states for the purpose of acquiring information as to the nature and extent of the arms buildup which was threatening the peace and security of the hemisphere. Since the Rio Treaty authorizes measures of self-defense and measures of collective action against threats to the peace, the power to investigate and obtain information on such threats obviously rests within the organization. The OAS had already recognized its powers of investigation in previous cases which had come before it where it had sent committees into troubled areas and had authorized pacific observation flights to check on military movements.[141]

Cuba, of course, could hardly claim that these flights, whether taken individually or collectively, were illegal intervention, for Cuba by its own conduct had excluded itself from the inter-American community, and probably from the international community of civilized states. Since it had done so, the Castro government could not rely on the principles of law, including that of non-intervention, which govern these communities, but could only expect to be dealt with on a political as distinguished from a legal basis.[142]

When confronted with proof of the presence of Soviet rocket bases in Cuba with nuclear missiles poised to strike throughout the hemisphere, the American republics were suddenly and rudely shocked into a posture of unity. Only a nuclear threat could produce sufficient solidarity for the Rio Treaty to be invoked and for authorization to be obtained for collective measures to meet the threat of the international communist movement to this hemisphere. In spite of extensive communist penetration into the political apparatus, the student movements, the labor organizations, the communications facilities, and even the military forces of nations of this hemisphere, the OAS has been exceedingly hesitant to take effective measures to combat this extracontinental intervention of Sino-Soviet origins. It has relied solely on weak resolutions calling for the eradication of international communism from the Western Hemisphere. Even as late as the October 2-3, 1962, informal meeting of foreign ministers, when confronted with the evidence of the influx of Soviet military personnel into Cuba the OAS hesitated to act, preferring to see in the troop movements only action for defense of Cuba against potential United States invasion.

If consideration is given to the fact that the organization failed to take a decisive step in 1954 when faced with communist intervention in Guatemala, and again failed to take a decisive step in 1961-62 when faced with clear evidence of the communist subversion of the Cuban revolution against the Batista regime, one must reluctantly come to the conclusion that the OAS is not a dynamic force acting to secure the peace and self-determination of the nations of the hemisphere. While it was heartening to view the sudden and dramatic unity which appeared during the Cuban missile crisis, any optimism must be tempered by the fact that this unity resulted only because there was a clear and present danger of direct aggression to all the members from the Soviet missiles. And even here there was some foot-dragging about authorizing a military invasion of Cuba to remove the missiles; some American states apparently felt that the principle of non-intervention is solely directed at the United States and not at the subversive intervention of international communism.

Whether the American nations will remain divided in their efforts to combat communism in the hemisphere lies in the laps of the gods. As this is written the Cuban crisis is far from over. Russia has (as far as can be ascertained by aerial surveillance) withdrawn some of the weapons described as offensive, and the OAS has lifted the quarantine. But the pledge of international inspection is still unfulfilled. Russian troops have not been withdrawn, and it is reported that their number is increasing and that they and the Cuban forces are being equipped with the most modern of conventional arms. International safeguards against the reintroduction of Soviet nuclear weapons are still lacking. Castro still dominates the Cuban scene, and consequently there remains in this hemisphere the problem of international communism with its shocking displays of the violations of all human rights and its unending acts of external subversion. But the members of the OAS still fail to honor their pledges to support the independence of any hemispheric nation against a foreign regime imposed by internal subversion, and they still refuse to take the necessary collective measures to deal with international communism, which endangers not only inter-American peace and security but also the peace and security of all the world.

CHAPTER XVIII

THE OAS, CIVIL STRIFE, AND THE MONROE DOCTRINE

A common denominator of political life in the Latin American republics has been the presence of internal revolutionary disturbance as rivals have competed for political power. As a consequence of this competition, plots, conspiracies, and movements against the government in power have been the order of the day in all of the republics at varying times, and these movements have often resulted in civil strife when opposing parties within a state have had recourse to arms for the purpose of obtaining power in the state or when a portion of the population of a state has risen in arms against the existing government. Hemispheric history is replete with interventions by foreign states in the affairs of a state torn asunder by or threatened with civil strife.[1] A foreign state may directly aid one or the other of the contending factions by use of the foreign state's armed forces to maintain or overthrow a government, or by the manipulation of its diplomatic or economic policy, including the supplying of arms or refusal to supply them, so as to favor one side or another. Or again a foreign state may act in a more indirect manner by fomenting civil strife to subvert a government of another state, generally by aiding, in a more or less covert way, private rebel or other groups in their movement to topple a government as well as by engaging in hostile propaganda against the government of another state.

INTERNATIONAL LAW AND CIVIL STRIFE

The prevalence of foreign interferences in time of civil strife has subjected such action to legal scrutiny. A divergence of opinion has resulted with respect to the duties of foreign states to a state wherein revolutionary turmoil exists. To a degree the obligations of American states to such a state have been clarified by the 1928 Habana Convention on the Duties and Rights of States in the Event of Civil Strife, which is correlated to the non-intervention principle,[2] and the 1957 Protocol to the Convention on Duties and Rights of States in the Event of Civil Strife,[3] which has not yet been widely ratified.[4]

International law looks upon civil strife as a domestic issue. It is considered an internal affair. A people are claiming a right to govern themselves as they desire, even through resort to revolution.[5] Moreover, the legitimate government is reacting against a violation of its domestic law, that is against an illegal use of force. Being a domestic question, civil strife is in no way of and by itself an international wrong or delict.[6] Consequently there can be no legitimate grounds for foreign intervention to assist in suppressing or aiding the internal strife, unless it is based on the consent of the state.[7] In order that consent may be recognized as a valid basis for legality of intervention, the consent must be legal. To be legal, it must be granted by the legal representative of the state.[8] To some jurists, a consent by government in time of serious civil conflict to a foreign intervention to maintain that government could hardly be called the consent of the state. The very fact of civil strife would show that the identity of the legal representative of the state was in doubt, for the consent would be made without the acquiescence of a large number of the state's citizens.[9] Nevertheless, it has been claimed to the contrary that if intervention takes place by invitation of one of the disputing parties it is a legal intervention.[10] Some, while declining to admit the legality of intervention at the invitation of the rebellious group, do admit its justification if the intervention is at the request of or in aid of the established government.[11] Others, such as Vattel, hold that a state may intervene to assist the faction which appears to have justice on its side.[12] In the nineteenth century, the Holy Alliance intervened unhesitatingly where revolutionary democratic movements in some states threatened the existing monarchical system.[13] They based their right to intervene on all of these contentions. Where a monarch had been deposed and sought to regain his throne, intervention was based on invitation by one of the disputing parties. Where the monarch was engaged in attempting to hold his throne in face of a liberal rebellion, intervention was based on the reasoning that a *de jure* government had an absolute claim; and in both cases, intervention was based on the idea of justice, which was equated with protection for the existing order menaced by republicanism and democracy.

Hall denounces all these contentions that there exists a legal basis on which foreign states can intervene in case of civil strife. He declares:

It is hard to see by what reasoning these views can be supported. As interventions, in so far as they purport to be made in compliance with an invitation, are independent of the reasons or pretexts which have already been discussed, it must be assumed that they are based either on simple friendship or upon a sentiment of justice. If intervention on the ground of mere friendship were allowed, it would be idle to speak seriously of the rights of independence. Supposing the intervention to be directed against the existing government, independence is violated by an attempt to prevent the regular organ of the state from managing the state affairs in its own way. Supposing it on the other hand to be directed against the rebels, the fact that it has been necessary to call in foreign help is enough to show that the issue of the conflict would without it be uncertain, and consequently that there is doubt as to which side would ultimately establish itself as the legal representative of the state. If, again, the intervention is based upon an opinion as to the merits of the question at issue, the intervening state takes upon itself to pass judgment in a matter which, having nothing to do with the relations of states, must be regarded as being for legal purposes beyond the range of its vision.[14]

According to this line of thought, neither faction on its own can speak as legal representative of the state as long as the result is uncertain so as to make legal foreign assistance for one or the other of the contestants. Hence, strict impartiality becomes the duty of foreign states in the presence of an internal strife in the territory of another state. Aid at the request of the *de jure* government as well as aid at the request of the revolutionaries is an illegal intervention in the internal affairs of the state.[15] Foreign intervention could only be legitimate if both parties requested it. In such a case the legality of the intervention would be based upon the total consent of the state—a condition which would be most unlikely to come about.

Another line of authority takes issue with this point of view. The right of a people to choose their own form of government and to do so by revolution is, of course, recognized, but various stages of development of civil strife are recognized at the same time. Until a stage of belligerency ensues, neutrality or impartiality is not required. To the contrary, the existing recognized government is to be favored as against the revolutionary group.

As civil strife may vary from mob riots to civil war, if all relationships are suspended, then under some circumstances failure to fulfil certain duties might well amount to intervention. On the other hand, if all relationships are not suspended, there may be instances where the fulfilment of a duty might be an act of intervention. In order to overcome this difficulty degrees of civil strife are observed. A mob outbreak, a riot, or other isolated instances of rebellion occurring in a nation in no way change the relation of other states with the government in which the incidents occur.[16] If the situation spreads and becomes of serious proportions, is organized, has leaders, and offers for a time effective resistance to the established government, then it becomes an insurgency.[17] When the revolt goes still farther and the insurgents control territory in the state and maintain a responsible government, then it evolves into civil war or a state of belligerency.[18] It is in the instance of insurgency and belligerency that the question of aid to one side or another as possible intervention becomes important.

A state of insurgency is an insurrection which has become war in a material sense although not in a legal sense.[19] It is an intermediate stage between a state of internal peace and a state of all-out civil war. When a foreign state recognizes a state of insurgency, it merely acknowledges the fact of the insurrection, but does not create any new international status between it and the parties to the strife. Recognition of insurgency is a domestic act "drawing the attention of the public to a state of fact in a foreign state which calls for special caution."[20] A status of insurgency, recognized or unrecognized, does not change the obligations owed by a foreign state to the state wherein civil strife prevails. A status of insurgency does not place upon the state the obligations of neutrality, hence the obligations which the outside state owes to the state in civil strife are owed to the *de jure* government, and no duty prevents a state from continuing its obligations to that government.[21] The fact that insurgency has occurred does not place the *de jure* government faced with the rebellion on a legal status different from that of any other *de jure* government, for this fact has no effect on the juridical status of the state. Thus no international law rule prohibits a grant of assistance by a foreign state to the government to enable the government to put down the revolt against its authority. Whether the foreign state does so is to be determined by its own policy, but if it does, it is not to be considered an unlawful intervention as would be the case if assistance were rendered to the rebels.[22]

A state may recognize a status of belligerency, as distinguished from insurgency, as prevailing in another state when civil strife disturbs to a considerable extent the relations of the foreign state with the state disrupted by internal hostilities and when the insurrection grows to such proportions as to have become public war in a legal sense.[23] It has been stated that in order that an insurrection may be recognized as having developed into a civil war the following prerequisites must be met:

It must be an armed struggle, carried on between two political bodies, each of which exercises *de facto* authority over persons within a determinated territory, and commands an army which is prepared to observe the ordinary laws of war. It requires, then, on the part of the insurgents an organization purporting to have the characteristics of a State, though not yet recognized as such. The armed insurgents must act under the direction of this organized civil authority. An organized army is not enough. And all this, of course, must take place within the territorial limits recognized by foreign States as part of the parent country.[24]

When a status of belligerency is recognized, then the equivalent of war has come into existence. The state recognizing the condition of belligerency must thereafter assume the obligations of neutrality just as if the two contending factions were two contending states in an international war.[25]

The recognition of belligerency does bestow benefits on the insurgents, for by such act they are permitted to obtain loans on the credit of the state; their ships have a right to enter ports of the recognizing state; they may maintain the right of visit and search at sea, confiscate contraband goods, and maintain blockades. On the other hand, recognition of belligerency burdens the titular government in that after such recognition it is treated equally with the rebels, thus changing the international legal status.[26] Such an action cannot, therefore, be lightly undertaken. International law places upon the state granting the recognition of belligerency the definite prerequisite that its relations with the state engaged in civil war are seriously disrupted or disturbed.[27]

Furthermore, even if the relationship between the foreign state and the state engaged in civil strife is seriously disrupted but the insurrection has not developed into a civil war, a recognition of belligerency would be an act of intervention. As stated by Oppenheim, a premature recognition of belligerency is an "illicit interference in the affairs of the state affected by civil disorders— an international wrong analogous to the premature recognition of a state or a government."[28] Mere military success of a revolting army would not, therefore, permit recognition of belligerency if that army was unable to maintain order and law in the territory under its control or if it was unwilling to observe the ordinary laws of war.[29]

If the requirements for a civil war are fulfilled and if the relationship between the foreign state and the state engaged in civil conflict is seriously disrupted, then a refusal to recognize belligerency would be an imposition of inequality and hardship upon the belligerent community and would also be an illegal intervention in the internal affairs of the disrupted state.

Therefore, although it is the generally accepted rule of international law that in the event of civil strife foreign intervention to aid one side or the other is illegal, at the same time it is acknowledged that prior to recognition of belligerency the lawful government is entitled to privileged treatment by a foreign state as compared with insurgents seeking to overthrow that government, for as long as the lawful sovereign authority has not been definitely supplanted in a portion of the state's territory by civil war, when international law notes a change of status, it alone can be regarded and treated as the subject of the rights ordinarily enjoyed by states. To treat it otherwise would be a clear act of illegal intervention.[30] After the international requirements for the recognition

of belligerency have been fulfilled, a duty of recognition of belligerency necessarily follows, and a refusal of recognition is interference with the right of
political self-determination of the people of a state and therefore constitutes
illegal intervention.

An exponent of the distinction between insurgency and belligerency in
relation to duties of foreign states—a distinction which requires neutrality of
foreign states only in times of belligerency—has stated:

> If international law is to continue to predicate its existence and strength upon an
> orderly system of sovereign states, each independent of the other and sovereign over
> its internal affairs, distinction must be preserved between the rights and duties of
> foreign states in time of civil and international war. Neutrality and non-intervention
> in time of unrecognized insurgency and in time of international warfare involve very
> different propositions. To apply to unrecognized and irresponsible rebels the same
> principles that are applicable to sovereign states and established governments is to
> encourage rebellion and disorder and to weaken public law and authority. The law
> cannot afford to do this.[31]

This latter position is the underlying theory of inter-American law as
embodied in the Habana Convention on Duties and Rights of States in the
Event of Civil Strife and the 1957 Protocol thereto, for in these documents
the distinction between insurgency and belligerency is maintained, and while
the former status exists, whether recognized or not, the obligations of the
ratifying states are not neutral or impartial, but favor the established government as against revolutionaries.[32] Only with the recognition of a status of
belligerency is neutrality required. Hence, it would appear under these instruments that aid rendered at the request of a government harassed by insurgency
would not constitute a delict, but aid to the insurgents is clearly outlawed.

The Habana Convention[33] provides that the contracting parties must use
the means at their disposal to prevent inhabitants of their territory—nationals
as well as aliens—from participating in civil strife, gathering elements for it,
or crossing the boundary or sailing from their territory for the purpose of
starting or promoting such civil strife.[34] This provision seems to follow the
rule of general international law. In times of peace all nations owe other
nations the duty to prevent their territory from being used as a base for hostile
activities against the legitimate government of a state. Insurgency or the recognition thereof does not change this duty, but rather demands that the internal
authorities exercise special precautions to make certain that this duty is not
breached.[35] Although a state is duty bound to prevent its territory from being
used by persons whose aim is to carry out antagonistic and unfriendly acts
against the government of another state, international law recognizes that complete prevention is often impossible. So an absolute prohibition is not established;
instead, responsibility is imposed on a state only to the extent of using "due
diligence" to prevent such activities on its soil.[36] Thus, failure to exercise due
diligence to prevent the state's territory from being used as a base for hostile
acts with a purpose of starting or promoting rebellion against another government is a delict under international law.[37] The Habana Convention uses words
somewhat more forceful than "due diligence," for it commands the American

states "to use all means at their command" to prevent their territory from being used for such hostile revolutionary acts.[38]

The 1957 Protocol[39] attempts to clarify, supplement, and strengthen the inter-American principles and rules applicable in the event of civil strife and commands, in Article V, with words somewhat similar to those of the Habana Convention, that each state

shall in areas subject to its jurisdiction and within the powers granted by its constitution, use all appropriate means to prevent any person, national or alien, from deliberately participating in the preparation, organization, or carrying out of a military enterprise that has as its purpose the starting, promoting or supporting of civil strife in another contracting State *whether or not the government of the latter has been recognized.* [Italics supplied][40]

The article then lists specifically certain acts which among others are to be considered as participation in the preparation, organization, or carrying out of a military enterprise. They are:

a) The contribution, supply or provision of arms and war material;
b) The equipment, training, collection, or transportation of members of a military expedition; or
c) The provision or receipt of money, by any method, intended for the military enterprise.

The pledge by the contracting parties to prevent persons within their territory from committing acts designed to start, promote, or support civil strife in an American state is obviously an aid to the established government in that it tends to promote internal stability at the expense of revolutionary disorder, and, according to Article V of the Protocol, the government is so favored whether recognized or not.

The Habana Convention also forbids traffic in arms except such as is intended for the government of the country when the belligerency of the rebels has not been recognized.[41] The Protocol contains added duties for the American states, enjoining them to keep under surveillance traffic in arms and war material believed to be intended for starting, promoting, or supporting civil strife in another American state; to suspend the exportation or importation of any shipment of arms and war material during the period of the investigation of the circumstances relating to the shipment where there is reason to believe that such arms and war material may be intended for starting, promoting, or supporting such civil strife; and to prohibit the exportation or importation of any shipment of arms and war material intended for starting, promoting, or supporting civil strife in another American state.[42]

In addition, the Habana Convention calls upon each contracting party to disarm and intern rebel forces coming into its territory and to prevent the equipping or arming of any vessel intended to operate in favor of the rebellion.[43] It is to be noted that these provisions apply against the forces in rebellion only. There is no prohibition directed to a state placing upon it the duty to disarm and intern forces of the titular government. With respect to this problem the practices of states have been contradictory. Government forces as well as rebel forces of a nation engaged in civil strife have in some instances been treated as forces of a country engaged in an international war; that is, upon their entrance into a neutral state they have been interned.[44] However, there have been instances in which government forces have been permitted to pass through the territory of another state and to return to their own country.[45]

There are two distinct situations that may be involved in incidents of this character. The first occurs when groups or individuals of government forces cross over into the territory of another state. In such a situation it has been contended that they should be disarmed, and thereafter, if they so desire, they should be permitted to return to their home state with their weapons. In such an instance, the state into which they have crossed is not obligated by neutrality, for these forces, belonging to the legitimate government, are not a danger to the government involved in civil conflict.

The second situation arises when the titular government requests passage through another state. Here again the foreign state may grant permission, although it is not obligated to do so. In either situation, it would seem that such action on the part of a foreign state could be tolerated only in time of a status of insurgency. If a status of belligerency has been legally recognized by the foreign state, then it would be incumbent upon that state to act as a neutral. The presence of such troops on neutral territory is an obvious danger to the other side of the conflict. Therefore the neutral duty of impartiality obligates the foreign state to disarm and intern them so as to insure that they will not further participate in the war. This applies equally to government troops and to insurgents.[46]

Although the Civil Strife Convention does not here speak in terms of belligerency or insurgency, demanding only the internment and disarming of rebel forces in time of civil strife, nevertheless, by the use of the words "rebel forces" it would seem that this article is referring to insurgency rather than belligerency, for in the latter status it is customary to refer to the two sides as belligerents. It is safe to conclude that the convention establishes the duty to intern rebels only in the instance of insurgency, and that when belligerency occurs the general international law rules which pertain to this problem are to be applied.

The same argument can be made in connection with Article 1, Paragraph 4, which requires a state to prevent in its territory the equipping or arming of any vessel for warlike purposes operating in favor of the rebellion. This article makes no mention of equipping government vessels of the state in conflict, nor does it distinguish between belligerency and insurgency. This article, too, would seem to be directed only to a status of insurgency, for under a status of belligerency, neutrality requires the prevention of the arming and equipping of belligerent men-of-war in neutral ports, as otherwise the neutral state would be indirectly assisting them in preparing for hostilities. It has long been recognized, however, that a neutral may grant temporary asylum to belligerent men-of-war without being obliged to disarm or detain them.[47]

Article 1, Paragraph 3 of the convention forbids traffic in arms and war material "except when intended for the government, while the belligerency of the rebels has not been recognized, in which latter case the rules of neutrality shall be applied." Article 2 of the Protocol sets forth a similar provision. Both the convention and the protocol definitely prohibit a foreign state from permitting arms to go to the rebels and, in addition, call upon the state to prevent persons within its jurisdiction from engaging in the traffic of arms with the rebels prior to a declaration of belligerency. During insurgency, general international law grants a privileged status to the government,[48] and these sections appear to be a codification of the rules of general international law on this point; for these provisions deny the foreign government the right to aid the insurgent group or groups and place upon it the duty to prevent persons within its territory from doing so. On the other hand, no duty is set forth to prevent a foreign government from supplying munitions and war materials to the government to assist it in quashing the rebellion. Although it would seem that a state has no duty to supply the legitimate government with arms to put down a rebellion or to permit such government to be supplied, it has a right to do so. It has a duty not to aid the insurgents and a right to aid the government. If there is a legal right to action, such action cannot be an illegal intervention.

A state may, under its domestic law, refuse to permit the shipment of arms to a legitimate government engaged in insurgency, for it may refuse to ship arms to a government not faced with civil strife. There is no general international law duty to supply arms to other friendly nations; that is a domestic issue governed by the internal municipal law of each state.[49]

After belligerency has been recognized and neutrality comes about, the neutral state in its corporate person must not directly aid either side by the sale of munitions, for it would then be violating its duty of impartiality. But general international law recognizes that the supply of such articles by subjects of neutrals is lawful. By municipal law, a neutral may prohibit its subjects from engaging in arms traffic, but that is an internal domestic question and not an obligation imposed by general international law.[50]

Consequently it would seem that in the main, the Convention on the Duties and Rights of States in the Event of Civil Strife, as well as the Protocol thereto, are codifications of some of the general international law rules which apply to insurgency and belligerency and both adopt the fact that the government of a state in civil strife is in a preferred position during a status of insurgency. They present no radically new legal norms to govern inter-American relationships in time of internal rebellion, but rather clarify and make definite through written agreement rules applicable to civil strife.

COLLECTIVE ACTION OF THE OAS AND CIVIL STRIFE

Civil strife has been involved in most of the cases[51] which have confronted the consultative organs of the OAS for collective action under the Rio Treaty in the face of a threat to or breach of the peace in the Americas.[52] The first group of such cases, dating from a period ranging from 1948 to 1955, which came before the Council for consideration set a pattern and furnish insights into and precedents of inter-American law. In these instances there had developed in the territories of various states groups of persons who were engaged in activities designed to overthrow the governments of other states.

In all of these cases except one the Council of the OAS convoked itself as Provisional Organ of Consultation under the Rio Treaty for purposes of collective action in the interests of hemispheric peace, although fortunately the taking of collective enforcement measures proved unnecessary.

The main purpose of the OAS is to strengthen the peace and security of the continent and not the internal peace and security of an individual state.[53] Accordingly, in the event of civil strife the OAS has no power to act unless the civil strife contains factors which endanger the peace of the Americas, and such factors would have to be of a nature which threatened the inviolability or the integrity of the territory or the sovereignty or political independence of an American state. The right of a people to establish within their own territory a government of their own choosing, so long as such action does not endanger other states or the peace of the Americas, is a long-established principle of inter-American relations,[54] and the OAS has no power to intervene either on behalf of the government or on behalf of the forces seeking to overthrow that government.

What, then, if the government of a state harassed or threatened by civil rebellion complains to the OAS that a foreign nation is engaged in subversive activities against that government in violation of international law and inter-American instruments such as the non-intervention agreement and the Convention on the Duties and Rights of States in the Event of Civil Strife? The issue then would no longer be an internal, domestic question but a dispute between states, and the OAS could take action under the Rio Treaty, viewing such activity on the part of the foreign state as a threat to the peace of the Americas affecting the political independence or the territorial integrity of an American state.[55]

And this is how the OAS has viewed the matter. In the first Costa Rican–Nicaraguan case, the OAS Investigating Committee found that the Costa Rican rebellion was organized mainly in Nicaraguan territory by a large group of Costa Rican political exiles; that these rebels had in Nicaragua prepared the expedition that had crossed the frontier into Costa Rica; and that the Nicaraguan government had failed to take adequate measures to prevent the revolutionary activities from being carried out against the Costa Rican government. Moreover, the committee found that the Caribbean Legion, a group organized on a military basis with the purpose of overthrowing certain American dictatorships inclusive of the government of Nicaragua, had received material and moral help from the Costa Rican government. This situation, wherein each government was aiding and abetting revolutionary groups to overthrow the government of the other, was called abnormal and dangerous to inter-American peace.[56]

The Council of the OAS approved a resolution requesting the two governments to abstain from hostile acts against each other and advised the Government of Nicaragua that it could and should have taken adequate measures at the proper time to prevent both the development in its territory of activities aimed at overthrowing the Costa Rican government and the departure from Nicaraguan territory of revolutionary armed elements that crossed into Costa Rica. Costa Rica was informed that it could and should have taken adequate measures to rid its territory of groups of nationals or foreigners organized on a military basis with the known intention of conspiring against the security of

Nicaragua and other sister republics and preparing to engage in hostilities against their governments. In addition, the two governments were requested by the Council to observe faithfully, by every available means, the principles and rules of non-intervention.[57]

In the second Costa Rican–Nicaraguan Case in 1955, the report of the Investigating Committee indicated that there had been a breach of the Civil Strife Convention and flatly declared that Costa Rica was the victim of acts of intervention "proceeding from abroad." The committee announced that there was foreign intervention in the preparation, financing, and furnishing of arms and ammunition and transportation facilities to the persons who entered Costa Rica by force. Many of the rebel forces and war materials used by them entered by way of the Costa Rican–Nicaraguan frontier. Clandestine radio stations operating outside Costa Rica incited the people of Costa Rica to support the rebel movement. Aircraft from abroad dropped arms and ammunition to the rebel forces in Costa Rica and aircraft from abroad landed on Costa Rican territory and also bombed and machine-gunned various towns of Costa Rica.[58]

In the Haitian–Dominican Republic–Cuban–Guatemalan case, the Council of the OAS found that a revolutionary conspiracy did exist between persons in Haiti and persons in the Dominican Republic, including Dominican government officials, for the purpose of overthrowing the Haitian government. The Council called upon the Dominican Republic to take measures to prevent its government officials from tolerating, instigating, encouraging, aiding, or fomenting subversive or seditious movements against other governments. With respect to the Dominican Republic's countercharges, the Council found that there existed within Cuba and Guatemala armed groups of various nationalities whose purpose was to overthrow the Dominican Republic by force, and that the governments of these two nations not only openly expressed their sympathy for the aims of these groups but in some instances lent them aid, thus violating the Convention on Rights and Duties of States in Event of Civil Strife and also the principle of non-intervention. These governments were told to adopt measures to prevent the existence in their territories of groups organized for the purpose of promoting or starting civil strife in another nation and to take adequate measures to insure absolute respect for the principle of non-intervention.[59]

From these cases the Council of the OAS has given a definition of aggression, and it would seem that a breach of the Civil Strife Convention is definitely an act of intervention and an act of aggression and is so recognized by the OAS. In the second Haitian–Dominican Republic case the Council made it clear that were the acts of foreign intervention in domestic revolutionary situations to persist and recur, they would bring about the applications of the procedures of the Rio Treaty to protect the principle of *non-intervention* and to insure the political independence of American states against *aggression* on the part of any state so intervening.[60]

The subversive actions in these cases violated almost all of the provisions of the Civil Strife Convention and were held to be not only breaches of this treaty but also illegal interventions. But this treaty does not speak to the point of revolutionary propaganda directed against a state, inciting a people of that state to revolt and overthrow their government. It is generally agreed at international law that hostile propaganda is a form of illegal intervention. Martens, for example, wrote: "Each state has a right to require that foreign powers shall not incite the people of its territory to rise against it."[61] And Stowell flatly asserts that calling on subjects of a foreign state to revolt is a "violation of the sovereign rights of a friendly state."[62] Accordingly there has come into being the rule of international law that each state has a duty to refrain from spreading propaganda in a friendly country hostile to the latter's government;[63] but aside from special treaty provisions, a state is under no responsibility with respect to private propaganda activities.[64] Some attempts have been made to codify into international law a rule outlawing hostile propaganda against another government, whether from private sources or government inspired and directed. The League of Nations passed a resolution in 1934 declaring "that it is the duty of every state neither to encourage nor tolerate on its territory any terrorist activity with a political purpose . . ." In the category of "terrorist" activity was included propaganda hostile to a foreign government.[65]

Nations which have an inclination to change government by means of revolution are fertile fields for intervention by propaganda, as skilfully directed propaganda may light the torch of antagonists to the existing government. Hence, the danger of hostile propaganda against a foreign country has long occupied the attention of the inter-American system and certain inter-American instruments have attempted to place a ban against hostile propaganda stemming from official or private sources. In 1935 a number of South American nations signed an agreement pledging that as far as radio broadcasts were concerned, they would control the sources and accuracy of the information broadcast, avoid defamatory emissions, and abstain from participation in the political and social tendencies operating in other adhering states.[66]

In December, 1936, the Inter-American Conference for the Maintenance of Peace, held at Buenos Aires, passed resolutions concerned with broadcasting, recommending in Resolution XV measures for the positive use of the radio to promote understanding across frontiers and warning signatories to avoid broadcasting likely to disturb peaceful relations or programs that would wound the national susceptibilities of foreign listeners.[67]

The 1954 Convention on Territorial Asylum, signed at the Tenth Inter-American Conference, provided for freedom of expression for all inhabitants of a state including asylees or refugees, but recognized that systematic propaganda by such asylees which would incite the use of force or violence against the government of another state would be grounds for complaint by that state.[68]

These instruments do show some intent to prohibit the dissemination of hostile propaganda by private groups, but still there is no treaty including all of the American republics which binds them not to tolerate in their respective territories private activities in the form of propaganda which have as their objective the disturbance of domestic peace of a neighboring country.

Nevertheless, the general international law rule that each state has a duty to refrain from spreading propaganda in a friendly country hostile to the latter's government, is, without doubt, the law of the inter-American system, for Article 7 of the Charter of Bogotá establishes the duty of each state to respect the rights enjoyed by every other state in accordance with international law, and the non-intervention clause of the Charter stipulates that the duty of non-intervention applies not only to armed force but also to "any other form of interference or attempted threat against the personalty of the state or against its political, economic and cultural elements."[69] It should be noted that the non-intervention principle is directed against state interventionary action, not against activities of private individuals.

Under both the Rio Treaty and the Charter of Bogotá, intervention by a state by propaganda can well be considered as an aggression which is not an armed attack, and under both of these, if the propaganda is of such a nature as to affect the sovereignty or political independence of a state it may be characterized as an act of aggression against all American states.

In 1949 the Ambassador of Haiti addressed the President of the Council of the OAS, calling his attention to certain facts in the relations between Haiti and the Dominican Republic which created a situation that might endanger the peace and which he characterized as a "moral aggression."[70] The Dominican Republic was permitting broadcasts over a Dominican radio station by an exiled Haitian citizen violently attacking the government of Haiti.

The Dominican government denied collaboration by Dominican officials in the hostile propaganda; pointed out that the radio station was not official but private; and stated that all the Dominican Republic had done was to grant political asylum to a Haitian exile and permit him to deliver certain talks on a private broadcasting station which, though possibly of a disagreeable character, were his personal responsibility. These facts were not thought to justify an application of the Rio Treaty.[71]

After surveying the situation, the Council concluded that the facts did not authorize a consultative meeting. The Council was apparently of the belief that the propaganda had not yet reached a stage where it could be considered as affecting the political independence of Haiti.[72] The Council could hardly have been impressed by the Dominican statement to the effect that it was only a private propaganda activity. In a tightly controlled dictatorship like that of the Dominican Republic at that time it is hard to conceive that all radio stations were not under absolute control of the government. Hence, any propaganda activities of hostile nature carried on by such a government-controlled organization can no longer be classified as private and therefore devoid of state responsibility. If an intermediary party or organization is subject to the direct or indirect control of the government, even though it does not possess an official character in a legal sense, its acts are the acts of the government and invoke the doctrine of state responsibility.[73]

A short time later the report of the Inter-American Peace Committee proclaimed in fourteen points a reaffirmation of certain standards and principles basic to inter-American peace and solidarity. Among these was the following:

To express, likewise, the desirability that the American nations within the limits of their constitutional powers, to avoid any systematic and hostile propaganda, *whatever its medium of expression* against other countries of the Continent or their respective governments. [Italics added][74]

In the later Haitian–Dominican Republic case both the Investigating Committee and the Council condemned hostile propaganda, and the Council specifically requested the governments of Cuba and Guatemala to make every effort to observe the above principle, which is sufficiently broad in scope to cover hostile propaganda activities governmental or private in nature; and the action of the Council indicates that when such activities reach a point at which they threaten the political independence of another state the OAS will act to prohibit such hostile propaganda.[75]

In the aforementioned cases of subversive intervention in which the Council took action as Provisional Organ of Consultation, it did so under Article 6 of the Rio Treaty which permits, and in case of aggression requires, collective action when the peace of the Americas is endangered and the inviolability or the integrity, the sovereignty, or the political independence of any American state is affected. Subversive intervention, which includes a wide range of activities stretching from toleration of rebel activities to official encouragement and instigation and material aid to revolutionary conspirators, has been labeled aggression and the OAS has resorted to Article 6.

Until the 1960 case between Venezuela and the Dominican Republic, the OAS was content to rely on persuasion rather than direct enforcement measures. But in 1960 the Meeting of Foreign Ministers as Organ of Consultation found the following acts to be intervention and aggression against Venezuela which affected the sovereignty of that state and endangered the peace of the Americas, thus justifying collective measures:

1. The attempt against the life of the President of Venezuela perpetrated on June 24, 1960, was part of a plot intended to overthrow the Government of that country.
2. The persons implicated in the aforementioned attempt and plot received moral support and material assistance from high officials of the Government of the Dominican Republic.
3. This assistance consisted principally of providing the persons implicated facilities to travel and to enter and reside in Dominican territory in connection with their subversive plans; of having facilitated the two flights of the plane of Venezuelan registry to and from the military air base of San Isidro, Dominican Republic; of providing arms for use in the coup against the Government of Venezuela and the electronic device and the explosive which were used in the attempt; as well as of having instructed the person who caused the explosion in the operation of the electronic device of that explosive and of having demonstrated to him the destructive force of the same.[76]

The Organ of Consultation ordered diplomatic and economic measures against the Dominican Republic under Articles 6 and 8 of the Rio Treaty, even though the aggression was not called an armed attack.[77] Apparently the OAS felt that no legal barriers prevented such measures.

Under the United Nations Charter the right of collective security measures without United Nations authorization would seem to exist only in an exercise of the right of collective self-defense.[78] Save for this single exception, it might be thought that the OAS could not resort to enforcement measures in other cases because Article 53 of the United Nations Charter declares that "no enforcement action shall be taken under regional arrangements or by regional agencies without the authorization of the Security Council." And the Charter obligates the members to refrain from the threat or use of force with the exception of an exercise of individual or collective self-defense unless the United Nations sanctions it. Nevertheless, the OAS did resort to enforcement measures of a lesser type, i.e., diplomatic and economic sanctions, in the face of this aggression. It has been the position of the OAS authorities all along that measures not involving physical violence can at any time be legally employed by the Organization without breaching the United Nations Charter, for it is contended that it is within the power of any state without violating its purposes, principles, or provisions, to break diplomatic, consular, and economic relations or to interrupt its communications with another state.[79]

Could the OAS authorize armed force as a collective measure against a state guilty of such subversive intervention? Article 51 of the United Nations Charter permits the use of armed force individually or collectively in the exercise of the right of self-defense against an armed attack, and Article 3 of the Rio Treaty declares that an armed attack by any state against an American state constitutes an attack against all the American states, and each of the parties to the treaty undertakes to assist in meeting the attack in the exercise of its inherent right of individual or collective self-defense recognized by Article 51 of the United Nations Charter.

Article 3 of the Rio Treaty speaks in terms of an armed attack against an American state, which may be interpreted as meaning an actual illegal armed attack and possibly an impending or imminent armed attack where the necessity for self-defense is "instant, overwhelming, leaving no choice of means and no moment of deliberation."[80] Subversive intervention by a state which would culminate in armed attack against another state could occur when the government of a state is responsible for launching a hostile rebel military expedition against another state by arming or otherwise assisting the revolutionary group in its fight against the government or by failing in its international duty to use due diligence or adequate means to prevent or repress the rebel attack to such an extent that its failure would show approval of the attack.

But would such an armed attack by a rebel group against a state, even though aided and abetted or approved by another state, be the type of armed attack contemplated by Article 3, which speaks of armed attack by *a state*? It can be and has been so contended in relation to "armed attack" as used by Article 51 of the United Nations Charter, although admittedly that Article speaks in terms of armed attack *against* a member state and does not specify *by* a state. Still, Dr. Josef L. Kunz declares in relation to Article 51 that it must be an armed attack made by a state, but he goes on to add "or with the approval of a state."[81] Dr. Ricardo Alfaro has defined force which would comprise "armed attack" as "any elements at the disposal of States which are capable of destroying life and property or of inflicting serious damage," comprising not only regular forces but also "irregular bands."[82] Moreover, the United States apparently took the position before the United Nations that Yugoslavian, Albanian, and Bulgarian assistance to guerilla forces fighting against the Greek government in the civil strife in that country amounted to armed attack, making Article 51 applicable.[83]

If this position is correct, then an attack by a rebel group can be imputed and attributed directly to the state which encouraged and supported the group's activities. The state thus attacked may exercise its right of individual self-defense against the offending state. Moreover, the other American republics are duty bound to come to the defense of the state attacked, although at this preliminary stage each state is free to determine the immediate measures which it will individually take.[84] The Organ of Consultation is called upon to meet without delay to examine these measures and agree upon collective measures that should be taken; these collective measures can include the use of armed force against the delinquent or measures of an economic or diplomatic nature.[85] Therefore, there are instances when the OAS might legally authorize armed force against subversive intervention; however, the Rio Treaty, although permitting the use of armed force, does not bind any nation to use it without its consent.[86]

But what if the subversive intervention against a state takes a form not containing any element of armed attack or imminent threat thereof, but consists of delictual and interventionary conduct of a more subtle type to bring about a government's overthrow through ideological aggression, inclusive of hostile propaganda, which can be just as dangerous and menacing to a state's security and to its political independence as an illegal use of force? When such indirect aggression takes place against a state engaged in civil strife or is used to promote civil strife, could it be maintained that the Organ of Consultation would be justified in authorizing the use of collective armed force against the delinquent if the circumstances warranted, and if the measure was thought to be the only possible one to stop the aggression, assure the security of the aggrieved state, and maintain hemispheric peace? If the very restrictive position is taken that the right of individual and collective self-defense permits the use of armed force only against an armed attack, then the answer must be in the negative.

But if the wider view is accepted that the right of self-defense extends not only to an illegal armed attack, but to other delictual conduct by a state which violates legal rights of another state,[87] then the members of the OAS through the Organ of Consultation could agree to use force against the delinquent state in the exercise of the right of collective self-defense to protect the wronged state and the community from irreparable harm where no other means are available, if the use of force in the circumstances is reasonable, limited to the necessity of protection, and proportionate to the danger. It would be optimistic today to expect protection of American rights from the United Nations. Thus, the prime condition to be considered with respect to legality of OAS use of force where the delinquent state's conduct itself does not involve such use or threat thereof would be that of proportionality, for other collective measures of a lesser type might be effective to afford protection.[88]

THE OAS AND THE MONROE DOCTRINE

In these cases involving intracontinental attempts at fomenting or aiding revolutionary overthrow by one American government against another, the OAS designated such individual action intervention and aggression prohibited by inter-American doctrine, calling for collective action in the interests of continental peace and security. These plots, counterplots, and overt attempts at military adventure directed against a country for the purpose of revolution when encouraged, instigated, or even tolerated by a government were heartily condemned whether the government being subjected to the overthrow was democratic or dictatorship. There can be discerned a tendency on the part of the OAS to attempt to maintain the status quo and stability not only internationally, but also with respect to the internal regime of a nation, at least to the extent that revolutionary movements should not be encouraged or aided or tolerated from abroad.

Until 1954 the subversive and seditious activities of the international communist movement had been of limited importance in the Western Hemisphere, but in that year the government of Guatemala showed serious symptoms of communist infiltration[89] and the Americas were confronted for the first time in many a year with a violation of the Monroe Doctrine, a non-American intervention in the hemisphere. It will be remembered that the United States in proclaiming that doctrine had declared that "we should consider any attempt on their [the European Powers] part to extend their system to any portion of this hemisphere as dangerous to our peace and safety . . . ," that "we could not view any interposition for the purpose of oppressing them [the American nations], or controlling in any other manner their destiny, by any European Power in any other light than as the manifestation of an unfriendly disposition toward the United States . . ." And further,

It is impossible that the allied Powers should extend their political system to any portion of either continent without endangering our peace and happiness; nor can one believe that our southern brethren, if left to themselves, would adopt it of their own accord. It is equally impossible, therefore, that we should behold such interposition in any form with indifference.[90]

And it should be recalled that the Monroe Doctrine was proclaimed against the machinations of the Holy Alliance, a group of nations seeking to impose upon Europe, and it was thought upon America also, their absolutist form of government—the totalitarianism of that day—as opposed to the republican democratic form.[91] About the only difference was that the Holy Alliance stood ready to prevent revolution against autocratic and hereditary monarchy by armed intervention. Today, at least until the 1962 missile crisis, the new form of totalitarianism has sought to pursue its objectives and the imposition of its autocracy in the Americas by subversive intervention which has been reduced to a science, a rationalized and precalculated routine, progressing step by step on the basis of experience and precedent, and this subversive intervention has consisted of the use of all forms of communication—inclusive of the diplomatic pouch—for the spread of hostile propaganda directed against governments and calling for revolutionary overthrow or for changes in internal and external policy to conform to the Russian or Red Chinese position. Aid is rendered to communist agitators and revolutionary nationalist groups and their activities are carefully manipulated against the government in power or against other governments so as to exploit to the most any given situation in such a way as to bring about discredit upon those governments. Governments and other national organizations, particularly minority parties, are infiltrated so that at a propitious time a communist take-over can be accomplished—either outright or concealed, but in any event subject to the control and direction of the Russo-Sino imperialist movement.[92]

COLLECTIVE MEASURES TO ENFORCE THE MONROE DOCTRINE

During World War II the Americas were concerned with totalitarian subversive intervention. At this time the threat came primarily from the other head of the double-headed dragon, nazism. In the early days of the war it soon became apparent that the individual existence of American states was involved and more was required than the right of each state to take sanctions against intervention by hostile propaganda. At a Meeting of Consultation of American Foreign Ministers held in Panama in 1939, a resolution was adopted recommending that the American states "take the necessary measures to eradicate from the Americas the spread of doctrines that tend to place in jeopardy the common inter-American democratic ideal."[93]

In 1940, the ministers met again in Habana and adopted a resolution making it mandatory that each government adopt measures

to prevent and suppress any activities directed, assisted or abetted by foreign governments, or foreign groups or individuals, which tend to subvert the domestic institutions, or to foment disorder in their internal political life, or to modify by pressure, propaganda, threats, or in any other manner, the free sovereign right of their peoples to be governed by their democratic systems.[94]

A second resolution recommended the adoption of effective prohibitions of every political activity by foreign individuals, associations, groups, or political parties, no matter what form they used to disguise or cloak such activities.[95] Both of the Habana resolutions provided for consultations.

The Habana resolutions differed from most of the resolutions theretofore adopted by the inter-American system. The first, for example, made action by each government mandatory rather than permissive;[96] furthermore, it expressly declared that all American states were equally concerned and responsible for the security of the hemisphere and indicated that all were to maintain a collective interest in the internal affairs of each state with reference to activities which constituted intervention by propaganda.

The second Habana resolution was unique in that if one American country was affected by failure of another to curtail foreign subversion, it permitted the government so affected to initiate the procedure of consultation to establish some basis of joint action in the matter.[97]

The purport of these resolutions was that nations can defeat modern methods of subversion used as intervention, but that the answer is not solely that of mutual non-intervention in each other's internal affairs. Necessity brought a shift to the realization that the safeguarding of the internal form of government against totalitarian subversive intervention could be carried out by international co-operation and consultation in which all the nations collectively recognized that a regime dominated by foreign totalitarianism was a threat to each and all of them and that therefore all had to maintain a collective interest in the internal affairs of each state.

The 1942 Meeting of Foreign Ministers created the Emergency Advisory Committee for Political Defense to implement inter-American policy against subversive Axis activities, which were said to be "acts of aggression of a non-military character, including systematic espionage, sabotage and subversive propaganda."[98] During the war this committee adopted and applied a collective nonrecognition policy against nazi-influenced regimes as a defense against Axis political aggression in the Americas when such regimes assumed power by the activities of subversive groups in order to alienate a country from its agreements for the common defense of the hemisphere.[99]

The resolutions creating this policy and machinery against non-American subversion were only wartime measures, but at the war's end, although intervention by nazi-fascist totalitarianism had been destroyed, there was unfortunately an increase in seditious activities by extracontinental communist totalitarianism. This danger was recognized at the Ninth Conference in 1948 in a resolution on the Preservation and Defense of Democracy in the Americas which declared: "That by its anti-democratic nature and interventionist tendency, the political activity of international communist or any other totalitarian doctrine is incompatible with the concept of American freedom."[100] Moreover, in the same resolution it was agreed that the American republics would adopt within their territories and in accordance with their constitutional provisions,

measures necessary to eradicate and prevent activities directed, assisted or instigated by foreign governments, organizations or individuals tending to overthrow their institutions by violence, to foment disorder in their domestic political life, or to disturb, by means of pressure, subversive propaganda, threats or by any other means, the free and sovereign right of their people to govern themselves in accordance with their democratic aspirations.[101]

A similar resolution in opposition to the subversive action of international communism and recommendation to the republics to take measures to meet threats therefrom was taken at the Fourth Meeting of Ministers of Foreign Affairs in 1951.[102]

Although the statements were made in conference resolutions only, they did indicate inter-American agreement in condemnation of international communism and constituted pledges to prevent its spread in each American republic. They were then formulated principles of inter-American conduct, but the application of these principles was left in each country in the hands of its government.

The Tenth Inter-American Conference wrestled again with the problem, in view of the threat to continental peace and security caused by the then existing government of Guatemala which had been infiltrated by the movement. The conference adopted a Declaration of Solidarity for the Preservation of the Political Integrity of the American States Against the Intervention of International Communism.[103] In this declaration the activities of the international communist movement are once again condemned as constituting intervention in American affairs. Recommendation is made that the American governments

take certain steps for the purpose of counteracting the subversive activities of
the movement. More important was the following:

That the domination or control of the political institutions of an American state by
the international communist movement, extending to this Hemisphere the political
system of an extracontinental power, would constitute a threat to the sovereignty
and political independence of the American states, endangering the peace of America,
and would call for a Meeting of Consultation to consider the adoption of appropriate
action in accordance with existing treaties.[104]

Article 25 of the Charter of Bogotá and Article 6 of the Rio Treaty establish the procedure which shall be followed in the event any *fact or situation*
threatens the sovereignty or political independence of the American states
endangering the peace of the Americas. This procedure consists of collective
measures by the American republics through the Organ of Consultation for the
common defense and for the maintenance of the peace and security of the
continent. Hence, the effect of this portion of the declaration is interpretive
in nature, designed to assure that the broad term "fact or situation" includes
the domination or control of the political institutions of an American state by
the international communist movement. It directs the Organ of Consultation
to order the necessary measures when it determines that international communism is established in a state of the hemisphere for the purpose of removing
this threat to the peace.

The Monroe Doctrine as probably envisaged by its framers signified that
the United States would take action against any European, and later any
non-American, nation to prevent intervention, aggression, or acquisition of
territory in the Western Hemisphere. The Rio Treaty is the final step to date
in the multilateralization or continentalization of the Monroe Doctrine, and by
its terms a system of collective security is created for the common defense of
the hemisphere in the face of a non-American hemispheric aggression, armed
or otherwise, or in the face of any other non-American fact or situation endangering the peace of the Americas and affecting the sovereignty or political independence of an American state. It is obvious that if Soviet Russia or any other
non-American state carries out its colonialist designs by aggression, which
includes subversive intervention against an American state, or endangers the
peace of the Americas, the OAS is empowered to take certain collective measures against Russia to assist the victim of the aggression, or to provide for the
common defense and for the maintenance of continental peace and security.

But the Rio Treaty is not concerned with aggression and threats to and
breaches of American peace by non-American states alone. Its provisions also
extend to inter-American peace and security and provide collective security
against an American state guilty of aggressive acts against a fellow American
state or of other acts which endanger American peace. The Caracas declaration
simply interprets this aspect of the Rio Treaty and permits the collective action
of the American states against any state of the Americas which comes under
the control or domination of the international communist movement on the
ground that this would constitute a threat to the sovereignty and political
independence of the American states, endangering the peace of the Americas.

Since the international communist movement is described as the political system of an extracontinental power the extension of which to the continent endangers continental peace, we have overtones of the Monroe Doctrine involved. But the corrective action here is not necessarily to be directed against the non-American state, but against the American state so controlled or dominated. Therefore, in effect there is present a new corollary of the Monroe Doctrine, i.e., a collective American counter-intervention in the affairs of an American state to remove a certain type of non-American intervention. This smacks in some degree of a former corollary, i.e., the Roosevelt corollary to the Monroe Doctrine.[105] Here, however, is a collective protective intervention to remove a non-American political system from control or domination of an American state in the interests of continental defense, peace, and security. Roosevelt's corollary would permit United States intervention in an American state to prevent a non-American intervention in the interests of continental peace and security.

This interpretation, which turns the Monroe Doctrine inward against an American state, especially against a political system which might lodge itself therein, was viewed with some trepidation by other American states. Mexico, for example, while condemning the subversive intervention of an American state by an extracontinental communist power, still believed that the declaration as adopted would possibly permit collective intervention in the domestic affairs of an American state, i.e., its right freely to choose its own institutions, under the pretense that the state was communist-dominated and hence a threat to the peace.[106] Mexico therefore abstained[107] despite the addition of Article II of the declaration, which was added to quiet such fears and which reads:

This declaration of foreign policy made by the American republics in relation to dangers originating outside this Hemisphere is designed to protect and not to impair the inalienable right of each American state freely to choose its own form of government and economic system and to live its own social and cultural life.

It has been maintained that this clause states that each American country continues free from threat of intervention if a local political party should succeed in imposing upon its people a national brand of communism.[108]

The basic principle behind this multilateralization of the Monroe Doctrine is sound, just as the principle behind the original pronouncement was sound. Both have the effect of extending protection to the external right of self-determination of the American states; i.e., the right of these states to organize and maintain themselves as independent states in the community of nations, as well as the internal right of self-determination of these self-same states, i.e., the right of the people to organize the internal affairs of the state as they see fit in the light of their traditions and aspirations.[109]

It cannot be gainsaid that the new social order of totalitarianism—international communism à la Russia—is based on the concept that it has a right to destroy the rights of all other states for what it deems to be the ultimate good of mankind.[110] It would be belaboring history to point out examples of instances since World War II where Russian imperialism has dominated in the guise of the international communist movement, and in such instances the external independence or self-determination of those dominated states exists no more.

Moreover, it is a truism to state that when the totalitarian communist movement takes over a country the right of the people to choose their own governmental forms, as well as their own social, economic, and cultural policies, also goes out of the window. Internal self-determination no longer exists.

It might be said that the Rio Treaty and the interpretive declaration permit the infringement of the right of self-determination in that collective action can be taken to judge, condemn, and overthrow an internal regime of an American state committed to the international communist movement. The collective security system of the Americas seeks to preserve the peace of the Americas, which involves protecting the sovereignty or independence of the American states against aggression, subversive or otherwise, and other facts or situations which affect that sovereignty and which endanger that peace. The collective security system, therefore, may be turned against a state controlled or dominated by the international communist movement on the ground that this is a threat or danger to the self-determination of the other American states, threatening continental peace and security. Even if the people of a state, through an exercise of self-determination, do away with the external self-determination of the state by placing it within the communist orbit, at the same time doing away with their internal rights of self-determination by the imposition of such a totalitarian dictatorship (a situation highly unlikely unless the state were riddled with subversive Soviet intervention in the first place, for in the words of the Monroe Doctrine "it is inconceivable that our southern brethren would adopt such a foreign system of their own accord"), or if the leaders of the state betrayed its people by selling out to communist control (a situation which has happened),[111] the OAS could still act to remove this cancer in the hemispheric body in the interests of self-defense and the maintenance of continental peace and security, to assure the continued self-determination or sovereignty of the American states as well as to return self-determination to the state where it has been lost and to its people.

The Caracas Declaration Against the Intervention of International Communism, from its language, would seem to be an interpretation of Article 6 of the Rio Treaty. The OAS has taken collective enforcement measures of a nonforceful character under Article 6 without United Nations Security Council authorization, but it has never recommended the use of armed force except as collective self-defense against an imminent threat of nuclear attack in the 1962 Cuban missile crisis.[112] But nonforceful actions may well not be strong enough to remove a regime dominated or controlled by international communism, and the question arises as to the legality of a collective use of armed force in such a situation when authorized by the OAS but not by the Security Council.

If the restrictive view is taken that armed force may be used individually or collectively only in the face of an armed attack or possibly in the case of a most imminent threat of armed attack,[113] then the OAS would be legally powerless to order a use of armed force against the threats to the hemisphere emanating from the nonforceful aggressions and subversive interventions of a communist-controlled American state. Only if that state were guilty of an armed aggression, committed directly under its aegis or indirectly by its support and aid of private revolutionary groups or in case of an imminent threat thereof, could the OAS authorize on its own the use of collective armed force.[114]

But a broader view of self-defense has been taken, i.e., that the right of self-defense as envisaged under the United Nations Charter and the Rio Treaty, as well as under international law generally, is not limited to an illegal use of force or imminent threat thereof alone, but also extends to delictual conduct of a state which seriously endangers the rights of other states upon which their security depends, in instances where no other means of protection are available to protect the wronged state or states from irreparable injury.[115] Following this view and since self-defense, collective or individual, may involve the use of armed force,[116] such collective action can be taken by the American states to protect their security against unlawful acts of other states, and it can hardly be denied that the indirect aggressions of a state dedicated to communist imperialism, even when not armed aggression, violate the right of political independence of the states against whom they are directed and consequently the American doctrine of non-intervention. As has been stated:

Through indirect action, via secret agents or internal groups supported by outside propaganda (the "ideological" aggression), money, arms, and, at the critical moment of the disturbances, by direct intimidation and political pressure, a state can put an end to the independent existence of another as effectively as with the classical, external military aggression.[117]

Such violation as it endangers the political independence of American states by the aggressive and totalitarian policies of a non-American ideology extended to the hemisphere, even when an American state aligns itself therewith, brings into play the Monroe Doctrine, a doctrine of self-defense when directed against an immediate danger of illegal non-American intervention, a danger to the real and legitimate interests of all of the American states.[118] Collective measures involving the use of armed force may be taken by the OAS against such illegal danger to remove it from the hemisphere in the exercise of collective self-defense.

Completely apart from the right of self-defense and conditions for its exercise, it would seem that the OAS as the inter-American community might well justify collective security action, even though it took the form of armed force and even though there was no Security Council authorization, in certain circumstances for the maintenance of the peace and security of the Americas. This would be a residual responsibility where the United Nations as the organization primarily responsible for world peace fails to take the necessary action to maintain it.[119] It must be obvious that because of the Soviet veto the Security Council could never take action to remove the threat of communist imperialism from the Western Hemisphere, and it would be the height of folly to pretend that given today's international condition the General Assembly could take effective action for this purpose. Thus, the Americas can hardly expect a United Nations remedy and there would be no necessity to place the problem before the United Nations, for there is no necessity to exhaust all remedies if there are no remedies to exhaust.[120] In the exercise of a residual responsibility for inter-American peace and security, collective enforcement measures against an

American state dominated by the international communist movement appear legitimate.

Despite the undoubted legal right of the OAS to take some measures against the international communist movement in the Americas in accordance with the Rio Treaty, the hemispheric body has been signally hesitant to make use of them. In the case of Guatemala, the communist issue was resolved without effective action by either the OAS or the United Nations, for that situation was taken care of by a not so neatly arranged overthrow of the Guatemalan government by a group of Guatemalan rebels.[121] Within five years the Americas were once again in the presence of the problem with the assumption of power in Cuba by Fidel Castro, who sought to export his revolution to other American states by means of subversion and indirect aggression. Despite the threats to other governments by such subversion, despite the establishment of a Cuban dictatorship increasingly communist which grossly violated rights of Cubans and foreigners, despite a flood of refugees, despite Russian and Chinese violation of the Monroe Doctrine, despite ruptures of diplomatic relations between Cuba and many other American states, despite an economic embargo by the United States on certain trade with Cuba, and despite an ill-starred Cuban invasion, the OAS still remained in a state of semiparalysis, contenting itself with a series of broad resolutions which stressed non-intervention, reaffirmed the principles of democracy, and futilely condemned Sino-Soviet intervention in the Americas.[122]

No thought was given to the opportunity to apply the Monroe Doctrine in the classic sense against the non-American intruders. And to turn it inward against the American state which had come to be dominated by the international communist movement caused Latin American consternation. For this notion brought to the fore all the old fears of intervention which could not be overcome by the communist threat in Cuba—which simply did not exist to many Latin Americans, who preferred to be self-blinded because of anti-Yankeeism or because of sympathy with Fidel and his stated aims.

In the face of Castro's open proclamation that he was and always had been a dedicated Marxist-Leninist and his ever increasing efforts to export his communist creed to other parts of the hemisphere, a Meeting of Foreign Ministers was called in January, 1962, to study measures that could be taken against communism in and communist subversion emanating from Cuba. The only collective enforcement measure resorted to under Article 8 of the Rio Treaty at this time was an arms embargo and a directive to the Council to consider the suspension of trade with Cuba in other items. As noted in the previous chapter, agreement could not be reached to take other measures against Cuba. Instead the Meeting of Foreign Ministers adopted a resolution excluding Cuba from participation in OAS organs on the ground of incompatibility. This Meeting did condemn communism and called for the establishment by the Council of a Committee of Experts to study the necessary security measures against communist subversion. Member governments were also called upon to co-operate in countering communist subversion.[123]

The accelerated buildup of Soviet military personnel and equipment in Cuba during the summer of 1962 caused increasing concern, but the United

States concluded that the weapons and men were defensive in nature and not of a sufficient offensive power to constitute a threat to the other parts of the hemisphere. However, President Kennedy opined that if Cuba sought to export its aggressive purposes by force or the threat of force against any nation of the hemisphere and if Cuba became an offensive military base then the United States would do whatever must be done to protect its own security and that of the continent. A resolution of Congress echoed his words. Such statements, of course, tend to involve the Monroe Doctrine but at the same time they are one step removed from it, for the Monroe Doctrine and the Caracas declaration consider the domination or control of the destiny of any American state by a non-American state or the extension thereto of a non-American absolutist political system in and of themselves as dangerous to the hemisphere and United States peace and security. Such domination and extension had already occurred in Cuba.

The American republics were shocked into a state of unity when they were confronted on October 22, 1962, with proof of the existence of Soviet rocket bases in Cuba with missiles poised to strike the hemisphere.[124] As in previous history, when confronted with an extra-continental intervention of evil and excessive proportion they sought refuge in solidarity and were able to invoke the necessary collective measures to remove this threat of hemispheric annihiliation.[125]

This indeed was the finest hour of the Monroe Doctrine. It was enforced as originally intended, not inwardly but outwardly against a non-American intervention threatening the peace and security of the continent. The United States set forth the policy when President Kennedy served notice on Soviet Russia that a nuclear missile launched from Cuba against any American nation would be considered as an attack against the United States and would require full retaliatory measures against the non-American perpetrator, Russia.[126] Moreover, the quarantine action was largely directed against the European Soviet bloc. But more important still was the fact that this was collective rather than unilateral action of the Americas to enforce the Monroe Doctrine and the Rio Treaty. The Latin Americans for the first time fully realized that the doctrine had become multilateral and continental, and that action inclusive of the use of armed force or threat thereof could be taken as a collective measure of self-defense under the Rio Treaty in the face of this non-American imminent threat of armed attack. The Monroe Doctrine stood as a doctrine of individual and collective self-defense to be directed against an immediate danger of illegal non-American intervention, a danger to the real and legitimate interests of all of the American states bound together by a proximate relationship. Thus, the Americas faced up to their greatest challenge and met it with a solid front.

Of course, Castro's communist Cuba is still with us to plague us. Moreover, there was some hesitancy over an inward application of the doctrine when the possibility existed of an armed invasion of Cuba, a fellow American state. But even here there was a large and substantial unity, and if the need had arisen to invade the island to dismantle the missiles, it is believed that unanimity would have been forthcoming at that time.

UNILATERAL MEASURES TO ENFORCE THE MONROE DOCTRINE

The absence of positive collective measures by the OAS[127] prior to the crisis of October, 1962, created a vacuum and brought about certain unilateral measures against Castro's Cuba which by words and deeds had acknowledged its acceptance of the international communist movement and placed itself within the bloc of iron curtain nations. Thus, the United States cut the Cuban sugar quota by which Cuba was guaranteed sale of half its yearly crop to the United States at an advantageous price; it placed an embargo on Cuba prohibiting the export of most United States products to that country; it set up a naval parol in the Caribbean to block a possible Cuban invasion of certain Caribbean countries; it ruptured diplomatic and consular relations with Cuba; and finally it aided and abetted an armed invasion of Cuba by Cuban exiles.[128] None of these actions were stated by the United States government to have been taken to enforce the Monroe Doctrine, but insofar as they might have been taken to weaken the regime in Cuba, to bring about its overthrow, or to force the Castro government to break with Russia they might be regarded as such. The big difficulty with such unilateral action if taken to coerce and compel another American nation from a legal point of view is the American doctrine of non-intervention.

The cut in the sugar quota and the embargo might be considered to be economic intervention if taken in an attempt to coerce and compel Cuba's government to change its domestic or external policies, and hence violative of the non-intervention principle of Article 15 of the Bogotá Charter and the more specific language of Article 16 which prohibits the use of coercive measures of an economic or political character to force the sovereign will of another nation and obtain from it advantages of any kind. At international law such economic intervention can, of course, be considered legitimate if conducted as reprisals for violation of international law.[129] And certainly Cuba had breached international law in its relations with the United States by engaging in a campaign of hostile propaganda amounting to warmongering against the United States,[130] by attacking United States naval vessels; by discriminatory economic policy against United States citizens; and by confiscating and intervening properties of United States citizens and the United States government in Cuba.[131] However, the strict non-intervention principle of the Americas serves to outlaw reprisals.[132]

The United States actions might be considered as retorsions, i.e., a reaction by a state to a violation by another state of its interests, as distinguished from its rights. In such an instance the offended state reacts by a violation of an interest of the offending state and such action is generally not forbidden by international law, inasmuch as neither state goes so far as to commit international wrong. However, even retorsions would seem forbidden by the non-intervention doctrine if taken to coerce another state to cease the unfriendly act.[133] In its stated reasons for reducing the sugar quota, the United States seemed to have in mind neither retorsion nor reprisal, neither retaliation nor coercion. The action was taken to protect the best interests of the United States for a continued supply of sugar, which, because of Cuban hostility and the fact that Cuba was committing increasing amounts of sugar to the communist bloc, would make uncertain its future ability to provide sugar for the United

States.[134] It might also be noted that Cuban officials stated on various occasions that the preferential sugar quota worked to the disadvantage of Cuba, and that it would be more advantageous if the United States did not buy Cuban sugar, for it enslaved the Cuban people.[135] In effect they seemed to be saying that the quota was economic aggression by the United States. But when it was cut off they called that action economic aggression also. They can hardly have it both ways.

The embargo on Cuba[136] appears to be a reprisal and hence an act of intervention, legal at general international law as a sanction against a lawbreaker but illegal under the American doctrine of non-intervention. In imposing the embargo the United States cited Cuba's "arbitrary, illegal and discriminatory economic measures which have injured thousands of American citizens, and have drastically altered the hitherto mutually beneficial pattern of trade between the United States and Cuba." For these reasons the United States declared:

The step has been reluctantly taken by the United States, in the exercise of its sovereignty and in order to carry out the responsibility of this Government to defend the legitimate economic interests of the people of this country against the discriminatory, aggressive, and injurious economic policies of the Castro regime.[137]

These statements would indicate that the United States was taking the action to attempt to coerce Cuba to return to legality, although there arises the possibility that the United States was engaging in an action of self-defense against the delicts of the Cuban government to defend and protect the legal rights of its citizens, and of itself. Cuba, of course, claimed economic aggression and intervention for the purpose of "obstructing the Revolutionary Government's industrialization program . . ." and "to reconvert Cuba into a colonial dependency."[138]

The United States was also accused of intervention by the action it took in sending naval units to the Caribbean area on patrol at the request of the governments of Nicaragua and Guatemala to protect them from the threat of an invasion from Cuba.[139] The United States in taking the action stated that the naval and air units would act within the territorial limits of the two countries to protect them against communist-directed invasion forces.[140] This in some quarters was said to be intervention in the affairs of the two nations, even though taken at the behest of the two governments, in that it was helping these governments to defend themselves against insurrection and consequently the United States was intervening in a situation of civil strife.[141] It has been seen that international law and inter-American treaties do not prohibit aid to the government in time of civil strife when a state of belligerency has not yet been attained. At this point neutrality is not required.[142] From this point of view the naval patrol could not have been considered intervention. Even if one follows the viewpoint that international law requires neutrality in any instance of civil strife and that aid should not be extended to either side, the United States action could hardly be considered intervention, for it was not taken to suppress internal revolt, but to help the two countries at their request to seek out and prevent intervention on the part of communist-directed elements, i.e., to protect them from invasion or imminent threat thereof from Cuban-backed armed groups.

This would then be an exercise of the right of collective self-defense.[143] To dismiss the threat would not accord with the facts of recent happenings which had seen Cuban involvement in armed invasions—for example, the case of Panama.

It is true, however, that if armed aggression or other type of aggression or threat thereof was present, the OAS was obligated to meet in consultation to agree upon measures that should be taken to assist the victim. At that time this duty was not met.[144]

The severance of diplomatic relations with a government may in instances be regarded as coercive procedure to effect a settlement of differences between states. If taken as a reaction against a violation of international law to influence the delinquent state to remedy the situation, it can be regarded as a nonforceful sanction.[145] Since general international law places no obligation upon a state to maintain diplomatic relations with another, the severance of diplomatic relations is not considered a violation.[146] It is a nonforceful procedure, and thus it is not prohibited by the United Nations Charter.[147] But as an act taken to sanction or to coerce the government of another state, it would appear to fall within the proscription against non-intervention under the Charter of Bogotá.[148] It is doubtful if the United States rupture can be so categorized as intervention under the Bogotá Charter, however, for the action was not taken in any spirit of coercion, but as a result of action by the Cuban government designed to limit United States Embassy and Consulate personnel, which the United States declared would so cripple the ability of the United States Mission to carry on its normal functions as to achieve an effective termination by Cuba of such relations.[149]

The armed invasion of Cuba by Cuban exiles bent on overthrow of the Castro government presents a more serious problem. In aiding and abetting these exiles within territory of the United States, in supplying them with war materials for revolutionary purposes, and in failing to use means at its disposal to prevent them from gathering elements for civil strife or crossing the boundary or sailing from the United States territory for such purpose, the United States was guilty of commissions and omissions which in previous cases had been called violative of the Civil Strife Convention and the doctrine of non-intervention and equated with aggression.[150]

Might some semblance of legality have been maintained by the United States here, had it withdrawn recognition from the Castro government and extended recognition to the Revolutionary Council as the government of Cuba? It could then have been argued that the United States aid granted to the revolutionaries was legitimate, not because they were revolutionaries, but because they were regarded by the United States as the legitimate government, and, according to a strong line of authority, aid to the legitimate government in a revolutionary situation is not forbidden by international law or the Inter-American Civil Strife Convention which speaks in terms of prohibiting aid to rebels, not to the government.[151] It might be said that the rupture of relations accomplished this purpose, but this does not appear to be the rule at international law, for a mere break of international relations is not considered equivalent to a withdrawal of recognition.[152]

Withdrawal of recognition of a government would be contrary to principles of international law until the requirements of conditions of recognition themselves cease to exist.[153] If the view is taken that recognition is conditioned only upon a government's effective control over national territory, and the Castro regime does exercise such effective control, then as long as such exists, no matter how it exists, recognition cannot legitimately be withdrawn. If added conditions are required for recognition, such as acquiescence of the people to the regime manifested in an adequate form and the capacity and willingness of the government to comply with international obligations, then recognition can be withdrawn when these conditions no longer exist. They no longer exist in Castro's Cuba, if acquiescence of the people means some form of popular approval expressed through the ballot.[154] But even following the latter view, it is doubtful whether recognition as Cuba's government could be extended to any new entity—the Revolutionary Council for example—which lacks any semblance of effective control over Cuba's territory, one of the conditions of the recognition of a new government. Thus recognition of the Revolutionary Council would have appeared a delict, and aid given it would amount to no more than aid to rebel groups, not to a legitimately recognized government.

Are there any legal grounds which could justify unilateral action against a government like that of Castro, which has embraced the international communist movement and which defies international and inter-American principles over and over again to commit international wrongs? General international law authorized self-help in the form of self-defense or sanctions against a delinquent state.[155] The United Nations Charter restricts the right of self-help insofar as the measures used take the form of armed force save as taken pursuant to a right of individual or collective self-defense or pursuant to collective decisions.[156] The Charter of Bogotá follows the United Nations Charter in this respect but makes even more radical change in international law by the almost absolute prohibition of unilateral intervention, forceful or nonforceful, as a method of enforcing international law.[157] And the collective intervention of the OAS is by no means a complete replacement of the individual action permitted by general international law as a sanction to uphold the law. It is not empowered to enforce the law in all instances of breach thereof. Action is authorized only in case of armed attack or other aggression or situation which endangers the peace of the Americas. As a result, a hiatus of international law is created in the Americas.

If a communist-dominated state commits acts of armed aggression against another American state, then of course the right of individual action is present in the form of self-defense by the state attacked and other American states are required to take some measures against the aggressor in the exercise of the right of collective self-defense. Such action, as well as collective action by the OAS, is made an exception to the non-intervention principle. But if the communist state's actions are aggressions which are not armed attack or which otherwise threaten the peace of the hemisphere or which are breaches of international law, then the non-intervention principle on its face curtails individual intervention even to enforce the Monroe Doctrine unless the position is taken that the right of self-defense exists under the United Nations Charter and the

Rio Treaty, not only against illegal armed attack but also against other violations of international law in circumstances where no other means of protection exist for the wronged state.[158] Now the Organ of Consultation cannot act if a breach of international law occurs if it does not amount to aggression or at least in some way threatens inter-American peace.[159] Moreover, the Organ of Consultation *may* not see fit to act even in the latter circumstances. Hence it is possible for a state to commit all sorts of international wrongs and delicts against another state, and the wronged state would have no remedy or protection if an absolute interpretation of the non-intervention principle is maintained coupled with the view that the right of self-defense exists only in case of armed attack. Indeed if the wronged state does more than just sit and take it, its actions may result in what would be called intervention or even aggression.

Professor Julius Stone has pointed out with respect to the United Nations Charter that the extreme view which would make illegal in all cases except self-defense for armed attack the unilateral use of force, regardless of the wrong which provokes it and even though no collective relief from the United Nations is available, is not necessarily the only interpretation which can be deduced from the Charter.[160] He points out that Article 2(4) prohibits the threat or use of force when directed against the territorial integrity or political independence of any state, or in any other manner inconsistent with the purposes of the United Nations. This language limits the prohibition itself and one can well argue that action, even forceful action taken by a state to protect and to defend its substantive rights such as its own political independence, its territorial integrity, or the lives and property of its citizens would not involve a threat or use of force against the territorial integrity or political independence of the delinquent state against which the measures were directed. Futhermore, it can hardly be said that protection of a state's legitimate interests is inconsistent with the purposes of the United Nations, particularly in view of the provision which requires disputes to be settled by peaceful means in such a manner that international peace and security *and justice* are not endangered.[161] The use of the word "justice" can hardly be reconciled with an absolute restriction of the use of force if a state cannot protect its legitimate interests, or receive protection for them, for then justice is not present. Thus he concludes from these and other articles of the United Nations Charter that "It is certainly not self-evident what obligations (if any) are imported where no such collective measures are available for the remedy of just grievances."[162]

Similar observations can be made concerning the non-intervention principle of the Charter of Bogotá. Though the Charter is couched in terms of absolute non-intervention for any purpose other than self-defense and collective measures by the OAS,[163] still it contains other expressed inter-American principles that are incompatible with a blanket proscription of intervention. International law is declared to be the standard of conduct of states, and international order consists of respect for the sovereignty and independence of states and the faithful fulfilment of international obligations.[164] Every American state has the duty to respect the rights enjoyed by every other state in accordance with international obligations.[165] Every American state has the duty to respect the rights enjoyed by every other state in accordance with international law.[166] The rights of sovereignty are to be exercised in accordance with international law.[167] And of much importance is the statement that the "right of each state to protect itself and to live its own life does not authorize it to commit unjust acts against another state."[168]

The right to be free of intervention would imply that a state must conduct itself in accordance with these principles which are stated as strongly and in the same context as the principle of non-intervention and which can hardly be reconciled with an absolute prohibition of non-intervention for the vindication or protection of rights when no other means are possible. The duty of non-intervention and the right to be free of intervention are corollaries of the doctrine of the independence of sovereign states. But in international law there are no perfect rights, no absolute rights, but all rights are to be asserted with due regard to the preservation of the independence, security, and prosperity of neighboring states. Rights which have been given for the common good of all states may not be perverted to menace international security.[169] All rights must be exercised prudently with ordinary precautions without abusing them or without exceeding their equitable limits. Hence under international law and inter-American law no state can expect to retain the right of sovereign decision called independence, when by its conduct it makes clear that it cannot or will not fulfil the international law obligations of an independent and sovereign state.

Since the enforcement powers of the OAS cannot and may not in all circumstances afford relief against the actions of a lawbreaking state, it seems extravagant to maintain that an injured state must submit tamely and for all time to great legal wrongs when no collective remedy from international organization is in sight. Surely the non-intervention doctrine was not meant to put a lawbreaker above and beyond the law, but that is what it does if it is conceived of as an absolute which prevents any resort to self-help in vindication or defense of rights against a transgressor in the absence of other means of protection.

It may also be reasoned that if collective measures of an international organization created by the treaty method fail to protect a member in its rights or if a treaty changes international law so as to create a vacuum with respect to the protection of such rights, then a reference back to general international law may be made. If a norm of particular international law established in a treaty does not work, the norm of international law must apply, for there is no power in a treaty to create a lacuna, where there existed a definite rule of the law of nations. Its signatories can change general international law, but if they fail in the attempt the general international law must reappear.[170]

If an extracontinental totalitarian nation is successful in its attempts at illegal subversion in an American state, then such subversion and the subversive efforts from the state so controlled or dominated against other American states present a serious threat to the peace and order of the inter-American community and require OAS collective action. But if the OAS finds itself unable to act and unable to protect the sovereignty, political independence, or the territorial integrity of the other American states and consequently the peace and security of the hemisphere, or unable to protect the legal rights of the aggrieved states, then the conclusion seems inescapable that the respective norms of international law are only suspended by treaty law and they can be revived if treaty law fails. There is no power in the OAS or other international organization to create a vacuum where there existed previously a definite rule of the law of nations. Under the general international law of the Americas, any nation or group of nations may resort to self-help to uphold the law to prevent an American state from being destroyed by noncontinental totalitarian subversion, and to protect itself and other states of the community in their rights to be free of such destructive subversion when particular international law fails to vindicate or protect their rights and hemispheric peace when there are no other means available for such proctection or vindication.

But over and above these legal arguments of a somewhat technical nature which may be used to authorize self-help against an errant state such as Cuba, is a broader and more sweeping concept — the concept of international community. Modern international law was born through the co-operative endeavor of a specific group of nations, namely, those which were formed upon the dissolution of the Roman Empire of the West.[171] These nations had common ideals, common aspirations, and a willingness to accept for the most part a set of rules which they felt should guide the relations among themselves. In the earliest period of general international law, the nations accepting the law made no claim of universality for it, recognizing that throughout the globe there existed human societies which for some reason or other were not eligible for membership in the society which was governed by international law.[172] The two main qualifications for membership were that a group of people seeking membership had to fulfil the requirements of "statehood," and that the state had to be "civilized".[173] The state, according to this concept, consisted of an association of a people within a demarcated territory, acting through law as promulgated by a sovereign government endowed with coercive power to secure obedience. The concept of civilization implied the state's willingness to subscribe to the principles of good faith in dealing with other nations; the giving of protection to the life, liberty, and property of foreigners more or less in accordance with the liberal traditions of western European nations; and, in a few cases, the fulfilment of minimum standards of civilization for the state's own nationals.

Those societies which did not fulfil these requirements were not included in the community of nations and were not dealt with according to the rules established for relations between members, but rather were dealt with on a political, as distinguished from a legal, basis — to wit, in whatever manner was expedient and not according to definite established principles based on a recognition of common standards of good faith, justice, tolerance, and humanitarianism.[174]

Cuba, in embracing the totalitarian principles of Russian colonialism, has placed herself outside the pale of the international community of civilized states and consequently outside the bounds of international and inter-American law. Both forms of twentieth century totalitarianism, fascism and communism, represent a new type of social order which has deliberately set itself apart from other states of the world and from the legal order established by general international law. These nations accept the view that the fundamental rights and duties of nations and the fundamental rights and duties of individuals which fall under the scope of established legal rights and legal duties are but mere privileges to be enjoyed upon sufferance according to the view of expediency held by those in power. A nation based upon such a philosophy refuses, of necessity, to recognize that general international law rules are binding on it, for its goal is not the same goal as that of civilized nations. It is not seeking order under law among nations, but rather order based on autocratic power. That Cuba is now a member of the Russian imperialist communist bloc can hardly be denied; that it is unwilling to govern its conduct by international law or by inter-American law has been demonstrated over and over again by its repeated violations of the fundamental principles thereof, and by the acts and proclamations of its government, which with startling clarity illustrate the fact that it has rejected and is unwilling to accept the underlying ethical concepts on which international law and inter-American law are based.[175] Hence Castro's Cuba can be regarded as outside both communities and therefore to be dealt with on a political as distinguished from a legal basis. Any attempt to extend to Cuba under Castro the advantages emanating from the doctrine of non-intervention or from other basic principles and rules of the inter-American regional system is to make parody and mockery of law and can only result in the weakening of law, for Cuba does not possess the civilized prerequisite for membership in the society of nations. International law should not be used as a basis for dealing with such a nation which refuses to abide by the principles.

At least two-thirds of the American states have seemingly recognized this concept as applicable to the OAS and the American juridical community, for at the January, 1962, Punta del Este Meeting of Foreign Ministers Cuba was excluded from participation in the inter-American system, despite the fact that no express provision existed for such exclusion in inter-American treaties.[176] The view was then taken that no such provision was necessary, since Cuba by her own action in adopting the principles of Marxism-Leninism, principles hostile to and incompatible with inter-American principles, had automatically excluded herself. Thus Cuba by her unwillingness to abide by inter-American principles and by her adoption of principles antithetic thereto has excluded herself from the American community, and was to be dealt with by the members of the community on a political basis, as distinguished from a legal basis. Cuba would appear to be no longer subject to inter-American obligations, but at the same time, she cannot be accorded inter-American legal rights. Cuba has ostracized herself, and this fact has been recognized by the community.

This reasoning accords with happenings after the Meeting, for since that time a more stringent embargo on United States–Cuban trade was ordered by the government of the United States. This action was taken by the United States to prevent the Castro regime from obtaining dollar income and thereby to reduce its capacity to engage in acts of aggression, subversion, or other activities endangering the security of the hemisphere. The United States government sought to present this action within a hemispheric context, i.e., as in accord with the decisions of the Foreign Ministers Meeting. However, it can hardly be considered as a part of the collective action taken by that body, for such a sweeping economic rupture was not ordered by the Meeting. It was, therefore, unilateral action, and although it was taken in an attempt to halt Cuba's illegal activities against her neighbors, it was still coercive and repressive in nature — hence, intervention. As intervention of a unilateral nature not apparently taken on grounds of collective self-defense, it was illegal under the non-intervention principle of the Charter of the OAS. But since Cuba has excluded herself from the inter-American system, the legal advantages of non-intervention are no longer applicable. Cuba is outside the law of the Americas.

Those who scoffed at the possibility of the extension of an extracontinental totalitarianism to the Americas and who stated that the Western Hemisphere was relatively immune to cold war pressures have been proved wrong. A non-American empire incompatible with the inter-American system and a threat to the sovereignty and political independence of every American state, hence a threat to hemispheric peace, is among us and remains among us despite the collective action of the OAS which terminated one threat — the threat to hemispheric security from the location of Soviet missiles and bombers with nuclear capability on Cuban soil. However, the policy of the United States is said to remain one of no toleration of a communist nation in this hemisphere and high administration authorities have repeated that Castro must go and have continued economic and political pressures on the island.[177]

In spite of these pressures, Russia, after it had apparently removed its missiles, continued to increase the supply of what it called conventional military weapons in Cuba, and failed to remove the Soviet military forces on the island. By February, 1963, public anxiety over this situation forced the United States government to reiterate that in its opinion the weapons being supplied to Castro were defensive in nature and consequently were no threat to the security of the United States or of the other nations of the hemisphere. The Kennedy administration stated that the Russian troop withdrawal remained "unfinished business," and promised that the United States would continue its surveillance of the island and would continue making representations to Moscow warning that the presence of Soviet troops in Cuba could not be tolerated indefinitely.[178]

On February 12, 1963, a classified report was presented to the OAS by the Committee of Experts which had been appointed to study communist subversion in the hemisphere. This report contradicted the stand of the Kennedy administration that the Soviet weapons in Cuba were purely defensive in nature. It declared that many types of destructive weapons were being smuggled from Cuba to communist groups in various Latin American countries, and that through the use of these weapons subversive elements were carrying on terroristic activities designed to overthrow legitimate democratic governments. It was pointed out, for example, that throughout the month of January, 1963, the Havana radio sent hourly calls for revolution in Venezuela and broadcast instructions to communist guerrillas and urban terrorist commandos in that country on how to use the weapons and funds sent from Havana to Venezuela. The result was a well-organized terrorist campaign with widespread loss of life and property in Venezuela.[179]

The report went on to say that until Brazil, Mexico, Chile, Bolivia, and

Uruguay broke diplomatic relations with Cuba, the job of curbing subversive activities originating in Havana would be impossible. It therefore urged the OAS to insist that these nations sever their ties with the island, and further urged that stronger measures should be invoked against Cuba.

Apparently fifteen members of the OAS believe that enforcement of the Monroe Doctrine to remove a regime dominated by international communism should not falter. The other five nations, for various reasons, are willing to back this stand only in ultimate cases when there is evidence of extracontinental direct aggression rather than indirect aggression through subversion directed from outside the hemisphere. The Monroe Doctrine would appear to be very much alive in a situation of intercontinental missiles loaded with nuclear warheads;[180] but in the face of lesser threats than atomic annihilation, there again appears among certain elements in the hemisphere a strong reluctance to enforce the doctrine.

Chapter XIX

ECONOMIC, SOCIAL, CULTURAL, AND JURIDICAL CO-OPERATION

INTERNATIONAL ECONOMIC RELATIONS PRIOR TO WORLD WAR II

The cardinal point of international economic relations of the nineteenth and early twentieth centuries was the fact that these operations took place in an international open society. There existed a generally recognized code of norms, principles, rules of behavior, and value ideas protecting international trade relations and claims deriving from them, as most of the trading nations of the world respected international law.[1] There were very few institutional arrangements to facilitate the movement of merchandise and services on a broad basis, but there was a generally accepted free monetary order, the gold standard, which provided a medium of exchange giving material guarantees to the claims deriving from economic intercourse.[2]

It is doubtful if the gold standard ever functioned with automatic perfection, but there can be little doubt that until World War I it did provide a working system for the establishment of international exchange stability. It had the advantage of simplicity and of preserving the economic sovereignty of each participating nation. It was based upon the assumption that a balance of payments disequilibrium would be met by a transfer of gold from the deficit to the surplus country. The loss of gold by the deficit country would, through its banking system, cause a fall in prices and ultimately a lowering of the cost of production. The gain of gold in the surplus country would create a rise in prices and costs in that nation. Thus price-cost adjustments were made through a causal sequence initiated by the gold flow, those adjustments in turn causing export-import relationships to move in a manner favorable to the restoration of external balance between the two countries.[3] That the gold standard succeeded so well over such a long period can largely be ascribed to the fact that the period of its operation was also one of almost unbroken expansion of trade and industry the world over. The shortcomings of the system were obscured by the favorable conditions under which it operated.

A certain amount of economic co-operation on an internationally institutionalized basis did exist long prior to World War I. As early as 1856, the International Danube Commission was established to deal with Danubian transportation problems.[4] In 1865 there came into existence the International Telegraphic Union,[5] which was followed in a few years by the Universal Postal Union.[6] International public agencies dealing with economic affairs soon covered communications, transportation, and agricultural research.

With the establishment of the League of Nations following World War I, there began the first important co-ordination of worldwide economic activity. Although handicapped because the United States was not a member, the League frequently dealt with economic matters and organized intergovernmental co-operation in financial and trade affairs.[7] But the political developments of the interwar period were not conducive to extensive international economic co-operation.

In the first place, when after World War I an attempt was made to restore the gold standard, it proved unequal to the demands made upon it and ultimately collapsed. A great many factors were involved in the suspension of the gold standard, including political insecurity in various nations which influenced international trade and payment relations.[8] Much of the political insecurity was due to the fact that national economic systems were faced with new types of claims. The populace of nations were demanding that each state be in some measure insulated from economic disturbances of the world at large, and this brought about the institution of restrictive and discriminatory methods of economic defense and economic warfare by many nations. In addition, people demanded of national economic systems that they guarantee full employment, economic security, and social justice.[9] The impersonal system of cosmopolitan trading was considered to be oppressive to the underprivileged, and governments began to control activities formerly reserved to individuals. This trend soon became reflected in the international field, bringing with it a shifting emphasis from private to public law.

The process of increasing dependence of economic life on the intervention of the national government meant that national frontiers were more and more lines which separated territories where conditions of supply and demand were uniform for all residents but different from those prevailing in neighboring territories. Economic affairs became almost completely a matter of government and administration, but this governmental influence was valid only over the territory which the political authority ruled. This merging of economy and government placed an economic and political barrier between its sphere of planned economy and the rest of the world.[10] The result was that by the end of World War II it was discovered that the concentration of economic power on the national level was bought at the price of almost complete international disintegration.[11] The overcoming of this chaotic condition required intergovernmental co-operation which planned the main movements of capital, goods, and interests, and caused the establishment of a great variety of regional and universal economic agencies.[12]

Since 1945 the objectives of international economic policy have, therefore, been considerably widened. Freedom of commerce is no longer the only or even the main reason for governmental concern in this field. Changing ideas regarding mutual relations among nations have brought into being an explicit recognition that matters such as higher standards of living, full employment, economic stability, balanced growth, attainment of national wealth, and economic and social progress are legitimate topics of joint international action. These objectives are now pursued within a consciously planned collective framework in accordance with principles laid down in multilateral treaties, or in pragmatic arrangements of a quasi-legal nature.[13]

ECONOMIC CO-OPERATION IN THE AMERICAS

Although close economic co-operation among the American republics is of rather recent origin, commercial problems of the hemisphere have received consideration from the very beginning of the inter-American conferences. It is significant that when the Pan American Union was born it was initially called "The Commercial Bureau of American Republics."[14] In order to facilitate commercial relations, the early conferences dealt with such matters as the simplification of customs formalities; consular regulations; uniformity of commercial statistics; promotion of tourist travel; commercial arbitration; improvement of river, sea, railroad, highway and aerial communication; uniform legislation on various types of commercial paper; simplification of passports, patents, and trademarks; commercial and maritime law; and the juridical personality of foreign companies.

But the conferences did not begin to deal with the more fundamental problems in the economic field until 1933, despite efforts, particularly on the part of Argentina, to urge their consideration at the Sixth Conference.[15] By the time the Seventh Conference met in Montevideo in 1933, the depression had seriously affected the economies of all the American nations. Currencies were depreciated, foreign investments were liquidated, international trade was restricted by higher tariffs and quotas, unemployment was rampant the world over.[16] It became increasingly clear that national economic problems could not be solved on a national scale.

Therefore the American states began, rather timidly at first, to consider such matters as commercial policy, as opposed to commercial procedures; the possibility of relaxing import and export controls; the possibility of concluding collective commercial treaties; agricultural co-operation; immigration and labor problems; financial problems; and the possibility of creating an inter-American economic and financial organization.

When war broke out in Europe in 1939, the First Meeting of Ministers of Foreign Affairs convened in Panama to consider any and all measures which might be taken to minimize the expected dislocations in the economic life of the American nations.[17] The first step toward economic co-operation taken by this meeting involved the creation of the Inter-American Financial and Economic Advisory Committee[18] consisting of twenty-one economic specialists, one for each of the American republics, with its seat in Washington. To this committee was assigned the duty of studying ways and means to protect the American economies and to promote long-term economic development. In addition the ministers agreed on certain general co-operative measures relating to assurance of continued maritime service without unjustified rate increases and providing for movement of capital and facilitation of credit, stabilization of prices, detention of belligerent vessels, freedom of communication, and development of land and air transportation.

The Second Meeting of Ministers of Foreign Affairs held at Habana in 1940,[19] under ever increasing world disturbance and disruption of international trade, resolved to extend inter-American economic co-operation and to secure the economic development of all nations in the Western Hemisphere, and agreed to seek means to diversify production and increase consumptive capacity in the hemisphere. To this end the ministers gave out a general declaration of the adherence of the republics to liberal principles of trade. The meeting extended the scope of activities of the Inter-American Financial and Economic Advisory

Committee by assigning to it the duty of making studies on measures for raising standards of living and health; for assuring equitable terms of trade; for distribution, as relief, of portions of exportable surpluses; and for broadening economic co-operation. This meeting affirmed the action of the Advisory Committee which had created the Inter-American Development Commission, whose purpose was to seek out development enterprises which could be financed co-operatively by two or more nations.

The Third Meeting of Ministers of Foreign Affairs was called in 1942[20] after direct involvement of some of the American nations in the war. At this meeting economic co-operation to prevent total disruption of national economies and to aid in the successful prosecution of the war was emphasized. A general hemispheric economic mobilization was proposed, including increased production of and guarantees of access to basic and strategic materials essential to both military and civilian needs. Internal finances were to be strengthened and credit facilities broadened. The need for increased co-operation in the field of transportation, involving expansion and co-ordination of existing port and airport facilities and acceleration of work on the Pan American Highway, was reaffirmed. With reference to the maintenance of internal economic stability, the ministers placed particular emphasis on the prevention of undue rises in prices of exports and in prices charged by processors or importers. To minimize disruption of the trade of the republics, they agreed upon an equitable priority and licensing system, export controls, price ceilings on raw materials and foodstuffs, and preferential treatment to nations at war, particularly for access to supplies of goods essential to defense. The ministers also proposed the calling of a meeting of Ministers of Finance for the purpose of establishing an international stabilization fund, both to secure a more efficient mobilization of foreign exchange for purposes of the common war effort and also for more long-range economic purposes. An even broader jurisdiction was given to the Inter-American Financial and Economic Advisory Committee and its various subsidiaries.

Problems of the transition from war to peace, as well as long-term accelerated development of the economic life of the Latin American countries, were of major concern to the Latin American governments when the Chapultepec Conference met in Mexico in 1945.[21] The representatives of each Latin American nation at the conference pointed out that a sudden reduction in the purchase of raw materials by the United States would have a disastrous effect upon its economic structure. The conference adopted a number of resolutions on continued wartime economic co-operation, on the transition from war to peace, and on the long-term development in the postwar period. It also adopted a resolution known as "The Economic Charter of the Americas,"[22] which constituted a declaration of policy and objectives of great economic importance, relative to raising of standards of living, equal access to trade and raw materials, international commercial policy, private agreements restrictive to international trade, elimination of excesses of economic nationalism, treatment of foreign enterprise and capital, international financial and economic proposals, measures for preventing unemployment, private enterprise, and industrial development. As a final measure, the conference transformed the wartime Financial and

Economic Advisory Committee into the present Inter-American Economic and Social Council, establishing it as a permanent organization subsidiary to the former Governing Board of the Pan American Union, now the Council of the OAS.

This new Economic and Social Council was authorized to organize provisionally until the Ninth International Conference should give it definite organic structure. Its functions were set forth as follows:[23]

1) To carry out recommendations of the International Conference of American States;

2) To serve as the coordinating agency for all official Inter-American economic and social activities;

3) To promote social progress and the raising of the standards of living for all the American peoples;

4) To undertake studies and other activities upon its own initiative or upon the request of any American government;

5) To maintain liaison with the corresponding agency of the general international organization (U.N.) when established and with existing or projected international economic and social agencies.

The need for economic co-operation was emphasized by most of the Latin American delegates at the 1947 Rio Conference on the Maintenance of Continental Peace and Security.[24] Several resolutions on economic topics were introduced, but as it was not feasible to incorporate an article on economic co-operation into the Rio Treaty, the delegates resolved that the Inter-American Economic and Social Council should prepare a draft treaty on economic co-operation for submission to the Ninth Conference.

Between November, 1945, when the Inter-American Economic and Social Council was established, and April, 1948, when the Ninth Inter-American Conference was held at Bogotá, the new Council prepared various studies concerning the production and trade of rubber, vegetable fibers, cacao, and vegetable oils. Other studies were made on the conservation of natural resources and on principles that should govern the investment of capital, and a proposal was drawn up for the economic agreement to be considered at Bogotá.

At the Ninth Conference, the Economic and Social Council was definitely established as a permanent organ of the Council of the OAS.[25] Its purpose, as set out in Article 63 of the Charter, is "... the promotion of economic and social welfare of the American nations through effective co-operation for the better utilization of their natural resources, the development of their agriculture and industry and the raising of the standards of living of their peoples."

Its seat is the Pan American Union in Washington, but it may hold meetings in any city in the hemisphere decided upon by a majority of the member states. Among the new functions given to it was the power to suggest to the Council of the OAS the advisability of holding specialized conferences on economic and social matters. In addition it may carry on such activities as may be assigned to it by the Conferences, the Meetings of Ministers of Foreign Affairs, or the Council of the Organization.

One of the problems immediately undertaken by the Economic and Social Council was the need to co-ordinate its work with that of the Economic Committee for Latin America established by the United Nations Economic and

Social Council.[26] Taking into account the fact that many of the functions assigned to both organizations were essentially analogous and that limitation on funds made it necessary to avoid duplication of work, the two organizations established a satisfactory working arrangement, agreeing that each should continue its work along lines compatible with its respective interests but always consult with the other when initiating any specific project so that ways of supplementing and complementing the work of both could be agreed upon. Consequently no specific separation of functions has ever been made between the two organizations.

The draft of the proposed economic agreement drawn up by the Inter-American Economic and Social Council, following the resolution on this subject by the Rio Meeting, was the object of much heated discussion at the Ninth Inter-American Conference at Bogotá.[27] The first chapter of the economic agreement contains a series of principles, dealing with the general obligation of American states to co-operate with one another in the solution of their economic problems and the desirability of further bilateral or multilateral agreements to increase economic development and industrialization.

But the first chapter also included the question of raw material prices, under which the American states would recognize the necessity of taking action to compensate for the alleged disparity existing at times between the prices of raw materials and manufactured goods. Most of the nations of Latin America are still heavily dependent upon the export of raw materials and suffer seriously from a fall in the price level of their primary products. Having learned that during the depression years and the war years only international co-operation would prevent the complete dislocation of their economies, they sought some safeguards against price fluctuations. Latin American exporters of primary products long for a kind of assistance from Washington which the domestic United States farmer has received from his government. The Latin Americans, however, seemed unmindful of the fact that the United States' relevant and sad farm policy experience spoke tellingly against them. When the delegates met at Bogotá, the large wartime dollar balances accumulated by Latin American nations had been practically exhausted, and this left those nations entirely dependent upon foreign markets for their foreign exchange requirements. Hence the Economic Agreement declared that "there should be taken into account the need to compensate for the disparity that is frequently noted between the prices of raw materials and the prices of manufactured products by establishing the necessary balance between them."

This proposal was accepted by all the delegations except that of the United States, which entered a formal reservation to it without clarifying explanation. The United States as the chief purchaser of these raw materials would have to act as a guarantor of these prices if the Latin American position is accepted that the United States should assume responsibility for organizing and implementing some scheme to achieve greater price stability. Until recently, United States policy was adamant against any institutional arrangement of this nature.

The basic solution to the problem of dependence upon raw materials prices in an international market as visualized by all of the other American republics is industrialization. Without a doubt a certain degree of industrial development is required if these areas are to raise the standard of living of their inhabitants, for economic diversification enhances prosperity. Economic diversification permits a greater degree of cultural development and provides more vocational openings for the youth of these nations, since many more different kinds of jobs are provided in an economically complex than in an economically simple economy. Thus industrialization has a great psychological and political appeal at the present time, and it is not surprising therefore to find that the remainder of the important clauses of the Economic Agreement of Bogotá relate primarily to the issue of industrialization.

Chapter Two of the agreement deals entirely with the subject of technical co-operation between the American republics. This chapter vests responsibility for the development of technical co-operation in the Inter-American Economic and Social Council, which is directed to prepare an inventory of the economic potential of the states, promote research, training, and studies, make available information and technical advice, and on request study specific proposals for the development of immigration and assist in preparing data on special projects for presentation to obtain public or private financing. To perform these responsibilities the Council is authorized to form a technical staff which is to be paid for from the Pan American Union budget, although studies of special projects are to be made for the account of the state requesting them.

It has long been the declared policy of the United States to aid the efforts of the people of economically underdeveloped areas to develop their resources and improve their working and living conditions by encouraging the exchange of technical knowledge and granting technical assistance on a noncommercial basis. This program was first carried on in Latin America beginning in 1942 through the Institute of Inter-American Affairs.[28] Its activities were expanded under Truman's Point Four Program.[29] Thus the United States was in accord with regard to the general provisions of Chapter Two of the Economic Agreement of Bogotá.

Chapter Three of the Bogotá Economic Agreement deals with financial co-operation. Underlying this chapter was Latin American displeasure over Washington's unwillingness to establish a Marshall Plan for the area. Also involved was Latin American disappointment over the fact that development funds were not as easy to obtain from the International Bank for Reconstruction and Development or the Export-Import Bank as Latin Americans had originally hoped.[30] This flowed partly from the application by these banks of strictly business principles, but also in considerable measure from the fact that neither bank normally makes loans covering the local currency requirements of projects. For the local currency requirements the borrowing nations must produce their own capital. In most Latin American countries such capital is not readily available and commands high interest rates, for local citizens with a capital supply are seldom willing to risk the unstable political conditions of Latin America, preferring to invest their savings abroad. Furthermore, these banks have tried to use their lending capacity as a leverage to induce monetary and fiscal reforms.[31] The borrowing countries, however, tend to resist proposed corrective measures which are never popular either with governmental officials or with the populace in general.

The Latin American nations have long sought to have some sort of inter-American bank to establish and promote inter-American credit, help stabilize currency, control foreign exchange, and stimulate trade. The Latin Americans felt that an investment and credit institution created exclusively for the American countries would be more effective than the World Bank or the Export-Import Bank.[32] This idea was put forward as early as 1889, but has been resisted by the United States. At Bogotá the United States took the position that the International Bank for Reconstruction and Development was in a position to assist in financing all feasible projects which were beyond the resources of private capital and that therefore no new inter-American financial or development institution was needed. The United States delegation declared that the Latin American countries should take every possible step to stimulate the development of local capital and should assume the responsibility for fostering their own economic growth. The language of Chapter Three of the Bogotá Agreement reflects, therefore, the United States and not the Latin American point of view, when it states that the signatories undertake to stimulate the local investment of national savings and foreign capital and to utilize the services of the International Monetary Fund, and agree that international financing should not be sought for local currency requirements.

The hardest fought chapter of the entire agreement was Chapter Four, which covered private investments. Throughout the conference the United States stressed the theme of the role of which private capital might play in the economic development of Latin America. For decades Latin America was the favorite outlet for United States private foreign investment. Such investment had promoted indigenous exports, produced import-displacing goods, served as a catalytic agent with respect to activating local enterprise, inculcated skills in the indigenous labor force, expanded and deepened the local tax base, and helped to improve the governmental climate within which both local and foreign capital could operate. Nevertheless, foreign capital was at times leery of Latin America in view of impediments created by all or a substantial number of the Latin American countries. These can be listed as follows:[33]

1. Political instability, involving frequent changes in personnel, policies, and laws, creates an atmosphere of uncertainty and insecurity and adds to the cost of operation. Actually, damage to property and loss of life have been relatively minor except in a few countries, but foreign investors have at times suffered because local managers or associates were out of favor with a new regime. Historically, this has been an important reason for the reluctance of some foreign enterprises to seem to become too closely identified with any local group.

2. The small size and limited population and resources of some of the countries restrict investment opportunities to a narrow field. Some of the problems relating to foreign investment arise from the very conspicuousness of a large foreign enterprise in a small country. Nor can some of the smaller countries absorb big doses of foreign capital without social and political stresses. For the fact that labor is national while ownership and/or management are foreign gives rise to the temptation to make the foreigners a scapegoat or political football.

3. Partly as a result of historical evolution and partly owing to the characteristics of segments of the population (high percentage of illiteracy, lack of tradition of self-government, persistence of aboriginal customs), Latin America has been accustomed to a larger measure of governmental intervention in political, social (including labor-management relations), and economic affairs than the United States. During the last two decades these tendencies have been accentuated, especially in the economic sphere. Examples are the general development corporation or single-industry institutes and enterprises established in various countries. Some of these have been created *ad hoc* to take over a formerly foreign-owned concern, whereas others (e.g., electric power organizations) provide a nucleus for expansion of the national activities in a given field. The pattern of likely future development of these activities varies greatly, depending upon the country and the nature of the industry. In some cases the tendency is to evolve toward a complete government monopoly. In other cases, official intervention has been limited to a restricted field, leaving ample opportunity to national and foreign private enterprises.

4. Foreigners are excluded from particular activities in some countries, and in others are not permitted to have majority control. In some countries and in some industries some degree of local financial and management participation may be desirable, but in some countries and in some types of activity local participation, or in any case majority participation, may be inadvisable, owing, among other reasons, to the need to maintain the quality of the product or the standard of service.

5. The threat of expropriation or nationalization, without either prompt or adequate compensation, remains an obstacle to investment in Latin America, especially in view of the reluctance of some of the countries to admit the right of any foreign government to make representation in cases of alleged denial of justice by the local authorities. The adoption by the United Nations General Assembly late in 1952 of the resolution on the "right to exploit freely natural wealth and resources" has increased the fears of many investors with regard to nationalization or outright confiscation.

6. In practice, creeping expropriation has been a more serious problem for large investors than outright nationalization. Some countries have harassed foreign-controlled enterprises with fines and discriminatory tax and labor requirements, or have refused to permit utilities to charge rates high enough to yield adequate returns. Not infrequently foreign enterprises have to compete with national concerns that are exempt from taxes or other burdens to which the foreign firms are subject. Foreign firms may also be subject to discriminatory application of exchange rates.

7. As some of the Latin American currencies are subject to controls and are not readily convertible, except at a discount on the black market, the exchange risk is one of the ever-present hazards of foreign investment, especially for small investors. All investors must take into account the problems and difficulties inherent in the delays and administrative complexities of exchange controls. This hazard is especially important to small investors who lack the resources to weather long delays and to protect themselves against sudden shifts in currency valuations.

8. Finally, the customs negotiations in connection with import of equipment and raw materials are often hazardous, expensive, complicated; and at times officials are corrupt.

Even where these problems have been minimized, the success of private American investments still gives rise to numerous political problems including accusations of corporate interference with domestic politics, the demand of local infant industries for protection against new competition, and the rather absurd claim on the part of left-wing parties in Latin America that by demanding high returns on foreign investment, plus the right of free convertibility, the foreign capitalists were in fact "decapitalizing" Latin America. Most Latin Americans were therefore strongly in favor of developing their economic potential through governmental development corporations financed by foreign and local governmental capital, with a considerable degree of government control in planning and operations.

Chapter Four of the Economic Pact begins with a declaration of the importance of private investment. Foreign capital, it is declared, shall receive equitable treatment. The states therefore agree not to take unjustified, unreasonable, or discriminatory measures that would impair the legally acquired rights or interests of the nationals of other countries in the enterprises, capital, skills, arts, or technology they have supplied. There is a declaration that foreign investment should be made not only for profit, but also with a view to the sound development of the country and the welfare of the persons directly dependent upon the enterprise; with respect to employment, just and equitable treatment should be accorded to all personnel, national and foreign, and the development of technical and administrative training of national personnel should be encouraged, although it is desirable to permit enterprises to employ and utilize the services of a reasonable number of technical experts and executive personnel, whatever their nationality may be.

It is stated that foreign capital is subject to national laws, and each state retains its right to establish regulations to prevent intervention by foreign corporations in local politics or other activities which may prejudice the national security or fundamental interests of the state.

The rule was laid down that the American states should not take discriminatory action against investments in such a way that deprivation of property rights legally acquired by foreign capital would be carried out under conditions different from those which the constitution or laws of each country establish for national property. This was as far as several of the Latin American delegations were willing to go with reference to the question of expropriation. But the United States had proposed that there be added the statement that "there should be no expropriation of foreign owned property except for clearly defined public purposes accompanied by prompt, adequate and effective compensation." Three elements in this proposed addition caused difficulty. The reference to "foreign owned property" seemed, in the minds of some delegations, to set up a special and more favorable regime for foreign owned property than for national, and in the final version of the treaty those words were omitted. Second, several delegations raised difficulties based upon their constitutional provisions with regard to the idea of expropriation only for clearly defined public purposes. In the final version, it was found necessary to eliminate this phrase. Finally, the reference to "prompt, adequate and effective compensation" was declared to be in conflict with the constitutional provisions of various Latin American nations, including Mexico, Guatemala, and Venezuela, and was therefore unacceptable to these nations. The United States pointed out that international law rules governing expropriation established the "prompt, adequate and effective compensation" criterion,[34] and declared that an additional reiteration of this rule would create an increasing degree of confidence by investors in Latin America.

The United States won its point by a vote of 14 to 5; Article 25 of the Economic Pact contains the statement: "Any expropriation shall be accompanied by payment of fair compensation in a prompt, adequate and effective manner." But there were a number of reservations to this section by the various delegations.

The nations declare their intention to develop uniform principles of corporate accounting and standards of fair disclosure to private investors. They undertake to liberalize their tax laws, to eliminate double taxation and avoid burdensome or discriminatory taxes, and to seek to conclude agreements against double taxation.

The remaining chapters of the Economic Agreement were less controversial. Chapter Five set forth various general principles and obligations as a basis for inter-American co-operation in industrial and economic development, and various undertakings in connection with the furnishing of materials, machinery, and equipment needed for economic development, particularly under conditions when such materials and equipment are in short supply. The other chapters contained provisions dealing with co-operative measures in connection with industrial and general economic development; provisions regarding commodity agreements, commercial preference, social guarantees regarding the rights of labor and certain related social questions; maritime transportation, freedom of transit through the territories of American states as a means of encouraging international trade; the encouragement of inter-American travel to aid in economic development; the utilization of orderly and friendly means for the settlement of all economic disputes between the American states; the co-ordination of the activities of the Inter-American Economic and Social Council with those of other international agencies to avoid duplication of effort; and the customary provisions relating to ratification, entry into force, and amendment of the treaty.

At the time of signing, fifteen reservations were made by ten different countries; two declarations by two different countries; and one joint statement by three different countries. The two declarations appear to constitute reservations, since they lessen the obligations of the declaring countries. Only a few countries have deposited their ratification of the treaty, and as the agreement is to enter into force with respect to those countries which have ratified it, when two-thirds of the signatories have done so, the Economic Pact of Bogotá has not as yet entered into force.

In addition to approving the Economic Pact, the conference also approved a number of resolutions of an economic character, several of which referred various unresolved economic questions to the Inter-American Economic and Social Council for further study and possible transmittal to a later economic conference for action.

Immediately after the Ninth Conference of American States, the Inter-American Economic and Social Council initiated studies for implementing several resolutions approved at that conference. The problems with which these resolutions dealt were to be included in the agenda of an Inter-American Economic Conference scheduled to take place in the latter part of 1948 or early 1949. The conference did not materialize, however, and the problems in question were discussed during the First Extraordinary Meeting of the Inter-American Economic and Social Council, which was held in Washington in the spring of 1950.[35] At this meeting, considerable attention was given also to discussion of the reservations to the economic agreement of Bogotá and to the then current problem of the possible effects on the trade of the American republics from the devaluation of most world currencies occurring in September, 1949.

The initiation of hostilities in Korea[36] created a greater need for close inter-American economic co-operation. Consequently during the latter part of 1950 and all of 1951 the Economic and Social Council shifted its attention more and more to emergency economic problems. During this period, it undertook a study of emergency problems in anticipation of the Fourth Meeting of Consultation of Ministers of Foreign Affairs,[37] Washington, 1951, and later worked intensively toward the implementation of the recommendations and resolutions approved at that meeting. The problems which the Council thus discussed included those connected with the supply of commodities essential to the defense effort; the needs of the civilian economies and the continuation of the economic development plans of the American republics; transportation problems and financial problems.

This emphasis on emergency problems was also reflected in the discussions of the Second Extraordinary Meeting of the Economic and Social Council which took place in Panama in August, 1951.[38] Considerable attention was given to emergency transportation; to freight and insurance matters; and to materials problems, especially in connection with systems of export allocations and priorities, inter-American study groups of materials in short supply, and inter-American policy relative to the International Materials Conference. At the same time, there was indicated a growing interest on the part of the Economic and Social Council in social studies, which found expression in the creation of special work groups and committees devoted to proposed activities in this field.

The Third Extraordinary Meeting of the Economic and Social Council, held in Caracas in February, 1953,[39] also dealt with emergency questions but tended at the same time to shift its attention toward longer-range problems. This tendency was reflected in the emphasis placed on social problems and in the detailed consideration of low-cost housing and related matters.

When the Tenth Conference convened in Caracas, it was evident that the Latin American nations were anxious to preserve the economic gains made during the preceding decade and to obtain from the United States maximum assurances as to assistance in maintaining a favorable level of prices and avoidance of restrictions to trade with the United States. It was also clear that many of them looked to the United States to provide assurances or make commitments which they thought would lead to solutions of their common economic problems.

In the field of commodities, there was continued wide concern over national instability caused by dependence upon the exportation of only a few products and the wide fluctuation of the world prices of such products. The theory was expressed that over more or less extended periods raw material export prices tended to decline in relation to the prices paid for imported manufactured goods. Various delegations declared that when opportunities developed for the raw-material producing nations to obtain higher prices in emergency or other special situations which would permit compensation for periods of low prices, limitations were imposed on the prices at which the raw materials could be sold in the principal markets. Concern was also expressed by some delegations lest policies and actions by the United States in disposing of agricultural surpluses might have a harmful effect on their own normal marketings.

Some of the representatives declared that the United States had the primary responsibility—even unilaterally if necessary—to reduce or eliminate its tariff or other barriers to the importation of Latin American products, thus opening a greater market and enabling Latin America to earn more dollars. With the expansion of trade during the last decade between the United States and Latin America, there was some sentiment that this movement should be given further stimulation by regional agreements, the benefits of which would not be extended outside the hemisphere.

The Tenth Conference adopted a number of economic resolutions of a general nature. They declared the economic solidarity of the Americas and the desirability of intensifying regional and inter-American trade; recommended that industrialized countries eliminate restrictions of all kinds on the importation of raw materials or semimanufactured products originating in the less developed American countries; urged the intensification of the industrialization of Latin American nations in order to create a better rounded inter-American economy; recommended that the American countries maintain and adopt suitable measures for the purpose of encouraging the flow of private investments; urged the nations to increase efforts to carry out agrarian reforms; requested the Council of the OAS to study the desirability and possibility of creating an Inter-American Specialized Organization for lead, copper, zinc, tin, and tungsten; and called for a Meeting of Ministers of Finance and Economy of the American States to consider concrete measures dealing with the various economic problems which face the Western Hemisphere.[40]

At the Tenth Conference, Chile proposed that the special meeting of the Ministers of Finance or Economy of the American Republics also be the Fourth Extraordinary Meeting of the Inter-American Economic and Social Council. The purpose of the meeting, as stated by the Chilean delegate, was to "study on the highest technical level the present difficulties and to make concrete recommendations to all governments." Rio de Janeiro was designated as the site of the conference, starting November 22, 1954.[41]

The main Latin American proposals at Rio concerned:

1. Consultation in connection with the disposal of United States agricultural surpluses.

2. Consideration of possible measures to stabilize prices of primary products, including the use of stockpiles to avoid extreme fluctuations in the prices of strategic and other mineral products.

3. Reduction of United States tariffs and avoidance of restrictions on the importation of Latin American products.

4. Consideration of special treatment with respect to trade for under-developed countries in order to encourage economic development.

5. Utilization by the United States of income taxes collected on the operation of United States firms in Latin America to promote economic development in that area.

6. Establishment of a regional development institution to provide loan and equity capital for private enterprise.

7. Increased credit facilities for Latin America by the International and Export-Import Banks.

8. The setting up of target amounts for yearly public and private investment, with public investment making good any deficit in the quota of private investment.

In spite of Latin American hopes that specific solutions rather than general pronouncements would be sought at Rio, not too much was accomplished. Many resolutions were passed, among them decisions to study transportation, to work together to improve harbor facilities, to co-operate in lessening the barriers to maximum flow of trade and commerce, to improve the development of resources, and to expand travel between countries of this hemisphere.

But the United States contended it did not have the resources to enter into any price-parity formulas with Latin America, or any plans which involved vast financial commitments. Furthermore, it was still strongly against any regional bank to finance projects for the nations of Latin America, agreeing only that it was willing to reassure these nations as to the availability of sufficient public foreign credit resources to meet new, foreseeable needs for the financing of sound projects for which private capital was not readily available and whose financing was within the debt-carrying capacity of the country which wished to secure the loan in question.

In 1956, at the suggestion of the Representative of Mexico, the OAS Council scheduled a commemorative meeting on the Isthmus of Panama to mark the 130th anniversary of the Congress of Panama called by Bolívar in 1826.[42] This commemorative meeting was followed by a meeting of the presidents of the American nations, who were invited by the Panamanian chief executive to leave their duties long enough to gather in Panama and give their personal sanction to the commemorative assembly. On July 22, 1956, the President of the United States[43] addressed the assembled Heads of the American states and suggested that the presidents of each of the American republics appoint a special representative to a committee which would prepare concrete recommendations for making the OAS a more effective instrument. These representatives would be charged with preparing practical suggestions in the economic, financial, social, and technical fields which the OAS might appropriately adopt. The President pointed particularly to consideration of ways in which the beneficial use of nuclear forces throughout the hemisphere could be hastened, and suggested that the OAS should establish a specialized agency to study this problem.

On August 13 the United States Department of State announced that the President had sent a note to each of the other American republics proposing that the committee convene in Washington, on a mutually agreeable date, and requested the other governments to make suggestions regarding the committee and its tasks. The first meeting was held on September 18-21, 1956. At that time the committee listed twelve items for "practical" action by the OAS, and also decided to hold a later meeting for action on these issues after further review by each nation.[44] Some of the Latin American nations were disappointed at the "narrowness" of the agenda, while other delegates were of the private opinion that the conference had done little in the economic or financial field beyond stating the general platitudes which had been repeated in every postwar meeting dealing with economic problems.

On August 8, 1958, the president of Brazil sent an *aide memoire* to the governments of the other American states that described in detail the views of the government of Brazil with respect to the nature, characteristics, objectives, and functioning of "Operation Pan America."[45] The *aide memoire* recognized that the responsibility for dealing with problems in economic development, international trade and finance, industrial technology and productivity, social development, regional planning, housing, education, technical co-operation, statistics, public health, and agriculture was a collective one, and that if solutions were not provided, the tensions and pressures generated by the economic inequalities existing among the American nations would undermine the hemisphere's political solidarity.

In order to advance the spirit of "Operation Pan America," the United States secretary of state invited the ministers of foreign affairs of the twenty-one American republics to meet informally in Washington to exchange views on inter-American relations and problems, particularly those of an economic nature. At this meeting,[46] held in September, 1958, the United States announced a reversal of its historic stand against participating in an Inter-American Development Bank. With this added incentive, the ministers of foreign affairs recommended that the Council of the OAS establish a special committee to prepare a blueprint designed to direct co-operative effort toward a more rapid development of the economies of the member countries of the OAS. The new Committee of Twenty-one held three meetings: in Washington in November-December, 1958; in Buenos Aires in May, 1959;[47] and in Bogotá in September, 1960.[48]

From the Bogotá Meeting came the Act of Bogotá,[49] a blueprint for the economic and social development of Latin America. The blueprint recognized that the kind of economic development programs which have hitherto been undertaken in Latin America are likely to be slow in having effects on social welfare, and that, therefore, more direct measures are needed to combat poverty, inadequate housing, and malnutrition.

The Act of Bogotá is divided into four chapters. The first, "Measures for Social Improvement," enumerates the steps that should be taken to improve conditions of rural life and land use, housing and community facilities, educational systems and training facilities, and public health. It calls for a review of land-tenure legislation, to promote a wider and more equitable distribution of land ownership; of agricultural-credit institutions; and of tax systems and fiscal policies to help assure equitable taxation and encourage the use of idle privately owned land. Other provisions relating to agriculture look to an acceleration in the formulation of projects and programs for land reclamation and settlement, for increasing the productivity of land already in use, and for the construction of farm-to-market and access roads, and to government service programs designed to help the small farmer.

Chapter II of the Act of Bogotá, "Creation of a Special Fund for Social Development," states that "the delegations of the governments of the Latin American Republics welcome the decision of the Government of the United States to establish a special inter-American fund for social development, with the Inter-American Development Bank to become the primary mechanism for the administration of the fund." The fund would contribute capital and technical assistance on flexible terms, including repayment of loans in local currency and the relending of repaid funds, under certain conditions, to support the efforts of the Latin American countries that are prepared to start or expand effective institutional improvements and to adopt measures to employ their own resources efficiently, with a view to achieving greater social progress and more balanced economic growth.

Under Chapter III, "Measures for Economic Development," the Act makes two recommendations: first, that special attention be given to an expansion of long-term lending, particularly in view of the instability of exchange earnings of countries that export primary products and of the unfavorable effect of the excessive accumulation of short- and medium-term debt on continuing and orderly economic development; and second, that urgent attention be given to the search for effective and practical ways of dealing with the instability of exchange earnings of countries that depend heavily on exports of primary products.

"Multilateral Cooperation of Social and Economic Progress," Chapter IV, recommends that the Inter-American Economic and Social Council organize annual consultative meetings beginning with a discussion by experts and ending with sessions at the ministerial level, to review the social and economic progress of the member countries and to exchange views on measures that might be taken to overcome the problems and promote further development. It also recommended that the OAS Council find ways of strengthening the Inter-American Economic and Social Council, to give it more technical, administrative, and financial flexibility for the fulfilment of its tasks.

Another important resolution adopted by the Committee of Twenty-one and subsequently approved by the Council of the OAS was "that an economic crisis that so seriously affects the development process of any American State as to threaten the social peace and welfare of its people is of primary concern to all the other American states." Accordingly the resolution provided that an emergency meeting of American foreign ministers could be convened at the request of any American state which might be faced by an urgent economic crisis that it could not satisfactorily cope with by its own unaided effort.

While the Committee of Twenty-one pondered how to solve old social and economic problems through a better use of new methods and techniques, a group of financial experts of the American nations gathered in Washington in January, 1959, to draft an appropriate agreement for submission to the members of the OAS relating to the establishment of the Inter-American Development Bank.[50] Now that the United States had at last agreed to a step which Latin America had been urging for over half a century, the most vital question to be settled was the amount of money the bank would be given to work with, and this, of course, depended primarily upon the sum the United States would place at its disposal. After originally suggesting a total capital of $850 million, the United States eventually raised the figure to $1 billion in view of the general feeling that more was needed. Eighty-five per cent of the bank's total resources, it was agreed, would be used for commercial type loans like those already made by the International Bank for Reconstruction and Development and the Export-Import Bank; the remaining 15 per cent would constitute a "Fund for Special Operations" to make "soft" loans in support of useful projects that were not necessarily self-liquidating. Provision was also made for a possible 50 per cent increase in the bank's capitalization after September 30, 1962. After congressional approval of these arrangements, the United States formally accepted membership in the bank in October, 1959, and the deposit of the ratification of the other American nations brought the institution formally into existence on December 30.[51]

The Inter-American Development Bank, even though it is not specifically provided for by the Charter of the OAS, is still considered an integral part of the OAS. Nevertheless, because of its unique function, it is a completely autonomous agency.

With the advent of a new administration in Washington, a new impetus was given to "Operation Pan America" by the call for an Alliance for Progress.[52] To implement the objectives of the Act of Bogotá, the United States suggested a cabinet-level economic conference in Uruguay as a special meeting of the Inter-American Economic and Social Council, during the month of August, 1961.[53]

This meeting, in the Act of Punta del Este,[54] offered a three-pronged approach to the economic problems of Latin America: aid, trade, and social reform. A minimum of twenty billion dollars in foreign aid was pledged for a ten-year period. More than half of this money is to come from the United States, much in low interest long-term loans, the rest from international financial agencies, Western Europe, and private capital. Although the United States delegation admitted that Congress was resistant to long-term commitments, it felt that in this instance Congress was back of the Alliance for Progress and would feel itself morally committed to continue what was promised at Uruguay.

The United States came to Uruguay with a willingness at least to consider stabilization of prices for certain basic commodities. In other words, as an importing country, it was willing to join in international agreements aimed at dividing up production and export markets among the various producing countries. It agreed, as an initial experiment, to join in two such arrangements—on coffee, which is the basic export of some of the Central American countries, Brazil, and Colombia, and on tin, which is Bolivia's main export.

It had been agreed at the Punta del Este meeting of August, 1961, that the operation of the Alliance for Progress would be evaluated each year at a conference called specifically to deal with the program's progress and its shortcomings. Consequently, early in October, 1962, top-level experts representing the twenty nations involved in the Alliance met for three weeks in Mexico City as a special meeting of the Inter-American Economic and Social Council to study the economic and social situation of Latin America since the inauguration of the Alliance; the progress of regional economic integration; the world market for Latin American basic export products; and organizational and administrative matters relating to the Alliance.

While the financial and economic experts admitted that certain initial steps had been taken involving long-rang economic plans for Latin America, still they were highly critical of the administrative procedures and red tape involved in obtaining Alliance aid. Furthermore, it was agreed that special United States technical assistance programs which were in being when the Alliance for Progress had been created had been phased out too quickly, leaving a hiatus which the Alliance had failed to fill. It was recognized that while the Alliance had been expected to encourage an ever increasing flow of private capital from the United States into Latin America, in practice the result had been just the opposite. Because of apprehension over threats of expropriation and confiscatory social and economic legislation aimed at private capital, and because of an ever increasing agitation from extreme left-wing parties in Latin America, a poor investment climate had been created, causing the flow of private capital to dwindle to a mere trickle, while the flight of Latin American capital in a number of the larger nations had equaled if not exceeded the total amount of assistance to those countries granted by the Alliance. In order to encourage an additional flow of private capital, the United States urged the Latin American nations to join it in mutual guarantee treaties which would insure private investors against financial loss through expropriation or war, a move which many Latin American politicians reject because it gives to foreign investors a preferential treatment over national private investors.

The findings and recommendations of the experts of the Inter-American Economic and Social Council were handed to a meeting of the ministers of finance and economics of the twenty member nations which followed upon the heels of the special preparatory session of the Inter-American Economic and Social Council.

The Latin American ministers of finance and economics, gathered in Mexico City in October, 1962, were highly critical of the Alliance, pointing out that the program had started with high hopes and expectations but had floundered badly. They admitted that although there had been some economic and social advances in Latin America during the first year of the program, still it was moving too slowly to assure its success as a positive evolutionary measure for the betterment of the masses in Latin America. The delegates from the United States countered by commenting that some of the program's critical flaws were directly traceable to the failure of the Latin American nations to impose the discipline and submit to the sacrifices which the Alliance demanded, including such basic issues as agrarian and tax reform and responsible fiscal,

monetary, and infra-structure policies. The United States delegation announced
that the United States was prepared to participate in increasing the Inter-
American Development Bank's callable resources by $1 billion, which would
mean an additional obligation of the United States of approximately $500 mil-
lion. The delegates also agreed to assist in replenishing the Bank's social progress
fund, from which various social advancements in health and education are
financed.

The Latin American ministers at Mexico City advocated the formation
of a solid Western Hemisphere bloc to meet the threat of discriminatory trading
brought on by the European Economic Community, pointing out that more
and more of the world's trade was being determined by large-scale regional
arrangements which would eventually bypass isolated unintegrated areas. The
United States resisted the formation of such a common market on the grounds
that it had too many other international commitments, but suggested that the
two regional groups now in existence in Latin America—the nine-nation Latin
American Free Trade Association and the five-nation Central American common
market—should continue to move as rapidly as possible to integrate their basic
economic activities. The United States also advocated a multilateral approach
on a commodity basis such as had been brought about in the worldwide coffee
agreement. It was also announced that the United States was planning to reduce
trade barriers affecting certain Latin American exports under the Trade Expansion Act passed by the United States Congress in 1962. Nevertheless, the dissatisfaction of the Latin American ministers was not assuaged. They complained
that the Alliance was not developing on a multilateral basis as had been anticipated, but at best was degenerating into a series of bilateral United States give-
away programs. They grumbled that the decline in prices for the continent's
basic products had brought the economy of nearly all Latin American countries
to the brink of collapse, a situation which created revolutionary instead of
evolutionary tendencies among the depressed classes. The United States therefore agreed that a two-man committee should be appointed with power to review
not only the Alliance for Progress program but the entire Pan American
system, with a view to recommending whatever structural modifications they
conceived to be necessary to turn the system into an efficient instrument in the
fight against underdevelopment. Two highly respected men, former President
Juscelino Kubitschek of Brazil and former President Alberto Lleras Camargo
of Colombia, agreed to serve and to report their findings and recommendations
directly to the OAS Council by March, 1963. The conference of ministers of
finance and economics ended on October 27, 1962, after designating Brazil as
the host country for the 1963 meeting.[55]

Successful inter-American co-operation in the economic field is, then, not
overly dependent upon principles of general or particular international law.
If a given problem is ripe for inter-American action, if a nation's internal policies are sufficiently elastic and capable of modification to make such action
possible, and if the governments definitely desire it, real progress will be made.
Where, however, these conditions do not exist, no possible machinery can do
much useful work. In other words, the success of inter-American economic
collaboration depends on the concrete conditions of each individual case and

on their appreciation by all of the governments concerned. The mere existence of inter-American machinery to deal with economic problems does not automatically mean that there will be a steady progress in law and order in the economic arena, for it is not the scientifically ascertained requirements of the general welfare of mankind but the interests and policies of individual states in this hemisphere that are the essential factors in determining inter-American economic collaboration.

SOCIAL CO-OPERATION IN THE HEMISPHERE

It is almost impossible to draw a clear line between an economic approach and a social approach to the attainment of conditions of internal prosperity and general well-being in any society, because there must be a large measure of fusion between economic development and social advancement. It can, perhaps, be said that inter-American social co-operation can be distinguished from economic co-operation in that the latter is concerned with national and international development relating to human, industrial, agricultural, and mineral resources, while the former is concerned with the physical, mental, and emotional well-being of the individual citizen in his ever changing environment.

It is not surprising, in view of the long tradition of individualism in this hemisphere, that only after World War II did the inter-American system assign major importance to the creation of machinery for international collaboration in the social fields. The exception was the problem of health, which, from the time of the Second Conference in 1901,[56] has appeared regularly on conference agendas. The present Pan American Health Organization, formerly the Pan American Sanitary Bureau, is the oldest international health organization in the world, having been founded in 1902.[57] It maintains close working relations with the national public health services of member countries and also serves as regional organization for the World Health Organization.[58] Its activities have ranged from unending fights against communicable diseases, the strengthening of national health programs and services, and the training of public health workers, to the sponsoring of programs for the eradication of hoof-and-mouth disease and tuberculosis in domestic animals.

During the last decade, the inter-American conferences have repeatedly emphasized the principle that economic development and social welfare are inseparable. The Charter of the OAS pledges the member states to "cooperate with one another to achieve just and decent living conditions for their entire populations."[59] The formidable task of implementing the expanded concepts of inter-American social policy and action is carried out through an intricate network of intergovernmental channels. Structurally these consist of the social and welfare system of the OAS including, in addition to the Pan American Health Organization, the Inter-American Economic and Social Council, the Inter-American Institute of Agricultural Sciences, the Inter-American Commission of Women, the Inter-American Children's Institute, and the Inter-American Indian Institute. These also consist of international organizations which have no direct organic relationship to the OAS, such as nongovernmental organizations or organizations adjunct to or complementary to the United Nations.

All persons would agree that programs to promote health, education, housing, and improved labor conditions are necessary to the overall growth of a country; but when such plans compete, as they must, for limited available resources, each one must be carefully assessed in terms of its contribution to economic development and a system of priorities must be established. In this task the OAS plays the role of catalyst: instead of passing judgment on the relative importance of each project in a nation's development program, the international organization brings together technicians and specialists who exchange views, experiences, and advice so that each government can establish its own system of priorities. The OAS also sponsors community development programs and other forms of technical assistance, carries on literacy and health campaigns, and runs training centers for technicians in agriculture, rural education, evaluation of natural resources, housing, statistics, social sciences, business administration, social services, and sanitation.

The projects developed and sponsored by the OAS are designed to help people solve their own problems—that is, to become contributing members of society rather than to depend upon society to take care of them. In addition to the promotion of general welfare, the OAS seeks to nurture through education and shared experience the feeling of interdependence of all the peoples of the Americas. This broad focus makes for an infinite variety of service proposals and it has, consequently, been necessary for the OAS to resist the temptation to embark on an unmanageable series of undertakings of insufficient impact or of questionable suitability. Instead of establishing inter-American bodies which have directly administered and managed field programs, doing jobs through their own personnel and with their own budgetary resources, the work of the OAS machinery has primarily been of a more modest nature. In the area of social co-operation, the OAS has tended to stress fact-finding, research into the nature and magnitude of problems, idea-sharing, sponsorship of consultation among experts and responsible officials of national governments, encouragement of standardization and harmonization of national social aims and policies, with a small measure of direct technical and educational aid thrown in.

While the reports of both the regular and the specialized inter-American conferences generally contain resounding pronouncements relating to the field of social co-operation, most of the American countries take the position that these objectives are directions addressed to the political and legislative departments of signatory governments, and that domestic administrators and judges are not legally bound thereby in the absence of internal implementing legislation. For example, at the August, 1961, Punta del Este meeting, the Alliance for Progress set ambitious social goals:[60] six years of free schooling for all children, literacy for fifty million now illiterate, eradication of malaria, large-scale public housing, potable water for more than half the population. The Act also pledges the Latin Americas to two basic and controversial structural reforms. One is agrarian reform, that is a redistribution of large land holdings now either in the hands of the government or of a small minority; the other is tax reform, "redistributing the national income in order to benefit those who are most in need." But as matters now stand, there is no international liability for actions inconsistent with these specific objectives, and for this reason there is little to add in a legal analysis of the OAS to the account already given in the section on organizational structure. Undoubtedly, inter-American social institutions have made impressive and increasingly important contributions to hemispheric social progress by means of new devices and special techniques, but their work is decidedly less than fully governed by international public law in terms of the conferment on inter-American social agencies of authority to make decisions, to order compliance, to command resources, and to initiate and conduct activities. In other words, the OAS in the field of social co-operation, has largely been confined to the work of helping governments to help themselves and encouraging member nations to help each other.

INTER-AMERICAN CULTURAL CO-OPERATION

During the colonial period there was almost no intercourse whatsoever between the English and Spanish colonies of this hemisphere. This state of affairs was due chiefly to the monopolistic and isolationist policy of the Spanish Crown, which barred all commercial or intellectual interchange between Spanish possessions and any other country. For a long period after the wars of independence little interest was evinced in establishing cultural interchange between North, Central, and South America. There were many reasons for this mutual lack of interest, the primary one being that neither Spanish America nor the United States had much to offer in the field of letters, arts, and sciences until the middle half of the nineteenth century. Added to this were the common barriers of language, racial and religious prejudices, and different temperamental and cultural traditions.[61] What little cultural exchange existed prior to the twentieth century was purely through person-to-person contact between the intellectuals of the different countries. This individualized contact between leading men of the Western Hemisphere brought about a recognition that international relations between the American republics must be founded on a broader basis than those of trade and commerce—that they must be predicated on an intelligent appreciation by the people of each country of the cultural values of the other nations.

While at the First Inter-American Conference (Washington, 1889-90) problems dealing with matters relating to education, literature, and the arts and sciences were not even brought up for discussion, the turn of the century brought with it a growing concern over intellectual co-operation. At the Second Inter-American Conference held in Mexico City (1901-2),[62] a recommendation was approved creating an international archeological commission; a convention relating to the exchange of official, scientific, literary and industrial publications was signed; and a convention on the practice of learned professions, under which citizens of any country were permitted to exercise their professions in the territory of any of the other signatory states, was drawn up.[63] The 1906 Conference at Rio de Janeiro referred specifically to this latter convention, confirming it and recommending its immediate ratification. At the Fourth Conference in Buenos Aires (1910),[64] a resolution was adopted recommending the interchange of professors and students. At these four early conferences consideration was also given to the question of copyrights, but the approach was primarily from the standpoint of the protection of property rights rather than the stimulation of intellectual exchange.[65]

Since the Fifth Conference in 1923,[66] resolutions, recommendations, and conventions in the field of intellectual co-operation have been passed in increasing numbers, either urging official action by the respective governments or encouraging unofficial entities to take an active part in the important task of promoting inter-American understanding. While most of these resolutions, recommendations, and conventions have emanated directly from the inter-American conferences, a number of them have resulted from meetings of a purely cultural nature, such as the First American Conference of National Committees on Intellectual Cooperation, which took place in Santiago, Chile, in 1939,[67] or the First Conference of Ministers and Directors of Education of the American Republics held in Panama in 1943.[68] The chief means by which the general policies agreed upon at the general conferences were carried into effect were the Pan American Scientific Congresses, of which the first was held in 1909;[69] the Division of Intellectual Cooperation of the Pan American Union, which functioned until 1948 as the central permanent body in this field;[70] and the Pan American Institute of Geography and History, created in 1929 as an organ of co-operation between geographic and historical societies.[71] Thus some of the documents resulting from these meetings promoted action and developed institutions that today play an important part in the life of the continent; others have been outmoded by time and the increasing complexity of situations; while there are still others that await attention and execution.

Beginning with the Charter of Bogotá and its complementary documents, there was evidence of a new concern with cultural co-operation. One of the essential purposes of the Organization of American States is declared to be the promotion of cultural development, and the Charter acknowledges that the spiritual unity of the continent is based on respect for the cultural values of the American countries and requires their close co-operation for the high purposes of civilization.[72] Furthermore, the member states agree to promote, in accordance with their constitutional provisions and their material resources, the exercise of the right to education, stating that elementary education shall be compulsory and wihout cost when provided by the state, and that higher education shall be available to all, without distinction as to race, nationality, sex, language, creed, or social condition.[73] Member states also undertake to facilitate free cultural interchange by every medium of expression.[74]

Probably the chief interest at Bogotá in cultural matters related to the creation of the Inter-American Cultural Council as an organ of the Council of the OAS. The Charter of Bogotá provides that the Inter-American Cultural Council is "to promote friendly relations and mutual understanding among the American peoples in order to strengthen the peaceful sentiments that have characterized the evolution of America, through the promotion of education, scientific and cultural exchange."[75] Provision is also made in the Charter for the organization and functioning of the Committee for Cultural Action, which serves as the permanent subcommittee of the Inter-American Cultural Council. The members of the Committee for Cultural Action must be specialists in educational or cultural matters, and the seat of the committee is Mexico City.

The first meeting of the Inter-American Cultural Council took place in September, 1951, in Mexico City.[76] Among other actions taken at this meeting, the Cultural Council requested the Pan American Union to prepare a preliminary draft of a treaty to be known as "The Cultural Charter of America," the purpose being to assemble in a single document the many cultural standards established in inter-American cultural resolutions, recommendations, and conventions reached at inter-American meetings—both general and specialized. It was suggested that this Draft Cultural Charter be presented to the Tenth Inter-American Conference.

As the work of the Pan American Union in this field was not completed by the time the American republics met in Caracas in 1954, the Tenth Conference resolved that the Pan American Union was to proceed with its work on the preliminary draft, taking into account American cultural values of differing origins (which are to be incorporated in a declaration of principles), the cultural ideals proclaimed in the Charter of Bogotá and in other declarations of cultural co-operation approved by American conferences and Meetings of Ministers of Foreign Affairs, and resolutions by other bodies reflecting the increased need for intellectual understanding.[77] When completed this preliminary draft was to be transmitted to the Committee for Cultural Action, the permanent organ of the Inter-American Cultural Council, for further consideration, and then to the Inter-American Cultural Council, which, if it approved the Charter, should present it to the Eleventh Conference of American States for signature and ratification.

The Tenth Conference also adopted a "Convention for the Promotion of Inter-American Cultural Relations"[78] which was signed by the delegates of all the countries at the conference. This Convention, which is a revision of a similar convention adopted in 1936 and ratified by seventeen American republics, was concerned with the further exchange of fellowships for postgraduate students, teachers, and other persons of equivalent cultural attainments; sought to promote more effective interchange of university professors and experts in special fields; and requested the Pan American Union to increase its co-ordinating functions designed to insure more satisfactory operation of the system of cultural exchange. This Caracas Cultural Convention will enter into force between ratifying states immediately as the respective instruments of ratification are deposited with the Pan American Union.

The many proposals submitted and the number of resolutions adopted by the Tenth Conference in the field of education reflect the importance which is attached to the need for promoting general education in the American republics. It was recognized that while the need may vary from country to country, the solution of educational problems is basic to the strengthening of democratic institutions and the realization of an ever increasing measure of social and economic welfare. The adoption of resolutions urging nations to intensify their national campaigns against illiteracy and endeavoring to co-ordinate them with the activities of the OAS in this field; recommending to the governments the establishment of special educational centers for the training of women in rural areas; requesting the Committee for Cultural Action to undertake studies on vocational education in member countries; recommending the recognition of the equivalence of academic degrees; and urging the governments to lend their support to the development of demonstration libraries were typical of ways and means sought by the conference to tie the continent more tightly together by increased educational advancement.

Prior to the Tenth Conference, various forums of the Organization of American States pointed out the need for a review of the status of existing and contemplated programs in the cultural field. The assessment would have as its purpose the selection of areas of cultural co-operation in which activities should be undertaken and the assigning of priorities. Policy guidance of this nature was considered essential to the development of sound, balanced programs on the part of the agencies of the OAS, and to the promotion of co-ordinated cultural action in national and regional spheres. While the Tenth Conference did not succeed in tracing as complete a blueprint for future action as was needed, it did reach some significant decisions affording guidance to the governments, the Council of the OAS, and the Inter-American Cultural Council in the preparation and carrying out of their cultural programs. The "Declaration on Cultural Cooperation"[79] (Resolution II) sets forth the areas in the educational, scientific, and cultural fields in which they are urged to intensify their efforts as well as the forms which such efforts should take. In Resolution VII,[80] entitled "Inter-American Cultural Organizations," the conference recommended greater utilization of the cultural organs of the OAS and an increased effort by the Council of the OAS to improve the functioning and co-ordination of its cultural organs; and listed a series of points emphasizing co-ordination and the establishment of priorities which the Inter-American Cultural Council should bear in mind in developing its program for the future.

As a supplement to action on the regional level, the Tenth Conference adopted a resolution (IX)[81] recommending to the republics that they encourage and facilitate the efforts of private organizations engaged in educational, scientific, and cultural exchange.

The Inter-American Cultural Council, at its First Meeting in Mexico City in 1951, had designated São Paulo, Brazil, as the site of its Second Meeting. When the government of Brazil informed the Council that, for various reasons, it would be impossible to offer the necessary facilities for the meeting to be held in São Paulo, Brazil, the Inter-American Cultural Council accepted an invitation from the government of Peru to hold it in Lima, where it took place from May 3 to 12, 1956.[82] At this meeting the Cultural Council passed a total of thirty-four resolutions and recommendations establishing a program of cultural action for the OAS and presenting a series of changes in the Statutes of the Inter-American Cultural Council for consideration by the Council of the OAS. It also assigned to the Committee for Cultural Action nineteen studies to be completed by the time of the Third Meeting of the Inter-American Cultural Council.

Under Article 75 of the Charter of the OAS, it was the duty of the Second Meeting of the Cultural Council to designate the site of the Third Meeting. The cities of Bogotá and Montevideo were proposed. Since, however, an absolute majority of votes could not be obtained as required by Article 26 of the Statutes of the Inter-American Cultural Council,[83] it was agreed to submit the question to the Council of the OAS for decision. At the end of 1957, the government of Uruguay informed the Secretary General of the Organization that it agreed in principle that the Third Meeting of the Cultural Council be held in Montevideo. Nevertheless, on April 10, 1959, it asked through its representative on the Council of the Organization to be relieved from that agreement. For that reason, the Council of the OAS accepted on July 8, 1959, the offer of the government of the United States to hold the meeting in San Juan, Puerto Rico, November 22 to December 2, 1959.[84]

During the Third Meeting the Cultural Council reviewed the activities of the General Secretariat of the OAS in education, social and natural sciences, philosophy, letters, music, and the visual arts, and the development of libraries and bibliographic services. It also examined the studies prepared by the Committee for Cultural Action since the Second Meeting, covering such topics as school organization and administration, the teaching of literature, prejudices hindering inter-American understanding and solidarity, pre-school education, inter-American exhibits, the promotion of literature, the re-education of maladjusted and abnormal youth, ownership of artistic property and copyright, the exchange of persons, and representative books of the Americas. At the end of the meeting it assigned twenty-one new or continued studies to its permanent committee.

The Cultural Council called for the establishment of a special OAS Council committee to study the possibility and advisability of creating an inter-American fund to give financial help to public or private agencies for building schools and universities and for other educational projects on all levels. It also recommended a Pan American seminar on the history, structure, functions, and aims of the university; continuance of seminars on social sciences; and new seminars on the teaching of natural sciences and mathematics.

Throughout the Third Meeting, it was pointed out that there had been neglect of the OAS cultural programs because of the organization's stepped up economic and technological activities which left but a slim budget for cultural affairs. The aims of the Cultural Council are generally accomplished through research and publications, exhibits and concerts, seminars, meetings and conferences, informational services, the interchange of persons and ideas, and direct technical assistance in solving specific cultural problems of member countries. All of these activities require adequate financing if progress is to be obtained in the OAS's objective of promoting by co-operative action the cultural advancement of its member countries. The Third Meeting therefore recommended, in addition to increased financing for cultural affairs, that there be an articulation of the programs of cultural development with those of economic development.

The guiding principle of inter-American cultural co-operation is to provide for international contacts other than those established through political and diplomatic agents. The Cultural Council tries to maintain direct contact between persons who have acquired special knowledge in cultural pursuits interesting to the inter-American community, thereby bringing together under the auspices of the OAS the people of the hemisphere rather than just their political leaders. But it must be recognized that many of the really vital cultural problems do not by their very nature lend themselves to easy settlement by formal meetings at which treaties are signed establishing a unified cultural compact for the area. It is generally possible to give effect to cultural aims programed by the Cultural Council only through the internal machinery of a member government.

This means that on the whole cultural co-operation is in the nature of mutual help rather than reciprocal contact. This tends to make the Cultural Council a clearinghouse rather than an agency through which the hemisphere administers its common cultural affairs under the rule of hemispherically binding law.

JURIDICAL CO-OPERATION IN THE AMERICAS

The importance of both codifying international law principles and establishing uniform principles of internal law has long been accepted by the American nations. At the Second International Conference of American States, held in Mexico in 1901-2, a treaty was signed that provided for the appointment of a Committee of Jurists to draft codes of public and private international law which should govern the relations among the American nations.[85] Although that committee was never formed, because of lack of ratification of the treaty, the idea did not die and at the Third Conference another treaty was signed providing for the creation of an International Commission of American Jurists composed of one representative of each of the ratifying countries.[86]

The Fifth Conference, held at Santiago, Chile, in 1923, reorganized the commission, increasing the number of delegates from one to two for each state, and directing that its studies and conclusions be submitted to the Sixth Conference. The commission met at Rio de Janeiro in 1927, and at this meeting adopted twelve projects which were presented to the Sixth Conference at Habana in 1928. Seven of those projects, including the Bustamante Code on Private International Law, served as the basis for treaties signed at this conference.[87]

Encouraged by the work of the International Commission of Jurists, the Habana Conference decided to increase the codification agencies by the establishment of three Permanent Commissions, one at Rio on Public International Law, another at Montevideo on Private International Law, and another at Habana on Comparative Legislation and Uniformity of Legislation. It was also recommended that when it was considered advisable, a Commission of Jurists might be constituted to draft a project of uniform civil legislation for all the American nations.

At the Seventh International Conference in 1933,[88] the representatives voted to abolish the three Permanent Commissions created at Habana and establish the Commission on Experts on the Codification of International Law, composed of seven members. The purpose of this commission was to act as a subcommittee of the International Commission of Jurists and to do the preparatory work for it. At the same time the Seventh Conference provided for the establishment of National Codification Commissions and, recognizing the need for a general secretariat for the administration of the work of codification, recommended the creation of a Juridical Office in the Pan American Union to serve in that capacity.

At Buenos Aires in 1936 and at Lima in 1938 attempts were made to co-ordinate the work of the different international commissions and national commissions. The Buenos Aires Conference re-established the three permanent commissions abolished by the Seventh Conference. The Eighth Conference, attempting to facilitate and speed the work of codification, again revised the procedure, placing special emphasis on the co-ordination of the labors of the different entities and determining the specific duties that each should perform. At the same time this conference created the Permanent Committee of Jurists for the Unification of the Civil and Commercial Laws of America, with head-quarters in Lima.[89]

The outbreak of war in Europe in 1939 led to the creation of the Inter-American Neutrality Committee, composed of seven experts in the field of international law. In 1942, at the Third Meeting of Consultation of Ministers of Foreign Affairs, the Neutrality Committee became the Inter-American Juridi-cal Committee, and among the duties assigned to it was that of "developing and coordinating the work of codification of international law."[90]

In spite of the vast amount of work done by certain codification agencies while they were in active operation, by the time the Inter-American Conference on Problems of War and Peace met in Mexico in 1945 it was realized that the system needed overhauling. The commissions were composed of jurists who were unable to devote all their time and attention to the work of codification because of their own professional activities. Furthermore, there was considerable duplication in the studies carried on by the various agencies, while there were vast gaps untouched by any of the agencies. The Commission of Experts for the Codification of International Law stated in its report submitted to the Eighth Conference that "the present system of codification suffers from excessive and unnecessary complication that, instead of helping and stimulating the work of codification, hinders it and makes it difficult." The Inter-American Juridical Committee in its report on the reorganization of the codification agencies, sub-mitted to the governments in 1944, declared, "The Committee has reached the conclusion that, to carry forward the work efficiently and systematically, it will first be necessary to coordinate the many agencies created at one time or another by the American governments to undertake the work of codification."[91] The Mexico City Conference therefore passed a resolution providing that the Inter-American System should be strengthened through the creation of new agencies or the elimination or adaptation of existing agencies, specifying and co-ordinat-ing their functions as among themselves and with the world organization.[92]

Under the authority of this resolution, the Governing Board prepared a draft on the establishment of an Inter-American Council of Jurists, which with almost no changes was adopted at Bogotá. Article 57 of the Charter of the OAS established the Inter-American Council of Jurists as one of the organs of the Council and its basic functions were set forth in Article 67: "to serve as an advisory body on juridical matters; to promote the development and codification of public and private international law; and to study the possibility of attaining uniformity in the legislation of the various American countries, insofar as it may appear desirable."

The Inter-American Juridical Committee is the permanent committee of the Council of Jurists. Its task is that of research and development of draft projects to be presented to the Council of Jurists for consideration. It is a nine-member committee whose personnel is selected from specific countries desig-nated by the Inter-American Conference. While the Council of Jurists meets when convoked by the Council of the OAS, generally every two or three years, the Inter-American Juridical Committee meets every year in Rio for a working session of at least three months.[93]

The Department of International Law of the Pan American Union is the Secretariat of the Council of Jurists, and the director of the Department is its executive secretary.[94] The director assists in the preparation of the agenda of meetings of the Council of Jurists, publishes the approved minutes and the definite texts formulated by the Council, publishes and transmits to the governments the studies and reports prepared by the Juridical Committee, and maintains contact with the members of the Council of Jurists during the periods between the meetings. The Department of International Law also acts as a clearinghouse of information for the Council of Jurists, in that it obtains opinions and observations on codification and unification of law by various national and international groups regarding studies prepared by the Juridical Committee.

The First Meeting of the Council of Jurists[95] was held in Rio de Janeiro in 1950 with an agenda whose main topics were based on resolutions of the Bogotá Conference. In pursuance of these resolutions, the Council of Jurists had been called upon to prepare a draft convention and report on the recognition of de facto governments, and also a draft agreement to eliminate the use of passports and to establish an American identification certificate. It found it impossible, however, to come to an agreement upon the fundamental conditions of recognition of de facto governments, and the topic was referred back to the Juridical Committee for further study. The Council had before it a report of its permanent committee pointing out the difficulties of the problem of the elimination of the use of passports under the existing political conditions. The decision was reached to refer the report, without comment, to the Inter-American Economic and Social Council, which had been entrusted with the preparation of the draft agreement jointly with the Council of Jurists.

The two other topics suggested by the Ninth Conference were the consideration of a draft statute providing for the creation and function of an Inter-American Court to Protect the Rights of Man, and a study of "The Right of Resistance." On the first the Juridical Committee's report stated that it was not feasible to create the proposed court because of the lack of substantive law on the subject and because the establishment of such a court would involve a radical transformation of the constitutional systems of the American states. This report was accepted and approved by the Council of Jurists and referred to the Council of the OAS. The Juridical Committee had also prepared a study on the "Right of Resistance" which stated that "the so-called 'right of resistance' is not yet recognized in international juridical order, and the latter does not have at its command adequate means to protect the exercise thereof." On this, the Council of Jurists did no more than accept the report of the Juridical Committee.

A fifth technical subject came before the Council of Jurists at the instance of the Council of the OAS. The latter, confronted in 1949 with a question as to its competence to discuss a case of diplomatic asylum, found itself in the presence of conflicting views on this point and adopted a resolution requesting the Council of Jurists to prepare a technical study of the question. The decision of the Council of Jurists was to forward to the Council of the OAS the relevant documents and to recommend to the Juridical Committee that it continue study of the subject.

At its first meeting the Council of Jurists also adopted a resolution on "Development and Codification of Public International Law and Private International Law and the Attainment of Uniformity of Legislation among the American States," which assigned various specific studies to the Juridical Committee and requested the executive secretary of the Council of the OAS to serve as liaison officer with the International Law Commission of the United Nations.

The Second Meeting of the Council of Jurists was held in Buenos Aires[96] in 1953. The issues of the recognition of *de facto* governments and the creation of an Inter-American Court to Protect the Rights of Man were again on the agenda. In neither case was the Council of Jurists prepared to take action. Over the protest of the delegates of Brazil and Cuba, the Council of Jurists held that to draw up a treaty on the subject of recognition would be premature, and it referred the question to the Tenth Inter-American Conference. In the matter of the Inter-American Court, the Council of Jurists reaffirmed the stand taken at its first meeting, and in addition over the objection of the delegate from Guatemala, referred the subject to the Council of the OAS for possible inclusion in the agenda of the Tenth Conference.

The Council of the OAS and the Fourth Meeting of Consultation of Ministers of Foreign Affairs had referred to the Council of Jurists the question of "strengthening the effective exercise of democracy." But as the Juridical Committee had been unable to undertake the preliminary studies, the Council of Jurists postponed consideration of the topic. Two other topics assigned by the Council of the OAS were carefully considered. A Draft Convention on the Regimen of Political Exiles, Asylees and Refugees, prepared by the Juridical Committee, was revised and approved by the delegations of all the participating countries except the United States. A Draft Convention on Diplomatic Asylum was also heatedly discussed, as the jurists were in disagreement over the provision which permitted the state granting asylum to have the final decision over the classification of whether or not the asylee fell within the scope of political delinquency. While the draft convention was adopted, dissents thereto were lodged by the delegations of Brazil, Peru, and the Dominican Republic. The United States refrained from signing, in accordance with its traditional position on the subject.

The Juridical Committee, acting in compliance with the resolution of the First Meeting of the Council of Jurists, had prepared a draft convention on the system of territorial waters and related questions and a second draft convention on the nationality and status of stateless persons. In neither case did the Council of Jurists feel it wise to approve the drafts without further study of the subject by the Juridical Committee. Moreover, in respect to the system of territorial waters, a difference of opinion arose as to the desirability of asserting that there existed a general principle of international law that the littoral state controlled the resources of the continental shelf.

Three topics in the field of private international law were discussed. The revision of the Bustamante Code, upon which the Juridical Committee had prepared a first and second revised report, was referred by the Council of Jurists back to the Juridical Committee for further study. A Draft Uniform Law on the International Sale of Personal Property was revised and then forwarded to the secretary general of the OAS with the request that it be submitted to the national codification commissions and other interested bodies for their observations. Similar action was taken with respect to a Draft Convention on International Co-operation in Judicial Procedures.

At the Third Meeting of the Council of Jurists, held in Mexico City in 1956,[97] the jurists took under consideration various items entrusted to them for study by the Tenth Inter-American Conference. Among its decisions the Council of Jurists requested its permanent committee to complete a study of the contribution the American continent had made to the development and codification of the principles of international law governing the responsibility of the state. It also approved, after debate, a draft convention on extradition, and transmitted the same to the Council of the OAS with clarifying statements and reservations by the Dominican Republic, Uruguay, the United States, Mexico, Peru, and Nicaragua. It prepared and submitted to the Council of the OAS a series of draft rules applicable to reservations to multilateral treaties, to be forwarded to member governments for comment, and it requested the Juridical Committee to continue its study of the problems arising from such reservations.

As requested by the Tenth Conference, the Council of Jurists set forth its opinion concerning the juridical regime of the sea, so that this could be studied by a scheduled inter-American specialized conference on the conservation of natural resources of the continental shelf and marine waters which was to be held in the Dominican Republic in March, 1956.

The Council of Jurists recommended that the American republics, to the extent practicable, adopt in their legislation the draft uniform law on inter-American commercial arbitration which it had approved, and requested the secretary general of the OAS to urge the respective American republics to give publicity to this draft law. It also requested the secretary general to ask the republics to entrust to the proper individual the study of the general problem of international co-operation in judicial matters and to ask the republics to submit a report on the principal problems with which they were confronted in the field of inter-American judicial co-operation, as well as their legislation and practices with relation to that subject. And the Council of Jurists concluded their third meeting by designating Santiago, Chile, as the seat of the Fourth Meeting.

This fourth meeting was held in 1959.[98] At that time the Council of Jurists submitted to the Council of the OAS for presentation, if it considers it appropriate, to the Eleventh Inter-American Conference, a draft of a protocol to the existing conventions on diplomatic asylum, and requested its permanent committee to prepare a study and a draft convention on political offenses supplementing the conventions on asylum. It also submitted to the Council of the OAS for transmission to the Eleventh Conference a draft convention on extradition.

The Council of Jurists resolved to continue the study of the possibility of revision of the Inter-American Code of Private International Law, generally referred to as the Bustamante Code, and urged governments which had made reservations to the code or which had not ratified the convention to indicate in detail the nature of the conflict that might exist between provisions of the code and those of their respective domestic legislation, and to propose, to the extent possible, the manner of resolving the conflict.

With reference to the immunity of state-owned vessels, it accepted the study of the Inter-American Juridical Committee stating that the Brussels Convention of April 10, 1926, and its protocol of May 24, 1934, contained the juridical principles universally accepted on the subject, and under these circumstances the promotion of a special inter-American regional law on the subject did not seem justified. Therefore it resolved to consider complete the study on this topic by the Inter-American Juridical Committee.

It prepared a group of rules to be considered by the Eleventh Inter-American Conference relating to reservations to multilateral treaties, and suggested to the Council of the OAS that it convoke a special session of the Inter-American Juridical Committee to cover such legal topics as might be needed by the Eleventh Conference for its consideration.

The Fourth Meeting also prepared a draft convention with various alternative provisions concerning the substantive materials pertinent to human rights— as well as the institutional and procedural parts of these rights, including the creation and functioning of an Inter-American Court of Human Rights and an Inter-American Commission for the Protection of Human Rights—which is to be submitted to the Eleventh Conference by the Council of the OAS. It assigned to the Juridical Committee for study the topic "possible juridical relationship between respect for human rights and the effective exercise of representative democracy, and the right to put into motion the machinery of existing American international law in force."

Since the beginning of this century, the inter-American system has wrestled with the problem of codification of international law. Some of the best legal minds of the continent have devoted years of earnest effort to the project, but on the whole the results have been meager, and one may well question whether the OAS's program for codification is self-evidently praise-worthy and worthy of continued political and juristic support.

Codification of inter-American international law entails two processes: first, the scientific determination of the law, and second, the achievement of acceptance of the law so defined by the American nations. In both of these processes there has been one major stumbling block. Each member of a gathering of inter-American jurists under the auspices of the OAS, whether it be in the Council of Jurists or the Juridical Committee, is bound to pay regard to the needs, the feelings, and the wishes of his government. Yet international law does not alter in accordance with the aspirations of the inhabitants of any particular country. It is a branch of legal science whose canons cannot be rewritten from day to day in accordance with any standards so shifting and variable. Instead of a scientific determination of the law, one finds inter-American codifying bodies directing their major efforts to drafts of treaties which embody rules which are acceptable to all parties—a process which is of questionable scientific integrity. And even in those few instances where a scientific determination of the law has been achieved, new uncertainties have arisen in that acceptance of the law so defined. As pointed out by Professor Julius Stone,[99] first, parties to the new treaties may attach reservations to their ratification and enter caveats on the rule as embodied in the treaty which they could not effectively impose against a customary rule. Second, once the rule is embodied in a treaty, its life may come to depend, in practice, on the life of the treaty. Third, any treaty formulation, whatever its pretensions to certainty and clarity, is subject inevitably to a vast network of doubt, conflict, and confusion which accompanies the process of interpretation of treaty texts. And finally, any treaty reformulation also exposes the former customary rules to all the hazards resulting from the chronic doubts affecting many elementary questions touching the legal nature and force of treaties.

All these factors have recently led to a recognition on the part of international legal publicists[100] that while it is imperative that the task of codification should be attempted it is of equal importance that it should be independent of governments, not only in its composition but also in other relevant aspects. Effective codification activities, even on a regional level, must operate on a plan which transcends national interests. How this can best be accomplished remains one of the major problems facing inter-American juridical co-operation.

Once the codifying agency, which is not composed of representatives of governments, has made a scientific determination of the law which is dictated by the interests of the inter-American community, by the rationally conceived interests of the American states and by the requirements of a progressive development of international law as an instrument of inter-American co-operation and as the protector of the rights of the individual as conceived as the ultimate subject and beneficiary of all law, then the problem arises as to the best manner in which to obtain acceptance of that law. As we have pointed out, the placing of such codification in treaty form can lead to further confusion. It might be necessary to do no more than publish the codification, with the hope that once a carefully documented nonpolitical instrument is available, it will directly influence the people of the hemisphere and will act as a restraining instrument against those governments who would seek to subvert international law for immediate political ends.

CHAPTER XX

EPILOGUE

It has been recognized[1] that there are five prerequisites necessary for an effective international organization: (1) a viable international community; (2) peaceful settlement of disputes; (3) rational pattern of membership in the organization; (4) ability to legislate for the members of the organization; and (5) enforcement of international legal obligations. Does the OAS fulfil these?

A VIABLE INTERNATIONAL COMMUNITY

Schwartzenberger[2] sets out the criterion by which a society may be distinguished from a community by stating that society is the means to an end, while community is an end in itself. Society is based on interest and fear, whereas a community requires self-sacrifice and love. One is founded on distrust, whereas the other presupposes mutual trust. The members of a society remain isolated in spite of their association. The members of a community are united in spite of their individual existence. Therefore a sense of community is much more than simply verbal attachment to any number of similar or identical values. Rather it is a matter of mutual sympathy and loyalties; of trust and consideration; of at least a partial identification in terms of self images and interests; of ability to predict each other's behavior and ability to act in accordance with that prediction. A perfect community requires perpetual attention, communication, perception of needs, and responsiveness. It cannot be a condition of static agreement, but must be a dynamic process—a process of social learning. It results in mutual responsiveness to the needs of the members, leading to appropriate political and economic action.

That there is an essential unity in the new world has been reiterated for more than a century. It has been assumed that there exist among the American states some sentiment of solidarity which sets them apart from the other nations of the world and some commonly shared values as to the proper role of man in society. It has been declared that the American nations form a group bound together by a combination of geographical, political, cultural, historical, and spiritual ties. In the words of Dr. Alfaro: "Pan Americanism as a primary conception is essentially a sentiment, a peculiar sentiment of unity, of solidarity, that has existed from the beginning of our international life and survives in spite of the many forces that have worked or do work against it."[3]

But of late there have arisen strong voices of dissent which claim there is no cohesive capacity in the centripetal forces of the Pan American system.[4] These dissenters point out that neither in political, cultural, nor economic aspects is there a true hemispheric unity of purpose. The continent is divided into two sharply differentiated cultural, politicial, and economic zones, which have opposing problems, interests, and aims. Furthermore, the essential norms of political co-operation have not formed bonds of solidarity sufficiently strong to create even a weak hemispheric community. The so-called Western Hemisphere Idea is in fact merely a recognition that there exists a loosely organized hemispheric society with which the American states co-operate only when there are immediate tangible benefits to be gained.

The validity of such accusations is hard to deny, and the most dangerous charge is that of lack of spiritual unity. For it is the strength and character of its spiritual unity that makes or unmakes an international community. The narrowing or enfeeblement of its spirit leads to ultimate community dissolution. But still it should be established that a viable inter-American community is of necessity a mixed concept. It involves both facts about the ideals which its members espouse and facts about their actual conduct and attitudes.

While Latin America and the United States may have divergent and at times inconsistent interests, in many instances they have accepted common standards of actions, have recognized and observed accepted rules, and have established institutions and procedures which have been followed for the good of the community even when immediate national interests might be injured.

To claim that the hemisphere is divided into two spheres is fallacious, for there exists as great a divergency among the Latin American nations themselves as there does between any one of them and the United States. The Latin American nations do not possess a common outlook, or highly similar views within a social democratic framework. Latin American economies tend to be competitive rather than complementary. Their governments run the spectrum from right to left in every possible sense, which makes international co-operation the more difficult. Their cultural orientations vary sharply from nation to nation, there is mistrust and hostility between them, and excessive nationalism has led to an inability to overcome bias and prejudice.

Certainly it cannot be said that the illiterate masses of Latin America or even the semiliterate masses of North America are driven by a spirit of inter-American co-operation. Nevertheless, there has always been an awareness among the leaders and the political elite in all the nations of this hemisphere that inter-American co-operation has been beneficial. This awareness has established a habit of international co-operation leading to the gradual enmeshing of American states in procedures of collective deliberations. These leaders recognize that although the inter-American system is not a perfectly functioning community, although it has serious weaknesses and has suffered defeats, potent forces still exist to challenge its members toward an ideal still imperfectly formed and realized.

In looking back over the history of the inter-American system, one cannot but be impressed by the fact that it has undergone a vast process of development leading to the recognition that there is a preponderance of uniting over dividing interests in this hemisphere. This history of past attainment makes possible a viable vision of present and future growth, but the long and tedious road which has led to today's OAS must act as a warning to those who expect too much of the organization and thereby pass from the illusion of easy progress to the complete denial of progress.

PEACEFUL SETTLEMENT OF DISPUTES

The OAS is concerned with all phases of hemispheric life: economic, social, cultural, humanitarian, and political. But the political field is the most important, for it is precisely in this area that international organization succeeds or fails.

Without international peace, all other forms of international co-operation are immaterial. A carefully planned program of functional amalgamation among member countries of the OAS may be a useful approach toward an eventual more far-reaching integration among them, but it should be recognized that functionalism does not guarantee peace in the Americas, which, in the long run, is the most compelling reason for the existence of the inter-American system.

The procedures which have evolved over the years of inter-American co-operation for the settlement of conflicts may seem at times confused by a multiplicity of declarations and an overabundance of unratified treaties. Nevertheless, as long as the nations of the Western Hemisphere were convinced that the main essential of inter-Americanism was to preserve its unity, they could secure the necessary collective action to act effectively in almost all cases of inter-American disharmony. The mere recognition of this ability to act collectively has held smoldering disputes in abeyance for many years. Because of historical conditions and traditions there remain latent problems in the Americas which may simmer and flare sporadically but which, with a little courage and a lot of perseverence, can eventually be settled without resort to armed force.

But the fateful question for the future of the OAS is whether it will prove effective in maintaining in this continent the ideal of democratic government. If it fails in this, even if it continues for a time its secondary activities in the economic, social, and cultural fields, the organization must collapse. The acid test will be whether the members of the OAS, in it and through it, will be able to stop the wave of Russian colonialism now established in this hemisphere.

The ideological tripolarization of the world into the communist camp, the anticommunist camp, and the noncommunist camp is something that cannot be lightly dismissed. Of the three ideologies only communism seeks immediate universalism. On the whole the anticommunist nations, most of which either are democracies or aspire to democratic government, are nonaggressive except in the ultimate instance where aggressiveness is necessary to protect their way of life. The noncommunist nations are seeking to establish a national identity and a national image and are also generally nonaggressive. In ringing proclamations and high-sounding ideals they staunchly proclaim a neutral position between communism and anticommunism; but when put to the final test, they generally crumble before the massive power and propaganda onslaught of communist imperialism. This poses a double threat both for the anticommunist nations and for all of mankind. Not only must the anticommunists guard against the aggressive and powerfully supported ideology of communism on a multitude of fronts in the anticommunist world, but some effort must be made to save the noncommunists from their own blindness, which can only lead them to succumbing to the ruthless and incredibly ingenious devices of Russian totalitarianism.

As long as many members of the OAS fail to come to grips with the substance of the communist problem, the OAS is sitting on a rumbling volcano. That a unified OAS could rid the hemisphere of communist imperialism and could prevent its further encroachment in this area of the world is unquestionable. That it has not done so to date does not nullify the organization, but its failure in face of the advancing enemy is seriously weakening it to a point where eventual resistance may come too late.

RATIONAL PATTERN OF MEMBERSHIP

Membership in the OAS is open only to the states of the Western Hemisphere willing to ratify the organization's Charter; consequently the OAS is strictly a regional organization. Whether a geographic region as vast as this hemisphere is truly a rational pattern for organizational membership is dependent on a number of factors. Most important of these is its historical growth. The OAS is not a hastily conceived modern alliance but rather a product of slow growth and established tradition. All the members of the inter-American system call themselves "Americans," whether they be from North America, Central America, or South America, and this feeling of uniqueness is an indication that cultural, social, and linguistic handicaps can be overcome by common objectives in a geographic region of great extremes and divergencies.

By limiting its membership, the OAS has been able to focus its attention upon common interests, develop international co-operation along lines directed by specific geographically localized conditions, and increase a sense of continental responsibility by recognizing that propinquity is a source of rapprochement through which the aims of liberty, well-being, and security can be attained.

ABILITY TO LEGISLATE

The political nature of the inter-American community has not rested on a juristic consensus sufficiently strong to embody powers of legislative competence like those of a federal union. Nonetheless, there has been a partial sharing of a sense of justice and of moral values on which law must ultimately rest, and from this there has developed unique experimental work in the inter-American legislative area.

Traditional intergovernmental arrangements established in treaties which preserved all the formal prerogatives of the signatories early proved unfruitful as a means of legislation for all nations of the hemisphere, so other techniques, experiments, and at times improvisations were tried. Conference resolutions and declarations, for example, were used as bases for organizational development, as methods of expressing customary American international law, as tools to induce greater co-operation among the American nations, and as moral, sociological, economic, and political formulations from which regional law developed. While at times there have been different expressions of legal rules and different interpretation of legal doctrine by the members of the OAS, this in no way defeated the existence of an operative normative order accepted by all or most of the members of the inter-American system. Whenever an American state deliberately and consciously broke away from broad areas of agreement on regional law which the other nations of the hemisphere supported, it has done so at a definite price to hemispheric unity.

The limitations of inter-American law do not stem from a lack of techniques adequate to the formulation of the law. They arise from two separate trends. On the one hand, the nations of this hemisphere are still reluctant to encroach upon their national sovereign power by granting greater power to the regional organization. Wishing for or proclaiming the rule of law in inter-American relations does not in fact create an inter-American international law. The American states know well that inter-American regional law is a creature of the members of the community, it is what they make it, and only when the member states realize that their major problems are transnational and need transnational solution, that any losses a member state may suffer in granting greater legislative power to the regional body will be balanced in the long run by advantages based on the overall protection and satisfactions a strong legal hemispheric regional order would continuously furnish them, will more legislative power be granted to the OAS.

The second trend limiting inter-American law is the fact that there is no escape even in this hemisphere from the battle of ideologies now in progress. This ideological battle is causing a deep schism in the ethical foundations of the inter-American community. Every system of law that arises from its own premises must rest on an ethic whose values transcend those of law. But the spiritual confusion in the world has become reflected in the thinking of Western Hemispheric leaders, thereby undermining the ethical basis of American regional law. More and more the political leaders of the American continent are supplanting the principles of solidarity and responsibility by the principles of disunity and irresponsibility.

ENFORCEMENT OF INTER-AMERICAN LEGAL OBLIGATIONS

Respect for the obligations accepted by members of any community is a prerequisite for community survival, and it is always necessary for a community to be able to take action against a member state which flagrantly disregards its community obligations. But no community could exist if it had to enforce all legal obligations, while on the other hand, no community has ever had rules of which the infringement was without some kind of penalty. The efficacy of law does not lie in the percentage of law violations which are punished. On the contrary, if a law is violated it is less efficacious than when it is not violated, for in the latter case it is followed because of its complete acceptance by those whom it controls.

The legal obligations accepted by the members of the OAS can be broadly divided into two categories—those which aim at the development of a sense of mutual well-being among member states and those which aim at maintaining hemispheric peace and security. The first category is a long-range objective which can be slowly nurtured over the years; the second requires instant collective action whenever a serious threat arises.

In developing a sense of mutual well-being, the organization has at its disposal many elastic and sometimes subtle forms of pressure which can be used to assure that member states will abide by their continental legal commitments. Such pressures may not be considered sanctions or enforcement actions in the usual sense of specific measures for securing compliance with the law by a delinquent nation, but the effect may be the same. Thus, the OAS can use the medium of publicity to mold hemispheric public opinion. Its organs may pass resolutions of appeal or reminder, or admonitions addressed to all members generally or when necessary to a specific member. It can give vent to expressions of regret at noncompliance or heap laurels upon those nations which have complied. Its power of investigation or discussion can also be used to promote acceptance of acknowledged obligations. There are, consequently, lodged within the organization, powers and incentives which can be used to promote its aims without resort to measures of a compulsory or insistent nature directed against its members.

But the field of hemispheric peace and security requires a stricter compliance with obligations by all participants, and here, to be successful, the organization has had to resort to other methods, although even in these cases the mere existence of the OAS equipped with means to handle disputes is of value, since the member states can turn to it with a knowledge that there is a forum where their grievances can be aired. The procedures for the settlement of intrahemispheric conflicts developed by the OAS have functioned effectively in almost all instances without resort to direct coercive action.

But it is in the field of extrahemispheric threats that the organization has faltered. If the member nations refuse to accept their obligation to take collective action to keep extracontinental totalitarianisms from this hemisphere, there arise dangerous implications for hemispheric security. No nation in this hemisphere can really be safe from internal aggression, and no nation can be sure that it will not be the next victim. In the long run justification for the OAS must rest on its capacity to provide peace, security, and law-enforcement; and to defend it in terms of success in functional matters is to beg the question.

The pursuit of continental unity of purpose may occasionally meet resistance and lead to strained relationships. Temporary disturbances of unity may nevertheless be only a stage in the necessary progress to greater unification. It is hoped that such is the case today in the inter-American system. But if the antagonisms in fundamental conviction continue, the road to a greater inter-American legal order is closed. The organization has faced great challenges in the past and has survived; perhaps it can again assert a policy of dynamism which can demonstrate the clarity of its vision, its determination, and the adaptability of its institutions so as to face the ideological imperatives before it. The outlook is gloomy—even, to put it mildly, alarming—but we can only hope for better developments than any present indications promise and work toward the expectation that genuine regional legal order will eventually flourish.

APPENDICES

APPENDIX A

CHARTER OF THE ORGANIZATION OF AMERICAN STATES
(CHARTER OF BOGOTA)

IN THE NAME OF THEIR PEOPLES
THE STATES
REPRESENTED AT THE NINTH INTERNATIONAL
CONFERENCE OF AMERICAN STATES,

CONVINCED that the historic mission of America is to offer to man a land of liberty, and a favorable environment for the development of his personality and the realization of his just aspirations;

CONSCIOUS that that mission has already inspired numerous agreements, whose essential value lies in the desire of the American peoples to live together in peace, and, through their mutual understanding and respect for the sovereignty of each one, to provide for the betterment of all, in independence, in equality and under law;

CONFIDENT that the true significance of American solidarity and good neighborliness can only mean the consolidation on this continent, within the framework of democratic institutions, of a system of individual liberty and social justice based on respect for the essential rights of man;

PERSUADED that their welfare and their contribution to the progress and the civilization of the world will increasingly require intensive continental co-operation;

RESOLVED to persevere in the noble undertaking that humanity has conferred upon the United Nations, whose principles and purposes they solemnly reaffirm;

CONVINCED that juridical organization is a necessary condition for security and peace founded on moral order and on justice; and

In accordance with Resolution IX of the Inter-American Conference on Problems of War and Peace, held at Mexico City,

Have Agreed Upon The Following

CHARTER OF THE ORGANIZATION OF AMERICAN STATES

Part One

CHAPTER I: NATURE AND PURPOSES

Article 1
The American States establish by this Charter the international organization that they have developed to achieve an order of peace and justice, to promote their solidarity, to strengthen their collaboration, and to defend their sovereignty, their territorial integrity and their independence. Within the

413

United Nations, the Organization of American States is a regional agency.

Article 2

All American States that ratify the present Charter are Members of the Organization.

Article 3

Any new political entity that arises from the union of several Member States and that, as such, ratifies the present Charter, shall become a Member of the Organization. The entry of the new political entity into the Organization shall result in the loss of membership of each one of the States which constitute it.

Article 4

The Organization of American States, in order to put into practice the principles on which it is founded and to fulfil its regional obligations under the Charter of the United Nations, proclaims the following essential purposes:

a) To strengthen the peace and security of the continent;

b) To prevent possible causes of difficulties and to ensure the pacific settlement of disputes that may arise among the Member States;

c) To provide for common action on the part of those States in the event of aggression;

d) To seek the solution of political, juridical and economic problems that may arise among them; and

e) To promote, by co-operative action, their economic, social and cultural development.

CHAPTER II: PRINCIPLES

Article 5

The American States reaffirm the following principles:

a) International law is the standard of conduct of States in their reciprocal relations;

b) International order consists essentially of respect for the personality, sovereignty and independence of States, and the faithful fulfilment of obligations derived from treaties and other sources of international law;

c) Good faith shall govern the relations between States;

d) The solidarity of the American States and the high aims which are sought through it require the political organization of those States on the basis of the effective exercise of representative democracy;

e) The American States condemn war of aggression: victory does not give rights;

f) An act of aggression against one American State is an act of aggression against all the other American States;

g) Controversies of an international character arising between two or more American States shall be settled by peaceful procedures;

h) Social justice and social security are bases of lasting peace;

i) Economic co-operation is essential to the common welfare and prosperity of the peoples of the continent;

j) The American States proclaim the fundamental rights of the individual without distinction as to race, nationality, creed or sex;

k) The spiritual unity of the continent is based on respect for the cultural values of the American countries and requires their close co-operation for the high purposes of civilization;

l) The education of peoples should be directed toward justice, freedom and peace.

CHAPTER III: FUNDAMENTAL RIGHTS AND DUTIES OF STATES

Article 6

States are juridically equal, enjoy equal rights and equal capacity to exercise these rights, and have equal duties. The rights of each State depend not upon its power to ensure the exercise thereof, but upon the mere fact of its existence as a person under international law.

Article 7

Every American State has the duty to respect the rights enjoyed by every other State in accordance with international law.

Article 8

The fundamental rights of States may not be impaired in any manner whatsoever.

Article 9

The political existence of the State is independent of recognition by other States. Even before being recognized, the State has the right to defend its integrity and independence, to provide for its preservation and prosperity, and consequently to organize itself as it sees fit, to legislate concerning its interests, to administer its services, and to determine the jurisdiction and competence of its courts. The exercise of these rights is limited only by the exercise of the rights of other States in accordance with international law.

Article 10

Recognition implies that the State granting it accepts the personality of the new State, with all the rights and duties that international law prescribes for the two States.

Article 11

The right of each State to protect itself and to live its own life does not authorize it to commit unjust acts against another State.

Article 12

The jurisdiction of States within the limits of their national territory is exercised equally over all the inhabitants, whether nationals or aliens.

Article 13

Each State has the right to develop its cultural, political and economic life freely and naturally. In this free development, the State shall respect the rights of the individual and the principles of universal morality.

Article 14

Respect for and the faithful observance of treaties constitute standards for the development of peaceful relations among States. International treaties and agreements should be public.

Article 15

No State or group of States has the right to intervene, directly or indirectly, for any reason whatever, in the internal or external affairs of any other State.

The foregoing principle prohibits not only armed force but also any other form of interference or attempted threat against the personality of the State or against its political, economic and cultural elements.

Article 16

No State may use or encourage the use of coercive measures of an economic or political character in order to force the sovereign will of another State and obtain from it advantages of any kind.

Article 17

The territory of a State is inviolable; it may not be the object, even temporarily, of military occupation or of other measures of force taken by another State, directly or indirectly, on any grounds whatever. No territorial acquisitions or special advantages obtained either by force or by other means of coercion shall be recognized.

Article 18

The American States bind themselves in their international relations not to have recourse to the use of force, except in the case of self-defense in accordance with existing treaties or in fulfilment thereof.

Article 19

Measures adopted for the maintenance of peace and security in accordance with existing treaties do not constitute a violation of the principles set forth in Articles 15 and 17.

CHAPTER IV: PACIFIC SETTLEMENT OF DISPUTES

Article 20

All international disputes that may arise between American States shall be submitted to the peaceful procedures set forth in this Charter, before being referred to the Security Council of the United Nations.

Article 21

The following are peaceful procedures: direct negotiation, good offices, mediation, investigation and conciliation, judicial settlement, arbitration, and those which the parties to the dispute may especially agree upon at any time.

Article 22

In the event that a dispute arises between two or more American States which, in the opinion of one of them, cannot be settled through the usual diplomatic channels, the Parties shall agree on some other peaceful procedure that will enable them to reach a solution.

Article 23

A special treaty will establish adequate procedures for the pacific settlement of disputes and will determine the appropriate means for their application, so that no dispute between American States shall fail of definitive settlement within a reasonable period.

CHAPTER V: COLLECTIVE SECURITY

Article 24

Every act of aggression by a State against the territorial integrity or the inviolability of the territory or against the sovereignty or political independence of an American State shall be considered an act of aggression against the other American States.

Article 25

If the inviolability or the integrity of the territory or the sovereignty or political independence of any American State should be affected by an armed attack or by an act of aggression that is not an armed attack, or by an extra-continental conflict, or by a conflict between two or more American States, or by any other fact or situation that might endanger the peace of America, the American States, in furtherance of the principles of continental solidarity or collective self-defense, shall apply the measures and procedures established in the special treaties on the subject.

CHAPTER VI: ECONOMIC STANDARDS

Article 26

The Member States agree to co-operate with one another, as far as their resources may permit and their laws may provide, in the broadest spirit of good neighborliness, in order to strengthen their economic structure, develop their agriculture and mining, promote their industry and increase their trade.

Article 27

If the economy of an American State is affected by serious conditions that cannot be satisfactorily remedied by its own unaided effort, such State may place its economic problems before the Inter-American Economic and Social Council to seek through consultation the most appropriate solution for such problems.

CHAPTER VII: SOCIAL STANDARDS

Article 28

The Member States agree to co-operate with one another to achieve just and decent living conditions for their entire populations.

Article 29

The Member States agree upon the desirability of developing their social legislation on the following basis:

a) All human beings, without distinction as to race, nationality, sex, creed or social condition, have the right to attain material well-being and spiritual growth under circumstances of liberty, dignity, equality of opportunity, and economic security;

b) Work is a right and a social duty; it shall not be considered as an article of commerce; it demands respect for freedom of association and for the dignity of the worker; and it is to be performed under conditions that ensure life, health and a decent standard of living, both during the working years and during old age, or when any circumstance deprives the individual of the possibility of working.

CHAPTER VIII: CULTURAL STANDARDS

Article 30

The Member States agree to promote, in accordance with their constitutional provisions and their material resources, the exercise of the right to education, on the following bases:

a) Elementary education shall be compulsory and, when provided by the State, shall be without cost;

b) Higher education shall be available to all, without distinction as to race, nationality, sex, language, creed or social condition.

Article 31

With due consideration for the national character of each State, the Member States undertake to facilitate free cultural interchange by every medium of expression.

Part Two

CHAPTER IX: THE ORGANS

Article 32

The Organization of American States accomplishes its purposes by means of:

a) The Inter-American Conference;

b) The Meeting of Consultation of Ministers of Foreign Affairs;

c) The Council;

d) The Pan American Union;

e) The Specialized Conferences; and

f) The Specialized Organizations.

CHAPTER X: THE INTER-AMERICAN CONFERENCE

Article 33

The Inter-American Conference is the supreme organ of the Organization of American States. It decides the general action and policy of the Organization and determines the structure and functions of its Organs, and has the authority to consider any matter relating to friendly relations among the American States. These functions shall be carried out in accordance with the provisions of this Charter and of other inter-American treaties.

Article 34

All Member States have the right to be represented at the Inter-American Conference. Each State has the right to one vote.

Article 35

The Conference shall convene every five years at the time fixed by the Council of the Organization, after consultation with the government of the country where the Conference is to be held.

Article 36

In special circumstances and with the approval of two-thirds of the American Governments, a special Inter-American Conference may be held, or the date of the next regular Conference may be changed.

Article 37

Each Inter-American Conference shall designate the place of meeting of the next Conference. If for any unforeseen reason the Conference cannot be held at the place designated, the Council of the Organization shall designate a new place.

Article 38

The program and regulations of the Inter-American Conference shall be prepared by the Council of the Organization and submitted to the Member States for consideration.

CHAPTER XI: THE MEETING OF CONSULTATION OF MINISTERS OF FOREIGN AFFAIRS

Article 39

The Meeting of Consultation of Ministers of Foreign Affairs shall be held in order to consider problems of an urgent nature and of common interest to the American States, and to serve as the Organ of Consultation.

Article 40

Any Member State may request that a Meeting of Consultation be called. The request shall be addressed to the Council of the Organization, which shall decide by an absolute majority whether a meeting should be held.

Article 41

The program and regulations of the Meeting of Consultation shall be prepared by the Council of the Organization and submitted to the Member States for consideration.

Article 42

If, for exceptional reasons, a Minister of Foreign Affairs is unable to attend the meeting, he shall be represented by a special delegate.

Article 43

In case of an armed attack within the territory of an American State or within the region of security delimited by treaties in force, a Meeting of Consultation shall be held without delay. Such Meeting shall be called immediately by the Chairman of the Council of the Organization, who shall at the same time call a meeting of the Council itself.

Article 44

An Advisory Defense Committee shall be established to advise the Organ of Consultation on problems of military cooperation that may arise in connection with the application of existing special treaties on collective security.

Article 45

The Advisory Defense Committee shall be composed of the highest military authorities of the American States participating in the Meeting of Consultation. Under exceptional circumstances the Governments may appoint substitutes. Each State shall be entitled to one vote.

Article 46

The Advisory Defense Committee shall be convoked under the same conditions as the Organ of Consultation, when the latter deals with matters relating to defense against aggression.

Article 47

The Committee shall also meet when the Conference or the Meeting of Consultation or the Governments, by a two-thirds majority of the Member States, assign to it technical studies or reports on specific subjects.

CHAPTER XII: THE COUNCIL

Article 48

The Council of the Organization of American States is composed of one Representative of each Member State of the Organization, especially appointed by the respective Government, with the rank of Ambassador. The appointment may be given to the diplomatic representative accredited to the Government of the country in which the Council has its seat. During the absence of the titular Representative, the Government may appoint an interim Representative.

Article 49

The Council shall elect a Chairman and a Vice Chairman, who shall serve for one year and shall not be eligible for election to either of those positions for the term immediately following.

Article 50

The Council takes cognizance, within the limits of the present Charter and of inter-American treaties and agreements, of any matter referred to it by the Inter-American Conference or the Meeting of Consultation of Ministers of Foreign Affairs.

Article 51

The Council shall be responsible for the proper discharge by the Pan American Union of the duties assigned to it.

Article 52

The Council shall serve provisionally as the Organ of Consultation when the circumstances contemplated in Article 43 of this Charter arise.

Article 53

It is also the duty of the Council:

a) To draft and submit to the Governments and to the Inter-American Conference proposals for the creation of new Specialized Organizations or for the combination, adaptation or elimination of existing ones, including matters relating to the financing and support thereof;

b) To draft recommendations to the Governments, the Inter-American Conference, the Specialized Conferences or the Specialized Organizations, for the coordination of the activities and programs of such organizations, after consultation with them;

c) To conclude agreements with the Inter-American Specialized Organizations to determine the relations that shall exist between the respective agency and the Organization;

d) To conclude agreements or special arrangements for cooperation with other American organizations of recognized international standing;

e) To promote and facilitate collaboration between the Organization of American States and the United Nations, as well as between Inter-American Specialized Organizations and similar international agencies;

f) To adopt resolutions that will enable the Secretary General to perform the duties envisaged in Article 84;

g) To perform the other duties assigned to it by the present Charter.

Article 54

The Council shall establish the bases for fixing the quota that each Government is to contribute to the maintenance of the Pan American Union, taking into account the ability to pay of the respective countries and their determination to contribute in an equitable manner. The budget, after approval by the Council, shall be transmitted to the Governments at least six months before the first day of the fiscal year, with a statement of the annual quota of each country. Decisions on budgetary matters require the approval of two-thirds of the members of the Council.

Article 55

The Council shall formulate its own regulations.

Article 56

The Council shall function at the seat of the Pan American Union.

Article 57

The following are organs of the Council of the Organization of American States:

a) The Inter-American Economic and Social Council;

b) The Inter-American Council of Jurists; and

c) The Inter-American Cultural Council.

Article 58

The organs referred to in the preceding article shall have technical autonomy within the limits of this Charter; but their decisions shall not encroach upon the sphere of action of the Council of the Organization.

Article 59

The organs of the Council of the Organization are composed of representatives of all the Member States of the Organization.

Article 60

The organs of the Council of the Organization shall, as far as possible, render to the Governments such technical services as the latter may request; and they shall advise the Council of the Organization on matters within their jurisdiction.

Article 61

The organs of the Council of the Organization shall, in agreement with the Council, establish cooperative relations with the corresponding organs of the United Nations and with the national or international agencies that function within their respective spheres of action.

Article 62

The Council of the Organization, with the advice of the appropriate bodies and after consultation with the Governments, shall formulate the statutes of its organs in accordance with and in the execution of the provisions of this Charter. The organs shall formulate their own regulations.

A) The Inter-American Economic and Social Council

Article 63

The Inter-American Economic and Social Council has for its principal purpose the promotion of the economic and social welfare of the American nations through effective cooperation for the better utilization of their natural resources, the development of their agriculture and industry and the raising of the standards of living of their peoples.

Article 64

To accomplish this purpose the Council shall:

a) Propose the means by which the American nations may give each other technical assistance in making studies and formulating and executing plans to carry out the purposes referred to in Article 26 and to develop and improve their social services;

b) Act as coordinating agency for all official inter-American activities of an economic and social nature;

c) Undertake studies on its own initiative or at the request of any Member State;

d) Assemble and prepare reports on economic and social matters for the use of the Member States;

e) Suggest to the Council of the Organization the advisability of holding specialized conferences on economic and social matters;

f) Carry on such other activities as may be assigned to it by the Inter-American Conference, the Meeting of Consultation of Ministers of Foreign Affairs, or the Council of the Organization.

Article 65

The Inter-American Economic and Social Council, composed of technical delegates appointed by each Member State, shall meet on its own initiative or on that of the Council of the Organization.

Article 66

The Inter-American Economic and Social Council shall function at the seat of the Pan American Union, but it may hold meetings in any American city by a majority decision of the Member States.

B) The Inter-American Council of Jurists

Article 67

The purpose of the Inter-American Council of Jurists is to serve as an advisory body on juridical matters; to promote the development and codification of public and private international law; and to study the possibility of attaining uniformity in the legislation of the various American countries, insofar as it may appear desirable.

Article 68

The Inter-American Juridical Committee of Rio de Janeiro shall be the permanent committee of the Inter-American Council of Jurists.

Article 69

The Juridical Committee shall be composed of jurists of the nine countries selected by the Inter-American Conference. The selection of the jurists shall be made by the Inter-American Council of Jurists from a panel submitted by each country chosen by the Conference. The Members of the Juridical Committee represent all Member States of the Organization. The Council of the Organization is empowered to fill any vacancies that occur during the intervals between Inter-American Conferences and between meetings of the Inter-American Council of Jurists.

Article 70

The Juridical Committee shall undertake such studies and preparatory work as are assigned to it by the Inter-American Council of Jurists, the Inter-American Conference, the Meeting of Consultation of Ministers of Foreign

Affairs, or the Council of the Organization. It may also undertake those studies and projects which, on its own initiative, it considers advisable.

Article 71

The Inter-American Council of Jurists and the Juridical Committee should seek the cooperation of national committees for the codification of international law, of institutes of international and comparative law, and of other specialized agencies.

Article 72

The Inter-American Council of Jurists shall meet when convened by the Council of the Organization, at the place determined by the Council of Jurists at its previous meeting.

C) The Inter-American Cultural Council

Article 73

The purpose of the Inter-American Cultural Council is to promote friendly relations and mutual understanding among the American peoples, in order to strengthen the peaceful sentiments that have characterized the evolution of America, through the promotion of educational, scientific and cultural exchange.

Article 74

To this end the principal functions of the Council shall be:

a) To sponsor inter-American cultural activities;

b) To collect and supply information on cultural activities carried on in and among the American States by private and official agencies both national and international in character;

c) To promote the adoption of basic educational programs adapted to the needs of all population groups in the American countries;

d) To promote, in addition, the adoption of special programs of training, education and culture for the indigenous groups of the American countries;

e) To cooperate in the protection, preservation and increase of the cultural heritage of the continent;

f) To promote cooperation among the American nations in the fields of education, science and culture, by means of the exchange of materials for research and study, as well as the exchange of teachers, students, specialists and, in general, such other persons and materials as are useful for the realization of these ends;

g) To encourage the education of the peoples for harmonious international relations;

h) To carry on such other activities as may be assigned to it by the Inter-American Conference, the Meeting of Consultation of Ministers of Foreign Affairs, or the Council of the Organization.

Article 75

The Inter-American Cultural Council shall determine the place of its next meeting and shall be convened by the Council of the Organization on the date chosen by the latter in agreement with the Government of the country selected as the seat of the meeting.

Article 76

There shall be a Committee for Cultural Action of which five States, chosen at each Inter-American Conference, shall be members. The individuals composing the Committee for Cultural Action shall be selected by the Inter-American Cultural Council from a panel submitted by each country chosen by the Conference, and they shall be specialists in education or cultural matters. When the Inter-American Cultural Council and the Inter-American Conference are not in session, the Council of the Organization may fill vacancies that arise and replace those countries that find it necessary to discontinue their cooperation.

Article 77

The Committee for Cultural Action shall function as the permanent committee of the Inter-American Cultural Council, for the purpose of preparing any studies that the latter may assign to it. With respect to these studies the Council shall have the final decision.

CHAPTER XIII: THE PAN AMERICAN UNION

Article 78

The Pan American Union is the central and permanent organ of the Organization of American States and the General Secretariat of the Organization. It shall perform the duties assigned to it in this Charter and such other duties as may be assigned to it in other inter-American treaties and agreements.

Article 79

There shall be a Secretary General of the Organization, who shall be elected by the Council for a ten-year term and who may not be reelected or be succeeded by a person of the same nationality. In the event of a vacancy in the office of Secretary General, the Council shall, within the next ninety days, elect a successor to fill the office for the remainder of the term, who may be reelected if the vacancy occurs during the second half of the term.

Article 80

The Secretary General shall direct the Pan American Union and be the legal representative thereof.

Article 81

The Secretary General shall participate with voice, but without vote, in the deliberations of the Inter-American Conference, the Meeting of Consultation of Ministers of Foreign Affairs, the Specialized Conferences, and the Council and its organs.

Article 82

The Pan American Union, through its technical and information offices, shall, under the direction of the Council, promote economic, social, juridical and cultural relations among all the Member States of the Organization.

Article 83

The Pan American Union shall also perform the following functions:

a) Transmit *ex officio* to Member States the convocation to the Inter-American Conference, the Meeting of Consultation of Ministers of Foreign Affairs, and the Specialized Conferences;

b) Advise the Council and its organs in the preparation of programs and regulations of the Inter-American Conference, the Meeting of Consultation of Ministers of Foreign Affairs, and the Specialized Conferences;

c) Place, to the extent of its ability, at the disposal of the Government of the country where a conference is to be held, the technical aid and personnel which such Government may request;

d) Serve as custodian of the documents and archives of the Inter-American Conference, of the Meeting of Consultation of Ministers of Foreign Affairs, and, insofar as possible, of the Specialized Conferences;

e) Serve as depository of the instruments of ratification of inter-American agreements;

f) Perform the functions entrusted to it by the Inter-American Conference, and the Meeting of Consultation of Ministers of Foreign Affairs;

g) Submit to the Council an annual report on the activities of the Organization;

h) Submit to the Inter-American Conference a report on the work accomplished by the Organs of the Organization since the previous Conference.

Article 84

It is the duty of the Secretary General:

a) To establish, with the approval of the Council, such technical and administrative offices of the Pan American Union as are necessary to accomplish its purposes;

b) To determine the number of department heads, officers and employees of the Pan American Union; to appoint them, regulate their powers and duties, and fix their compensation, in accordance with general standards established by the Council.

Article 85

There shall be an Assistant Secretary General, elected by the Council for a term of ten years and eligible for reelection. In the event of a vacancy in the office of Assistant Secretary General, the Council shall, within the next ninety days, elect a successor to fill such office for the remainder of the term.

Article 86

The Assistant Secretary General shall be the Secretary of the Council. He shall perform the duties of the Secretary General during the temporary absence or disability of the latter, or during the ninety-day vacancy referred to in Article 79. He shall also serve as advisory officer to the Secretary General, with the power to act as his delegate in all matters that the Secretary General may entrust to him.

Article 87

The Council, by a two-thirds vote of its members, may remove the Secretary General or the Assistant Secretary General whenever the proper functioning of the Organization so demands.

Article 88

The heads of the respective departments of the Pan American Union, appointed by the Secretary General, shall be the Executive Secretaries of the Inter-American Economic and Social Council, the Council of Jurists and the Cultural Council.

Article 89

In the performance of their duties the personnel shall not seek or receive instructions from any government or from any other authority outside the Pan

American Union. They shall refrain from any action that might reflect upon their position as international officials responsible only to the Union.

Article 90

Every Member of the Organization of American States pledges itself to respect the exclusively international character of the responsibilities of the Secretary General and the personnel, and not to seek to influence them in the discharge of their duties.

Article 91

In selecting its personnel the Pan American Union shall give first consideration to efficiency, competence and integrity; but at the same time importance shall be given to the necessity of recruiting personnel on as broad a geographical basis as possible.

Article 92

The seat of the Pan American Union is the city of Washington.

CHAPTER XIV: THE SPECIALIZED CONFERENCES

Article 93

The Specialized Conferences shall meet to deal with special technical matters or to develop specific aspects of inter-American cooperation, when it is so decided by the Inter-American Conference or the Meeting of Consultation of Ministers of Foreign Affairs; when inter-American agreements so provide; or when the Council of the Organization considers it necessary, either on its own initiative or at the request of one of its organs or of one of the Specialized Organizations.

Article 94

The program and regulations of the Specialized Conferences shall be prepared by the organs of the Council of the Organization or by the Specialized Organizations concerned; they shall be submitted to the Member Governments for consideration and transmitted to the Council for its information.

CHAPTER XV: THE SPECIALIZED ORGANIZATIONS

Article 95

For the purposes of the present Charter, Inter-American Specialized Organizations are the intergovernmental organizations established by multilateral agreements and having specific functions with respect to technical matters of common interest to the American States.

Article 96

The Council shall, for the purposes stated in Article 53, maintain a register of the Organizations that fulfill the conditions set forth in the foregoing Article.

Article 97

The Specialized Organizations shall enjoy the fullest technical autonomy and shall take into account the recommendations of the Council, in conformity with the provisions of the present Charter.

Article 98

The Specialized Organizations shall submit to the Council periodic reports on the progress of their work and on their annual budgets and expenses.

Article 99

Agreements between the Council and the Specialized Organizations contemplated in paragraph c) of Article 53 may provide that such Organizations transmit their budgets to the Council for approval. Arrangements may also be made for the Pan American Union to receive the quotas of the contributing countries and distribute them in accordance with the said agreements.

Article 100

The Specialized Organizations shall establish cooperative relations with world agencies of the same character in order to coordinate their activities. In concluding agreements with international agencies of a world-wide character, the Inter-American Specialized Organizations shall preserve their identity and their status as integral parts of the Organization of American States, even when they perform regional functions of international agencies.

Article 101

In determining the geographic location of the Specialized Organizations the interests of all the American States shall be taken into account.

Part Three

CHAPTER XVI: THE UNITED NATIONS

Article 102

None of the provisions of this Charter shall be construed as impairing the rights and obligations of the Member States under the Charter of the United Nations.

CHAPTER XVII: MISCELLANEOUS PROVISIONS

Article 103

The Organization of American States shall enjoy in the territory of each Member such legal capacity, privileges and immunities as are necessary for the exercise of its functions and the accomplishment of its purposes.

Article 104

The Representatives of the Governments on the Council of the Organization, the representatives on the organs of the Council, the personnel of their delegations, as well as the Secretary General and the Assistant Secretary General of the Organization, shall enjoy the privileges and immunities necessary for the independent performance of their duties.

Article 105

The juridical status of the Inter-American Specialized Organizations and the privileges and immunities that should be granted to them and to their personnel, as well as to the officials of the Pan American Union, shall be determined in each case through agreements between the respective organizations and the Governments concerned.

Article 106

Correspondence of the Organization of American States, including printed matter and parcels, bearing the frank thereof, shall be carried free of charge in the mails of the Member States.

Article 107

The Organization of American States does not recognize any restriction on the eligibility of men and women to participate in the activities of the various Organs and to hold positions therein.

CHAPTER XVIII: RATIFICATION AND ENTRY INTO FORCE

Article 108

The present Charter shall remain open for signature by the American States and shall be ratified in accordance with their respective constitutional procedures. The original instrument, the Spanish, English, Portuguese and French texts of which are equally authentic, shall be deposited with the Pan American Union, which shall transmit certified copies thereof to the Governments for purposes of ratification. The instruments of ratification shall be deposited with the Pan American Union, which shall notify the signatory States of such deposit.

Article 109

The present Charter shall enter into force among the ratifying States when two-thirds of the Signatory States have deposited their ratifications. It shall enter into force with respect to the remaining States in the order in which they deposit their ratifications.

Article 110

The present Charter shall be registered with the Secretariat of the United Nations through the Pan American Union.

Article 111

Amendments to the present Charter may be adopted only at an Inter-American Conference convened for that purpose. Amendments shall enter into force in accordance with the terms and procedure set forth in Article 109.

Article 112

The present Charter shall remain in force indefinitely, but may be denounced by any Member State upon written notification to the Pan American Union, which shall communicate to all the others each notice of denunciation received. After two years from the date on which the Pan American Union receives a notice of denunciation, the present Charter shall cease to be in force with respect to the denouncing State, which shall cease to belong to the Organization after it has fulfilled the obligations arising from the present Charter.

IN WITNESS WHEREOF the undersigned Plenipotentiaries, whose full powers have been presented and found to be in good and due form, sign the present Charter at the City of Bogotá, Colombia, on the dates that appear opposite their respective signatures.

INTER-AMERICAN TREATY OF RECIPROCAL ASSISTANCE
(RIO TREATY)

In the name of their Peoples, the Governments represented at the Inter-American Conference for the Maintenance of Continental Peace and Security, desirous of consolidating and strengthening their relations of friendship and good neighborliness, and

Considering:

That Resolution VIII of the Inter-American Conference on Problems of War and Peace, which met in Mexico City, recommended the conclusion of a treaty to prevent and repel threats and acts of aggression against any of the countries of America;

That the High Contracting Parties reiterate their will to remain united in an inter-American system consistent with the purposes and principles of the United Nations, and reaffirm the existence of the agreement which they have concluded concerning those matters relating to the maintenance of international peace and security which are appropriate for regional action;

That the High Contracting Parties reaffirm their adherence to the principles of inter-American solidarity and cooperation, and especially to those set forth in the preamble and declarations of the Act of Chapultepec, all of which should be understood to be accepted as standards of their mutual relations and as the juridical basis of the Inter-American System;

That the American States propose, in order to improve the procedures for the pacific settlement of their controversies, to conclude the treaty concerning the "Inter-American Peace System" envisaged in Resolutions IX and XXXIX of the Inter-American Conference on Problems of War and Peace;

That the obligation of mutual assistance and common defense of the American Republics is essentially related to their democratic ideals and to their will to cooperate permanently in the fulfillment of the principles and purposes of a policy of peace;

That the American regional community affirms as a manifest truth that juridical organization is a necessary prerequisite of security and peace, and that peace is founded on justice and moral order and, consequently, on the international recognition and protection of human rights and freedoms, on the indispensable well-being of the people, and on the effectiveness of democracy for the international realization of justice and security.

Have resolved, in conformity with the objectives stated above, to conclude the following Treaty, in order to assure peace, through adequate means, to provide for effective reciprocal assistance to meet armed attacks against any American State, and in order to deal with threats of aggression against any of them:

Article 1

The High Contracting Parties formally condemn war and undertake in their international relations not to resort to the threat or the use of force in any manner inconsistent with the provisions of the Charter of the United Nations or of this treaty.

Article 2

As a consequence of the principle set forth in the preceding Article, the High Contracting Parties undertake to submit every controversy which may arise between them to methods of peaceful settlement and to endeavor to settle any such controversy among themselves by means of the procedures in force in the Inter-American System before referring it to the General Assembly or the Security Council of the United Nations.

Article 3

1. The High Contracting Parties agree that an armed attack by any State against an American State shall be considered as an attack against all the American States and, consequently, each one of the said Contracting Parties undertakes to assist in meeting the attack in the exercise of the inherent right of individual or collective self-defense recognized by Article 51 of the Charter of the United Nations.

2. On the request of the State or States directly attacked and until the decision of the Organ of Consultation of the Inter-American System, each one of the Contracting Parties may determine the immediate measures which it may individually take in fulfillment of the obligation contained in the preceding paragraph and in accordance with the principle of continental solidarity. The Organ of Consultation shall meet without delay for the purpose of examining those measures and agreeing upon the measures of a collective character that should be taken.

3. The provisions of this Article shall be applied in case of any armed attack which takes place within the region described in Article 4 or within the territory of an American State. When the attack takes place outside of the said areas, the provisions of Article 6 shall be applied.

4. Measures of self-defense provided for under this Article may be taken until the Security Council of the United Nations has taken the measures necessary to maintain international peace and security.

Article 4

The region to which this Treaty refers is bounded as follows: beginning at the North Pole; thence due south to a point 74 degrees north latitude, 10 degrees west longitude; thence by a rhumb line to a point 47 degrees 30 minutes north latitude, 50 degrees west longitude; thence by a rhumb line to a point 35 degrees north latitude, 60 degrees west longitude; thence due south to a point in 20 degrees north latitude; thence by a rhumb line to a point 5 degrees north latitude, 24 degrees west longitude; thence due south to the South Pole; thence due north to a point 30 degrees south latitude, 90 degrees west longitude; thence by a rhumb line to a point on the Equator at 97 degrees west longitude; thence by a rhumb line to a point 15 degrees north latitude, 120 degrees west longitude; thence by a rhumb line to a point 50 degrees north latitude, 170 degrees east longitude; thence due north to a point in 54 degrees north latitude; thence by a rhumb line to a point 65 degrees 30 minutes north latitude, 168 degrees 58 minutes 5 seconds west longitude; thence due north to the North Pole.

Article 5

The High Contracting Parties shall immediately send to the Security Council of the United Nations, in conformity with Articles 51 and 54 of the Charter of the United Nations, complete information concerning the activities undertaken or in contemplation in the exercise of the right of self-defense or for the purpose of maintaining inter-American peace and security.

Article 6

If the inviolability or the integrity of the territory or the sovereignty or political independence of any American State should be affected by an aggression which is not an armed attack or by an extra-continental or intra-continental conflict, or by any other fact or situation that might endanger the peace of America, the Organ of Consultation shall meet immediately in order to agree on the measures which must be taken in case of aggression to assist the victim of the aggression or, in any case, the measures which should be taken for the common defense and for the maintenance of the peace and security of the Continent.

Article 7

In the case of a conflict between two or more American States, without prejudice to the right of self-defense in conformity with Article 51 of the Charter of the United Nations, the High Contracting Parties, meeting in consultation shall call upon the contending States to suspend hostilities and restore matters to the *statu quo ante bellum,* and shall take in addition all other necessary measures to re-establish or maintain inter-American peace and security and for the solution of the conflict by peaceful means. The rejection of the pacifying action will be considered in the determination of the aggressor and in the application of the measures which the consultative meeting may agree upon.

Article 8

For the purposes of this treaty, the measures on which the Organ of Consultation may agree will comprise one or more of the following: recall of chiefs of diplomatic missions; breaking of diplomatic relations; breaking of consular relations; partial or complete interruption of economic relations or of rail, sea, air, postal, telegraphic, telephonic, and radiotelephonic or radiotelegraphic communications; and use of armed force.

Article 9

In addition to other acts which the Organ of Consultation may characterize as aggression, the following shall be considered as such:

a. Unprovoked armed attack by a State against the territory, the people, or the land, sea, or air forces of another State;

b. Invasion, by the armed forces of a State, of the territory of an American State, through the trespassing of boundaries demarcated in accordance with a treaty, judicial decision, or arbitral award, or, in the absence of frontiers thus demarcated, invasion affecting a region which is under the effective jurisdiction of another State.

Article 10

None of the provisions of this Treaty shall be construed as impairing the rights and obligations of the High Contracting Parties under the Charter of the United Nations.

Article 11

The consultations to which this Treaty refers shall be carried out by means of the Meetings of Ministers of Foreign Affairs of the American Republics which have ratified the Treaty, or in the manner or by the organ which in the future may be agreed upon.

Article 12

The Governing Board of the Pan American Union may act provisionally as an organ of consultation until the meeting of the Organ of Consultation referred to in the preceding Article takes place.

Article 13

The consultations shall be initiated at the request addressed to the Governing Board of the Pan American Union by any of the Signatory States which has ratified the Treaty.

Article 14

In the voting referred to in this Treaty only the representatives of the Signatory States which have ratified the Treaty may take part.

Article 15

The Governing Board of the Pan American Union shall act in all matters concerning this Treaty as an organ of liaison among the Signatory States which have ratified this Treaty and between these States and the United Nations.

Article 16

The decisions of the Governing Board of the Pan American Union referred to in Articles 13 and 15 above shall be taken by an absolute majority of the Members entitled to vote.

Article 17

The Organ of Consultation shall take its decisions by a vote of two-thirds of Signatory States which have ratified the Treaty.

Article 18

In the case of a situation or dispute between American States, the parties directly interested shall be excluded from the voting referred to in the two preceding Articles.

Article 19

To constitute a quorum in all the meetings referred to in the previous Articles, it shall be necessary that the number of States represented shall be at least equal to the number of votes necessary for the taking of the decision.

Article 20

Decisions which require the application of the measures specified in Article 8 shall be binding upon all the Signatory States which have ratified this Treaty, with the sole exception that no State shall be required to use armed force without its consent.

Article 21

The measures agreed upon by the Organ of Consultation shall be executed through the procedures and agencies now existing or those which may in the future be established.

Article 22

This Treaty shall come into effect between the States which ratify it as soon as the ratifications of two-thirds of the Signatory States have been deposited.

Article 23

This Treaty is open for signature by the American States at the city of Rio de Janeiro, and shall be ratified by the Signatory States as soon as possible in accordance with their respective constitutional processes. The ratifications shall be deposited with the Pan American Union, which shall notify the Signatory States of each deposit. Such notification shall be considered as an exchange of ratifications.

Article 24

The present Treaty shall be registered with the Secretariat of the United Nations through the Pan American Union, when two-thirds of the Signatory States have deposited their ratifications.

Article 25

This Treaty shall remain in force indefinitely, but may be denounced by any High Contracting Party by a notification in writing to the Pan American Union, which shall inform all the other High Contracting parties of each notification of denunciation received. After the expiration of two years from the date of the receipt by the Pan American Union of a notification of denunciation by any High Contracting Party, the present Treaty shall cease to be in force with respect to such State, but shall remain in full force and effect with respect to all the other High Contracting Parties.

Article 26

The principles and fundamental provisions of this Treaty shall be incorporated in the Organic Pact of the Inter-American System.

IN WITNESS WHEREOF, the undersigned Plenipotentiaries, having deposited their full powers found to be in due and proper form, sign this Treaty on behalf of their respective Governments, on the dates appearing opposite their signatures.

DONE in the city of Rio de Janeiro, in four texts respectively in the English, French, Portuguese and Spanish languages, on the second of September nineteen hundred forty-seven.

NOTES

1. On the beginnings of Pan America and its historical antecedents see Bemis, The Latin American Policy of the United States, Chs. II, III, IV, V, and VI (1943); Fenwick, The Inter-American Regional System, Ch. I (1949); Gil, Evolucion del Pan Americanismo 19-37 (1933); Lockey, Pan-Americanism, Its Beginnings (1920); IV Moore, Collected Papers, 13-22, 437-48 (1944); Perkins, The Monroe Doctrine 1823-1826 (1932); Sanchez i Sanchez, Curso de Derecho Internacional Publico Americano 167-81 (1943); Whitaker, The United States and the Independence of Latin America 1800-1830 (1941); Whitaker, The Western Hemisphere Idea: Its Rise and Decline, Chs. I and II (1954); Ypes, El Panamericanismo y el Derecho Internacional 3-62 (1930); Alvarez, "Latin America and International Law," 3 Am. J. Int. L. 269 (1909).

2. Following the Napoleonic Wars the members of the Quadruple Alliance bound themselves together to support each other mutually in matters requiring common action, e.g., to prevent further French aggression should there be a violation by France of the new frontier; to exercise surveillance over the Napoleonic family and prevent any one of them from acceding to the throne of France, since it was felt that French aggression would ensue should such an accession occur; and to act jointly should revolution occur in France. An ambassadorial conference was created composed of the ambassadors of the members of the alliance, which supervised political conditions in France and threatened to take over further duties afield from the French scene. The Holy Alliance was an outgrowth of the Quadruple Alliance, the latter being composed of the four great powers who led the coalition against Napoleonic France: Great Britain, Russia, Austria, and Prussia. The British sovereign, however, was constitutionally prevented from joining and binding his government to the Holy Alliance, although the other monarchs of Europe—except the Pope, who was not an hereditary prince and who declined, and the Sultan of Turkey, who was not a Christian—adhered to the Alliance. On the activities of the Holy Alliance see Butler and Maccoby, The Development of International Law 356 et seq. (1928); Thomas & Thomas, Non-Intervention: The Law and Its Import in the Americas 8-10 (1956); Bemis, op. cit. supra note 1, Ch. IV.

3. The belief has been expressed that the nations of the Holy Alliance really had no immediate designs on the New World, but that Monroe thought they had and thought there was serious danger. Perkins, Hands Off; A History of the Monroe Doctrine 54 and 60 (1941).

On the background and history of the promulgation of the Monroe Doctrine see the following: VI Moore, A Digest of International Law Ch. 20 (1906); Perkins, Hands Off, op. cit. supra note 3, Ch. II; Perkins, The Monroe Doctrine 1823-1826, op. cit. supra note 1; Stuart, Latin America and the United States Ch. II (4th ed. 1943); Higgins, "The Monroe Doctrine," 1924 Brit. Y. B. Int. L. 102.

4. The terms of the doctrine are set forth in VI Moore's Digest, id. at 401.

5. See Stuart, op. cit. supra note 3, at 55.

6. Alvarez, supra note 1, at 311-12.

7. On the aftermath and repercussions of the Monroe Doctrine, see Perkins, The Monroe Doctrine 1823-1826, op. cit. supra note 1, Chs. VI and VII; Thomas & Thomas, op. cit. supra note 2, Ch. II; Alvarez, supra note 1, at 311.

8. Lockey, op. cit. supra note 1, Ch. VII, describes such projects and even earlier proposals for an inter-American community.

9. See Alvarez, supra note 1, at 276; Wilgus, The Development of Hispanic America 680-81 (1941).

10. As quoted in Alvarez, The Monroe Doctrine 113 (1924).

11. Id. at 113-14.

12. As quoted in Lockey, op. cit. supra note 1, at 284; see also I Antokoletz, Derecho Internacional Publico 336 (1944).

13. Lecuna and Bierck, I Selected Writings of Bolivar 1810-1822, 118 (1951).

14. The treaties may be found in Alvarez, The Monroe Doctrine, op. cit. supra note 10, at 135-41.

15. E.g., Art. 3, Additional Treaty of Perpetual Union, League and Confederation, between Colombia and Peru, signed at Lima, July 6, 1822, id. at 136-37.

16. Lockey, op. cit. supra note 1, at 312.

17. Circular Invitation Addressed by Simón Bolívar to the Governments of Colombia, Mexico, Central America, the United Provinces of Buenos Aires, Chile and Brazil, Lima, December 7, 1824, as set forth in International Conferences of American States 1889-1928, edited by Scott, at XIX-XX (1931).

18. Regarding the countries invited and their attitudes toward the Congress see Lockey, op. cit. supra note 1, at 312-16, Ch. X and XI.

19. Accounts and summaries of the Congress of Panama may be found in I Antokoletz, op. cit. supra note 12, at 338-42; Bemis, John Quincy Adams and the Foundations of

American Foreign Policy 543-65 (1949); Gil, *op. cit. supra* note 1, at 23-29; Moore, *op. cit. supra* note 1, at 15-18; Whitaker, The United States and the Independence of Latin America, *op. cit. supra* note 1, at 564-84; Ypes, *op. cit. supra* note 1, Ch. I; Collins, "The Congress of Bolivar," VI Hispanic American Historical Rev. 194 (1926); Hackett, "The Development of J. Q. Adams' Policy with Respect to an American Confederation and the Pan American Congress, 1822-1865," VIII Hispanic American Historical Rev. 496 (1928); Reinhold, "New Research on the First Pan American Conference Held at Panama in 1826," XVIII Hispanic American Historical Rev. 342 (1938).

20. "Treaty of Perpetual Union, League and Confederation between the Republics of Colombia, Central America, Peru and the United Mexican States, July 15, 1826," International Conference of American States, *op. cit. supra* note 17, at XXIV-XXIX.

21. *Id.*, Arts. 1 and 2.
22. *Id.*, Art. 3.
23. *Id.*, Art. 11.
24. *Id.*, Art. 13.
25. *Id.*, Art. 14.
26. *Id.*, Art. 17.
27. *Id.*, Art. 18.
28. *Id.*, Art. 19.
29. *Id.*, Art. 29.
30. *Id.*, Art. 10.
31. *Id.*, Arts. 4, 5, and 6.
32. *Id.*, Art. 26.
33. *Id.*, Art. 27.
34. *Id.*, Arts. 23 and 24.
35. *Id.*, Art. 25.

36. Whitaker, The Western Hemisphere Idea, *op. cit. supra* note 1, at 41-48 describes the reasons well and succinctly.

37. The Treaty of Confederation of the Congress of Lima, 1847, as signed by Peru, Bolivia, Chile, Ecuador, and New Granada, February 8, 1848, is set forth in Alvarez, The Monroe Doctrine, *op. cit. supra* note 10, at 170-75; The Continental Treaty between Peru, Chile and Ecuador signed at Santiago, September 15, 1856, *id.* at 176-78; The Treaty of Union and Defensive Alliance between Bolivia, the United States of Colombia, Chile, Ecuador, Peru, Salvador, and Venezuela signed at Lima, January 23, 1865, *id.*, at 179-81.

Summaries and accounts of these conferences may be found in I Antokoletz, *op. cit. supra* note 12, at 342-46; Sanchez i Sanchez, *op. cit. supra* note 1, at 175-81; Whitaker, The Western Hemisphere Idea, *op. cit. supra* note 1, at 49-60; Ypes, *op. cit. supra* note 1, at 33-52; Alvarez, *supra* note 1, at 280-89; Frazer, "The Role of the Lima Congress, 1864-1865, in the Development of Pan Americanism," XXIX Hispanic American Historical Rev. 319 (1949); Nuermberger, "The Continental Treaties of 1865," XX Hispanic American Historical Rev. 32 (1940).

38. See IV Moore's Collected Papers, *op. cit. supra* note 1, at 18-19.
39. See Alvarez, *supra* note 1, at 283.
40. *Id.* at 280-82; Whitaker, The Western Hemisphere Idea, *op. cit. supra* note 1, at 52.
41. *Ibid.*
42. See Alvarez, *id.* at 283.
43. Art. 23, The Continental Treaty, *supra* note 37.
44. See Alvarez, *op. cit. supra* note 1, at 285.
45. I Antokoletz, *op. cit. supra* note 12, at 345.
46. See Whitaker, The Western Hemisphere Idea, *op. cit. supra* note 1, at 58.
47. *Id.* at 58-60; Ypes, *op. cit. supra* note 1, at 51-52.
48. As quoted by Ypes, *id.* at 50 and in Whitaker, *id.* at 288.
49. See Alvarez, *supra* note 1, at 288.

50. Whitaker in the Western Hemisphere Idea, *op. cit. supra* note 1, at 61-74, discusses this Latin American sentiment as seen through the eyes of certain Latin American intellectuals such as Alberdi, Saramiento, and others.

51. The background of the first Pan American Conference and the attitude of the United States may be found in Whitaker, *id.*, at 74-85; Ypes, *op. cit. supra* note 1, at 90-95; Alvarez, *supra* note 1, at 325-26; Wilgus, "James G. Blaine and the Pan American Movement," V Hispanic American Historical Rev. 662 (1922).

52. "An Act Authorizing the President of the United States To Arrange a Conference Between The United States of America and The Republics of Mexico, Central and South America, Hayti, San Domingo, and The Empire of Brazil," 25 U.S. Stat. 155; also set forth in International Conferences of American States, *op. cit. supra* note 17, at 3-4.

53. International Conferences of American States, *id.*, at 5-6.

54. The Reports, Recommendations and Resolutions Adopted by the Conference are set forth in International Conferences of American States, *id.*, at 11-47. For discussion of the Conference see Sanchez i Sanchez, *op. cit. supra* note 1, 189-201; Ypes, *op. cit. supra* note 1, 90-104; Alvarez, *supra* note 1, 325-29; Elguera, "Reminiscences of the First International Conference of American States," LXXIV PAU Bull. 263 (1940).

55. International Conferences of American States, *id.*, at 40-41, f.n. 4. Chile in particular opposed such a plan for she felt that it might endanger her interests regarding questions not yet decided arising from the War of the Pacific. See Alvarez, *id.* at 328.

56. Report of Committee on Customs Regulation, Bureau of Information, International Conferences of American States, *id.* at 36.

57. Documents pertaining to these conferences will be found in International Conferences of American States, *id.*, at 51-206; these conferences are discussed in the following studies: Sanchez i Sanchez, *op. cit. supra* note 1, 201-25; Ypes, *op. cit. supra* note 1, at 105-6; Wilgus, "The Second International American Conference at Mexico City," XI Hispanic American Historical Rev. 27 (1931); Wilgus, "The Third International American Conference at Rio de Janeiro, 1906," XII Hispanic American Historical Rev. 420 (1932).

58. See *infra* on the constitutional basis of the system, pp. 39-41, and on collective security, pp. 205-11, Ch. XV.

59. See the much quoted statement made by Secretary Olney in 1895 which begins "Today the United States is practically sovereign on this continent..." as set forth in VI Moore's Digest of International Law 553 (1906). On this era of intervention see Thomas & Thomas, *op. cit. supra* note 2, at 19-54.

60. Quintanilla, A Latin American Speaks 156 (1943).

61. VI Moore's Digest, *op. cit. supra* note 3, sec. 967.

62. As incorporated by Gantenbein, The Evolution of Our Latin American Policy 361-62 (1950).

63. On the Roosevelt Corollary see Thomas & Thomas, *op. cit. supra* note 2, at 33-34.

64. "The Drago Doctrine: Letter of Dr. Luis M. Drago, Minister of Foreign Relations of the Argentine Republic, to Mr. Merou, Argentine Minister to the United States, December 29, 1902," Foreign Relations of the United States 1 (1903); quoted also in Alvarez, The Monroe Doctrine, *op. cit. supra* note 10, 187 at 190-91. On the Drago Doctrine see Drago, "State Loans and Their Relation to International Policy," 1 Am. J. Int. L. 692 (1907); Hershey, "The Calvo and Drago Doctrines," 1 Am. J. Int. L. 26 (1907).

65. See Whitaker, The Western Hemisphere Idea, *op. cit. supra* note 1, Ch. V.

66. *Id.* at 95-107.

67. Thomas & Thomas, *op. cit. supra* note 2, at 342.

68. See Ball, The Problem of Inter-American Organization 66 (1944).

69. *Ibid.* See also Callorda, "Idea de una Liga que Responda a los Conceptos Panamericanos del Congreso de Bolivar," X Revista de derecho internacional de Cuba 77 at 80 (1926).

70. Ball, *id.*, at 67.

71. See Thomas & Thomas, *op. cit. supra* note 2, at 35, 45-47, 53, 248-49.

72. Papers Relating to the Foreign Relations of the United States: The Lansing Papers (1914-1920), vol. II, 495-96 (1940). For discussion of the Wilson Pact see Bemis, *op cit. supra* note 1, Ch. XI; Whitaker, The Western Hemisphere Idea, *op. cit. supra* note 1, at 120-31.

CHAPTER II

1. All of the Latin American nations were League of Nations members at one time or another. On Latin America and the League of Nations see Kelchner, Latin American Relations with the League of Nations (1929); Wilgus, The Development of Hispanic America 813-15 (1941); de Oliveira Lima, "Pan-Americanism and the League of Nations," IV Hispanic American Historical Rev. 239 (1921); Duggan, "Latin America, The League and The United States," VII For. Affairs 281 (1934).

2. "Fifth International Conference of American States, Santiago, Mar. 25-May 3, 1923," International Conferences of American States 1889-1928 (edited by Scott) 209-91 (1931).

3. Brums's ideas are contained in his work entitled: The Peace of America; American Solidarity; World Solidarity; Association of American Countries (1923). The text of the project is found in that part entitled: Association of American Countries, *id.* at 55 *et seq.*

4. The proposal was made by the Uruguayan delegation. See "Statement of Delegate of Uruguay in the First Committee," Quinta Conferencia Internacional Americana, Actas de las Sesiones de las Comisiones de la Conferencia, 169 (1923). The proposal appeared on the program of the Conference as Topic IX in the following terms: "Consideration of measures tending toward closer association of the Republics of the American Continent

with a view to promoting common interests." International Conferences, *op. cit. supra* note 2, at 211.

5. See discussion in the First Committee, Quinta Conferencia, *id.* at 167.

6. For a summary of the U.S. attitude see Perkins, Hands Off; A History of the Monroe Doctrine, 331-33 (1941).

7. International Conferences of American States, *op. cit. supra* note 2, at 267-68.

8. On the court project see "Proposed Treaty Presented by the Delegation of Costa Rica regarding the Creation of a Permanent Court of American Justice," *id.* at 452-54.

9. "Resolution, Consideration of the Rights of Aliens Resident within the Jurisdiction of Any of the American Republics," *id.* at 282.

10. See Gil, Evolucion del Panamericanismo 97-98 (1933).

11. Ball, The Problem of Inter-American Organization 19 (1944); Kunz, "The Pan American Union in the Field of International Administration," 31 Iowa L. Rev. 58 at 62-63 (1945). See also *infra* on Historical Evolution of the Council, pp. 96-101.

12. "Resolution, Organization of the Pan American Union, Art. V," International Conferences of American States, *op. cit. supra* note 2, at 270.

13. Ball, *op. cit. supra* note 11, at 19.

14. *Supra* note 12.

15. Kunz, *supra* note 11.

16. International Conferences of American States, *op. cit. supra* note 2, at 285.

17. "Observations on the Monroe Doctrine," Address delivered before the American Bar Association at Minneapolis, Minn., Aug. 30, 1923, 17 Am. J. Int. L. 611 at 616 (1923).

18. For summary of this effort see Thomas & Thomas, Non-Intervention: The Law and Its Import in the Americas, Ch. II, 55-64 (1956).

19. "Resolution, Codification of American International Law," International Conferences of American States, *op. cit. supra* note 2, at 245-46.

20. Project 2 of the Commission's twelve projects for codification entitled "States: Existence-Equality-Recognition" contained this recommendation. International Commission of American Jurists, 1927 Meeting, Ministry of State for Foreign Affairs, Rio de Janeiro, vol. 4, 1927; Commissão Internacional de Jurisconsultos (Sessões de Rio de Janeiro de 18 de abril a 20 de maio de 1927) Direito Publico Internacional, União Pan-Americana, 1927. See also Scott, "The Gradual and Progressive Codification of International Law," 21 Am. J. Int. L. 417 (1927).

21. The results of the Sixth International Conference of American States, Habana, Jan. 16-Feb. 20, 1928, are set forth in International Conferences of American States *op. cit. supra* note 2 at 295 *et seq.* See also Actas de las Sesiones Plenarias de la Sexta Conferencia Internacional Americana (1933). For discussion of the Conference see Scott, "The Sixth International Conference of American States, Held at Havana, Jan. 16-Feb. 20, 1928, A Survey," International Conciliation, No. 241, June, 1928; Scott, "The Sixth Pan American Conference," 22 Am. J. Int. L. 351 (1928).

22. Thomas & Thomas, *op. cit. supra* note 18 at 60.

23. The discourses of the delegates are set forth in the Actas de las Sesiones Plenarias, *op. cit. supra* note 21 at 103-12. On the various attitudes of the delegates see Rivero Reyes, "Deberes y Derechos de los Estados," 31 Revista de Derecho Internacional 70 at 72-78 (1937).

24. Actas de las Sesiones, *id.* at 107-8.

25. "Resolution, Future Codification of International Law" and "Resolution, Fundamental Bases of International Law and the State," International Conferences of American States, *op. cit. supra* note 2, at 439-42.

26. "Seventh International Conference of American States, Montevideo. Dec. 3-26, 1933," International Conferences of American States, First Supp. 1933-1940, 3 *et seq.* And see Manger, "The Seventh International Conference of American States," PAU Bull., vol. LXVIII, No. 4, April, 1934, p. 271; Scott, "Seventh International Conference of American States," 28 Am. J. Int. L. 219 (1934).

27. This statement was made by President Franklin D. Roosevelt in his inaugural address, Mar. 4, 1933. II Rosenman, The Public Papers and Addresses of Franklin D. Roosevelt, 14 (1938).

28. See Thomas & Thomas, *op. cit. supra* note 18, at 27.

29. See statement of Sr. Portell Vila (Cuba), quoted in Septima Conferencia Internacional Americana, Segunda y Octava Comisiones, Actas y Antecedentes, Montevideo, 1933 at 113.

30. "Convention on Rights and Duties of States," International Conferences, 1st Supp., *op. cit. supra* note 26, at 121-23.

31. *Id.* at 123-24.

32. *Ibid.*

33. Thomas & Thomas, *op. cit. supra* note 18, at Ch. II, Era of Intervention, Nicaragua 39-44.

34. *Id.,* Cuba at 21-28.

35. *Id.,* Haiti at 36-39.

36. *Id.,* Panama at 28-32.

37. *Id.,* Dominican Republic, 32-36.

38. "Inter-American Conference for the Maintenance of Peace, Buenos Aires, Dec. 1-23, 1936," International Conferences, 1st. Supp., *op. cit. supra* note 26, at 129 *et seq.*

39. *Id.,* at 191-92.

40. *Id.,* at 188-90.

41. For further elaboration see *infra* pp. 208-9. And see Ball, *op. cit. supra* note 11, at 52-54; Blackmer, United States Policy and the Inter-American Peace System 1889-1952, 60-62, 71-72 (1952); Fenwick, "The Inter-American Conference for the Maintenance of Peace," 31 Am. J. Int. L. 201 (1937); Inman, "An Appraisal of the Buenos Aires Conference," World Affairs, C, no. 1, March, 1937, 50; Jessup, "The Inter-American Conference for the Maintenance of Peace," 31 Am. J. Int. L. 85 (1937); Rippy, "The Conference of Buenos Aires; a Retrospective View," World Affairs, C, no. 1, March, 1937, 46.

42. "Eighth International Conference of American States, Lima, Dec. 9-27, 1938," International Conferences, 1st Supp., *op. cit. supra* note 26, at 215 *et seq.* For discussion of the Conference see Rowe, "The Eighth International Conference of American States," PAU Bull., vol. LXXIII, No. 4, April, 1938, 216.

43. International Conferences, *id.,* at 309-10.

44. Declaration on the Principles of the Solidarity of America (Declaration of Lima) *id.,* at 308-9. See Fenwick, "The Monroe Doctrine and the Declaration of Lima," 33 Am. J. Int. L. 257 (1939).

45. "Report on the Meeting of the Ministers of Foreign Affairs, Panama, Sept. 23-Oct. 3, 1939, Submitted to the Governing Board of the P.A.U. by the Director General," PAU Cong. & Conf. Series, no. 29; International Conferences, 1st Supp. *op. cit. supra* note 26, at 315 *et seq.*

46. "General Declaration of Neutrality of the American Republics," Director General's Report, *id.* at 14-16.

47. "Declaration of Panama," *id.* at 19-21.

48. The safety zone did not include Canada. It varied from 250 miles to 1,250 miles in width. For discussion of the Declaration of Panama and the security zone see Brown, "Protective Jurisdiction," 34 Am. J. Int. L. 112 (1940); Fenwick, "The Declaration of Panama," *id.* at 116; Wright, "Rights and Duties under International Law as Affected by the United States Neutrality Act and the Resolutions of Panama," *id.,* at 238.

49. See I Memoirs of Cordell Hull, 690-92 (1948).

50. "Second Meeting of the Ministers of Foreign Affairs of the American Republics, Habana, July 21-30, 1940," International Conferences, 1st Supp. *op. cit. supra* note 26, at 343, *et seq.* Report on the Second Meeting of the Ministers of Foreign Affairs of the American Republics, Submitted to the Governing Board of the PAU by the Director General, PAU Cong. & Conf. Series No. 32 (1940).

51. "Act of Habana Concerning the Provisional Administration of European Colonies and Possessions in the Americas," International Conferences, *id.* at 373-77.

52. In 1811 the Congress of the United States passed a No-Transfer Resolution to forestall possible British occupation of the Floridas, at that time territory of Spain although the United States had recently taken possession of most of West Florida. The resolution declared:

Taking into view the peculiar situation of Spain and her American provinces; and considering the influence which the destiny of the territory adjoining the southern border of the United States may have upon their security, tranquility, and commerce: Therefore, Resolved by the Senate and House of Representatives of the United States of America in Congress assembled, that the United States, under the peculiar circumstances of the existing crisis, cannot without serious inquietude see any part of the said territory pass into the hands of any foreign Power; and that a due regard to their own safety compels them to provide under certain contingencies, for the temporary occupation of the said territory; they, at the same time, declare that the said territory shall, in their hands, remain subject to a future negotiation.

Bemis, The Latin American Policy of the United States at 29 (1943). The no-transfer doctrine was later extended to Cuba, the United States asserting that the island should not be transferred to any other nation. The United States declared that they could not see any state other than Spain in possession of Cuba. See I Hyde, International Law Chiefly as Interpreted and Applied by the United States, sec. 79, f.n. 1 (2d ed. 1947). The no-transfer doctrine was integrated with the Monroe Doctrine although not included in the original pronouncement. See Bemis, *id.* at 30, 66, 88, 116.

53. See the various recommendations and resolutions, International Conferences, 1st Supp., *op. cit. supra* note 26, at 351-56.

54. "Economic and Financial Cooperation," *id.* at 368-70.

55. "Reciprocal Assistance and Cooperation for the Defense of the Nations of the Americas," *id.* at 360-61.

56. Report on the Third Meeting of the Ministers of Foreign Affairs of the American Republics, Rio de Janeiro, Jan. 15-28, 1942, Submitted to the Governering Board of the PAU by the Director General, PAU Cong. & Conf. Series, no. 36 (1942).

57. *Id.* at 7.

58. For a short discussion of the obligations subscribed to by the American States at the Meeting of Foreign Ministers, Habana, see Fenwick, "The Third Meeting of Ministers of Foreign Affairs at Rio de Janeiro," 36 Am. J. Int. L. 169 at 176-77 (1942).

59. See Smith, Yankee Diplomacy 51 (1953).

60. These three nations put forth a joint resolution to the effect that none of the American republics could continue to maintain political, commercial, and financial relations with the Axis. Fenwick, *supra* note 58.

61. "Breaking of Diplomatic Relations," Director General's Report on the Third Meeting, *op. cit. supra* note 56, at 32.

62. See Bemis, *op. cit. supra* note 52, at 374. These two nations did announce that they would not treat the American republics at war as belligerents. *Id.* at 377.

63. On the reasons of Chile's refusal see Smith, *op. cit. supra* note 59, at 56. And see Duggan, The Americas (1949) where the author declares at 87 that the Chilean delegate at the Meeting sought to bargain with the United States for Chile's acceptance of the rupture resolution. Chile sought to get from the United States large amounts of financial assistance and military and civilian supples. Smith, *ibid.,* is of the opinion that Chile was not prepared for such an important step as rupture of relations, due to political conditions in the country at the time. The death of the president had made elections necessary in February, 1942, and the provisional regime did not feel that it could, prior to the elections, change the policy of the nation so drastically.

64. Summaries of Argentina's relations with Pan-Americanism and with the United States are set forth in Bemis, *op. cit. supra* note 52, Chs. XV, XVI, XVII, XXI XXII; Blackmer, *op. cit. supra* note 41, at 109-30; Smith, *op. cit. supra* note 59.

65. *Supra* Ch. I, pp. 4, 11.

66. *Id.* at 16-17 on the Drago Doctrine, and see *infra* pp. 172-73.

67. Whitaker in The Western Hemisphere Idea (1954) advances this thesis at 88.

68. Smith, *op. cit. supra* note 59, at 15.

69. Bemis, *op. cit. supra* note 52, at 265.

70. *Ibid.*

71. I Hull, *op. cit. supra* note 49, at 317 (1948).

72. Bemis, *op. cit. supra* note 52, summarizes the background of the Anti-War Treaty at 264-70. For text of the Treaty see International Conferences, 1st Supp. *op. cit. supra* note 26, Appendix C at 496-99.

73. I Hull, *op. cit. supra* note 49, at 325-41.

74. "Adherence to and Ratification of Peace Instruments," International Conferences, 1st Supp. *op. cit. supra* note 26, at 19-20.

75. Smith, *op. cit. supra* note 59, at 23.

76. "Convention on Rights and Duties of States," International Conferences, 1st. Supp. *op. cit. supra* note 26 at 121-24. The non-intervention principle is contained in Art. 8.

77. Bemis, *op. cit. supra* note 52, at 276.

78. *Ibid.*

79. See Bemis, *id.* at 284-93; Blackmer, *op. cit. supra* note 41, at 112-13; Smith, *op. cit. supra* note 59, at 26-36.

80. Art. II, "Convention for the Maintenance, Preservation and Reestablishment of Peace," International Conferences 1st. Supp. *op. cit. supra* note 26 at 188-90. The Buenos Aires Conference tended to demonstrate a divergence of opinion among the American republics concerning the type of inter-American regional system which should be created. By and large the nations of the extreme southern portion of the hemisphere distant from the United States fell into the Argentine orbit and seemed to favor a loosely knit, voluntary organization co-ordinated closely with the League of Nations. The United States and Brazil were satisfied with the system as it existed except that they wanted additional procedures of regularized consultation which might meet and take solidary action for the American community whenever emergencies, particularly non-American in character, threatened hemi-

spheric peace. On the other hand the Caribbean nations had noted the weakness of the League of Nations. Knowing that they were in danger because of their location in the center of the continent, fearing the threat of war from Europe, and motivated also by some fear of the United States, the Caribbean countries hoped for a formalistic and binding hemispheric relationship to achieve a greater voice in inter-American affairs and some measure of United States protection. See Smith, *op. cit. supra* note 59, at 35.

81. I Hull, *op. cit. supra* note 49, at 602.

82. The Argentine Foreign Minister did not head that country's delegation, although he did deliver an opening speech and then two days later left for Chile. Hull thought that he left the Conference "to kill it." *Id.* at 605.

83. *Id.* at 607.

84. International Conferences 1st Supp. *op. cit. supra* note 26, at 308-9.

85. *Ibid.*

86. See Smith, *op. cit. supra* note 59, at 43-44.

87. *Id.* at 46. See also Blackmer, *op. cit. supra* note 41, at 114.

88. II Hull, *op. cit. supra* note 49, at 1380-84, sets forth the background of the Chilean rupture. See also Duggan, *op. cit. supra* note 63, at 89-90.

89. On this phase of inter-American history see II Hull, *id.,* Chs. 99 and 100. See also Welles, Where Are We Heading? Ch. IV (1946).

90. Welles, *id.* at 198-204.

91. *Id.* at 204; "Inter-American Conference on Problems of War and Peace, Mexico City, Feb. 21-Mar. 8, 1945," Report Submitted to the Governing Board of the Pan American Union by the Director General, PAU Cong. & Conf. Series no. 47, 1947, p. 23.

92. II Hull, *op. cit. supra* note 49, at 1403-4.

93. *Id.* at 1405; and see Smith, *op. cit. supra* note 59, at 126-27.

94. Smith, *id.* at 127.

95. Director General's Report, *op. cit. supra* note 91, at 23-24.

96. *Ibid.* On the Conference see Canyes, "The Inter-American System and the Conference of Chapultepec," 39 Am. J. Int. L. 504 (1945); Kunz, "The Inter-American Conference on Problems of War and Peace at Mexico City and the Problem of the Reorganization of the Inter-American System," *id.* at 527.

97. "Resolution LIX, On the Communication Addressed by the Argentine Government to the Pan American Union," Director General's Report, *op. cit. supra* note 91, at 97.

98. *Id.* at 98.

99. PAU Bull., vol. LXXXIX, May, 1945, 261-63; Dept. of State Bull., vol. XII, April 8, 1945, 611-13.

100. Dept. of State Bull., vol. XII, April 15, 1945, 670.

101. Blackmer, *op. cit. supra* note 41, at 124.

102. *Id.* at 142-43; Kunz, *supra* note 96, at 527.

103. Director General's Report, *op. cit. supra* note 91, at 1.

104. "Reciprocal Assistance and American Solidarity," *id.,* at 30-33.

105. Uruguay, because of her proximity to Argentina, was most insistent on an agreement to sanction American aggressors. On this concern as to Argentine intentions and their influence as to reciprocal assistance against American aggression see Smith, *op. cit. supra* note 59, at 130; Duggan, *op. cit. supra* note 63, at 109-10.

106. "Resolution IX, Reorganization, Consolidation and Strengthening of the Inter-American System," Director General's Report, *op. cit. supra* note 91, at 33-38. And see, Canyes, *supra* note 96, at 511-14; Kunz, *supra* note 96.

107. See *infra* Regional Agency, p. 51, for Latin American attitudes and reactions on the Dumbarton Oaks Proposals.

108. Director General's Report. *op. cit. supra* note 91, at 36-38.

109. Plaza, "Latin America's Contribution to the United Nations Organization," International Conciliation, No. 419 (March, 1946) 150. The author discusses that which Latin America was determined to obtain at 153-57.

110. *Id.* at 153.

111. Whitaker, *op. cit. supra* note 67, at 158-73 states the differing views of Latin America and the United States toward regionalism succinctly and well.

112. *Id.* at 172; see also Duggan, *op. cit. supra* note 63, at 116-22.

113. Duggan, *id.* at 120.

114. *Ibid;* Blackmer, *op. cit. supra* note 41, at 155.

115. Smith, *op. cit. supra* note 59, at 137.

116. See *infra,* Regional Agency pp. 48-53.

117. Plaza, *supra* note 109, at 156. And see "Announcement of Secretary of State Stettinius" at the Conference stating the intention of inviting the other American republics to a conference for such a purpose. Dept. of State Bull., vol. XII (May 20, 1945), 930.

118. Inter-American Conference for the Maintenance of Continental Peace and Security, Quitandinha, Brazil, Aug. 15-Sept. 2, 1947, Report of the Delegation of the U.S.A. 59 *et seq.* (1948).

119. Ninth International Conference of American States, Bogotá, Colombia, Mar. 30-May 2, 1948, Report of the Delegation of the United States, 166 *et seq.* (1948).

120. *Id.* at 186 *et seq.*

CHAPTER III

1. The Charter of the Organization of American States (Charter of Bogotá) is set forth in Ninth International Conference of American States, Bogotá, Colombia, Mar. 30-May 2, 1948, Report of the Delegation of the United States, at 166-86 (1948).

2. "Report of Committee on Customs Regulations, Bureau of Information, First International Conference of American States, Washington, Oct. 2, 1889-April 19, 1890," as set forth in International Conferences of American States 36-40 (edited by Scott, 1931).

3. "Resolution, Pan American Union and a Project of a Convention, Fourth International Conference of American States, Buenos Aires, July 12-Aug. 30, 1910," International Conferences, *id.* at 176-79. See Kunz, "The Pan American Union in the Field of International Administration," 31 Iowa L. Rev. 58 at 62 (1945).

4. "Resolution, Organization of the Pan American Union, Fifth International Conference of American States, Santiago, Mar. 25-May 3, 1923," International Conferences, *id.* at 271.

5. *Ibid.*

6. Sixth International Conference of American States, Habana, Jan. 16-Feb. 20, 1928, International Conferences, *id.* at 398-403.

7. Pan American Union, *id.* at 397-98.

8. Art. XIV of the Convention, *op. cit. supra* note 6, at 403 provided that the Convention was to become operative after ratification by all the twenty-one American republics. Some sixteen states finally ratified it. PAU, Tratados y Convenciones Interamericanos, Firmas, ratificaciones y depositos con notas explicativas 33 (Segunda Edicion, 1957).

9. The reasons are summed up by Lleras, "Report on the Ninth International Conference of American States," I Annals of OAS 1 at 9-10 (1949); and by Kunz, *supra* note 3, at 76.

10. "Resolution IX, Reorganization, Consolidation and Strengthening of the Inter-American System," as set forth in Inter-American Conference on Problems of War and Peace, Mexico City, Feb. 21-Mar. 8, 1945, Report Submitted to the Governing Board of the Pan American Union by the Director General, 33-38, PAU Cong. & Conf. Series, no. 47 (1945). For discussion see Canyes, "The Inter-American System and the Conference of Chapultepec," 39 Am. J. Int. L. 504 (1945); Kunz, "The Inter-American Conference on Problems of War and Peace at Mexico City and the Problem of the Reorganization of the Inter-American System," 39 Am. J. Int. L. 527 (1945).

11. The Charter of the United Nations is set forth in Basic Documents of the United Nations 1 *et seq.* (edited by Sohn, 1956).

12. Canyes, *supra* note 10.

13. Inter-American Conference for the Maintenance of Continental Security, Quitandinha, Brazil, Aug. 15-Sept. 2, 1947, Report of the Delegation of the United States of America 59 *et seq.* (1948).

14. See note 1, *supra.*

15. *Id.* at 186 *et seq.*

16. *Id.* at 166.

17. Preamble, *id.* at 166-67. Although the preamble begins with "in the name of their peoples," it is obvious that this is not a grant of power from the peoples to a central authority as is the case of the Constitution of the United States. Moreover, the preamble also speaks of "the States represented" as having agreed to the charter. Lleras in his Report on the Ninth Conference, *supra* note 9, at 20, declares that the use of the terminology "in the name of their peoples" is simply an affirmation of the "democratic principle . . . as opposed to the concept of the State as something antecedent and superior to the rights of the individual."

18. On the binding force of treaties see Fenwick, International Law 430-31 (3rd ed. 1948); I Oppenheim's International Law 800-81 (Lauterpacht 8th ed. 1955); Thomas & Thomas, International Treaties 52 *et seq.* (Monograph, 1950); Research in International Law under the auspicies of the Harvard Law School, Part III, Law of Treaties, Art. 20 in 29 Am. J. Int. L. Supp. 657 at 661 (1935); for comment on Art. 20 see *id.* at 977-92; Kunz, "The Meaning and Range of the Norm *Pacta Sunt Servanda,*" 39 Am. J. Int. L. 180 (1945).

19. 3 Annals of OAS 393 (1951).

20. 9 Annals of OAS 37 (1957). It will be observed that an interim period existed

from the time of the signing of the Charter in 1948 to the time of its coming into force in 1951, and still another interim period until 1956 when it finally came into force as to all the states. This was contemplated by the delegates at Bogotá. Hence a procedure was established by resolution providing for a functioning of the organs on an interim basis in a manner similar to that established in the Charter. It was declared:

> 1. The agencies that have hitherto functioned as Organs of the System of the Union of American Republics shall immediately adopt the nomenclature and provisions established in the Charter of the Organization of American States. 2. The new Organs provided for in the Charter shall be established on a provisional basis, in accordance with the Charter.

Final Act, Ninth International Conference, Resolution XL, *op. cit. supra* note 1, at 273.
    21. Art. 111, Charter of Bogotá, Ninth Conference *id.* at 186.
    22. *Supra* note 13. And see *infra* pp. 205-11 on collective security for discussion.
    23. *Supra* note 15. And see *infra* pp. 203-5 on peaceful settlement of disputes for discussion.
    24. Art. 25, Charter of Bogotá.
    25. Chapter IV of the Charter of Bogotá entitled "Pacific Settlement of Disputes."
    26. Art. 23, Charter of Bogotá.
    27. See e. g. reservation made by certain states when they signed the Pact, Ninth International Conference, *op. cit. supra* note 1, at 199 *et seq.*
    28. As of June, 1961, the following states had ratified: Costa Rica, Dominican Republic, El Salvador, Haiti, Honduras, Mexico, Nicaragua, Panama, and Uruguay. See PAU, Inter-American Treaties and Conventions 44 (Treaty Series No. 9, 1961).
    29. Unlike the Charter of Bogotá and the Rio Treaty, it was provided by Art. LIII of the Pact of Bogotá that its provisions were to come into effect between the parties in the order in which they deposit their ratifications.
    30. Art. LVIII of the Pact of Bogotá lists the treaties which are to cease to be in force upon ratification.
    31. Resolution XIV, Committee on Methods for the Peaceful Solution of Conflicts, International Conferences of American States, 1st Supp. 1933-1940 360 (1940). For discussion of the Inter-American Peace Committee see *infra* pp. 125-27.
    32. See Chapter XV of the Charter of Bogotá on the Specialized Organizations.
    33. On international organization in general and its historical development see Cheever and Haviland, Organizing for Peace 18-42 (1954); Mangone, A Short History of International Organization (1954); Schwarzenberger, Power Politics 93-99, 232-50 (2d ed. 1951); Wright, The Study of International Relations 199-211 (1955); Jenks, "Some Constitutional Problems of International Organizations," 22 Brit. Y. B. Int. L. 11 (1945); Lowenstein, "Sovereignty and International Co-operation," 48 Am. J. Int. L. 222 (1954). For a complete bibliography on international organization see Sohn, Cases and Materials on World Law 1-6 (1950).
    34. See *infra* Ch. VII on functions of OAS.
    35. For discussion see Thomas and Thomas, Non-Intervention: The Law and Its Import in the Americas 109-11 (1956).
    36. Schwarzenberger in his Manual of International Law (1947) at p. 119 uses the term "quasi governmental" in speaking of agencies of international organization.
    37. *Supra* note 2.
    38. Resolution, Reorganization of the "Union of American Republics," Fourth International Conference of American States, International Conferences, *op. cit. supra* note 2, at 172-76.
    39. *Supra* note 10.
    40. Ninth International Conference of American States, *op. cit. supra* note 1, at 95.
    41. Fenwick, "The Ninth International Conference of American States," 42 Am. J. Int. L. 553 at 555 (1948). High-sounding and lofty names such as "Organic Charter of the Pan American Union," "Charter of the American Regional Community," and "Pact for the Organization of an Association of American Nations" were submitted. None of them found favor. It was believed that to use in the title the words "Pan American Union" would serve to perpetuate the confusion between the association itself and one of its institutions. See Lleras, *supra* note 9, at 15-16.
    42. Argentina was strongly in opposition to the use of any name suggesting a superstate. See Ninth International Conference, *op. cit. supra* note 1, at 14. And see Fenwick, *ibid.;* and Lleras, *ibid.*
    43. On the federal state see I Oppenheim, *op. cit. supra* note 18, at 175-78; Ross, Constitution of the United Nations 193-94 (1950); Schwarzenberger, *op. cit. supra* note 33,

at 76-79, 88-89; Vinacke, International Organization, Ch. 4 (1934); I Willoughby on the Constitution of the United States 129-40 (2d ed. 1929).

44. See Lleras, *op. cit. supra* note 9 at 18-19 on the debate at Bogotá over the nature of the OAS. He declares at 18:

> What could a superstate be except a force superior to the autonomous and unilateral will of each State? But is it not well known that such a force exists, in every international organization, and that the principle underlying every association of nations is that of placing a limit upon the individual act of each State for the purpose of subjecting it to the bilateral or multilateral action called for by the international contract? Cannot a superstate, in international relations be also (and only) what the state is in relation to individuals?

Lleras continues at 19:

> There was certainly no fear [at Bogotá] that the voluntary delegation of power and sovereignty by a group of States would have as its natural consequence a power superior to that which resides in each individual power and sovereignty; the fear rather was that an ambiguous basis would be established for the eventual creation in America, not of a superstate, but of a single state.

45. Ross is of the opinion that the world organization, the United Nations, cannot be considered as a confederation or, as he calls it, a federation because the United Nations is an agency supposedly universal in nature potentially to be composed of all nations. Therefore, it cannot be said that it protects the community externally. Ross, *op. cit. supra* note 43, at 195-96. This objection cannot be made as to the OAS for, as a regional organization, it was created in part to protect the members externally, i.e., from threats to the peace and aggressions from without the hemisphere as well as to maintain peace internally among the member states.

46. This is not always true, for the states of the United States under the Articles of Confederation 1781-89 did for all practical purposes lose their international personality. They lost control of their foreign affairs to the United States, the central government which acquired international personality. See Fenwick, *op. cit. supra* note 18, at 121. He further points out here that the international personality of the states was latent inasmuch as they could regain control of their foreign affairs by dissolving the union.

On confederation see I Oppenheim, *op. cit. supra* note 18, at 173-74; Vinacke, *op. cit. supra* note 43; I Willoughby, *op. cit. supra* note 43. Wright points out that the difference between a federation and a confederation is relative and that they have both been classified as federal governments. Although the distinction is often made that confederations act only on states while federation signifies a federal government acting within its powers to govern individuals, he mentions that international organizations often have functions which extend over into the field of individual interests, and if these functions are implemented effectively by the organization, the organization may become a federation. As such, Wright believes that the United Nations has the potentiality of becoming a federation. See Wright, *op. cit. supra* note 33 at 204-5. Chapter VII of the Charter of Bogotá sets out principles of co-operation to achieve a decent standard of living conditions and to develop certain human rights. These functions apply to individuals. To the extent that these functions of the OAS are accepted and implemented by the OAS it might be said that it approaches a federation, although the problem still exists that it will be the individual states implementing OAS action. The OAS will not act directly on the individual.

47. Schwartzenberger, *op. cit. supra* note 33, at 244-50 discusses briefly former confederations of states, their lack of power and impotence.

48. For discussion of legal personality of international organizations see Kelsen, The Law of the United Nations 329 *et seq.* (1950); Corbett, "What Is the League of Nations?" 1932 Brit. Y. B. Int. L. 119; Friedmann, "International Public Corporations," 6 Mod. L. Rev. 185 (1943); Jenks, "The Legal Personality of International Organizations," 22 Brit. Y. B. Int. L. 267 (1945); Penfield, "The Legal Status of the Pan American Union," 2 Am. J. Int. L. 257 (1926); Rapisardi-Mirabelli, "La théorie générale des unions internationales," 7 Recueil des Cours 345 (1925).

49. Fitzmaurice, "The Law and Procedure of the International Court of Justice," 27 Brit. Y. B. Int. L. 7 at 24-27 (1950).

50. See *infra* pp. 89-93, 101-7 on the powers of these organs and *infra* pp. 249-50 on maintenance of peace and security.

51. Travis, "The Organization of American States: A Guide to the Future," X Western

Political Quarterly 491 (1957) concludes at 503-4 that the OAS possesses legal personality on the regional level.

52. Reparation for Injuries Suffered in the Service of the United Nations, Advisory Opinion, I. C. J. Reports 1949, p. 174 at 179. For discussion of this case see Wright, "The Jural Personality of the United Nations," 43 Am. J. Int. L. 509 (1949).

53. Advisory Opinion, *id.* at 178-79.

54. Jenks, "The Legal Personality of International Organizations," *supra* note 48.

55. In connection with this article, the General Assembly on Feb. 13, 1946, approved a convention, Privileges and Immunities of the United Nations as set forth in Sohn, *op cit. supra* note 11, at 268-74. See also Liang, "Legal Status of the United Nations in the United States of America," 2 Int. L. Q. 577 (1949).

56. Art. 104 requires privileges and immunities necessary for the independent performance of their duties to be granted to the representatives of the governments on the Council and the organs of the Council and the personnel of their delegations as well as the secretary general and the assistant secretary general.

57. Art. 105 declares that the juridical status of the specialized organizations and the officials of the Pan American Union shall be determined through agreements between the respective organs and the governments concerned.

58. Documents and Notes on Privileges and Immunities with Special Reference to the Organization of American States, Pan American Union Division of Law and Treaties, 1954, p. 44 *et seq.* For reports of the Committee on Privileges and Immunities see *id.* at 30 *et seq.* and 38 *et seq.* See also 1948 Inter-American Jur. Y. B. 120; and Colburn, "Privileges and Immunities of the Organization of American States," 1949 Inter-American Jur. Y. B. 96.

59. Documents and Notes on Privileges and Immunities, *id.* at 64.

60. 2 Annals of OAS 29-30 (1950).

61. Art. 15 of the Agreement states: "The present Agreement shall be subject to the approval of the appropriate authorities in the respective countries." Note the agreement requires approval but not necessarily ratification. The drafting committee was of the opinion that if necessary in a nation it should be formally ratified, but felt that in some nations the agreement could be effectuated by the executive power without the need of formal ratification. Thus "approval" was required which would permit each government to facilitate it in the manner it thought desirable. See Report of the Committee on Privileges and Immunities of the OAS, *op. cit. supra* note 58, at 31.

62. *Id.* at 30.

63. "The Specialized Conferences and the Specialized Organizations are not included within the scope of this Agreement." Art. 1, par. 2 of the Agreement.

64. Art. 2. This Article does permit express waiver of immunity from legal process, but even in case of waiver the property and assets of the organization are not subject to any measure of execution.

65. Agreement on Privilege and Immunities, Arts. 3 and 4.

66. *Id.* Art. 5.

67. *Id.* Art. 6.

68. *Id.* Art. 9.

69. *Id.* Art. 10.

70. As of 1961 only Costa Rica, Cuba, Ecuador, Haiti, Peru, and Nicaragua had ratified. PAU, Inter-American Treaties and Conventions 101 (Treaty Ser. No. 9, 1961).

71. 59 Stat. 669; also set forth in Documents and Notes on Privileges and Immunities *op. cit. supra* note 58, at 84.

72. Section 8 of the Act, Documents and Notes, *ibid.*

73. Executive Order 9698, *id.* at 98. The Inter-American Defense Board has also been so designated, *id.* at 99.

74. It is clear that the Pan American Union does possess these competences. In recent years it has instituted legal proceedings in the Federal District Court of the District of Columbia. See 5 Annals of the OAS 36 (1953). Moreover, in years before the reorganization at Bogotá it possessed such powers. See Kunz, *supra* note 3, at 79. But see Penfield, *supra* note 48, who believed that the funds in the hands of the Union were the common property of the members of the organization and not the property of the Pan American Union as an entity.

75. Section 8(b) of the Act, *supra* note 71.

76. *Supra* note 59.

77. See Report of the House of Representatives Committee on Foreign Affairs Regarding the USA-OAS Bilateral Agreements, Documents on Privileges and Immunities, *op. cit. supra* note 58, at 55; and Report of Senate Committee on Foreign Relations Regarding USA-OAS Bilateral Agreement, *id.* at 60.

78. Ninth International Conference of American States, *op. cit. supra* note 1, at 272.

79. Art. 25, Bogotá Charter.

80. See Lleras, *supra* note 9, at 21-23; and Fenwick, "The Inter-American Regional System: Fifty Years of Progress," 50 Am. J. Int. L. 18 at 27 (1956).

81. UNCIO, Interim Report to Committee III/4 by Subcommittee III/4/A, Doc. 533, III/4/A/9 p. 3 (Documents, XII, p. 850).

82. UNCIO, Summary Report of Fifth Meeting of Committee III/4, June 8, 1945, Doc. 889/III/4/12 p. 1 (Documents, XII, p. 701).

On the problem of regionalism and regional arrangements vis-à-vis the United Nations see Aranha, "Regional Systems and the Future of the United Nations," 26 For. Affairs 415 (1948); Bebr, "Regional Organizations: A United Nations Problem," 49 Am. J. Int. L. 166 (1955); Liang, "Regional Arrangements and International Security," 31 Grotius Soc. Trans. 216 (1946); Starke, "Regionalism as a Problem of International Law," in Lipsky, Law and Politics in the World Community 114 (1953); van Kleffens, "Regionalism and Political Facts," 43 Am. J. Int. L. 666 (1949).

83. On conflict of jurisdiction between the United Nations and the OAS see the Guatemala case *infra* pp. 302-13.

84. Eagleton in International Government (3rd ed. 1957) lists the reasons for regionalism at 557. Arguments in favor point out that development toward a world system of government is best attainable gradually through the experience of smaller groups with closer interests; that threats to peace originate generally between neighboring states and hence the peoples in the area being most vitally affected are most willing to take the necessary security measures and with more dispatch and efficiency; that many problems are local and therefore local people are best able to handle them; that in each region there would be a dominant power, thus constituting a balance of power under the leadership of the great powers; and finally that homogeneity of interests brings about a natural trend toward regionalism.

Arguments against regionalism declare that international problems are worldwide in nature; that even though disputes may originate locally they tend to develop into world wars and thus the world community must take an interest; that regional groupings are enlarged alliances which lead to bigger wars; that the regions vary as to power so that a balance of power could hardly ensue; that the smaller states of a regional system will be dominated by the great power in the region and if more than one great power exists the matter would be even more complicated; that there is little reason to believe that nations in a region could work with more co-operation and efficiency than all nations in a universal system; that security enforcement through a regional organization would divide any potential strength that could be massed against an aggressor; that economic sanctions could not effectively be used in a region since in order to be effective such sanctions must be universal.

85. See Ball and Killough, International Relations 446 (1956); and Bebr, *supra* note 82, at 167.

86. On the reaction of the Americas to the Dumbarton Oaks Proposals and their efforts to salvage the Inter-American System see Kunz, "Individual and Collective Self-Defense in Article 51 of the Charter of the United Nations," 41 Am. J. Int. L. 872 (1947); Padilla, "The American System and the World Organization," 24 Foreign Affairs 99 (1945); Plaza, "Latin America's Contribution to the United Nations Organization," 1946, Int. Concil. No. 419 p. 150. Reid, "Regionalism under the United Nations Charter," *id.* at 120; Rowe, "Regional Arrangements and the United Nations," Bull. PAU, vol. 79 (1945) p. 429.

87. Ch. VII, Section C of paragraph 1 of the Dumbarton Oaks Proposals for the Establishment of a General International Organization as set forth in Sohn, *op. cit. supra* note 11, at 1146.

88. *Ibid.*

89. *Id.* par. 2.

90. See Act of Chapultepec, Director General's Report, *op. cit. supra* note 10, at 30-33.

91. See *infra* pp. 250-60 on individual and collective self-defense.

92. See Ball and Killough, *op. cit. supra* note 85, at 449.

93. See *infra* pp. 205-11 on the Rio Treaty.

94. But see the Guatemala case *infra* pp. 302-13.

95. See Paddleford, "Recent Developments in Regional Organizations," Proceedings of Am. Soc. Int. L. 1955 p. 23. At p. 37 he cites the Chairman of Committee III/14 at the San Francisco Conference as adopting this constitution.

96. See Goodrich and Hambro, Charter of the United Nations 314-15 (2d and rev. ed. 1949).

97. Ninth International Conference, *op. cit. supra* note 1, at 33-34. The OAS has, however, co-operated well with the world organization. See Whitaker, "Development of American Regionalism," Int. Concil. No. 469, Mar. 1951, 123 at 157.

98. Ball, *op. cit. supra* note 85, at 449.

CHAPTER IV

1. See, e.g., "Art. V, Resolution on the Organization of the Pan American Union, Fifth International Conference of American States, Santiago, Mar. 25-May 3, 1923," International Conferences of American States, 1889-1928, 268-71 at 270; "Art. I, Convention, Pan American Union," Sixth International Conference of American States, Habana, Jan. 16-Feb. 20, 1928, *id.*, 398-403, at 399. See also Ninth International Conference of American States, Bogotá, Colombia, Mar. 30-May 2, 1948, Report of the Delegation of the United States 95 at 97 (1948); Kunz, "The Pan American Union in the Field of International Administration," 31 Iowa L. Rev. 58 at 78 (1945).

2. Art. 4, Rio Treaty. Although this zone is defined for purposes of collective security of the hemisphere, it can well be assumed that this in effect delineates the boundaries of the region.

3. Kunz, in his article, "The Bogotá Charter of the Organization of American States," 42 Am. J. Int. L. (1948) takes the position, at 571, that only sovereign states are admissible.

Art. 3 makes it clear that states of a federal union are not admissible, for, if two or more independent states now existing form a new political entity, i.e., a state, the original component parts lose their membership upon entry into the organization of the new entity by ratification of the Charter. As to an entity under complete colonial status, a great stretch of the imagination would have to take place to bring it within the definition of "state."

4. International Conferences of American States 1933-40, 1st Supp. at 122 (1940). This is the definition in general of the term "state" in international law. See Fenwick, International Law 104-6 (3rd ed. 1948); I Oppenheim's International Law, sec. 64 (Lauterpacht 8th ed. 1955); Ross, A Textbook of International Law 33-36 (1947).

5. The status of Cuba, Panama, the Dominican Republic, and Haiti as full sovereign states in earlier times has been subject to doubt because of certain obligations imposed upon these countries by treaties with the United States, which, some claimed, made them dependents or protectorates of the United States. Nevertheless they were admitted to the Inter-American System. Such treaty obligations have now been abrogated, thus the states involved are fully sovereign. On the earlier status of these nations and the removal of the restrictions see Fenwick, *id.* at 111-13; Hershey, The Essentials of International Public Law 108 (1921); I Hyde, International Law Chiefly as Interpreted and Applied by the United States 56-84 (2d ed. 1947); Thomas and Thomas, Non-Intervention: The Law and Its Import in the Americas 21-39 (1956).

6. Goodrich and Hambro, Charter of the United Nations 124-25; Kelsen, The Law of the United Nations 59-60 (1950); Ross, The Constitution of the United Nations 43 (1950).

7. For example, the Commonwealth of Puerto Rico has been granted internal self-government, although the United States retains control over external affairs and matters of defense. On the status of Puerto Rico, see "Puerto Rico, A Study in Democratic Government," The Annals of the American Academy of Political Science, January, 1953; Hayden and Rivlin, Non-Self-Governing Territories: Status of Puerto Rico (Woodrow Wilson Foundation, Sept., 1954).

8. It is doubtful whether a hard and fast requirement of a political structure conforming to a republic has ever existed, for at the time of the First International Conference of American States, in 1889, Brazil was still an empire and she was invited; see Kunz, *supra* note 1, at 78.

9. All of the republics have now ratified the Charter of Bogotá. The last nation to ratify was Uruguay, which deposited its ratification September 1, 1955. PAU, Inter-American Treaties and Conventions, Signatures, ratifications and deposits with explanatory notes 42 (2d ed. 1957).

10. Ninth International Conference, *op. cit. supra* note 1, at 16.

11. An interesting and difficult problem could possibly arise under Article 3. Assume the creation of a new federal state from two or more formerly sovereign American states, members of the OAS. It could occur that the new federal state would fail to ratify. According to the strict wording of Article 3, the former sovereign states of the new federation do not lose membership until the entry of the new political entity into the organization. Query, could the original membership of the component parts now not fully sovereign states continue in view of the fact that no provision is made for expulsion?

12. Art. 2, Draft Organic Pact of the Inter-American System, Ninth International Conference, *op. cit. supra* note 1, at 97.

13. Ninth International Conference, *id.* at 15. Because certain American territories are in the process of shedding their colonial status and will soon emerge as new hemispheric states, some dissatisfaction has been expressed over the Charter's provisions which permit new American states to be admitted to the OAS automatically upon their unilateral act of ratification. Thus Guatemala, noting that the Charter does not establish any procedure for the verification of the minimum requirements for membership such as the new territory's character as a state, its geographic location within the hemisphere, the compatibility or incompatibility with the inter-American system of its possible ties with the former metropolitan country or with other extracontinental states, and also noting that the Charter does not establish any form that a judgment on these issues by the American community should take, has requested the Council of the OAS to make pertinent studies of this problem and to draw up standards for admittance procedures. At its meeting in May, 1962, the Council referred the question to its Committee on Juridical and Political Affairs. PAU, Explanatory Note and Memorandum from the Delegation of Guatemala on the Need to Establish a Procedure for the Admission of New States to the Organization of American States, OEA/Ser. G/V, C-d-985 (English) Rev., May 16, 1962. And see discussion *infra* p. 57 on possible procedures to be followed for admittance in case necessity arises.

14. Kelsen, *op. cit. supra* note 6, at 58.

15. If the issue ever became important in the OAS, which is unlikely, and an actual dispute arose, the matter of decision might ultimately have to be decided by an Inter-American Conference or a Meeting of Ministers of Foreign Affairs. See *infra* p. 57 on admitting a new community as a state into the OAS.

16. Arts. 3 and 4, UN Charter, Basic Documents of the United Nations 1 at 3 (edited by Sohn 1956).

17. Art. 108, Charter of Bogotá.

18. The phrasing was taken from Article 23 of the Rio Treaty. For discussion see Inter-American Conference for the Maintenance of Continental Peace and Security, Quitandinha, Brazil, Aug. 15-Sept. 2, 1947, Report of the Delegation of the United States of America 37 (1948).

19. See *infra* pp. 251, 267 on renunciation of use of force and condemnation of aggression.

20. Ninth International Conference, *op. cit. supra* note 1, at 15.

21. Art. 4(2), UN Charter, *op. cit. supra* note 16. See also Conditions of Admission of a State to Membership in the United Nations, Advisory Opinion of the International Court of Justice, May 28, 1948, I.C.J. Reports 57-115 (1948).

22. Goodrich and Hambro, *op. cit. supra* note 6, at 135-37; Ross, *op. cit. supra* note 6, at 46.

23. Aufricht, "Principles and Practices of Recognition by International Organizations," 43 Am. J. Int. L. 679 (1949).

24. See *supra* note 14.

25. See *infra* Ch. V on discussion of the functions of the Inter-American Conference.

26. See *infra* Ch. V on discussion of the powers of the Meetings of Ministers of Foreign Affairs under Article 39 of the Bogotá Charter.

27. It is to be hoped that the organ so deciding will confine itself to juridical considerations as to the legal meaning of the word "state," and as to whether the applicant meets the qualifications. Such consideration is particularly to be hoped for in view of the fact that the American states have defined what is meant by a state as noted above. See *supra* note 4. In any event the problem will probably not arise in the OAS given today's conditions. In the United Nations the struggles over admissions of new members have been political, caused by the power struggle of the two competing blocs who are trying to gain ascendancy and mastery in that organization through the admission or nonadmission of members favoring one or the other bloc.

28. For example, a situation similiar to the Chinese representation question in the United Nations.

29. See *infra* Ch. XI on the principles of recognition.

30. See Jenks, "Some Constitutional Problems of International Organizations," 22 Brit. Y. B. Int. L. 11 at 24-27 (1945).

31. Art. 6, UN Charter, *op. cit. supra* note 16.

32. Art. 5, UN Charter, *ibid.*

33. Kelsen, *op. cit. supra* note 6, at 710-12.

34. Report of Rapporteur of Committee I/2 as amended June 19 [24], 1945, UNCIO Doc. 1178 I/2/72 (2); 7 UNCIO Docs., pp. 329-32.

35. See Jenks, *supra* note 30, at 25.

36. *Supra* note 34.

37. Jenks, *supra* note 30 at 26.

38. See Art. 3, Draft Organic Pact of the Inter-American System, Ninth International Conference, *op. cit. supra* note 1, at 97. And see *id.* at 16.

39. On the Punta del Este Meeting see PAU, Final Act Eighth Meeting of Consultation of Ministers of Foreign Affairs Serving as Organ of Consultation in Application of the Inter-American Treaty of Reciprocal Assistance, Punta del Este, Uruguay, January 22-31, 1962, OEA/Ser.C/II.8 (English) 1962; XLVI Dept. State Bull. 267-83 (Feb. 19, 1962); N. Y. Times, Jan. 26, 28, 31, Feb. 1, 4 (1962); Time, p. 23, vol. LXXIX, No. 7, Latin American ed., 1962. On the concept of community and international law see *infra* pp. 188-89. Fenwick justifies the exclusion of the Castro government of Cuba from the OAS on the basis of the rule of international law that violation of a treaty by one party justifies the release from treaty obligations by the other party. He is of the opinion that this rule applies equally to a multilateral treaty, but that the members in taking the decision should act by a large majority and should consider the seriousness of the violation. See Fenwick, "The Issues at Punta del Este: Non-Intervention v. Collective Security," 56 Am. J. Int. L. 469 at 474 (1962).

40. Art. 112, Charter of Bogotá.

41. Resolution Pan American Union, Sixth International Conference, *op. cit. supra* note 1, at 397-98. See Kunz, *supra* note 1, at 78; and Kunz, *supra* note 3, at 571.

42. See Jenks, *supra* note 30, at 23-24.

43. See Discussion in Committee I/2, June 17, 1945, UNCIO Doc. 1086, I/2/77; 7 UNCIO Docs. pp. 262-67, 274. Report of Rapporteur of Committee I/2, as amended, June 19 [24] 1945, UNCIO Doc. 1178, I/2/76(2); 7 UNCIO Docs., pp. 327-29. Discussion in Committee I, June 19, 1945, UNCIO Doc. 1167, I/10; 6 UNCIO Docs., pp. 122-23.

44. Ninth International Conference, *op. cit. supra* note 1, at 16.

45. For something on the legal confusion created in the United Nations, see Thomas and Thomas, *op. cit. supra* note 5, at 156-58.

CHAPTER V

1. Charter of Bogotá, Arts. 33, 39, 93. For discussion of the international conference in general, see Dunn, The Practice and Procedure of International Conferences (1929); Middlebush and Hill, Elements of International Relations 179-82 (1940); Potter, An Introduction to the Study of International Organization Ch. XII, 188-209 (3rd ed. 1928); Schwarzenberger, Power Politics 240-43 (2d ed. 1951); Vandenbosch & Hogan, The United Nations: Background, Organization, Functions, Activities 29-31 (1952); Vinacke, International Organization 140-77 (1934).

2. *Supra* Ch. I.

3. A collection of the documents and results of the first six conferences will be found in The International Conferences of American States 1889-1928 (edited by Scott, 1931); conferences held between 1933 and 1940 will be found in the International Conferences of American States, First Supplement 1933-1940 (1940). The Ninth Conference is set forth in The Report of the Delegation of the United States, Ninth International Conference of American States, Bogotá, Colombia, March 30-May 2, 1948, at 166 *et seq.* The Tenth Conference is contained in Report of the Delegation of the United States, Tenth Inter-American Conference, Caracas, Venezuela, March 1-28, 1954, at 76 *et seq.*

4. See Whitaker, "Development of American Regionalism, The Organization of American States," International Conciliation, No. 469 March, 1951, 123 at 129; Fenwick, "The Ninth International Conference of American States," 42 Am. J. Int. L. 553 at 557 (1948).

5. "International Conference of American States on Conciliation and Arbitration, Washington, Dec. 10, 1928-Jan. 5, 1929," International Conferences 1889-1928, *op. cit. supra* note 3 at 455 *et seq.*

6. International Conferences, 1st Supp., *op. cit. supra* note 3 at 129 *et seq.*

7. As contained in the Report Submitted to the Governing Board of the PAU by the Director General (Cong. & Conf. Series No. 47, PAU, 1945).

8. Report of the Delegation of the United States of America, Inter-American Conference for the Maintenance of Continental Peace and Security, Quitandinha, Brazil, August 15-Sept. 2, 1947.

9. Art. 36, Charter of Bogotá. See also Report of Delegation of USA, *op. cit. supra* note 3 at 17.

10. See *infra* pp. 79 *et seq.* on the Meetings of Foreign Ministers.

11. Art. 111, Charter of Bogotá.

12. See *supra* Ch. III, pp. 35-36. For discussion of the Inter-American Conference, see Lleras, "Report on the Ninth International Conference of American States," I Annals of OAS 1 at 33-34 (1949); Report of Delegation of U.S.A., *op. cit. supra* note 3 at 17-19; Whitaker, *supra* note 4, at 139-40.

13. Charter of Bogotá, Arts. 33 and 111.

14. *Id.,* Art. 33.

15. The question of establishing peace between Paraguay and Bolivia was discussed at the Seventh Conference in 1933 and the conference activities aided in bringing about an armistice of short duration between the belligerents. See "Resolution LXIX, Peace in the Chaco, Seventh International Conference of American States," International Conferences, 1st Supp., *op. cit. supra* note 3 at 84. See also Wilgus, The Development of Hispanic America, 755 (1941).

16. Report of Delegation of U.S.A., *op. cit. supra* note 3 at 186 *et seq.*

17. Rio Treaty, Arts. 3, 6, 8, 11, and 12.

18. "XCIII, Declaration of Solidarity for the Preservation of the Political Integrity of the American States against the Intervention of International Communism," Report of Delegation of U.S.A., Tenth Conference, *op. cit. supra* note 3 at 157.

19. On international legislation in general see I Hudson, International Legislation, "Introduction," xiii—1x (1931); see also Eagleton, International Government 183-209 (3rd ed. 1950).

20. See "Resolution VIII on Reciprocal Assistance and American Solidarity," Report of the Director General, *op. cit. supra* note 7 at 30. See also Sanders, "Sovereignty and Interdependence in the New World," 18 Dept. State Bull. 155 at 165 (1948); Fenwick, "The Inter-American Regional System," 39 Am. Pol. Sci. Rev. 490 at 496 (1945).

21. "The effect of a treaty depends on whether or not the treaty is subject to ratification. . . . As a rule . . . , the responsibility for final decision is too great to be undertaken by a diplomatic representative. The government of a state may wish to reserve to itself the last word on the subject, or may be constitutionally required to leave the matter with another branch of the government, as, for example, parliament or congress. Thus a ratification clause is included in most treaties. If a treaty is subject to ratification, signature means no more than that the delegates have agreed upon a text and are willing to accept it and refer it to their governments for such action as those governments may choose to take in regard to acceptance or rejection of the treaty." Thomas & Thomas, International Treaties 33 (monograph 1950).

22. Formal ratification is accepted procedure for inter-American treaties and conventions. See Fenwick, International Law 435 (3rd ed. 1948); Fenwick, *supra* note 20 at 496.

23. These computations are based on the 1957 publication of the Pan American Union, Inter-American Treaties and Conventions, Signatures, ratifications and deposits with explanatory notes.

24. *Id.* at 42.

25. *Id.* at 81.

26. On this problem of ratification after signature by conference delegates in other international organizations see Eagleton, *op. cit. supra* note 19 at 193-94.

27. PAU, Handbook for Delegates to the Ninth International Conference of American States, Bogotá, Colombia, March 30, 1948, at 20 (1947); Fenwick, *supra* note 20 at 496.

28. Fenwick, *ibid.;* Sanders, *supra* note 20 at 165.

29. Eighth International Conference of American States, Lima, December 9-27, 1938, International Conferences, 1st Supp, *op. cit. supra* note 3 at 215 *et seq.*

30. At least such was the attitude of the United States. Argentina apparently adopted no such attitude as to the Declaration of Lima. See Smith, Yankee Diplomacy 43-45 (1953).

31. See Note, "The Binding Force of League Resolutions," XVI Brit. Y. B. Int. L. 157 (1935), where issue is taken with the position that League of Nations Resolutions could be considered binding to an extent to bring about a change in international law. See also I Podesta Costa, Derecho Internacional Publico 367 (3rd ed. 1955).

32. Report of the Director General, *op. cit. supra* note 7 at 30.

33. Fenwick, *op. cit. supra* note 22 at 205.

34. *Id.* at 79. Fenwick declares that such resolutions and declarations "have been regarded *de facto* as creating binding obligations . . . "

35. V Hackworth, A Digest of International Law 33 (1927).

36. Fawcett, in "The Legal Character of International Agreements," XXX Brit. Y. B. Int. L. 382 (1953), establishes that no particular form is necessary to validity. That which is requisite is an intention of the parties to create legal obligations between them. For examples of various types of international agreements see II Accioly, Tratado de Derecho

Internacional Publico 412-15 (1946); III Antokoletz, Derecho Internacional Publico 252-54 (4th ed. 1944); Jones, "International Agreements Other Than 'Interstate Treaties'—Modern Developments," XXI Brit. Y. B. Int. L. 111 at 115 (1944).

37. See Jessup, A Modern Law of Nations 126 (1948); Jones, Full Powers and Ratification 133 (1946); I Oppenheim, International Law 906 (8th ed. Lauterpacht, 1955); Blix, "The Requirement of Ratification," XXX Brit. Y. B. Int. L. 352 (1953); McDougal & Lans, "Treaties and Congressional-Executive or Presidential Agreements: Interchangeable Instruments of National Policy," 54 Yale L. J. 181, 534 at 321 (1945).

38. Hudson, op. cit. supra note 19 at xiii.

39. Starke, An Introduction to International Law 306 (3rd ed. 1954). Blix, supra note 37 discusses in a lucid and complete manner the practices of states, decided cases, and the opinions of writers concerning the requirement of ratification. He concludes that treaties enter into force in accordance with the express or clearly implied intentions of the parties, or in case of doubt by signature. In his opinion ratification is not needed unless the parties expressly or impliedly so intend, and when ratification is intended it is set forth expressly or by very clear implication.

40. See Fenwick, supra note 20 at 496.

41. Sanders, supra note 20 at 165.

42. See line of authority cited supra notes 38 and 39.

43. See "Harvard Draft Convention on the Law of Treaties, Article 7(d)" and comment thereon with citation of authorities, 29 Am. J. Int. L. 657 at 763 et seq. (1935).

Article 5 of the Habana Convention on Treaties declares: "Treaties are obligatory only after ratification ... even though the condition is not stipulated in the full powers of the negotiators or does not appear in the treaty itself." International Conferences 1889-1928, op. cit. supra note 3 at 417.

Antokoletz is of the opinion that ratification is an essential element even though the treaty is silent in this respect. III Antokoletz, op. cit. supra note 36 at 257. Accioly and Podesta Costa are in accord. II Accioly, op. cit. supra note 36 at 437; I Podesta Costa, op. cit. supra note 31 at 373. Oppenheim is generally in accord although he recognizes certain exceptions. I Oppenheim, op. cit. supra note 37 at 906.

44. Ratification is actually a procedure carried out by the executive power of a state, usually the head of state. However, because of constitutional requirements necessitating consent or approval of the legislative body the term "ratification" has been sometimes used to describe the action of the state. Some authors, therefore, call ratification by the executive international ratification and the approval by the legislative organ of the state constitutional ratification. Blix, supra note 37 at 352.

45. This view has come into international law in the twentieth century and some still doubt that international law requires approval of a treaty by the legislative branch to render the treaty valid. See for example Fitzmaurice, "Do Treaties Need Ratification?" XV Brit. Y. B. Int. L. 113 at 134 (1934). See also McDougal & Lans, supra note 37 at 323-31. Jessup is of the opinion that the constitutional law of the state determines whether an agreement comes into force without ratification. Jessup, op. cit. supra note 37 at 126. Jones takes the position that if the constitutional law of the other contracting party requires ratification the treaty cannot be invoked unless ratification has been forthcoming. Jones, op. cit. supra note 36 at 133. Fenwick, op. cit. supra note 22 at 436, states that a majority of writers believe that a treaty which has not been ratified with observance of constitutional requirements is invalid.

46. Constitution of the U.S.A., Art. II, Sec. 2.

47. Their constitutional validity is well established by the Supreme Court of the United States in such cases as U.S. v. Belmont, 301 U.S. 324 (1937) and U.S. v. Pink, 315 U.S. 203 (1942). McDougal and Lans, supra note 37, point out at 324 that U.S. adherence to international organizations in the past was almost always carried out by executive agreements. At 272 they say that declarations of Inter-American Conferences which attempt to create obligations have been treated as executive agreements with no submission to the U.S. Senate.

48. See Schwartz, American Constitutional Law 107-8 (1955).

49. I Oppenheim, op. cit. supra note 37 at 906.

50. McDougal & Lans, supra note 37 at 320 seem of the opinion that under U.S. practice ratification by the President is generally necessary, but that it may be informal and no particular form need be followed.

Blix, supra note 37 at 357, speaks to the effect that the consent of the parties can be established not only by formal ratification by the executive, but also by proclamations, by publication, or by an exchange of telegrams or of notes.

However, ratification may not come about in a tacit manner, i.e., arising from implication by the inactivity of the state. It would seem that a ratification must be in writing, expressing confirmation of the treaty, and have finality. Jones, *op. cit. supra* note 37 at 357. Accioly comments that ratification can be tacit, but through unequivocal acts such as a beginning of execution of the treaty. I Accioly, *op. cit. supra* note 36 at 411.

51. For discussion, see Gomez Otalora, "Treaties and Executive Agreements in Latin America" (Unpublished Comment, 1959).

Most jurists of Latin America seem to believe that international agreements are subject to legislative approval for validity. For example, Tena Ramirez in his work, Derecho Constitucional Mexicano (3rd ed. 1955), states emphatically at 420 that executive agreements are subject to the approval of the Senate because the Mexican Constitution, unlike the Constitution of the United States, provides that the Senate shall have this power not only in connection with international treaties but also in connection with any "diplomatic convention."

However, Antokoletz recognizes that not all international agreements require legislative approval in Argentina. Such approval is necessary for all such agreements that directly or indirectly affect a constitutional principle or that create new international obligations, or that pertain to public monies. III Antokoletz, *op. cit. supra* note 36 at 258.

Podesta Costa asserts that since 1930 the executive power of Argentina has ratified certain international agreements without congressional consent when such agreements do not concern matters essentially legislative in character. I Podesta Costa, *op. cit. supra* note 31 at 374, f.n. 1.

52. See I Podesta Costa, *id.* at 30.

53. "Report of Committee on Customs Regulations Bureau of Information, First International Conference of American States," International Conferences 1889-1928, *op. cit. supra* note 3 at 36.

54. Schmeckebier, International Organizations in which the United States Participates 78-79 (1935); Kunz, "The Pan-American Union in the Field of International Administration," 31 Iowa L. Rev. 58 at 76-79 (1945); McDougal & Lans, *supra* note 37 at 271.

If this resolution was ratified by a mere exchange of notes by the Foreign Ministers of the republics only and with no submission to the legislative branches for approval, it lends force to an argument that executive agreements are recognized in Latin America.

55. *Supra* note 53 at 39.

56. See I Podesta Costa, *op. sit. supra* note 31 at 30.

57. See *infra* p. 78 on conference voting.

58. For comment on recommendations of international organizations see Thomas & Thomas, Non-Intervention: The Law and Its Import in the Americas 109-10, 117-18 (1956); Fenwick, *supra* note 20 at 496.

59. See Lleras, *supra* note 12 at 33; Sanders, *supra* note 20 at 158.

60. *Supra* note 53.

61. See in particular *infra* on the development of the Pan-American Union and the Governing Board pp. 96-101, 128-29.

62. See Kunz, "The Bogotá Charter of the Organization of American States," 42 Am. J. Int. L. 568 (1948).

63. Art. 38.

64. "Report of the PAU on the Tenth Inter-American Conference," 6 Annals of OAS 4 (Special Number 1954).

65. *Ibid.* The text of the Permanent Regulations of the Inter-American Conference are set forth in Appendix C, *id.* at 133-42.

66. See Report of Delegation of U.S.A., Ninth Conference, *op. cit. supra* note 3 at 18.

67. *Id.* at 5.

68. The Committee on Preparation for the Eleventh Inter-American Conference has proposed amendments to the Regulations of the Inter-American Conference. The Council resolved to transmit the committee's proposals to the governments of the member states for their observations. Among the proposals are amendments to Chapter II which would broaden the participation of observers by permitting invitations to be sent to American states not members of the OAS and to interested non-American states as well as to representatives of the UN, its specialized agencies, and other international organizations. See Proyecto de Modificaciones al Reglamento de la Conferencia Inter-Americana, Acta de la Sesión Ordinaria Celebrada el 4 de Junio de 1958, Consejo de la Organización de los Estados Americanos, Unión Pan Americana, Serie del Consejo, C-a-284 (aprobada) 4 Junio 1958; Acta de la Sesión Extraordinaria Celebrada en la Mañana del 2 Julio de 1959; Consejo de la Organización de los Estados Americanos, Unión Pan Americana, 82 *et seq.*, Serie del Consejo C-2-328 (aprobada) 2 Julio 1959.

69. See *infra* on the Specialized Conferences pp. 93-95.

70. Art. 8, Conference Regulations.

71. Art. 9, Conference Regulations.

72. Art. 10, Conference Regulations.

73. An addition to Article 11 has been provided by the proposed amendments to the Regulations of the Inter-American Conference, *supra* note 68, which would permit the changes in the agenda to be initiated at the conference by a two-thirds vote if unforeseen circumstances arise and if the change is of such an urgent and important character as to justify its consideration.

74. Arts. 12 and 13, Conference Regulations.

75. *Ibid.*

76. This has been changed to seven working days by the proposed amendments, *supra* note 68.

77. Art. 13, Conference Regulations.

78. Art. 14, Conference Regulations.

79. Arts. 20, 21, 24, Conference Regulations.

80. Art. 20, Conference Regulations.

81. Art. 21, Conference Regulations.

82. Art. 24, Conference Regulations. His duties are set forth in Art. 25.

83. Art. 27, Conference Regulations.

84. Art. 28, Conference Regulations.

85. Art. 29, Conference Regulations.

86. Art. 30, Conference Regulations.

87. Art. 31, Conference Regulations.

88. Art. 33, Conference Regulations.

89. Art. 34, Conference Regulations.

90. Art. 39, Conference Regulations.

91. Art. 41, Conference Regulations.

92. Art. 42, Conference Regulations.

93. Art. 53, Conference Regulations.

94. On the principle of equality of states, see *infra* pp. 149-56; see Fenwick, "The Voting Procedure in Inter-American Conferences," 1948 Inter-American Juridical Y. B. 91. For bibliography on the problem of voting in international assemblies, see Sohn, Cases and Materials on World Law 316-17 (1950).

95. Art. 43, Conference Regulations. For exceptions to the majority vote see Art. 52 which requires a two-thirds vote to suspend the rules to proceed to consideration of a given matter, and Art. 12 which requires two-thirds vote at the preliminary session for admission of a proposal of a draft of a treaty or a convention which has not been submitted in time.

96. For comment see Fenwick *supra* note 94 at 91-92.

97. Arts. 57, 58, and 59, Conference Regulations. See slight change in Articles 57 and 59 effectuated by proposed amendments, *supra* note 68.

98. Art. 62, Conference Regulations.

99. Art. 63, Conference Regulations.

100. Art. 64, Conference Regulations.

101. Art. 66, Conference Regulations.

102. *Ibid.*

103. Art. 61, Conference Regulations.

104. Art. 64, Conference Regulations.

105. Art. 67, Conference Regulations.

106. Art. 68, Conference Regulations.

107. Art. 68, Conference Regulations.

108. Art. 39, Charter of Bogotá. For discussion of this organ see Lleras, *supra* note 12 at 33-36; Kunz, *supra* note 62 at 575-76; Report of Delegation of U.S.A., Ninth Conference, *op. cit. supra* note 3 at 17-19; PAU, Handbook for Delegates to the Ninth International Conference of American States, Bogotá, Colombia, March 30, 1948, at pp. 30-31 (1947). Historical background of the procedure of consultation and the consultative organ is discussed in Blackmer, United States Policy and the Inter-American Peace System 1889-1952, at pp. 71-106 (1952); Ball, The Problem of Inter-American Organization 52-69 (1944).

109. International Conferences, 1st Supp., *op. cit. supra* note 3 at 188.

110. *Id.* at 309.

111. PAU, Report on the Meeting of the Ministers of Foreign Affairs of the American Republics, Panama, September 23-October 3, 1939 (Cong. & Conf. Series No. 29, 1939).

112. PAU, Report on the Second Meeting of the Ministers of Foreign Affairs of the American Republics, Habana, July 21-30, 1940 (Cong. & Conf. Series No. 32, 1940).

113. PAU, Report on the Third Meeting of the Ministers of Foreign Affairs of the American Republics, Rio de Janeiro, January 15-28, 1942 (Cong. & Conf. Series No. 36, 1942).

114. "Fourth Meeting of Consultation of Ministers of Foreign Affairs, Washington, D.C., March 26 to April 7, 1951," 3 Annals of OAS 126-57 (1951).

115. On the Santiago Meeting, see XLI Dept. State Bull. 136, 299, and 342 (1959); on the San José Meetings see PAU, 1960 Annual Report of the Secretary General of the OAS 16 (1961); on the Punta del Este Meeting see XLV Dept. State Bull. 1069-1071 1961); N. Y. Times, Jan. 26, 28, 31, Feb. 1, 4 (1962).

116. *Supra* note 110.

117. *Id.* at 307.

118. Declaration of Panama, Report on the Panama Meeting *op. cit. supra* note 111 at 19-21.

119. Reciprocal Assistance and Cooperation for the Defense of the Nations of the Americas, Report on the Habana Meeting, *op. cit. supra* note 112 at 35.

120. Continental Solidarity in Observance of Treaties, Rio de Janeiro Meeting, *op. cit. supra* note 113 at 50.

121. Note 111, *supra.*

122. Note 112, *supra.*

123. Note 113, *supra.*

124. Report on the Third Meeting, *id.* at 20-21.

125. On the Fourth Meeting see *supra* note 114. And see Fenwick, "The Fourth Meeting of Consultation of Ministers of Foreign Affairs," 45 Am. J. Int. L. 335 (1951).

126. See "U.S. Supports Call for Meeting of OAS Foreign Ministers," XLI Dept. State Bull. 128 (1959).

127. "Declaration of Santiago," XLI Dept. State Bull. 342 (1959); "Resolution on Inter-American Peace Committee," XLI Dept. State Bull. 343 (1959).

128. On the Sixth and Seventh Meetings see PAU, Annual Report of the Secretary General 1960, pp. 6 *et seq.* (1961).

129. See *infra* pp. 101 *et seq.* on powers of Council.

130. 3 Annals of OAS 128-31 (1951).

131. *Id.* at 129.

132. See Report of Delegation of U.S.A., Ninth Conference, *op. cit. supra* note 3 at 18.

133. See statement of Dr. L. S. Rowe, *supra* note 124.

134. Art. 40, Charter of Bogotá.

135. *Ibid.*

136. Art. 4, Regulations.

137. Arts. 8 and 9, Regulations.

138. Art. 10, Regulations.

139. Art. 21, Regulations.

140. Art. 23, Regulations.

141. Art. 22, Regulations.

142. Art. 24, Regulations.

143. Art. 25, Regulations.

144. Arts. 15 and 16, Regulations.

145. Art. 15, Regulations.

146. Art. 11, Regulations.

147. *Ibid.*

148. Art. 17, Regulations.

149. Art. 19, Regulations.

150. Art. 13, Regulations.

151. Art. 12, Regulations.

152. *Ibid.*

153. Art. 26, Regulations.

154. Art. 28, Regulations.

155. *Ibid.*

156. Art. 29, Regulations.

157. See Report of the Delegation of the U.S.A., Inter-American Conference for the Maintenance of Continental Peace and Security, Quitandinha, Brazil, August 15-September 2, 1947, p. 29 (1948).

158. Art. 39, Charter of Bogotá.

159. See Report of Delegation of the U.S.A., Conference for the Maintenance of Continental Peace and Security, *op. cit. supra* note 157 at 28-29.

160. *Ibid.*

161. Report of Delegation of U.S.A., Ninth Conference, *op. cit. supra* note 3 at 22.

162. See *infra* pp. 264-69 on collective security.

163. See *supra* pp. 48-53, and *infra* pp. 269-71.

164. On voting in inter-American assemblies, see Fenwick, *supra* note 94, and see PAU, Report of the Director General on the Results of the Conference (Inter-American Conference for the Maintenance of Continental Peace and Security) 48-49 (1947).

165. PAU, Consultation on the Principal Points of the Treaty to be Signed at Rio de Janeiro 2 (1947).

166. All but Argentina, which desired a unanimous vote, and Uruguay, which favored a majority vote only. *Id.* at 8.

167. The latter were Brazil, Chile, Cuba, Mexico, Panama, U.S.A. *Id.* at 9.

168. See Report of Delegation of U.S.A., Inter-American Conference for the Maintenance of Continental Peace and Security, *op. cit. supra* note 157 at 33.

169. *Id.* at 32. See also Report of the Director General, Results of the Conference, *op. cit. supra* note 164 at 47-48.

170. Report of Delegation of U.S.A., *id.* at 31-32.

171. Art. 19, Rio Treaty.

172. Under Art. 53, the UN Charter, it is required that authorization of the Security Council must first be obtained prior to the taking of enforcement action by a regional agency, except of course for that action taken to meet an armed attack in the exercise of the individual or collective right of self-defense. It has been stated that when the American states decide to take enforcement action under the Rio Treaty by a two-thirds vote and then request authorization from the Security Council, "the position of those American States, members of the Council, on the question of granting such authorization would be determined by the two-thirds binding vote of American States in the decision under the treaty." Report of Delegation of U.S.A., *op. cit. supra* note 157 at 34.

173. Art. 12, Rio Treaty.

174. See *infra* pp. 298-302.

On July 29, 1960, in preparation for the Sixth Meeting of Consultation of Ministers of Foreign Affairs, which was the first meeting as Organ of Consultation under the Rio Treaty, the Council approved Regulations of the Meeting of Consultation of Ministers of Foreign Affairs acting as Organ of Consultation pursuant to the Inter-American Treaty of Reciprocal Assistance. These regulations are contained in PAU, Sexta Reunion de Consulta de Ministro de Relaciones Exteriores, San José, Costa Rica, 16 a 21 de Agosto de 1960, Actas y Documentos, OEA/Ser.F/III.6 (1961) at 6-15. Provisions of the Rio Treaty as to voting and quorum are incorporated herein as well as certain articles of the Regulations of the Council governing the sessions' debates. In addition the regulations deal with the convocation, place and date of the meeting, its members and functionaires, its officers, and its committees.

175. See *infra* on the Council pp. 101-7.

176. See the 1954 Guatemalan case *infra* pp. 302-13 and the controversy between Venezuela and the Dominican Republic *infra* pp. 318-19.

177. For general discussion of the Specialized Conferences see Report of Delegation of U.S.A., Ninth Conference, *op. cit. supra* note 3 at 17-19; Lleras, *supra* note 12 at 41-42; Handbook for Delegates to the Ninth Conference, *op. cit. supra* note 27 at 31-33.

178. Handbook for Delegates to the Ninth Conference, *id.* at 31.

179. See, e.g., Report on the Activities of the Organization of American States 1948-1953 submitted by the Pan American Union to the Tenth Inter-American Conference, Ch. V, pp. 145-56 (1953).

180. "Standards for the Exercise of the Authority of the Council with Respect to Specialized Conferences," 1 Annals of OAS 280-84 (1949). The standards so formulated are summarized and commented upon in Report on the Activities of the Organization of American States *id.* at 146-49. These standards were restricted to the duties of the Council and its organs in relation to Specialized Conferences. In order to make them applicable to relations between such conferences and other organs of the OAS, Proposed Amendments to the Standards for the Exercise of the Authority of the Council with Respect to Specialized Conferences were drawn up and approved by the Council. 6 Annals of OAS 148-50 (1954). These Amendments were submitted to the Tenth Inter-American Conference for adoption by the organization as a whole. *Id.* at 148. Resolution LV of the Conference called upon the Council to continue, in co-operation with other organs and with the governments, its studies regarding the standards and authorized the Council to adopt after consultation the necessary standards with respect to all the Specialized Conferences. 6 Annals of OAS 26, 84 (Special Number, 1954).

181. See Ch. III, Standards, 1 Annals of the OAS 282 (1949); and amendments to Chapter III, Proposed Amendments to the Standards, 6 Annals of OAS 148 (1954).

182. Standards, *ibid.*

183. Standards, Chapter V (3), *ibid.;* Proposed Amendments, *supra* note 181 at 149.

184. Standards, Chapter V (c), *ibid.*

185. Standards, Chapter IX, *ibid.*

CHAPTER VI

1. This modification reflected the fact that the Governing Board had ceased to be a mere Board of Directors of the Pan American Union. It had over the years come to be an executive body with varied functions of a political, advisory, and co-ordinating character.

2. "Resolución, Reorganization of the International Bureau of the American Republics, Second International Conference of American States, Mexico City, October 22, 1901-January 31, 1902," International Conferences of American States 1889-1929, 92 *et seq.* (edited by Scott, 1931).

3. "Resolution, Reorganization of the Bureau of the American Republics, Third International Conference of American States, Rio de Janeiro, July 23-August 27, 1906," *id.* at 125 *et seq.*

4. "Resolution, Reorganization of the Bureau of the American Republics, Fourth International Conference of American States, Buenos Aires, July 12-August 30, 1910," *id.* 172.

5. See Ball, The Problem of Inter-American Organization 19 (1944); and Kunz, "The Pan-American Union in the Field of International Administration," 31 Iowa L. Rev. 58 at 63 (1945).

6. *Ibid.*

7. "Resolution, Organization of the Pan-American Union, Fifth International Conference of American States, Santiago, March 25-May 3, 1923," International Conferences of American States, *op. cit. supra* note 2 at 268 *et seq.*

8. *Ibid.*

9. "Resolution, Measures for the Closer Association of the American Republics—Questions Arising Out of an Encroachment by a Non-American Power on the Rights of an American Nation," *id.* at 267-68.

10. "Resolution, Organization of the Governing Board of the Pan-American Union," *id.* at 271.

11. "Convention, Pan American Union, Sixth International Conference of American States, Habana, January 16-February 20, 1928," *id.* at 398 *et seq.*

12. "Resolution, Pan American Union," *id.* at 397-98.

13. The Convention required the ratification of the twenty-one American republics. Only sixteen ratified it. It was, of course, superseded by the Charter of Bogotá.

14. Paragraph 3 of the Resolution, *supra* note 12; and Art. VI of the Convention, *supra* note 11.

15. For discussion of history and evolution of the Governing Board see Ball, *op. cit. supra* note 5 at 15-23; Freeman, "The Political Powers of the OAS Council," Law and Politics in the World Community 252 (compiled and edited by Lipsky, 1953); Kunz, *supra* note 5; Sanders, Sovereignty and Interdependence in the New World, Department of State Publication 3054, Inter-American Series 35, 159-63 (1948).

16. Freeman, *id.* at 255 sets forth Costa Rican proposals in this direction, and at 258, Colombian and Dominican proposals.

17. Art. VI of the Convention, *supra* note 11.

18. *Ibid.*

19. "Convention for the Maintenance, Preservation and Reestablishment of Peace, Inter-American Conference for the Maintenance of Peace, Buenos Aires, December 1-23, 1936," International Conferences of American States, First Supplement 1933-1940, 188 (1940).

20. "Declaration of Lima, Eighth International Conference of American States, Lima, December 9-27, 1938," *id.* at 308 *et seq.*

21. "Procedure of Consultation," PAU, Report on the Second Meeting of the Ministers of Foreign Affairs of the American Republics, Habana, July 21-30, 1940, p. 36 (Cong. & Conf. Series, No. 32, 1940).

22. "Peaceful Solution of Conflicts," *id.* at 34-35.

23. "Reorganization, Consolidation and Strengthening of the Inter-American System," PAU, Inter-American Conference on Problems of War and Peace, Mexico City, February 21-March 8, 1945, pp. 33 *et seq.* (Cong. & Conf. Series No. 47, 1945).

24. See Sanders, *supra* note 15 at 162.

25. See note 23, *supra.*

26. Art. 12, Inter-American Treaty of Reciprocal Assistance, Report of Delegation of U.S.A., Inter-American Conference for the Maintenance of Continental Peace and Security, Quitandinha, Brazil, August 15-September 2, 1947, p. 62 (1948).

27. Argentina desired the Council to possess administrative powers only, contending that a grant of political power to this body would permit it to invade the sphere of action of the conferences, would permit intervention by the organization into the internal affairs of the member states, and would tend toward the creation of a superstate. Chile maintained that political functions should not be granted to the Council, and that those already granted should be retracted. This delegation wished to create a special organ of consultation in security matters. This organ would be composed of the American diplomatic corps accredited to an American nation, the country to be chosen in rotation every five years by the Inter-American Conference. Panama sustained a similar thesis, stating that all political powers should be granted to a special council of solidarity with headquarters in one of the other American Republics. See Report of the Delegation of the U.S.A., Ninth International Conference of American States, Bogotá, Colombia, March 30-May 2, 1948, p. 21 (1948).

28. Art. 39, Charter of Bogotá.

29. Art. 11, Rio Treaty.

30. Art. 25 of the Charter of Bogotá provides:

If the inviolability or the integrity of the territory or the sovereignty or political independence of any American State should be affected by an armed attack or by an act of aggression that is not an armed attack, or by an extra-continental conflict, or by a conflict between two or more American States, or by any other fact or situation that might endanger the peace of America, the American States, in furtherance of the principles of continental solidarity or collective self-defense, shall apply the measures and procedures established in the special treaties on the subject.

31. See Report of the Delegation of the U.S.A., Inter-American Conference for the Maintenance of Continental Peace and Security, *op. cit. supra* note 26 at 29.

32. *Ibid.*

33. On cases arising and discussions of actions taken see PAU, Applications of the Inter-American Treaty of Reciprocal Assistance 1948-1956 (1957). See also *infra* Ch. XVII for discussion of the various cases.

34. This is borne out by remarks of the Uruguayan delegate inserted in the record of the 3rd committee and generally accepted by the members of the committee. See Freeman, *supra* note 15 at 267; see also PAU, Opinion on the Scope of Powers of the Council of the Organization of American States (OEA/Sec. 1/VI. 2 C.I.J. 59 English 1961) wherein it is stated at page 10 that the Council is the Provisional Organ of Consultation, not just the Council acting in a provisional capacity. Therefore its actions are valid in themselves and need not be submitted to a higher organ for ratification.

35. For remarks on the Haiti–Dominican Republic Case see Fenwick, "Application of the Treaty of Rio de Janeiro to the Controversy Between Costa Rica and Nicaragua," 43 Am. J. Int. L. 329 at 322 (1949).

36. Freeman, *supra* note 15, agrees with this point of view at p. 274, as does Fenwick. See Fenwick, "The Competence of the Council of the Organization of American States," 1949 Inter-American Juridical Yearbook 21 at 32.

37. "Annual Report of the Secretary General of the OAS for the Fiscal Year 1949-1950," 3 Annals of OAS 1 at 7-8. And see PAU, Opinion on Scope of Powers of the OAS *op. cit. supra* note 34 at 11-12 substantiating this viewpoint although previously the Juridical Committee had taken a contrary view.

38. *Ibid.*

39. See Fenwick, *supra* note 36 at 32; Freeman, *supra* note 15 at 275.

40. See Report of Delegation of U.S.A., Ninth Conference, *op. cit. supra* note 27 at 22.

41. As quoted in Freeman, *supra* note 15 at 265.

42. *Ibid.*

43. Fenwick notes a clear violation here and speaks to the effect that if this type of procedure is to be maintained modification of the treaty should be made. Fenwick, *supra* note 36 at 32.

44. See Freeman, *supra* note 15 at 277. And see competence of the Council in this respect as outlined by the Juridical Committee in its opinion on the powers of the Council of the OAS *op. cit. supra* note 34 at 7-8.

45. See Applications of the Inter-American Treaty of Reciprocal Assistance, *op. cit.* *supra* note 33 at 151; Resolution of the Council Postponing the Meeting, *id.* at 154.

46. See *infra* the 1960 Venezuelan–Dominican Republic Case, pp. 318-19; see *supra* pp. 80, 93 and *infra* pp. 325-27 on the Eighth Meeting of Ministers of Foreign Affairs.

47. See Fenwick, *supra* note 36 at 34-35; Freeman, *supra* note 15 at 272-74.

48. See "Asylum and Safe-Conduct for the Ex-President of Venezuela," 1 Annals of OAS 216 (1949).

49. *Id.* at 217.

50. *Ibid.*

51. "Annual Report of Secretary General for Fiscal Year July 1, 1948-June 30, 1949," 2 Annals of OAS 31 (1950).

52. Consideration was given to this by the First Meeting of the Council of Jurists, see Amplitud de las Facultades del Consejo de la Organización de los Estados Americanos, Documentos Considerados por el Consejo Interamericano de Jurisconsultos en su Primera Reunión, Rio de Janeiro, mayo 22-junio 15, 1950 y Sometidos al Consejo de la Organización. At this first meeting it was resolved to continue the discussion of the subject at the second meeting of the Council of Jurists to be held in Buenos Aires. *Id.* at 162. See also PAU, Report of the Executive Secretary of the Inter-American Council of Jurists 12-17 (1950), and see PAU, Opinion on the Scope of the Powers of the Council of the OAS *op. cit. supra* note 34. Here the Inter-American Juridical Committee in 1961 sets forth its ideas on the Council's competence in certain areas and requests that the Council or the Council of Jurists or the Committee be authorized to prepare a draft resolution on the powers of the Council.

53. See Annual Report, *supra* note 51 at 31.

54. *Id.* at 31, and PAU, Opinion on the Scope of Powers of the Council of the OAS, *op. cit. supra* note 34 at 13.

55. *Ibid.* Fenwick, *supra* note 36 at 35.

56. Fenwick, *ibid.*

57. For summary of the powers of the Council in the nonpolitical field see Report of Delegation of U.S.A., Ninth Conference, *op. cit. supra* note 26 at 23-24.

58. Art. 84, Charter of Bogotá.

59. Art. 79, Charter of Bogotá.

60. Art. 85, Charter of Bogotá.

61. Art. 87, Charter of Bogotá.

62. Art. 82, Charter of Bogotá. But see *infra* p. 133 on the easy manner in which new agencies not provided for in the Charter have been attached to the OAS.

63. Art. 58, Charter of Bogotá.

64. Art. 62, Charter of Bogotá.

65. Art. 53, Charter of Bogotá.

66. The bases of financing were approved by the Council in 1949. Under the approved system, the maximum annual quota to be assigned to any one state is set at 66 per cent of the total assessment. The remainder is apportioned on the basis of the capacity of each member to pay and that capacity is determined by the position of each state, in relation to other American states, on the current United Nations scale of contributions. 2 Annals of OAS 161-62 (1950). As of 1960, only Chile, Colombia, and the United States had paid in full. The total delinquency of the Latin American nations by the end of 1962 amounted to $8.5 million and the OAS had a previous deficit of $2.4 million.

67. Arts. 55 and 38, Charter of Bogotá.

68. Art. 41, Charter of Bogotá.

69. Art. 35, Charter of Bogotá.

70. Art. 37, Charter of Bogotá.

71. Art. 93, Charter of Bogotá.

72. For discussion see *infra* pp. 289, 294-95.

73. See note 23, *supra.*

74. See Blackmer, United States Policy and the Inter-American Peace System 1889-1952, 147 (1952); Handbook for Delegates to the Ninth Conference of American States, Bogotá, Colombia, March 30, 1948, 37 (1947).

75. Handbook for Delegates to the Ninth Conference, *id.* at 38.

76. *Ibid.*

77. Report of Delegation of U.S.A., Ninth Conference, *op. cit. supra* note 27 at 20.

78. And see Art. 1 of the Regulations of the Council of the Organization of American States, 9 Annals of OAS 186-93 (1957). The full text of the Regulations of the Council is set out here incorporating all amendments made to July 3, 1957.

79. Art. 35 of the Regulations.

80. Arts. 13 and 16, Rio Treaty.
81. Arts. 15 and 16, Rio Treaty.
82. Art. 16, Rio Treaty.
83. Art. 14, Rio Treaty.
84. Art. 18, Rio Treaty.
85. See Report of Delegation of U.S.A., *op. cit. supra* note 26 at 32.
86. Art. 17, Rio Treaty.
87. See Report of Delegation of U.S.A., *op. cit. supra* note 26 at 32-33.
88. Art. 54, Charter of Bogotá, Art. 82, Council Regulations.
89. Arts. 20 and 21, Council Regulations.
90. Arts. 84 and 88, Council Regulations.
91. Arts. 86 and 88, Council Regulations. A motion for closure of a debate in the Council may only be had upon a two-thirds vote. Art. 34, Council Regulations.
92. Art. 49, Charter of Bogotá; Art. 17, Council Regulations.
93. Art. 86, Charter of Bogotá.
94. Art. 56 of the Charter of Bogotá requires the Council to function at the seat of the Pan American Union. Art. 92 of the Charter makes the seat of the Pan American Union the City of Washington, D.C.
95. Art. 7, Council Regulations.
96. Art. 11, Council Regulations.
97. Art. 9, Council Regulations.
98. Art. 56, Council Regulations.
99. Art. 44, Council Regulations.
100. Art. 45, Council Regulations.
101. Art. 57, Council Regulations.
102. Art. 46, Council Regulations.
103. Art. 47, Council Regulations.
104. Art. 57.
105. Art. 58, Charter of Bogotá.
106. See "Report on the Status of the Council," 6 Annals of OAS 107 at 108 (1954). Each Council has "a maximum of authority in the formulation of its program and in determining the manner in which it should be carried out. The term 'dependent organ' is used more in the sense of describing the position of the Councils in the organizational set up, rather than implying any position of inferiority or subordination." Handbook for Delegates to the Ninth Conference, *op. cit. supra* note 74 at 41.
107. Art. 60.
108. Art. 61, Charter of Bogotá.
109. Art. 62, Charter of Bogotá.
110. PAU, Report on the Meeting of the Ministers of Foreign Affairs of the American Republics, Panama, September 23-October 3, 1939, at pp. 11-13 (Cong. & Conf. Series No. 29, 1939).
111. *Supra* note 23 at 36.
112. "Statutes of the Inter-American Economic and Social Council," 7 Annals of OAS 172 *et seq.* (1955). The previous statutes are set forth in 2 Annals of OAS 155 *et seq.* (1950).
113. See "Report on the Status of the Council," *supra* note 106 at 108. Art. 64 of the Charter of Bogotá delineates the functions as the manner in which the purpose of this Council is to be accomplished. See also Art. 27 of the Charter.

The actual work in the economic and social field will be discussed *infra* Ch. XIX on economic and social co-operation.

114. "Report on the Status of the Council," *supra* note 106 at 109.
115. "Composition and Operation of the Inter-American Economic and Social Council," 5 Annals of OAS 143-44 (1953).
116. "Report on the Status of the Council," *supra* note 106 at 109.
117. *Ibid.*
118. *Id.* at 109-10.
119. Art. 2 of the Statutes, *supra*, note 112 declares:

To accomplish that purpose the Council shall:
a) Propose the means by which the American states may cooperate among themselves to carry out studies and to formulate and execute plans directed toward the best utilization of their natural resources; toward their agricultural, industrial, and commercial development; toward improving their social services; and, in general, toward the raising of the standard of living of their peoples;

b) Propose the means by which the American states may cooperate among themselves to provide technical assistance;

c) Act as coordinating agency for all official inter-American economic and social activities;

d) Suggest to the Council of the Organization the advisability of holding specialized conferences on economic and social matters and

e) Carry on any other activities entrusted to it by the Inter-American Conference, the Meeting of Consultation of Ministers of Foreign Affairs, or the Council of the Organization.

Art. 3 of the Statutes declares:

The Inter-American Economic and Social Council shall also exercise the functions entrusted to it by agreements and conventions in force on the date of adoption of these Statutes or those signed and put into effect later.

120. Statutes, Art. 30.

121. Art. 1, Regulations. The "Revised Regulations of the Inter-American Economic and Social Council" may be found in 8 Annals of OAS 271 *et seq.* (1956).

122. Statutes, Art. 10.

123. Regulations, Art. 1.

124. Report on the Status of the Council, *supra* note 106 at 110.

125. Art. 66.

126. Art. 65, Charter of Bogotá.

127. Art. 15, Statutes; Art. 19, Regulations.

128. See Chapter V, Regulations on Special Meetings.

129. Chapter VI, Regulations.

130. Chapter VII, Regulations.

131. Chapter XIV, Regulations.

132. Art. 32 of the Regulations. If the Council decides that the formality of a resolution is not necessary, the approved decision shall be entered in the minutes.

133. Art. 20, Regulations.

134. Chapter IX, Regulations. Matters concerned with budget estimates of the organ are determined by approval of two-thirds of the members.

135. Art. 55 of the Regulations.

136. Art. 56, Regulations. The standing committees are: Committee on Economic Cooperation, Committee on Social Cooperation, Committee on Technical Cooperation, and Committee on Preparations for Economic and Social Meetings. PAU, Annual Report of the Secretary General 1956-1957, 24 (1957).

137. Chapter XII, Regulations. Some of the special committees are: Special Committee on Bananas, Special Committee on Coffee, Permanent Executive Committee of the Inter-American Travel Congresses, Permanent Executive Committee of the Pan-American Highway Congresses, Permanent Technical Committee on Ports, and Special Committee of Experts to Consider the Financial Requirements Arising from Execution of Agrarian Reform Plans, PAU, 1960, Annual Report of the Secretary General of the OAS 31 (1961).

138. Chapter X, Regulations; Chapter XVI, Regulations.

139. PAU, 1960 Annual Report of the Secretary General, *op cit. supra* note 137 at 4, 32; PAU, Statutes of Inter-American Economic and Social Council (OEA/Ser. H/I.1) 1962.

140. Art. 71, Charter of Bogotá.

141. Art. 4, "Statutes of the Inter-American Council of Jurists," PAU, Handbook— Fourth Meeting of the Inter-American Council of Jurists, Santiago de Chile, August 24, 1959, pp. 75 *et seq.* (1959).

142. Art. 60, Charter of Bogotá. Art. 5, Statutes of the Inter-American Council of Jurists.

143. Art. 17, Statutes of the Inter-American Council of Jurists.

144. Art. 25, Statutes of the Inter-American Council of Jurists.

145. Art. 59, Charter of Bogotá; Art. 7, Statutes of the Inter-American Council of Jurists.

146. See "Annual Report of the Secretary General of the Organization of American States 1949-1950," 3 Annals of OAS at 15 (1951).

147. See PAU, Second Meeting of the Inter-American Council of Jurists, Report of the Executive Secretary of the Inter-American Council of Jurists 28-29 (1953).

148. Art. 9, Statutes of the Inter-American Council of Jurists.

149. Art. 10, Statutes of the Inter-American Council of Jurists.

150. Art. 23, "Regulations of the Inter-American Council of Jurists," PAU, Handbook, Fourth Meeting, *op. cit. supra* note 141 at 71 *et seq.*

151. Art. 68, Charter of Bogotá.

152. Art. 69, Charter of Bogotá.

153. Art. 70, Charter of Bogotá.

154. See 2 Annals of OAS 33-34 (1950).

155. See 3 Annals of OAS 351 (1951).

156. This background is well summarized in a report, "Membership of the Inter-American Juridical Committee," 3 Annals of OAS 351-54 (1951).

157. "Resolution V, General Declaration of Neutrality of the American Republics," Report on the Meeting of Ministers of Foreign Affairs, Panama, *op. cit. supra* note 110 at pp. 14-16.

158. See "Membership of the Inter-American Juridical Committee," *supra* note 156 at 352.

159. "Resolution XXVI, Inter-American Juridical Committee," PAU, Report of the Third Meeting of the Ministers of Foreign Affairs, Rio de Janeiro, January 15-28, 1942, pp. 53-54 (Cong. & Conf. Series No. 36, 1942).

160. *Ibid.*

161. "Resolution V, General Declaration of the American Republics," *supra* note 157.

162. See "Membership of the Inter-American Juridical Committee," *supra* note 156 at 352.

163. As set out in Report of Delegation of U.S.A. Ninth Conference *op. cit. supra* note 31 at 230-31.

164. This was done after consultation with the governments, 4 Annals of OAS 147-48 (1952).

165. For discussion see "Functioning of the Inter-American Juridical Committee," 6 Annals of OAS 118-21 (1954).

166. "Resolution LI, Inter-American Juridical Committee," 6 Annals of OAS 82 (Special Number, 1954).

167. Report of the Delegation of the U.S.A. Tenth Inter-American Conference, Caracas, Venezuela, March 1-28, 1954, pp. 39-40 (1955).

168. Resolution LI, Tenth Conference, *supra* note 166.

169. *Ibid.* "Resolution LII, Membership of the Inter-American Juridical Committee," *id.* at 82-83 selected Chile, Argentina, Brazil, Colombia, Peru, Venezuela, Mexico, United States, and Dominican Republic as the nine countries from which the membership of the committee would be drawn.

170. Resolution LI, Tenth Conference, *id.* at 82.

171. *Ibid.* These changes have been made. See PAU, Handbook, Fourth Meeting *op. cit. supra* note 141 at 54-60 and Appendices.

172. Art. 57, Charter of Bogotá.

173. Art. 73, Charter of Bogotá.

174. Art. 74, Charter of Bogotá.

175. Art. 59, Charter of Bogotá.

176. Art. 11, Statutes of the Inter-American Cultural Council as set forth in PAU, Statutes of the Inter-American Cultural Council and Principles and Standards to Govern the Committee for Cultural Action (1957).

177. Art. 12, Statutes of the Inter-American Cultural Council.

178. Art. 75, Charter of Bogotá.

179. Art. 26, Statutes of the Inter-American Cultural Council.

180. "Art. 17, Regulations of the Inter-American Cultural Council," 8 Annals of OAS 228 *et seq.* (1956).

181. Art. 5, Statutes of the Inter-American Cultural Council.

182. Art. 6, Statutes of the Inter-American Cultural Council.

183. Art. 76, Charter of Bogotá.

184. *Ibid.*

185. Art. 27.

186. "Art. 12, Regulations of the Committee for Cultural Action," 8 Annals of OAS 230 *et seq.* (1956).

187. *Id.* Art. 21.

188. *Id.* Art. 22.

189. On this background see "Annual Report of the Secretary General of the Organization of American States 1949-1950," 3 Annals of OAS 59-62 (1951); 3 Annals of OAS

390-92 (1951); 4 Annals of OAS 248-56 (1952); PAU, Report of the Activities of the Organization of American States 1948-1953, 73 *et seq.* (1953).

190. Report of the First Meeting of the Cultural Council is set forth in 4 Annals of OAS 148 *et seq.* (1952).

191. See Report of Delegation of U.S.A., Ninth Conference, *op. cit. supra* note 31 at 40.

192. *Id.* at 122.

193. See 8 Annals of OAS 204 *et seq.* (1956); 9 Annals of OAS 117 *et seq.* (1957).

194. Arts. 44 and 45, Charter of Bogotá. The number of military authorities to represent each state is not stipulated, but Article 45 grants each state only one vote.

195. Art. 46, Charter of Bogotá.

196. See Report of the Delegation of the U.S.A., Ninth Conference, *op. cit. supra* note 31 at 27.

197. Art. 47, Charter of Bogotá.

198. "Resolution IV, Creation of a Permanent Military Agency," Inter-American Conference on Problems of War and Peace *op. cit. supra* note 23 at 26.

199. See Arts. 58, 60, 61, 62, 63, 64, and 65, Draft Organic Pact of the Inter-American System, Report of the Delegation of U.S.A., Ninth Conference *op. cit. supra* note 31 at 107-8.

200. *Id.* at 26.

201. "Resolution XXXIX, Inter-American Defense Board," PAU, Report of the Third Meeting, *op. cit. supra* note 159 at 59.

202. Inter-American Defense Board, Background and Regulations of the Inter-American Defense Board (1949).

203. For discussion and summary see 2 Annals of OAS 93-95 (1950); 3 Annals of OAS 25-26 (1951).

204. 2 Annals of OAS 325-27 (1950).

205. 3 Annals of OAS 143 at 144 (1951).

206. See PAU, Annual Report of the Secretary General to the Council of the Organization 1957-1958 p. 118 (1958).

207. Resolution XIV, Report on the Second Meeting of the Ministers of Foreign Affairs, *op. cit. supra* note 21 at 34-35; see Stowell, "The Habana Conference and Inter-American Cooperation," 35 Am. J. Int. L. 123 (1941).

208. For discussion see Fenwick, "The Inter-American Peace Committee," 43 Am. J. Int. L. 770 (1949); Report on the Activities of the Organization of American States 1948-1953, *op. cit. supra* note 189 at 17-18; "Annual Report of the Secretary General 1948-1949," 2 Annals of OAS 22-23 (1950). Blackmer, United States Policy and the Inter-American System 1889-1952, 191-93 (1952).

209. "Annual Report of Secretary General 1948-1949," *id.* at 23.

210. *Ibid.*

211. See *infra* on these cases, pp. 299-302.

212. 1 Annals of OAS 325 f.n. 1. (1949). The Statute of the Inter-American Peace Committee was approved on May 24, 1950. The text of this original statute may be found in 2 Annals of OAS 320-21 (1950).

213. See Article LVIII, Pact of Bogotá, which lists the former treaties, protocols, and conventions which are to cease to be effective upon ratification of the Pact. The Resolution creating the Inter-American Peace Committee is not mentioned.

214. See Report on the Activities of the Organization of American States 1948-1953 *op. cit. supra* note 189 at 17-18.

215. Report of the Delegation of the U.S.A. Tenth Conference *op. cit. supra* note 167 at 13-14.

216. Resolution CII, Final Act *id.* at 163-64.

217. For text of the Statutes see PAU, Statutes of the Inter-American Peace Committee (1956).

218. Art. 1, Statutes.

219. Art. 15, Statutes.

220. Art. 16, Statutes.

221. Art. 17, Statutes.

222. *Ibid.*

223. Art. 18, Statutes.

224. Art. 22, Statutes.

225. *Ibid.*

226. Art. 3, Statutes.

227. See Annual Report of the Secretary General *supra* note 208 at 23.

228. Art. 5, Statutes.

229. Art. 6, Statutes.
230. Art. 7, Statutes.
231. Art. 8, Statutes.
232. Art. 11, Statutes.
233. Art. 12, Statutes.
234. Art. 14, Statutes.
235. Art. 21, Statutes.
236. Art. 19, Statutes.
237. Art. 23, Statutes.
238. "Resolution on Inter-American Peace Committee," text set forth in XLI Dept. State Bull. 343-44 (1959).
239. Original Statute of 1950 *supra* note 212.
240. "Report of Committee on Customs Regulations, Bureau of Information, First International Conference of American States, October 2, 1889-April 19, 1890," International Conference of American States, *op. cit. supra* note 2 at 36 *et seq.*
241. "Reorganization of the International Bureau of the American Republics, Second International Conference of American States, October 22, 1901-January 31, 1902," *id.* at 92 *et seq.*
242. "Reorganization of the Union of American Republics, Fourth International Conference of American States, July 12-August 30, 1910," *id.* at 172 *et seq.*
243. See Historical Evolution of the Council *supra* pp. 96-101. For background of the Pan American Union as it developed prior to the Bogotá Charter see Ball, *op. cit. supra* note 5 at 15-24; Kunz, *supra* note 5.
244. See note 240 *supra.*
245. See *supra* on the Council footnote 1. As to the continued close connection between the Council and the Pan American Union, the Council still retains supervisory authority of the Union, the directors of the corresponding divisions of the Union serve as executive secretaries of the Council and its permanent organs. The Council elects the secretary general and the assistant secretary general, the former participating in the Meetings of the Council without vote, and the latter is secretary of the Council.
246. Provisional Regulations of the Pan American Union were adopted in 1949. They may be found in 1 Annals of OAS 220-26 (1949). With some changes the Regulations of the Pan American Union were approved by the Council in 1957. The full text of these regulations is contained in 9 Annals of OAS 124-33 (1957). Certain reorganization of the Pan American Union was carried out in 1958. These changes are set forth in PAU, Annual Report of the Secretary General to the Council of the Organization 1957-1958, pp. 14, 124-25 (1958). See also 10 Annals of OAS 59-62 (1958).
247. Charter of Bogotá, Art. 92.
248. Charter of Bogotá, Art. 82.
249. Charter of Bogotá, Art. 88.
250. Charter of Bogotá, Art. 80.
251. Regulations of the Pan American Union, Art. 8.
252. Charter of Bogotá, Art. 79.
253. Kunz, *supra* note 5 at 67.
254. Charter of Bogotá, Art. 79.
255. The duties of the secretary general are set forth in Arts. 81, 84, and 88 of the Charter of Bogotá. See also Arts. 8-14 of the Regulations of the Pan American Union.
256. Charter of Bogotá, Art. 85.
257. Charter of Bogotá, Art. 86.
258. Charter of Bogotá, Art. 87.
259. The Department of Economic and Social Affairs is divided into five divisions: the Housing Program, Division of Economic Research, Division of Labor and Social Affairs, Division of Industry and Technology, and the Travel Division. It is placed under a director who also serves as the executive secretary of the Inter-American Economic and Social Council. This department initiates and develops programs related to inter-American social and economic problems; conducts studies of problems concerning various fields such as the national economies of the American states, agriculture, and conservation. Data is collected and published on housing, labor, social security; and information is disseminated for travelers to the Americas. In addition technical papers are prepared related to the activities of the Economic and Social Council. The department maintains liaison with the economic staff of the United Nations and other international organizations.
260. The director of the Department of Cultural Affairs serves as executive secretary for the Inter-American Cultural Council and the department is the Secretariat for the Committee for Cultural Action. The department is composed of the Music and Visual

Arts Sections, and the Divisions of Education, Philosophy and Letters, Science Development, and the Columbus Memorial Library. Its purpose is to broaden the scope of, to co-ordinate, and to integrate inter-American cultural activities. It promotes active co-operation in the fields of philosophy and science and provides information and technical advice in music and visual arts. It also studies educational problems of the hemisphere and supplies information with respect thereto. The Columbus Memorial Library is a valuable reference source containing volumes, pamphlets, maps, newspapers, and periodicals of the Americas.

261. The Department of Legal Affairs is composed of the General Legal Division and the Codification Division. Its director is the executive secretary of the Inter-American Council of Jurists. The department also serves as secretariat for the Inter-American Juridical Committee and for the Inter-American Commission of Women. The activities of this department in the main concern the study, compilation, and interpretation of juridical matters of the hemisphere. It publishes various works on inter-American law, including the status of inter-American treaties; undertakes the preliminary work for all the official conferences; compiles the official texts of treaties, conventions, and other documents in English, Spanish, Portuguese, and French. It is also concerned with codification of public and private international law, and maintains contact with other groups interested in juridical problems.

262. The Department of Technical Cooperation with two divisions, the Division of Technical Cooperation and Assistance and the Division of Fellowships, is responsible for directing and co-ordinating the activities of the Program of Technical Cooperation, the OAS Fellowship Program, and the Direct Technical Assistance Program.

263. The Department of Statistics, whose director is secretary general of the Inter-American Statistical Institute, furnishes statistical information to other organs of the OAS and serves as a vehicle for the dissemination of statistical information concerning the hemisphere.

264. The Department of Public Information, with its General Information Division, Press Division, Division of Radio and Television, and Americas Division, has charge of publicity and the spread of information on the OAS and its members.

265. See 10 Annals of OAS 61 (1958).

266. The Office of Conference and Secretariat Services, with a Division of Official Records and a Division of Council Secretariat Services, organizes and co-ordinates the services required in connection with meetings of the Council of the OAS, committees, and official conferences. The work includes translation and interpretation services, the issuance, registration, and archiving of official records, the preparation of reference documents and minutes, and the physical arrangement for meetings.

The Office of Financial Services, the director of which is the treasurer of the Pan American Union, is divided into the Fiscal Division, Internal Audit Division, and General Services Division. This department has in large part taken over the functions of the former Department of Administrative Affairs and is charged with fiscal, budgetary, accounting, and treasury problems. Finally, the Office of Publication Services with a Sales and Promotion Division, Graphic Services Division, Production and Distribution Divisions, was also formerly under the Department of Administrative Affairs. The names of its divisions indicate the services it performs.

267. Art. 18, Regulations of the Pan-American Union.

268. See PAU, Annual Report of the Secretary General, 1960, at 107 (1961).

269. Art. 91, Charter of Bogotá.

270. Art. 90, Charter of Bogotá.

271. A listing and discussion of most of these organizations may be found in Masters, Handbook of International Organizations in the Americas (1945). For criticism of the organizational setup as it existed before the Charter of Bogotá see Sanders, *supra* note 15 at 163-64; Kunz, "The Bogotá Charter and the Organization of American States," 42 Am. J. Int. L. 568 at 582-86 (1948); Report of the Delegation of the U.S.A., Ninth Conference, *op. cit. supra* note 27 at 28-32.

272. Resolution IX, Art. 10, Inter-American Conference on War and Peace, *op. cit. supra* note 23 at 38. And see the Governing Board Report on Specialized Organizations (PAU 1947 mim.). See also PAU, Handbook for Delegates to the Ninth Conference of American States, Bogotá, Colombia, March 30, 1948 pp. 42-44, 60-72 (1947).

273. Some agencies were eliminated by the creation of the organs of the Council. Thus, the establishment of the Juridical Council did away with five agencies concerned with the study of legal problems: the Committee of Experts on Codification of International Law, Permanent Committee on Public International Law, Permanent Committee on Private International Law, Permanent Committee on Comparative Legislation and the Unification of Legislation, Permanent Committee of Jurists for the Unification of Civil and Commercial Law of the Americas. Art. 11, paragraph 2, of the Economic Agreement called for the

absorption of existing inter-American organizations having similar functions by the Economic and Social Council. For additional discussion of action taken by the Ninth Conference re such organizations see Kunz, *supra* note 271.

274. Charter of Bogotá, Art. 53 and Arts. 96-99.

275. Resolution III of the Final Act is contained in the Report of the Delegation of the U.S.A., *op. cit. supra* note 27 at 231.

276. Private unofficial organizations do not form a part of the OAS, although close collaboration may be maintained with them. (Art. 53 d).

277. Art. 96, Charter of Bogotá.

278. Art. 97, Charter of Bogotá.

279. Arts. 98 and 99, Charter of Bogotá.

280. Art. 99, Charter of Bogotá.

281. Art. 100, Charter of Bogotá.

282. See Report of the Activities of the OAS 1948-1953, *op. cit. supra* note 189 at 13, 157-58.

283. "Standards for the Study of Inter-American Organizations" as contained in PAU, Organismos Especializados Inter-Americanos y Otros Vinculados a la O. E. A. 4-8 (1958). A summary of the Standards will be found in 2 Annals of OAS 36-37 (1950).

284. Section I of the Standards.

285. 1960 Annual Report of Secretary General, *supra* note 268 p. 2.

286. "Standards and Procedures to be Applied in Concluding Agreements of Special Arrangements between the Council of the Organization and Nongovernmental Organizations and in Establishing Cooperation Between the Organs of the Council and Nongovernmental Organizations," 4 Annals of OAS 222-25 (1952). A previous set of Standards promulgated in 1949, 1 Annals of OAS 284-85 (1949), was superseded by these provisions.

287. Section VII (2) of the Standards.

288. See Report of the Activities of the OAS, *op. cit. supra* note 189 at 21-22.

289. Section VII (1) of the Standards. The 1952 Standards were amended in part in 1954. See 6 Annals of OAS 169-71 (1954). For a listing of nongovernmental organizations with which arrangements have been concluded see PAU, Organizations with which the Organization of American States Has Established Cooperative Relations (1959).

290. See 1960 Annual Report, *supra* note 268 at 2-3, 19-21, 61-62, 32-34.

CHAPTER VII

1. See Ross, Constitution of the United Nations 108-36 (1950) for a discussion of the ends, functions, and principles of the United Nations.

2. See discussion of Lleras in "Report on the Ninth Conference of American States," 1 Annals of OAS 31-32 (1949), and see Goodrich and Hambro, Charter of the United Nations 319 (2d ed. 1949).

3. Of course the thought, in part, behind co-operation for economic, social, and cultural development of the Americas will tend to create conditions of internal stability in the nations. See Lleras, The Bogotá Conference 8-10 (PAU, No. 62 Cong. & Conf. Series, 1948).

4. Article 6 of the Rio Treaty speaks specifically of extracontinental as well as intracontinental conflicts.

5. Ross, *op. cit. supra* note 1 at 110; Fenwick, International Law 178 (3rd ed. 1948); Schwarzenberger, Power Politics 429 (2d ed. 1951).

6. Lleras, *supra* note 2 at 20.

7. This function is more clearly expressed in Chapter V of the Charter entitled Collective Security. It finds its most perfect expression in the Rio Treaty.

8. See Chapter IV of the Charter entitled Pacific Settlement of Disputes and the Pact of Bogotá.

9. See, e.g., Ball, The Problem of Inter-American Organization 44 (1944).

10. Article 67 of the Charter places upon the Inter-American Council of Jurists the duty to serve as an advisory body on juridical matters; to promote the *development* and *codification* of public and private international law; and to study the possibility of attaining uniformity in the legislation of the various American countries.

11. On the issue of development and codification of international law see Yuen-Li Liang, "The General Assembly and the Progressive Development and Codification of International Law," 42 Am. J. Int. Law 66 (1948); Goodrich and Hambro, *op. cit. supra* note 2 at 175-77; Fenwick, *op. cit. supra* note 5 at 192.

12. Kelsen, The Law of the United Nations 20-22 (1950).

13. Alfaro, Commentary on Pan American Problems 5 (1938).

14. Functional co-operation has come to mean international co-operation in economic, social, cultural, and educational matters. For discussion see Schwarzenberger, *op. cit. supra* note 5 at 565.

15. Ross in speaking of the "purposes" of the United Nations declares that the purposes are to an end, to perform the functions while applying the principles. See his discussion on the purposes. Ross, *op. cit. supra* note 1 at 108-9.

16. For historical background of the basic inter-American principles and rights and duties of American states see Thomas & Thomas, Non-Intervention: The Law and Its Import in the Americas 57-64 (1956); De Leuchsenring. "El Principio de la No Intervención en el Instituto Americano de Derecho Internacional y en la Comisión de Jurisconsultos Americanos," 13 Revista de Derecho Internacional 367 (1928); Root, "The Declaration of the Rights and Duties of Nations Adopted by the American Institute of International Law," 10 Am. J. Int. L. 211 (1916); Rivero Reyes, "Deberes y Derechos de los Estados," 31 Revista de Derecho Internacional 70 (1937); Garcia-Amador, "Los Principios Americanos Concernientes a los Derechos y Deberes de los Estados," 44 Revista de Derecho Internacional 210 (1943). And see "Convention on Rights and Duties of States, Seventh International Conference of American States, Montevideo, Dec. 3-26, 1933," The International Conferences of American States, First Supp. 1933-1940 at 121-23 (1940). For discussion see Scott, "Seventh International Conference of American States," 28 Am. J. Int. L. 219 (1934).

17. Chapter IV, Charter of Bogotá.

18. Chapter V, Charter of Bogotá.

19. Chapters VI, VII, VIII, Charter of Bogotá.

20. This distinction is maintained by Kunz in an article entitled "The Bogotá Charter of the Organization of American States," 42 Am. J. Int. L. 568 at 572 (1948).

21. See Thomas & Thomas, *op. cit. supra* note 16 at 104 and 362-63.

22. *Id.* at 118-21. And see discussion *supra* Chapter III pp. 43-45.

23. *Ibid.*

24. For similar classifications see PAU, Manual of Inter-American Relations 1-14 (Cong. & Conf. Series No. 26, 1953); PAU, Handbook for Delegates to the Ninth International Conference of American States 20-26 (1947). And see discussion of the juridical political principles in Castañeda, "Pan Americanism and Regionalism: A Mexican View," 10 Int. Org. 373 (1956) and Sanders, "Sovereignty and Interdependence in the New World," 18 Dept. State Bull. 155 at 165-73 (1948).

25. On the concept of American international law see *infra* Ch. XII.

CHAPTER VIII

1. "Resolution XXVII, Inter-American Conference for the Maintenance of Peace, Buenos Aires, Dec. 1-23, 1936," International Conferences of American States, First Supp. 1933-1940 160 (1940). See also Article 3 of the earlier "Convention on Rights and Duties of States, Seventh International Conference of American States, Montevideo, Dec. 3-26, 1933," *id.* at 121-23.

2. Resolution XI (3), PAU, Report Submitted to the Governing Board of the Pan American Union by the Director General, Inter-American Conference on Problems of War and Peace, Mexico City, Feb. 21-March 8, 1945 at 39 (1945).

3. Resolution VIII (g), *id.* at 30-31.

4. Resolution XXXII, Report of the Delegation of U.S.A., Ninth International Conference of American States, Bogotá, Colombia, March 30-May 2, 1948 at 266-67 (1948).

5. Resolution XCIII, Report of the Delegation of the U.S.A., Tenth Inter-American Conference, Caracas, Venezuela, March 1-28, 1954 at 156-57 (1955).

6. Although it is convenient to speak of the right of independence, it is not in actuality correct according to Kelsen, for he points out that independence is an essential characteristic of a state, not a right. See Kelsen, "The Draft Declaration on Rights and Duties of States," 44 Am. J. Int. L. 259 at 267 (1950). But see Fenwick, International Law 249-50 (3rd ed. 1948) who speaks of a "right of independence." In the inter-American community it would seem that the members attempt through the OAS to guarantee mutually the independence of each American state, at least against extinguishment by force or aggression. Hence, it may well be spoken of as a right in the inter-American community. See *infra,* discussion on reciprocal assistance and collective security pp. 205-11. For further discussions of sovereignty and independence of states see Schwarzenberger, Power Politics Ch. V (2d ed. 1951); I Oppenheim, International Law 286-97 (8th ed., Lauterpacht, 1955); Kelsen, "The Principle of Sovereign Equality of States as a Basis for International Organization," 53 Yale L. J. 207 (1944); Van Kleffens, "Sovereignty in International Law," 82 Recueil des Cours 5 (1953).

7. I Oppenheim, *ibid.*
8. See *supra* Ch. I.
9. Van Kleffens, *supra* note 6 at 82 where he states that "... the sovereign state in the sense of an omnipotent completely self-determining entity does not exist and has never existed."
10. Kelsen, Principles of International Law 110-12, 152 (1952); Fenwick, *op. cit. supra* note 6 at 250.
11. Kelsen, *ibid.*
12. Schwarzenberger, A Manual of International Law 58 (1947); Thomas & Thomas, International Treaties 7 (Monograph, 1950).
13. Thomas & Thomas, Non-Intervention: The Law and Its Import in the Americas 74-91 (1956).
14. See *infra* pp. 184-85.
15. See *infra* pp. 203-5.
16. See *infra* pp. 205-11.
17. This is exceedingly doubtful. See *infra* Ch. XIV.
18. Lasswell & Kaplan, Power and Society 74 (1950).
19. For discussion of enforcement measures see *infra* pp. 269-74.
20. Lasswell & Kaplan, *op. cit. supra* note 18 at 55; Thomas & Thomas, *op. cit. supra* note 13 at 108-9.
21. Thomas & Thomas, *ibid.*
22. *Ibid.*
23. See *supra* Ch. III.
24. On the principle of equality as applicable specifically to the inter-American system see Herrera, "Evolution of Equality in the Inter-American System," 61 Pol. Sci. Q. 90 (1946). On the principle in general at international law see Dickinson, The Equality of States in International Law (1920); Goebel, The Equality of States (1953); Hicks, "The Equality of States and The Hague Conferences," 2 Am. J. Int. L. 530 (1908); Lande, "Revindication of the Principle of Equality of States," 62 Pol. Sci. Q. 258-398 (1947); Thomas & Thomas, "Equality of States in International Law—Fact or Fiction?" 37 Va. L. Rev. 791 (1951). Weinschel, "The Doctrine of the Equality of States and Its Recent Modifications," 45 Am. J. Int. L. 416 (1951).
25. See Thomas & Thomas, *op. cit. supra* note 13 at 15, 56-57.
26. I Calvo, Le Droit International Publique et Privé 286 (1885) as translated and quoted in Dickinson, *op. cit. supra* note 24 at 100-101.
27. U.S. For. Rel. 1903, p. 2. See also Drago, "State Loans in their Relation to International Policy," 1 Am. J. Int. L. 692 (1907).
28. Convention on Rights and Duties of States, Seventh Conference, *op. cit. supra* note 1.
29. Fenwick, *op. cit. supra* note 6 at 220; Kelsen, *supra* note 6 at 209.
30. Dickinson, *op. cit. supra* note 24.
31. *Id.* at 4, 103-9, 334-35.
32. *Ibid.*
33. Baker, "The Equality of States in International Law," Brit. Y. B. Int. L. 1923-24, 1, 6; McNair, "Equality in International Law," 26 Mich. L. Rev. 131 at 136-37 (1927).
34. Fenwick, *op. cit. supra* note 6 at 221, n. 37.
35. Friedman, Legal Theory 9 (1949).
36. Cahn, The Sense of Injustice 14 (1949).
37. Brierly, The Law of Nations 64 (2d ed. 1936).
38. Dickinson, *op. cit. supra* note 24 at 280.
39. See Ross, A Textbook of International Law 246-47 (1947); Hindmarsh, "Self-Help in Time of Peace," 26 Am. J. Int. L. 315 (1952); Maccoby, "Reprisals as Measures of Redress Short of War," 11 Cambridge L. J. 60 (1924).
40. See *infra* discussion of self-defense pp. 162, 250-60.
41. See *infra* discussion of collective security pp. 250-68.
42. Pact of Bogotá, Arts. II, XXXII.
43. Pact of Bogotá, Art. L.
44. Pact of Bogotá, Arts. V, VI, and VII.
45. Such reprisals would of course be a violation of the non-intervention principle which binds the American states. See *infra* discussion on non-intervention pp. 162-64.
46. See *infra* discussion of the Pact of Bogotá, Ch. XVI.
47. I Oppenheim, *op. cit. supra* note 6 at 22-23.
48. See *supra* on the legislative function of the Conference pp. 65-73.
49. Butler and Maccoby, The Development of International Law 259-60 (1928).

50. Dickinson, *op. cit. supra* note 24 at 280.
51. Thomas & Thomas, *supra* note 24 at 809-23.
52. See *supra* on representation and voting in these organs pp. 78, 88-89, 91-92, 111-12.
53. See *infra* on collective security pp. 249-50.
54. Art. 54, Charter of Bogotá.

CHAPTER IX

1. The principle was of course known at international law prior to the independence of the American republics, but the practices of European states indicated that intervention was more nearly the rule. For early history of the principle see Thomas & Thomas, Non-Intervention: The Law and Its Import in the Americas 3-14 (1956).

2. Samuel Flagg Bemis is of the opinion that the American principle of non-intervention sprang from two sources: the foreign policy of the United States, and the principles evolved by Latin American jurists and statesmen in opposition to non-American interventions as well as interventions by the United States. Bemis, The Latin American Policy of the United States 227 (1943).

3. See, e.g., I Antokoletz, Tratado de Derecho Internacional Público 572-73 (1944); I Accioly, Tratado de Derecho Internacional Publico 280 (1945).

4. See *supra* Chs. I and II on interventions in Latin America.

5. See Bordwell, "Calvo and the 'Calvo Doctrine,'" 18 The Greenbag 377 at 379-80 (1906).

6. On the Monroe Doctrine and U.S. interventions see *supra* Chs. I and II.

7. See *supra* Ch. I for discussions of the Congress of Panama.

8. "Instructions That Are to Govern the Conduct of the Ministers Plenipotentiary from Perú to the General Congress on the Isthmus of Panamá. Issued by General Bolívar, May 15, 1825," International Conferences of American States 1889-1928, xxi-xxiv, Art. 13 at xxiii (edited by Scott, 1931).

9. Art. 5 of the treaty, *id.* at xxiv-xxix at xxv.

10. Art. 2(2), 2 Archivo Diplomatico Peruano 302-3 (1938) as quoted in Irizary y Puente, "The Doctrines of Recognition and Intervention in Latin America," 28 Tulane L. Rev. 313 at 327 (1954).

11. Calvo, Le Droit International Theorique et Pratique (1896).

12. Drago, "State Loans and Their Relation to International Policy," 1 Am. J. Int. L. 692 (1907); Hershey, "The Calvo and Drago Doctrines," 1 Am. J. Int. L. 26 (1907).

13. Bemis, *op. cit. supra* note 2 at 328.

14. A summary of the work of the Commission of Jurists as pertaining to non-intervention will be found in Thomas & Thomas, *op. cit. supra* note 1 at 57-59.

15. On the various attitudes of the delegates at the Sixth Conference on this matter see Rivero Reyes, "Deberes y Derechos de los Estados," 31 Revista de Derecho Internacional 7 at 72-78 (1938).

16. "Convention on Rights and Duties of States, Seventh International Conference of American States, Montevideo, December 3-26, 1933," The International Conferences of American States, First Supp. 1933-1940, at 121-23 (1940).

17. *Id.* at 123-24.

18. *Id.* at 191-92.

19. Thomas & Thomas, *op. cit. supra* note 1 at 71.

20. Stowell, Intervention in International Law 318 (1921); I Ruiz Moreno, Derecho Internacional Publico 187 (1940). But see jurists who declare that intervention does not occur unless there is present the use or threat of use of armed force. I Oppenheim, International Law 305 (8th ed., Lauterpacht, 1955); Kelsen, Principles of International Law 64 (1952); Brierly, The Law of Nations 247 (2d ed. 1938).

21. See Lawrence, Principles of International Law 124 (5th ed. 1913); Westlake asserts that a tender of advice, though imprudent, is not intervention. I Westlake, International Law 307 (1904).

22. See Stowell, *op. cit. supra* note 20 at 318.

23. See, e.g., Hall, A Treatise on International Law 279 (6th ed. 1909) and I Oppenheim, *op. cit. supra* note 20 at 306.

24. Kelsen, *op. cit. supra* note 20 at 110-12, 152.

25. See Thomas & Thomas, *op. cit. supra* note 1 at 91-97.

26. See, e.g., Bowett, Self-Defense in International Law Ch. I (1958); Brierly, *op. cit. supra* note 20 at 253; I Westlake, *op. cit. supra* note 21 at 299-304; Lawrence, *op. cit. supra* note 21 at 117-18, 121-22; Ross, A Textbook of International Law 244 (1947); and I Hyde, International Law Chiefly as Interpreted and Applied by the United States, sec. 70 (2d

ed. 1947). "The Case of the Neptune," IV Moore's International Adjudications 372, 441-43 (1931), as well as the International Tribunal Nuremburg, cmd 6964, p. 28 (1946), both recognized self-defense, but both cases limited it drastically as justification. On elements of the right of self-defense and the meaning thereof see *infra* collective security pp. 250-60.

27. Lawrence, *id.* at 117-18; and I Hyde, *ibid.*

28. See Thomas & Thomas, *op. cit. supra* note 1 at 70-71.

29. Kelsen, *op. cit. supra* note 20 at 7-9, 22-23. See Hindmarsh, "Self-Help in Time of Peace," 26 Am. J. Int. L. 315 (1932).

30. Kelsen, *id.* at 23-25. Some jurists refuse to subscribe to the theory of war as a sanction or as a delict; thus, there are contrary views as to the legal character of war. See Kelsen's discussion pro and con, *id.* 33-38. He, of course, subscribes to the *bellum justum* doctrine.

31. Ross, *op. cit. supra* note 26 at 246.

32. *Ibid.*

33. For discussion of the various forms of reprisals see Thomas & Thomas, *op. cit. supra* note 1 at 86-87.

34. *Id.* at 88-91.

35. I Oppenheim, *op. cit. supra* note 20 at 308; Hall, *op. cit. supra* note 23 at 55, see also p. 282.

36. See Thomas & Thomas, *op. cit. supra* note 1 at 131.

37. Art. 15, Charter of Bogotá.

38. On retorsion as intervention see Thomas & Thomas, *op. cit. supra* note 1 at 87.

39. For discussion under the U.N. Charter see Thomas & Thomas, *id.* at 132-38.

40. As to the legal personality of the OAS see *supra* Ch. III.

41. Art. 19, Charter of Bogotá. Non-intervention is a principle upon which the OAS is founded, and the OAS by Art. 4 must practice the basic principle to carry out its purposes.

42. See *infra* on collective security p. 207.

43. See, e.g., Lauterpacht, "The International Protection of Human Rights," 70 Recueil des Cours 14 at 21 (1947).

44. Lleras, "Report on the Ninth International Conference of American States," 1 Annals of OAS 25-27 (1949); Record, U.N. General Assembly, 3rd Sess., Pt. II, April 30, 1949, Doc. A/P V 203, p. 46.

45. For example, Preuss, "Article 2, Paragraph 7 of the Charter of the United Nations and Matters of Domestic Jurisdiction," 74 Recueil des Cours 553 (1949).

46. See *supra* Ch. III.

47. Travis, "The Organization of American States: A Guide to the Future," X Western Political Quarterly 491 at 503-5 (1957).

48. The preamble of the Charter states that juridical organization is a necessary condition for security and peace founded on moral order and justice. Article 1 declares that the organization is established to achieve an order of peace and justice. Since justice and international law are not identical, these articles do not necessarily spell out the fact that a basic purpose of the OAS is to protect international law. However, these articles coupled with Article 5(a) and (b) would seem to stipulate that the OAS is an entity devoted to the maintenance of an order of international law and justice. See *infra* pp. 199-202.

49. Kelsen, "Limitations on the Functions of the United Nations," 55 Yale L. J. 997 (1945-46).

CHAPTER X

1. See *supra* discussion on sovereignty, Ch. VIII.

2. I Oppenheim, International Law 287-88 (8th ed., Lauterpacht, 1955).

3. *Id.* sec. 319; 1 Accioly, Tratado de Derecho Internacional Publico sec. 382 (1945).

4. Roth, The Minimum Standard of International Law Applied to Aliens 62 (1949).

5. On the minimum standard rule see Roth, *id.* at 81 *et seq.;* Borchard, Diplomatic Protection of Citizens Abroad 177 (1915); Root, 4 Proceedings Am. Soc. Int. L. 16 (1910); II Hyde, International Law Chiefly as Interpreted and Applied by the United States secs. 266, 267 (2d rev. ed. 1945); "Harvard Draft Convention on Responsibility of States by Reason of Damage Caused on their Territory to the Persons and Property of Foreigners," 53 Am. J. Int. L. Supp. 133 (1929).

6. Fenwick, International Law 279 (3rd ed. 1948).

7. See *supra* on sanctions at international law, Ch. IX.

8. Grotius, De Jure Belli Ac Pacis, Bk. III, Ch. II, V at p. 627 of Classics of International Law (Scott ed., 1929).

9. "Hence a sovereign should not interfere in the suits of his subject in foreign countries, nor grant there his protection except in cases where justice has been denied, or the decision is clearly and palpably unjust, or the proper procedure has not been observed, or finally, in cases where his subjects, or foreigners in general, have been discriminated against." Vattel, The Law of Nations or the Principles of Natural Law (Text of 1758) Bk. II, Ch. VII, sec. 84 as set forth in Classics of International Law, Vol. III, p. 139(1916).

10. See Lissitzyn, "The Meaning of the Term 'Denial of Justice,'" 30 Am. J. Int. L. 632 (1936); Freeman, The International Responsibility of States for Denial of Justice, Chs. V-VII (1938); II Hyde, op. cit. supra note 5 at sec. 381 et seq. These authorities discuss the various meanings attached to the term "denial of justice."

11. Northrop, The Meeting of East and West 43 (1946); 32 Am. J. Int. L. Supp. 181, 198 (1938).

12. See Ypes, Le Panaméricanisme au point de vue historique, juridique et politique 121-23 (1936). As to the equality of treatment doctrine see Roth, op. cit. supra note 4 at 62 et seq.

13. International Conferences of American States 1889-1928, p. 45 (Scott ed., 1931). And along similar lines see "Convention Relative to the Rights of Aliens" signed and ratified by several Latin American states, but not by the United States. International Conferences, id. at 90-91.

14. International Conferences of American States, First Supp. 1933-1940, p. 121 (1940).

15. Id. at 123.

16. Art. 12, Charter of Bogotá. For discussion on this matter at the Bogotá Conference see Report of the Delegation of the U.S.A., Ninth International Conference of American States 36 (1948).

17. Id. at 36-37. For summaries of other inter-American instruments pertaining to the status of aliens, their rights and duties, see PAU, Manual of Inter-American Relations 101-5 (1953).

18. I Calvo, Le Droit International Theorique et Pratique, sec. 205 (1896). See on the Calvo Doctrine, Hershey, "The Calvo and Drago Doctrines," 1 Am. J. Int. L. 26 (1907); Bordwell, "Calvo and the 'Calvo Doctrine,'" 18 The Green Bag 377 (1906).

19. For summaries and interpretations of the Calvo Doctrine see Hershey, id. at 31; Borchard, op. cit. supra note 4 at 837, 842; Podesta Costa, Manual de Derecho Internacional Publico 207 (2d ed. 1947); Freeman, "Recent Aspects of the Calvo Doctrine and the Challenge to International Law," 40 Am. J. Int. L. 121 at 133 (1946).

20. See Lipstein, "The Place of the Calvo Clause in International Law," 22 Brit. Y. B. Int. L. 130 (1945). The Calvo Doctrine gave birth to the Calvo Clause, which is a stipulation utilized by some nations in contracts entered into between the state and foreign individuals whereby the alien agrees that disputes which may arise out of the contract are to be submitted to local courts and are to give rise to no international claims. See Hyde, "Attempts by Contract to Restrict Interposition," 21 Am. J. Int. L. 298 (1927). Some states have included language of the Calvo Clause in their Constitutions, e.g., Guatemala, El Salvador, Nicaragua, Honduras, Peru, Venezuela, and Mexico. See II Hyde, op. cit. supra note 5, sec. 305. A complete work on the Calvo Clause, is Shea, The Calvo Clause (1955).

21. For a discussion of the Drago Doctrine see Drago, "State Loans and Their Relation to International Policy," 1 Am. J. Int. L. 692 (1907); Hershey, op. cit. supra note 18.

22. Sanchez i Sanchez, Curso de Derecho Internacional Publico Americano sec. 202 (1943).

23. International Conferences, op. cit. supra note 13 at 135-36.

24. Borchard, op. cit. supra note 5 at 318-21.

25. II Malloy's Treaties 2254 (1910); II Scott, The Hague Peace Conferences 357 (1909). For discussion see II Hyde, op. cit. supra note 5, sec. 309; Borchard, op. cit. supra note 5 at 321-22.

26. International Conferences, First Supp., op. cit. supra note 14 at 122.

27. Id. at 191. See also the Argentine project, which if adopted would have proscribed armed force and diplomatic intervention for pecuniary claims. Id. at 165.

28. International Conferences, First Supp., op. cit. supra note 14 at 191.

29. See Bowett, Self-Defence in International Law Ch. 5 (1958).

30. Art. VII, Pact of Bogotá.

31. Report of Delegation of the U.S.A., Ninth Conference, op. cit. supra note 16 at 50.

32. Id. at 200.

33. Hyde would apparently state that intervention, diplomatic or armed, to protect persons or property of nationals would be interposition only. I Hyde, op. cit. supra note 5 at 246 (text and n. 2). See also Fenwick, "Intervention: Individual and Collective," 39 Am. J. Int. L. 645 at 645-46 (1945); Freeman supra note 19 at 136 and 137.

34. PAU, Inter-American Juridical Committee, Instrument Relating to Violations of the Principles of Nonintervention, sec. i, draft instrument on violations of the principle of nonintervention pp. 15-17 (1959).

35. *Id.* at 26.

CHAPTER XI

1. Fenwick, International Law 136 *et seq.* (3rd ed. 1948).

2. The Convention on Rights and Duties of States, Montevideo, 1933, declares in Art. I:

The State as a person of international law should possess the following qualifications: a) a permanent population; b) a defined territory; c) government; and d) capacity to enter into relations with other States.

International Conferences of American States, First Supp. 1933-1940, 121-23 (1940).

3. For lists of the jurists on one side or the other see Chen, The International Law of Recognition 13-17 (1951), and Lauterpacht, Recognition in International Law Chs. IV and V (1948).

4. Fenwick, *op. cit. supra* note 1 at 141, n. 27.

5. I Oppenheim, International Law 12 (5th ed., 1937).

6. See Chen, *op. cit. supra* note 3 at 31.

7. For such a view see Le Normand, La Reconnaissance Internationale et ses Diverses Applications 37 (1899).

8. See Chen, *op. cit. supra* note 3 at 77-78 and 133-71.

9. See note 2, *supra.*

10. I Oppenheim, International Law 146-148 (8th ed., Lauterpacht, 1955); Lauterpacht, *op. cit. supra* note 3, Ch. XX; Chen, *op. cit. supra* note 3 at 189.

11. Under the modern constitutive theory there may be a withdrawal of recognition when a state ceases to possess the qualifications of statehood. Lauterpacht, *id.* at 349-52; Kelsen, Principles of International Law 274-75 (1952).

12. Kelsen, *id.* at 275.

13. On recognition of governments see Chen, *op. cit. supra* note 3 at 97-130; Lauterpacht, *op. cit. supra* note 3 at 87-114; Kelsen, *op. cit. supra* note 11 at 279-88; Jimenez de Arechaga, Reconocimiento de Gobiernos (1947); Sepulveda, La Teoria y la Practica del Reconocimiento de Gobiernos (1954); Dennis, "Revolution, Recognition and Intervention," 9 For. Affairs 54 (1930).

14. I Phillimore, Commentaries upon International Law 553 (1879); I Wheaton, Elements of International Law 55 (4th ed., Keith, 1959).

15. For example, the premature recognition of the United States by France in 1778 which resulted in war between Great Britain and France. See I Moore, A Digest of International Law 73 (1906); Sharp, Non-Recognition as a Legal Obligation 1775-1934, p. 18 (1934). The United States' recognition of Panama was premature, and by the act of recognition the United States actually prevented the parent state, Colombia, from quashing the revolution. See I Moore, *id.* at 78 *et seq.*; I Manning, Diplomatic Correspondence of the United States Concerning the Independence of the Latin American Nations 87, 194 (1925).

16. Lauterpacht, *op. cit. supra* note 3 at 26; Chen, *op. cit. supra* note 3 at 54-62.

17. See Harcourt, Letters of Historicus on Some Questions of International Law 24 (1863); Lorimer, "La Doctrine de la Reconnaissance," 16 Revue de Droit Internationale et de Legislation Comparée 333 at 339 (1884); I Hyde, International Law Chiefly as Interpreted and Applied by the United States 17 (2d ed. 1945); Hall, A Treatise on International Law 48 (1924).

18. See Thomas & Thomas, Non-Intervention: The Law and Its Import in the Americas 241-43 (1956).

19. *Id.* at 245 *et seq.*

20. Early in 1907, Carlos Tobar of Ecuador advocated that governments coming into power by revolutions contrary to the constitution should not be recognized by the other American republics. See Anderson, El Gobierno De Facto 26 (1925); Stowell, "The Doctrine of Constitutional Legitimacy," 55 Am. J. Int. L. 302 (1931). See on the adoption of this principle for a time by the Central American republics and the added test advocated by President Wilson, "The General Treaty of Peace and Amity, Washington 1907," II Malloy, Treaties of the United States 2397 (1910); I Hackworth, Digest of International Law 181 (1940); Alvarez, "La Doctrina de Wilson sobre el No Reconocimiento de los Gobiernos Surgidos," 3 Annuario de la Sociedad Cubana de Derecho Internacional 225 (1919). In

1923 another Treaty of Peace and Amity was signed by the Central American nations embodying Wilson's doctrine. For text of Article II of the Treaty see I Hackworth, *ibid*.

A recent attempt was made to obtain a more uniform policy on recognition when Venezuela, Costa Rica, the Dominican Republic, and Honduras submitted to the Council of the OAS a resolution calling for a convocation of a Meeting of Consultation of Ministers of Foreign Affairs, pursuant to Article 39 of the OAS Charter, to consider the position that should be taken by the governments of the member states with regard to recognizing regimes which came into being by coups d'état. The resolution did not receive the necessary eleven votes. An alternative resolution was then presented by the United States, which sought Council agreement on the "desirability" of calling a ministerial conference that would study the whole question of coups d'état and would provide for joint inter-American action whenever necessary. This resolution was sent to a committee for further study without other action being taken. OEA/Ser.G/V/C-d-1012, 1014 August 10, August 22 (1962).

21. See resolutions of Guatemala to this effect as summarized in Thomas & Thomas, *op. cit. supra* note 18 at 252-53.

22. But consider the doctrine of Genaro Estrada of Mexico, who would seek to abolish the institution of express recognition. For discussion see Jessup, "The Estrada Doctrine," 25 Am. J. Int. L. 119 (1931); I Ulloa, Derecho Internacional Publico sec. 212 (1946).

23. This assumes that the other requisites of a state are met, that is, a territory and a people.

24. Thomas Jefferson stated, "It accords with our principles to acknowledge any government to be rightful which is formed by the will of the nation substantially declared." I Moore, *op. cit. supra* note 15 at 120; III Jefferson's Works 489 (4th ed. 1939).

25. See, e.g., Podesta Costa, Manual de Derecho Internacional Publico 74-75 (2d ed. 1947); I Antokoletz, Tratado de Derecho Internacional Público Ch. VII (4th ed. 1944); I Bustamante, Derecho Internacional Publico, sec. 207 (1933); Ursúa, Derecho Internacional Publico sec. 69 (1938).

26. Some unity among the American states was forthcoming during World War II as to a common policy of recognition or nonrecognition of new governments. In effect recognition of a new government was conditioned on the requisite that the new government observe its continental commitments. See the activities of the Emergency Advisory Committee for Political Defense of the Continent, Spaeth and Sanders, "The Emergency Advisory Committee for Political Defense," 38 Am. J. Int. L. 218 (1944). Recognition of certain governments in Bolivia and Argentina was withheld for a time by most of the republics. See Thomas & Thomas, *op. cit. supra* note 18 at 251, and see *supra* Ch. II. Following the war there have been attempts to formulate common prerequisites for recognition in accordance with Resolution XXXIV of the Bogotá Conference. The Inter-American Juridical Committee prepared a draft treaty on the subject, but the Inter-American Council of Jurists thought that the time was not ripe for a convention on the subject; see Freeman, "The First Meeting of the Inter-American Council of Jurists," 44 Am. J. Int. L. 374 (1950); 5 Annals of OAS 151 *et seq.* (1953); Thomas & Thomas, *id.* at 253-54.

27. See *supra* Ch. IV.

28. Aufricht, "Principles and Practices of Recognition by International Organizations," 43 Am. J. Int. L. 679 (1949).

29. *Supra* note 2.

30. Charter of Bogotá, Arts. 5(a), (b) and 14.

31. Lauterpacht, *op. cit. supra* note 3 at 380; Note, "Implied Recognition," 21 Brit. Y. B. Int. L. 123 at 145 (1944).

32. Bull. PAU, vol. LXXXI, Oct. 1947.

33. See *infra* on civil strife pp. 339-45.

34. See I Oppenheim, International Law 693 (7th ed., Lauterpacht, 1952).

35. I Oppenheim, *op. cit. supra* note 10 at 566-67.

36. *Id.* at 142.

37. Fenwick, *op. cit. supra* note 1 at 358-61.

38. See McMahon, Conquest and Modern International Law Ch. IV (1939) for a survey of modern opinion as to legality of the right of conquest.

39. See Lauterpacht, *op. cit. supra* note 3 at 420-21; Tucker, "The Principle of Effectiveness in International Law," in Lipsky, Law and Politics in the World Community 31 at 42-47 (1953).

40. Graske, "Some Aspects of Treaty Interpretation in the United States 1931-1935," 10 Tulane L. Rev. 246 (1936); Brierly, "Some Considerations on the Obsolescence of Treaties," 11 Trans. of Grotius Soc. 11 (1926). Today under the U.N. Charter, which has attempted to abolish the use of force, the position of international law has seemingly changed, and consent given under forceful duress would vitiate the treaty. I Oppenheim,

op. cit. supra note 10, sec. 499. Such would clearly be true under the non-intervention principle of the Americas, see Thomas & Thomas, *op. cit. supra* note 18 at 94-96.

41. The Latin American nations attempted to proscribe the right of conquest even earlier. The Congress of Panama, in Article 22 of the Treaty of Union, League and Perpetual Confederation, would have guaranteed boundaries by placing them under the protection of the Confederation. The Santiago Conference of 1856 provided in the Continental Treaty, by the terms of Article 13, a legal duty of nonrecognition of territorial changes. Mutual territorial guarantees were contained in the Treaty of Union and Defensive Alliance signed at the Lima Conference in 1865. See *infra* Ch. I on these early conferences and treaties. See Langer, Seizure of Territory Chs. VII, XI, XII, and XIII (1947) on the efforts of the American nations to repudiate the forcible acquisition of territory. McMahon, *op. cit. supra* note 38 in Ch. VI discusses "Pan American Treaty Limitations on Conquest."

42. "Recommendation, The Right of Conquest," International Conferences of American States 1889-1928 pp. 44-45 (edited by Scott, 1931); and see "Plan of Arbitration," *id.* at 40-43.

43. McMahon, *op. cit. supra* note 38 at 124.

44. These territorial questions were questions not yet decided, growing out of the War of the Pacific, 1879-1883, with Chile against Peru and Bolivia. The outcome of this war deprived Bolivia of her seacoast and Peru of certain territory. See Alvarez, "Latin America and International Law," 3 Am. J. Int. L. 269 at 328 (1909).

45. See International Conferences of American States, *op. cit. supra* note 42 at 40-41, n. 4.

46. This community sentiment crystallized to a degree by a resolution of the Sixth Conference, 1928, condemning aggression and pledging the American states to employ pacific means to settle their controversies. *Id.* at 441-42.

47. For discussion see Langer, *op. cit. supra* note 41 at 56-61; Wright, "The Stimson Note of January 7, 1932," 26 Am. J. Int. L. 342 (1932); McNair, "The Stimson Doctrine of Non-Recognition," 14 Brit. Y. B. Int. L. 65 (1933).

48. As quoted in Langer, *op. cit. supra* note 41 at 68. For discussion of the Chaco affair see *id.* at 67-68; Woolsey, "Settlement of the Chaco Dispute," 33 Am. J. Int. L. 126 (1939).

49. Woolsey, "The Leticia Dispute," 27 Am. J. Int. L. 313 (1933).

50. McMahon, *op. cit. supra* note 38 at 178.

51. International Conferences of American States, First Supp., *op. cit. supra* note 2 at 496-99.

52. *Id.* at 122.

53. PAU, Report on the Second Meeting of the Ministers of Foreign Affairs of the American Republics, Habana, July 21-30, 1940 p. 22 (1940).

54. "Declaration of Principles of Inter-American Solidarity and Cooperation," International Conferences of American States, First Supp., *op. cit. supra* note 2 at 160.

55. "Non-Recognition of Acquisition of Territory by Force," *id.* at 254.

56. "Act of Chapultepec and Declaration of Mexico," PAU, Inter-American Conference on Problems of War and Peace, Mexico City, Feb. 21-Mar. 8, 1945 pp. 30, 39 (Cong. & Conf. Series No. 47, 1945).

57. Rio Treaty, Art. 1.

58. *Id.* Art. 3.

59. *Id.* Arts. 6, 20. For discussion of these principles see *infra* on collective security pp. 269-71.

CHAPTER XII

1. I Oppenheim, International Law 15-17, 25 (Lauterpacht, 8th ed. 1955).

2. Thomas & Thomas, International Treaties 52-54 (Monograph, 1950).

3. Alvarez, Le Droit International Américain 137 (1910); I Antokoletz, Tratado de Derecho Internacional Público 327 (4th ed. 1944); and Ulloa, Derecho Internacional Publico 70 (1938).

4. U.N. Secretariat Memo: The Codification of International Law in the Inter-American System with Special Reference to the Methods of Codification. A/AC. 10/8 (1947).

5. Urrutia, Le Continent Américain et le Droit International 199 (1928).

6. For statements of these principles and the various occasions on which they were set forth see PAU, Manual of Inter-American Relations 4-5 (Cong. & Conf. Series No. 26, 1953).

7. Arts. 7 and 9.

8. On the supremacy of international law see Brierly, The Law of Nations 50-57 (5th ed. 1955); Garner, "Limitations on National Sovereignty in International Relations," 19 Am. Pol. Sci. Rev. 1 (1925); Kelsen, The Principle of Sovereign Equality as a Basis for International Organization 207 (1944); Van Kleffens, "Sovereignty in International Law," 82 Recueil des Cours 5 (1953).

9. Schwarzenberger, A Manual of International Law 58 (1947); Schuman, "Treaties," 15 Encyclopedia of Social Sciences 96 (1937).

10. Alvarez, Le Droit International Américain, Son Fondement—Sa Nature (1910); Alvarez, "Latin America and International Law," 3 Am. J. Int. L. 269 (1909); Alvarez, "American International Law," 3 Proc. Am. Soc. Int. L. 206 (1909); Alvarez, International Law and Related Subjects from the Point of View of the American Continent (1922).

11. Manoel Alvarado de Souza Sá Vianna, De la Non-Existence d'un Droit International Américain (1912); Manoel Alvarado de Souza Sá Vianna, Elementos de Direito Internacional 84-180 (1908).

12. I Antokoletz, op. cit. supra note 3 at 315-28.

13. Jacobini, A Study of the Philosophy of International Law as Seen in Works of Latin American Writers 121-36 (1954).

14. Id. at 124.

15. Alvarez, Despues de la Guerra 181 (1943).

16. Colombian-Peruvian Asylum Case, Judgment of November 20, 1950: I.C.J. Reports 1950, p. 266, Dissenting Opinion by Judge Alvarez at p. 294.

17. Ibid. It has been suggested that American international law may be subdivided even further, i.e., into Central American and Caribbean law. For discussion see Sanchez i Sanchez, Curso de Derecho Internacional Publico Americano 163-64 (1943).

18. Jacobini, op. cit. supra note 13 at 128. Certain specific rules of American international law mentioned by Alvarez are (1) the principle of uti possidetis, which signifies in the Americas that as of 1810 and thereafter the Latin American nations as they became independent established their colonial boundaries as their national boundaries; (2) res nullius does not exist in the Americas; (3) the equality of states; (4) the Drago Doctrine; (5) defense of the hemisphere; (6) acceptance of codification of international law; (7) recognition of the legal status of rebels and the right of asylum; (8) recognition of the principle of ius soli. See Jacobini, id. at 129. Some of these principles are now obsolete. In the main the principles existing today are included in the Principles and Rights and Duties of States chapters of the Charter of Bogotá plus certain others.

19. See Thomas, Communism versus International Law Chs. 1 and 2 (1953).

20. Root, "The Need of Popular Understanding of International Law," 1 Am. J. Int. L. 1 (1907).

21. Alvarez, "Le Développement du Droit des Gens dans le Nouveau-Monde," XXV Transactions of the Grotius Society 169 (1939).

22. Alvarez, "American International Law," 3 Proc. Am. Soc. Int. L. 206 at 209 (1909).

23. Lauterpacht, The Function of Law in the International Community 286 (1933).

24. See e.g. I Oppenheim, op. cit. supra note 1 at 5, 27-28, and criticism by Kunz, "General International Law and the Law of International Organization," 47 Am. J. Int. L. 456, n. 1 (1953).

25. See Walker, The Science of International Law, Ch. 1, sec. 1 (1893); Hall, International Law 5 (1880); I Westlake, International Law, 16 (1910).

26. See I Calvo, Le Droit International Théorique et Pratique 154 (1887); I Anzolotti, Corso di Diritto Internazionale 43 (2d ed. 1923); Diena, Diritto Internazionale 18 (2d ed. 1914); Cavaglieri, Lezioni di Diritto Internazionale (Parte Generale) 56-57 (1925); Heilborn, Grundebegroffe des Volkerrechts 70, 71 (1912).

27. Colombian-Peruvian Asylum Case, Judgment of November 20, 1950; I.C.J. Reports 1950, p. 266.

28. Id. at 276.

29. Id. at 276-77.

30. Brierly, The Law of Nations 39 (3rd ed. 1947).

31. Sir John Fischer Williams, Some Aspects of International Law 44 (1939).

32. Colombian-Peruvian Asylum Case, Judgment of November 20, 1950; I.C.J. Reports 1950, p. 266, Dissenting Opinion by Judge Alvarez, p. 295.

33. Id., Dissenting Opinion by Judge Azevedo, at 336.

34. Id., Dissenting Opinion by Judge Caicedo Castilla, at 370.

35. Id., Dissenting Opinion by Judge Read, at 316.

36. Kelsen, General Theory of Law and State 363 et seq. (1946), and see Von Verdross, "The Charter of the United Nations and General International Law," as contained in Lipsky, Law and Politics in the World Community 153 (1953).

37. Thomas & Thomas, *op. cit. supra* note 2.

38. See Starke, "Regionalism as a Problem of International Law," as contained in Lipsky, Law and Politics in the World Community 114 at 116-18 (1953). See also Jacobini, *op. cit. supra* note 13 at 134.

39. See discussion of Von Verdross as to the U.N., *supra* note 36, at 156.

40. See Thomas & Thomas, Non-Intervention: The Law and Its Import in the Americas 124, 134, 209 (1956). See also Von Verdross, *id.* at 156; Kunz, *supra* note 24 at 458.

41. See for example Von Verdross, "Forbidden Treaties in International Law," 31 Am. J. Int. L. 511 (1937).

42. On the effect of treaties on third states see *infra* pp. 274-76.

43. Fenwick, International Law 277 (1924).

44. V Hackworth, Digest of International Law 222 (1943); "Research in International Law, Draft Convention on the Law of Treaties, Harvard Law School, Comment," 29 Am. J. Int. L. Supp. 653, 925 (1935).

45. See on the abuse of rights, Gutteridge, "Abuse of Rights," 5 Camb. L. J. 22 (1935).

46. I Oppenheim, *op. cit. supra* note 1, at 370-71.

47. *Supra* Ch. V.

48. See, e.g., Fitzmaurice, "The United Nations and the Rule of Law," 38 Transactions of the Grotius Society 135 (1953).

49. On the use of the term "justice" and "international law" in various articles of the U.N. Charter particularly Art. 1(1), Kelsen declares that the use of both terms, if they are considered identical, is superfluity. He goes on to say that it is more probable that they are not identical and then concludes that they are in opposition to each other. This creates difficulty, for in case of conflict the question becomes one of which the U.N. shall maintain. Kelsen, The Law of the United Nations 17 (1950). But see Stone, Legal Controls of International Conflict (1954) who at pp. 50-56 takes issue with Kelsen's statements and concludes that there is in reality no conflict between the two principles, and that a reference to justice does not weaken international law. See also Chakste, "Justice and Law in the Charter of the United Nations," 42 Am. J. Int. L. 590 (1948).

50. Stone, *ibid.*

51. Art. 5(a) and (b), Charter of Bogotá.

52. Art. 4, Charter of Bogotá.

53. Thomas & Thomas, *op. cit. supra* note 40 at 85-91.

54. See *supra* Ch. IX.

55. *Ibid.* And see *infra* Ch. XV.

56. *Infra* on the enforcement measures as sanctions pp. 271-74.

57. Arts. 3 and 6, The Rio Treaty.

58. See *supra* pp. 188-89. With respect to the U.N. Charter it is not so clear that the members are bound to the observance of international law, for there is nothing in the Charter from which can be spelled an agreement that all members are to be governed by rules of international law. Thomas & Thomas, *op. cit. supra* note 40 at 105.

59. For discussion of this matter as relating to the United Nations see Kelsen, *op. cit. supra* note 49 at 17; Ross, Constitution of the United Nations 116-18 (1950).

60. On the collective measures see *infra* pp. 269-71.

61. Art. 6, The Rio Treaty.

CHAPTER XIII

1. These same obligations are placed upon the members of the United Nations. Arts. 2(4) and 2(3) U.N. Charter. See Schwarzenberger, Power Politics 454 (2d ed. 1951).

2. See *supra* Ch. I.

3. See *infra* pp. 277-81.

4. "Treaty to Avoid or Prevent Conflicts Between the American States," International Conferences of American States 1889-1928, 285 *et seq.* (Scott ed., 1931).

5. "Resolution, Aggression," *id.* at 441-42.

6. International Conferences of American States, First Supp., 1933-1940, 496-99.

7. Art. 11, *id.* at 122.

8. For summaries of the principles see PAU, Manual of Inter-American Relations 5-8, 10-12 (Cong. & Conf. Series No. 26, 1953).

9. Art. 1, Rio Treaty.

10. Art. 15, Charter of Bogotá.

11. Art. 17, Charter of Bogotá.

12. Art. 18, Charter of Bogotá.

13. Art. 2, Rio Treaty; Art. 5(g) and Art. 20, Charter of Bogotá.

14. The U.N. is concerned only with disputes which are a threat to the peace, while the OAS is concerned with all disputes. See Thomas and Thomas, Non-Intervention: The Law and Its Import in the Americas 131, 139 (1956).

15. Arts. 15 and 16, Charter of Bogotá.

16. See infra pp. 250-60.

17. See infra pp. 264-71.

18. On the principle of collective security see Levi, World Organization 68 et seq. (1950); Ball & Killough, International Relations 331 et seq. (1956); Ross, Constitution of the United Nations 137 et seq. (1950); Schwarzenberger, op. cit. supra note 1 at 455-56, 492-533.

19. The Charter of Bogotá declares as a principle: "An act of aggression against one American state is an act of aggression against all the other American states." Art. 5(f). And see Arts 24 and 25 of the Charter as well as the preamble, and Arts. 3 and 6 of the Rio Treaty.

20. Ross, op. cit. supra note 18 at 137-40.

21. Art. 3, Rio Treaty, and see infra pp. 250-60.

22. Ibid.

23. Art. 6, Rio Treaty, and see infra pp. 264-71. Ross actually would not call the action under stages 1 and 2 collective action. See Ross, op. cit. supra note 18 at 138.

24. Sanctions in the form of reprisals even involving the use of force are recognized by general international law, although particular international law has circumscribed such use of force. In 1907, the Second Hague Convention proscribed the use of armed force to collect debts unless the debtor nation refused to arbitrate or refused to carry out the award after arbitration. Scott, Les Conventions et Declarations de La Haye de 1899 et 1907, p. 89 (1918); I Scott, The Hague Peace Conferences Ch. 8 (1909). The Pact of Paris of 1928 prohibited even more broadly reprisals or sanctions by armed force, for it enjoined the contracting parties to settle all disputes by peaceful means. Treaty for the Renunciation of War (Kellogg-Briand Pact), U.S. Treaty Series, No. 796.

25. Allegations have been made that there is a right to come to the aid of another state illegally attacked, but there would appear to be no assertion that there is a duty. For discussion see Thomas and Thomas, op. cit. supra note 14 at 88-91.

26. See Schwarzenberger, op. cit. supra note 1 at 455 and 493-94.

27. Id. at 493.

28. See, e.g., Hall, A Treatise on International Law 288 (6th ed. 1909); see also Bluntschli, Das Moderne Volkerrecht der Civilisirten Staaten, secs. 474-80 (3rd ed. 1878); Lowenstein, Political Reconstruction 14 (1946).

29. Rosbrugh, "The Sanction of International Law," 14 Am. J. Int. L. 26 (1920).

30. Fenwick, "Intervention: Individual and Collective," 39 Am. J. Int. L. 645 (1945).

31. Thomas & Thomas, op. cit. supra note 14 at 91.

32. Id. at 88 et seq.

33. See Ross, A Textbook of International Law 246-47 (1947); Hindmarsh, "Self-Help in Time of Peace," 26 Am. J. Int. L. 315 (1932).

34. See Chs. I and II, supra.

35. Scelle, Manuel de Droit International Public 580 (1948).

36. See infra pp. 271-74.

37. "Adherence to and Ratification of Peace Instruments, Seventh International Conference of American States," International Conferences of American States, First Supp., op. cit. supra note 6 at 19-20.

38. This treaty is set forth in International Conferences, id. at 496 et seq.

39. Fenwick, "Inter-American Conference for the Maintenance of Peace," 31 Am. J. Int. L. 201 (1937).

40. For text of treaty, see International Conferences of American States, First Supp., op. cit. supra note 6 at 188 et seq.

41. Id. at 192 et seq.

42. "Resolutions CVII and CIX, Eighth Conference," id. at 307 and 308-9.

43. Id. at 360.

44. Id. at 361.

45. PAU, Report of the Third Meeting of the Ministers of Foreign Affairs of the American Republics, Rio de Janeiro, January 15-28, 1942, pp. 32 and 44 et seq. (Cong. & Conf. Series No. 36, 1942).

46. PAU, Inter-American Conference on Problems of War and Peace, Mexico City, February 21-March 8, 1945, p. 32 (Cong. & Conf. Series No. 47, 1945).

CHAPTER XIV

1. On the beginnings of Pan America and its historical antecedents see Bemis, The Latin American Policy of the United States Chs. II, III, IV, V, and VI (1943); Gil, Evolución del Pan Americanismo 19-37 (1933); Lockey, Pan-Americanism, Its Beginnings (1920); Sanchez i Sanchez, Curso de Derecho Internacional Público Americano 157-81 (1943); Whitaker, The Western Hemisphere Idea: Its Rise and Decline Chs. I and II (1954); Ypes, El Panamericanismo y el Derecho Internacional 3-62 (1930); Alvarez, "Latin America and International Law," 3 Am. J. Int. L. 269 (1909).

2. For example, all of the American republics have adopted a constitutional structure similar to that of the United States, which embodies a republican-democratic form of government. See Fitzgibbon, The Constitutions of the Americas (1948). An excellent article by Jaffin, "New World Constitutional Harmony: A Pan-Ameri-canadian Panorama," 42 Col. L. Rev. 523 (1942) traces and explains American constitutional ideology. See discussion by Whitaker, id. at 1-21 for a discussion of the early ideological background of the hemispheric movement. Many Latin American jurists proclaim democracy and liberty as a unifying force in the Americas and as bases of inter-American solidarity, see, e.g., Ypes, id. at 432; Alvarez, Le Développement du Droit des Gens dans le Nouveau-Monde, XXV Transactions of the Grotius Society 169 (1939).

3. See Kelsen, Principles of International Law 18-23 (1959) and Kunz, "Sanctions in International Law," 54 Am. J. Int. L. 324 (1960) for a discussion of international delicts and sanctions therefor.

4. Quintanilla, A Latin American Speaks 219-36 (1943); Thomas, Communism versus International Law 51-55 (1953).

5. Forster, Two Cheers for Democracy 69 (1951); Mayo, Democracy and Marxism 254-60 (1955); Padilla, Free Men of America 68-78 (1943).

6. "Democracy in a World of Tensions," a symposium prepared for Unesco Paris, p. 62 (1951).

7. "It is impossible that the allied Powers should extend their political system to any portion of either continent without endangering our peace and happiness; nor can one believe that our southern brethren, if left to themselves, would adopt it of their own accord. It is equally impossible therefore, that we should behold such interposition in any form with indifference." Monroe Doctrine as set forth in VI Moore, A Digest of International Law 401 (1906). For summary of the background of the Monroe Doctrine see Thomas & Thomas, Non-Intervention: The Law and Its Import in the Americas 10-14 (1956).

8. Accounts and summaries of the Congress of Panama may be found in I Antokoletz, Tratado de Derecho Internacional Público 338-42 (1944); Bemis, John Quincy Adams and the Foundations of American Foreign Policy 543-65 (1949); Collins, "The Congress of Bolivar," VI Hispanic American Historical Rev. 194 (1926).

9. Art. 29, "Treaty of Perpetual Union, League and Confederation between the Republics of Colombia, Central America, Perú and the United Mexican States, July 15, 1826." International Conferences of American States 1889-1898, at xxiv-xxix (Scott ed. 1931).

10. Only Gran Colombia ratified the treaty and it did so with reservation.

11. The attitude of Latin America to non-intervention and the reasons therefor are contained in Thomas & Thomas, op. cit. supra note 7 Chs. II and III.

12. Thomas & Thomas, id. at 7.

13. Hershey, Essentials of International Public Law and Organization (1935) claims at p. 243 n. that the principle of non-intervention appears to have first been put forth by Kant in his Essay on Perpetual Peace published in 1795. Hershey fails, however, to mention the fact that Kant's seemingly absolute prohibition of intervention and his stand for unfettered internal sovereignty might be considered as modified by his statement that the civil constitution in every state should be republican.

14. For a statement of this thesis of Kant, see Lowenstein, Political Reconstruction 17-20 (1946).

15. Hall asserts the principle as follows: "Thus a state may place itself under any form of government that it wishes and may frame its social institutions upon any model. To foreign states the political or social doctrines which may be exemplified in it ... are legally immaterial." Hall, A Treatise on International Law 43-44 (6th ed. 1909).

16. See citations in note 11, supra.

17. Art. 8, "Convention on Rights and Duties of States, Seventh International Conference of American States," International Conferences of American States, First Supp. 1933-1940, 121-23 (1940); Art. 1, "Additional Protocol Relative to Non-Intervention, Inter-American Conference for the Maintenance of Peace," id. at 191-92; Art. 15, Charter

of the Organization of American States as set forth in Ninth International Conference of American States (Report of the Delegation of the United States with Related Documents), Dept. of State Pub. 3263 at pp. 167-70 (1948).

18. Burr & Hussey, Documents on Inter-American Cooperation, 1810-1881, Document No. 19 (1954).

19. *Id.* Document No. 23.

20. I Ulloa, Congreso Americano de Lima clxx (1938).

21. Anderson, El Gobierno de Facto 26 (1925); Garcia, "Estudios sobre la Doctrina Tobar," vol. 20, Trabajos del Cuarto Congreso Cientifico (1° Pan-Americano) celebrado en Santiago de Chile del 25 de Diciembre de 1908 al 5 de Enero 1909, pp. 326-29 (1912); Stowell, "The Doctrine of Constitutional Legitimacy," 25 Am. J. Int. L. 302 (1931).

22. General Treaty of Peace and Amity, 1907, II Malloy, Treaties of the United States 2397 (1910). General Treaty of Peace and Amity, 1923, 17 Am. J. Int. L. Supp. (Off. Doc.) 117 (1923).

23. Thomas & Thomas, *op. cit. supra* note 7 at 248-49.

24. The terms of the Wilson Pact may be found in Papers Relating to the Foreign Relations of the United States, The Lansing Papers (1914-1920), vol. II 495-96 (1940).

25. Résumés of all of these statements and declarations are contained in PAU, Manual of Inter-American Relations, Conferences and Organization Series No. 26 at 74-80 (1953).

26. See Spaeth & Sanders, "The Emergency Advisory Committee for Political Defense," 38 Am. J. Int. L. 218 (1944).

27. Second Annual Report Emergency Advisory Committee for Political Defense 16 (1944).

28. Smith, Yankee Diplomacy 97-98 (1953).

29. Fenwick, "Intervention: Individual and Collective," 39 Am. J. Int. L. 645 at 660 (1945).

30. See, e.g., a project of convention submitted by Ecuador on the abolition of the recognition of *de facto* governments as set forth in PAU, Handbook for Delegates to the Ninth International Conference of American States 87-88 (1947).

31. *Id.* at 88-89.

32. PAU, Inter-American Juridical Committee Report and Draft Convention on Recognition of *De Facto* Governments 9 (1950).

33. Resolution XXXVIII, Defense and Preservation of Democracy in America, PAU, Inter-American Conference on Problems of War and Peace, Report Submitted to the Governing Board of the Pan American Union by the Director General p. 67 (Cong. & Conf. Series No. 47, 1945).

34. Fenwick, "The Problems of the Recognition of *De Facto* Governments," 1948 Inter-American Juridical Y. B. 18 at 33.

35. PAU, Consultation of the Government of Uruguay and Replies of the Governments on the Parallelism between Democracy and Peace, the International Rights of Man and Collective Action in Defense of those Principles (May, 1946).

36. *Ibid.*

37. *Ibid.* Selte-Camara Filho, "A Doutrina Larreta," 3 Boletim da Sociedade de Direito Internacional 18 (1946).

38. Ninth International Conference of American States, *op. cit. supra* note 17, at 15.

39. The Charter of the OAS may be found in Ninth International Conference of American States, *id.* at 166 *et seq.*

40. Pollux, "The Interpretation of the Charter," 23 Brit. Y. B. Int. L. 54 (1946).

41. Goodrich & Hambro, Charter of the United Nations 89 (rev. ed. 1949).

42. "A legal obligation to behave in a certain way is established if a sanction is attached to the contrary behavior." Kelsen, The Law of the United Nations 9 (1950).

43. On the OAS and its constitutional background see Thomas & Thomas, *op. cit. supra* note 7, at 114.

44. The Inter-American Treaty of Reciprocal Assistance is set forth in Inter-American Conference for the Maintenance of Continental Peace and Security, Report of the Delegation of the United States of America, Dept. State Pub. 3016 at 59 *et seq.* (1948).

45. Green, "General Principles of Law and Human Rights," 8 Current Legal Problems 162 (1955).

46. Arts. 24, 25, and 27 of the Treaty as contained in International Conferences of American States, *op. cit. supra* note 9, at xxviii.

47. Marshall, "No Compromise on Essential Freedoms," 19 Dept. State Bull. 432 (Oct. 3, 1948).

48. Résumés of these resolutions may be found in PAU, Manual of Inter-American Relations, *op. cit. supra* note 25, at 113-14.

49. Resolution XL, PAU, Inter-American Conference on Problems of War and Peace, *op. cit. supra* note 33, at 69.

50. PAU, Inter-American Judicial Committee Report to the Inter-American Council of Jurists concerning Resolution XXXI of the Conference of Bogotá 2 (1949).

51. Ninth International Conference of American States, *op. cit. supra* note 17, at 13.

52. See Art. 6, Rio Treaty, *supra* note 44.

53. Final Act, Res. XXX, as contained in Ninth International Conference of American States, *op. cit. supra* note 17, at 260 *et seq.*

54. De Visscher, Theory and Reality in Public International Law 122 (tr. P. E. Corbett, 1957); Lauterpacht, International Law and Human Rights 123 (1950); Fenwick, "Pan American Action for the Protection of Human Rights," 248 The Annals of the American Academy of Political and Social Science 52 (1946).

55. Wright, "Human Rights and World Order," 389 International Conciliation 239 (1943); Thomson, Equality 79 (1949).

56. Accioly, "Principes Généraux de La Responsabilité Internationale d'après La Doctrine et La Jurisprudence," 96 Recueil des Cours 353 at 356 (1959).

57. Res. XXXI, Ninth International Conference of American States, *op. cit. supra* note 17, at 266.

58. PAU, Inter-American Council of Jurists, Inter-American Court to Protect the Rights of Man 2 (1953).

59. PAU, Tenth Inter-American Conference—Final Act, Res. XXVIII, p. 34 (1954).

60. For discussion of the Rio Treaty's Article 6 and measures to be taken see Thomas & Thomas, "The Organization of American States and Collective Security," 13 S. W. L. J. 177 at 196 *et seq.* (1959) and see *infra* Ch. XV.

61. These cases may be found in PAU, Applications of the Inter-American Treaty of Reciprocal Assistance 1948-1956 at pp. 19-148 (1957).

62. An excellent and detailed discussion of these cases and OAS action with reference thereto may be found in Furniss, "The Inter-American System and Recent Caribbean Disputes," 4 Int. Org. 585 (1950).

63. Report of the Investigating Committee of the Organ of Consultation Relative to the Petition of the Dominican Republic, Applications of the Inter-American Treaty of Reciprocal Assistance, *op. cit. supra* note 61, at 120-21.

64. See for example the resolution of the Council acting provisionally as Organ of Consultation in the second Haiti–Dominican Republic case, *id.* at 128.

65. *Ibid.*

66. On the Guatemalan affair see Taylor, "The Guatemalan Affair: A Critique of U.S. Foreign Policy," 50 Am. Pol. Sci. Rev. 421 (1956).

67. PAU, Tenth Inter-American Conference, Final Act, p. 94 (1954). For short discussion of the U.S. position see Tenth Inter-American Conference, Report of the Delegation of the U.S.A., Dept. State Pub. 5692, pp. 7-9 (1954).

68. On the impact of the Cuban revolution see Benton, "The Communist Threat at Our Back Door," N. Y. Times Mag., July 17, 1960, p. 10; Szulc, "Castro Tries to Export Fidelismo," N. Y. Times Mag., Nov. 27, 1960, p. 19.

69. These cases and Council consideration thereof are set forth in PAU, Aplicaciones del Tratado Interamericano de Asistencia Reciproca 1948-1960 pp. 259 *et seq.*

70. *Id.* at 301, 346.

71. *Id.* at 387-90. See Stebbins, The United States in World Affairs 352-56 (1959), for reasons behind the convocation of the Meeting. See also *infra* p. 317.

72. On the background of the Santiago Meeting see 41 Dept. State Bull. 299 *et seq.* (Aug. 31, 1959); N. Y. Times August 13, 1959.

73. N. Y. Times, August 16, 1959. For a summation of the ideas of the Foreign Minister of Venezuela at the Meeting see Compton, "What About Intervention?" Americas, vol. 11, Nov. 1959 p. 3 at 6.

74. The Declaration of Santiago is set forth in 41 Dept. State Bull. 342-43 (Sept. 7, 1959).

75. *Ibid.*

76. *Ibid.*

77. For discussion of the Inter-American Peace Committee see Fenwick, "The Inter-American Peace Committee," 43 Am. J. Int. L. 770 (1949); Report of the Delegation of the U.S.A., Tenth Inter-American Conference, *op. cit. supra*, note 67, at 13-14. For text of the Statutes of the Committee see PAU, Statutes of the Inter-American Peace Committee (1956).

78. Resolution on Inter-American Peace Committee is set forth in 41 Dept. State Bull. 343-44 (Sept. 7, 1959).

79. PAU, Final Act of the Fourth Meeting of the Inter-American Council of Jurists, Santiago, Chile, August 24-September 9, 1959, "Draft Convention on Human Rights" p. 48 (1960).

80. Article 79 of the draft, id. at 72.

81. Resolution VIII, Fifth Meeting of Consultation of Ministers of Foreign Affairs, Santiago, Chile, Aug. 1959. OAS Official Records OEA/Ser.C./II.5. See also Sorensen, "Federal States and the International Protection of Human Rights," 46 Am. J. Int. L. 195 (1952).

82. Op. cit. supra note 79 at 87.

83. Id.

84. PAU, La Organización de los Estados Americanos 1954-1959, p. 12 (OEA/Ser. D/II.2, 1959).

85. PAU, Draft Statute of the Inter-American Commission on Human Rights, OEA/Ser.G/C-sa-371(3) (1960), and Amended Draft Statute of the Inter-American Commission on Human Rights, OEA/Ser.G/III/C-32-373(3) (1960).

86. PAU, 1960 Annual Report of the Secretary General of the OAS, 20 (1961).

87. Id.

88. PAU, Inter-American Commission on Human Rights, Report on the Work Accomplished During its Second Session, April 10-26, 1961 (OEA/Ser.L/V/II 2, Doc. 24, 1961). Report on the Work Accomplished During its Third Session, October 2-November 4, 1961 (OEA/Ser.L/V/II.3, Doc. 32, 1961). Prior to its fourth meeting in April, 1963, the commission continued to hear testimony on violation of human rights in Cuba and prepared a special report on this situation. The government of Nicaragua refused to permit the commission to make an on-the-spot study of conditions in that country following allegations that in 1963 the Nicaraguan government was engaging in practices detrimental to human rights.

89. PAU, Acta Final, Quinta Reunión de Consulta de Ministros de Relaciones Exteriores, Santiago de Chile, 12 a 18 de Agosto de 1959, p. 12 (OEA/Ser.C/II.5, Español, 1960).

90. PAU, Report of the Special Committee to Study Resolutions IX and X of the Fifth Meeting of Consultation of Ministers of Foreign Affairs, submitted to the Council of the OAS at the meeting held on Dec. 15, 1959 (C-1-447, Rev. 2, 1959).

91. Id. Art. IX.

92. Id. Art. X.

93. Id. Arts. XI-XIII.

94. Id. Arts. XVII and XVIII.

95. Id. Arts. XX-XXIII.

96. N. Y. Times, Feb. 6, 12, 16, 1960.

97. N. Y. Times, June 9, 1960.

98. For discussion of the continuing Caribbean tensions, see infra pp. 316 et seq.

99. PAU, Aplicaciones del Tratado Interamericano de Asistencia Reciproca, op. cit. supra note 69, at 393 et seq.

100. N. Y. Times, July 12, 16, 18, 19, 20, 30, Aug. 16, 21, 1960.

101. N. Y. Times, Aug. 19, 21, 23, 1960.

102. 43 Dept. State Bull. 358 (Sept. 5, 1960).

103. Id. at 355-58.

104. N. Y. Times, Aug. 19, 1960.

105. N. Y. Times, Aug. 21, 1960.

106. Art. 39, Charter of OAS.

107. See note 68 supra.

108. N. Y. Times, Aug. 24, 1960.

109. Statements made by Secretary Herter, 43 Dept. State Bull. 395-407 (Sept. 12, 1960).

110. Declarations of San José, Costa Rica, id. at 407-98; see also N. Y. Times, Aug. 27, 29, 1960.

111. N. Y. Times, Aug. 30, 1960.

112. N. Y. Times, Aug. 24, 1960.

113. On the Punta del Este Meeting, see PAU, Final Act Eighth Meeting of Consultation of Ministers of Foreign Affairs Serving as Organ of Consultation in Application of the Inter-American Treaty of Reciprocal Assistance, Punta del Este, Uruguay, January 22-31, 1962, OEA/Ser.C/II.8 (English) 1962; 46 Dept. State Bull. 267-83 (Feb. 19, 1962); N. Y. Times, Jan. 26, 28, 31, Feb. 1, 4 (1962). See also supra pp. 59-60 and infra pp. 326-27, 360.

114. Art. III, declaration against the intervention of international communism of the Tenth Inter-American Conference, *supra* note 67.

115. Irizarry y Puente, "The Doctrines of Recognition and Intervention in Latin America," 28 Tulane L. Rev. 313 at 341 (1954).

116. Declaration of Santiago, *supra* note 74.

117. Art. 2, Paragraph 4 of the U.N. Charter prohibits the members from using or threatening to use force. Art. 51, of the Charter makes an exception and permits such use in the right of individual or collective self-defense. Otherwise by the terms of Art. 53 regional agencies may take no enforcement action unless authorized by the Security Council. On the right of self-defense under the Rio Treaty and the U.N. Charter see Thomas & Thomas, *supra* note 60, at 178 *et seq.*, and infra Ch. XV.

118. Shakespeare, Hamlet Act III, Sc. 2, Line 20.

CHAPTER XV

1. *Supra* Ch. XIII on Collective Security and Reciprocal Assistance.

2. Inter-American Conference on War and Peace, Mexico City, February 21-March 8, 1945, Report Submitted to the Governing Board of the Pan American Union by the Director General 32 (1945).

3. The provisions of the Rio Treaty are found in Inter-American Conference for the Maintenance of Continental Peace and Security, Quitandinha, Brazil, August 15-September 2, 1947, Report of the Delegation of the U.S.A. 59-65 (1948). Discussion of the treaty may be found in the following: *id.* at 1-42; Inter-American Conference for the Maintenance of Continental Peace and Security, Rio de Janeiro, Report on Results of Conference, Submitted to the Governing Board of the Pan-American Union by the Director General (1947); Blackmer, United States Policy and the Inter-American Peace System 1889-1952, 161-70 (1952); Thomas & Thomas, Non-Intervention: The Law and Its Import in the Americas 183-95, 210-11 (1956); Garcia Mora, "The Law of the Inter-American Treaty of Reciprocal Assistance," 20 Fordham L. Rev. 1 (1951); Kunz, "The Inter-American Treaty of Reciprocal Assistance," 42 Am. J. Int. L. 111 (1948).

4. The Charter of the Organization of American States (Charter of Bogotá) is set forth in the Ninth International Conference of American States, Bogotá, Colombia, March 30-May 2, 1948, Report of the Delegation of the U.S.A. and Related Documents, 166-86 (1948).

5. On regional arrangements see *supra* Ch. III pp. 48-53.

6. Such a distinction was thought necessary to make the treaty fully consistent with the U.N. Charter. But see *infra* pp. 250-52, 258, 264. It should be noted that the Act of Chapultepec made no distinction between action to be taken upon occurrence of armed attack or other aggressions. It simply spoke of "threats and acts of aggression." See Report of the Delegation of U.S.A., *op. cit. supra* note 3 at 15-16.

7. As to the Organ of Consultation and the Provisional Organ of Consultation and their powers see *supra* pp. 89-93, 101-7.

8. See, e.g., Kelsen, Principles of International Law 60 (1952); Kelsen, The Law of the United Nations 792 (1950); Kunz, "Individual and Collective Self-Defense in Article 51 of the Charter of the United Nations," 41 Am. J. Int. L. 872 (1947). Ross, A Textbook of International Law 244 (1947).

9. With reference to the German invasion of Norway, the International Military Tribunal stated that preventive action in foreign countries was justified only in cases of "an instant and overwhelming necessity for self-defense, leaving no choice of means and no moment of deliberation." The International Military Tribunal Nuremberg, cmd. 6964, p. 28 (1946).

10. See, e.g., Bowett, Self-Defence in International Law, Ch. I (1958). Cheng, General Principles of International Law as Applied by International Courts and Tribunals 94 *et seq.* (1953); I Hyde, International Law Chiefly as Interpreted and Applied by the United States, sec. 70 (1947); I Schwarzenberger, A Manual of International Law 172-73 (4th ed. 1960). The violation of the essential rights of a state which would justify self-defense are, according to Bowett, the following: the right of territorial integrity, the right of political independence, the right of protection over nationals, and certain economic rights. Bowett, *id.* Part I and as summed up in the conclusion at p. 270.

11. Bowett, *id.* at 3-4.

12. U.N. Charter, Art. 2 (4).

13. Rio Treaty, Art. 1. And see Art. 18 of the Charter of Bogotá, wherein it is provided that the American states bind themselves not to have recourse to the use of force except in the case of self-defense in accordance with existing treaties or in fulfilment thereof.

14. For example, Kelsen and Beckett are of the opinion that the right of self-defense under the Charter is limited to action *after* an armed attack has occurred. Beckett, The North Atlantic Treaty 13 (1950); Kelsen, The Law of the United Nations 791 *et. seq.* (1950). Kunz also takes this position; Kunz, *supra* note 3 at 878.

15. For such reasoning see Kunz, *id.* at 876.

16. See Bowett, *op. cit. supra* note 10, Chs. IX and X; Stone, Aggression and World Order, Ch. 5 (1958).

17. Bowett, *id.* Ch. IX.

18. *Id.* at 188.

19. *Id.* at 185 and 186. Stone reaches a similar view in his interpretation of Art. 2 (4), and other articles of the U.N. Charter. Stone, *op. cit. supra* note 16 at 94-97. Rights of territorial integrity and political independence are not absolute, but relative, and when a state violates essential legal rights of another, it can hardly claim absolute inviolability of its own political independence and territorial integrity from a legitimate action of self-defense by the wronged state to protect its own security, i.e., its right of political independence and territorial integrity, in the absence of other means of protection. Moreover, it is doubtful that such rights of self-defense conflict with the "Purposes" of the United Nations as set forth in Article I of the Charter, which are concerned primarily with the maintenance of international peace by the members and the organization. A defense by a state of its legitimate interests can hardly be said to be inconsistent with these purposes, particularly where the U.N. or other international organization fails to achieve the "Purposes." See Bowett, *ibid.*

20. Cheng, *op. cit. supra* note 10 at 101.

21. 2 Annals of the OAS 231 at 252 (1950). And see discussion of this statement 3 Annals of the OAS 11 (1951).

22. It has been said that no duty of self-defense is imposed, probably on the ground that an obligation cannot be created which would force a person or a state to defend himself or itself. Kunz, for example, says that there is a right but no duty of self-defense, *op. cit. supra* note 3 at 115. But Article 3 of the Rio Treaty declares that each one of the contracting parties (which would include any American state subjected to attack) "undertakes to assist in meeting the attack in the exercise of an inherent right of individual or collective self-defense." *Quaere,* do these words spell out an obligation? It is so stated in the Report of the Delegation of the U.S.A., *op. cit. supra* note 3, at 21. It can be argued that an attack on any state of the hemisphere creates such a danger to the peace that all states, including the attacked state, are obligated to meet it, such obligation not being for the protection of the victim alone, but for the protection of all.

23. Report on Results of Conference, *op. cit. supra* note 3, at 34.

24. *Id.* at 40-41.

25. Rio Treaty, Art. 13.

26. Bogotá Charter, Art. 43.

27. Rio Treaty, Art. 20.

28. See Report on the Results of the Conference, *op. cit. supra* note 3, at 22.

29. See Report of the Delegation of the U.S.A., *op. cit. supra* note 3, at 22; Blackmer, *op. cit. supra* note 3, at 168.

30. Rio Treaty, Art. 17.

31. Rio Treaty, Art. 20.

32. Stone, Legal Controls of International Conflict 245 (1954), declares categorically that no right of self-defense exists by reason of an armed attack upon a third state. See also, Kelsen, The Law of the United Nations 792 (1950).

33. For this thesis see Bowett, *op. cit supra* note 10, Ch. X.

34. Bowett cites provisions of systems of municipal law which bear out this principle and internationalists who make the analogy. *Id.* at 201-2.

35. See citations to Kelsen, *op. cit. supra* note 8.

36. But see pp. 269-71 *infra* on the measures as "enforcement measures."

37. Bowett, *op. cit. supra* note 10 at 23-25.

38. That self-defense at international law is to be exercised only against delictual conduct appears to be almost universally accepted. See citations to authorities *supra* notes 8 and 10.

39. Kunz, *supra* note 8 at 878.

40. See Alfaro, "Memorandum on the Question of Defining Aggression," Yearbook of the International Law Commission 1951, vol. II, U.N. Doc. No. A/cN.4/L. 8 at p. 36 where he criticizes the use of the word "unprovoked" as introducing into the determination of the aggressor the "vague, imprecise, and uncertain element of provocation."

41. See *id.* at 37-38, where Alfaro defines "force" which would comprise "armed attack":

The term force is used in a broad sense to signify any elements at the disposal of states which are capable of destroying life and property, or of inflicting serious damage. It comprises land, sea and air forces, regular armies as well as irregular bands and any and all kinds of weapons, contrivances, explosives, toxic or asphyxiating gases, employed for the destruction of life and property in land, naval, air, chemical or bacteriological warfare.

He goes on to say in defining armed aggression against the territory and people of states or governments:

Aggression is bound to be conceived as perpetrated against the territory and against the people under the jurisdiction of the state victim, and aimed at the submission or destruction of any forces opposing resistance to the aggression. This aim implies the possibility of destroying life and property, a destruction of which the victim is the people of the state attacked. Aggression against the territory and the people of a state or government must comprise any acts of violence perpetrated against its land, sea or air forces, or against its vessels or aircraft, whatever their character; or against structures vital to public life and health, as for instance, water works and protective dams; or against the whole of the population, through the use of any weapons or the commission of any acts likely to endanger combatants and non-combatants.

42. See also *id.* at 36.
43. See authorities cited *supra* note 8.
44. See Bowett, *op. cit. supra* note 10, Ch. X.
45. In Article 3 of the Rio Treaty which speaks of the individual and collective right of self-defense and requires certain *measures* to be taken. Article 6 is concerned with aggressions which are not armed attack and other facts or situations endangering the peace of the Americas and affecting the territorial integrity, sovereignty, etc., of an American state and which require certain *measures* to be taken. Article 8 sets forth the *measures* for both Article 3 and Article 6 inclusive of the use of armed force.
46. Kunz is of the opinion that requirements of proportionality and reasonableness are lacking from the right of collective self-defense under Article 51 of the U.N. Charter. See Kunz, *supra* note 8, at 877-78.
47. *Id.* at 876.
48. It may be noted that there was some agitation at the Conference for the Maintenance of Continental Peace and Security that distinctions should be drawn beween obligations and procedures in case of aggression by a non-American state against an American state and those in the event of aggressions between American states. See, e.g., Report of the Delegation of the U.S.A., *op. cit. supra* note 3, at 17.
49. See pp. 274-76 *infra* concerning the Rio Treaty and nonmembers. Kunz declares specifically that in case of armed attack within the region, the Rio Treaty applies even though the attack is against a nonmember such as Canada. Kunz, *supra* note 3, at 116. See also in this respect, "Radio Address by Senator Vandenberg, Sept. 4, 1947," 17 Dept. State Bull. 502, 504 (1947).
50. See "Address by Senator Vandenberg," *ibid.*; Kunz, *ibid.* See also Report of the Delegation of the U.S.A., *op. cit. supra* note 3, at 21; Report on Results of Conference, *op. cit. supra* note 3, at 36.
51. See note 49, *supra.*
52. *Ibid.*
53. Report on Results of Conference, *op. cit. supra* note 3, at 37.
54. See pp. 48-52 *supra* on regional arrangements.
55. See pp. 270-71 *infra.*
56. See *supra* pp. 250-60 for discussion of this theory of self-defense.
57. See Bowett, *op. cit. supra* note 10, at 19-20 and 215-33.
58. See Thomas & Thomas, *op. cit. supra* note 3, at 173. See also McDougal and Gardner, "The Veto and the Charter: An Interpretation for Survival," 60 Yale L. J. 258 (1951).
59. Rio Treaty, Art. 20.
60. *Ibid.*
61. For discussion of the problem of aggression and its definition, see Stone, Aggression and World Order (1958); Wright, "The Prevention of Aggression," 50 Am. J. Int. L. 514, 526 (1956). See also on the question of defining aggression, Yearbook of the International Law Commission, 1951, vol. II, Documents of the third session including the report of the Commission to the General Assembly, pp. 28-42, 131-33.

62. See Gould, An Introduction to International Law 606 (1907); Stone, *id.* at 58-61, 66-68. But see Wright, *id.* at 526-27, who is of the opinion that aggression means the use of armed force or threat thereof.

63. Yearbook of International Law Commission, *op. cit. supra* note 61, at 126.

64. Applications of the Inter-American Treaty of Reciprocal Assistance 1948-1956, p. 126 (1957).

65. 3 Annals of the OAS 10-11 (1951).

66. Rio Treaty, Art. 17.

67. Rio Treaty, Art. 20.

68. See Report on Results of Conference, *op. cit. supra* note 3, at 40-41; and Report of the Delegation of the U.S.A., *op. cit. supra* note 3, at 26-27.

69. Report on Results of Conference, *id.* at 42; Report of Delegation of U.S.A., *id.* at 27.

70. Garcia Mora, *supra* note 3, at 14, criticizes Article 7 and declares that it seems to have been added as an afterthought.

71. See, e.g., Kelsen, The Law of the United Nations (1950) who, at 724, characterizes such measures under the U.N. Charter as enforcement measures.

72. Kelsen would apparently say that all such measures of a coercive nature are enforcement measures; hence, measures of a diplomatic or economic nature as well as of armed force would be forbidden by Article 53. Kelsen, *id.* at 327, 724.

73. Report on Results of Conference, *op. cit. supra* note 3, at 41-42.

74. Such reasoning, of course, reaches a rather anomalous result in that measures meant to be of an enforcement and coercive character under the U.N. Charter when taken by the Security Council are not so considered when taken by a regional agency like the OAS. For practices of the American states before the United Nations which indicate that the Report of the Director General is the correct interpretation insofar as the OAS is concerned see *infra* pp. 350-51 on the action taken before the United Nations following the imposition of measures against the Dominican Republic.

75. See Hindmarsh, "Self Help in Time of Peace," 26 Am. J. Int. L. 315 (1932); Kelsen, Principles of International Law 22-23 (1952).

76. Treaties are one method used to bring about a change in the general international legal relationships between the signatories. Our inquiry here is not related to the legality of the measures established by the treaty, but seeks merely to discover whether or not the measures in these particular treaties fall within the sphere of true sanctions.

77. See Kelsen, The Law of the United Nations 724 (1950).

78. See Thomas and Thomas, *op. cit. supra* note 3, at 140. But see criticism by Kunz of the authors' concept of measures of the OAS as having a limited character of sanctions. Kunz, "Book Review," 50 Am. J. Int. L. 974 (1956).

79. See note 4 *supra*. See also Padilla, "The American System and World Organizations," 24 Foreign Affairs 199 (1945); Reid, "Regionalism under the United Nations Charter," 419 Int. Concil. 123 (1946).

80. U.N. Charter Art. 2 (3).

81. See Thomas & Thomas, *op. cit. supra* note 3, at 159-60.

82. See, e.g., Garcia Mora, *supra* note 3, at 11 n. 61.

83. *Supra* pp. 260-64.

84. *Ibid.*

85. Schwarzenberger, A Manual of International Law 68 (3rd ed. 1952).

86. Schwarzenberger, International Law as Applied by International Courts and Tribunals 194 (2d ed. 1941). See also Kelsen, *op. cit. supra* note 75, at 345; Thomas & Thomas, International Treaties 64 (Monograph 1950).

87. Kelsen, *id.* at 349.

88. *Ibid.*

89. Thomas & Thomas, *op. cit. supra* note 3, at 170-71, 178-79.

90. See discussion *supra* on these matters pp. 254-60, 264-68.

91. U.N. Charter, Art. 2 (3) (4).

CHAPTER XVI

1. The Plan of Arbitration from which a formal treaty with almost identical wording was drawn up after the conference is contained in International Conferences of American States 1889-1928 (edited by Scott) at pp. 40-41 (1931).

2. *Id.* at 100-104.

3. Nine Latin American states signed this treaty but only six ratified. *Id.* at 100, n. 1, 104.

4. *Id.* at 61-62.

5. *Id.* at 104-5.
6. *Id.* at 104, n. 2.
7. *Id.* at 132-33.
8. *Id.* at 183-85.
9. Including the United States. *Id.* at 183, n. 1, and see also PAU, Tratados y Convenciones Interamericanos 19 (Serie Sobre Tratados No. 9, 1961).

10. For discussion of these treaties see the following: Alfaro, Commentary on Pan American Problems 38-54 (1938); Blackmer, United States Policy and the Inter-American Peace System 1889-1952, pp. 39-46 (1952); PAU, Handbook for Delegates to the Ninth International Conference of American States, Bogotá, Colombia, March 30, 1948, pp. 47-51 (1947); Fenwick, "The Coordination of Inter-American Peace Agreements," 38 Am. J. Int. L. 8 (1944); Hudson, "The Inter-American Treaties of Pacific Settlement," 15 For. Aff. 163 (1936-37); Murdock, "Arbitration and Conciliation in Pan America," 23 Am. J. Int. L. 282 (1929); Myers, "Acceptance of the General Treaty of Inter-American Arbitration," 20 Am. J. Int. L. 57 (1926).

11. International Conferences of American States 1889-1928, *op. cit. supra* note 1 at 285-88. This treaty was finally adhered to by all of the republics except Argentina. See Tratados y Convenciones Interamericanos, *op. cit. supra* note 9 at 20.

12. International Conferences of American States 1889-1928, *id.* at 455. Some eighteen states adhered to this treaty. Tratados y Convenciones Interamericanos, *id.* at 57.

13. International Conferences of American States, *id.* at 458. Sixteen states ratified this treaty, many with reservations. Tratados y Convenciones Interamericanos, *id.* at 58.

14. International Conferences of American States, First Supp., 1933-1940 at 496 (1940). Nineteen states adhered to the Pact. Tratados y Convenciones Interamericanos, *id.* at 62.

15. See Art. V of the Pact.

16. Art. VI of the Pact.

17. International Conferences of American States, First Supp., *id.* at 120-21. Only nine states ratified this Protocol. Tratados y Convenciones Interamericanos, *op. cit. supra* note 9 at 41.

18. International Conferences of American States, First Supp., *id.* at 199. Fifteen states ratified the treaty. Tratados y Convenciones Interamericanos, *id.* at 71.

19. International Conferences of American States, First Supp., *id.* at 197. Fourteen states ratified this convention. Tratados y Convenciones Interamericanos, *id.* at 70.

20. International Conferences of American States, First Supp., *id.* at 192. Fourteen states ratified the convention. Tratados y Convenciones Interamericanos, *id.* at 72.

21. It would seem that only one dispute, the Haitian–Dominican Republic frontier dispute 1937, was settled within this inter-American framework of treaties of peaceful settlement. This dispute was settled through the application of the Gondra Treaty and the Conciliation Convention. See Manger, "A Quarter Century of Pan American Progress," PAU Bulletin, vol. 79, 490 (1945) and see "Settlement of the Dominican-Haitian Controversy," PAU Bulletin, vol. 72, 152 (1938). Inter-American disputes were settled peacefully but by other procedures.

22. Mexico, as early as 1933, at the Seventh Conference proposed a Code of Peace which would have organized all provisions for peaceful settlement into one instrument. This Code would have created an American Court of International Justice with jurisdiction over matters permitting judicial settlement. The parties were obligated to submit their disputes to this court, to a Permanent Commission of Conciliaion, or to arbitration. The court was to be empowered to decide its competency. Arbitration was a procedure for decision of juridical as well as nonjuridical disputes with a binding award. The proposed Code is contained in Septima Conferencia Internacional Americana, Primera, Segunda y Octava Comisiones, Actos y Antecedentes, pp. 82-91 (Montevideo, 1933). The Conference referred it to later consideration of the American republics through the Pan American Union. Resolution XXXV and the text of the Code are to be found in International Conferences of American States, *op. cit. supra* at note 14, pp. 50-65. For later history of the Code and its referral by Conferences for further study see Resolution XXVIII Buenos Aires Conference, 1936, *id.* at 161; Resolution XV, Lima Conference, 1938, *id.* at 244-45.

Resolution IX, Paragraph 10, of the Mexico City Conference called for a consolidation, simplification, and extension of existing peace instruments, and Resolution XXXIX of the same Conference recommended to the Inter-American Juridical Committee to prepare a draft of a Peace System to accomplish the above-mentioned ends. PAU, Inter-American Conference on Problems of War and Peace, Mexico City, February 21-March 8, 1945, Report Submitted to the Governing Board of the Pan American Union by the Director General, pp. 33 and 68 respectively (1945).

The Juridical Committee thereafter formulated a draft and transmitted it to the governments for consideration. This draft followed rather closely the procedures of judicial settlement of the U.N. Charter, permitting the parties much flexibility as to choice of procedures. No obligation to submit to arbitration or judicial settlement was set forth and both procedures were limited to juridical disputes. Actually the greatest reliance for peaceful settlement was placed on the procedure of consultation of all the American states. For text of this draft see Ninth International Conference of American States, Bogotá, Colombia, March 30-May 2, 1948, Report of the Delegation of U.S.A., pp. 121-32 (Dept. State Pub. 3263, 1948). This first draft was followed by a second, a definitive project which was submitted to the Bogotá Conference. This draft contained a system of more rigid procedures which would lead to final decision in all cases and included general compulsory arbitration of juridical and nonjuridical disputes. The procedure of consultation was eliminated. See, Ninth International Conference, *id.* at 132-41. The Pact of Bogotá incorporates the more rigid procedure of this final draft.

23. Charter of Bogotá, Article 4(b), Ninth International Conference, *id.* at 167.

24. The text of the Pact is contained in Ninth International Conference of American States, *id.* at 186 *et seq.* For discussion of the Pact see *id.* at 41-51; Accioly, "O Pacto de Bogotá," 1948 Inter-American Juridical Yearbook 3; Blackmer, *op. cit. supra* note 10 at 179-87; Cordova," El Tratado Americano de Soluciones Pacificas—Pacto de Bogotá," 1948 Inter-American Juridical Yearbook 10; Fenwick, "The Pact of Bogotá and other Juridical Decisions of the Ninth Conference," PAU, The Results of Bogotá 17 (Cong. & Conf. Series No. 62, 1948); Kunz, "The Pact of Bogotá," 3 Arbitration Journal, New Series 147 (1948); Lleras, "Report on the Ninth International Conference of American States," 1 Annals of the OAS 44-53 (1949).

25. Arts. LII and LIII of the Pact.

26. Art. LVIII.

27. Art. II.

28. Art. IV.

29. Art. 2(a) of the Arbitration Treaty, see note 13 *supra.*

30. See Kelsen, Principles of International Law 190-201 (1959). Ross also expounds this view in Constitution of the United Nations 120-21 (1950). See also Brierly, "Matters of the Domestic Jurisdiction," 6 Brit. Yearbook Int. L. 8 (1925); Bentwich, "The Limits of the Domestic Jurisdiction of the State," 31 Trans. Grotius Soc. 59 (1945); Goodrich, "The United Nations and Domestic Jurisdiction," 3 Int. Org. 14 (1949).

31. See Nationality Decrees Issued in Tunis and Morocco, Permanent Court of International Justice, Advisory Opinion Feb. 7, 1923, P.C.I.J. Ser. B, No. 4.

32. Art. XXXIV.

33. See Reservations of the U.S.A., Ninth International Conference, *op. cit. supra* note 22 at 200.

34. *Id.* at 199, 200.

35. Art. XXXIV.

36. These views are discussed *supra* Ch. X.

37. Art. XXXIV.

38. See note 33 *supra.*

39. See *supra* Ch. XVI on individual and collective self-defense.

40. Art. 7, Inter-American Treaty of Reciprocal Assistance, Inter-American Conference for the Maintenance of Continental Peace and Security, Quitandinha, Brazil, Aug. 15-Sept. 2, 1947. Report of the Delegation of the U.S.A. pp. 61-62 (1948).

41. Art. IX.

42. Art. X.

43. Art. XI, Art. XII.

44. Art. XIII.

45. Art. XIV.

46. See, e.g., Brierly, The Law of Nations 293 (5th ed. 1955); II Oppenheim, International Law 8-11 (Lauterpacht 7th ed. 1952).

47. On investigation and conciliation see Brierly, *id.* at 293-94; II Oppenheim, *id.* at 12-20; Hyde, "The Place of Commissions of Inquiry and Conciliation Treaties in the Peaceful Settlement of International Disputes," 1929 Brit. Yearbook Int. L. 96; Metzger, "The Settlement of International Disputes by Non-Judicial Methods," 48 Am. J. Int. L. 408 (1954).

48. Art. XV.

49. Art. XVII.

50. Art. XIX.

51. Art. XVIII.
52. Art. XXII.
53. Art. XXVI.
54. Art. XXV.
55. Art. XXVII.
56. *Ibid.*
57. Art. XXVIII.
58. Art. XVI.
59. *Ibid.*
60. Art. XX.
61. For text of the Convention for the Establishment of a Central American Court of Justice see 2 Am. J. Int. L. Supplement 231-43 (1908). The Court ended its endeavors in 1918. In 1922 another treaty, the Convention for the Establishing of an International Central American Tribunal, was signed. This treaty sought to re-establish a Central American Court with more limited jurisdiction. A tribunal was never organized, however. For text of this Convention see Conference on Central American Affairs, Washington, 1923, pp. 287-95. See Hudson, "The Central American Court of Justice," 26 Am. J. Int. L. 768 (1932); Scott, "The Closing of the Central American Court of Justice," 12 Am. J. Int. L. 458 (1918).
62. The Costa Rican proposal is contained in International Conferences of American States, 1889-1928, *op. cit. supra* note 1 at 452.
63. See Ypes, El Panamericanismo y el Derecho Internacional 415-27 (1930).
64. *Supra* note 22.
65. See Resolution IV and n. 1, International Conferences of American States, First Supp., *op. cit. supra* note 14 at 144.
66. See Resolution XXV, *id.* at 253-54.
67. Resolution XXXI, Ninth International Conference, *op. cit. supra* note 22 at 266. The Juridical Committee found it impossible to create such a statute in the time allotted and suggested that until a treaty of human rights had come into being that it would be premature to establish a court for the protection of such rights. PAU, Inter-American Council of Jurists, Inter-American Court to Protect the Rights of Man (1953). The Tenth Conference called for the Council to continue studies on such a court so that the matter could be considered at the Eleventh Conference. Resolution XXIX, Final Conference Documents, Tenth Inter-American Conference, Caracas, Venezuela, March 1-28, 1954, Report of the Delegation of the U.S.A., 104. And see Resolution C, on Inter-American Court of Justice, *id.* at 162 where the Council was called upon to ascertain the position of the American states with respect to the idea of constituting such a court and if a majority was favorable to prepare a draft through the Council of Jurists and the juridical committee for submission to the Eleventh Conference. See "Corte Interamericana de Justicia," 1952-1954 Inter-American Juridical Yearbook 63 and 1955-1957 Inter-American Juridical Yearbook 97. See also *supra* Ch. XIV on recent proposals for a court to protect human rights.
68. 1 Annals of the OAS 51-52 (1949).
69. Art. III.
70. Art. XXXII.
71. Art. XXXIII.
72. Art. XXXIV.
73. For exhaustive discussion of justiciable and nonjusticiable questions see Lauterpacht, The Function of Law in the International Community (1933).
74. See, e.g., Eagleton, International Government 224-25 (3rd ed. 1957); I Hyde, International Law, Chiefly as Interpreted and Applied by the United States 113 (1st ed., 1922).
75. This is pointed up by Schwarzenberger in I A Manual of International Law 234 (4th ed. 1960); and see also Brierly, *op. cit. supra* note 46 at 286-87.
76. Brierly, *ibid.*; Kelsen, *op. cit. supra* note 30 at 380-86; Ross, A Textbook of International Law 278-79 (1947).
77. Schwarzenberger, for example, includes matters within the domestic jurisdiction under a heading, "political disputes," Power Politics 466-67 (2d ed. 1951).
78. Art. XXXVI of the Pact states: "The parties may agree, moreover, to have the controversy decided *ex aequo et bono.*" The power to decide *ex aequo et bono* is in reality a power to modify or abrogate legal rights, a power to decide according to free discretionary principles not according to settled rules of law. As such it is legislation.
79. See Brierly, *op. cit. supra* note 46 at 287; Kelsen, The Law of the United Nations 478-79 (1950); Schwarzenberger, *op. cit. supra* note 77 at 96, 236; Ross, *op. cit. supra* note 76 at 279-80. But see Lauterpacht, *op. cit. supra* note 73 at 372-74 where he states

the belief that all disputes are juridical and refuses to accept an argument that a state should be able to disregard the law and in effect put itself outside the law, by itself, by disregarding legal claims and calling the dispute nonjuridical. And see Ross's criticism of the Lauterpacht thesis *id.* at 282-83.

80. Ninth International Conference of American States, *op. cit. supra* note 22 at 43.

81. See Kelsen, *op. cit. supra* note 79 at 481.

82. *Id.* at 481-82. See also Lauterpacht, *op. cit. supra* note 73 at 372-73.

83. On arbitration in general see Carlston, The Process of International Arbitration (1946); Simpson and Fox, International Arbitration (1959); Ralston, The Law and Procedure of International Tribunals (1926); Jully, "Arbitration and Judicial Settlement, Recent Trends," 48 Am. J. Int. L. 380 (1954).

84. 36 Stat. 2199; 2 Malloy, Treaties 220 (1910).

85. See Eagleton, International Government 215 (3rd ed. 1957). Arbitration then differs from conciliation in that a conciliation commission is not limited to a decision on international law and the awards of such commission are not binding. *Id.* at 226.

86. Art. XXXVIII.

87. Fenwick, *supra* note 24 at 20.

88. See Kunz, *supra* note 24 at 154.

89. *Ibid.*

90. Art. XLI.

91. Art. XLVI.

92. Art. XLVIII.

93. Art. XLVII.

94. Art. L.

95. See *supra* Rio Treaty pp. 269-71.

96. Art. L.

97. United States Declaration Recognizing the Compulsory Jurisdiction of the International Court of Justice, Sohn, Cases and Materials on World Law 169 (1950); and see Reservation 3 of the United States to the Pact of Bogotá, Ninth International Conference of American States, *op. cit. supra* note 22 at 200.

98. Ninth International Conference, *id.* at 200.

99. *Id.* at 49.

100. If the court interprets nonjuridical disputes on the basis mentioned above, i.e., where one party is not content to demand its legal rights but demands satisfaction of its claim on other than existing legal rules, then, of course, that party may by so doing effectively oust the court of jurisdiction for it has no jurisdiction over nonjuridical or political disputes. See *supra* discussion on political disputes pp. 290-92.

101. Ninth International Conference, *op. cit. supra* note 22 at 200. The U.S. delegation declared: ". . . It was the opinion of the Delegation that arbitration of other cases, those not based on a claim of legal right, might result in decisions having the effect of altering existing legal relationships. While not denying that arbitration might, in appropriate cases, be a suitable method of effectuating the process of peaceful change in international relationships, the Delegation felt impelled to insist that this procedure be resorted to only when the circumstances of a given case appear to make it appropriate. The undertaking of an advance commitment of this character, of unlimited scope, was deemed likely to imperil existing legal relationships which constitute a stabilizing influence of major importance in international relations." *Id.* at 49-50.

102. *Id.* at 199-200.

103. Art. LIII.

104. Tratados y Convenciones Interamericanos, *op. cit. supra* note 9 at 44.

105. For example, there was included on the program of the Tenth Inter-American Conference a proposal to explore the "Possibilities of Revision of the Inter-American Treaty on Pacific Settlement (Pact of Bogotá)." Unfortunately the same conflicts of opinion manifested themselves again with respect to certain features of the Pact. The Mexican Delegation opposed revision at all. A compromise was reached with a proposal that the Council of the OAS should ascertain the suitability of proceeding to revise the Pact, and that if the decision was in the affirmative then the Inter-American Council of Jurists and the Juridical Committee should study the possibility of the revision and formulate preliminary drafts. Resolution XCIX, Final Conference Documents, Tenth Inter-American Conference. Caracas, Venezuela, March 1-28, 1954, Report of the Delegation of the U.S.A., 161-62 (1955). The survey was made. Twelve governments voiced an opinion. In favor of revision were Brazil, Ecuador, United States, and Venezuela. Opposed were Chile, Mexico, and Peru. The others were not definite. As a result the Council on March 6, 1957, concluded that a majority of the member states did not give a favorable opinion for the

necessity of revision, "El Tratado Americano de Soluciones Pacificas (Pacto de Bogotá)," 1955-1957 Inter-American Juridical Yearbook 96 at 97.

CHAPTER XVII

1. On this case see PAU, Applications of the Inter-American Treaty of Reciprocal Assistance 1948-1956, pp. 19-57 (1957); Ball, "Recent Developments in Inter-American Relations," 1949 Y. B. World Affairs 105; Fenwick, "Application of the Treaty of Rio de Janeiro to the Controversy Between Costa Rica and Nicaragua," 43 Am. J. Int. L. 329 (1949); Furniss, "The Inter-American System and Recent Caribbean Disputes," 4 Int. Org. 585 (1950); "O.A.S.—Council of the Organization," 3 Int. Org. 239 (1949); Peace in the Americas, A Resumé of Measures Undertaken Through the OAS to Preserve the Peace, Dept. State Pub. 3964, Int. Org. and Conf. Series, II Am. Rep. 6 (1950).

2. See *supra* pp. 264-71 for discussion of Art. 6.

3. For report of committee and its resolution, see PAU, Applications of the Inter-American Treaty of Reciprocal Assistance, *op. cit. supra* note 1 at 23.

4. *Id.* at 48-50.

5. See *supra* pp. 101-7 on powers of Council.

6. On these cases see PAU, Applications of the Inter-American Treaty of Reciprocal Assistance, *op. cit. supra* note 1 at 61-148; Furniss, *supra* note 1; Hall, "Actions of the Council of the Organization of American States under the Rio Pact," 32 S. W. Soc. Sci. Q. 69 (1951); Peace in the Americas, *op. cit. supra* note 1.

7. 22 Dept. State Bull. 280 (Feb. 20, 1950).

8. 23 Dept. State Bull. 19 (July 3, 1950).

9. Applications of the Inter-American Treaty of Reciprocal Assistance, *op. cit. supra* note 1 at 124 *et seq.*

10. Fenwick, "The Competence of the Council of the Organization of American States," 1949 Inter-Am. Juridical Y. B. 21 at 25.

11. *Supra* pp. 101-6 on the powers of the Council.

12. For Reports of the Special Committee for the Caribbean, see Applications of the Inter-American Treaty of Reciprocal Assistance, *op. cit. supra* note 1 at 155 *et seq.*

13. See *supra* pp. 125-28 on the Inter-American Peace Committee.

14. Much has been written on the affair. On the problem of communist infiltration in Guatemala see James, Red Design for the Americas; Guatemalan Prelude (1954); Martz, Communist Infiltration of Guatemala (1955); Intervention of International Communism in Guatemala, Dept. State Pub. 5556, Inter-Am. Series 48 (1954); Taylor, "The Guatemalan Affair: A Critique of United States Foreign Policy," 50 Am. Pol. Sci. Rev. 787 (1956). The view of the Guatemalan government of President Arbenz is presented by Toriello, La Batalla de Guatemala (1955). For résumés of this affair and discussion of specific aspects see Fenwick, "Juridical Questions Involved in the Guatemalan Revolution," 48 Am. J. Int. L. 597 (1954); "Guatemalan Question," 8 Int. Org. 514 (1954); Gillin & Silvert, "Ambiguities in Guatemala," 34 For. Aff. 469 (1956); Green, "The Double Standard of the United Nations," 1957 Y. B. World Affairs 104 at 129-33; Haas, Latin America and the United Nations 105-12 (1956); Masur, "Foreign Policy Ideologies in the Caribbean," in Wilgus, The Caribbean: Its Political Problems 12 at 20-24 (1956); McKey "The Organization of American States and the United Nations: Rivals or Partners?" 31 Dept. State Bull. 115 (1954); Swift, "International Peace and Security," 1954 Annual Rev. U.N. Aff. 1 at 25 (1955); Whitaker, "Guatemala, OAS and U.S.," 33 For. Pol. Bull. No. 24, pp. 4-7 (1954).

15. S/3232; SCOR, IX, Supp. for April-June, 1954, pp. 11-13. The Guatemalan Question and Security Council Documents may be found in Sohn, Cases and Materials on United Nations Law 371 *et seq.* (1956).

16. SCOR, IX, Mtg. 675, pp. 1-41.

17. Sohn, *op. cit. supra* note 15 at 376.

18. See Goodrich & Simons, The United Nations and the Maintenance of International Peace and Security 230-31 (1955). It is of course up to the Security Council to decide upon the existence of a dispute in such a case and until it does the constitutional controversy can never really be decided.

19. Mavrommatis Palestine Concessions (Jurisdiction) Case, Judgment of the Permanent Court of International Justice, 30 August 1924. PCIJ, Series A, No. 2, pp. 10-21. The Interim Committee of the General Assembly for purposes of Art. 27(3) of the U.N. Charter defined a dispute as follows:

Whenever the State or States bringing the matter before the Security Council allege that the actions of another State or States constitute a breach of an international obligation or are endangering or are likely to endanger the maintenance of international peace and security, or that such actions demonstrate preparation to commit a breach of international obligations or to endanger the maintenance of international peace and security, and the State or States which are the subject of these allegations contest, or do not admit, the facts alleged or inferences to be drawn from such allegations.

GAOR, III, Supp. 10, pp. 7-8. And see further attempts to define a dispute by the Interim Committee, GAOR, V, Supp. 14, pp. 6-7. For other definitions of "dispute" see Goodrich & Simons, *op. cit. supra* note 18, *ibid.;* Goodrich & Hambro, Charter of the United Nations 249 (rev. ed., 1949); Kelsen, The Law of the United Nations 262-63 (1950).

20. Sohn, *op. cit. supra* note 15 at 380.

21. *Id.* at 386-88.

22. SCOR, IX, Mtg., pp. 1-34.

23. S/3241; SCOR, IX, Supp. for April-June, 1954, pp. 14-15.

24. Sohn, *op. cit. supra* note 15 at 394.

25. See *supra* pp. 125-28 for discussion of the Inter-American Peace Committee.

26. "The Effect of Objections to Treaty Reservations," Note, 60 Yale L. Rev. 728 (1951).

27. Fenwick, "Reservations to Multilateral Treaties," 45 Am. J. Int. L. 145 (1951).

28. Article 38 of the Charter of the OAS provides that the regulations of the Inter-American Conferences shall be prepared by the Council, submitted to the member states for consideration, and finally approved by the Council. Among the regulations for the Tenth Conference was the following: "All the member states of the Organization have the right to be represented at the Inter-American Conference by the delegates whom they appoint thereto." Hence, it follows that by appointing a delegate to the Conference, Guatemala tacitly acknowledged membership in the Organization, and, as no question of the right of appointing a delegation was raised by other members, they assumed the membership of Guatemala.

It should also be pointed out that Guatemala's reservation to the OAS instruments did not attempt to limit its obligations under those instruments in a case like the one at hand. The reservation simply proclaimed that the treaties should not be considered an impediment to Guatemalan assertion of rights to Belize (British Honduras).

29. See, e.g., Fenwick, *supra* note 14 at 598.

It can also be argued with considerable force that a nation within a particular region where a regional agency exists impliedly consents to collective action by that agency by ratifying the U.N. Charter even though the nation has not expressly consented to the pact of the regional agency if in accord with Art. 52(1) of the U.N. Charter it is a "matter" appropriate for regional action. The concept underlying Chapter 8 of the U.N. Charter as to regional arrangements and action is that of common action for peace and security within the region between states situated within the region and does not refer to signatories or ratifiers of the regional pact only. See Thomas & Thomas, Non-Intervention: The Law and Its Import in the Americas 160 (1956).

30. See *supra* on regionalism pp. 48-53.

31. Difficulty of proof of United States implication has been noted, although many journalists assigned it a role in the overthrow of the Arbenz government and the thought is prevalent in Latin American quarters that the United States played a decisive part. See, Grant, "Guatemala and United States Foreign Policy," 9 Journal of Int. Affairs 69 (1955) and see Taylor, *supra* note 14 at 793 and 797.

32. See *supra* on regionalism pp. 48-53.

33. On this phase of the Peace Committee's action see OAS, Informe de la Comisión Interamericana de Paz sobre la Controversia entre Guatemala, Honduras and Nicaragua, Doc. CIP-313/54 pp. 6-14.

34. N. Y. Times, July 10, 1954.

35. Applications of the Inter-American Treaty of Reciprocal Assistance, *op. cit. supra* note 1 at 151. The ten states were: Nicaragua, Cuba, United States, Haiti, Brazil, Peru, Honduras, Panama, Dominican Republic, Costa Rica.

36. *Id.* at 153.

37. 6 Annals of the OAS 160 (1954).

38. *Ibid.* Applications of the Inter-American Treaty of Reciprocal Assistance, *op. cit. supra* note 1 at 153-54.

39. Such measures if not involving armed force are apparently considered as measures of pacific settlement only by OAS interpretation. Only the use of armed force is con-

sidered "enforcement measures" which would of course require prior Security Council approval for use by a regional agency except in the case of self-defense. See *supra* on Rio Treaty pp. 270-71.

40. See, e.g., Travis, "The Organization of American States: A Guide to the Future," 10 Western Pol. Q. 491 at 502-3 (1957).

41. See *supra* pp. 229, 240-41.

42. Article 6 of the Rio Treaty obligates all members to meet immediately to agree on measures which must be taken in case of aggression, or, in any case the measures which should be taken for the common defense and for the maintenance of the peace and security of the continent in the event the political independence of any American state should be affected by aggression or by any other fact or situation endangering American peace.

43. Toriello, Foreign Minister of Guatemala, cleverly exploited the dispute between Guatemala and the United Fruit Co., a United States corporation. See Toriello, *op. cit. supra* note 14. To the United States, however, the problem was communism in Guatemala. See "The Problem is Communism," Time, June 7, 1954 p. 35.

44. James, *op. cit. supra* note 14 at 304-6.

45. Taylor, *supra* note 14 at 795.

46. James, *op. cit. supra* note 14 at 306-10.

47. OAS Doc. C-a-153, Corr., Acta de la Sesión Extraordinaria celebrado el 28 de Junio de 1954, pp. 794-800.

48. See Martz, *op. cit. supra* note 14 at 99 *et seq.* for events leading up to and reasons for the fall of the Arbenz government.

49. See PAU, Applications of the Inter-American Treaty of Reciprocal Assistance, *op. cit. supra* note 1 at 159-224.

50. See *supra* pp. 254-60.

51. See *infra* pp. 338-45.

52. For the activities of the OAS on this case see PAU, Applications of the Inter-American Treaty of Reciprocal Assistance, *op. cit. supra* note 1 at 227-37.

53. This protocol may be found in 36 Am. J. Int. L. Off. Doc. 168 (1942). For a short background of the border controversy and the activities of the Third Meeting of Ministers of Foreign Affairs in its settlement see Fenwick, "The Third Meeting of Ministers of Foreign Affairs at Rio de Janeiro," 36 Am. J. Int. L. 169 at 190-91 (1942). See also Woolsey, "The Ecuador-Peru Boundary Controversy," 31 Am. J. Int. L. 97 (1937).

54. The guarantor states are Argentina, Brazil, Chile, and the United States.

55. Report of this case before the OAS is found in PAU, Aplicaciones del Tratado Interamericano de Asistencia Reciproca 1948-1960, pp. 219-92 (1960).

56. On the background of the dispute, events leading up to the submission to the arbitration, Nicaragua's refusal to accept the award, and Nicaragua's reasons for such refusal see U.S. For. Rel. 1918, pp. 11-34.

57. Case concerning the Arbitral Award made by the King of Spain on 23 December 1906, Judgment 18 November 1960, I.C.J. Reports 1960, p. 192.

58. Hall, *supra* note 6; Lleras, "The Inter-American System Today," 282 Annals of the Am. Ac. of Pol. & Soc. Sci. 97 (1952).

59. On the import of the Cuban revolution see Benton, "The Communist Threat at our Back Door," N. Y. Times Mag., July 17, 1960, p. 10; Szulc, "Castro Tries to Export 'Fidelismo,'" N. Y. Times Mag., Nov. 27, 1960, p. 19.

60. These cases and OAS consideration thereof are set forth in PAU, Aplicaciones del Tratado Interamericano de Asistencia Reciproca, *op. cit. supra* note 55 at 259 *et seq.*

61. *Id.* at 301, 346.

62. *Id.* at 387-90. See also Stebbins, The United States in World Affairs 352-56 (1959).

63. On the background of the Santiago Meeting see 41 Dept. State Bull. 279 *et seq.* (Aug. 31, 1959); N. Y. Times, Aug. 13, 1959.

64. For the resolution and declarations of the Santiago Meeting see 41 Dept. State Bull. 342-44 (Sept. 7, 1959).

65. N. Y. Times, Feb. 6, 9, 12, 16, 1960.

66. N. Y. Times, June 9, 1960.

67. N. Y. Times, Jan. 5, 1961.

68. PAU, Aplicaciones del Tratado Interamericano de Asistencia Reciproca, *op. cit. supra* note 55, at 393 *et seq.*

69. N. Y. Times, July 7, 1960.

70 N. Y. Times, July 10-13, 1960.

71. *Ibid.*

72. N. Y. Times, June 12, July 16, 18, 20, 1960.

73. N. Y. Times, July 19, 30, Aug. 16, 21, 1960.

74. N. Y. Times, Aug. 19, 21, 23, 1960.

75. 43 Dept. State Bull. 358 (Sept. 5, 1960).

76. Art. 39, Charter of OAS.

77. Declaration of San José, Costa Rica, 43 Dept. State Bull. 407-8 (Sept. 12, 1960).

78. N. Y. Times, Jan. 5, 1961.

79. N. Y. Times, Aug. 18, 1961 contains an article which requests re-establishment of diplomatic relations with the Dominican Republic by the other American States. Such request was made by General Rafael Trujillo, Jr.

80. N. Y. Times, June 6, 7, 8, 9, 10, July 16, Sept. 7, 1961.

81. 43 Dept. State Bull. 715 (Nov. 7, 1960).

82. 43 Dept. State Bull. 787 *et seq.* (Nov. 21, 1960).

83. On these disturbances see Time, vol. 76, No. 22, Nov. 28, 1960, pp. 28-31; Hispanic American Report, vol. 13, No. 11, Jan. 1961, pp. 776-77, 780-82, 783, 784, 841-43.

84. Time, *id.* at 15, Hispanic American Report, *ibid.*

85. United Nations Review, vol. 8, No. 2, Feb. 1961, pp. 26-31; The News of the Week in Review, N. Y. Times, Nov. 20, 1960.

86. *Id.* at 26.

87. *Ibid.*

88. *Ibid.*

89. 44 Dept. State Bull. 103 (Jan. 23, 1961).

90. Statements of the U.S. representative before the Security Council, *id.* at 104-14.

91. United Nations Review, *supra* note 85 at 28.

92. *Id.* at 29.

93. *Id.* at 31.

94. Text of the U.S. statement is contained in N. Y. Times, April 4, 1961.

95. N. Y. Times, Apr. 16, 17, 18, 19, 20, 1961. Reports on this situation and U.S. involvement therein are contained in the news media of the period such as Time, vol. 77, No. 18, Apr. 28, 1961, pp. 11-13, 19-23; U.S. News and World Report, vol. 50, No. 18, May 1, 1961, pp. 37-47; vol. 50, No. 20, May 15, 1961, pp. 44-47; Hispanic American Report, vol. 14, No. 4, June, 1961, pp. 309-16, 368-71.

96. Summary of the U.N. actions is found in United Nations Review, vol. 8, No. 5, May 1961, pp. 9-10. See also 44 Dept. State Bull. 667-85 (May 8, 1961).

97. N. Y. Times, Apr. 18, 1961.

98. *Ibid.*

99. N. Y. Times, Apr. 19, 1961.

100. *Ibid.*

101. *Ibid.*

102. See United Nations Review, *supra* note 96.

103. "United States & Soviet Union Exchange Messages in Regard to Events in Cuba," 44 Dept. State Bull. 661-67 (May 8, 1961).

104. "The Lesson of Cuba," *id.* at 659.

105. N. Y. Times, April 27, 30, 1961.

106. 45 Dept. State Bull. (Dec. 25, 1961) contains an account of the Council action at pp. 1069-71.

107. See *supra* p. 106.

108. On the Punta del Este Meeting see PAU, Final Act, Eighth Meeting of Consultation of Ministers of Foreign Affairs Serving as Organ of Consultation in Application of the Inter-American Treaty of Reciprocal Assistance, Punta del Este, Uruguay, January 22-31, 1962, OEA/Ser. C/II.8 (English) 1962; 46 Dept. State Bull. 267-83 (Feb. 19, 1962); N. Y. Times, Jan. 26, 28, 31, Feb. 1, 4, 14, 16, 1962; Time, vol. LXXIX, No. 7, Latin American ed., p. 23 (1962).

109. See *supra* pp. 59-60.

110. On March 8, 1962, the Council of the OAS voted to establish such a committee to be composed of seven experts on security matters. N. Y. Times, Mar. 9, 1962.

111. N. Y. Times, Feb. 16, 28, 1962.

112. 47 Dept. State Bull. 450 (Sept. 24, 1962); *id.* 481-82 (Oct. 1, 1962).

113. *Id.* at 481.

114. "Joint Resolution Expressing the Determination of the United States With Respect to Cuba," as set forth in 47 Dept. State Bull. 597 (Oct. 22, 1962).

115. 47 Dept. State Bull. 560-61 (Oct. 15, 1962).

116. See, e.g., statements made by Under Secretary of State Ball and Secretary of State Rusk in 47 Dept. State Bull. 591-98 (Oct. 22, 1962).

117. 47 Dept. State Bull. 541 (Oct. 8, 1962).

118. For reports on this informal meeting see N. Y. Times, Oct. 2, 3, 7, 1962.

119. The text of the communiqué may be found in 47 Dept. State Bull. 598-600 (Oct. 22, 1962).

120. N. Y. Times, Oct. 4, 5, 14, 1962.

121. The address of the President, "The Soviet Threat to the Americas," is contained in 47 Dept. State Bull. 715-20 (Nov. 12, 1962).

122. PAU, Convocation of the Organ of Consultation in Accordance with the Provisions of the Inter-American Treaty of Reciprocal Assistance, at the Request of the United States Government, Council Series OEA/Ser. G/V, C-d-1023 (English), 23 Oct. 1962.

123. The text of the resolution is contained in PAU, The Council of the Organization of American States Acting Provisionally as Organ of Consultation, Council Series OEA/Ser. G/V, C-d-1024 (English) Rev., 23 Oct. 1962, as well as in 47 Dept. State Bull. 722-3 (Nov. 12, 1962).

124. *Ibid.*

125. N. Y. Times, Oct. 24, 28, 1962.

126. 47 Dept State Bull. 717 (Oct. 12, 1962).

127. *Id.* at 724.

128. N. Y. Times, Oct. 28, 29, 1962. An excellent summary of the Cuban crisis is contained in the N. Y. Times, Nov. 3, 1962.

129. N. Y. Times, Nov. 1, 1962.

130. N. Y. Times, Nov. 21, 1962.

131. *Ibid.*

132. See *supra* pp. 318, 325-27.

133. See statement by Secretary of State Rusk to the special meeting of the OAS Council, Oct. 23, 1962, 47 Dept. State Bull. 721 (Nov. 12, 1962).

134. Certain Expenses of the United Nations (Article 17, paragraph 2 of the Charter), Advisory Opinion of 20 July, 1962; I.C.J. Reports 1962, p. 251. See *supra* pp. 270-71.

135. The President stated that actions were taken in the defense of United States security and the security of the Western Hemisphere. The interdiction against the delivery of the offensive weapons used the words "to prevent the missiles in Cuba with offensive capability from ever becoming an active threat to the peace and security of the Continent," as well as "to defend the security of the United States." Secretary of State Rusk spoke of the offensive nature of the weapons and stated that no country of the hemisphere "can feel secure from direct attack." The OAS resolution spoke of the obligation of the American states to meet armed attacks against them and to deal with threats of aggression against them through reciprocal assistance. See also, Oliver, The Inter-American Security System and the Cuban Crisis, The Hammarskjold's Forums, p. 27 (Nov. 19, 1962), and Larson, Letter to the N. Y. Times, Nov. 12, 1962.

136. See *supra* pp. 250-60, 264-71.

137. *The Case of the Steamer Caroline* as reproduced in Jennings, "The Caroline and McCleod Cases," 32 Am. J. Int. L. 82 at 89 (1938).

138. Statement of Secretary of State Rusk, 47 Dept. State Bull. 720-22 (Nov. 12, 1962). 1962).

139. N. Y. Times, Oct. 25, 1962.

140. For discussion of pacific blockade see Brierly, The Law of Nations 322 (5th ed. 1955); II Oppenheim, International Law 144-49 (7th ed., Lauterpacht, 1952); and see *supra* pp. 162-64.

141. See *supra* pp. 298-302, 313-14.

142. See *infra* pp. 368-70.

CHAPTER XVIII

1. See Thomas & Thomas, Non-Intervention: The Law and Its Import in the Americas, Ch. II, "The Era of Intervention in the Americas" (1956).

2. PAU, Treaties and Conventions Signed at the Sixth International Conference of American States, Habana, Cuba, January 16-February 20, 1928, pp. 19-20 (1950).

3. 1955-1957 Inter-American Juridical Yearbook 161-67 (1958).

4. As of 1961 ten states had signed the protocol but only seven had ratified. The seven ratifiers are: Argentina, Costa Rica, Cuba, the Dominican Republic, El Salvador, Haiti, Honduras. The three nations which only signed are: Brazil, Peru, and the United States. See PAU, Inter-American Treaties and Conventions 101 (Treaty Series No. 9, Rev. 1961).

5. I Hyde, International Law Chiefly as Interpreted and Applied by the United States, sec. 73 (2d ed. 1947).

6. *Ibid.;* Padelford, "International Law and the Spanish Civil War," 31 Am. J. Int. L. 226 at 228 (1937); Smith, "Some Problems of the Spanish Civil War," 18 Brit. Y. B. Int. L. 17 at 23 (1937).

7. Intervention under consent of the state is not true intervention, for intervention signifies a coercion of the will of the state by another, an imposition of will. If consent is freely given there is no coercion, no imposition of will, hence no intervention. See Thomas & Thomas, *op. cit. supra* note 1 at 71 *et seq.* and at 91 *et seq.*

8. Thomas & Thomas, *id.* at 93-94.

9. See, e.g., Winfield, "The Grounds of Intervention in International Law," 1924 Brit. Y. B. Int. L. 149 at 157-58.

10. I Phillimore, Commentaries upon International Law, CCCXCIII (3rd ed. 1879).

11. Woolsey, International Law, sec. 42 (6th ed. 1897).

12. Vattel, The Law of Nations or the Principles of Natural Law, Bk. II, Ch. IV, sec. 56 (1758), III Classics of International Law (1916).

13. Thomas & Thomas, *op. cit. supra* note 1 at 8-10.

14. Hall, International Law 287 (6th ed. 1909).

15. See I Hyde, *op. cit. supra* note 5; Garcia Mora, "International Law and the Law of Hostile Military Expeditions," 27 Fordham L. Rev. 309 (1958-59); Wright, "United States Intervention in the Lebanon," 53 Am. J. Int. L. 112 at 121-22 (1959).

16. Goebel, "The International Responsibility of States for Injuries Sustained by Aliens on Account of Mob Violence, Insurrections and Civil War," 8 Am. J. Int. L. 802 (1914).

17. Hershey, The Essentials of International Public Law and Organization 201-3 (rev. ed. 1935); I Hyde, *op. cit. supra* note 5 at sec. 50.

18. Hershey, *id.* at 203-6; Hyde, *id.* at sec. 47.

19. Hershey, *id.* at 203; The Three Friends, 166 U.S. 1 at 36-66 (1877).

20. Chen and Green, The International Law of Recognition 400 (1951).

21. Wilson, "Insurgency and International Maritime Law," 1 Am. J. Int. L. 46 at 59-60 (1907).

22. Garner, in "Questions of International Law in the Spanish Civil Strife," 31 Am. J. Int. L. 66 at 67-78 (1937), states this view very emphatically. See also Briggs, The Law of Nations: Cases, Documents, Notes, 992, 999-1000 (2d ed. 1952); Eagleton, International Government 71-72 (3rd ed. 1957); Jessup, "The Spanish Rebellion and International Law," 15 For. Aff. 260 at 265-68 (1936-37); Padelford, International Law and Diplomacy in the Spanish Civil Strife 1-8 (1939); Pfankuchen, A Documentary Textbook of International Law 953-54 (1960). And see 2 Podesta Costa, Derecho Internacional Publico 265 (3rd ed. 1955).

23. I Hyde, *op. cit. supra* note 5, secs. 47 and 49; Hershey, *op. cit. supra* note 17 at 203.

24. Beale, "The Recognition of the Cuban Belligerency," 9 Harv. L. Rev. 406 at 407 (1896).

25. Garner, *op. cit. supra* note 22; III Hyde, *op. cit. supra* note 5, sec. 885; Walker, "Recognition of Belligerency and Grant of Belligerent Rights," 23 Trans. Grotius Soc. 177 (1938).

26. Hershey, *op. cit. supra* note 17 at 204. But see the Inter-American Convention on Maritime Law which prohibits delivery to belligerents by neutrals of ships of war, munitions, or other war materials as well as grant of loans or other credits to belligerents. PAU, Treaties and Conventions Signed at the Sixth International Conference of American States, *op. cit. supra* note 2 at 14-18.

27. Garner, "Recognition of Belligerency," 32 Am. J. Int. L. 106 (1938); Wiesse, Le Droit International Applique aux Guerres Civiles 180 (1898).

28. II Oppenheim, International Law 249 (Lauterpacht, 7th ed., 1952).

29. Beale, *supra* note 24 at 406.

30. Lauterpacht, Recognition in International Law 229 (1947).

31. Padelford, *supra* note 6 at 586. Lauterpacht in general accepts the principle that until belligerency is recognized the government is entitled to privileged treatment and no duty of impartiality is required. However, he limits the privileges or assistance that can be granted the government by a foreign state. He declares that the presumptions in favor of the established government do not go beyond the duty not to grant the insurgents premature recognition as a government, and an outside state may not permit its terrtiory to become a base of operations against the lawful government. Apart from this, any unilateral extended grant of advantages to the lawful government amounts, even prior to the recognition of belligerency of the insurgents, to interference and to a denial of the right of the nation to decide for itself, by a physical contest, if necessary, between the rival forces and their views on the nature and form of internal government. Such language,

of course, abolishes a distinction between insurgency and belligerency insofar as the privileged treatment of the government in time of insurgency is concerned, requiring what is in effect neutrality in insurgency as well as belligerency. Wright shares the same opinion, see Wright, *supra* note 15.

32. See Jessup, *supra* note 22 at 265; Pfankuchen, *op. cit. supra* note 22 at 953.

33. For a discussion of this convention see Podesta Costa, "La Revision de la Convencion Interamericana sobre Derechos y Deberes de los Estados en Caso de Luchas Civiles," 1949 Inter-American Juridical Y. B. 9; Hernandez, "Algunas Ideas a Proposito de la Conveniencia de Revision de la Convencion de la Habana sobre los Derechos y Deberes de los Estados en Caso de Luchas Civiles," *id.* at 114; Accioly, "O Principio de Não-intervenção e a Convenção de Havana sobre Lutas Civis," *id.* at 3.

34. Habana Convention, Art. 1, par. 1, *supra* note 2.

35. Chen and Green, The International Law of Recognition 401 (1951).

36. Fenwick, International Law 301 (3rd ed. 1948).

37. See, e.g., Garcia Mora, *supra* note 15 at 311, where it is declared that inaction by a state in preventing the operation from its territory of a hostile military expedition against another state raises a logical presumption of governmental complicity in the hostile attack. Even if a state's tolerance of the organization can be regarded as complete disinterestedness in the outcome, it would appear to be a delict, for where there is a duty on the part of a state to act and that state omits to do the act with knowledge of what the consequences of that omission will be, it intends the consequences just as truly as it intended to omit what it should have done. See Thomas & Thomas, *op. cit. supra* note 1 at 217.

38. The term "due diligence" is ambiguous and later treaties have sought to substitute a more ascertainable standard such as "to employ the means at its disposal" or, as in the Habana Convention, "to use all means at their command." None of these terms impose an absolute obligation upon a state, however. See Garcia Mora, *id.* at 321-22.

39. See *supra* note 3.

40. "All appropriate means," while not appearing quite so strong as "to use all means at their command," would seem to be practically synonymous.

41. Habana Convention, Art. 1, par. 3, *supra* note 2.

42. Protocol, Art. 1, *supra* note 3.

43. Habana Convention, Art. 1, par. 2 and par. 3, *supra* note 2.

44. Podesta Costa, *supra* note 33 at 12.

45. *Ibid.*

46. See Spaight, War Rights on Land, secs. 485-501 (1911).

47. II Oppenheim, International Law 727 (Lauterpacht, 7th ed., 1952).

48. See *supra* p. 340.

49. See Thomas & Thomas, *op. cit. supra* note 1 at 218, 222.

50. *Id.* at 219-20.

51. The Ecuador-Peru Case and the Nicaragua-Honduras Case both involved boundary disputes. The 1962 Cuban missile crisis involved a threat of armed attack. See *supra* pp. 314-16, 330-37.

52. These cases are all summarized in the previous chapter. For full report see PAU, Aplicaciones del Tratado Interamericano de Asistencia Reciproca 1948-1960 (3rd ed. 1960).

53. See *supra* p. 138.

54. See *supra* p. 215.

55. See *supra* pp. 264-68.

56. See Conclusions of the Committee, PAU, Applications of the Inter-American Treaty of Reciprocal Assistance 1948-1956, pp. 26, 27 (1957).

57. *Id.* at 27-28.

58. *Id.* at 187-89. And see the strong reservation of the Ambassador of Ecuador who condemned the committee for failing to identify the authors of the "foreign intervention." *Id.* at 190.

59. *Id.* at 125-27.

60. *Id.* at 126. And see Annual Report of the Secretary General of the OAS for 1949-1950 wherein it is pointed out that such subversive actions as in the Haiti-Dominican Case are aggression and intervention. 3 Annals of the OAS 10-11 (1951).

61. Martens, Traité de Droit International, vol. I, Sec. 74 (1883).

62. Stowell, Intervention in International Law 378 (1921).

63. Paradisi, "L'amitie internationale: Les phases critiques de son ancienne historie," 78 Recueil des Cours 329 (1951).

64. Garcia Mora, "International Responsibility for Subversive Activities and Hostile Propaganda by Private Persons Against Foreign States," 35 Ind. L. J. 306 (1960); Wright,

"Subversive Intervention," 54 Am. J. Int. L. 521 (1960). Garcia Mora is of the belief that treaty law has now changed general international law so as to place some obligation upon states to suppress private hostile propoganda. *Id.* at 324. See also on private revolutionary activities, Lauterpacht, "Revolutionary Activities by Private Persons against Foreign States," 22 Am. J. Int. L. 105 (1928); Pruess, "International Responsibility for Hostile Propaganda against Foreign States," 28 Am. J. Int. L. 649 (1934).

65. League of Nations, Official Journal, Minutes of Council, pp. 1755-66, Dec. 1934. And see a draft convention of the League, "Convention for the Prevention and Punishment of Terrorism," 7 Hudson, International Legislation 862 (1941).

66. "South American Regional Agreement on Radio Communications, April 10, 1935," 7 Hudson, *id.* at 47.

67. International Conferences of American States, First Supp. 1933-1940, p. 152 (1940).

68. PAU, Convention on Territorial Asylum, Treaty Series, OAS, Off. Doc. Ser. A/10 (SEPF) (1961). This has been signed by twenty countries but ratified by only seven.

69. Art. 15.

70. PAU, Applications of the Inter-American Treaty of Reciprocal Assistance 1948-1956, *op. cit. supra* note 56 at 62.

71. *Id.* at 63-67.

72. Moreover the two governments indicated that they were ready to arrive at a friendly settlement and the case was handed over to the Inter-American Peace Committee. *Id.* at 67.

73. See Thomas & Thomas, *op. cit. supra* note 1 at 275.

74. 1 Annals of the OAS 393 (1949).

75. Applications of the Inter-American Treaty of Reciprocal Assistance, *op. cit. supra* note 56 at 96, 100-101, 125, 126.

76. 43 Dept. State Bull. 358 (1960).

77. *Ibid.*

78. Art. 51, U.N. Charter, and see *supra* pp. 254-60.

79. See *supra* p. 270. This view has apparently been adopted by the Security Council, for following the application of enforcement measures against the Dominican Republic, the OAS reported the action to the Security Council with no request for authorization. The USSR introduced a resolution which would have given the Security Council approval of the OAS action, rather than simply to take note of it, on the grounds that enforcement measures could not be taken under Article 53 by regional agencies without such approval. The American representatives dissented and the Council voted 9 to 0 with two abstentions (the Soviet Union and Poland) simply to take note of the action. See 7 U.N. Rev. 68-69 (Oct. 1960).

80. See *supra* pp. 250-54.

81. Kunz, "Individual and Collective Self-Defense in Article 51 of the Charter of the United Nations," 41 Am. J. Int. L. 872 (1947).

82. Alfaro, "Memorandum on the Question of Defining Aggression," Yearbook of the International Law Commission, 1951, Vol. II, U.N. Doc. No. A/cN.4/L.8 at 37-38. And see Brownlie, "International Law and the Activities of Armed Bands," 7 Int. and Comp. L. Q. 712 at 731-33 (1958). It is here declared that a "coordinated and general campaign by powerful bands of irregulars, with obvious or easily proven complicity of the government of the state from which they operate would constitute an armed attack," although mere negligence by a state in permitting a band to operate from its terriory probably would not. Stowell calls the state encouragement of such private expeditions a "constructive attack" by the state within whose territory the preparation takes place. Stowell, Intervention in International Law 373 (1921).

83. For example, the U.S. Deputy Representative pointed out that the failure of the Security Council to take action to protect Greek territorial integrity did not preclude individual or collective action by states willing to act. See U.N. Doc. S/P.V/180, pp. 56-65.

84. Art. 3, Rio Treaty.

85. *Ibid.*

86. Art. 20, Rio Treaty.

87. Bowett, Self-Defence in International Law, Chs. I, III, IX, X (1958).

88. See *supra* pp. 254-60, 264-68.

89. For discussion of the Guatemalan Case see *supra* pp. 302-13.

90. VI Moore, A Digest of International Law 401 (1906).

91. On the background of the Monroe Doctrine see Perkins, The Monroe Doctrine 1823-1836 (1932). For a brief historical discussion see Thomas & Thomas, *op. cit. supra* note 1 at 8-14.

92. See U.S. Statement on the Monroe Doctrine of July 14, 1960, in reply to Premier

Khrushchev, declaring that the doctrine is as valid today as in the days of Monroe to prevent the extension to the hemisphere of any despotic political system contrary to the independence of the American states, and labeling international communism the "new imperialism," N. Y. Times, July 15, 1960.

93. "Panama Resolution XI, Final Act," 34 Am. J. Int. L. Supp. 1-20 (1940).

94. "Habana Resolution VI, Final Act," 35 Am. J. Int. L. Supp. 1-32 (1941).

95. "Habana Resolution VII," *ibid.*

96. "... each one of the governments of the American republics *shall* adopt within its territory all necessary measures..." (italics supplied). See Cowles, "Joint Action to Protect an American State from Axis Subversive Activity," 36 Am. J. Int. L. 242 (1942).

97. It would seem that the recommendation for each nation to curtail subversive propaganda was mandatory upon those nations wherein wide-scale activities occurred, despite the use of the word "recommends," which usually indicates that states are free to act or not to act.

98. Resolution XVII, PAU, Report on the Third Meeting of the Ministers of Foreign Affairs of the American Republics 44 at 46 (Cong. and Conf. Series No. 36, 1942).

99. See *supra* pp. 28, 217-18.

100. Resolution XXXII incorporated in Ninth International Conference of American States, Bogotá, Colombia, 266 at 269, Report of the Delegation of the U.S.A., Dept. State Pub. 3263 (Int. Org. and Conf. Series 2, Am. Reps. 3, 1948).

101. *Ibid.*

102. Resolution VII, PAU, Fourth Meeting of Consultation of Ministers of Foreign Affairs, Washington, D.C., March 26-April 7, 1951, Final Act 11-13 (1951).

103. Resolution XCIII, Tenth Inter-American Conference, Caracas, Venezuela, March 1-28, 1954, pp. 156-57. Report of the Delegation of the U.S.A., Dept. State Pub. 5692 (Int. Org. and Conf. Series 11, Am. Rep. 14, 1955).

104. *Ibid.*

105. For discussion of the corollary and reasons therefor see I Hyde, *op. cit. supra* note 5, sec. 92.

106. For the Mexican viewpoint and the Mexican proposed amendment to the Declaration against International Communism see PAU, Decima Conferencia Interamericana, Actas y Documentos, Volumen II, pp. 135-38, 314-17 (1958). See also on the Declaration, Fenwick, "Intervention at the Caracas Conference," 48 Am. J. Int. L. 451 (1954); Fenwick, "Tenth Inter-American Conference: Some Issues of Inter-American Regional Law," *id.* at 464.

107. Argentina also abstained and Guatemala voted against the declaration.

108. Irizarry y Puente, "The Doctrine of Recognition and Intervention in Latin America," 28 Tulane L. Rev. 313 at 341 (1954).

109. Thomas & Thomas, *op. cit. supra* note 1 at 14.

110. Carmen, Soviet Imperialism 155 (1950). Chakste, "Soviet Concept of the State, International Law, and Sovereignty," 43 Am. J. Int. L. 21 (1949); Taracouzio, The Soviet Union and International Law 12 (1935).

111. For example, the Castro betrayal of the Cuban Revolution and his sellout of Cuba to Russia, Red China, and communism.

112. See *supra* pp. 318, 326-27.

113. See *supra* p. 250.

114. See *supra* pp. 258, 265.

115. See Bowett, *op. cit supra* note 87.

116. *Id.* at 24. The primary question, of course, would be that of proportionality. Can it be reasoned that in today's world the use of force against a subversive intervention (not involving the use of force) of the imperialist communist movement is proportional?

117. Pompe, Aggressive War 53 (1953).

118. See Bowett, *op. cit. supra* note 87 at 208-12. The Monroe Doctrine as a statement of long-run policy of the hemisphere is a statement of self-preservation and the right of self-defense can hardly be justified on a basis of self-preservation. See Thomas & Thomas, *op. cit. supra* note 1 at 81-85. But if viewed as a reaction against delictual action where the danger to legal rights of the American states, actual or imminent, is involved then an exercise of the right of self-defense can be invoked.

119. See Bowett, *id.* at 241-43.

120. For example, it is the rule in cases where a state has denied justice to an alien that the alien must exhaust all local remedies available to him before his state of citizenship may claim against the delinquent state. But the alien is not required to exhaust justice in such state if there is no justice to exhaust. See Panevezy-Saldutiskis Ry. Case, 1939, Pubs. Perm. Court of Int'l. Justice, Series A/B, No. 76, 18; II Hyde, *op. cit. supra* note 5, sec. 283.

121. See *supra* pp. 302-13.
122. See *supra* pp. 316 *et seq.*
123. Full discussion of the Punta del Este Meeting is set forth *supra* pp. 325-27.
124. On the Cuban missile crisis and its immediate background, see *supra* pp. 328-37.
125. See *supra* Chs. I and II.
126. Address by President Kennedy, "The Soviet Threat to the Americas," 47 Dept. State Bull. 715 at 718 (Nov. 12, 1962).
127. See *supra* p. 319 for discussion of the resolution against the intervention of international communism taken at San José by the Meeting of Foreign Ministers which was not a collective security measure and which failed to condemn Cuba.
128. For discussion see *supra* p. 316 *et seq.*
129. See Thomas & Thomas, *op. cit. supra* note 1 at 85-88, discussing economic reprisals as intervention.
130. See Wright, "The Crime of Warmongering," 42 Am. J. Int. L. 128 (1948).
131. For Cuban action against the United States see Press Release, "United States Submits to Inter-American Peace Committee Memorandum on Provocative Actions of Cuban Government," 43 Dept. State Bull. 79 (July 18, 1960); and Press Release, "United States Institutes Controls on Exports to Cuba," 43 Dept. State Bull. 715 (Nov. 7, 1960).
132. See Thomas & Thomas, *op. cit. supra* note 1 at 140.
133. *Id.* at 87-88.
134. Press Release, "President Reduces Cuban Sugar Quota for Balance of 1960," 43 Dept. State Bull. 140 (July 25, 1960).
135. See text of a U.S. Aide Memoire delivered on June 4, 1960, to the Foreign Ministry of Cuba, 42 Dept. State Bull. 994 (June 20, 1960).
136. For reasons for the embargo see Press Release, "United States Institutes Controls on Exports to Cuba," *supra* note 131.
137. *Ibid.*
138. Remarks of Cuba's Foreign Minister to the United Nations as quoted in statements by the U.S. Representatives and contained in 43 Dept. State Bull. 789 (Nov. 21, 1960).
139. XIII Hispanic American Reports 842 (Jan., 1961).
140. *Id.* at 777, 782, 841-43.
141. See *supra* pp. 320, 339.
142. See *supra* pp. 340 *et seq.*
143. Potter, "Legal Aspects of the Beirut Landing," 52 Am. J. Int. L. 727 (1958); Wright, "United States Intervention in the Lebanon," 53 Am. J. Int. L. 112 (1959).
144. Arts. 3 and 6 of the Rio Treaty. Charges were made by Costa Rican officials that the invasion was Cuban backed. See XIII Hispanic American Reports 783 (Jan., 1961).
145. Royal Institute of International Affairs, International Sanctions 20 (1938). The rupture of diplomatic and consular relations is considered as a collective measure under the U.N. Charter, Article 41, and the Rio Treaty, Article 8.
146. I Oppenheim, *op. cit. supra* note 28 at 693.
147. Thomas & Thomas, *op. cit. supra* note 1 at 132.
148. *Id.* at 140.
149. See U.S. statement for reasons behind the break, 44 Dept. State Bull. 103 (Jan. 23, 1961).
150. See *supra* p. 268.
151. See *supra* p. 341.
152. I Oppenheim, *op. cit. supra* note 28 at 693.
153. Lauterpacht, *op. cit. supra* note 30 at 349, 352-55 (1947). See also Chen and Green, *op. cit. supra* note 20 at 259 *et seq.*
154. See *supra* Ch. XI for discussion of conditions of recognition.
155. *Supra* pp. 161-63.
156. See *supra* pp. 250-52.
157. See *supra* pp. 164-65.
158. Bowett, *op. cit. supra* note 87.
159. Collective action is confined to such circumstances by the Rio Treaty.
160. Professor Stone's thesis in this respect is set forth in Ch. V of his work, Aggression and World Order (1958).
161. Art. 2 (3), U.N. Charter.
162. Stone, *op. cit. supra* note 160 at 96. Art. 19 of the Charter of Bogotá excepts measures for the maintenance of peace in accordance with existing treaties from the non-intervention principle.
163. *Supra* pp. 269-71.
164. Art. 5(a), Charter of Bogotá.

165. Art. 5(b), Charter of Bogotá.
166. Art. 7, Charter of Bogotá.
167. Art. 9, Charter of Bogotá.
168. Art. 11, Charter of Bogotá.
169. Lauterpacht, The Function of Law in the International Community 286 (1933); Campion, La Theorie de l'Abus des Droits 303-10 (1925); Gutteridge, "Abuse of Rights," 5 Camb. L. J. 22, 25 (1935).
170. Von Verdross, "The Charter of the United Nations and General International Law" in Lipsky, Law and Politics in the World Community 153 at 156 (1953); Kunz, "General International Law and the Law of International Obligation," 47 Am. J. Int. L. 456 at 458-59 (1953).
171. Thomas, Communism versus International Law 16 (1953).
172. Moller, International Law in Peace and War 10 (1931).
173. Dickinson, The Law of Nations 9 (1929).
174. Fiore states it thus:

Full and entire juridical equality ought to be limited to those states among which there have developed the fundamental juridical ideas essential to the co-existence of states in society. A state which does not find itself in a position to fulfil its international duties to other states, either as a result of traditional prejudices, of its internal organization, or its customs and religious beliefs, can only demand the full enjoyment of international rights in perfect equality on condition that it change its internal organization so as to enable it to fulfil its international duties by giving substantial guaranties on the subject.

I Fiore, Trattato di Diritto Internazionale Publico (4th ed. 1904). See also I Lorimer, Institutes of the Law of Nations 101, 157 (1883); and I Ward, Law of Nations xi (1795).
175. See, e.g., Castro's statement that he did not "feel obligated" by the Rio Treaty since "the revolution did not sign it." N. Y. Times, Aug. 28, 1960. For other attacks on the OAS by Cuban leaders see "Text of U.S. Supplemental Paper at the San Jose Conference on Cuba and Communism," N.Y. Times, Aug. 23, 1960; and "Castro Challenges OAS," N. Y. Times, Aug. 25, 1960.
176. See supra pp. 59-60.
177. N. Y. Times, Nov. 25, 1962.
178. N. Y. Times (Western Edition), Feb. 13, 1963.
179. Dallas Morning News, Feb. 14, 1963; N. Y. Times (Western Edition), Feb 13, 1963.
180. See discussions relating to the Monroe Doctrine and its place today, Plank, "Monroe's Doctrine and Castro's," N. Y. Times Magazine, Oct. 7, 1962, p. 30; Commager, "Can Monroe Doctrine Be Used?" Dallas Morning News, Oct. 14, 1962, p. 27.

CHAPTER XIX

1. Viner, Studies in the Theory of International Trade 21 (1937); Mander, Foundations of Modern World Society 371 (2d ed., 1947).
2. Gordon, International Trade: Goods, People and Ideas 312 (1958).
3. Johnson, International Trade and Economic Growth 65 (1958).
4. Cheever and Haviland, Organizing for Peace 26 (1954); Chamberlain, The Regime of International Rivers: Danube and Rhine 43 (1920).
5. Mander, op. cit. supra note 1 at 535.
6. Sly, "The Genesis of the Universal Postal Union," 233 International Conciliation (Oct. 1927).
7. Rappard, "Postwar Efforts for Freer Trade," 9 Geneva Studies, No. 2 (March, 1938).
8. Friedmann, "Some Impacts of Social Organization on International Law," 50 Am. J. Int. L. 475 (1956).
9. Jenks, The Common Law of Mankind 255 (1958).
10. Condliffe, "International Trade and Economic Nationalism," 476 International Conciliation (Dec., 1951).
11. Alexandrowicz, International Economic Organizations 32 (1953).
12. Tinbergen, International Economic Integration 7 (1954).
13. Brown, The United States and the Restoration of World Trade 50 (1950).
14. Ball, The Problem of Inter-American Organization 16 (1944); Baquero Lazcano, La Unión Panamericana Actual Secretaria de la Q.E.A. 4 (1956).
15. Alvarez, Le Panaméricanisme et la Sixième Conférence Panaméricaine 20 (1928).
16. International Conference of American States: Seventh; Minutes and Antecedents with General Index (Montevideo, 1933).

17. Rowe, "Meeting of the Ministers of Foreign Affairs of the American Republics," 73 Bulletin of the Pan American Union 690 (1939).

18. Ball, *op. cit. supra* note 14 at 33.

19. Trueblood, "The Havana Conference of 1940," 16 Foreign Policy Assn. Reports 158 (Sept., 1940).

20. Fenwick, "The Third Meeting of Ministers of Foreign Affairs at Rio de Janeiro," 36 Am. J. Int. L. 159 (1942).

21. Canyes, "The Inter-American System and the Conference of Chapultepec," 39 Am. J. Int. L. 501 (1945). Kunz, "The Inter-American Conference on Problems of War and Peace at Mexico City," 39 Am. J. Int. L. 527 (1945).

22. Sanders, Sovereignty and Interdependence in the New World: Comments on the Inter-American System 174 (Dept. State Pub. 3054; Inter-American Series 35, 1948).

23. Masters, "International Agencies in the Western Hemisphere," 39 Am. J. Int. L. 713 (1945); Report of the Delegation of the United States of America to the Inter-American Conference on Problems of War and Peace, Mexico City, Mexico. February 24-March 8, 1945 (Dept. State Pub. 2497, Conference Series 85, 1946).

24. Inter-American Conference for the Maintenance of Continental Peace and Security, Quitandinha, Brazil, August 15-September 2, 1947. Report of the Delegation of the United States of America (Dept. State Pub. 3016, Int. Org. and Conf. II, American Republics 1, 1948).

25. Ninth International Conference of American States, Bogotá, Colombia, March 30-May 2, 1948. Report of the Delegation of the United States of America with Related Documents. (Dept. State Pub. 3263, Int. Org. and Conf. Series II, American Republics 3, 1948); Fenwick, "The Ninth International Conference of American States" 42 Am. J. Int. L. 553 (1948).

26. Houston, Latin America in the United Nations 223 (1956); Urquipo, "Organismos Internacionales: La Comisión Económica para América Latina," 18 Cuadernos de Política Internacional 75 (1954).

27. Oreamuno, "The Bases of Inter-American Economic Cooperation" Social Science 216 (1953); Lleras, "Report on the Ninth International Conference of American States," 1 Annals of the OAS 1 at 31 (1949); Report of Delegation, *op. cit. supra* note 25 at 64; "Economic Agreement of Bogotá," 1 Annals of the OAS 99 (1949) is the complete text of the Agreement.

28. U.S. Technical Cooperation Administration, Point 4; What It Is; How It Works 5 (1953).

29. Point Four is a U.S. program of technical assistance to underdeveloped countries on a noncommercial basis. It is carried on by the Foreign Operations Administration. The name under which this program has become known was first used by President Truman in his inaugural address on Jan. 20, 1949, when it was defined as the fourth major point in U.S. foreign policy. Authority for the program was provided by the Act for International Development in 1950. Continuation of the program was authorized by the Mutual Security Acts of 1951 and 1952. Under the Eisenhower administration the original name was dropped in official documents and it became known as the Technical Assistance or Technical Cooperation Program; Rowe, Eleven Years of Point 4 in Latin America 2 (1953); Glick, The Administration of Technical Assistance: Growth in the Americas 140 (1957).

30. Tew, International Monetary Cooperation 1945-1960, Ch. 8 (1960); Ropke, "Economic Order and International Law," 86 Recueil des Cours 207 (1954).

31. Pan American Union, Basic Inter-American Economic Problems: General Observations 6 (1958).

32. Carlson, "The Economic Picture in the United States and Latin America: Background Papers," in The Final Report of the Sixteenth American Assembly 115 (1959); Rist, "Long-Term Financing Institutions of the Western Hemisphere," in International Banking and Foreign Trade 27 (1956).

33. Wolf and Sufrin, Capital Formation and Foreign Investment in Underdeveloped Areas 52 (1955); Schultz, "Latin American Economic Policy Lessons," 56 Proc. American Economic Review 425 (1956); Zook, Economic Development and International Trade (1959); Behrendt, Inter-American Economic Relations: Problems and Prospects 22 (1948).

34. Thomas & Thomas, Non-Intervention: The Law and Its Import in the Americas, Ch. XV (1956).

35. "Annual Report of the Secretary General of the Organization of American States for the Fiscal Year 1949-1950," 3 Annals of the OAS 43 (1951).

36. But see Thorning, "Latin American Reaction to the Korean Situation," 114 World Affairs 14 (1951).

37. "Fourth Meeting of Consultation of Ministers of Foreign Affairs," 3 Annals of the OAS 126 (1951); Kunz, "Fourth Meeting of Consultation of Ministers of Foreign Affairs of American States," 45 Am. J. Int. L. 740 (1951).

38. "Inter-American Economic and Social Council: Second Extraordinary Meeting," 3 Annals of the OAS 366 (1951).

39. "Inter-American Economic and Social Council: Third Extraordinary Meeting," 5 Annals of the OAS 124 (1953).

40. "Tenth Inter-American Conference: Report of the Pan American Union on the Conference," 6 Annals of the OAS 13 (1954).

41. "Organization of American States: Inter-American Economic and Social Council," 10 International Organization 332 (1956).

42. "Meeting Commemorating The Congress of Panama of 1826," 8 Annals of the OAS 192 (1956).

43. N. Y. Times, July 23, 1956; Fenwick, "The Meeting of Presidents at Panama," 51 Am. J. Int. L. 83 (1957).

44. An economic conference of the OAS was held in Buenos Aires from August 15 to September 4, 1957. This conference adopted the Economic Declaration of Buenos Aires, which again was merely a collection of pious platitudes declaring that it was the purpose of the American governments to increase trade among themselves, to reduce trade barriers, to extend international co-operation, to expand the flow of public capital to the countries of the Americas, and to establish better communications and sound monetary and financial conditions. 9 Annals of the OAS 213 (1957).

45. De Souza e Silva, "Operação Pan-Americana: Antecedentes e Perspectivas." 3 Revista Brasileira de Política Internacional, No. 9, p. 41 (1960).

46. Muniz, "Significado da Operação Pan-Americana," 2 Revista Brasileira de Política Internacional, No. 7, p. 5 (1959); "The Hemisphere Starts a Bank," 11 Americas 2 (June 1959).

47. N.Y. Times, May 3-10, 1959.

48. N.Y. Times, Sept. 4-12, 1960.

49. Pan American Union, Act of Bogotá: Measures for Social Improvement and Economic Development within the Framework of Operation Pan America (1951).

50. Smith, "The Inter-American Development Bank," 19 Fed. Bar J. 374 (1959); N.Y. Times, June 20, 1961.

51. Salera, "Economic Relations Between the United States and Latin America" 14 Year Book of World Affairs 92 (1960); 12 International Financial News Survey 269 (March 4, 1960); id. at 282 (March 11, 1960).

52. N.Y. Times, March 16, 1961; 45 Dept. State Bull. 355 (1961).

53. "The OAS in Action: The Task at Montevideo," 13 Americas 31 (Aug., 1961).

54. N.Y. Times, Aug. 1-30, 1961; 45 Dept. State Bull. 388 (1961).

55. Ibid. Pan American Union, Instability in World Markets for Primary Products: General Background (1958); N.Y. Times, Oct. 21, 22, 24, 28, 1962.

56. International Conferences of American States 1889-1928, p. 94 (Scott ed., 1931).

57. Moll, "The Pan American Sanitary Bureau: Its Origin, Development and Achievements," 19 Boletin de la Oficina Sanitaria Panamericana 1219 (1940).

58. Brockington, World Health 170 (1958).

59. Charter of the OAS, Art. 28.

60. 45 Dept. State Bull. 388 (1961).

61. Padilla, Free Men of America 90 (1943).

62. Scott, op. cit. supra note 56 at 74, 79, 98.

63. Id. at 134.

64. Id. at 190.

65. Id. at 14, 71, 136, 180.

66. Id. at 229, 230, 242, 259, 412.

67. The International Conferences of American States, First Supp. 1933-1940, p. 420 (1941).

68. N.Y. Times, June 15, 1943.

69. International Conferences of American States, op. cit. supra note 56 at 422.

70. Pan American Union, Report of the Division of Intellectual Cooperation (1941).

71. Op. cit. supra note 67 at 315, Pan American Institute of Geography and History, Memorandum on the Creation and Working of the Pan American Institute of Geography and History (1939).

72. Charter of the OAS, Art. 5 (k).

73. Id. Art. 30.

74. Id. Art. 31.

75. *Id.* Art. 73.
76. 4 Annals of the OAS 148 (1952).
77. "Final Act of the Tenth Inter-American Conference, Resolution III," 6 Annals of the OAS 49 (1954).
78. U.S. Dept. State, Tenth Inter-American Conference 185 (Pub. 5692; Int. Org. and Conf. Series II, American Republics 14, 1955).
79. *Id.* at 81.
80. *Id.* at 88.
81. *Id.* at 90.
82. 8 Annals of the OAS 205 (1956).
83. 9 Annals of the OAS 117 (1957).
84. OAS Official Records, OEA/Ser.C/V.3, Third Meeting of the Inter-American Cultural Council: Final Act (1961).
85. International Conferences of American States, *op cit. supra* note 56 at 69. See also: Alvarez, Report to the Institute of International Law: Méthodes de la Codification du Droit International 9 (1947).
86. Scott *id.* at 114.
87. *Id.* at 325, 385, 415, 416, 420, 424, 428.
88. International Conferences of American States, *op. cit. supra* note 67 at 84.
89. Pan American Union: Informe Sobre los Resultados de La Octava Conferencia Internacional Americana 11 (1939).
90. Fenwick, *supra* note 20 at 169.
91. Pan American Union, Handbook: First Meeting of the Inter-American Council of Jurists 186 (1950).
92. Pan American Union, Inter-American Conference on Problems of War and Peace, Resolutiion IX, p. 33 (1945).
93. Murdock and Gobbi, "Inter-American Juridical Committee," 9 Am. J. Comp. L. 596 (1960)
94. Pan American Union: Report on the Activities of the Organization of American States 1948-1953 submitted to the Tenth Conference 73 (1953).
95. Pan American Union, Final Act of the First Meeting of the Inter-American Council of Jurists ii (1950).
96. Pan American Union, Report of the Executive Secretary of the Inter-American Council of Jurists on the Second Meeting of the Inter-American Council of Jurists (1953).
97. Pan American Union, Final Act of the Third Meeting of the Inter-American Council of Jurists 5 (1956).
98. Pan American Union, Handbook: Fourth Meeting of the Inter-American Council of Jurists (1959); *id.,* Final Act of the Fourth Meeting of the Inter-American Council of Jurists (1959).
99. Stone, "On the Vocation of the International Law Commission," 57 Columbia Law Review 16 at 19 (1957).
100. *Id.* at 47; Lauterpacht, "Codification and Development of International Law," 49 Am. J. Int. L. 16 (1955); Hurst, "A Plea for the Codification of International Law on New Lines," 32 Trans. Grotius Soc. 135 (1944); Rodgers, "What Parts of International Law May Be Codified?" 20 Am. J. Int. L. 437 (1926); Alvarez *supra* note 85 at 81; 2 Scelle, Précis de Droit des Gens 536 (1934).

CHAPTER XX

1. Potter, "The Indispensable and the Impossible," 55 Am. J. Int. L. 122 (1961).
2. Schwarzenberger, Power Politics 12 (2d ed., 1951).
3. Alfaro, Commentary on Pan American Problems 5 (1938).
4. Castañeda, "Pan Americanism and Regionalism: A Mexican View," 10 Int. Org. 373 (1956).

INDEX

INDEX

Abuse of rights, 367

Accioly, 452, 454, 470, 471, 481, 488, 497

Act of Bogotá (1960), 386-87, 388

Act of Chapultepec (1945): collective sanctions in, 29; and collective security, 29, 210, 249, 258; enforcement measures in, 51; and Habana declaration, 29; on independence, 145; influence on United Nations Charter, 31; and Rio Treaty, 31; Truman on, 31; as wartime measure, 29

Act of Habana (1940), 82, 210-11

Act of Punta del Este (1961), 388

Adams, John Quincy, 437-38

Additional Protocol Relative to Non-Intervention (1936): Calvo Doctrine and, 174; Drago Doctrine and, 174; stated, 159; and U.S., 23, 159.

Additional Protocol to the General Convention of Inter-American Conciliation, (1933), 279, 281

Administrative agency: governing board as, 96-98

Advisory Defense Committee: OAS Charter on, 123-25

Advisory Opinion on Certain Expenses of the United Nations: International Court of Justice, 333

Agenda: of Inter-American conferences, see Inter-American conferences; of Meeting of Ministers of Foreign Affairs, see Meeting of Ministers of Foreign Affairs

Agreement on Privileges and Immunities of the OAS (1948), 45-48

Aggression: aid to victim of, 101, 137; Alfaro on, 141; Anti-War Treaty on, 186; and breach of diplomatic relations, 184; charged by Guatemala, 302-3; in civil strife situations, 347; and collective self-defense, 24, 137, 359-60; communist, 356-62; condemnation of, 142, 186; defense against, 123-25, 142; definition of, 257, 269-70; and direct action, 148; by Dominican Republic, 107, 236; enforcement measures against, 148; European threats of, 3, 9; extracontinental, 138, 211, 356-62; in general, 90, 147, 201, 210, 251-54, 258, 263, 273, 276; Hispanic American treaties on, 10; hostile propaganda as, 349; and independence, 146; indirect, 268, 352, 359; Inter-American Defense Board and, 124-25; investigation

of, 105; not involving use of force, 264-68; meaning of, 267-68; moral, 103, 299, 349; OAS powers over, 102-4, 166; Peace Committee to study, 128; and preparation for collective action, 124; and Rio Treaty, 43-44, 50, 101; Sixth Conference on, 185; and subversive intervention, 268; territorial integrity endangered by, 103; versus dispute, 303; United States against Mexico, 8-9

Air surveillance of Cuba, 339

Albania, 351

Alberdi, 216, 438

Alcorta, 186

Alexandrowicz, 501

Alfaro, 141, 351, 405, 467, 484, 485, 487, 504

Aliens: and denial of justice, 170; duty of receiving state to, 15, 16, 169-71; equality of treatment, 169-72, 174-75; exhaustion of local remedies, 170; Fifth Conference on, 19; irreparable injury to, 174; jurisdiction over, 142, 144, 169-75; liability for injury to, 170; privileged position in international law, 169-72; standard of justice, 169-72; status of, 7, 146

Alliance for Progress, 327, 388-90, 392

Alvarez, 11, 189-97, 437, 438, 439, 473, 475, 476, 479, 501, 504

Alvaro, 498

Amendment: of Charter of OAS, 73, 74; of treaties, 38

American community. See Community; Inter-American community; Organization of American States; Pan-Americanism

American Court of International Justice, 487

American Declaration of the Rights and Duties of Man (1948): and democracy, 244; Inter-American Commission of Human Rights on, 234; objectives of, 223-26

American international law, 68, 74, 409; axiological approach, 191; characteristics of, 189-99; Commission of Jurists on, 158; and democracy, 192, 219; on forcible acquisition of territory, 185-86; and general international law, 197-99; non-intervention and, 157, 159-61; and OAS, 199-202; on right of asylum, 194-96; specific rules of, 144, 194-96, 476; thesis of Judge Alvarez, 189-97

American League of Nations: Alfaro on,